# America's 60 Families

## BY FERDINAND LUNDBERG

*Author of "Imperial Hearst"*

# Foreword

In this work we are not concerned with the methods, legal or illegal, by which the great American fortunes of today were created. These fortunes exist. Their potentialities for good or evil are not altered whether we accept Gustavus Meyers' account of their formation or whether we give credence to the late John D. Rockefeller's simple statement: "God gave me my money."

What this book purports to do is to furnish replies, naming names and quoting book, chapter, and verse, to two blunt questions: Who owns and controls these large fortunes today, and how are these fortunes used? To answer this second question it is necessary, of course, to examine the role of great wealth in politics, industry, education, science, literature and the arts, journalism, social life and philanthropy.

The reader is warned that this work is not predicated on the premise of James W. Gerard, who in August, 1930, named fifty-nine men and women that, he said, "ran" America. In Mr. Gerard's list were many persons deemed by the author of slight importance, many of them merely secondary deputies of great wealth and some of them persons whom Mr. Gerard undoubtedly flattered by including in his select list. The factor determining the inclusion of persons in this narrative has at all times been pecuniary power, directly or indirectly manifested.

This work will consider incidentally the various arguments brought forward by the apologists of great fortunes. These arguments are to the effect that huge fortunes are necessary so that industry may be financed; that the benefactions of great wealth permit advances in science, encourage writers and artists, etc.; that the lavish expenditures of wealthy persons "give employment" to many people; and that in any case these big fortunes are dissipated within a few generations.

More and more it is becoming plain that the major political and social problem of today and of the next decade centers about the taxation of great wealth. It is hoped that this book, the first objective study of the general social role of great fortunes, will shed at least a modicum of light upon this paramount issue.

F. L.

# Contents

gives a New Year's Eve party. Mrs. Joseph E. Davies brings coals
to Newcastle in Moscow. Average cost of social affairs. What the
"patrons" of symphony orchestras and opera get in return. The ex-
cessive generosity of John B. Ryan. Christmas parties at the George
F. Baker mansion. Jewels of fabulous worth and who owns them.
The Romanov-Donahue gems. Emerald collectors. The bathrooms
of the mighty and how they are glorified. The swimming pool, an
irreplaceable adjunct to the millionaire's estate. Hetty Green's son
collects stamps at $18,000. Country demesnes: Hearst's *San Simeon,
St. Donat's, Wyntoon;* Du Ponts' *Winterthur, Longwood, Ne-
mours, Henry Clay, Chevannes, Owl's Nest, Louviers, Guyencourt,
Granogue, Centerville;* Vanderbilts' *Biltmore, The Breakers, Mar-
ble House;* the Rockefellers' *Kijkuit* (Pocantico), *Golf House, The
Casements, Villa Turicum, Geralda Farm;* the Morgans' *Wall Hall
Castle.* Estates incorporated to evade taxes. Vincent Astor's estates.
Gardens worth a king's ransom and their millionaire owners.
Islands the private property of many wealthy families. Yachts. Du
Ponts world's largest collective owner of yachts. Other yacht owners,
their yachts and their costs. Pipe organs and for whom built. Private railway cars and railroads on many estates. Horses, polo, horse
shows, and their wealthy adherents. The Jockey Club. Automobiles.
Fleets of them owned by each family. Airplanes, a new thrill for millionaires. Gloria Morgan Vanderbilt and other costly children.
Clothes, men's and women's. A composite Park Avenue family
budget. What rich babies cost. E. F. Hutton's remedy for the depression. Self-justification.

## XII. THE "NEW DEAL"—AND AFTER                        447

The "New Deal's" reception by political factions of Right and Left.
"New Deal" born of crisis. Why its defenders found it to their liking. The "New Deal" subject to criticism despite some progressive
ingredients. Not radical nor revolutionary. Are "New Deal" motives
philanthropic? Lowest 1936 wage averages paid in industries supporting Roosevelt campaigns. "New Deal" represents one camp of
great wealth pitted against another: light goods and merchandising *versus* heavy industry and banking. Why "New Deal" policies
attract labor leaders and farmers. Republicans afraid to disclose
true "New Deal" aims. Forced to invent false radical issue. Nothing
in Roosevelt career to presage Presidential passion for "forgotten
man." Nominated by political deal. Du Ponts in recent elections.

Roosevelt always backed by wealth. Revealed bias toward *status quo* in bank crisis. His task as he saw it. Spectacular early "New Deal" measures: suspension of the gold standard, the AAA, the NIRA and Section 7A. Public works program stimulates buying power. Measures designed to hamper banks and heavy industry. Banking Act, sought by Rockefellers, hurts Morgans. Securities Exchange Act hinders stock promoters. Wheeler-Rayburn Act. The "death sentence." Source of opposition the same in all measures. "New Deal" tax rates analyzed. Facts behind Roosevelt's tax proposals. Loopholes in gift and philanthropic provisions. Novel measures used by the rich to cut tax liability. "New Deal" unconventional only in "experiments." Value of TVA, Resettlement Administration, Social Security Act, WPA cultural projects. Progressive policies in tariff revisions, neutrality. Policies in Latin America, Russia. Repeal of Prohibition most popular accomplishment. President fails to support measures he champions: Tugwell Bill, Child Labor Amendment. Why cry of "Dictator" is raised. Rockefeller and Astor hostility. Administration assails A. W. Mellon Charitable and Educational Trust and establishes a precedent. "New Deal" labor policy foisted on it. John L. Lewis, Roosevelt, and the CIO. Administration favoritism to wealthy partisans in labor disputes. Campaign contributors in 1936 show split between heavy and light industrialists and their allies. "Economic royalists" in Democratic ranks. Democratic Convention book sales. Other money-raising devices. Avalanche of hostile Republican money offset by unprecedented labor funds thrown to Roosevelt. Defections from Roosevelt camp. Roosevelt cool toward CIO, endorses legislation favoring his backers. President's court proposal not inherently progressive. Possible course of "New Deal" program. The task before the country today briefly discussed.

# America's 60 Families

# I

## Golden Dynasties and Their Treasures

THE United States is owned and dominated today by a hierarchy of its sixty richest families, buttressed by no more than ninety families of lesser wealth. Outside this plutocratic circle there are perhaps three hundred and fifty other families, less defined in development and in wealth, but accounting for most of the incomes of $100,000 or more that do not accrue to members of the inner circle.

These families are the living center of the modern industrial oligarchy which dominates the United States, functioning discreetly under a *de jure* democratic form of government behind which a *de facto* government, absolutist and plutocratic in its lineaments, has gradually taken form since the Civil War. This *de facto* government is actually the government of the United States—informal, invisible, shadowy. It is the government of money in a dollar democracy.

Our concern is mainly with the sixty families, although from time to time members of the surrounding ninety odd will enter the narrative. Under their acquisitive fingers, and in their possession, the sixty families hold the richest nation ever fashioned in the workshop of history. The whole long procession of states, nations, and empires that strained and sweated up to the threshold of the Industrial Revolution amassed much less material wealth than the United States alone possesses. The vaunted Roman Empire, for example, could be placed in the land area west of the Mississippi, with room to spare; all Europe is, indeed, only slightly larger than is the United States.

Bigness alone, however, means little; China, too, is very big. But in the economically decisive requisites of accumulated capital and equipment, technical knowledge and facilities, natural resources and man power, the United States is unique. Yet most of its people are,

3

paradoxically, very poor; most of them own nothing beyond a few sticks of furniture and the clothes on their backs.

The outstanding American proprietors of today tower historically over the proud aristocracy that surrounded Louis XIV, Czar Nicholas, Kaiser Wilhelm, and the Emperor Franz Joseph, and wield vastly greater power. The might of Cardinal Richelieu, Metternich, Bismarck, or Disraeli was no greater than that of private citizens, undistinguished by titles, like J. P. Morgan, Andrew W. Mellon, John D. Rockefeller, Henry Ford, and the Du Ponts. It was essentially the decision of these latter and their political deputies (so far as a single decision carried weight after the initial lines were drawn) that dictated the outcome of the World War, the greatest armed conflict in all history. Napoleon could have done no more.

The war, which raised wealthy Americans to the pinnacle of world power, obliterated huge sections of Europe's master class, and set other sections adrift. In Germany and Austria-Hungary the dominant élite of wealth—landowners, bankers, and industrialists—were virtually pauperized overnight. In France and England, seriously weakened, increasingly timorous, they staggered under tax burdens, and even yet are bedeviled by grave problems upon whose tranquil solution depends their future well-being. In Russia they were simply annihilated.

Of the world's wealthy ruling classes, those of America and England alone retain the full substance, as well as the insignia and panoply, of wealth and power. Alone do they still speak confidently and act decisively for themselves, not driven to utilize bizarre intermediaries like a Hitler, a Mussolini, or a Mikado to hypnotize the multitude; they are not challenged, as in France, by powerful domestic political coalitions of the economically disfranchised. This fortunate situation is, perhaps, purely temporary; it may be undermined by the next general war.

Instead of decreasing in wealth and power during the crisis of 1929–1933 America's sixty richest families were actually strengthened in relation to the hordes of citizens reduced to beggary. And even though many people have since been lifted from extreme low economic levels by some restoration of employment, the grotesque, basic inequalities, issuing from no fundamental differences in skill or merit, remain as great as ever. Paralleling re-employment, which has reduced the aggregate of joblessness from about twenty million in 1932 to about ten million in 1937, fantastic dividend and interest payments have been automatically returned to the top income group, which at its maximum comprises no more than six thousand adults.

The United States, it is apparent even to the blind, is a nightmare of contradictions. It has not only nurtured the wealthiest class history has ever known, but it has also spawned an immense, possibly permanent, army of paupers—the unemployed. One naturally expects to find millions of impoverished in backward economies such as India, China, Japan, or czarist Russia. In the advanced economic and cultural environment of North America, with all its natural resources, the phenomenon is little short of incredible. In the light of the nation's professed ideals it is tragically absurd.

The situation, for which the people themselves are in great measure to blame, is skilfully glossed over and colored by cunning apologists in press and pulpit, school and legislative hall. These briefly triumphant marionettes are able to show, to their own and to their patrons' satisfaction, that great wealth was garnered while society was being served in oblique and mysterious fashions; that it has been so administered, by ostensibly high-minded heirs of the early economic freebooters, as to constitute a great stimulus to social progress. The outstanding example of such a social servitor is presented in John D. Rockefeller, Jr.

Although editorial writers nourish such illusions with carefree abandon, the more realistic of the magnates have seldom seen themselves in other than a predatory role, even though they have admitted this only privately. The elder J. P. Morgan delighted, it is said, jestingly to trace his ancestry back to Henry Morgan, the seventeenth-century Caribbean pirate; in token of this he named his yacht the *Corsair* and painted it an anarchistic black. This gave rise to the whispered legend in Wall Street that on the high seas J. P. Morgan flew the skull and crossbones and placed the American flag in a secondary position. The present J. P. Morgan has retained the name of the *Corsair* for his black-painted private transatlantic steam yacht, but the Wall Street myth spinners aver, with a nice feeling for distinctions, that he flies the Union Jack followed, respectively, by the Jolly Roger and the Stars and Stripes.

The name of Rockefeller has come to be associated in the public mind, thanks to the magic of sedulously controlled publicity, with the giving of money. What merit there is in this reputation we shall explore later, but at the moment we may recall that the present John D. Rockefeller, by accident of birth, is the richest man in the world. His family, too, is the richest, closely approached in wealth only by the Mitsui family of Japan and the Ford family of America.

Rockefeller's Federal tax for the normal * year of 1924 was $6,279,-669, indicating a taxable income of $15,000,000. This last represented five per cent on capital of $300,000,000, or less than one-third of the fortune conceded by Wall Street authorities to be under his control. The Rockefellers, however, have vast sums concentrated in tax-exempt securities, notably in New York State and City bonds, and systematically obtain tax reductions by a policy of non-commercial investment, i.e., "philanthropy." On the basis of capital of about $1,000,000,000 under his ownership (exclusive of "philanthropic" funds under his control, which retain for him a large measure of influence in corporate, philanthropic, and educational affairs), the personal income of Mr. Rockefeller in 1924 may have been $30,000,000 to $50,000,000.

The annual revenue of the late Czar of Russia varied from only $10,000,000 to $12,000,000, little of which he could utilize at his discretion owing to the convention that he support his many relatives and maintain in traditional splendor his collection of palaces.[1] And, like Mr. Rockefeller, he was a conspicuous and publicly heralded "philanthropist."

The estate of Queen Victoria of England, much of it London slum real estate, was valued at £9,000,000 (about $45,000,000), and some or most of this now belongs to the King, producing an income of about $2,225,000 provided the original capital has not been increased by compounding of earnings.[2] From the Duchy of Lancaster the King annually receives £85,000 ($425,000) and from the Civil List, authorized by Parliament from the public revenues, about £370,000 ($1,850,000).[3] At most the income of the King is $4,500,000, and a

* See note 7, chapter II.

portion of what he receives from the Civil List is earmarked in advance for royal charities. The public treasury, in brief, supplies him with the means with which to bestow alms. But his is no more peculiar than the position of Mr. Rockefeller, who is able to pose as an altruist and benefactor of mankind because the law permits him to exploit for personal profit the nation's petroleum resources and forces of production.

Europe's wealthiest aristocrat until the World War was the Archduke Frederick of Austria, whose estate before 1914 was valued as high as $750,000,000. But no Europeans or Asiatics have ever been so wealthy as the Rockefeller, Ford, Harkness, Vanderbilt, Mellon, and Du Pont families of America.

Whenever a figure like the elder Rockefeller dies newspaper writers compare his wealth with that of certain Indian princes, said to be fabulously rich. In contrast with the American millionaires the Indian princes, however, are mere paupers. Their wealth is frozen in jewels and land, and cannot be readily liquidated or transferred into other vehicles; moreover, their society does not utilize on a large scale the wealth-producing technology of the West. But the securities of the American millionaires can be exchanged in a flash for any currency in the world, for land, for other stocks and bonds. The wealth of the Indian princes is immobile, static; the wealth of their American counterparts is mobile, dynamic. In the money markets of the world the feudal wealth of the Indian princes is of no consequence.

The uprush of the American fortunes, led by the monolithic Rockefeller accumulation, emphasizes that although the United States was once a great political democracy it has not remained one. Citizens may still be equals at the polls, where little is decided; but they are not equals at the bank tellers' wickets, where much is decided. The United States has produced, in the Standard Oil Company, the Aluminum Company of America, E. I. du Pont de Nemours and Company, the Ford Motor Company, and other industrial enterprises, what are essentially feudal, dictatorially ruled, dynastic fiefs that make the old crown properties of Romanovs, Hohenzollerns, Hapsburgs, and Hanovers seem, by comparison, like will-o'-the-wisps, insecure and insubstantial.

## II

Concentration of industrial and financial control in the capacious
hands of the wealthy—by means of majority ownership, legal device, and diffusion of fractional and disfranchised ownership among
thousands of impotent stockholders, bondholders, insurance policyholders, and bank depositors—has been given close, authoritative
study from various approaches.[4] But concentration of control has
also come about by more simple and obvious processes that have
been largely ignored, perhaps because of the absence of technical
intricacies to challenge the research specialist, perhaps because the
very lack of historical novelty in the processes has allowed them to
pass by virtually unnoticed.

Without minimizing the significance of control by the dominant
owning clique through corporate devices, it is nevertheless true that
corporations are merely the instruments or tools of control behind
which the living masters hide in discreet anonymity. The corporations do not represent the locus of control, nor do they, even when
viewed synoptically as in the valuable Rochester and Laidler studies,
reveal the full extent of control and concentration by a small group
working through partnerships.

The control points of private wealth in industrial capitalistic society, as in feudal society, remain the partnership, the family, and
the family alliance. It is the family that, in almost all cases, guides
the banks and the banking partnerships which, as Anna Rochester
shows, control the corporations.

The family today, in no slighter degree than two or three cen-
turies ago or in imperial Rome, is supreme in the governance of
wealth—amassing it, standing watch over it, and keeping it intact
from generation to generation. Because it is (unlike that relatively
new device, the corporation) a private entity which in the strictest
legality may resist public scrutiny, the family lends itself admirably
to alliances of a formal character and serves as an instrument for
confidential financial transactions. By definition the family is a sacro-
sanct institution, and no agency of government may pry into it
without offending inculcated prejudice. The partnership, it is true,
offers some refuge, and is certainly more of a private affair than is the

corporation; but it, too, is now quite open to political inquiry. The family alone provides a safe retreat from democratic processes, not outside the law, but, for practical financial purposes, above the law.

## III

For many decades American families of great wealth have been immeasurably and steadily reinforced by scores of marriages among their members. The joint fortunes have been passed on to children who themselves paired off with the progeny of other wealthy unions. There has also been much marriage between European and American ruling class families, but this has been less meaningful socially, politically, and economically than the unions of American millionaires with each other, for the Europeans, mostly impoverished noblemen, have only in a few cases brought an increase in fortune to their American partners. The chief assets of the Europeans have been hereditary titles, leisure-class manners, perhaps a shabby estate or two, and passports into the world of snobbery. American dollars have served very concretely, however, to re-establish, *via* marriage, hundreds of decadent European estates, an ironic contribution of American democracy to the peoples of Europe; Gustavus Myers estimated in 1909 that five hundred such marriages had taken place. By now the aggregate is easily six or eight times as great.

Marriages between wealthy Americans have, by all odds, been the more significant. Any tendency toward dispersal of great wealth that might be expected from its supposed distribution among numerous offspring of unions between rich and poor has been more than offset by the actual marriage of wealth with wealth. The wealthiest Americans, with few exceptions, are already joined by a multiplicity of family ties, just as they are joined by interlocking directorates and mutual participations in economic and social undertakings. The "community of interest" of the rich to which the elder J. P. Morgan made profound public obeisance has become, to a startling degree, a joint family interest.

The continuation of intermarriage among millionaire families will, other factors remaining unchanged, in a generation or two give rise to a situation wherein all the big American proprietors will be blood relatives—first, second, or third cousins. Already there are many persons with the blood of the Rockefellers, Stillmans, and Vanderbilts, and of the Harknesses, Whitneys, Paynes, and Stillmans. There are others with the blue blood of Europe blended in their veins with the blood of John D. Rockefeller, Sr., of John Jacob Astor I, of Cornelius Vanderbilt I, of Marshall Field, of E. H. Manville, and of many more of their class.

The Rockefellers have contracted numerous marriages of financial import. Mrs. John D. Rockefeller, Jr., is the daughter of the late Senator Nelson W. Aldrich, wealthy Rhode Island merchant and public utilities lord. Winthrop W. Aldrich, her brother, is thus the brother-in-law of Rockefeller. That such an alliance has economic and financial signification is attested by the strategic presence of Aldrich as chairman of the Rockefeller-controlled Chase National Bank, largest banking institution in the country. The grandfathers of the junior Rockefeller's children are the deceased senior Rockefeller and the late Senator Aldrich, who in his day was successively the legislative "whip" of first the Morgan and then the Rockefeller factions in the United States Senate.

Isabel G. Stillman, daughter of James Stillman, became Mrs. Percy A. Rockefeller and S. Elsie Stillman became Mrs. William G. Rockefeller. Thus was biologically cemented the financial alliance that existed between William Rockefeller, brother of John D., and the ruler of the National City Bank of New York. Geraldine Stillman Rockefeller became Mrs. Marcellus Hartley Dodge, linking the Rockefellers and Stillmans by marriage to the $50,000,000 fortune garnered by the Remington Arms Company in the Civil War and by the Phelps Dodge Corporation in later years. J. Stillman Rockefeller, son of William G. Rockefeller and grandnephew of John D. Rockefeller, married Nancy C. S. Carnegie, grandniece of Andrew Carnegie; in 1930 a son born of this union was named Andrew Carnegie Rockefeller.

Edith Rockefeller, sister of Rockefeller, Jr., married Harold F. McCormick, heir to an International Harvester Company fortune. Their son, Fowler, a grandson of Rockefeller, Sr., and Cyrus H. McCormick, inventor of the reaper, more recently married Fifi Stillman, divorced wife of James A. Stillman and mother of Mrs. Henry P. Davison, Jr., the wife of a current Morgan partner. Nelson

A. Rockefeller, son of Rockefeller, Jr., married a daughter of G. B. Roberts, former president of the Pennsylvania Railroad. Emma, daughter of William G. Rockefeller and Elsie Stillman Rockefeller, married David Hunter McAlpin. Their son, William Rockefeller McAlpin, more recently married Marion Angell, daughter of the president emeritus of Yale University.

These are only a few examples of the interlocking of the Rockefellers with families of wealth; some Rockefeller marriages, to be sure, have taken place outside of the pecuniary circle. The rich families with which the Rockefellers have interlocked in turn have been interlocked by marriages with other wealthy families, so that one can trace an almost unbroken line of biological relationships from the Rockefellers through one-half of the wealthiest sixty families of the nation. Mary E. Stillman, for example, became Mrs. Edward S. Harkness (Standard Oil). Anne Stillman is, as we have observed, Mrs. Henry P. Davison, Jr. The Stillmans also married into the Pratt (Standard Oil) family.

The powerful Whitneys, partners with the Rockefellers, the Harknesses, and the Pratts in the original Standard Oil Trust, likewise fused their wealth with wealth by marriage. William C. Whitney, lieutenant of the elder Rockefeller, married Flora Payne, heiress to the fortune of another Rockefeller partner. The Harknesses and Flaglers (Standard Oil) were likewise joined by marriage, and the reigning head of this Standard Oil line is Harry Harkness Flagler.

An examination of Vanderbilt marriages discloses the same drift. A Vanderbilt married Virginia Fair, daughter of Senator James Fair of California, thus bringing the Fair accumulation, based upon the fabulous Ophir silver mine, into the Vanderbilt orbit. James Watson Webb, descendant of Commodore Cornelius Vanderbilt, married Electra Havemeyer (American Sugar Refining Company), who is now Electra H. Webb and reputed one of the wealthiest women in America. A daughter of Cornelius Vanderbilt II became Mrs. Harry Payne Whitney, wife of a Standard Oil princeling, and a daughter of William Henry Vanderbilt married Hamilton McKay Twombly; upon her husband's death she, too, became one of America's wealthiest women.

These dynastic alliances are so numerous, and intertwine at so many points with one another, that to survey them all would turn this into a genealogical study. Among various of the many dynastic marriages that have consolidated the winnings of the original robber barons of America we may briefly note, however, those that brought Mary L. Duke, heiress to the tobacco fortune, into the Biddle family, as Mrs. Anthony Drexel Biddle, while her brother married Biddle's sister; Lillie Harriman into the Havemeyer family and Cornelia Harriman into the Gerry family; Marjorie G. Gould into the Drexel family; a granddaughter of George F. Baker into the Schiff family; a Deering (International Harvester Company) into the McCormick family (International Harvester); Ruth Hanna (coal, iron, and steel) into the McCormick family; Doris Duke into the Stotesbury circle by marriage to James H. R. Cromwell, former husband of Delphine Dodge (automobiles) and son of Mrs. E. T. Stotesbury, wife of the senior Morgan partner in Philadelphia; Margaret Mellon into the Laughlin (steel) family; Marjorie Post (Postum) and Edna Woolworth (5-and-10 cent stores) into the Hutton family, and so on.

The marriage of wealth with wealth has gone a good deal farther even than these citations indicate. Selecting at random from the past fifteen years we find that Gilbert W. Kahn, son of Otto H. Kahn, married a daughter of George Whelan, head of the United Cigar Stores; Mrs. Edith Stuyvesant Vanderbilt, widow of George W. Vanderbilt, married the wealthy Peter Goelet Gerry, of Rhode Island, himself the offspring of two big fortunes; Mrs. Rachel Littleton Vanderbilt, half sister of Martin W. Littleton, corporation attorney, and divorced wife of Cornelius Vanderbilt, Jr., married Jasper Morgan, nephew of J. P. Morgan; Margaret D. Kahn, daughter of Otto Kahn, married John Barry Ryan, Jr., grandson of Thomas Fortune Ryan; Margaret Carnegie Perkins, grandniece of Andrew Carnegie, married John Speer Laughlin, of the Jones and Laughlin steel dynasty; Esther du Pont, daughter of Lammot du Pont, married Campbell Weir (steel); W. A. Harriman, son of E. H. Harriman, married Marie Norton Whitney, divorced wife of Cornelius Vanderbilt Whitney, who is the son of Harry Payne Whitney.

In only a few cases do great fortunes appear to have been reared initially upon a dynastic basis. One such general accumulation is centered about the banking house of Kuhn, Loeb and Company, founded in the middle of the nineteenth century as a mercantile organization by Abraham Kuhn and Solomon Loeb. Jacob H. Schiff came from Germany, married Teresa, Loeb's daughter, and induced the partners to set up in Wall Street as a private bank. Paul M. Warburg, of a Hamburg German-Jewish banking house, also came to this country, became a partner, and married Nina J. Loeb. Felix M. Warburg, his brother, married Frieda Schiff, and the dissimilar strains of the original partners were mingled through the Warburgs, whose spokesman today is the politically aggressive James P. Warburg, son of Paul M. Warburg and Nina J. Loeb, and cousin of the surviving Schiffs. Otto H. Kahn, a partner, married Addie Wolff, daughter of another early partner.

In later years the Warburg-Kuhn-Loeb-Schiff-Kahn dynasty has been linked in marriage, as we have noted, to the huge George F. Baker and Thomas Fortune Ryan accumulations, which are in turn linked by marriage to other notable fortunes.

Except for the early Standard Oil intermarriages, there has thus far been little intermarriage among the principal heirs of the largest fortunes, and in only a few cases do marriages of convenience appear to have taken place. A sound psychological reason for the marriage of wealth with wealth is simply that the rich are suspicious, when it comes to contracting marriage, of the motives of those who are not rich. They are afraid of fortune-hunters, and properly so, for there have been many cases in which outsiders have obtained legal claims to the family funds through marriage and have grossly abused their rights.

Propinquity has also led to the marriage of wealthy couples, for few persons of wealth maintain social relationships with the non-wealthy. But, whatever the reason, the great fortunes are interlinked by marriage, no less than by common property holdings, so that it is quite arbitrary in many cases to speak of a person as representing a single fortune.

President Franklin D. Roosevelt, stung by the diatribes of newspapers owned or controlled by men of wealth, irately referred in 1936 to these men, in a figurative sense, as "economic royalists." But it is in a strictly literal sense that hundreds of the offspring of the wealthy families are members of nobility or royalty. Few are the

very wealthy families of America that have not at least one representative in the *Almanach de Gotha* or *Burke's Peerage*. Thus Anita Stewart, sister of William Rhinelander Stewart, is the Princess de Bra-
ganza, consort of the late pretender to the throne of Portugal. The
daughter of Bessie Rockefeller married the Marqués George de Cuevas; the Cuevas children, great-grandchildren of the elder Rockefeller, are Spanish grandees in their own right.

William Waldorf Astor voluntarily expatriated himself (although
retaining his American property holdings) and was transmuted by
the sorcery of money into an English Lord. He was succeeded by the
present William Waldorf, Viscount Astor of Hever Castle, who has
four sons and one daughter who, although born British nobles, are
descendants of the miserly John Jacob Astor I, flute importer, real
estate speculator, and fur dealer. The Astors have climbed high
socially in England; they have even entered the fringes of the royal
family, for Rachel Spender-Clay, granddaughter of the first Lord
Astor, in 1929 married the Hon. David Bowes-Lyon, brother of
Elizabeth, the present Queen of England.

The sister of Vincent Astor became the Princess Serge Obolen-
sky. Anna Gould married successively Count Boni de Castellane and
the Duke de Talleyrand. Millicent Rogers (Standard Oil) was first
the Countess von Salm and then became the wife of a wealthy Ar-
gentinian. The daughter of Levi Z. Leiter, Chicago partner of Marshall Field I, married Lord Curzon, later Viceroy of India. Clara
Huntington, adopted daughter of Collis P. Huntington, railroad
baron, became the Princess Hatzfeldt-Wildenburg. Barbara Hutton
(Woolworth), after divorcing Prince Alexis Mdivani, became the
Countess Haugwitz-Reventlow. Ethel Field, daughter of Marshall
Field I, became Lady Beatty, consort of Admiral of the Fleet Earl
Beatty and mother of the present peer.

Vivien Gould married Lord Decies. Gladys Vanderbilt married
Count Lâszló Széchényi. The Széchényi union brought forth five
children, of Vanderbilt and noble Magyar lineage. Consuelo Vanderbilt became the Duchess of Marlborough; although this union was
dissolved, it produced two children, the present Duke of Marlborough
and Lord Ivor Spencer Churchill. Estelle Manville, daughter of
Hiram E. Manville (asbestos), married Count Folke Bernadotte,

nephew of the King of Sweden; their child is the Count of Visborg. The Honorable Dorothy Paget, whose mother was a daughter of William C. Whitney (Standard Oil), is a first cousin of "Jock" and "Sonny" Whitney. Her father, Almeric Hugh Paget, is Lord Queensborough.

European nobles of American lineage probably enjoy more opulent incomes than their peers who lack American forebears and dowries. It is one of the many ironies of the situation that the United States should be pumping forth dividends and rents to support persons in stations so alien to the American concept of social status. It is no less ironical that the children of these transatlantic unions, permanently in residence abroad, draw from American enterprises immense revenues the like of which the average American of this and succeeding generations—no matter how intelligent, crafty, dishonest, or creative—may never reasonably expect to attain. Not only does American labor produce revenue for the support of the ornate estates of America, but it also supports many remote castles in Europe.

The Fords, the Mellons, and the Du Ponts have been less conspicuous than these others in their marriages although Andrew Mellon, like many another American magnate, married and had his children by a wealthy English woman. Perhaps the most meaningful of transatlantic marriages, after all, have been these between wealthy British commoners and Americans, which join the purely moneyed classes of the two nations by sentimental ties as the House of Morgan and international trade join them by financial and economic ties. The McCormicks, Astors, Fields, and others have contracted such unions with British commoners; they are too numerous to detail here.

The Du Ponts have married among themselves when they have not entered wedlock with obscure persons; the Ford family has not yet been sufficiently long established in the possession of wealth to contract marriages of economic coloring. Marriages of first cousins among the Du Ponts became so frequent, indeed, according to a recent biographer, that the head of this essentially feudal dynasty forbade further inbreeding. The marriage in 1937 of Ethel du Pont, daughter of Eugene du Pont, to Franklin D. Roosevelt, Jr., son of the President, himself heir to an old colonial land fortune now of modest size, constituted the first Du Pont union with one of the foremost old-line aristocratic families of America.

The designation Du Ponts refers to a single family of several hundred contemporaries, about a dozen of whom receive extraordinarily large revenues from the General Motors Corporation, the United States Rubber Company, and from E. I. du Pont de Nemours and Company. As a family the Du Ponts rank seventh in size of taxable income in the United States, according to the 1924 norm, although few individual Du Ponts of the main line of descent appear to draw much more than $1,000,000 taxable income annually. What they may draw from tax-exempt sources is, of course, unknown. The Du Ponts have been infinitely resourceful in keeping down their tax bills by legalistic legerdemain.

The *Social Register* (1934), for example, lists 73 adult Du Ponts, in contrast with only 53 Goulds, 31 Mellons, 29 Hannas, 28 Harrimans, 27 Rockefellers, 22 Winthrops, 21 Vanderbilts, 18 Drexels, 16 Harknesses, 7 Archbolds, and so on.

In the Du Pont clan are Mr. and Mrs. Eugene du Pont II, Mr. and Mrs. Eugene du Pont III, Mr. and Mrs. Lammot du Pont, Mr. and Mrs. Irénée du Pont, Mr. and Mrs. A. Felix du Pont, Mr. and Mrs. Richard du Pont, Mr. and Mrs. Victor du Pont, Mr. and Mrs. Victor du Pont, Jr.; there are also Mr. and Mrs. Henry Belin du Pont, Mr. and Mrs. E. Paul du Pont, Mr. and Mrs. Archibald du Pont, Mrs. William Laird, sister of Pierre, and her two daughters, Mrs. Ellason Downs and Mrs. Robert N. Downs, Mr. and Mrs. Philip Francis du Pont, Mrs. Porter Schutt (the former Phyllis du Pont), Mr. and Mrs. Lammot Copeland, Mr. and Mrs. Eugene E. du Pont, Mr. and Mrs. William du Pont, Irénée du Pont, Jr., Mrs. Ellen du Pont Meeds, Mrs. Henderson Weir, etc.; and there are the Misses Lydia, Ruth Ellen, Pauline Louise, Octavia, Alexandrine, Lucile Evelina, Murton, and Nancy du Pont. This is only a very partial list.

All these dynasties, to be sure, include many members that do not bear the family name. Selecting one at random, neither the largest nor the smallest, we find that it comprises 140 members in all its branches. This is the Pratt (Standard Oil) family of Brooklyn. Among the many Pratts are Mr. and Mrs. Frederic Bayley Pratt,

Mrs. Charles M. Pratt, Mr. and Mrs. Harold Irving Pratt, Jr., former
Congresswoman Ruth Baker Pratt, Mr. and Mrs. John T. Pratt, Mr.
and Mrs. Samuel Croft Register II, Mr. and Mrs. Richardson Pratt,
Mr. and Mrs. Theodore Pratt, Mrs. George Dupont Pratt, Mr. and
Mrs. George D. Pratt, Jr., Mr. and Mrs. James Ramsey Hunt, Mr.
and Mrs. Richard Stockton Emmett, Mrs. Pratt McLane, Mr. and
Mrs. David R. Wilmerding, Mr. and Mrs. Herbert L. Pratt, Jr., Mr.
and Mrs. Charles Pratt, Sherman Pratt, Mr. and Mrs. Elliott Pratt,
Mr. and Mrs. James Jackson, Jr., Mr. and Mrs. Robert H. Thayer,
Mr. and Mrs. Edwin H. B. Pratt, and about thirty children.

In the J. P. Morgan family are Mrs. Paul Pennoyer, *née* Frances
Morgan; Miss Virginia Morgan Pennoyer; Mrs. George Nichols, *née*
Jane Morgan; Miss Jane N. Nichols, and eleven young grandchildren. The father of the present J. P. Morgan, who died in 1913, has
sixteen living grandchildren.

## IV

Marriage has in some cases, naturally, shielded family wealth
behind commonplace names.

Thus we find, in addition to Electra H. Webb, a woman who,
under the undistinguished name of H. S. Wilks, paid a 1924 tax on
income of more than $500,000. She is Mrs. Matthew Astor Wilks,
daughter of the fabulous Hetty Green, and married into a subsidiary
branch of the Astor family. Ella Wendel, who died in 1931 possessed
of $75,000,000 worth of New York real estate, was also related to the
Astors, for the stepmother of the original John Jacob Astor bore six
children by his father, and one child, Elizabeth Astor, in 1799 married John Wendel, founder of a line that made its fortune quietly
sitting on real estate and allowing the tenants and community growth
to enhance its value in accord with the traditional Astor policy.

Ailsa Mellon married David K. E. Bruce, son of former Senator
William Cabell Bruce of Maryland. The former Caroline S. Astor
became Mrs. M. Orme Wilson. Jessie Woolworth became Mrs. James
P. Donahue, and Helena Woolworth acquired the name McCann
through marriage to a nephew of Richard Croker, Tammany boss.
Certain Woolworth heirs of the youngest generation are, therefore,
named Donahue and McCann; others bear the names of Betts and

Guest. Josephine Hartford, granddaughter of the founder of the Great Atlantic and Pacific Tea Company, was first Mrs. Oliver O'Donnell and then Mrs. Vadim Markaroff. Some women of the Rockefeller, Morgan, Vanderbilt, Harkness, and other clans have also assumed unpublicized names by marriage.

To be sure, not all members of the wealthy families contract marriages within the pecuniary circle, but when any member steps outside the bounds to select a mate the uproar the newspapers create suffices to indicate the unusualness of the event. James A. ("Bud") Stillman, Jr., married a daughter of his mother's cook; Leonard Kip Rhinelander married the daughter of a Negro taxicab driver; Ellin Mackay married Irving Berlin, the Broadway song writer; Mathilde McCormick married a Swiss riding master. In every such case so extraordinary did newspaper editors consider it that a sentimental attachment could transcend monetary considerations, that they behaved like maniacs in exploiting the "stories."

Very many men of diverse names who hold leading positions in American industry are, unknown to the multitude, connected by marriage with the large fortunes. Thus James A. Farrell, for many years president of the United States Steel Corporation, was married to a daughter of the late Anthony N. Brady, public utilities magnate. Another Brady daughter married Francis P. Garvan, a Tammany Assistant District Attorney who soon after his marriage became President Wilson's Assistant Attorney General and Alien Property Custodian. In the latter position he supervised the transfer of German chemical patents from confiscated companies to the Chemical Foundation for less than $300,000; Garvan is still head of the Chemical Foundation as well as dean of the law school at Fordham University. Walter C. Teagle, president of the Standard Oil Company of New Jersey, is a grandson of John D. Rockefeller's first business partner, Morris B. Clark.

Most of the desirable jobs throughout the biggest corporations and banks, indeed, are filled to an astonishing extent by men who are either collateral descendants of the wealthy families, married to direct or collateral descendants, or connected by blood relationship with persons directly or indirectly related. This situation, very often resembling flagrant nepotism, notoriously in the insurance companies, appears likely to assume increasing social significance as it becomes more and more impossible for aggressive persons without family connections to achieve promotion and enlarge their functional capacities. The Rockefeller sons, nephews, and cousins, for example, are strewn throughout the Rockefeller enterprises in positions which they could never have hoped to attain so easily, whatever their abilities, without family sponsorship.

The families themselves see nothing extraordinary in this trend. Henry Ford, in talking to newspaper reporters upon the elevation of his only son, Edsel, to the presidency of the Ford Motor Company, naively exclaimed that he thought the "real story" lay in the fact that a youngster just out of his teens should show such ability that he was placed in charge of a billion-dollar enterprise! Morgan partnerships, once open to any man of the requisite abilities, are now often reserved for the sons of partners. Two sons of J. P. Morgan are partners; one son of Thomas W. Lamont is a partner; a son of Henry P. Davison, a former partner, has been made a partner, and F. Trubee Davison, another son, has been placed in charge of the American Museum of Natural History after having been Assistant Secretary of War under President Hoover.

Rarely are the families rebuffed as was Mrs. Moses Taylor, a large hereditary stockholder of the National City Bank, by Charles E. Mitchell, president of the bank, in 1929. Riding high on the crest of the boom, Mitchell grandly refused to place a Taylor nephew in the bank and thundered that the bank was carrying its full quota of Taylors and Pynes. Mrs. Taylor left in a rage and dumped her bank stock on the market—just before the crash. The incident is reported to have saved her millions of dollars and to have embarrassed the bank in the market manipulation of its own stock preliminary to the proposed acquisition of the Corn Exchange Bank.

Scratch any big corporation executive and the chances are even that one will find an in-law of the wealthiest families. There is, of course, an immediate, practical reason for placing members of the family, and distant relatives, too, upon the pay rolls of enterprises in which other people have invested. The reason is that the jobs keep these individuals from making claims upon their wealthier relatives and from engaging in activities that bring contumely or censure down upon the vested repute of the family.

Although a few of the present owners of big fortunes are the architects of these fortunes, in most cases the present generation in possession of immense resources has simply inherited. This fact is emphasized and underscored, so that the most unperceptive may see it, by the number of women regnant over stupendous incomes, although they have never engaged in finance, industry, or commerce, have never invented anything, have never played any role whatever in production. They are social pensioners who by no stretch of imagination could be said to have given society any commensurate return for the preposterous incomes which they find it impossible to expend rationally.

In 1936 the following nineteen American women, some of tender years, were all in absolute possession of fortunes of $25,000,000 or more that gave a return of more than $1,000,000 annually: Mary Katherine Reynolds (tobacco), Doris Duke Cromwell (tobacco), Mary Duke Biddle (tobacco and banking), Mrs. Joseph E. Davies (Postum), Helena Woolworth McCann and Jessie Woolworth Donahue (5-and-10 cent stores), Countess Barbara Hutton Mdivani Haugwitz-Reventlow (5-and-10 cent stores), Mrs. H. S. Wilks (stocks and realty), Mrs. Payne Whitney (petroleum), Mrs. Charles Shipman Payson, née Joan Whitney (petroleum), Gertrude Vanderbilt Whitney (petroleum and railroads), Mrs. Moses Taylor (National City Bank), Mrs. Andrew Carnegie (steel), Mrs. Margaret C. Miller, née Louise Carnegie (steel), Mrs. Alexander Hamilton Rice,* née Eleanor Elkins and later married to a Widener (tobacco, utilities), Mrs. Horace E. Dodge (automobiles), Mrs. Matilda Wilson (automobiles), Isabel Dodge Sloan (automobiles), and Mrs. John T. Dorrance (Campbell Soup).[5] The gigantic fortune of Mrs. H. S. Wilks, consisting originally of half the holdings of Hetty Green and all those of the late Matthew Astor Wilks, was increased by $28,000,-000 to nearly $75,000,000 in 1936, when she was named the sole beneficiary in the will of her brother, E. H. R. Green, who left his wife a relatively small income.

* Died, 1937.

The income-tax returns for 1924 * portray scores of other women, and even infants, in receipt of Gargantuan revenues, although in some cases possession of fortunes was not absolute; family income was distributed in many instances so as to reduce the whole tax liability. But the cases where possession was absolute, numbering in all several hundred, prove beyond question (what was always known to the sophisticated) that accumulated wealth is not a reward for any tangible contribution to society made by the possessor. Many of these women inherited from husbands and fathers who also had never, even by casuistic interpretation, made any more than a dubiously ornamental contribution to society.

A valuable study showing that American fortunes have arrived at a period of stability and that their owners are largely born to the purple like so many lords, dukes, and earls, was completed in 1925 by Professor Pitrim Sorokin of Harvard University.⁸ Most American millionaires now living were sired by merchants, manufacturers, bankers, financiers, businessmen, or inactive capitalists, Sorokin found. These latecomers did not, in other words, buffet their way out of a fairly matched individualistic rough-and-tumble bearing their newly gained riches.

Sorokin discovered that "the percentage of living millionaires whose fathers followed 'money-making' occupations is much higher than that of the deceased group. This fact, taken together with some further data, gives a basis to state that the wealthy class of the United States is becoming less and less open, more and more closed, and is tending to be transformed into a castelike group."

Among millionaires of the last generation Sorokin discovered that 38.8 per cent had started poor whereas among living millionaires only 19.6 per cent started life in humble circumstances. Of the older generation 29.7 per cent began life as millionaires whereas of the present generation no less than 52.7 per cent were independently wealthy upon attaining their majorities and 31.5 per cent sprouted from comfortably prosperous surroundings.

The present marked tendency toward intrafamily transmission of occupation and status among the rich means, according to this conservative authority, that class differentiation is becoming more and

* See note 7, chapter II.

more hereditary in the United States. "American society is being transformed—at least in its upper stratum—into a society with rigid classes and well-outlined class divisions," he says.

If this is true of the upper class it can be no less true of the lower classes, who may not hope to attain, through individual effort, what others now possess and retain with a deathlike grip. Modern capitalism has become, like feudalism before it, a family affair.

# II

## The Sixty Families

As FAMILIES have grown and intertwined, as incomes have been apportioned among many dynastic heirs, the tremendous revenues accruing to the family entities have eluded proper notice. It has been assumed that the relative profusion of large individual incomes betokens a rather wide dispersal of great wealth, at least throughout the upper class. This is not the case, however, as is disclosed both when fortunes are analyzed from a family standpoint and when a count is made of the numerous nonwealthy, relics of a more prosperous day, that clutter the *Social Register*.

Although the Rockefeller and Ford fortunes exceed $1,000,000,000 each, there are several families whose accumulations closely approach these in magnitude. And the Rockefeller fortune is only one large segment of the vast Standard Oil Trust, representing no more than one quarter of the original joint participation. Other great Standard Oil fortunes, to mention only the inner conclave, are those of the Harknesses, Whitneys, Paynes, Flaglers, Rogers, Bedfords, and Pratts. In the outer conclave are the Pierces, Archbolds, Folgers, Chesebroughs, and Cutlers. The Jennings, the Benjamins, and some other families are also part of the Standard Oil alliance.

One may deduce the taxable net incomes from the 1924 tax returns, and the entire accumulation represented by such incomes at five per cent, but in so doing it must be remembered that the large fortunes have unknown reserve funds in tax-exempt securities and utilize legal loopholes, such as family corporations, to escape their full tax assessments. Estimates and appraisals from authoritative corollary sources, which will be cited, show that one can achieve a general approximation by multiplying by three the size of the fortunes and income indicated by the tax returns, providing for legal

23

deductions up to fifteen per cent of income for noncommercial investments, for paper losses, for tax-exempt income, and for some of the deductions based upon miscellaneous technicalities.

The table (pages 26-27), assembled on the above basis (working back to income from the rate of tax indicated by each individual payment) and checked against official appraisals and declarations, some of which are cited later, sets forth the number of members of each of the sixty richest families that in 1924 paid Federal income taxes, *under the family name,* on the aggregate amount of taxable income shown (persons not using the family name are arbitrarily omitted or classified with the family whose name they use; there are a few omissions which will be mentioned).

The reader should take special note of the names in the accompanying tabulation and should observe their recurrence throughout the narrative. These are the principal subjects of our inquiry. These, with few exceptions, constitute the living core of American capitalism.

The tax figures in the following were taken from *The New York Times,* September 1 to 15, 1925. Each individual income was first ascertained from each individual tax before it was added into the family group. As all these families have diversified holdings, the indicated source of income refers only to the primary source. Where evidence could not be found that large 1924 incomes recurred annually the families were excluded. Nonrecurring income is most frequently obtained from realized capital gains, i. e., profits from properties sold.

Certain omissions stem from the fact that some fortunes are entirely concentrated in tax-exempt securities and portions of others are so invested. The late Senator James G. Couzens of Michigan, one of the original Ford investors, who died in 1936 leaving an estate officially appraised at more than $30,000,000, is not included in the tabulation because his holdings were almost entirely of government securities and he regularly paid only a very small income tax. Henry L. Doherty, the public utilities operator, paid no tax for 1924, nor did J. Ogden Armour, Louis F. Swift, John R. Thompson, Jr., and some others.

The composition of the investment portfolios of the families would, of course, determine the precise amount of the fortune traceable through the tax returns. Two persons with identical incomes, one derived from a fortune concentrated fifty per cent in tax-exempt securities and another from a fortune invested to the extent of twenty-five per cent in tax-exempt securities, would pay different Federal taxes. It is manifestly impossible to delve into the composition of investments, but where prominent families appear toward the end of the list, families like the Goulds, Hills, and Drexels, whose claims to great wealth are well known—it is probable that large proportions of their invisible holdings are in tax-exempt securities. They may also be held in family corporations, of which there are many reporting under neutral names.

Another difficulty that interposes in attempting to spread a statistical panorama of the great fortunes is that rates of profit from investments vary. Investments bring in from three per cent to several hundred per cent, although high percentages of the latter variety are only occasional. Du Pont profits during the war were several hundred per cent; some of R. Stanley Dollar's shipping investments after the war, based upon fat politically-invoked government subsidies, yielded a return of several thousand per cent. It should be remembered, of course, that in dealing with the fortunes we are concerned with entities that are in flux, that are subject to constantly changing valuations.

The inability to produce precise figures on fortunes, rather than approximations, results, then, from no fault in plan or method, but rather from the extreme secrecy with which statistics on fortunes are guarded and from the very nature of fortunes. In individual instances the multiplication by three of the net fortune upon whose income a tax was paid may result in some distortion, but this appears to be the only way in which to obtain a general approximation; and as the method gives generally accurate results, the picture as a whole is not overdrawn. Rather is it very conservative. The absence of detailed figures about these accumulations, in an age which literally flaunts a chaos of statistics about subjects of little general interest, is clearly the fault of a government that at most times has been peculiarly sensitive to the wishes of millionaires.

Apart from the omissions of revenues from tax-exempt securities,

| FAMILY AND NUMBER OF TAX RETURNS | PRIMARY SOURCE OF WEALTH | AGGREGATE 1924 TAX | APPROXIMATE NET AGGREGATE INCOME TAXED | NET AGGREGATE FORTUNE TAXED | GROSS ADJUSTED FORTUNE AFTER MULTIPLYING BY 3 | MAXIMUM ESTIMATED FORTUNE |
|---|---|---|---|---|---|---|
| 1. 21 Rockefellers | Standard Oil | $73,309,989 | $17,955,000 | $359,100,000 | $1,077,300,000 | $2,500,000,000 |
| 2. 34 Morgan Inner Group | J. P. Morgan & Co. | 4,796,263 | 12,620,000 | 276,000,000‡ | 728,000,000‡ | ........ |
| *(Including Morgan partners and families and eight leading Morgan corporation executives)* | | | | | | |
| 3. 2 Fords | Ford Motor Co. | 4,766,863 | 11,000,000 | 220,000,000 | 660,000,000 | 1,000,000,000 |
| 4. 5 Harknesses | Standard Oil | 2,776,735 | 7,550,000 | 150,200,000 | 450,600,000 | 800,000,000 |
| 5. 3 Mellons | Aluminum Company | 3,237,876 | 7,500,000 | 150,000,000 | 450,000,000 | 1,000,000,000 |
| 6. 22 Vanderbilts | N. Y. Central R. R. | 2,148,892 | 6,005,000 | 120,100,000 | 360,300,000 | 800,000,000 |
| 7. 4 Whitneys | Standard Oil | 2,143,992 | 5,375,000 | 107,500,000 | 322,000,000 | 750,000,000 |
| 8. 28 Standard Oil Group | Standard Oil | 1,737,857 | 5,435,000 | 118,700,000 | 356,000,000 | ........ |
| *(Including Archbolds, Rogerses, Bedfords, Cutlers, Flaglers, Pratts and Benjamins, but excepting others)* | | | | | | |
| 9. 20 Du Ponts | E. I. du Pont de Nemours | 1,294,651 | 3,925,000 | 79,500,000 | 238,500,000 | 1,000,000,000 |
| 10. 8 McCormicks | Int. Harvester and Chi. Tribune | 1,332,517 | 3,520,000 | 70,400,000 | 211,200,000 | ........ |
| 11. 2 Bakers | 1st National Bank | 1,575,482 | 3,500,000 | 70,000,000 | 210,000,000 | 500,000,000 |
| 12. 5 Fishers | General Motors | 1,424,583 | 3,225,000 | 64,500,000 | 193,500,000 | 500,000,000 |
| 13. 6 Guggenheims | Amer. Smelting & Rfg. Co. | 817,836 | 2,185,000 | 63,700,000 | 190,100,000 | 500,000,000 |
| 14. 6 Fields | Marshall Field & Co. | 1,197,605 | 3,000,000 | 60,000,000 | 180,000,000 | ........ |
| 15. 5 Curtis-Boks | Curtis Pub. Co. | 1,303,228 | 2,900,000 | 58,000,000 | 174,000,000 | ........ |
| 16. 3 Dukes | Am. Tobacco Co. | 1,045,544 | 2,600,000 | 52,000,000 | 156,000,000 | ........ |
| 17. 3 Berwinds | Berwind-White Coal Co. | 906,495 | 2,500,000 | 50,000,000 | 150,000,000 | ........ |
| 18. 17 Lehmans | Lehman Brothers | 672,897 | 2,150,000 | 43,000,000 | 129,000,000‡ | ........ |
| 19. 3 Wideners | Am. Tob. & Pub. Utilities | 772,720 | 1,975,000 | 39,500,000 | 118,500,000 | ........ |
| 20. 7 Reynolds | R. J. Reynolds Tobacco Co. | 652,824 | 1,950,000 | 39,000,000 | 117,000,000 | ........ |
| 21. 3 Astors | Real Estate | 783,002 | 1,900,000 | 38,000,000 | 114,000,000 | 300,000,000 |
| 22. 6 Winthrops | Miscellaneous | 651,188 | 1,735,000 | 34,700,000 | 104,100,000 | ........ |
| 23. 3 Stillmans | National City Bank | 623,614 | 1,700,000 | 34,000,000 | 102,000,000 | 500,000,000 |
| 24. 3 Timkens | Timken Roller Bearing Co. | 781,435 | 1,850,000 | 37,000,000 | 111,000,000 | ........ |
| 25. 4 Pitcairns | Pittsburgh Plate Glass Co. | 752,545 | 1,666,000 | 33,200,000 | 99,600,000 | ........ |
| 26. 8 Warburgs | Kuhn, Loeb & Co. | 598,246 | 1,620,000 | 32,400,000 | 97,200,000‡ | ........ |
| 27. 4 Metcalfs | Rhode Island textile mills | 623,817 | 1,510,000 | 30,200,000 | 90,600,000 | ........ |

| # | Name | Business | Taxes Paid | | | | |
|---|---|---|---|---|---|---|---|
| 28. | 3 Clarks | Singer Sewing Mach. Co. | 583,087 | 1,475,000 | 30,000,000 | 90,000,000 | ........ |
| 29. | 16 Phipps | Carnegie Steel Co. | 431,969 | 1,485,000 | 29,700,000 | 89,100,000 | 600,000,000 |
| 30. | 4 Kahns | Kuhn, Loeb & Co. | 565,668 | 1,440,000 | 28,800,000 | 86,400,000‡ | ........ |
| 31. | 2 Greens | Stocks and real estate | 443,021 | 1,200,000 | 24,000,000 | 72,000,000 | ........ |
| 32. | 2 Pattersons | Chicago Tribune, Inc. | 365,211 | 1,015,000 | 20,300,000 | 60,900,000 | ........ |
| 33. | 3 Tafts | Real Estate | 329,689 | 900,000 | 18,000,000 | 54,000,000 | ........ |
| 34. | 3 Deerings | International Harvester | 315,701 | 825,000 | 16,500,000 | 49,500,000 | ........ |
| 35. | 6 De Forests | Corp. law practice | 202,013 | 685,000 | 13,700,000 | 41,100,000‡ | ........ |
| 36. | 5 Goulds | Railroads | 154,563 | 565,000 | 11,300,000 | 33,900,000 | 400,000,000 |
| 37. | 3 Hills | Railroads | 226,827 | 366,000 | 7,200,000 | 21,600,000 | 150,000,000 |
| 38. | 2 Drexels | J. P. Morgan & Co. | 131,616 | 350,000 | 7,000,000 | 21,000,000 | 100,000,000 |

FAMILY TAXES PAID BY INDIVIDUALS

| # | Name | Business | Taxes Paid | | | |
|---|---|---|---|---|---|---|
| 39. | Thomas Fortune Ryan*† | Stock market | 791,851 | 1,800,000 | 36,000,000 | 108,000,000 |
| 40. | H. Foster (Cleveland) | Auto Parts | 569,894 | 1,700,000 | 34,000,000 | 106,000,000 |
| 41. | Eldridge Johnson | Victor Phonograph | 542,627 | 1,250,000 | 25,000,000 | 75,000,000 |
| 42. | Arthur Curtiss James | Copper and railroads | 521,388 | 1,200,000 | 24,000,000 | 72,000,000 |
| 43. | C. W. Nash | Automobiles | 459,776 | 1,100,000 | 22,000,000 | 66,000,000 |
| 44. | Mortimer Schiff | Kuhn, Loeb & Co. | 459,410 | 1,100,000 | 22,000,000 | 66,000,000 |
| 45. | James A. Patten | Wheat market | 425,348 | 1,000,000 | 20,000,000 | 60,000,000‡ |
| 46. | Charles Hayden* | Stock market | 427,979 | 1,000,000 | 20,000,000 | 60,000,000 |
| 47. | Orlando F. Weber | Allied Chemical & Dye Corp. | 406,582 | 900,000 | 18,000,000 | 54,000,000 |
| 48. | George Blumenthal | Lazard Frères | 415,621 | 900,000 | 18,000,000 | 54,000,000‡ |
| 49. | Ogden L. Mills | Mining | 372,827 | 800,000 | 16,000,000 | 48,000,000 |
| 50. | Michael Friedsam*† | Merchandising | 292,396 | 700,000 | 14,000,000 | 42,000,000 |
| 51. | Edward B. McLean | Mining | 281,125 | 700,000 | 14,000,000 | 42,000,000 |
| 52. | Eugene Higgins | New York real estate | 279,265 | 700,000 | 14,000,000 | 42,000,000 |
| 53. | Alexander S. Cochran*† | Textiles | 271,542 | 700,000 | 14,000,000 | 42,000,000 |
| 54. | Mrs. L. N. Kirkwood | | 268,556 | 625,000 | 12,500,000 | 37,500,000 |
| 55. | Helen Tyson | | 258,086 | 600,000 | 12,000,000 | 36,000,000 |
| 56. | Archer D. Huntington*† | Railroads | 226,353 | 575,000 | 11,500,000 | 34,500,000 |
| 57. | James J. Storrow*† | Lee Higginson & Co. | 222,571 | 575,000 | 11,500,000 | 34,500,000‡ |
| 58. | Julius Rosenwald*† | Sears, Roebuck & Co. | 208,812 | 500,000 | 10,000,000 | 30,000,000 |
| 59. | Bernard M. Baruch | Stock market | 268,142 | 625,000 | 12,500,000 | 37,500,000 |
| 60. | S. S. Kresge | Merchandising | 188,608 | 500,000 | 10,000,000 | 30,000,000 |

*Deceased.  †Fortune left to family.  ‡ Partly theoretical as income consisted in varying measure of fees.

there are other omissions from the tabulation—some purposeful, because, although the individual incomes were large, they did not compare at all with the vast family concentrations or with the biggest individual payments. In certain cases, on the other hand, it was impossible to allocate income to any single family. For example, income of the Hutton-Post-Woolworth-McCann-Donahue group, emanating from three distinct fortunes, could not be attributed to any single family, and the individual segments of each of these fortunes were not large enough to be included with our biggest families. The Hutton-Post-Woolworth-McCann-Donahue combination belongs, however, among our sixty leading families. Seven persons in this group (and this does not by any means include all) paid taxes on a gross indicated fortune of $165,600,000.

Certain of the less wealthy family dynasties, that resemble the richest families in every respect except the size of their accumulations, have been left out of the tabulation although they will appear now and then in our narrative. Among these are the Aldriches; the Candlers (Coca-Cola); the Cannons (textiles); the Dollars (shipping); the Huntingtons (shipping); the Swifts (packing); the Fleischmanns (yeast and distilling); the Pulitzers (publishing); the Goelets (real estate and the Chemical Bank and Trust Company); the Grays (tobacco); the Bradys (public utilities); the Harrimans (railroads); the Heinzes (pickles); the Kresses (retail stores); the Lewisohns (copper); the Hearsts (publishing and mining); the Manvilles (asbestos); the Elkins; the Mills-Reids (mining and publishing); the McFaddens and McLeans, both of Philadelphia; the McClintics; the Phillipses, of Rhode Island; the Twomblys; the Weyerhaeusers (lumber and shipping); the Cudahys (packing), and quite a few others.

Some omissions have been made necessary by the studiously haphazard way in which the tax figures were issued. The legislation enabling the publication of the figures even in jumbled form was understandably very unpopular with the rich, who were able to get it repealed before the 1925 figures were issued; public opinion would be greatly embittered, to be sure, if the monotonous yearly recurrence of stupendous individual revenues could be observed. The assembling of the figures for each family was therefore not without difficulty, for they could not be presented by the newspapers in orderly fashion, even had the newspapers so desired to present them. No attempt was made to include in the tabulation the collateral descendants of the large fortune-builders; were they included (and it would be necessary to obtain the co-operation of the Bureau of Internal Revenue for this to be done) each accumulation would be projected on a greatly enlarged scale. It is well to take note of this important fact.

Both the Dorrance (Campbell Soup) and Hartford (Great Atlantic and Pacific Tea) tax payments appear to have been overlooked by the journalists who combed the confused lists issued by the Bureau of Internal Revenue. Purposely omitted from our tabulation are individual fortunes not placed on a family basis, and among these are the accumulations of George W. Eastman of the Eastman Kodak Company, Andrew Carnegie (evidently concentrated in tax-exempt securities), Charles M. Schwab (whom Clarence W. Barron appraised at $40,000,000 after examining Schwab's records), H. C. Frick, Frederick H. Prince, Harvey S. Firestone, Edward L. Doheny, Harry F. Sinclair, E. L. Cord, Walter P. Chrysler, Samuel Zemurray, Leonor F. Loree, Earl D. Babst, and Harrison Williams. These men or their heirs, however, belong in the top circle of wealth for one reason or the other, although their individual power is decidedly limited. Whether their fortunes will eventually be placed on a permanent family basis is not yet certain.

The broad picture is shown, however, in the tabulation. Only the Morgan group represents a nonfamily collection of incomes. As the Morgan incomes do not derive in a primary sense from property ownership they will be given special notice.

The conservative character of the results obtained by multiplying the taxed fortunes by three, in order to obtain the size of the whole fortune, may be illustrated. The estate of Thomas Fortune Ryan, who died in 1928, was officially appraised at approximately $135,000,000, and this may be compared with $108,000,000, his indicated total fortune in 1924. Allowing for the rise in securities values between 1924 and the time of the appraisal, the figure for 1924 would seem to be almost exact. The largest individual estate ever appraised in New York was that of Payne Whitney, who died in 1927 worth $186,000,000, which may be compared with the valuation in the foregoing table of $322,000,000 on the joint fortune of four Whitneys.

Payne Whitney's share in the group of four, on the basis of a tax payment of $1,676,626, is computed at approximately $220,000,000. The fortune of six members of the Field family is given at $180,000,000 in the tabulation, which may be compared with $120,000,000 as the appraised approximate value of the estate of Marshall Field I in 1906.

J. P. Morgan's Federal tax in 1924 was $574,379 on about $1,500,000 of income. This in turn was five per cent on $30,000,000 and multiplying this by three we obtain $90,000,000. The estate he inherited in 1913 was officially valued at $77,465,975.38, but about $20,000,000 of cash had to be disbursed for specific bequests to various members of the family and was replaced only by the sale of the Morgan art collection which had been lent—not given, as a gullible public had fondly supposed—to the Metropolitan Museum of Art; there was, of course, a futile storm of public indignation when the younger Morgan calmly repossessed himself of his father's art treasure. It is not too much to assume an appreciation of only $13,500,000 in this fortune from 1913 to 1924.

The taxable Phipps fortune is set at $29,700,000 in our tabulation and the multiplied fortune at $89,100,000. Yet Clarence W. Barron, the late editor of *The Wall Street Journal*, gave credence to the report that the Phippses actually represent $600,000,000.[1] If Barron's information was correct, it would indicate a tremendous nontaxable revenue accruing to the Phippses, who were among the original participants in the Carnegie Steel Company.

John T. Dorrance, head of the Campbell Soup Company, made a fine art of concealing his wealth. Until his death in 1930 it was not known that he was worth $120,000,000 and would leave the third largest estate of record outside New York until Richard B. Mellon left $200,000,000. The estate consisted of $80,000,000 of Campbell Soup Company stock and $35,000,000 of United States government bonds. As the Campbell Soup Company was privately owned, revenues of stockholders could be concealed; they could be disbursed in part as nontaxable stock dividends or could simply be transferred into surplus, enhancing the value of the shares but involving no taxable money transfer.

But even by surveying estates that have been made public one does not gain precise knowledge of the greatest fortunes. The former holdings of John D. Rockefeller, Sr., were transferred privately to his son, who will presumably pass them on with similar discreetness to his own children. And even the recorded estates often represent merely residuary fragments. Huge sums have been transferred to relatives, to privately controlled foundations, and to family corporations in very many cases before the death of the owner. This accounts for the relatively modest size of estates left by men like Otto H. Kahn, who was popularly said to be "broke."

One special factor that makes the fortunes seem unduly small when projected from the 1924 tax figures and contrasted with official appraisals was the amazing administration of the Treasury Department by Andrew W. Mellon. Under this very wealthy man the widest latitude in the interpretation of tax laws was allowed people of wealth, as was subsequently revealed in a Senate investigation. It may therefore be that a closer approximation to the actual fortunes would be obtained by multiplying the taxed fortunes of 1924 by four.

For contemporary purposes, moreover, it would be best to regard most of the 1924 fortunes as enhanced by 25 per cent, for it is the opinion of conservative economists that the secular rate of increase in wealth in the United States is 2 per cent annually; and the fortunes grow with the country.

Certain of the individuals in the 1924 Federal tax list are now dead, but this does not alter significantly the status of the fortunes which, in almost all cases, were passed on to children or other relatives. To discuss the details of transfer would unnecessarily complicate the exposition.

## II

Very few persons of great wealth classify as newly rich. The only comparatively recent fortune of the first magnitude is that of Henry Ford, and its formidable proportions were discernible as long ago as 1917. The Dorrance fortune was created between 1910 and 1920, and the only other large, relatively recent accumulation appears to be that of the five Fisher brothers of Detroit, who were worth $196,-500,000 on the basis of 1924 tax figures and were reported by Barron to represent $1,000,000,000. Walter P. Chrysler, motorcar manufacturer, has survived the intense competition in the automotive industry furnished by the Morgans, Du Ponts, Fishers, and Fords; but it is not yet entirely clear whether he will emerge with his holdings intact and whether they will be large. The Hartford and Woolworth fortunes are of prewar vintage.

The only noteworthy postwar fortune belongs to Floyd B. Odlum, a Morgan corporation executive formerly with the Electric Bond and Share Company, and it is probably not very large. Odlum formed the Atlas Corporation, an investment trust, on the basis of a $40,000 investment in 1924. This enterprise now participates in nearly every industry, having acquired its equities at extreme depression lows. *The New York Times* of April 23, 1933, reported that Atlas Corporation then owned assets aggregating $100,000,000. Atlas assets are valued now at more than double this sum; the corporation is probably the biggest investment trust in the world. Odlum has been designated, with some truth, the sole newcomer to win in the great postwar boom and collapse.

It is a common popular error to suppose that men like Owen D. Young, of the General Electric Company; Walter S. Gifford, of the American Telephone and Telegraph Company; Thomas W. Lamont, of J. P. Morgan and Company; Albert H. Wiggin, until recently head of the Chase National Bank; Alfred P. Sloan, Jr., of General Motors; and Walter C. Teagle, of the Standard Oil Company of New Jersey, are leaders in the entourage of great wealth. Such figures, carefully publicized, are merely executives for the main groups of banking capital that represent the golden dynasties. These men have no independent power; they do not speak for themselves any more than do actors on a stage.

The importance of men like Lamont, Wiggin, and Sloan should not, however, be underestimated. Each has considerable wealth in his own right and before the World War would, perhaps, have been considered on his way to becoming a nabob of the first degree; but the power of each has been vastly greater than his personal wealth would indicate simply because it is concentrated power individually delegated to them by many wealthier men. Only the vastness of other accumulations has thrown their personal accumulations into second and third place. These men, however, cannot be judged on a quantitative basis; they must be approached from the qualitative standpoint. They are the virtuosi of capitalism, who do the work while beneficiaries of trust funds gamble at Biarritz or chase elephants through Africa.

An extraordinarily complex and resourceful personality like Thomas W. Lamont, who has been the brains of J. P. Morgan and Company throughout the postwar period and was a mentor of Woodrow Wilson in Wilson's second administration as well as of President Herbert Hoover throughout his fateful single term in the White House, has exercised more power for twenty years in the western hemisphere, has put into effect more final decisions from which there has been no appeal, than any other person. Lamont, in short, has been the First Consul *de facto* in the invisible Directory of postwar high finance and politics, a man consulted by presidents, prime ministers, governors of central banks, the directing intelligence behind the Dawes and Young Plans. Lamont is Protean; he is a diplomat, an editor, a writer, a publisher, a politician, a statesman —an international presence as well as a financier. He will be given more attention later.

Just as few new fortunes have been brought to port in the past twenty years, so have few foundered, despite economic storms. In the depression of 1920–21 the Armour fortune shrank seriously, but $25,000,000 was recouped through the accidental medium of a once worthless oil company stock into which the late Ogden Armour had placed a small sum on speculation. In the more recent collapse of 1929–33 the inherited fortune of Clarence W. Mackay underwent considerable downward revision. The Nash fortune appears to have been reduced also. The Lees and Higginsons of Boston, secondary figures, were seriously involved in the debacle of Ivar Kreuger, international adventurer who was himself never wealthy but was merely striving in time-sanctioned ways to achieve riches. Samuel Insull was only a corporation promoter for a Chicago group headed by the Fields; he had no independent status, as was shown when the Morgan banks foreclosed on the Insull properties. The Van Sweringens were mere bubbles inflated by J. P. Morgan and Company.

These partial casualties aside, no great private accumulations have been more than passingly embarrassed for many decades. It is a far cry to the days of Daniel Drew and John W. Gates when the quotations of the stock market could pronounce doom on a multimillionaire, although they can still embarrass a mere millionaire. Conversely, few who were poor in 1921 are not still in the same harsh circumstances. The rigid state of affairs lends point to the conclusions of Professor Sorokin that may have seemed premature in 1925.

### III

The big fortunes of America are mobilized in protective phalanxes that recall feudal dynastic alignments wherein many small but powerful families pledged allegiance to one dominant family of more than average strength, courage, daring, and intelligence, and obtained mutual benefits.

The Morgans may be likened to American Bourbons who have slowly, remorselessly, broken down the power of scores that refused to bend the knee, surrounding themselves with a host that accepts Morgan leadership. The Rockefellers may be likened to the Hapsburgs; the Mellons to the Hohenzollerns, the Du Ponts to the Romanovs, etc. Whereas the titled dynasties of feudal Europe divided the continent territorially, their untitled American capitalist counterparts have divided their continent by industries. This division was, of course, not conscious at first. A distinct advantage enjoyed by the American millionaires, incidentally, is that their power is not recognized by titles which would serve continually to remind the average citizen of their exalted status.

The private banking partnerships and the informal alliance are the ramparts behind which the dominant families deploy. In order of importance these private banking partnerships are J. P. Morgan and Company; Kuhn, Loeb and Company; Brown Brothers Harriman and Company; Lehman Brothers; Dillon, Read and Company; Bonbright and Company (Morgan); Lazard Frères; J. and W. Seligman; Speyer and Company; Goldman, Sachs and Company; Hallgarten and Company, and Ladenburg, Thalmann and Company.

Certain families operate without benefit of partnership. The Mellons, for example, work directly through the big commercial banks of Pittsburgh, which they control. The Du Ponts have a family holding company, the Christiana Corporation, which, according to John J. Raskob, gives them the largest industrial participation of any family in the United States. J. P. Morgan and Company, however, includes the Du Ponts among its supporting families. The Rockefellers function through the Chase National Bank of New York, largest commercial bank in the nation. Ford has the Ford Motor Company and enters the money market through the National City Bank. The Warburgs and Schiffs function through Kuhn, Loeb and Company, the Lehmans through the partnership of Lehman Brothers. A few families function primarily through their own law firms; two that do this are the Clark family of the Singer Sewing Machine fortune and the Taft family (Cincinnati real estate).

As we have observed, Morgan is not the wealthiest of our wealthy men. He derives his unique and perhaps unprecedented power from the massed resources of the many families and their corporations that stand behind him. The allegiance of these families was gradually won over a period of many decades by Morgan prestige, earned by a demonstrated ability in ruthless financial statesmanship and political intrigue exercised on behalf of the rich. The individual partners of J. P. Morgan and Company are not, by strict standards, independently wealthy, but they are men gifted in many ways and possessed of extraordinary financial acumen that is placed at the service of the Morgan clients; they are, too, adept in making oddly assorted but potent connections throughout the political and social fabric. Their rewards are fees, commissions, and opportunities to participate individually and collectively in big financial coups. Some of them, like the late Dwight W. Morrow, are not exclusively money-minded, and probably get their principal recompense in the satisfaction of participating in consequential intrigues. Contrary to the impression even in relatively well-informed quarters, the versatile Morgan partners themselves own very little stock in corporations, as was proved by recent corporation reports to the Federal Securities and Exchange Commission. It is the Morgan clients that own the stock; J. P. Morgan and Company merely sees that the big stockholders are served in accordance with expectations.

J. P. Morgan and Company delights to baffle inquiring senators and the public alike by pointing out blandly, of late through the slyly debonair T. W. Lamont, how slight are the holdings of the partners in various corporations. The most salient instance in which the Morgans referred to their puny participation was in rejoinder to the weighty charge that they maneuvered America into the World War, when J. P. Morgan and Company was purchasing agent for the Allies at a commission of one per cent. Of the hundreds of firms dealt with, the Morgan partners stress, always with tongue in cheek (it is to be hoped), that they held shares in only eleven, and these shares amounted to no more than three per cent of all outstanding.

The House of Morgan does not need to own much property; it has, instead, a technique which it merchandises, and thus escapes the very real risks of property ownership.

Whereas J. P. Morgan and Company has often been sternly criticized, the record shows that in recent decades its clients, excepting the Du Ponts, have scarcely been mentioned in condemnation. The banking firm, absorbing the blows of public opinion, acts as a great buffer between the public and the ultimate beneficiaries of collective acts and policies that stir up public resentment.

The Morgan firm and its affiliated commercial banks act, broadly, on behalf of such tremendous accumulations as those of the Vanderbilts, Goulds, Drexels, Wideners, Berwinds, Phippses, Hills, Dukes, Ryans, McCormicks, Bakers, Du Ponts, Fishers, Fields, Jameses, and others. All these families, it should now be clear, own more wealth than the individuals they deputize to watch over their interests. In general, they leave most of the supervision of fiscal affairs to J. P. Morgan and Company, or act upon Morgan advice, knowing it to be in their own interest. From time to time there are, to be sure, minor shifts of allegiance as between the Morgans and the Rockefellers, or the Morgans and the Mellons, but only some colossal blunder by J. P. Morgan and Company in serving its clients could lessen its power substantially. (Had Germany won the war, for example, J. P. Morgan and Company would surely have gone on the rocks.) The massed voting power of the stocks and bonds of its client families is utilized, except in unusual instances, in accord with the formal decision of the Morgan partners in meeting assembled.

J. P. Morgan and Company has branches in Philadelphia, London, and Paris. The principal commercial banks in which it exercises dominance are the Guaranty Trust Company of New York, the

Bankers Trust Company, the First National Bank of New York, and the New York Trust Company. Guaranty Trust is the third largest bank in the nation, trailing after Chase National and National City, respectively. But the four Morgan commercial banks collectively outweigh both Chase National and National City in total assets, deposits, and resources.

Neither the Morgan firm nor its partners own much stock in any of these banks. There are Morgan partners or executives on all their boards, however, and the final decision on their operation, as all of Wall Street knows, is made by the Morgan partners. Naturally, J. P. Morgan and Company, desirous of minimizing the public conception of its power, denies this. Except for the Bakers at the First National, the Morgan banks' executives are hired men who on their own account represent no vast accumulation. Significantly, Morgan partners preponderate on the executive committees of the banks, excepting the First National. Thomas W. Lamont is chairman of the executive committee of the Guaranty Trust Company.

The total extent of Morgan power in American industry and finance defies statistical measurement. We can, however, list 35 banks, insurance companies, etc., and 60 nonfinancial corporations. . . . If we include companies tied in a similar way . . . we find another $16,200,000,000 of assets, in 16 banks, insurance companies, etc., and in 26 miscellaneous corporations.

These 51 banks, etc., and 86 nonbanking corporations with their combined assets of $46,200,000,000 include foreign corporations with over three billion of assets. The American total—nearly 43 billion—represents nearly one-sixth the total wealth of all corporations in the United States.

But like a medieval fortress, this inner stronghold is surrounded by open stretches on which maneuvers can take place only with the knowledge and good will of the ruling lord. Morgan control shades off into Morgan dominance and dominance shades off into Morgan influence. . . . We can list over 80 banks and other corporations with $16,500,000,000 of assets, mostly in some degree under Morgan influence. . . . These various connections, with their varying degrees of control, dominance and influence, bring roughly $77,600,000,000 of corporation assets into some relation to the Morgan groups. . . . The total within the United States—over $72,000,000,000 as of January 1, 1932—is more than one-fourth of American corporate wealth.[2]

At least thirty-six large nonbanking corporations with assets totaling about $22,000,000,000 have some direct connection with the John D. Rockefeller interests.[3]

Aligned with the Mellons are various Pennsylvania and Ohio families, small but nevertheless collectively powerful owing to the leadership of the Mellons, with their extensive personal stake.

We find the Mellon group dominant in about 35 banks and insurance companies and in about 40 nonfinancial corporations having total combined assets of $4,250,000,000. . . . The Mellon group is directly or indirectly represented . . . in other banks and corporations having about $13,000,000,000 of total assets. This larger group includes eleven banks and corporations clearly under Morgan influence, with assets of $6,000,000,000; and three companies close to Kuhn, Loeb & Co., with assets of $4,000,000,000; and 29 other banks and corporations with assets of $2,900,000,000.[4]

Kuhn, Loeb partners hold few directorships and exercise their influence in nonfinancial corporations chiefly through giving technical financial advice. But by a long-established relationship they are a definite power not only in several railroads but in a few other companies, including Western Union Telegraph Co., Westinghouse Electric & Manufacturing Co. (with Mellon, and now with Rockefeller also), U. S. Rubber Co. (now with Du Pont), and Hudson and Manhattan R. R. Co. . . .[5]

Both the Schiff and Warburg families are represented by Kuhn, Loeb and Company, which participates in the Bank of Manhattan and the Chemical Bank and Trust Company. In the former the two families are associated with the moderately wealthy Stephen Baker group and in the latter with the Gerry-Goelets. Both these institutions are classed as independent, i. e., they are free of the Morgans and the Rockefellers.

Lehman Brothers is fully as important as Kuhn, Loeb and Company, both because of its mercantile connections and its eminence in New York State politics. The partners of this firm, representing the Governor of New York State and the numerous other members of the Lehman family, whose combined fortune at 1924 levels was at least $129,000,000, or sixteenth in the nation, own approximately twenty per cent of the stock of the Corn Exchange Bank and Trust Company, a large commercial institution with much prestige and many branches. This bank is in a position to become to the Lehmans what Chase is to the Rockefellers and the "Big Four" is to J. P. Morgan and Company. The Commercial National Bank and Trust Company of New York, a $100,000,000 enterprise; the Lehman Corporation, a $100,000,000 investment trust; and the Pan-American Trust Company (the old Harbor State Bank) are also dominated by the Lehmans. The second largest interest in this last, newly reorganized and expanded institution is held by the National Bank of Mexico, biggest commercial bank below the Rio Grande. The power of the Lehmans, like that of the Mellons before 1920, is hardly appreciated; like the power of the Morgans, it undoubtedly exceeds the size of their personal holdings. By marriage the Lehmans are linked to the Lazard Frères partners.

The National City Bank, second largest in the country, is in certain respects the most remarkable of all Wall Street institutions. It is not uniquely connected with any private partnership and, instead of representing one or two dominant families, since the Rockefeller group left it, it has represented a coalition of moderately powerful families, no one of which gives full allegiance to any financial overlord, and each one of which insistently presses for its own desires, often irrespective of the wishes of the Wall Street community. This circumstance has made National City something of a buccaneer in recent Wall Street history, when other banks have evinced a disposition to settle down to the quietly lucrative practices of the experienced English banks. Until 1929 the National City group was intent upon defending its pre-eminence against the Chase National Bank, but has not been able to withstand the Rockefeller influence in Chase.

For many years National City was ruled as a family stronghold by the Stillman, Pyne, Taylor, Dodge, and William and Percy Rockefeller families. It was long known as a Rockefeller institution, because the close partners of John D. Rockefeller—men like John D. Archbold and Henry H. Rogers—used it as a bludgeon in their wars of aggrandizement. This use of the bank was conspicuous in the great copper war early this century when the forces of F. Augustus Heinze were vanquished.

In time the principal Rockefeller allegiance was transferred to the smaller Equitable Trust Company and then in 1929, to the Chase. The William Rockefeller faction remained, however, with the Stillmans, Taylors, and Pynes, in the National City Bank. The Pratts took over the Brooklyn Trust Company as their instrument of personal action, although they still listen closely to counsel from the other Rockefeller clansmen.

As National City in the postwar years came to represent a diverse coalition Henry Ford, ever suspicious of banking capital owing to its many abortive attempts to ruin him, began using it for his commercial business. He is believed in Wall Street to hold National City stock indirectly, but his spokesmen strenuously deny this. The Fords, however, are known to hold stock in large Detroit banks that are National City correspondents.

National City's leading stockholder is A. P. Giannini, the Italian-American who is the outstanding factor in California banking. Although his share in National City, held through the Transamerica Corporation, is as extensive as that of the Rockefellers in Chase National, his influence in National City is not comparable to that of the Rockefellers in their bank, for Giannini lacks the backing of many wealthy families or informal alliances.

The second largest stockholder in National City is J. P. Morgan and Company which obtained its National City interest largely by a fluke. J. P. Morgan and Company, traditionally ready to make personal loans to non-Morgan commercial bank chieftains (thus bringing them under its wing), in 1929 lent money to Charles E. Mitchell, former National City chairman, on the security of his National City stock. When Mitchell could not liquidate the loan, the collateral was quietly pre-empted by J. P. Morgan and Company. Morgan's prewar interest in National City had previously been relinquished.

The Stillman and William Rockefeller clique is the third largest National City stockholding factor.

National City is unique in that it has more than seventy-five foreign branches scattered over the globe; no other American bank has even five. National City has, consequently, corralled the business of the large importing and exporting interests and has been a significant factor in inducing the State Department from time to time to adopt or to modify aggressive diplomatic attitudes.

Over and above all others, most of the important copper and other nonferrous metal interests came to look to this institution for banking guidance, largely because copper is the institution's main economic foundation. Ever since 1895 the National City has acted for the Anaconda Copper Mining Company (Amalgamated Copper Company), which in 1929 produced more than forty per cent of the world's copper. The bank's copper dominance has brought into its orbit, partially or entirely, such mining lords as William Randolph Hearst, the Guggenheims, the Lewisohns, the Phelps-Dodges, the Nichols, and others.

The realty-owning Goelets, as we have observed, bulk large in the Chemical Bank and Trust Company. They are also important stockholders in the Fulton Trust Company, largest of institutions that supervise personal trusts. The big Central Hanover Bank and Trust Company is ruled by William Woodward, race-track sportsman, who inherited it from his father; it is the only one of the prewar personal banking institutions left unattached to an outstanding bloc.

The Irving Trust Company operates on behalf of many relatively small groups that, however, are strong in union. Its dominant voice appears to be the Skinner textile family, and the bank is consequently a force in the textile field; but the Du Ponts are said recently to have become heavy stockholders. The Equitable Trust Company was owned by Chase National, was sold to Charles Hayden, and is now owned by the Manufacturers Trust Company; the Farmers Loan and Trust Company is owned by National City. Excepting the very old and conservative Bank of New York and Trust Company, which functions largely on behalf of the scions of the pre-Civil War land fortunes, and the staid Fifth Avenue Bank, favorite of dowagers, this virtually exhausts the New York banking field.

Leading Philadelphia, Chicago, and Boston banks are no more than appendages of these institutions, operating independently only in strictly local affairs, a fact officially established as long ago as 1912 during the Pujo Money-Trust investigation.

All the financially dominant families are held together in their banking allegiances by a share in a single major type of enterprise or economic province. Their banks specialize in some single basic industry, or cluster of related industries, although fingers may stray into many other profitable economic pies. J. P. Morgan and Company and its affiliated banks have long dominated the provinces of steel, coal, and railroads. The Rockefellers control the province of petroleum through the Chase National Bank. The Corn Exchange Bank has become identified, in the main, with huge retail merchandising enterprises, but it is also the banker for the very important Allied Chemical and Dye Corporation in which Eugene Meyer is a large stockholder. The Mellon banks are based primarily on a monopoly of aluminum, with petroleum, steel, coal, and railroads of subsidiary interest.

All these groups, true enough, maintain positions throughout the industrial fabric. But each belongs principally to that sphere in which it wields virtually exclusive power. It has been only in certain of the newer industries, such as electric light and power, aviation, radio, bus transportation, chemicals, and automobiles, that in recent years the separate groups have maneuvered against each other. Each knows too well the punitive forces controlled by the others to hazard a major role where another group has a virtual monopoly.

Added to the families standing behind these massive financial phalanxes are the noncommercial foundations and insurance companies which intensify industrial, financial, and political strength in the controllers of their finances. The institutional foundations, which may be termed impersonal fortunes, are endowed schools, universities, religious establishments, social service organizations, hospitals, and similar undertakings. They are vital not only to financial but to social control; the management and discretionary utilization of their funds is in the hands of various of the Wall Street agencies of banking capital, mostly of the Rockefellers and the Morgans.

Finally, to suggest the vast amount of power wielded by such an aggregation as J. P. Morgan and Company, let us briefly scan the Morgan-controlled American Telephone and Telegraph Company.

The assets of A. T. & T., according to Berle and Means,[6] exceed in value the wealth of twenty-one states of the Union taken together. Its assets, say the same authorities, are greater than those of 8,000 average-sized corporations.

J. P. Morgan and Company would, of course, deny that it controls

A. T. & T., whose advertising stresses that no individual owns so much as one per cent of its stock. Working control, however, resides in a small Wall Street group, whose own stock is buttressed by shares under the control of brokers, although held "for account of others." Undisputed control—a consequence of the extensive public dispersal of more than half the company's shares—is exercised by the board of directors, and it is obviously a Morgan board. As of April 4, 1928, the second largest stockholder was George F. Baker, Sr. (Morgan), the seventh was Kidder, Peabody and Company (since reorganized by J. P. Morgan and Company), and the fifteenth and sixteenth were the estates of Mrs. A. M. Harkness and Edward S. Harkness. The twenty largest stockholders held 4.6 per cent of stock, but—there was no one among the myriad small stockholders strong enough to dispute their sway. The twenty largest stockholders of United States Steel, an acknowledged Morgan corporation (acknowledged perhaps because it is not a public utility and therefore not so sensitive to criticism), held only 1.7 per cent of stock at the same time.

Briefly, the greater the fractional distribution of share ownership among small stockholders, as Berle and Means illustrate with great detail in their epochal work, the more secure is the control of the managing directorship. Such control, even without ownership, is very valuable, for it is the directors that determine *who shall get the orders for the vast amount of materials consumed by the corporate giant and who shall receive on deposit its huge working capital.* It is control of other people's money that brings the greatest profits at the least risk.

The Morgan men on the A. T. & T. board are George F. Baker,* president of the First National Bank of New York; Samuel A. Welldon, vice-president of the First National Bank of New York; John W. Davis, chief counsel for J. P. Morgan and Company; and Myron C. Taylor, chairman of the finance committee of the United States Steel Corporation. The Rockefellers are represented by Winthrop W. Aldrich, chairman of the Chase National Bank. A Boston group closely identified with J. P. Morgan and Company is represented by Charles Francis Adams, director of the Union Trust Company of Boston and numerous corporations, former Secretary of the Navy,

* Died, 1937.

and father-in-law of Henry Sturgis Morgan, J. P. Morgan's son; W. Cameron Forbes, of J. M. Forbes and Company, a Boston enterprise, and former Governor General of the Philippines; George P. Gardner, director of the Morgan-controlled General Electric Company; Thomas Nelson Perkins, lawyer; and Philip Stockton, director of the First National Bank of Boston. The presidents of three railroads dependent upon J. P. Morgan and Company for financing, two insurance company heads, and James F. Bell, of General Mills, Inc., fill out the board with three A. T. & T. executives who have little to say outside the technical field.

But A. T. & T., despite its mammoth size, is only one corner of the Morgan empire that includes the United States Steel Corporation, the General Electric Company, the Consolidated Edison Company of New York, the United Gas Improvement Company of Philadelphia, the American and Foreign Power Company, the Electric Bond and Share Company, the Niagara Hudson Power Corporation, the United Corporation, Standard Brands, Inc., Montgomery Ward and Company, International Telephone and Telegraph Corporation, the American Can Company, the Kennecott Copper Corporation, the Newmont Mining Corporation, the Chesapeake and Ohio Railroad, the New York Central Railroad, General Motors Corporation, E. I. du Pont de Nemours and Company, and many others.

## IV

Only in comparison with the social plight of the mass of citizens do the figures on the large fortunes assume their correct relative dimensions. In 1892 there were only 4,047 fortunes of $1,000,000 or more; in 1914 there were 7,509, and in the next year, owing to the incidence of war profits, there were 10,450. The aggregate, according to Internal Revenue Bureau figures, rose to 11,800 in 1917, there to remain for several years. But in the 1929 boom the aggregate of $1,000,000 fortunes was pushed up to 38,889. Since then there has been a recession to about the 1917 level.

Incomes on $1,000,000 of capital or its equivalent increased by seventy-one per cent from 1914 to 1924 [7] and by four hundred per cent from 1914 to 1929.

Incomes of $1,000,000 derived from $20,000,000 or more of capital totaled only sixty in 1914 but increased to seventy-five in 1924 and to five hundred and thirteen in 1929—an advance of seven hundred per cent over 1914. But in the 1914-29 period gross national income increased only seventy-three per cent, so that the proportionate participation of the richest class in national revenue was very much greater in 1929 than in 1914. In the same fifteen-year period population increased by twenty-four per cent, which meant many more individual claimants to a share in the national income.

Despite the great boom in production during the war and postwar period, only 7,369,788 citizens had taxable income ($2,000 or more) in 1924 out of a nation of 70,000,000 adults. By 1929, with national income increasing by leaps and bounds, the number of income-tax payers was reduced by one-half. Even if five adult dependents are arbitrarily allocated to each taxpayer, there remains at least one-half the adult population which did not figure even indirectly in 1924 income-tax returns, i. e., had no taxable income.

Robert R. Doane, formerly a member of the staff of the National Bureau of Economic Research, has shown how much is retained under exceptionally favorable circumstances by each income class after all expenditures.[8] His findings, based upon 1929 data, follow:

| Income Class | Percentage of Income Saved | Percentage Distribution in Total Income |
|---|---|---|
| $1,000,000 and over | 74.4 | 8.3 |
| 500,000 to $1,000,000 | 71.2 | 4.5 |
| 300,000 to 500,000 | 67.2 | 4.1 |
| 150,000 to 300,000 | 43.4 | 4.8 |
| 100,000 to 150,000 | 35.1 | 2.6 |
| 50,000 to 100,000 | 31.4 | 5.7 |
| 25,000 to 50,000 | 30. | 7.7 |
| 10,000 to 25,000 | 21.8 | 10.6 |
| 5,000 to 10,000 | 13.9 | 7.5 |
| 3,000 to 5,000 | 11.2 | 14.5 |
| 2,000 to 3,000 | 10.6 | 11.5 |
| 1,000 to 2,000 | 4.8 | 14.3 |
| 1,000 and less | 2.6 | 3.9 |
| | | 100. |

This tabulation, based on Doane's computations, suggests that capital accumulations giving annual revenue of $300,000 or more are increased in a favorable year by more than fifty per cent of net revenue. Accumulations of $25,000 to $300,000 are increased by thirty to 43.4 per cent of net revenue. In short, the big fortunes tend to reproduce themselves on an enlarging scale, through the compounding of revenues which it is not possible for the few beneficiaries to expend on consumers' goods. At the same time, only a small fraction of the lower income group is able to better its economic status, and then only slightly. Expansion of fortunes does not proceed always at the above rate because capital investment is limited by the market, which in turn is restricted by the economic debility of the masses. But the tendency is well illustrated by Doane's figures, from which it is plain that the big fortunes, as a general rule, are automatically driven by swollen revenues to enlarge themselves from year to year.

Although incomes above $50,000 accounted for thirty per cent of individual savings in 1929, Bureau of Internal Revenue figures show that only 38,889 persons, or .05 of one per cent of the adult population, received such incomes. (Left out of consideration are incomes from wholly tax-exempt sources which are relatively few in number and not of public record.) These savings, concentrated in few hands, obviously had greater mobility and individual weight than the diffuse savings of the lower income groups which were, moreover, placed in the keeping of banks and insurance companies managed by representatives of the higher income strata. Incomes of $25,000 and more, reported in the boom year by only 102,578 persons, or .15 of one per cent of all adults, accounted for 37.7 per cent of individual savings.

Doane brings out very clearly that the bulk of gross revenue in the income classes below $5,000 was expended for food, clothing, housing, transportation, and medical care.

In 1929, Doane shows, about ninety-nine per cent of all citizens had gross incomes of $5,000 or less, and eighty-three per cent of all the liquid wealth was possessed by the one per cent that received $5,000 or more annually.[9] It is obvious that even in boom times very many Americans, much like chattel slaves, receive, in the richest

economic environment ever known to man, little more than enough
to reproduce and sustain themselves.

There are differences in types of income. This is illustrated in the
Department of Commerce estimate of national income for 1929 at
approximately $78,576,000,000, whereas income taxes for the same
year were paid in the same year on only $25,000,000,000 of income.
The figure for national income covered all types of money transfers
and was not income at all from an individual standpoint.

Of this national income $51,000,000,000 went into wages and sala-
ries. Were it not that most wages and salaries have to be expended
immediately for necessities, this would seem like a fair apportionment. No less than 35 per cent of the gross national income, or $27,-
500,000,000, consisted of unearned or property revenues—dividends,
interest, rent, royalties, and entrepreneurial withdrawals. It was
largely from these categories that the wealthy drew their income,
although bank depositors and insurance policyholders of the poorer
classes shared in interest payments. But the wealthy also dipped in
their hands for other payments, drawing huge—theoretically earned
—salaries and bonuses and commissions whose proportions they
themselves determined by the voting power of their stocks.

Total national savings in 1929 were about $2,400,000,000. Of this
total $1,423,000,000, or more than fifty per cent, was for the account
of corporations and only $979,000,000 was for individual account,
with the bulk of individual savings concentrated, as Doane shows,
in the income classes above $5,000.

While almost all income in the lower groups had to be released
upon receipt for necessities, less than twenty-five per cent of revenues
in the income group above $1,000,000 yearly sufficed, Doane shows,
for food, housing, transportation, health services, education, recreation, "philanthropy," clothing, and amusement. This was so even
though expenditures in the higher income group are customarily
made on a scale which, to persons unused to opulence, must seem
lavish. From the standpoint of the average citizen personal expenditures of the wealthy are, indeed, lavish; from the standpoint of the
need of society for these funds the personal expenditures are, it is
equally clear, criminal; but in relation to the grand revenue accruing
to the possessors of great wealth the personal expenditures are very

modest, almost frugal. Persons of limited means who scrimp to save from fifty to seventy-five per cent of income are properly termed misers, and are regarded with pitying scorn; but the rich of today enjoy the doubly paradoxical distinction of being spendthrifts, misers, and philanthropists simultaneously.

However one approaches the problem of income distribution, one is confronted with substantially the same conclusion: fewer than twenty per cent of the people possess nearly everything while eighty per cent own practically nothing except chattels. Wealth itself has become monopolized.

Not only does this contradiction bespeak extreme social weakness in the majority, but it also argues tremendous social strength in a minority—strength which it is virtually impossible to challenge peremptorily in our highly complex society. Authorities of conservative outlook may be consulted for information about the general condition which exists.[10]

Of 1,300,000 Americans who died in 1933 only ten thousand, or .77 of one per cent, left taxable estates of $50,000 or more, the average estate value being $80,000. There were 43,000,000 persons gainfully employed in the country in 1933 but upon only 3,600,000 could income taxes be effectively levied despite a lowering of the tax base to $1,000. These conditions are not of recent origin; they are merely present in an aggravated form.

With respect to the carefully nourished myth that the seignorial holdings of the upper income groups are steadily disintegrating, that they are being given away when they are not being dissipated, Robert H. Jackson, counsel of the Internal Revenue Bureau, in testimony before the Senate Finance Committee, August, 1935, declared:

"It is often asserted that large wealth is dissipated in three generations. . . . It was doubtless once true that all a grandfather saved from the fruits of his labor could be spent by a grandson. It is probably true today of very moderate fortunes. It is not true of large invested fortunes under present conditions. They not only perpetuate themselves, they grow.

"This is because they are now so large. A riotous-living heir to one of our larger fortunes would exhaust himself before he could exhaust the income alone of the estate. Furthermore, such estates are largely perpetuated in trusts, and every legal and economic obstacle to their dissipation is employed. . . . Most of the large estates as at present managed, we find, not only perpetuate themselves but are larger as they pass from generation to generation. . . ."

Very recent concrete proof of the truth of Jackson's analysis was given on August 4, 1937, when an accounting was made to the New York courts by the trustees of the estate of William Rockefeller, brother of John D. Rockefeller. William Rockefeller left $50,000,000 in 1922, stipulating that a portion of income be divided among four children and fourteen grandchildren and that the principal itself be reserved for his great-grandchildren. From 1922 to 1937 the children and grandchildren drew income of $9,514,834 from the estate, which increased in value by $13,947,361 in the fifteen-year period. It is expected that about fifty great-grandchildren will inherit in 1950 an estate which will be valued at $75,000,000 to $100,000,000 after the payment of income to children and grandchildren.

William Rockefeller, therefore, leaves fifty millionaires, who, if they keep the funds in trust, may expect to leave similarly magnified fortunes to their children, grandchildren, and great-grandchildren. Until Rockefeller's attorneys drew this will it had not been generally known that one could legally transmit wealth to the fourth generation, but law to the persons in power is merely something to be manipulated. Unless extraordinary events intervene, after 1950 there will be two great Rockefeller dynasties every member of which will be a millionaire or a multi-millionaire.

Even though the provision made by William Rockefeller was commented upon as unusual by the newspapers, it is not extraordinary. "The modern strategy of finance capital in tying up family trusts," says Professor Jerome Davis in *Capitalism and Its Culture*, "makes the rise of an hereditary caste inevitable. John J. Gray, former analyst and examiner of the Interstate Commerce Commission, says: 'I know of but one large fortune probated in forty years not so tied up for about one hundred years.'"

# III

# The Politics of Pecuniary Aggrandizement:

# 1896-1912

GOVERNMENT has been the indispensable handmaiden of private wealth since the origin of society. And far from having embellished history with a significant exception, the government of the United States, without the camouflage of custom or tradition, ritual or dogma, Church or Aristocracy, has actually done more to prove the truth of this generalization than have all the governments of Europe.

So perfect, so thorough, has been the collaboration of politics and private fortune since the founding of the American colonies that it is difficult to ascertain from the data of any given period where political intrigue on behalf of specific private interest has terminated. Very early in the New World the vague idea of public welfare was seized upon to cloak the clear-cut material aims of a restricted few. The apology heard in due course was the familiar *laissez-faire* rationalization of European capitalism that the general good is subsumed in unfettered individual enterprise.

The first fortunes on the virgin continent were out-and-out political creations—huge tracts of land and lucrative trading privileges arbitrarily bestowed by the British and Dutch crowns upon favorite individuals and companies; what are now whole eastern cities, counties, and states were once simply private demesnes. The early royal grants—forerunners of tariffs; ship and airplane subsidies; doles to banks and railroads by the Reconstruction Finance Corporation; war contracts let on a cost-plus basis; public-utility franchises; imperial grants of vast stretches of public lands to railroads, mining, and land companies; tax-exempt securities, etc.—were the sole property titles of the newly created landed aristocrats.

50

The fomenters and directors of the war against England did not, by and large, give their economic allegiance to the land. They owned commodities, small factories, stocks, bonds, and bills, or were desirous of effecting such ownership and introducing nationalistic mercantile capitalism into America. The constitutional government they erected, under the leadership notably of James Madison and Alexander Hamilton, was consciously designed to fortify the newer forms of property and at the same time to retard popular political movements.[1]

The Constitution, written in the furtive atmosphere of a *coup d'état* during secret deliberations of a convention called merely to regulate commerce, was received with hostility by the populace, which forced the precipitate addition of the first ten amendments. The document provided for a government of ostensible checks and balances (but really, as a wit has said, of all checks and no balances), and at the same time guaranteed the utmost freedom, unchecked and unbalanced, to propertied interests. In short, the government itself was tightly laced into a strait jacket, while private economic enterprise was given unprecedented freedom to establish and develop a strong informal government outside the bounds of formal government— a *de facto* government beyond and behind the government *de jure*.

"The result . . . is a modern government that is about five times as inflexible, and much less democratic, than the government of Great Britain." [2]

Through the decades leading to the Civil War the fuel of political strife was provided by the propertied classes, who not only bickered incessantly among themselves about the priority of the landed province over the commercial province, and vice versa, but also provoked in the economically disfranchised farmers and mechanics resentment mirrored most broadly in the Jacksonian Democracy. When a series of political defeats at the hands of the northern industrialists and merchants eventually became ominously foreboding, the Southern planter faction did not hesitate to draw the sword. The Civil War began as a counterrevolution, but ended as a revolution.

The triumph of the North in the war, forever dislodging the landed gentry from political power, brought sweeping authority to the tariff-minded industrialists—authority that has since been seriously disputed, and then in purely parliamentary fashion, only by the

Western agrarians under William Jennings Bryan, who had mistaken their true class interests when they helped crush the South. From 1865 to 1896 the essentially revolutionary rule of the industrialists was unbroken.

The evolutionary phase in which the dominion of the industrialists regularized itself and shaded off into the rule of finance capitalists began to assume shape in 1896.

Marcus Alonzo Hanna, commissar extraordinary of John D. Rockefeller, became the political architect of the new era, whose unique characteristics have been a tremendous drive into foreign markets, unprecedented industrial consolidation, expansion of the mass-production industries to a staggering degree, the unexampled application of technology to production, and the fateful gravitation of the nation's producing resources as well as its political apparatus into the hands of bank capitalists. But although nascent finance capital made its first bid for dominance with the national emergence of Hanna, not until 1920, with the election of Warren G. Harding to the presidency, did it seize upon undivided suzerainty.

In the three decades preceding the advent of Hanna in Washington, the grip of the new special interests upon government had been extemporaneous, unorganized, individualistic; under Hanna the hold was made conscious, formal, and systematic, to be exercised with careful premeditation on behalf of the whole clique of big industrial proprietors. Before Hanna the fledgling industrialists had prompted the two dominant political parties in hoarsely contradictory and discordant voices from the outside (although they did have obliging friends in office); under Hanna the industrialists and bankers moved in, a consolidated body, and constituted themselves the two political parties. Before Hanna the unconstitutional control by the industrialists had been furtive, half ashamed, and vehemently denied even in the face of the most damning evidence; under Hanna the control was for the first time brazenly admitted and, cynically or sincerely, justified on the pretense that it was in the national interest. Control, it became obvious to the magnates, had to be wielded openly, as a prescriptive right of big capital, rather than covertly; otherwise, the rising chorus of protest might develop into an overwhelming mass movement.

After Hanna crude bribery by men of wealth was no longer a prime essential to the control of government; first, because the men placed in the highest public offices from McKinley through Hoover were all the political creations of the wealthy; and, second, because the community of wealth had finally obtained the rich treasure trove it had been ceaselessly seeking in the maze of frauds and trickeries that extended from the Civil War to the end of the century. This treasure was simply the public domain, consisting of vast lands owned by the citizenry. In 1860 more than half the land area of the nation was held in trust for the people by the government, but by 1900 fully nine-tenths of it had been given away, under the stimulus of corrupt payments, to railroads, mining syndicates, speculative land enterprises, and homesteaders. Whatever of more than average value fell into the hands of the latter innocents was soon taken away by mortgage or by fraud, by force or by wit, by hook or by crook. It is a challenging fact that most of the natural resources owned today by the United States Steel Corporation, the Aluminum Corporation, the Standard Oil Company, the railroads, and, in fact, nearly all private corporations, were in 1860 communally owned under political auspices.

Every great fortune that rolled out of the nineteenth century was rooted in fraud; and the literature and documentation in proof of this broad statement is voluminous.[3] "In their absorbing passion for the accumulation of wealth," says David Saville Muzzey, a cool historian, "men were plundering the resources of the country like burglars looting a palace."[4] Fraud and trickery were the revolutionary devices resorted to by the northern industrialists to complete the job begun by Grant's cannon and bayonets; by fraud a realm oozing riches, and far surpassing in value the Russian Empire seized by the Bolsheviks, was wrested from the American people in the years 1860-1900. Whereas in the Civil War it was the Southern planters who were mowed down and summarily divorced from their property, in the postwar decades it was the farmers, laborers, professionals, and small merchants who were indirectly expropriated by unscrupulous, revolutionary improvisation upon the Constitutional machinery. That there was universal popular approval for the dismemberment of the public domain does not alter the fact that it was the common people,

ever slow to comprehend their true economic interest, who were
despoiled.

It cannot be contended that the opening of the public domain to
private exploitation, the erection of a protective tariff that grew
higher with the years, and the enactment of many other special
measures of value to fortune seekers were without material benefit
for the nation. The stimulus given cupidity and avarice by loose
governmental policies did bring about a rapid construction of a
crude but serviceable society. But the price exacted by the industrialists for their entrepreneurial activity savors of the price wrung by Me-
phistopheles from Faust. The industrialists simply claimed, in exchange for material improvements, the nation's soul in perpetuity.

The Standard Oil Company was conniving with the chieftains
of both parties before 1880. John D. Rockefeller habitually contributed large funds to the Republicans in return for lucrative concessions; Colonel Oliver H. Payne, his partner, gave liberally to the
Democrats, and did not hesitate to call upon them peremptorily for
delivery of the political *quid pro quo*.[5] James A. Garfield, the successful candidate for the presidency in 1880, anxiously asked an associate "if Mr. Rockefeller would be willing to assist."[6] Rockefeller
gave heavily for the Garfield campaign, and Mark Hanna, the statesman of Standard Oil, sent four checks for $1,000 each to the Ohio
State Republican Committee.[7] "It was the settled policy of the company to use its money everywhere and anywhere, in state and national councils, to produce results." [8]

Some years later Henry Havemeyer, sugar magnate and son of a
former Tammany mayor of New York, told the United States Industrial Commission that he habitually contributed to both parties.
"We get a good deal of protection for our contributions," he said
laconically. Havemeyer was head of the American Sugar Refining
Company, which in 1909 became notorious when it was convicted
and fined $2,000,000 for having systematically cheated the customs
office over a long period.

That the ingenious Hanna, with his Rockefeller tutelage, brought
into American politics a new technique rather than a new philosophy
may be seen from the size of the funds that have snared American
votes since 1860. After Hanna started sculpturing political contours

with pecuniary tools the election funds merely became larger (but the stakes, too, were larger) and subject to more careful bookkeeping. From 1860 onward the national party funds in presidential years alone have been as follows (figures down through 1908 from the New York *World,* October 28, 1924):

|  | REPUBLICANS | DEMOCRATS |
|---|---|---|
| 1860 | $100,000 | $50,000 |
| 1864 | 150,000 | 50,000 |
| 1868 | 150,000 | 75,000 |
| 1872 | 250,000 | 50,000 |
| 1876 | 950,000 | 900,000 |
| 1880 | 1,100,000 | 355,000 |
| 1884 | 1,300,000 | 1,400,000 |
| 1888 | 1,350,000 | 855,000 |
| 1892 | 1,850,000 | 2,350,000 |
| 1896 | 16,000,000 | 425,000 |
| 1900 | 9,500,000 | 425,000 |
| 1904 | 3,500,000 | 1,250,000 |
| 1908 | 1,700,000 | 750,000 |
| 1912 | *1,071,548 | *1,134,848 |
| 1916 | †2,500,000 | †2,000,000 |
| 1920 | ‡9,700,738 | ‡2,537,750 |
| 1924 | §4,370,409 | §903,908 |
| 1928 | xx9,433,604 | xx7,152,511 |
| 1932 | ††2,900,052 | ††2,245,975 |
| 1936 | ‡‡8,892,971 | ‡‡5,671,118 |

The two administrations of Democratic Grover Cleveland (1884-1888; 1892-1896) were more tightly interlocked with the community of industrial wealth, both in personnel and in general policy, than any which preceded; they foreshadowed, tentatively, what was to come under succeeding Republican administrations. Significantly, the slush funds of the Democrats in the years of the two Cleveland triumphs exceeded those of the Republicans.

* Sen. Priv. & Elec. Com., 1913, p. 1504
† N. Y. *Times,* Sept. 7, 1924
‡ Kenyon Committee Report, 1920
§ Borah Committee Report, 1924
xx N. Y. *Herald Tribune,* March 1, 1929
†† N. Y. *Times,* Dec. 13, 1933
‡‡ N. Y. *Times,* Mar. 5, 1937

Cleveland's Secretary of the Navy was William C. Whitney of
New York. The husband of Oliver H. Payne's daughter, he was the
father of Harry Payne Whitney, Payne Whitney, Lady Almeric
Paget, and Mrs. Willard D. Straight (now Mrs. Leonard K. Elmhirst). He began his ascent to riches in 1872 as an inspector of New
York schools; in 1875 he became City Corporation Counsel. Originally an anti-Tammany man, he was metamorphosed into the confidential Rockefeller link to Boss Richard Croker of Tammany Hall,
and for years was Croker's chief mentor and political guide.[9] He was
the Rockefeller pipeline into the Cleveland Cabinet. ". . . Grover
Cleveland said more than once to friends that he owed his nomination to Whitney."[10] Whitney spent a small fortune on Cleveland's
three presidential campaigns, and was a prime example of those magnates who rose to pecuniary eminence not through any economic
contribution of their own but through their political positions and
their willingness to use these positions for private gain. Of such
politicians there have been not a few, and among them were Thomas
Fortune Ryan, Oliver H. Payne, Anthony N. Brady, William Elkins,
and Peter A. B. Widener.

Whitney achieved wealth, in partnership with Ryan, by pyramiding securities of the Metropolitan Street Railway, which owned the
Broadway and other franchises in New York. *The World,* under the
able Pulitzer, had revealed the corrupt circumstances under which
the so-called "boodle" aldermen in 1884 voted this francise to one
Jake Sharp. The revelation upset the deal, but the franchise remained,
and was quietly appropriated by Whitney, Ryan, and Brady, who
added to it, in collaboration with Tammany, many other franchises.
The eventual, inevitable collapse of the Metropolitan Street Railway,
into which a wide circle of Democratic insiders had been invited,
including William Randolph Hearst, brought severe losses after the
turn of the century to thousands of small investors.[11] By that time the
Ryan-Whitney-Brady gang had joined the Rockefellers in the exploitation of the Third Avenue Railway Company, allied with the
Metropolitan Street Railway through the Metropolitan Securities
Company.

During his second term Cleveland accepted fiscal advice from J. P.
Morgan and August P. Belmont, both frequent callers at the White

House and in correspondence with its occupant.[12] These two bankers induced Cleveland to issue to them government bonds in exchange for gold, which was immediately bought back from the Treasury by the jocund Wall Street banks, thereby necessitating more bond issues. Cleveland sold the bonds privately to the bankers, who promptly resold them at heavily advanced prices. Negotiations with the government for the bond issues were conducted· on behalf of J. P. Morgan and Company by its attorney, F. L. Stetson, who had been Cleveland's law partner.

Pulitzer's hard-hitting *World* ended the lucrative deviltry by demanding public bids and offering to buy $1,000,000 of government securities at top prices. This forced the introduction of public bidding, but not before Cleveland had sold $162,000,000 of securities to the bankers, who netted profits of more than fifteen per cent.

Cleveland's most revelatory action on behalf of Wall Street came, however, in 1894 when he trampled upon the Constitution by sending Federal troops into Chicago, unsolicited by the Governor of Illinois, under the pretense of protecting the mails but really to break the Pullman strike. The troops caused the first violence.

After Cleveland left the presidency he was, at the suggestion of J. P. Morgan, made a trustee of the Harriman-Ryan Equitable Life Assurance Society, when the company needed an eminent sponsor during the insurance scandals of 1905. In 1900, recent testimony indicates, Cleveland was a participant in a stock market pool with Oliver H. Payne, William C. Whitney, and Calvin Brice, Senator from Ohio (1890-1897) and promoter of the Nickel Plate Railroad.[13]

## II

McKinley, like Taft and Harding, came from Ohio, the seat of the Standard Oil empire. From the time his affable personality first attracted Hanna in 1876, he enjoyed Rockefeller support. In 1891 Hanna procured for Congressman McKinley, whose name graced the highest tariff yet enacted, the governorship of Ohio.

Hanna's Rockefeller affiliation, in 1891, was intimate and of long standing. Rockefeller, who received his early schooling in Owego County, New York, became a schoolmate of Hanna's at Central High School, Cleveland. Hanna's coal and iron business for many years was closely allied with the Pennsylvania Railroad, from which Standard Oil got some of its juiciest secret freight rebates and in which the Rockefellers came to own stock; at Rockefeller's personal request Hanna at an early date relinquished to Standard Oil a petroleum enterprise in which he held an interest; friends and relatives of Hanna's were direct investors in the closely held Standard Oil Trust; and, emphasizing the Hanna-Rockefeller political juxtaposition even more positively, on November 21, 1890, Hanna, at Rockefeller's solicitation, wrote to David K. Watson, Attorney General of Ohio, and ordered him, upon pain of political destruction, to proceed circumspectly about pushing a dissolution suit against Standard Oil.[14] Watson stubbornly went ahead with the litigation, was offered a $100,000 bribe by Standard Oil, spurned it, and was ushered into political oblivion. His successor, Francis S. Monnett, was offered $400,000 to quash the same action; he, too, refused and was removed. The litigation was stopped in 1900 by a subservient attorney general placed in office by Hanna to handle this particular job. The Rockefellers, incidentally, habitually smashed unpurchasable public officials, just as the Morgan-Widener-Yerkes traction ring in Illinois smashed Governor John P. Altgeld for declining to approve perpetual traction franchises in Chicago.

Many of Hanna's political favorites, notably Joseph B. Foraker, as it later came to light, were simply Standard Oil stipendiaries. Hanna himself had ample personal means.

McKinley became as thoroughly implicated as his preceptor in the destinies of Standard Oil. In 1893, while Governor of Ohio, he went bankrupt, but was secretly salvaged by a syndicate comprising Mark Hanna, Myron T. Herrick, Samuel Mather, Charles Taft, Henry C. Frick, Andrew Carnegie, and others.[15] Hanna frequently lent money to Governors Foraker and McKinley while they were in office.[16] After his elevation to the White House, McKinley, to make room for Hanna in the Senate, designated as his Secretary of State the octogenarian Senator John Sherman, of Ohio. Sherman did not remain long in office, because it soon became sadly evident that he was not in full possession of his mental powers.

But Sherman had well served the Rockefellers and other Wall Street denizens in his long political career. It was Senator Sherman who in 1875 put through the Specie Resumption Act; and Henry L. Stoddard, New York Republican newspaper publisher for many decades, notes in his memoirs that Sherman's "relations with the First National Bank of New York [Baker] were so close during the resumption crisis that that institution was popularly called 'Fort Sherman.' "

At Hanna's elevation to the Senate in 1897 by the Rockefeller-controlled Ohio Legislature there was the usual raucous accusation of fraud which followed nearly every election; but the Senate, firm in the grip of Boss Aldrich of Rhode Island and Hale of Maine, refused to investigate, even though one Ohio legislator swore that he had been given $1,750 for his vote, and even displayed bank notes he said he had been given.[17]

The installation of men in high offices by corrupt means was no novelty; especially was it no novelty in Ohio. Oliver H. Payne, the Senator's son, had seated himself at a desk in the Ohio Legislature, and, like a gambling-house croupier, gravely apportioned $65,000 for the votes that sent his father to the United States Senate to act for the glory of Standard Oil.[18]

Wall Street, despite the gold-embossed bona fides of McKinley, favored the nomination in 1896 of Levi P. Morton, Vice-President of the United States from 1889 to 1893, president of the Morton Trust Company, Governor of New York, and long entangled in many shady deals. Morton was touted by the Morgan clique, but McKinley captured the Republican nomination through Hanna's shrewd planning. It was not, however, until Hanna on August 15, 1896, met James J. Hill, railroad factotum of the Morgan camp, that the entire financial community rallied behind McKinley. Hill offered to introduce Hanna in Wall Street, and in five days the two henchmen collected all that was necessary to buy decisive blocs of votes and to regiment the opinion of an ignorant electorate.[19]

The meeting between Hanna and one of Morgan's many scouts was hardly accidental, for Rockefeller shortly before had transformed himself into a bank capitalist. Starting as a mercantile capitalist, then becoming an industrial capitalist, John D. Rockefeller early in the nineties veered with the trend and bought stock in the National City Bank of New York, then the largest financial house in the country. For more than two decades the name of James Stillman, president of the National City Bank, was to be synonymous with the name of Rockefeller.

The precise proportions of the Republican slush fund of 1896 never became known, although the *Evening World* set the figure at $16,-000,000. The magnates, frightened by the threat of the grim-faced Bryanites, threw money about like sailors in a brothel. Herbert Croly, Hanna's biographer, estimates the election fund at $3,500,000, but his surmise related only to the national committee collections; funds were independently dispatched by the magnates to the state and county committees, and were personally conveyed to senatorial and congressional candidates. It is an established fact that vast sums about which the general public seldom hears are used to prostitute virtually all elections.[20]

The Standard Oil Company flung $250,000 into the political caldron.[21] ". . . In 1896 every bank and trust company in New York but one, and most of the insurance companies, made contributions to the Republican national committee," the late Cornelius Bliss, Sr., Republican treasurer and Secretary of the Interior under McKinley, told Judge Charles H. Duell of New York, assistant Republican treasurer in 1904.[22] Each of the three leading insurance companies —the New York Life (Morgan), the Mutual Life (Rockefeller), and the Equitable Life (Ryan-Harriman)—generously coughed up their policyholders' funds.[23] Life insurance at that time was much more of a "racket" than it is now under comparatively stringent laws. The insurance companies, as it was revealed later in the Hughes investigation (forced by the trumpetings of Pulitzer's *World*), made a fine art of political and miscellaneous venality. The Mutual in 1904 disbursed $364,254 for corruption, the Equitable $172,698, and the New York $204,109; the Equitable had been giving $30,000 annually to the New York State Republican Committee for several years.[24]

"The men whose hands went deepest into their pockets understood in general that if the Republicans won, the politics of the country would be managed in the interest of business—a consequence that was acknowledged by all the Republican speakers and by none so frankly as by Mark Hanna."[25]

Under the triumphant McKinley the antitrust law, of course, remained a dead letter, for no one was more endangered by it than the Standard Oil Company. Monetary policy under McKinley was also precisely what the magnates had ordered, gaining formal expression in the Gold Standard Act. Tariffs in the Dingley Tariff Act were jacked up to 49½-52 per cent, in accord with the desires of Big Business. Vital legislation in the McKinley Administration passed through the hands of Senator Nelson W. Aldrich, chairman of the powerful Senate Finance Committee, who placed his blessing upon the Dingley Act.

Seven Presidents served under Aldrich, Republican Senate whip. Destined to become young Rockefeller's father-in-law, Aldrich had as unsavory a record as one could conceive. *McClure's Magazine,* February, 1905, revealed that the whole Rhode Island political machine, dominated by Aldrich and General Charles R. Brayton, was corrupt in every detail; that the majority of state senators were bought; that Brayton, Aldrich, and Marsden J. Perry manipulated the legislature, gave themselves perpetual public-utility franchises, and passed unrepealable laws worth millions to themselves. When Aldrich gave up his wholesale grocery business in 1881 to enter the Senate he was worth $50,000; when he died, after thirty years in politics, he was worth $12,000,000.[26]

The war with Spain, precipitated by journalistic stimuli, distracted the country from its multiplying social grievances in the first years of the McKinley Administration, but McKinley was scarcely hustled into the war against his will. In 1896 he exchanged letters with Whitelaw Reid, owner of the New York *Tribune,* and both agreed that the United States would have Cuba; but both favored the postponement of an armed struggle with Spain. Assistant Secretary of the Navy Theodore Roosevelt and Senator Henry Cabot Lodge, both of whom enjoyed political life only by virtue of J. P. Morgan's pleasure, were the nucleus of a jingoistic Washington cabal that boldly espoused the war and, indeed, worked indefatigably to provoke it.[27] Secretary Roosevelt from his first day in office feverishly prepared the Navy for this particular conflict, and it was Roosevelt who secretly, and on his own responsibility, ordered Dewey's descent on

Manila, although the status of the Philippines was not an avowed issue.

All the magnates deplored the war—in public. But although Morgan and Carnegie professed themselves against the war, Lodge and Roosevelt did as much as Hearst and Pulitzer to bring it on. And Senator Joseph B. Foraker and Representative Joseph Bailey, both in time disclosed as outright hirelings of the Standard Oil Company, daily, while the decision hung in the balance, demanded a declaration of war.

The inner motivation with respect to this war has not yet been brought to light in documentary form. But these facts are certain: Rockefeller's paid henchmen on the floor of Congress wanted the war; Hearst and Pulitzer demanded it; Roosevelt and Lodge forced it; McKinley and Hanna acquiesced in it; and the Rockefeller-Stillman National City Bank benefited most directly from it, for Cuba, the Philippines, and, indeed, all of Latin America soon afterward became dotted with National City branches, and the Cuban sugar industry gravitated into National City's hands. Moreover, all of Wall Street, its eyes upon South America's rich mineral resources, wanted the Isthmian Canal built; and Cuba and Porto Rico bore a strategic relation to the control of such a canal.

The National City Bank during McKinley's incumbency was, significantly, more closely involved in Administration affairs than any other bank, and Lyman J. Gage, the Secretary of the Treasury, was widely looked upon as a National City man.[28] Gage took Frank A. Vanderlip, financial editor of the Chicago *Tribune,* to Washington as his assistant. From this post Vanderlip stepped into the National City Bank, eventually assuming the presidency of the institution. Gage, upon leaving the treasury, was made president of the United States Trust Company by James Stillman.

After the brief hostilities, the process of trust building to which Hanna was wholeheartedly committed began in deadly earnest. In 1899 alone there were launched no fewer than ninety-two corporate trusts, including the Standard Oil Company of New Jersey. Nothing like it had ever been seen before.

The new combinations, however, were not "trusts" in the old sense of the term. They were really holding companies which, thanks to purposely contrived state laws, were enabled to do anything under the sun. The old Standard Oil Company and about a dozen others, including the American Sugar Refining Company, were the "trusts" from which the name derived. Rockefeller's enterprise was actually named the Standard Oil Trust; it was a device whereby the Rockefeller partners, holding the shares of forty affiliated concerns under trust agreements, voted the stock without consulting the actual owners.

The practice in the new holding-company era was for a banking group, usually led by J. P. Morgan and Company, to induce the dominant families of competing enterprises to exchange their holdings for cash or for stocks and bonds in a consolidated enterprise. Securities of the new companies were then peddled like fish to a gullible public properly primed by glowing newspaper and magazine articles. The proceeds went to original owners of the constituent companies and, in the form of fat commissions and fees, to the bankers. The Morgan syndicate that floated the United States Steel Corporation in 1901 exacted a fee of $62,500,000 according to the United States Bureau of Corporations, whereas the tangible value of the entire property was only $682,000,000; the new securities had a face value, however, of $1,400,000,000. Similar fees were charged for merging companies into the General Electric Company, the International Harvester Company, and the American Telephone and Telegraph Company.

Most of the new securities, as in the case of United States Steel, represented at least half "water," which made it impossible for many corporations, United States Steel included, to show even conservative earnings on the overcapitalization; many of the new contrivances simply exploded in the bankruptcy courts during the ensuing three decades. Even where the combinations endured, the securities frequently sank in market value toward the zero mark. Small investors, again prompted by florid newspaper accounts, cleared out like frightened geese, with heavy losses, while the manipulators and original owners retrieved the depreciated holdings at far less than their true potential value.

The business operated with the planned precision of a great military campaign, and the gains of the promoters in the period 1899-1909 exceeded in value the plunder of many great wars.

The census of 1900, with McKinley's first term ending, showed that 185 of the new combinations, with $3,000,000,000 of capital, controlled one-third the manufacturing resources of the nation.[29] The securities of one hundred of these companies in October, 1903, on the other hand, showed a shrinkage of forty-seven per cent in market value from the high prices of 1899 and 1900.[30] United States Steel sank from $40 to $8 a share, with a corresponding loss to thousands of investors.

## III

McKinley triumphed again in 1900 because the tinsel of a victorious war and a new tropical colonial empire draped his Administration, and there were impressionable spirits who imagined that they, too, would one day partake of the feast of the magnates. Again the President was backed by Hanna and the 1896 synthesis of rival financial forces, although the harmonious coalition was soon to disintegrate.

The composition of McKinley's Cabinet reflected the coalition that twice elected him. John Sherman was a Rockefeller-Hanna man from his boots up. John Hay, who succeeded as Secretary of State, was a Republican stalwart, former secretary of Abraham Lincoln. Cornelius N. Bliss, Secretary of the Interior, was a Morgan-Ryan slush-fund supervisor and a director of the Equitable Life Assurance Society. Elihu Root, who took the portfolio of war in 1899, was Ryan's attorney and became Morgan's; he had been Tammany Boss Tweed's lawyer and as such had been reprimanded by the trial court in the Tweed scandal for improper activities. Philander C. Knox was a Frick-Mellon man, a director in several Mellon banks that had long financed Frick's coke business, and the reorganizer of the Carnegie Steel Corporation as a holding company. "Mr. Frick's closest political associate was Philander C. Knox and far-reaching consequences were attributable to their mutual fidelity." [31] Frick personally solicited of McKinley the Cabinet post for Knox.[32] Gage, as we have seen, was a Rockefeller-Stillman man.

Knox and Root sat in the Cabinets of three Presidents, faithful janizaries of the economic royalists. They later invaded the Senate to continue their boring from within. E. H. Harriman it was who gave away the secret of Root's popularity in high circles when he said, "Other attorneys tell us what we can't do; Mr. Root tells us what we can do."

Joseph H. Choate, Rockefeller's ablest attorney, who for years contested State and Federal dissolution suits against Standard Oil, was made Ambassador to Great Britain by McKinley; the aging Hay eventually succeeded him. As the rise of international finance capitalism made certain ambassadorial posts of vital importance we find after the 1890's that nearly all the ambassadors to London, Paris, Tokyo, Berlin, Rome, and lesser foreign capitals are the trusted deputies of the Morgan, Rockefeller, Mellon, and other banking camps.

In 1900 the Standard Oil Company again gave the Republicans $250,000 over its name. The insurance companies, as usual, freely disposed of policyholders' funds, of which they had more than the capital goods industries could immediately absorb. All the magnates again deluged the Republican Party with money, underwriting its success at the polls.

The Democrats, to be sure, notwithstanding Bryan and his Populistic cohorts, were not without the backing of private wealth in the campaigns of 1896 and 1900. William Randolph Hearst, heir to gold, silver, and copper mines, discovered that he could create a profitable sensation by supporting Bryan, whom most metropolitan newspapers vilified hysterically. Hearst in 1896 offered to match, dollar for dollar, the contributions of his readers, who sent in $40,000. Marcus Daly, head of the Anaconda silver enterprise and, with William A. Clark and F. Augustus Heinze, one of a group that corrupted Montana to the core, in 1896 raised $289,000 for the Democrats, whose prattle boomed speculation in silver shares.[33] Four years later Bryan was borne aloft again by the same dubious elements.*

The assassination of the re-elected McKinley by an anarchist in September, 1901, befogged, temporarily, what had been a serene prospect for the votaries of Mammon. J. P. Morgan was thoroughly unnerved by the news.[34] The Rockefellers, too, were stricken, for "they took the best medical advice after McKinley was shot and

* See Appendix C, page 500

determined that his chances for getting well were not good," according to James R. Phillips, Jr., president of the Butte and Consolidated Mining Company and an associate of Archbold, Rogers, and William Rockefeller in Amalgamated Copper. "They therefore sold out all their speculative holdings." [35]

Only as recently as Inauguration Day, a fitting occasion, J. P. Morgan and Company had announced itself the syndicate manager for the Brobdingnagian United States Steel Corporation, so there was cause for Morgan's worry.

Not only was there consternation at McKinley's untimely death, but there were misgivings about Vice-President Theodore Roosevelt, who automatically became President. Roosevelt had done a good deal of bold talking about reform; but there need have been no questioning of his essential conservatism. In many ways it was a blessing for the magnates that Roosevelt replaced McKinley, for the new President's purely verbal radicalism was to hold in check the rising tide of social discontent as the reckless pyramiding of fortunes continued. McKinley had never been resilient enough to pretend hostility to the magnates while privately capitulating to their demands; but Roosevelt, a virtuoso at deception, is even today looked back upon as a great liberal and reformer.

Roosevelt had been boosted from the bottom to the top of his political career by the Morgan clique, but it was some time before the bull-headed Morgan learned to discount his gestures. He was in the vice-presidency, as a matter of solemn fact, because he was scheduled for political oblivion. His antics as Governor of New York had displeased many powerful personages, among them J. P. Morgan. As the latter's henchmen alone had advanced the Roosevelt political fortunes, Morgan had justification for being dissatisfied.

Roosevelt, after having served in the New York Legislature, had been nominated for the mayoralty of New York in 1886 by Chauncey Depew, president of the Vanderbilt's New York Central Railroad; the nomination was approved by Elihu Root and Levi P. Morton.[36] In 1897 Roosevelt became Assistant Secretary of the Navy upon recommendation from the same quarters but not before he had served as a Civil Service Commissioner under Presidents Harrison and Cleveland, and as Police Commissioner of New York City.

Roosevelt's emergence as a press-created hero of the Spanish-American War was the only role not written for him in advance. His war reputation was joyfully capitalized, for in 1898 Thomas C. Platt, boss of New York State, was instructed by Depew to support him for the governorship of New York.[37] The word of the New York Central Railroad was law; Roosevelt was placed in nomination at Saratoga by Depew, and was seconded by Elihu Root, not the least of whose accomplishments had been the writing, with Joseph H. Choate, of the New York State Constitution of 1893 that disfranchised a large area of New York City. The Roosevelt campaign was forwarded by State Republican Chairman Benjamin B. Odell, who succeeded as Governor and whom E. H. Harriman was brutally to stigmatize during the insurance investigations as his personal "creature." [38] Roosevelt won the election on the issue of "patriotism."

"The campaign for Governor marked the first occasion on which the financial interests of the East contributed funds toward the election of Roosevelt. They did so again in 1900 and 1904. Donations were received from the Mutual, Equitable, and New York insurance companies as well as from the Metropolitan and Third Avenue Railways. Tom Platt boasted that he had collected $10,000 from J. P. Morgan. . . . The respectables were behind Roosevelt." [39]

As Governor of New York, Roosevelt proved he was no maverick. After he had prepared his second message to the Legislature in December, 1899, he responded to the promptings of Harriman's agent, Odell, and greatly modified it.[40]

An even more revelatory course was flashed into view by the redoubtable New York *World,* which on March 13, 1900, flatly accused the Governor of having abused his power by shielding Thomas Fortune Ryan and the devious Elihu Root, then sitting in McKinley's Cabinet, from the consequences of an unlawful act. The facts were these: Root was counsel to the State Trust Company when the bank made illegal loans in the amount of $5,000,000. One loan of $435,000 went to L. F. Payn, State Superintendent of Banks and Insurance, Wall Street's major link to the Albany lobby, and Jay Gould's former chief lobbyist and bribe dispenser. Another loan of $2,000,000 went to Daniel H. Shea, an office boy employed by Thomas Fortune Ryan, a director of the bank. Root, said *The World,* had passed upon the legality of the loans; but Roosevelt did nothing to bring Root, Payn, or Ryan to answer before the law. Indeed, Roosevelt later was glad to welcome Root into his Presidential Cabinet.

Governor Roosevelt also winked at the notorious Erie Canal frauds.

Roosevelt, however, annoyed J. P. Morgan very decidedly by sponsoring the tax on franchises, which intruded theoretically upon the public utilities swindle. He also came to be feared as a formidable rival by Platt, who proposed to get rid of him by making him Vice-President. Roosevelt threatened to become a stumbling block to Platt "in the green valley of New York State politics." [41] At the Republican convention of 1900, convinced that he was stranded politically, Roosevelt allowed himself to be sponsored for the vice-presidency by the wily Platt and the sinister Quay of Pennsylvania. His nomination was formally seconded by Depew, an accredited delegate. Quay, suspicious of the powers that had fallen to the Hanna-Rockefeller group and himself synchronized with the Mellon-Frick element, wished to encumber the Administration by saddling it with a supposedly headstrong person; Quay's machine might, perhaps, also guide this person. As it worked out, Frick himself became one of Roosevelt's private advisers and was subsequently offered a place on the Isthmian Canal Commission. McKinley and Hanna both objected to having the orally fiery Rough Rider on the 1900 ticket, but to no avail.[42] They succeeded only in making Roosevelt believe Standard Oil was inimical to his career.

By the time Roosevelt took the presidential oath the Morgan coterie was reasonably reassured about his intentions, for as Vice-President Elect the new Chief Executive had given a private dinner in December, 1900, in honor of no lesser personage than J. P. Morgan. This function "dispelled lingering doubts induced by Roosevelt's fight for the franchise tax as governor. It enabled Mr. Morgan to proceed with entire confidence with his plans for the organization of the United States Steel Corporation." [43]

No sooner was he inducted into the presidency than Roosevelt entered into an agreement with Senators Aldrich and Hale, and their followers of the industrialist Republican Senate bloc, to continue without change the McKinley policies. In return he was promised their co-operation.

When Roosevelt's two terms are weighed it becomes patent that during this period, and with Roosevelt's collaboration, J. P. Morgan and Company and its clients made the greatest progress in their history. The evidence in support of this conclusion is crushing.

Roosevelt summoned the masters of the nation for advice on his initial message to Congress. The men who closely scrutinized his first state paper included A. J. Cassatt, president of the Pennsylvania Railroad, Nelson W. Aldrich, "Morgan's floor broker in the Senate," Mark Hanna, Elihu Root, and Philander C. Knox. With all the big clans represented, omissions and emendations desired by their spokesmen were promptly accepted.[44] The presidential message as delivered was so ambiguous that there was speculation about its meaning throughout the country for many weeks. Its positive aspects were all in line with Wall Street predilections except for the recommendation that a new Department of Commerce and Labor be established; the Rockefellers did not like this, but Roosevelt, after 1900, did not like the Rockefellers. The "trusts" were mentioned; but that was all. The digging of an Isthmian Canal was recommended, and the reduction of sugar duties. Lower sugar tariffs were ardently sought only by the American Sugar Refining Company.

Roosevelt, throughout his term of high office, like a dutiful schoolboy, submitted all official proclamations to the magnates and accepted their rescripts. "He submitted a draft of his third annual message to James Stillman, president of the National City Bank, and promised to make changes in the passages referring to the currency question. He even invited Morgan himself to the White House. 'I should like very much to see you to talk over certain financial matters,' he wrote him on October 8, 1903." [45]

From 1902 to 1905 Roosevelt, as was disclosed by the Senate Privileges and Elections Committee slush-fund investigation of 1912, secretly corresponded with Harriman about appointments, public pronouncements, campaign contributions, and like matters. Harriman, a power in New York State, had a large voice in the Legislature and the office of Governor Odell. He was, moreover, allied with Kuhn, Loeb and Company, and was a factor, along with Thomas Fortune Ryan, in the Equitable Life Assurance Society.

The sense of security that reigned in the breasts of the money-masters as the new President meekly took advice, and retained the corporation lawyers that were the pivots of the McKinley Cabinet, was apparently dispelled in February, 1902, when Roosevelt peremptorily ordered Attorney General Knox to file suit against the Northern Securities Company as a violator of the antitrust law. Knox, upon Roosevelt's solicitation, rendered the opinion that this great railroad combination violated the law. Coming from a Frick-Mellon man about a Morgan company his opinion suggests a maneuver behind the scenes. Knox had no principled objection to combinations.

The Northern Securities Company, incorporated some months before by J. P. Morgan and Company, represented an ambitious plan to consolidate the Northern Pacific, Great Northern, and Chicago, Burlington, and Quincy Railroads. On the day of incorporation there was a conference in the Morgan offices attended by the weighty parties to the transaction, who were George F. Baker, E. H. Harriman, James J. Hill, James Stillman, William Rockefeller, and C. S. Mellen, Morgan deputy in charge of the New Haven Railroad.

J. P. Morgan was said to have been thunderstruck by Roosevelt's fiat; he sought an audience with the President, and when he asked if the similar United States Steel organization was also to be assailed Roosevelt is said to have replied, "Not unless we find out . . . they have done something that we regard as wrong." [46] Roosevelt never did find anything wrong with United States Steel.

Elihu Root stepped out of the Cabinet to act as the Morgan-Hill defense counsel for Northern Securities, and succeeded in obtaining a purely technical dissolution decree from the Supreme Court on March 14, 1904. Justice Oliver Wendell Holmes, in a dissenting minority opinion, with delicate irony insinuated that, as the Sherman Act was a criminal statute and as the law had been admittedly violated, Morgan, Harriman, Hill, Stillman, and their colleagues could be prosecuted as common felons rather than merely spanked with a dissolution order. "No one, Roosevelt least of all, had any desire to start such prosecution . . . the 1904 campaign was approaching." [47]

The true nature of this celebrated government "victory" over J. P. Morgan and Company was disclosed by the late Senator Robert M. LaFollette, who wrote, "The government's attorneys in preparing the decree omitted to provide for the dissolution of the combination and conspiracy between the competing and parallel lines; and likewise omitted from the decree the provision that these competing lines be required thereafter to operate independently each through its own board of directors. The effect of the abortive decree was to leave the combination in full force and operation through a holding company or trust agreement. This defeated the very purpose for which the action was brought and left the Government nothing. Furthermore, the decision entered in that case operated to increase the capital stock of the monopoly one hundred million dollars as a burden upon transportation."

What Roosevelt's motives were in ordering the prosecution one cannot say. Perhaps Morgan secretly wanted the suit, for by the terms of the decree the Morgan-Hill ownership in the railroads was increased at the expense of Harriman. Certain it is that Roosevelt's dramatic act, notwithstanding its trivial outcome, established him in the popular fancy as a foe of entrenched wealth; certain it is that this popular misconception, strengthened by an immediate speaking tour, proved to be a decided political asset; and it is no less certain that this was the last time, as well as the first, that Roosevelt crossed swords in more than rhetorical fashion with J. P. Morgan and Co. Roosevelt's conduct thereafter was as though, having shown his independence for all to see, he could now let J. P. Morgan do as he pleased.

Roosevelt went out of his way, in a theatrical fashion, to strengthen the popular impression that he was hostile to Morgan. After the Northern Securities litigation, at a dinner of the Gridiron Club, an organization of Washington journalists, he pugnaciously shook his fist under Morgan's nose and said harshly, "And if you don't let us do this, those who come after us will rise and bring you to ruin." Reports of the affair could not, under the rules of the club, be written, but intimations were permitted to leak out; and editors thereupon spun out the great myth of Morgan's enmity toward Roosevelt, who was supposed to reciprocate it with interest.

While Roosevelt and Morgan shadow-boxed for public delectation, the Rockefellers were becoming increasingly suspicious of the new White House occupant, and quite justifiably. They tried to block establishment of the new Department of Commerce and Labor with its Bureau of Corporations, but Roosevelt tripped them up with a celerity that displayed the power of the presidency—if put to use. He ended the clamor inspired by the Rockefellers by calling in newspapermen and telling them that John D. Rockefeller had sent to nine senators, including Hale, Spooner, Elkins, and Kean, telegrams which read: "We are opposed to the antitrust legislation. Our counsel will see you. It must be stopped."

The Roosevelt-Rockefeller feud lent color to the popular misapprehension that the President was hostile to great wealth. But the mere composition of Roosevelt's Cabinets showed that he bore no ill will toward the "plunderbund." After the Northern Securities comedy Root returned as Secretary of State. George von L. Meyer, a director of the Old Colony Trust Company of Boston and an undercover agent of Morgan's, was Postmaster-General from 1907 to 1909, when he took the portfolio of Navy under Taft. Paul Morton, president of the Santa Fe Railroad and, later, president of the Equitable Life, was Secretary of the Navy for a few months in 1904 when Roosevelt and Harriman, a major stockholder in Equitable Life and the dominant influence in Santa Fe, carried on a profound intrigue over Western territorial judicial and executive appointments. In 1909 Robert Bacon, Morgan partner with whom Roosevelt in his first term corresponded about affairs of state, moved up from Assistant Secretary to Secretary of State as Root stepped into the Senate. William Howard Taft, who had distinguished himself by his antilabor decisions on the Ohio bench, took over the War Department in 1904. Leslie M. Shaw, a wealthy Iowa banker, was Secretary of the Treasury from 1902 to 1907. For a brief interval Herbert L. Satterlee, Morgan's son-in-law, was Assistant Secretary of the Navy.

Harriman, Morgan, Ryan, Mellon, and Frick all had their errand boys at the President's elbow, but there was never a Rockefeller man in Roosevelt's Cabinet, and this alone was enough to nettle Standard Oil.

## IV

The Panama Canal project, conceived under McKinley but born under Roosevelt's ministrations, involved powerful financial factions. It had always been understood in Washington that if an Isthmian canal ever was built, it would cross Nicaragua, where the United States had acquired canal rights. A French company began digging early in the 1880's across what is now Panama, but had long since abandoned work. In time, the chief creditor of this company became Philippe Bunau-Varilla, publisher of *Le Matin,* of Paris, and a speculator with a police record. Elihu Root privately referred to him as a member of "the penitentiary gang." Bunau-Varilla, who knew a thing or two, in 1896 retained as his lawyer William Nelson Cromwell, of New York.

The Republican convention of 1900 had been on the verge of formally endorsing the Nicaraguan route, but Cromwell—by giving $60,000 directly to Mark Hanna for the Republican campaign of 1900 [48] and charging the sum to the French company—blocked the endorsement.[49] Hanna declaimed convincingly in the Senate on behalf of the hitherto unacceptable Panama project and Congress on June 28, 1902, passed the Spooner bill favoring Panama; but Senator Morgan of Alabama charged corruption, and recalled that Congress in 1899 had authorized the Nicaraguan Canal as traversing "the most practicable route." Theodore Roosevelt, incidentally, had earlier gone on record as favoring the Nicaraguan route.

The abrupt abandonment of the Nicaraguan route by the Republican convention of 1900 constituted the first public recognition in North America that a canal along any other route was feasible. But there was a juicy plum for private sharpers imbedded in the Panama project; there was nothing extraneous in the Nicaraguan plan.

In May, 1901, the Isthmian Canal Commission, appointed by President McKinley to forward Cromwell's scheme, appraised the unexercised rights of the moribund French company at $40,000,000. By a strange coincidence this was just what the French company claimed. Originally it had asked $109,141,500, but had scaled its price down because the engineering cost of a Panama Canal was estimated at $144,233,000 as against $189,864,052 for a Nicaraguan Canal; the reduced price of the Panama rights enabled the Republicans to bellow that the costs of both projects were the same.

The sum of $40,000,000 was eventually transferred by the government, through J. P. Morgan and Company, to the unidentified stockholders of the French company. "These rights, such as they were, could doubtless have been bought for a much smaller sum, had there been a counter offer." [50] The money was paid, however, only after the government, with Roosevelt directing the conspiracy from behind the scenes, as he boasted many years later, had called upon the Navy to protect the synthetic revolution which terminated the sovereignty of Colombia over Panama.

Credit for the revolution was publicly taken by Bunau-Varilla who, with Cromwell, actually plotted the whole affair. Indeed, the New York *World* of July 5, 1903, foretold and gave the date of the revolt which took place as scheduled on November 3, 1903. Bunau-Varilla, who emerged as an official of the new Republic, was apprised in advance *via* Washington of the movements of American warships toward Panama, and informed his co-conspirators.[51]

Two Congressional investigations failed to disclose the identity of the stockholders of the French company who got the $40,000,000 windfall, although Roosevelt, to appease critics, averred that Cromwell had privately given him the names. The suspicion was voiced that, if there were indeed stockholders, they were not the original investors for whom partial repayment had been solicited as an act of simple justice, but speculative chiselers who had bought up the depreciated canal shares in Paris for a song. This theory was based upon more than conjecture, for the Panama Canal Company of America, successor to the original company, was formed in 1899 by August Belmont, Kuhn, Loeb and Company, Levi P. Morton, and clerks in Cromwell's law office.[52] This new company got $15,000,000 of the $40,000,000 collected by J. P. Morgan and Company. Who behind the façade of the company shared with Cromwell and Bunau-Varilla was never established on the record, but from all appearances the whole Panama affair was a gamble on a shoestring for big stakes in which all the leading politicians of finance shared. Cromwell repeatedly refused to name the stockholders when called upon to do so by Congress. In ensuing decades he continued to make substantial cash contributions to the Republican Party, and became an attorney for some of the largest corporations.

The final cost of the Panama Canal was much greater than the estimated cost of the projected Nicaraguan Canal. The United States agreed to give the bastard Republic of Panama $10,000,000 and, after

1913, $250,000 annually. Under the treaty of 1922, Colombia had to be paid $25,000,000. When this payment was proposed during the Wilson Administration, Roosevelt himself fumed that it could be justified only "upon the ground that this nation had played the part of a thief, or a receiver of stolen goods."

The somber coloring of the Panama Canal imbroglio did not become thoroughly apparent until Pulitzer's *World* toward the end of Roosevelt's second Administration flatly charged that the Cromwell deal was corrupt.[53]

Roosevelt had Pulitzer and his newspaper twice indicted for criminal libel, and flooded the World Building with secret-service agents who tapped telephones, opened mail, and carried on intimidating espionage.[54] The first indictment, brought in Washington, named the Indianapolis *News* as well as *The World*. But in Indianapolis Judge Albert Barnes Anderson upheld the defendants' contention that they should not be dragged to Washington, and significantly observed, "There are many very peculiar circumstances about the history of this Panama Canal or Panama Canal business."

The second indictment, procured in New York by District Attorney Henry L. Stimson, alleged that President Roosevelt, Charles P. Taft, Elihu Root, Douglas Robinson (the President's brother-in-law), William Nelson Cromwell, and J. P. Morgan had been libeled by *The World*. This action was quashed by Federal Judge Charles M. Hough, who declared that the President had "prostituted" his power in suing *The World*. The United States Supreme Court on January 3, 1911, unanimously upheld Judge Hough, and sitting on the court were Holmes, appointed by Roosevelt, and Hughes, appointed by Taft.

*The World's* allegations, coming just as Taft was about to assume the presidency, prevented William Nelson Cromwell from being appointed Attorney General. Cromwell was seriously mentioned for this high post, which had already been ornamented by Philander Knox and was later to boast the incumbency of A. Mitchell Palmer and Harry M. Daugherty.

Roosevelt's first term ended without having produced any constructive social legislation, but with the country convinced that the President was an enemy of Wall Street. Late in 1903, Senator Lodge,

Morgan spokesman in Bosto:.'s political purlieus, informed the President that J. P. Morgan and other financiers had agreed to support him for re-election in the 1904 campaign.[55] John Cudahy and J. Ogden Armour, the meat packers, tactfully declared in favor of Roosevelt, who had just brought suit against them for price-fixing.

The political collaboration of the magnates with their apparent foe in the White House would seem strange were it not that Roosevelt had a technique in these matters. He would lodge charges against a few conspicuous trusts, those of his political enemies by preference, and allow the others to go their way. As to Morgan, who Roosevelt had publicly implied was one of "the criminal rich," "the banker usually got what he wanted." [56]

## V

The Republican slush fund of 1904 was of the customary elephantine proportions; but it has more clinical value for the historian than its earlier counterparts because details of its composition are preserved in the records of the Senate Privileges and Elections Committee investigation of 1912.

The identities of its contributors bespoke the crafty pecuniary influences behind Roosevelt and his predecessor in the White House, although Roosevelt in 1912 tried to disavow knowledge of the situation when called upon to explain. But the damning Harriman letters, unfortunately for him, proved he was aware of what was going on.

E. H. Harriman regarded himself as Roosevelt's confidential campaign manager in 1904. The President and Harriman for several years had been on exceedingly intimate terms. On June 2, 1904, Harriman wrote to the Chief Executive: "I have not yet been able to get at Messrs. Dodge, Hughitt, and Frick, but hope to be able to accomplish it in the first part of the next week." On September 23, 1904, Roosevelt wrote to the railroad manipulator: "There were one or two points in my letter of acceptance which I should have liked to discuss with you before putting it out."

Again on October 14, the President wrote: "A suggestion has come to me in a roundabout way that you do not think it wise to come on to see me in these closing weeks of the campaign, but that you are reluctant to refuse, inasmuch as I have asked you. Now, my dear sir, you and I are practical men, and you are on the ground and know conditions better than I do. If you think there is any danger of your visit causing me trouble, or if you think there is nothing special I should be informed about, or no matter in which I could give aid, why, of course, give up the visit for the time being, and then a few weeks hence, before I write my message, I shall get you to come down to discuss certain Governmental matters not connected with the campaign."

Harriman on October 20, 1904, wrote: "Would like to speak with you personally on long-distance telephone."

After the election, Roosevelt and Harriman continued a lively correspondence about the appointment of an Arizona territorial Governor and Chief Justice who would be friendly to the railroad interests. Even more remote appointments were of interest to Harriman, for on December 28, 1903, he wrote to Roosevelt: "I have been requested to endorse M. W. C. Ralston as candidate for naval officer at San Francisco, which I cheerfully do."

In 1905, government suits against Harriman's Central Pacific Railroad and Southern Pacific Railroad, which had consolidated competing lines, were abruptly dismissed by the Attorney General. The complaints, based upon Interstate Commerce Commission Report No. 943, showed flagrant violation of the Sherman Act. The termination of this and subsequent litigation amply rewarded Harriman for his political outlays in 1904. The government lost a later suit against the same companies, because it had drawn a faulty bill of complaint. Roosevelt's critics charged that the complaint had been incorrectly drawn by design.

The happy relations between Roosevelt and Harriman ended in 1906, as a reflex to the inner struggle for control of the Equitable Life Assurance Society and to the ensuing insurance scandals. The insurance companies bore an intimate relation both to the Republican and to the Democratic Parties; they were the central switchboards of finance capital because they held vast resources and controlled some of the major commercial banks of New York.

James Hazen Hyde, a young wastrel, had inherited from his father

502 shares, or fifty-one per cent, of the Equitable Life Assurance Society. By a special trust agreement the dividends on these shares were limited to $3,514 a year in all so that the company might misrepresent itself as mutualized. The shares, however, gave ironclad control of resources of several hundred millions as well as of many big banks and trust companies; and, as the subsequent public inquiry showed, this control could be used to dispose almost at will of huge funds.

In February, 1905, James W. Alexander, president, and thirty-five other officers of the company, requested the board of directors to give stockholders the right to vote, implying that Hyde was not reliable so far as their interests were concerned. After months of recrimination and intrigue the board in April, 1905, appointed a committee consisting of Henry C. Frick, E. H. Harriman, Cornelius N. Bliss, James J. Hill and Darius O. Mills, all of them directors, to investigate. The committee's report arraigned the Hyde regime and cited certain abuses.

Young Hyde, intimidated by the proceedings, sold his shares to Thomas Fortune Ryan for $2,500,000, although he had once been offered as much as $7,000,000. Hill had offered him $5,000,000. These shares, and not the abuses, were the real occasion for all the excitement.

Ryan's quiet coup enraged Harriman, who peremptorily served notice that unless Ryan sold him half the shares at cost the Harriman political apparatus in Albany would rip open the entire insurance situation. Ryan capitulated, but strange rumors had seeped into the office of the New York *World,* which demanded a general legislative investigation of all the insurance companies. The fat was in the fire. The State Legislature had to call an inquiry. Despite maneuvering to make it a whitewash, the steady publicity given by *The World* kept it straight. When at the outset it was discovered that no competent lawyer would dare conduct the hearings, *The World* itself put the issue up to Charles Evans Hughes, then in his early forties. Hughes, a corporation attorney who had himself acted as counsel for Alexander of Equitable Life, apparently was able to recognize opportunity, for he at once accepted the position of counsel to the committee.

Moving through Root* and Roosevelt, Ryan ruined Harriman politically, but not before the public had its nostrils assailed for months by the Hughes disclosures.

The insurance company funds were used by officers and directors for their pet speculative enterprises; the margin for private speculative accounts of officers and directors was supplied by the companies; J. P. Morgan and Company kept the New York Life Insurance Company from purchasing superior securities so that it might instead be stocked up with nearly $150,000,000 of less desirable issues emitted through the banking firm's syndicates; officers and directors acquired securities from syndicates and resold them to the companies at advanced prices; friends and relatives of officers and directors were fastened like barnacles in superfluous jobs throughout the companies; salaries and commissions to insiders were exorbitant; vast funds were misdirected over a period of decades to lobbying for laws that would permit a continuation or an extension of malpractices in all states; legislators were bought and paid for in wholesale fashion; and policyholders received only a fraction of value for their money.

The poorest earnings ratios were shown by the biggest companies— the Mutual Life (Rockefeller), New York Life (Morgan), and Equitable Life Assurance Society (Ryan-Harriman). Among the statesmen on the secret insurance company pay roll were Senator Chauncey M. Depew (Republican) and Senator David B. Hill; Depew received $20,000 annually although he was not even an attorney for the companies.

The personalities behind the scandal consisted of the richest men

* Elihu Root was brought into the life-insurance situation in a quiet advisory capacity before the scandal became public and while he was in the Cabinet, according to Henry Morgenthau, *All In a Life Time*, p. 82. Morgenthau, a large-scale New York real-estate operator, was president at the time of the Central Realty, Bond and Trust Company, in which Anthony N. Brady, Henry O. Havemeyer, James Stillman, and the Mutual Life Insurance Company (Rockefeller) owned stock, and Morgenthau functioned for the insurance companies in realty transactions. He relates that he was picked by Alexander to build the fire under Hyde by collecting voting proxies from several thousand policyholders of Equitable Life, and that this was done through the United States Express Company. Stillman warned Morgenthau not to bring general reflection upon the financial community, and Morgenthau outlined the entire situation for Stillman and Root before proceeding. Harriman, too, was consulted. Virtually everybody of importance in politics and finance, then and later, was involved in some way in the insurance situation.

in the country. Among the trustees of the Equitable Life Assurance
Society in 1905 were James J. Hill, Henry Clay Frick, Alfred G. Van-
derbilt, John Jacob Astor, Marcellus Hartley Dodge, Chauncey M.
Depew, Cornelius N. Bliss, Levi P. Morton, George J. Gould, T.
Jefferson Coolidge, John A. Stewart, Jacob H. Schiff, August Belmont, and E. H. Harriman. Trustees of the Mutual Life Insurance
Company included Cornelius Vanderbilt, George F. Baker, Henry
H. Rogers, Augustus D. Juilliard, George S. Bowdoin (Morgan partner), Adrian Iselin, Jr., William Rockefeller, Elbridge T. Gerry, H.
McK. Twombley, Stuyvesant Fish, and James Speyer. Trustees of
the New York Life Insurance Company included George W. Perkins, Norman B. Ream, Oscar S. Straus, Clarence H. Mackay, Darwin P. Kingsley, John A. McCall, and James Stillman.

The investigation brought out that the central pivot of political
corruption was George W. Perkins, partner of J. P. Morgan and
Company, vice-president of the New York Life Insurance Company,
and keeper of the so-called "Yellow-Dog Fund" maintained in common by the companies and administered from the shady "House of
Mirth" in Albany. Perkins won a decision, 4 to 3, before the New York
Court of Appeals on his plea that a charge of grand larceny relating
to his transfer of $48,500 of New York Life Insurance Company
funds to the Republican Party be dismissed. This accusation had
been irregularly lodged by District Attorney William Travers Jerome
in police-court proceedings rather than by grand jury indictment.
*The World* stormed, and Perkins was indicted for forgery on the
company's books; but this charge also came to nothing as Jerome
refused to prosecute. Since 1902 Perkins, incidentally, had been in
very friendly correspondence with Roosevelt.

One product of the investigation was a more stringent statute that
apparently made certain malpractices impossible, but all the companies continued under the same auspices and in most cases with
the same officers. The present directors of the four largest insurance
companies are all either primary or secondary figures in the Morgan,
Rockefeller, Mellon, Du Pont, National City, and Kuhn, Loeb and
Company camps, for the fundamental law of the land has not
changed since 1905.

The companies were required by a new law to mutualize, and formally complied. But as the Pujo Committee of the House of Representatives found in 1912, "the so-called control of life insurance companies by policyholders through mutualization is a farce . . . its only result is to keep in office a self-constituted, self-perpetuating management."

The companies were also ordered to divest themselves of control of banks and trust companies. They fulfilled the order by turning over bank control to the leading financial lords. J. P. Morgan and Company acquired from the Equitable and the Mutual Life Insurance Company several banks which were combined with the Bankers Trust Company and the Guaranty Trust Company, then already under Morgan control. J. P. Morgan and Company also acquired from the insurance companies shares in the First National Bank and the National City Bank, assuming a direct interest in these institutions for the first time. Viewed from this aspect the insurance scandal was a blessing to Morgan, for without it he could never have hoped to pry loose these bank stocks.

In 1910 Morgan paid $3,000,000 for the Harriman-Ryan shares in the Equitable Life Assurance Society, whose par value was only $51,000 and whose dividends amounted to one-eighth of one per cent of the cost. But, as Louis D. Brandeis has observed, this stock "gave control of $504,000,000 of assets."

That the insurance situation still presents suspicious aspects despite reforms is shown by a long dispatch to *The New York Times* from Albany, March 17, 1937, which began as follows:

"A proposal for a sweeping legislative investigation of life insurance companies produced a series of lively exchanges here today at a public hearing conducted by the Senate Insurance Committee. Several of the Senators sitting on the committee assailed practices of insurance companies and declared the investigation was essential. Words like 'petty larceny,' 'racket' and 'fleecing the policy holders' were heard. . . !"

One of the chief complaints still made against the insurance companies is that they pay their top officials annual salaries ranging from $200,000 to $300,000 for duties so standardized they could be performed by intelligent clerks. The entire system of life insurance is also the object of severe criticism.*

The sequel to the Harriman-Ryan feud was dramatic, and Harriman held the losing cards.

In 1907 there drifted into the office of *The World* a copy of a long letter written by Harriman early in 1906 to Sidney Webster, a Republican factotum.[57] Harriman set forth in this communication that he had been unwillingly sucked into the insurance imbroglio and that he had unsuccessfully backed Depew for an ambassadorship. He had, he said, thrown fifty thousand votes to Roosevelt, making a difference of one hundred thousand votes in the outcome.

Harriman's letter closed as follows: "Ryan's success in all his manipulations of traction deals, tobacco companies, manipulations of the State Trust Company into the Morton Trust Company, and the Shoe and Leather Bank into the Western National Bank and then again into the Bank of Commerce, thus covering up his tracks, has been done by the adroit mind of Elihu Root, and this present situation has been brought about by the conditions and circumstances which have brought together the Ryan-Root-Roosevelt element. Where do I stand?"

Publication of this missive pointed the finger of suspicion at Roosevelt, who hastily revealed correspondence tending to show Harriman had first approached the President. As Harriman's posthumously published correspondence proved, however, Roosevelt withheld his own letter wherein he had first called upon Harriman to advance his political fortunes.

The President, moreover, had before this set forces into motion against Harriman by having the Interstate Commerce Commission investigate the Harriman railroads, disclosing many abuses and allowing himself to appear again before the public as a foe of entrenched wealth. In due course the I.C.C. investigation disclosed that Harriman's Union Pacific Railroad had irregularly issued $375,158,183 of securities, only $46,500,000 of which were refunded or redeemed up to 1912 and about $362,000,000 of whose proceeds were used to purchase securities of other railroads, giving Harriman twenty-seven

* See *Life Insurance—A Legalized Racket*, by Mort and E. A. Gilbert (Farrar and Rinehart, 1936).

railroad directorships and extraordinary powers. Harriman, it was shown, deliberately ruined the Chicago and Alton Railroad.

At his death in 1909, Harriman left $100,000,000 to his wife, who passed it on to two sons, but a formidable Morgan antagonist, a client of Kuhn, Loeb and Company, was effectively broken in a political sense by the President.

Although Harriman bestirred himself in 1904, the lead in mobilizing funds for the electoral struggle was taken by the Morgan group, with Standard Oil chipping in generously but playing a double game by giving the Democrats reinforced secret assistance. John D. Archbold, vice-president of Standard Oil, talked over the Republican tariff attitude with Cornelius N. Bliss, and during the conversation insisted that Roosevelt be informed of the Standard Oil contribution because, said Archbold, he wanted it "gratefully received." [58] Archbold also wanted assurances conveyed that Standard Oil was not hostile to the President.

On behalf of the Morgan group E. T. Stotesbury, Morgan partner, collected $146,759 in Philadelphia; S. T. Wainwright, of the Wainwright Coal Company, collected $101,700 in Pittsburgh; Senator John F. Dryden, of New Jersey, founder and president of the Prudential Insurance Company (originally named the Widows' and Orphans' Friendly Society), collected $70,000; a special committee under Perkins collected $100,000, mostly from the insurance companies; George von L. Meyer, of the Old Colony Trust Company of Boston, and destined for a chair in the second Roosevelt Cabinet and the Taft Cabinet, collected $105,727 in New England. "The Meyer Committee," C. S. Mellen confided to C. W. Barron in 1913, "was organized in the interest of J. P. Morgan and Company and has been in that firm's control from the beginning and is so now." [59] Mellen, Senator Lodge, and T. Jefferson Coolidge, Sr., president of the Burlington Railroad and former Ambassador to France, were members of this committee.

Harriman took $250,000 from the coffers of his various railroads for the Roosevelt campaign. But the largest individual contribution did not come to light until 1922, when litigation over the estate of George J. Gould, a Harriman-Stillman collaborator, disclosed that the Gould family in 1904 had given the Republicans $500,000.[60] Gould at the time was directing many railroad manipulations, and had reason to fear railroad legislation and White House initiative. The Senate Committee in 1912 found that he contributed only $100,000, and the discrepancy between this figure and the sum he actually did contribute suggests that other similar discrepancies may exist.

Aside from Gould's long-secret donation the biggest individual contributions, as revealed, were as follows:[61]

$150,000

J. P. Morgan and Company, the Metropolitan Life Insurance Company, the Mutual Life Insurance Company, and the New York Life Insurance Company.[62]

$100,000

John D. Rockefeller and Henry H. Rogers, jointly; E. H. Harriman and Chauncey M. Depew.

$50,000

C. S. Mellen, Jacob H. Schiff, Percy Rockefeller, Henry Clay Frick,* James Hazen Hyde.

$25,000 to $50,000

James Speyer, private banker; Robert Mather; Whitelaw Reid, son-in-law of D. O. Mills, mining magnate, and publisher of the New York *Tribune;* R. C. Lake of Missouri.

$5,000 to $25,000

James Stillman, N. W. Kendall, Clarence H. Mackay, M. A. Hanna, Simon and Murry Guggenheim, Adolph Lewisohn, Andrew Carnegie, A. D. Juilliard, Isaac N. Seligman, Frank Munsey, D. O. Mills, H. McK. Twombly, Robert Bacon, John Jacob Astor, John Hay, T. Coleman du Pont, William Nelson Cromwell, Nicholas Murray Butler, the American Can Company, the International Harvester Company, the Cuba Mail Steamship Company, the Hawaiian Sugar Planters Association, Chicago, Milwaukee and St. Paul Railway, the Bethlehem Steel Corporation, the United States Steel Corporation, etc.

$1,000 to $5,000

Joseph H. Choate, C. W. Post, O. C. Barber, Cornelius Vanderbilt, International Nickel Company, Remington Typewriter Company,

* George Harvey, in his biography of Henry Clay Frick (p. 298), says that Frick gave more than $100,000 to the Republicans in 1904.

St. Joseph Lead Company, General Electric Company, the American Locomotive Company, and hundreds of additional similar individuals and corporations.

The detailed figures on Democratic contributions for 1904, when Judge Alton B. Parker was the Democratic candidate, were destroyed. But significant shreds of data were salvaged by the Senate Privileges and Elections Committee. August Belmont, private banker, gave $250,000,[63] and was a member of the party's executive committee. Thomas Fortune Ryan, whose agents infested the successive Roosevelt Cabinets, gave $450,000.[64] Ryan, incidentally, was one formidable figure whom the fire-breathing Roosevelt never tackled. Henry Havemeyer gave $10,000, but his company contributed to the Republicans.

Belmont and Ryan persuaded Parker to declare in favor of the gold standard, thereby creating a sensation because the Democratic platform contained no declaration for gold. Parker's statement amounted to an official repudiation of Bryanism and an endorsement by the Democrats of the Gold Standard Act of the McKinley Administration.

Wall Street generally understood that Parker had been selected at the behest of Rockefeller, with whom Ryan was closely associated in the Metropolitan Securities Company. Oliver H. Payne tried, on the other hand, to induce Hanna to oppose Roosevelt for the Republican nomination, thereby scaring the President and making him more embittered than ever against Standard Oil, but Hanna was unresponsive, broken in health and spirit by McKinley's violent end. Parker's nomination was boisterously contested by William Randolph Hearst, himself seeking the presidency by means fair and foul, and the support given to his rival so angered Hearst that his resentment led to many later journalistic revelations of Rockefeller transgressions. It was Heart's agents who stole the Archbold correspondence whose eventual publication justified public suspicion of the Rockefellers' professed uprightness. .

Thoroughly informed testimony about the role of the Rockefeller junta in blessing the obscure Parker with the nomination came from Thomas W. Lawson, Boston financier and stock-market manipulator, who told the Senate under oath in 1912 that H. H. Rogers of Standard Oil "practically gave their agents at the convention *carte blanche* to nominate Mr. Parker." [65] Lawson had been unhappily associated with Rogers and Archbold in speculations with Amalgamated Copper Company. Additional testimony is obtained from James R. Philipps, Jr., who, with no ax of vengeance to grind, on April 7, 1904, confided to C. W. Barron, proprietor of the *Wall Street Journal*, that "Standard Oil will support Parker as the Democratic nominee." [66] But the disappearance of the Democratic records makes it impossible to ascertain the sum of money contributed by Standard Oil. Possibly a part of the huge Belmont-Ryan contribution came from Rockefeller.

After his re-election Roosevelt began to speak more freely about social questions; but the tide of revolt, too, was swelling, especially in the West where Governor Robert M. LaFollette of Wisconsin was ending the first stage of his long uphill fight against privilege. Too much significance cannot be attached to the appearance of La-Follette in the Senate in 1905, for thereafter the machinations of anti-social vested wealth were at least to be subjected to adverse criticism in the highest parliamentary forum.

"The President, so often torn by anxiety for the future, was led to radicalism by his desire to perpetuate the existing order." [67] He was radical in utterance at any rate, and his most penetrating biographer* makes it clear that he was dissembling. Roosevelt, it was noted, would "progress to a certain point in his program to ward off socialism and unrest, and then make energetic efforts to appease the right wing." He was in unholy communion with "the criminal rich" even as he oratorically flogged them.

There was every reason for the President to take up the catch-words of Bryanism and Populism, for the country since the Civil War had exhibited with increasing starkness the paradoxical contradiction of profound and apparently intensifying poverty within the lower mass while increasingly heavy tribute flowed to the upper stratum.

By the second Roosevelt term, most of the public domain having been pre-empted, the social safety valve of an open frontier was

---

* Walter F. McCaleb, sometime fellow in history, the University of Chicago.

definitely closed. This safety valve for decades had relieved the slowly growing pressure of social restlessness and discontent that was reflected late in the nineteenth century in the appearance of Henry George's *Progress and Poverty* and Edward Bellamy's *Looking Backward;* in the Knights of Labor struggle and the Populist movement; in the Homestead and Pullman strikes; and in numerous other dynamic symptoms of profound economic maladjustment.

Furthermore, the mailed fist of government upon a people accustomed to a certain degree of freedom had, paradoxically, grown heavier as chattel slavery was abolished and popular suffrage was broadened. Under the post-Civil War industrial regime, which spread the wages system, the power of the President was progressively enhanced by usage, as expressed in the greatly increased invocation of the veto; and the functions of the Supreme Court, its members all presidential appointees, were gradually broadened to give it supremacy over a corrupted Congress that did not fight back as did free British Parliaments once opposed by the throne. Before the Civil War the Supreme Court nullified only one act of Congress. But from 1860 to 1930 it voided no fewer than fifty-eight, and did not really attain its full stride as a legislative *saboteur* until the decade 1930-1940.

Theodore Roosevelt, who used the veto forty times, was properly disturbed by what he saw as he gazed about the land. In 1906 he wrote in alarm to Senator Lodge: "The labor men are very ugly and no one can tell how far such discontent will spread."

The sharpest intellectual portent of underlying discontent was the school of magazines that attained great circulation by exposing variegated social evils, tidings of which the newspapers for the most part, excepting Pulitzer's *World,* religiously suppressed. The President irately dubbed the contributors to these irreverent publications "muckrakers." This designation in time became a badge of honor, for the offenders were, without exception, the ablest, most honest, most fearless journalists of the day.

Despite the commotion raised by the muckrakers there was only a languid legislative reflex to it in Roosevelt's second term. Although he had a Republican Congress and controlled patronage, the President, who could talk so glibly, seemed unable to get any but Wall

Street measures over the hurdles. The Hepburn bill was passed, giving the I.C.C. authority to establish railroad rates, but the fight against it was led by Senator Lodge, the President's closest friend, and Senator Aldrich. LaFollette believed the Hepburn bill too weak, but he fought Lodge. When Senators Aldrich, Spooner, Lodge, and Knox (who replaced the deceased Quay) were unable to kill the measure they amended it to provide for judicial review and revision of rates. This left everything as it had been. Incidentally, Senator Knox's new seat in the Senate had cost $500,000.* [68]

After the passage of the Hepburn bill "Roosevelt once more belabored trusts with his big stick, but, with his free hand he was signaling the 'boys' back of him, saying under his breath, 'Don't get excited, this is for public consumption.' " [69] Referring to the Hepburn bill and other similar measures, McCaleb says, "The result of Roosevelt's sponsored legislation is today become the very bulwark of the worst combinations with which the country is afflicted." [70]

Roosevelt retained his popularity, however, by filing suit against the Tobacco Trust and the Standard Oil Company. The American Tobacco Company, like Standard Oil, was under Rockefeller domination, although Thomas Fortune Ryan and James B. Duke were also important factors in it. The litigation against these companies amounted to political reprisal by Roosevelt for real and imagined Rockefeller opposition, and it strengthened the Morgan-Mellon-Frick element to the extent that the Rockefellers were weakened.

The Standard Oil litigation led to the "dissolution" of the company in 1911 by the Supreme Court; but the constituent parts prospered and in 1929 the Rockefellers began the job of gradually putting them together again. In a separate court action Judge K. M. Landis gave the public abnormal satisfaction in 1907 by fining Standard Oil $29,000,000, but his ruling was set aside.

Roosevelt privately said of his antitrust tactics during his second term: "As a matter of fact, I have let up in every case where I have had any possible excuse for so doing." [71] He confined himself to bring-

---

* The $500,000 that bought Knox's seat in the Senate was provided by A. J. Cassatt, president of the Pennsylvania Railroad, John D. Archbold, vice-president of the Standard Oil Company, and Henry Clay Frick, director of the United States Steel Corporation.—Oswald Garrison Villard, *Prophets True and False*, p. 251.

ing suits against a few outstanding combinations, but "even when verdicts were rendered in favor of the Government, no real results ever flowed from the decisions." Government counsel, as LaFollette observed, usually sabotaged the Federal cases.

In his message of December, 1906, the President asked for income and inheritance taxes (for which Pulitzer had agitated in 1884); for Federal licensing of corporations; for the prohibition of corporation political funds; for maximum working hours for railway employees; and for the curtailment of judicial injunction powers in labor disputes. Congress dutifully proscribed corporation political contributions (but the corporation men were still permitted to contribute), and set seventeen hours as the maximum safe period of labor for railroad workers! The rest of the President's message was sardonically ignored.

LaFollette was joined in his insurgency by Senator Albert J. Beveridge, of Indiana, a quondam imperialist who gradually came to understand the ominous drift of political affairs. It was Beveridge and LaFollette who, aided by public opinion which had been outraged by stockyard conditions as portrayed in Upton Sinclair's *The Jungle,* forced through the Pure Food and Drug Act. Whittling by the reactionaries under Aldrich, however, made the measure woefully ineffective. Beveridge again, without any assistance from the White House, vainly attempted to obtain a general prohibition of child labor; Lodge stood out in the opposition although Beveridge in the course of a three-day speech said, "The evidence is before the Senate of the slow murder of these children, not by tens or hundreds, but by the thousands." Spooner warned that it was unconstitutional to interfere with the exploitation of children. A second child-labor bill written by Beveridge was throttled in committee.

The Aldrich-Vreeland currency bill, first proposed by Roosevelt, allowed national banks to form associations and borrow from the government up to ninety per cent of their pooled assets; it was passed even though LaFollette filibustered eighteen hours in a vain attempt to prevent what was really the underwriting of finance capital by the central government. Attempts to outlaw anti-labor injunctions and an effort by Beveridge and LaFollette to form a tariff commission of experts were brought to naught by Aldrich and his hatchet men, with the White House doing nothing.

Throughout his tenure Roosevelt continued to demand and receive funds for the building of a huge Navy intended merely to underwrite foreign economic conquests of Wall Street; in 1907 he theatrically sent the fleet around the world. In defiance of the expressed injunction of the Constitution he expanded the powers of the presidency in the field of diplomacy. In his first term, for example, he ordered the seizure of the Dominican customs for the benefit of European creditors who applied pressure through J. P. Morgan and Company. At the beginning of his second term he arranged with Japan and England, unknown to the Senate or to the nation, a secret informal agreement respecting the Pacific Ocean. In doing this, as Dr. Beard believes, he laid the groundwork for American participation on the side of England and Japan in the World War.

The President arbitrarily intruded in the European parceling out of Chinese commercial privileges by insisting upon American "rights," and shortly afterward, in 1909, J. P. Morgan and Company assumed the leadership of an American syndicate for Chinese railway financing. This step led to the Chinese financial consortiums of 1910 and 1920, in both of which Morgans represented the American participation. Losses of not quite fifty per cent were sustained by Americans who lapped up Chinese securities ladled out by this syndicate.

The large measure of Morgan influence in the White House under Roosevelt was most convincingly illustrated during the panic of 1907. It was freely charged later, and President Roosevelt himself hinted it, that the panic was aggravated, if not started, solely to permit the United States Steel Corporation to gobble up the Tennessee Coal and Iron Corporation in contravention of the Sherman Act. Tennessee Coal was not then very important, but it was known to possess ore deposits among the richest in the world.

If there was a conspiracy, and the preponderance of evidence suggests that there unquestionably was, it was a joint venture of the Morgan and Rockefeller groups to apportion special economic domains. The Rockefeller and Morgan groups in this period were intertwined in a number of ventures, and busily traded and bartered positions one with the other.

The recorded story of the Tennessee Coal and Iron seizure, and the ruin of F. Augustus Heinze, begins at the General Convention of the Protestant Episcopal Church, at Richmond, in the fall of 1907. Toward the close of the convention the stock market sickened and dropped, and certain brokerage houses were known to be in danger. Wall Street and its troubadours in the press blamed President Roosevelt because he had recently alluded bellicosely to the "malefactors of great wealth."

Morgan, an Episcopal elder, sang "lustily" on the train to New York from the convention, according to Bishop Lawrence of Massachusetts [72]—surely bizarre conduct at a moment of financial crisis! But an odd reason for Morgan's musical elation was not long in fitting itself into a peculiar series of events. This reason was, apparently, the crash a few days earlier, on October 16, of the stock of United Copper, a company owned by Heinze, president of the Mercantile National Bank; Heinze promptly resigned from the bank. On the same day Otto Heinze and Company, brokers, went under the gong, and in distant Butte a Heinze bank gave up the ghost. "These disturbing events, presumably, had been described in telegrams received by Morgan at Richmond." [73] Yet Morgan sang lustily.

The academic historians, in analyzing the "Bankers' Panic" of 1907, have ignored the significance of Heinze's downfall, as well as other incidents, although all the facts in the case point unmistakably to the conclusion that the doom of Heinze and United Copper was a *quid pro quo* exacted by the Rockefellers for permitting Morgan to swallow Tennessee Coal and Iron. Heinze for years had been a hornet in the hide of Rockefeller-controlled Amalgamated Copper, formed in 1899 as the "Copper Trust" to control the Anaconda Copper Mining Company, and various other metallurgical enterprises. Directors of Amalgamated Copper were William Rockefeller, William G. Rockefeller, James Stillman, Henry H. Rogers, and Robert Bacon, Morgan partner and close friend of President Roosevelt who in the second Roosevelt Administration became a Cabinet member.

Amalgamated Copper was a high-cost producer. United Copper was a low-cost producer which could, and did, freely undersell Amalgamated in all markets. Between 1901 and 1904 Amalgamated Copper common, of a par value of $150,000,000, declined sharply, and the enterprise was severely and repeatedly criticized adversely by Clarence W. Barron in the bulletins of the Boston News Bureau. On April 4, 1903, Barron revealed that Amalgamated Copper "people" had told him with respect to Heinze, "We are going to settle this, but we are going to settle it in our own way." * Settlement day came on October 16, 1907, when the raid conducted by a widespread group of brokers forced the price of United Copper stock down so far that its value as collateral was severely reduced and Heinze bank loans were immediately liquidated. Heinze was ruined.

Further reasons for Morgan jubilation developed on October 23, 1907, for on that day the Knickerbocker Trust Company failed. As soon as the Knickerbocker closed its doors Secretary of the Treasury George B. Cortelyou, who in 1909 was to enter upon a twenty-five-year tenure as head of the Morgan-Rockefeller Consolidated Gas Company of New York, hurried into private conference with Morgan. The next day call money was melodramatically marked up to one hundred per cent, and was then cut down to ten per cent when President Roosevelt placed $25,000,000 of Treasury funds in the hands of J. P. Morgan and Company, giving Morgan tight control of the money market.

The stage was set; the government was collaborating.

On the day Knickerbocker Trust failed, a story appeared in the New York *Evening Sun,* according to testimony before the Stanley Congressional Committee in 1911, to the effect that there was also a run on the Trust Company of America. It was a fabricated yarn, but the morning *Sun* had carried a suggestive story that Oakleigh Thorne, president of the Trust Company of America, might resign. The first *Sun* story directed suspicion toward the Trust Company of America; the second *Sun* story strengthened the earlier suspicion.

There was logic behind this, for *The Sun* at the time was published by William Laffan, who was personally subsidized by J. P. Morgan. Laffan founded the *Evening Sun* in 1887 and in 1897 took over the morning *Sun* from W. L. Dana, purchasing full ownership in 1902

---

* John Moody, *The Truth About the Trusts,* (1904), p. 36. This standard manual gives in full detail the background of the Heinze-Rockefeller feud.

with Morgan money. An art connoisseur and Morgan's adviser on esthetic matters, Laffan died in 1909; Morgan's will in 1913 established in Laffan's honor the Laffan Professorship of Assyriology and Babylonian Literature at Yale University.

The morning after the *Evening Sun* sounded the false alarm, October 24, 1907, a front-page story appeared in *The New York Times*, published by Adolph Ochs, relating that there had been a terrific run on the Trust Company of America and that worried bankers had met in all-night conference. The information was false; there had been no run. As brought out before the Stanley Committee, this article was planted in the unsuspecting *Times* by none other than George W. Perkins, who wrote a statement purporting to give the gist of banking sentiment, stipulating to the *Times* representative, like his editors impressed by the Morgan power, that neither the name of Perkins nor of J. P. Morgan and Company be mentioned. Perkins' inflammatory statement began: "The chief sore point is the Trust Company of America."

Perkins' essay was considered so "injudicious" by Melville E. Stone, head of the Associated Press, that, despite Morgan prestige and Morgan friendliness toward the Associated Press, he could not bring himself to release it to the country.[74] At the time, however, there was every reason for the *Times* to regard Perkins as a friendly collaborator: mortgages on the Times Building were held by various of the insurance companies.

The day the *Times* blazoned forth the fictitious story frenzied depositors withdrew $13,500,000 from the Trust Company of America, in contrast with normal withdrawals of $1,586,000 the day before.

The bankers' nocturnal meeting between the appearance of the two false newspaper stories had, indeed, been called by J. P. Morgan and Company on the pretense that the Trust Company of America was in danger. Thorne, upon being told that the meeting concerned his bank, was dumbfounded, knowing the institution was perfectly sound; but the canard in the *Times* forced the issue inexorably.

Thorne soon learned what the bankers' game was. Among the securities possessed by his bank was a big block of Tennessee Coal and Iron stock, held against a small loan of $482,700 to a Rockefeller group including Oliver H. Payne, L. C. Hanna (a brother of Mark

Hanna), J. B. Duke, E. J. Berwind, and Anthony N. Brady. J. P. Morgan and Company, controlling the money market with government money, stipulated that aid to the beleaguered bank was contingent upon the release of this stock in exchange for bonds of the United States Steel Corporation. Indeed, all banks holding loans on Tennessee stock were ordered by J. P. Morgan to give up this stock.[75]

Thorne himself owned 12,500 Tennessee Coal shares which were unpledged, and he had to agree to release these along with the other shares before he could obtain a required $30,000,000 on the excellent collateral which his bank offered. Henry Clay Frick, Elbert Gary, and J. P. Morgan personally rounded up $30,375,875 of shares of Tennessee Coal and Iron from all sources, mostly banks and brokerage houses, giving full ownership to United States Steel.

But before the Steel Corporation could with impunity swallow Tennessee Coal and Iron and its rich ore deposits it was necessary to obtain the formal assent of the White House, which had the authority to institute antitrust proceedings. It was also necessary to make the deal palatable to public opinion. Therefore, on Sunday, October 28, 1907, it was agreed by Morgan, Frick, and Gary that Roosevelt must be consulted before the spurious emergency consolidation took place. Frick and Gary went to Washington, and the next morning they told Roosevelt that a big "house," which they pointedly offered to name, was in danger of failing. Roosevelt, curiously enough, asked them not to name this "house," although the newspapers had been screaming about the apparently imperiled Trust Company of America.

This odd request relieved the two Morgan emissaries of identifying the alleged endangered enterprise and protected Roosevelt from any accusation that he had permitted the steel merger for insufficient reasons. Had the President insisted on knowing the name of the house Gary and Frick had in mind, they could only have mentioned the insignificant brokerage firm of Moore and Schley. The prospect of the failure of such an enterprise would not have justified the President's suspension of the antitrust law in order to "save the country." The difficulties of this brokerage house simply enabled Gary and Frick falsely to imply to Roosevelt that an institution of much greater moment was in danger, and also to imply to the public that this conference with the President concerned the thoroughly solvent Trust Company of America about which there was so much manufactured alarm.

Roosevelt, officially knowing nothing, but possibly thoroughly informed about the inner nature of the entire transaction which he alone had made possible by giving J. P. Morgan and Company control of the money market, assured his callers he would not institute antitrust proceedings. The panic in Wall Street subsided. United States Steel got the coveted Tennessee Coal and Iron shares. Rockefeller and Stillman got rid of Heinze. The pressure on the Trust Company of America abated. And everybody was happy, including the public which read about Mr. Morgan's heroic rescue and the felicitations sent by the President to the financiers.

Gary admitted to the Stanley Committee that the Trust Company of America had never been in danger. Its supposed insolvency merely provided an excuse for shifting desirable stock into Morgan's hands. A subcommittee of the Senate Judiciary Committee, steered by Aldrich, decided in 1908, however, that there had been no conspiracy. But Roosevelt, when later confronted with all the evidence, admitted that the Senate committee had been deceived. If this is true then Roosevelt himself deceived the committee, for he himself took and significantly spirited away the records of the Bureau of Corporations relating to the case when they were demanded by the Senate Committee.[76]

A fair measured conclusion drawn from all the evidence would seem to be that Roosevelt was informed about the plans of his closest political associates to ruin Heinze and grab Tennessee Coal and Iron, that he lent all the power of his high office to the conspiracy in the full knowledge of what he was doing, and that he destroyed the direct evidence of his complicity.

Not without reason has the United States Steel-Tennessee Coal transaction been called "theft." [77] But, despite the findings of the Stanley Committee, the United States Steel Corporation kept the valuable Tennessee Coal and Iron property. When dissolution proceedings against United States Steel (instituted by President Taft on the basis of the evidence uncovered by the Stanley Committee), reached the Supreme Court that august body, in one of its most tortuous decisions, decided that "reasonable" combination was not precluded by the antitrust law.

Before he relinquished his office to Taft there were other incidents in which the "malefactors of great wealth" found Roosevelt equally obliging.

The President on August 22, 1907, directed Attorney General Bonaparte to cancel preparations for a dissolution suit against the International Harvester Company. Just before the order was issued Perkins, the Morgan partner who organized this company in 1902, visited Roosevelt and remonstrated against the litigation. In 1912 it was freely charged by the Taft forces that the President had capitulated to the threats of Perkins, a director of International Harvester who had also been a director of Northern Securities Company. Notwithstanding his notorious implication in the insurance scandals, Perkins became, in collaboration with Frank Munsey, the newspaper and magazine publisher, Roosevelt's chief political mentor and financier.

On March 11, 1907, Roosevelt personally assured J. P. Morgan, visiting at the White House, that the suits filed against the Harriman lines did not presage a general assault upon railroad combinations; Morgan apparently had uppermost in mind the New York, New Haven and Hartford Railroad. In the same year the President assured C. S. Mellen of the New Haven Railroad that the company might acquire an interest in the Boston and Maine, thereby providing the basis for an antitrust suit that President Taft properly dismissed because Roosevelt himself had invalidated the government's contentions by giving the New Haven, through Mellen, permission to retain the Long Island steamboat line.[78] The absorption of the Boston and Maine was contrary to the wishes of this road's individual stockholders, who fought for more than twenty years against a union that meant only losses for themselves and profits for the New Haven and J. P. Morgan and Company.

The Rockefeller faction, for some undisclosed reason, obtained a valuable favor through William J. Matheson, vice-president of the Rockefeller-controlled Corn Products Refining Company, who dropped in at the White House one day in 1907 and induced Roosevelt to stop Harvey W. Wiley, chief chemist of the Department of Agriculture, from requiring the company to cease advertising Karo as a syrup. Wiley had wanted it called a glucose.[79]

Although the Rockefellers were out in the cold during Roosevelt's incumbency as far as White House favors were concerned, they were playing a large political role, as revealed by the Senate Privileges and Elections Committee investigation of 1912. This inquiry was forced upon the Senate, for since 1908 the Hearst newspapers had been publishing fragments of letters stolen from the files of John D. Archbold in the Standard Oil Company offices.

Archbold himself admitted to the Senate committee that he gave $25,000 in 1904 to Senator Boies Penrose and $100,000 to Cornelius Bliss, as well as moneys to Senators Nathan B. Scott and Stephen B. Elkins of West Virginia. Penrose, as a member of the United States Industrial Committee appointed by McKinley to conduct a survey of corporations, secretly brought to Archbold a copy of the Committee's report, which recommended the disclosure of the names of all corporation stockholders. At Archbold's suggestion, Penrose had this revolutionary recommendation deleted.

Archbold's correspondence, which, like Harriman's, is too extensive to quote in full, showed that in 1898 Standard Oil had given $2,000 to W. C. Stone, former Lieutenant Governor of Pennsylvania and later Congressman; that it had given sums of $5,000 to Representative John P. Elkins, of Pennsylvania; that Representative Joseph C. Sibley, of Pennsylvania, president of the Rockefeller-controlled Galena Signal Oil Company, regularly took Standard Oil advice about pending legislation and committee appointments, and also frequently accepted money; that Senator Joseph B. Foraker habitually accepted large sums of money for specified and unspecified purposes; that Senators Bailey of Texas, McLaurin of South Carolina, and Quay of Pennsylvania were on the Standard Oil pay roll; and that in general Standard Oil was pumping money out with a muscular hand. The evidence suggests that Sibley in the House and Foraker in the Senate were the Rockefeller paymasters in Washington. Sibley, indeed, from time to time mentioned in his letters various friendly Representatives that were in dire need of "loans."

Foraker, the letters made clear, used money not only to defeat and to pass bills in the Senate, but also to influence decisions in the Ohio courts and actions by Ohio's legislative and administrative officers. Until Hearst made the first Foraker letters public in 1908, it should be remembered that Foraker was a serious contender for the Republican presidential nomination. He made the nominating speech for McKinley in 1896.

Under date of January 25, 1902, Foraker asked Archbold for $50,000 with which to acquire a secret share in the influential *Ohio State Journal* of Columbus, but the attempt on the Columbus newspaper failed. Foraker returned Archbold's bank draft.

An example of Foraker's legislative functions is disclosed by an Archbold letter of February 25, 1902: "Again, my dear Senator, I venture to write you a word regarding the bill introduced by Senator Jones, of Arkansas, known as S. 649, intended to amend the act to protect trade and commerce against unlawful restraint and monopolies, etc., introduced by him December 4. It really seems as though this bill is very unnecessarily severe and even vicious. Is it not much better to test the application of the Sherman law instead of resorting to a measure of this kind? I hope you will feel so about it, and I will be greatly pleased to have a word from you on the subject. . . ."

The Jones bill came to naught.

## VI

President William Howard Taft, as it turned out, was entirely satisfactory to no one; that is probably why he was sidetracked in 1912. He was placed in the presidency by Roosevelt, who was evidently under the impression that he himself would be able to exercise presidential power through a docile creation, much as Hanna had worked through McKinley. Taft, a conservative of conservatives, was ruggedly honest, however, according to his own lights, as McKinley had unquestionably been. Neither Taft nor McKinley posed as a liberal. They sincerely admired the Wall Street crowd which Roosevelt personally found distasteful.

The essential difference between the Taft and Roosevelt Administrations, as far as the overlords of money were concerned, was that whereas Roosevelt favored J. P. Morgan and Company and bore down on John D. Rockefeller, Taft redressed the balance by hindering J. P. Morgan and Company and helping the sorely beset Rockefeller clique. The Du Ponts, who had run aground politically under Roosevelt, also found a friend in Taft.

No sooner was Taft's candidacy announced than John D. Rockefeller publicly declared for him as against Bryan, who was running for the third hopeless time on the Democratic ticket.[80] Everybody who had rallied around Roosevelt in 1904, and some who had supported Parker, got behind Taft. The 1908 slush fund was not, however, as large as its three predecessors. Indeed, it was the smallest Republican slush fund since 1888.

The Taft family itself made the biggest contribution to the fight—$110,000, but Charles P. Taft, the candidate's half brother, a successful corporation lawyer, could well afford to part with the money. According to data unearthed by the Senate Privileges and Elections Committee in 1912, Andrew Carnegie and J. P. Morgan and Company gave $20,000 each; Alexander Smith Cochran, textile manufacturer and Morgan client, and E. T. Stotesbury, Morgan partner, put up $15,000 each; Frank Munsey, Jacob H. Schiff, J. P. Morgan, and Whitelaw Reid each gave $10,000; and Simon Guggenheim, J. and W. Seligman and Co., George F. Baker, Adolph Busch, James Speyer, and George W. Perkins gave $5,000 each. Perkins also sent $15,000 into West Virginia for the State campaign, and other sums elsewhere. Henry Clay Frick gave more than $50,000, according to George Harvey, but the Senate Committee missed this contribution as it probably missed many others.

T. Coleman du Pont, who was rumored to have given $70,000 in 1904, which never appeared on the record, in 1908 tendered the Republicans a check for $20,000, but it was delicately refused because there was a suit pending against his company for allegedly defrauding the War Department on gunpowder contracts. Taft eased up on this litigation, begun when a Du Pont employee, for personal revenge, told what the company had been doing. The Democrats, too, had grown finicky, perhaps because of the letters Hearst was publishing, and returned a check for $10,000 to the American Sugar Refining Company, involved in litigation with the government over manipulated weighing machines.

The Democratic national campaign cost $750,000, and the biggest contributor was Herman Ridder, newspaper publisher, who gave

$37,000. Tammany Hall gave $10,000. William A. Clark, the mining magnate, gave $4,000. Small businessmen and lawyers gave amounts below $5,000. After the election, the Standard Oil Company gave $5,000 to defray accumulated debts.

Taft's victory placed him at the head of a country very different from the one Roosevelt had inherited. In 1900, for example, there were 149 trusts of $4,000,000,000 capitalization; when the "trust-busting" Roosevelt breezed out of the White House, there were 10,020, with $31,000,000,000 of capitalization.[81]

Roosevelt's outstanding contribution was that he made the government infinitely more efficient than it had ever been before. The civil service was extended, forest lands and water-power sites were reclaimed, irrigation projects were launched, and the Navy was made into an effective bill collector at foreign ports. The money spent to elect Roosevelt had brought not only special favors to the major contributors but had also given them the best government, from the standpoint of businesslike operation, they had ever had.*

President Taft could never see why he was not permitted to hobnob openly with the magnates, whose company he enjoyed. His advisers had a daily job trying to keep him away from the members of the "plunderbund" and of keeping their White House visits secret. Taft liked to play golf with Henry Clay Frick, but Mrs. Taft had to use all her influence to keep him from golfing with John D. Rockefeller, of whom Taft was frankly very fond.[82] J. P. Morgan, however, often called at Beverly, Taft's summer home, without being

---

* That aspect of Roosevelt's regime which liberal historians consider of a constructive nature has, however, been rather successfully called into question by H. C. Hansbrough in *The Wreck: An Historical and Critical Study of the Administrations of Theodore Roosevelt and William Howard Taft* (1913). This critic contends that the Roosevelt land-conservation program was designed in part, at least, to close the public domain so that settlers would move to privately owned railroad lands (p. 52). The railroads, Hansbrough brings out, financed the conservation movement outside the government and paid $45,000 a year to a periodical, *The Talisman,* so that it would favor conservation. "This," says Hansbrough, "was the milk in the reform cocoanut." An active Washington conservation lobby was also financed by the railroads. Roosevelt's policy of trust "regulation," Hansbrough also brings out, was originated by George W. Perkins, who lectured and wrote on it a year before it was enunciated by Roosevelt. The Hansbrough volume contains the correspondence between Herbert Knox Smith, head of the Bureau of Corporations, Perkins, and Oscar Straus, relative to the quashing of litigation against the International Harvester Company (pp. 62-69).

detected.[83] On one occasion Morgan offended Taft's sense of propriety by requesting the President to come to his New York home for a conference at which Senator Aldrich was to be present. Taft suggested that Morgan come to Washington if he wanted to see him.[84]

Taft, quite clearly, did not have the conspiratorial attitude of Roosevelt, of whom Representative Sibley wrote to Archbold under date of January 9, 1904, that he had acquiesced when "Aldrich told him also that he did not know as it would do for Mr. Archbold to come over, as it might cause comment. . . ."[85]

In April, 1911, Senator Aldrich, his daughter Abby, and John D. Rockefeller, Jr., Abby's husband, paid a clandestine visit to the White House for lunch and were cautiously brought in by a back entrance; Taft requested that no entry be made of the arrivals in the White House register for prying journalists to see.[86]

Legislatively, the Taft Administration's accomplishments merely bolstered up the positions of the magnates. Taft's first message, in which he promised tariff reform in consonance with the Republican platform pledge, was perfunctory. It took two minutes to read.

Instead of tariff reform Congress produced the Payne-Aldrich Act, which boosted the tariffs on more than six hundred items and made it possible for American manufacturers, ensconced behind a protective wall, to raise prices to extortionate levels although wages had not moved up correspondingly since the passage of the Dingley Act. The House bill was quickly revised by Aldrich, Hale, Lodge, and Reed Smoot of Utah, sitting on the Senate Finance Committee. Aldrich spent forty-eight hours writing up the rates, the while the lobby outside his office swarmed with the agents of the corporations all clamoring for higher tariffs. Duties on trivial items were reduced.

Beveridge and LaFollette fought without success against the bill; the Senate, like the Supreme Court, was packed with corporation men. LaFollette showed that the tariff reductions amounted to only $45,000 and the increases to $10,000,000. Protected by the old tariff, he proved, the Rockefeller-Ryan American Tobacco Company was making a steady fifty per cent annual profit on its capital and in ten years had abnormally profited to the extent of $180,000,000 at the expense of the public.

Taft nevertheless signed the bill, first describing it as bad but then reversing himself and saying it was the best tariff bill ever written.

The Cabinet under Taft held only corporation lawyers. Knox had resigned his Senate seat to become Secretary of State. George W. Wickersham, Taft's Attorney General, prepared a new railroad bill designed to wipe out the Interstate Commerce Commission. La-Follette and Albert Cummins, however, whittled away at this measure, behind which the Administration stood, until it was no longer recognizable. The Commerce Commission was saved.

Taft bestirred himself in bringing antitrust suits, but directed them against the Morgan camp. Late in 1911, after the hearings of the Stanley Committee, the ax fell on United States Steel. All in all, Taft brought forty-five suits, against only twenty-five by Roosevelt, and yet Roosevelt is remembered as the "trust-buster."

It was the instigation of the suit against United States Steel that finally swung Roosevelt against Taft; Roosevelt complained that Taft, as a Cabinet member, had approved the union of Tennessee Coal and Iron with United States Steel. It was also the bringing of this suit, and another against the International Harvester Company, that set Morgan, standing in back of Roosevelt, against the re-election of Taft. But, with the Stanley Committee's report before the public, Taft had no alternative but to proceed as he did.

The Rockefellers could, of course, do nothing about the pending suit against Standard Oil, which was ordered "dissolved" by the Supreme Court in 1911. Chief Justice Edward White in his decision said the company had been operating in defiance of law for the nineteen years since an Ohio court had ordered it dissolved in 1892.

The unhappy Taft experienced an increasingly hostile press as his Administration matured, and in June, 1910, he ascribed this to the tariff, which, he declared, "did not cut low enough the rate on print paper. . . ."[87]

The general imperialistic foreign policy of McKinley and Roosevelt was continued under Taft, who himself was responsible for giving it the name of "dollar diplomacy." Intervention abroad in favor of Wall Street interests gained momentum under the guiding hand of Secretary of State Philander C. Knox.

Taft threw a very special favor in the way of the Rockefellers' National City Bank and became personally responsible for the sinister flowering of bank securities affiliates when, after a secret White House conference in 1911 with Frank A. Vanderlip, president of the National City Bank, and Henry P. Davison, Morgan partner, he ordered suppressed an important opinion of Solicitor General Frederick W. Lehmann, who held that securities affiliates were illegal. Lehmann's opinion was not made known until February 24, 1933, when it was discovered during the inquiry into Wall Street irregularities by the Senate Banking and Currency Committee.[88] Irreparable injury to the public interest was done for two decades by these securities affiliates which sprang up like locusts around nearly all large commercial banks. As the Senate showed in 1933, they traded in the stock of the parent banks, rigged the securities markets, and sold dubious securities to an unsuspecting public.

When the National City Company was formed as the first securities affiliate the directors of the parent bank were J. Ogden Armour, Cleveland H. Dodge, Henry C. Frick, Joseph P. Grace (Latin American shipping), Robert S. Lovett (chairman of the Union Pacific Railroad), Cyrus H. McCormick, J. P. Morgan the younger, William Rockefeller, Jacob H. Schiff, Moses Taylor, Frank Trumbull (chairman of the Chesapeake and Ohio Railroad), Edwin S. Marston (president of the Farmers Loan and Trust Company), William D. Sloane (son-in-law of William H. Vanderbilt), James A. Stillman, James Stillman, and Frank A. Vanderlip.

The Taft Administration would hardly have been well rounded had there not been at least one resounding scandal involving the overlords of wealth, although the long-deferred revelation of the suppressed Lehmann opinion suggests that there were indeed more than a few Wall Street skeletons in Taft's political closets. The affair which came to light during Taft's incumbency as the Ballinger scandal involved an attempt of the Guggenheims and J. P. Morgan and Company to alienate valuable Alaskan mineral lands from the public domain. Secretary of the Interior Richard A. Ballinger had been an attorney for some of the Guggenheim interests before he took office.

A controversy broke out between Ballinger and Chief Forester Gifford Pinchot over the disposition of the lands, to which fraudulent claims had been filed by the Guggenheims in concert with J. P. Morgan and Company; Ballinger had reopened some of these lands to private exploitation in deference to the spurious claims. Taft promptly ousted Pinchot, but stood by Ballinger until public clamor became too great, and then permitted him to resign. The claims, valued at from $75,000,000 to $100,000,000, were later voided by the courts. Other than this, there never was a definite conclusion to the issue.

Taft also stepped forward on behalf of Charles Heike, secretary and treasurer of the American Sugar Refining Company, who with lesser employees had been convicted in the resounding weighing-machine scandal. Henry O. Havemeyer, president, fortunately died before the prosecution began. Heike, about to serve a term in the penitentiary, was freed by Taft. "The poorer men went to jail." [89]

The Administration had nothing to do with the Pujo Committee investigation launched by the House of Representatives in 1912. This committee revealed that J. P. Morgan, George F. Baker, and James Stillman, by means of virtual shoestrings, controlled in an absolute sense the money market of the nation. Under Morgan domination were companies with an aggregate capitalization of $17,273,000,-000, including the United States Steel Corporation, the International Harvester Company, the International Mercantile Marine, the American Telephone and Telegraph Company, the New Haven Railroad, the New York Life and Equitable Life insurance companies, and many others.

The partners of J. P. Morgan and Company and the directors of Stillman's National City Bank (Rockefeller) and Baker's First National Bank together held, according to the final report of the Pujo Committee:

One hundred and eighteen directorships in 34 banks and trust companies having total resources of $2,679,000,000 and total deposits of $1,983,000,000. Thirty directorships in 10 insurance companies, having total assets of $2,293,000,000. One hundred and five director-ships in 32 transportation systems having a total capitalization of $11,784,000,000 and a total mileage (excluding express companies and steamship lines) of 150,200. Sixty-three directorships in 24 producing and trading corporations having a total capitalization of $3,339,-000,000. Twenty-five directorships in 12 public-utility corporations having a total capitalization of $2,150,000,000. In all, 341 directorships in 112 corporations having aggregate resources or capitalization of $22,245,000,000.

Louis D. Brandeis, reviewing this report, proved that it actually understated the magnitude of resources controlled by this triumvirate of finance capitalists. He found that the great danger was not that these men owned all these resources but that they controlled them by means of "other people's money"—the essence of finance capitalism. Such control made for recklessness of operation, since the very great losses that were sustained from time to time bore most heavily on moderately circumstanced citizens. Such control also made possible the reaping of enormous profits by manipulation, profits in which the actual owners of property usually did not share. The consequences against which Brandeis specifically warned did not descend on the nation until 1929-33.

# IV

# The Politics of Pecuniary Aggrandizement:

## 1912-1920

J. P. MORGAN and Company played the leading role in the national election of 1912. Stellar supporting roles were taken by the National City Bank of New York, Thomas Fortune Ryan, George Harvey, Jacob H. Schiff, Cleveland H. Dodge, and Cyrus McCormick.

Taft and Roosevelt were the only contenders for the nomination at the Republican convention, with Roosevelt's personal popularity pitted against Taft's control of patronage. Patronage won, but not before Roosevelt had dramatized himself skilfully by waging fierce primary and convention fights.

Roosevelt's preconvention backers were George W. Perkins and Frank Munsey. These two, indeed, encouraged Roosevelt to contest Taft's nomination; they also induced him not to compromise at the convention.[1] Since 1895 Perkins and Munsey had been inseparable; and Munsey, although still widely remembered as a newspaper publisher, was actually one of the biggest stock-market operators ever to set foot in Wall Street. He made most of his $40,000,000 fortune in Wall Street speculations conducted through Perkins. In reciprocation for the latter's services Munsey functioned in the newspaper field for J. P. Morgan and Company—buying, selling, creating, and suppressing newspapers in consonance with J. P. Morgan's shifting needs.

Munsey's first big market killing took place in the International Harvester merger of 1902 after Perkins put him in on the ground floor. A novice at the game, Munsey made a fortune overnight. Until he met Perkins in 1895 Munsey, significantly indeed, was often near bankruptcy. But after falling in with the Morgan henchman he branched right out into newspaper publishing, which required much capital.

Munsey was brought into the original United States Steel syndicate, was ushered out before Steel common collapsed, and resumed buy· ing, unquestionably at Perkins' suggestion, after J. P. Morgan and Company had "pegged" the market at slightly more than $8 a share,— using Treasury funds during the panic of 1907. Munsey, in short, was an "insider."

From 1907 to 1911, it was brought out by the Stanley Committee, Munsey was the biggest stockholder in United States Steel, and utilized *Munsey's Magazine*, which then enjoyed a large national circulation, to praise both the company and its stock in a series of "idolatrous" articles written by himself on the basis of facts and figures supplied by the Steel Corporation. The facts and figures, as the Committee proved, were incorrect and misleading.

At times Munsey owned 500,000 to 1,100,000 shares of United States Steel, valued at $30,000,000 to $50,000,000. But when Perkins resigned from J. P. Morgan and Company on January 1, 1911, to assume a larger political role than he had ever played as director of the "Yellow-Dog Fund" of the insurance companies, Munsey's market operations significantly came to an end.[2]

"As they grew older he [Munsey] and Perkins saw each other more often, journeyed to Europe together, and found the close association of brothers in the Roosevelt presidential campaign of 1912."[3] And when Perkins died in June, 1920, Munsey said in a personal eulogy published in the New York *Sun,* which he had acquired from the Morgan-Laffan interests: "I have known Mr. Perkins for more than a quarter century. He had been much in my life; I much in his."

Before his death, however, Perkins brought out of obscurity Will H. Hays, a small-town Indiana lawyer. Perkins was the "principal factor" in selecting Hays as Republican National Chairman.[4]

In 1908 Munsey backed Taft, along with J. P. Morgan and Company, Roosevelt, and Perkins; but as Morgan, Roosevelt, and Perkins turned against Taft, Munsey also turned. The Munsey-Morgan newspapers became exceedingly hostile when suit was brought against the Steel Corporation in October, 1911. Taft merely rubbed salt into the wounds of Munsey as well as of Perkins when he also sued the

International Harvester Company, through whose formation both had made their first big money.

In 1910 Munsey was prompted by Perkins to give $25,000 to the ill-starred New York gubernatorial campaign of Henry L. Stimson, who came from a wealthy family. After his defeat for the governorship, Stimson was made Secretary of War by Taft upon the recommendation of Elihu Root. Under Coolidge he was first the special envoy of the United States to Nicaragua, and then was appointed Governor General of the Philippines. In the Morgan-controlled Hoover Administration Stimson became Secretary of State.

Munsey gave $67,166 to Roosevelt's 1912 preconvention campaign and Perkins gave $123,000, according to the findings of the Senate Privileges and Elections Committee (Clapp Committee). William Flinn, Pittsburgh Republican boss who took orders from Mellon and Frick, gave $144,000, although Mellon and Frick were even then backing Taft; Dan R. Hanna, Mark Hanna's son, gave $77,000; Alexander Smith Cochran, textile manufacturer and Morgan client, gave $25,000; George Emlen Roosevelt, investment banker related to the former President, gave $10,000; and Herbert L. Satterlee, Morgan's son-in-law, gave $600.

The chief contributors to Taft's preconvention fund were Andrew W. Mellon and Richard B. Mellon, $2,500 each; James Laughlin, Jr., and Henry A. Laughlin, of Jones and Laughlin Steel Company, $5,000 each; Julius Rosenwald, $5,000; George T. Oliver, Pittsburgh newspaper publisher financed by Mellon and Frick, $7,000; George Westinghouse, of the Westinghouse Electric and Manufacturing Company, $1,000; H. C. McEldowney, Mellon bank official, $500; Henry Chalfant, steel manufacturer, $1,000; Andrew Carnegie, $1,000; H. M. Byllesby, investment banker, $1,000; Isaac N. Seligman, New York investment banker, $500; Clarence H. Mackay, owner of the Postal Telegraph-Cable Company, $1,000; and Jacob H. Schiff, of Kuhn, Loeb and Company, $500.

Gifford and Amos Pinchot each gave $10,000 to LaFollette's preconvention fund before the announcement of Roosevelt's candidacy, after which they switched to the "Rough Rider"; William Flinn gave the LaFollette fund $1,000 before Roosevelt entered the field. Charles R. Crane of Chicago, head of the so-called Bathtub Trust, gave La-

Follette $23,500, and Rudolph Spreckels, California sugar magnate and civic reformer, gave him $3,000.

Dark forces bored busily from within the Democratic Party. Of a preconvention fund of $50,000 for Senator Oscar W. Underwood of Alabama, $35,000 was supplied in a lump by the sinister, self-effacing Thomas Fortune Ryan of the Rockefeller camp, who also gave $77,000 to the $146,000 preconvention fund of Governor Judson Harmon, of Ohio, another presidential aspirant. James J. Hill of the Morgan forces gave Harmon $15,000. Ryan's control of the Underwood, Harmon, and Tammany delegations in the Democratic convention was to be wielded to nominate Woodrow Wilson, whom Ryan supported as well from other directions, although on the convention floor he gave nominal support to Champ Clark. The luckless Clark, Speaker of the House and favorite of the subsidized Democratic press, had a relatively small known preconvention fund derived mostly from regional political bosses, with whom he was popular, and from William Randolph Hearst, who gave him $8,500.

The financial genius behind Woodrow Wilson was Cleveland H. Dodge, of the National City Bank, who surreptitiously exercised the most pervasive influence of any unofficial person in the two Wilson Administrations. Dodge gathered $85,000 for Wilson's preconvention campaign, and of this sum he contributed $51,000. Cyrus H. McCormick and Jacob H. Schiff supplied the balance. Schiff was the senior partner of Kuhn, Loeb and Company, and McCormick was head of the International Harvester Company.

Charles R. Crane gave $10,000; William F. McCombs, Wilson's campaign manager and by his own admission a confidential agent for Thomas Fortune Ryan and Charles F. Murphy,[5] $11,000; Henry Morgenthau, New York realty operator who became Wilson's Minister to Turkey, $20,000; and Samuel Untermyer, ambitious New York lawyer, $7,000.

Roosevelt was defeated for the Republican nomination at the Chicago convention when the legitimate credentials of most of his delegates, won at primaries, were blandly ruled out by the credentials committee under Root and Aldrich. Root bore a fresh personal grievance against Roosevelt, who, he believed, should have thrown the presidency to him in 1908; Aldrich had definitely aligned himself with the Rockefellers. The Mellon-Frick influence was also now exerted against Roosevelt through Secretary of State Knox.

"George Perkins and Frank Munsey influenced the politics of this country in 1912 more than any men with whose activities at the time I am familiar," says Henry L. Stoddard, former publisher of the New York *Evening Mail* (secretly financed by Perkins).[6] "There certainly would have been no national Progressive Party but for those two men; there probably would not have been a Roosevelt candidacy for nomination in the convention against Taft but for them." [7]

Stoddard was present in the Auditorium Annex Hotel, Chicago, after Roosevelt's convention defeat, when Munsey and Perkins both urged the former President, now grown reluctant to jeopardize his reputation further, to seek election on a third party ticket.[8] In that hotel room was born the Progressive Party, which rallied to its standard thousands of sincere liberals.

Roosevelt, ever irresolute, would not, as Stoddard makes clear, have contested Taft's nomination and candidacy had it not been for the insistence of Munsey and Perkins. "William L. Ward, George Perkins, and Frank Munsey were the directing heads" of Roosevelt's fight for anti-Taft delegates.[9] Perkins, indeed, was the floor manager of the struggle, in the course of which Munsey was offered for $200,000 a block of accredited delegates' votes sufficient to assure Roosevelt's nomination.[10] Munsey refused the offer, and in view of the vast sums subsequently spent by him and Perkins to forward the Progressive campaign and insure Taft's defeat, the suspicion seems justified that the two were not overanxious to have Roosevelt win. The notion that Perkins and Munsey may have wanted Wilson to win, or any Democratic candidate other than Bryan, is partly substantiated by the fact that Perkins put a good deal of cash behind the Wilson campaign through Cleveland H. Dodge. Dodge and Perkins financed, to the extent of $35,500, the Trenton *True American,* a newspaper that circulated nationally with Wilson propaganda.[11]

As soon as Roosevelt signified that he would again challenge Taft the President's defeat was inevitable. Throughout the three-cornered fight Roosevelt had Munsey and Perkins constantly at his heels, supplying money, going over his speeches, bringing people from

Wall Street in to help, and, in general, carrying the entire burden of the campaign against Taft. There was nothing distinctive about the platforms of the three parties once their common planks were eliminated, as is aptly observed by David Saville Muzzey, the historian. An attempt was made, however, to make the Progressive platform unique by including a strong antitrust plank, but this was ruled out by George W. Perkins, chairman of the party's executive committee.[12] Amos Pinchot thereupon precipitated a fierce struggle behind the scenes, calling upon Roosevelt to repudiate Perkins.[13] This Roosevelt refused to do. Pinchot, perhaps was a little naïve, for Perkins and J. P. Morgan and Company were the substance of the Progressive Party; everything else was trimming.

Senator Beveridge was induced to join the Progressive insurgents (some, at least, were insurgents) upon the promise of Perkins and Munsey that the new party would be placed upon a permanent basis and would continue the good fight after the election.[14] Yet three months after the campaign Munsey was publicly suggesting that the Progressive Party, which had polled more votes than the Republican Party, be merged with it; and Perkins was turning aside with evasive jests Beveridge's perturbed inquiries.[15]

And when the moment came to bury the synthetic Progressive Party, Munsey and Perkins left the task to Roosevelt, thus escaping the appearance of breaking faith with Beveridge.

Roosevelt tried to sneak back into the Republican fold right after the election, and his antics led Beveridge to make this bitter statement: "I think that history has not one single example of a party or a movement which was used so cold-bloodedly and wrecked so cynically and selfishly as the Progressive Party has been used and wrecked." [16]

Beveridge in 1912 suddenly attained great public stature when the Senate Privileges and Elections Committee, ignoring palpably venal senators and maliciously singling him out because of his liberalism, asked him to explain the receipt of $30,000 from George W. Perkins in 1904. Beveridge, by affidavits and witnesses, proved he had returned the $30,000 at once. The committee members, intent upon besmirching a foe, pressed Beveridge to produce a telegram he had then received from Perkins. This Beveridge was loath to do. When the committee insisted Beveridge handed over the message, which read:

LETTER AND TELEGRAM RECEIVED. AN HONEST MAN IS THE NO-
BLEST WORK OF GOD. GEORGE.

Beveridge was made the chairman and keynote speaker of the Progressive Convention which nominated the hand-picked Roosevelt.

Roosevelt's most celebrated 1912 campaign speech was delivered at Columbus, where he endorsed the judicial recall and lost the support of middle-of-the-road voters. But immediately thereafter he indicated that he favored judicial reform merely as a long-range possibility; this qualification made Western liberals and agrarians suspicious and threw them, pell-mell, behind Wilson. The speech, incidentally, like all those Roosevelt ever made on public questions, was revised in advance by the magnates. The hidden editor, in this case, was E. C. Converse, president of the Bankers Trust Company of New York (Morgan).

Munsey's cash contribution to the Progressive Party brought his total political outlay for 1912 to $229,255.72. Perkins made their joint contribution more than $500,000, and Munsey expended $1,000,-000 in cash additionally to acquire from Henry Einstein the New York *Press* so that Roosevelt would have a New York City morning newspaper. Perkins and Munsey, as the Clapp Committee learned from Roosevelt himself, also underwrote the heavy expense of Roosevelt's campaign train. In short, most of Roosevelt's campaign fund was supplied by the two Morgan hatchet men who were seeking Taft's scalp.

Munsey and Perkins, as it afterward came out, however, had not used only their own money for Roosevelt. They received funds in secret from James Stillman, Elbert H. Gary, head of United States Steel, Daniel G. Reid, founder of the American Can Company and a director in many Morgan railroads and banks, Charles F. Brooker, vice-president of the New Haven Railroad, and Robert L. Bacon, former Morgan partner.

Champ Clark was maneuvered out of the Democratic nomination at Baltimore after a tediously prolonged casting of ballots under the two-thirds rule. Clark led from the beginning, but the tide was inadvertently turned to Wilson by Bryan, who was seeking the nomination a fourth time.

Bryan denounced Clark ostensibly because the latter was openly supported by Hearst, Thomas Fortune Ryan, August Belmont, and Tammany Hall. But Bryan, in his three attempts at the presidency, had been only too willing to accept Tammany and Hearst support, as well as the support of W. A. Clark, Montana copper king. Bryan did not realize, apparently, that the vote would quickly swing to Wilson, once Clark was eliminated. Ryan had carefully lubricated the convention mechanism for just this eventuality.

Soon after Bryan's denunciation Senator Underwood arose for Alabama and cast its Ryan-financed votes for Wilson. This started the drift to Wilson which swept into its current the Ryan-financed Ohio delegation as well.

When the turn of Nebraska came Bryan, not sensing the direction of the wind, cast its votes for Wilson, although the delegation had been pledged to Clark at the primaries. The votes of the New York delegation, under Rockefeller-Ryan-Tammany control, and cast earlier for Harmon, were now swung to Clark, thus putting the curse on him in the eyes of the Bryanites and prolonging the balloting. Charles F. Murphy, the Tammany leader, as we shall see when we scrutinize the work of George W. Harvey, was induced by a ruse to vote for Clark. Had he thrown Tammany's vote to Wilson he would have opened wide the door for Bryan.

Wilson's nomination represented a personal triumph for Cleveland H. Dodge, director of the National City Bank, scion of the Dodge copper and munitions fortune, and inheritor of the invisible mantle that passed from Mark Hanna to George W. Perkins. The nomination represented no less a triumph for Ryan, Harvey, and J. P. Morgan and Company. Sitting with Dodge as co-directors of the National City Bank at the time were the younger J. P. Morgan, now the head of the firm, Jacob Schiff, William Rockefeller, J. Ogden Armour, and James Stillman. In short, except for George F. Baker, everyone whom the Pujo Committee had termed rulers of the "Money Trust" was in this bank.

But before the complicated machinery which gave Wilson the Democratic nomination was set into motion, Dodge arranged a significant meeting between the presidential aspirant and James Stillman and William Rockefeller at Beechwood, the estate of Frank A. Vanderlip, president of the National City Bank.[17] What was said has not, of course, been placed upon the record yet, and perhaps never will be; but the connection of Wilson with the National City Bank, we know, was very close and has an important bearing upon crucial decisions during Wilson's White House occupancy.

During the campaign Vanderlip supplied the fiscal and monetary views for Wilson's speeches through William Gibbs McAdoo, who acted as go-between.[18] Wilson annoyed Vanderlip by refusing to receive him in person; the candidate was obviously afraid to be seen with financiers.[19]

After his nomination Wilson was prompted by Perry Belmont, banker, corporation director, brother of August Belmont, and contributor to Champ Clark's fund, to declare in favor of the free passage of American coastwise vessels through the Panama Canal, despite the British contention that this would contravene the Hay-Pauncefote Treaty of 1901. Belmont's recommendation was incorporated verbatim in a Wilson speech, although the source was not mentioned.[20]

For nearly twenty years before his nomination Woodrow Wilson had moved in the shadow of Wall Street. The magnates knew as much about him in 1912 as they had known about McKinley or Taft when they were nominated; they knew a great deal more about him than they had known about Roosevelt in 1901. Dodge and McCormick had been Wilson's classmates at Princeton University, class of 1879. When Wilson returned to Princeton as a professor in 1890, Dodge and McCormick were, by reason of their wealth, university trustees. Discerning Wilson's unquestioned abilities, they set about doing all they could to advance his career.

In 1898 Wilson, his salary unsatisfactory, besieged with offers of many university presidencies, threatened to resign. Dodge and McCormick thereupon constituted themselves his financial guardians, and agreed to raise the additional informal stipendium that kept him at Princeton. The contributors to this private fund were Dodge, McCormick, and Moses Taylor Pyne and Percy R. Pyne, of the family that founded the National City Bank.[21] In 1902 this same group arranged Wilson's election as president of the university. The induction of the new president was witnessed by Morgan, Harvey, Walter Hines Page, Grover Cleveland, then a Princeton trustee, Thomas B. Reed, Speaker of the House, Dodge, the Pynes, and McCormick.

Dodge and Wilson corresponded constantly through the years on intimate terms, the latter habitually addressing the banker as "Dear Cleve." [22] Dodge at all times acted as Wilson's agent in approaching wealthy persons like Mrs. Russell Sage and Andrew Carnegie for university gifts; by 1910 Dodge stood as close to Wilson as Hanna in 1896 had stood to McKinley.

In 1902 a potent figure burst into Wilson's life in the person of George W. Harvey, who as president of Harper and Brothers, then undergoing reorganization by J. P. Morgan and Company, was impressed by Wilson's *History of the American People,* published by Harper's.[23] Harvey was a Morgan-Ryan henchman from his boots up, and ran *The North American Review* from 1899 to 1926 as his personal organ for the propagation of Wall Street points of view.

Acutely sensitive politically owing to his long training under Thomas Fortune Ryan and William C. Whitney, Harvey almost immediately visualized Wilson as a man of presidential caliber, and began extolling him in the Wall Street counting rooms. So successful was he that early in 1904 Wilson was summoned to meet a powerful clique in a private dining room at Delmonico's, an event related in the memoirs of Edward P. Mitchell, for many decades the editor of the New York *Sun.* The hosts were Thomas Fortune Ryan, William Laffan, Morgan's deputy in charge of the rigidly Republican *Sun,* Dr. John A. Wyeth, president of the Southern Society of New York, and Francis L. Stetson.[24] In the course of the evening the ubiquitous Elihu Root, Republican Cabinet member, casually strolled in to inspect the Democratic prospect.

Neither Laffan nor Ryan was favorably impressed. But Harvey, undeterred, felt sure he had discovered a future Chief Executive. Again in 1906, at a Lotos Club dinner, with all the magnates present, including Morgan, Harvey boldly proposed the Princetonian for the presidency. He also began beating the tom-tom for him in *Harper's*

*Weekly,* which on March 10, 1906, saluted Wilson as a Democratic presidential prospect for 1908.

Harvey went in person to the Democratic convention of that year to procure the nomination for his protégé.[25] During the deliberations Wilson waited nervously at Princeton for news, as his biographer relates; but Bryan snared the nomination for the third time, and was to prove for the third time that it was impossible to get into the White House without the consent of the reigning families. On May 15, 1909, *Harper's Weekly* predicted that Wilson would be elected Governor of New Jersey in 1910 and President of the United States in 1912.

Harvey is worthy of brief attention if the factors that made Wilson a President of the United States are to be understood. Harvey owed his eminence to Thomas Fortune Ryan and William C. Whitney, with whom he worked in close harmony while he was managing editor of the New York *World,* during the second Cleveland presidential campaign.[26] In 1891 he resigned from *The World* to become advertising manager and publicity agent for the Whitney-Ryan Metropolitan Street Railway, then engaged in giving the public a forced diet of bogus securities. So successful was Harvey in getting "puffs" about the Metropolitan inserted into the newspapers that he was made an insider in many Whitney-Ryan stock-market pools. His sole function was, indeed, simply to see that the newspapers printed matter that made their readers accept arguments in favor of the wholesale traction mergers then going on, and come into the stock market for a thorough trimming. For more than a decade Harvey worked this greasy game, and eventually came to the favorable attention of J. P. Morgan and Company.

Another detail of Harvey's background, which dovetailed with his profitable Whitney-Ryan association, made it possible for him to function decisively in forwarding the political fortunes of Wilson. Back in the 1880's, while employed by *The World,* Harvey had been a resident of New Jersey. In 1887 he resigned from *The World* and accepted the managing editorship of the Newark *Journal,* owned by James Smith, Jr. Harvey remained in Newark about a year before returning to the wider opportunities offered by *The World,* and in 1888 became aide-de-camp of the Governor of New Jersey, gaining the appellation of "Colonel." With this sunburst insignia clinging to him and while still editing *The World*, he became in 1890 the State Commissioner of Banking and Insurance of New Jersey.

Harvey's New Jersey connections made him invaluable to Whitney and Ryan, then insinuating themselves into New Jersey traction, electric, and gas companies. It was, indeed, the year after he met Whitney and Ryan that he went to Newark. In 1892 he introduced his former Newark employer, James Smith, Jr., to William C. Whitney, the invisible power behind the Cleveland Administration;[27] and Whitney, by a judicious use of money, induced the New Jersey State Legislature to send Smith to the United States Senate, where he sat, a Whitney-Ryan agent, until 1899.

Smith was not ungrateful to Harvey for having gained him this political preferment, which enabled him to become the Democratic boss of New Jersey. After listening to Harvey's representations, he procured for Wilson the gubernatorial nomination on the first ballot of the Trenton Democratic State Convention in October, 1910. It was common talk in political circles that Dodge had been forced to give Smith $75,000 to get Wilson nominated.[28] Wilson also had to promise, through Harvey, to make Smith a Senator again in 1912; but Wilson was to repudiate this agreement when the time came for its fulfillment, giving the Dodge-Harvey propaganda agents the opportunity to boast that the great Princeton democrat had repudiated the "bosses."

Wilson carried New Jersey in the general movement of popular revulsion against the Taft Administration marked by the Democratic congressional victories of 1910. His campaign was financed by Dodge, although the general public knew nothing of it. Wilson, truth to tell, was a "natural" candidate. The Harvey propaganda, for example, transmuted what had been a feud among the Princeton faculty members into a glorious, but unsuccessful, struggle by Wilson to "democratize" the university by doing away with campus eating clubs!

Throughout Wilson's gubernatorial term *Harper's Weekly* sedulously boomed him for the presidency. But eventually the open support of this periodical, known far and wide as a Morgan publication, became embarrassing, and Wilson asked Harvey to be less fervid in his support. "Then I will sing low," said Harvey.[29] Reports that there had been a quarrel with Harvey, helpful to Wilson among the Western Democrats, were then circulated. So realistic did Harvey make his sudden hostility appear that Wilson became alarmed and dispatched two abject letters of apology.[30] Despite the supposed antagonism between the two men, which gave inordinate satisfaction to liberal Wilsonians, *Harper's* continued to push the Wilson cause, albeit quietly.

At the convention of 1912 Harvey ostentatiously supported Clark, but Harvey's authorized biographer makes it clear that he did so merely to confuse Bryan. [31] It was Harvey who got Alabama to vote for Wilson immediately after Bryan's denunciation of Clark;[32] and it was Harvey who induced Murphy, the Tammany chieftain, to stand firm against Wilson.[32]

Harvey, indeed, duped Murphy by telling him flatly that Wilson as President would do nothing for Tammany.[33] With Wilson's cynical treatment of James Smith, Jr., fresh in mind, Murphy could well believe this. Murphy, moreover, assumed that Harvey, who had done so much to create Wilson politically, knew his man. Much to the satisfaction of the Wilson forces, he stuck grimly by Clark throughout the subsequent balloting.

That Murphy at this time was under the control of Thomas Fortune Ryan has been very positively established on the record. In 1912 Ryan gave Murphy at least $10,000 and at the same time Anthony N. Brady gave the Tammany chief at least $25,000.[34] Such contributions to Tammany were regularly made by Ryan and Brady.

William G. McAdoo, traction promoter and, later, Wilson's Secretary of the Treasury, was brought into the fight for Wilson by William F. McCombs, a Ryan agent. A former pupil under Wilson at Princeton and a graduate of the Princeton Law School, McCombs hopped on the band wagon after Wilson had been elected Governor of New Jersey. He was chairman of the Democratic National Committee by 1912, at the age of thirty-five, firmly re-established with Wilson on the basis of their former academic relationship.

McAdoo was already celebrated for his promotion of the Hudson and Manhattan Railroad, which connected New York and New Jersey by tunnel under the Hudson. Long before 1912 McAdoo had become an integral part of the New York public-utilities network, shown by John Moody's standard *Truth About the Trusts* (1904) to have been dominated by Ryan and the Rockefellers through National City Bank since the beginning of the century.*

Brady in 1901 gave McAdoo's Hudson and Manhattan Railroad project financial backing; the Guaranty Trust Company (Morgan) also put up money.[85] The Bradys were so impressed by McAdoo's abilities that in 1919 Nicholas and James Brady, sons of the quondam Albany grocery clerk, offered McAdoo, then resigning as Secretary of the Treasury, the lucrative receivership of the Brooklyn Rapid Transit Company.[86] McAdoo had to reject this offer; he was about to move to California, there to become counsel to E. L. Doheny, owner of the Mexican Petroleum Company.

But it was Ryan's man, McCombs, who obtained political preferment for McAdoo. First McCombs got McAdoo elected president, over the heads of more eligible persons, of the Southern Society of New York, a semipolitical body. Then he contrived to have McAdoo twice re-elected. McCombs introduced McAdoo to Wilson when the latter was Governor of New Jersey after McAdoo had signified a desire to talk to the New Jersey Governor about certain public-utilities regulations that affected the Hudson and Manhattan Railroad in New Jersey.[87]

So successful was Wilson's campaign on behalf of "The New Freedom" that the general public contributed large sums in small individual amounts to his campaign finances. When Wilson testified before the Clapp Committee he was able to say righteously that McCormick and Dodge had recalled their contributions to his campaign. These tidings created a favorable impression, even though McCormick and Dodge had been impelled to recall their contributions by the uproar that followed the Clapp Committee's preconvention fund revelations.

Although the nature and extent of the Roosevelt campaign contributions were spread on the record, details of the Taft and Wilson postconvention campaign funds have been lost; Charles P. Taft, however, gave $150,000 to his brother's campaign. Information about other contributions, placed in the hands of the Clerk of the House of Representatives in accordance with an Act of Congress, was soon

* See Appendix A: "The Public-Utilities Background of Wilson's Backers."

afterward thoughtfully destroyed—because Congress had not yet stipulated that it should be made a permanent matter of record!

After the 1912 disclosures extraordinarily large individual contributions to the political parties, while not unknown, became less numerous. Yet the money continued to gush forth from essentially the same inexhaustible sources. A factor in the new technique of making political contributions was the income-tax law enacted in the first Wilson Administration. To reduce taxes, corporations in general increased the salaries of their officials to outrageous levels, with the understanding that they show "public spirit" by donating a portion of their income to political parties and controlled charities. And after 1912 the magnates also pressed their families into service in making political contributions, so that now wives, sons, daughters, sisters, cousins, aunts, and uncles, as well as major and minor employees, patriotically help swell political slush funds. Since 1916 thousands of contributions ranging from $500 to $5,000 have come from persons easily traceable to the inner circle of the dominant families.

## II

Woodrow Wilson took office ominously, one might say, as a reformer and a liberal.

Wall Street was not disturbed. As George Harvey later wrote, vested wealth accepted Wilson's election "without serious misgivings"; the capitalists, he said, "felt no animosity toward Mr. Wilson for such of his utterances as they regarded as radical and menacing to their interests. He had simply played the political game."

The first Wilson Administration brought various superficial reforms. The Underwood Tariff Act scaled down the rates of the Payne-Aldrich Tariff by ten per cent. An income-tax law was attached as an amendment to the new tariff bill in accordance with the terms of a new Constitutional amendment. The schedule provided for a levy of one per cent on incomes of more than $3,000 and a graduated surtax on incomes of more than $20,000; the surtax amounted to only six per cent on incomes of more than $500,000. Liberals hailed the new tax law as a brake on the fortunes, but the fortunes were all too firmly established. The Adamson Law set an eight-hour day for railroad workers, but it was passed in the face of a threatened general railroad strike.

In his first message to Congress the President gave liberals a thrill by intoning, "We must abolish everything that bears even the semblance of privilege or any kind of artificial advantage."

The Clayton Antitrust Act was passed in deference to the pretense of newspapers and politicians that the Sherman Act was unworkable. Such a conclusion was hardly warranted, for there never was waged a sincere prosecution under the Sherman Act. The Clayton Act was, not without design, even less of a bar to monopoly than its predecessor. The Wilson Administration also established the Federal Trade Commission, successor to the old Bureau of Corporations.

The Federal Reserve Act was passed in the first Wilson term, and, although the class paternity of this measure impugns it before history, it is technically one of the most constructive laws ever enacted. As with all laws, however, its operation depended upon the social bias of its administrators, and the administration of the Reserve System has reposed from the beginning in Wall Street hands.

The Federal Reserve Act was the offshoot of a bill originally presented in the Senate by the dubious Aldrich, whose measure incorporated the collective wisdom of a monetary commission under his chairmanship. The ideas of the commission in turn emanated from the fertile brains of the Wall Street clique, whose deputies worked out the details in 1908 at the remote Jekyll Island Club, Jekyll Island, off the Georgia coast, during an ostensible duckhunting expedition.[38] Among those present were Paul M. Warburg, partner of Kuhn, Loeb and Company; Henry P. Davison, partner of J. P. Morgan and Company; Frank A. Vanderlip, president of the National City Bank; Dr. Piatt Andrew, special assistant to the Senate Monetary Commission; and Benjamin Strong, vice-president of the Bankers Trust Company (Morgan).

The protracted Jekyll Island conference took place in the atmosphere of an elaborate conspiracy. The trip to Georgia was made in a private car chartered by Aldrich, and the travelers all used assumed names so that the train crew would not establish their identities.[39] For a long time there was no public knowledge that such a conclave had been held.

The financiers wanted a central bank on the European model, to facilitate the large-scale manipulation of the national economy. An instrument was desired that would function as had the United States Bank, smashed by President Andrew Jackson because it concentrated immense monetary power in private hands.

But when Aldrich introduced the scenario produced by the Jekyll Island duck hunters it was immediately hooted down as a nefarious Wall Street enterprise and, for the time being, came to naught.

The task of the liberal Wilson Administration was to place essentially the Jekyll Island measure on the statute books, but in an eccentric guise. The job of drawing up such a bill was given to Paul M. Warburg, one of the Jekyll Island plotters. Warburg collaborated with all the big financiers, as his own memoirs reveal, and when Administration views were needed he conferred with Colonel Edward M. House, Wilson's roving commissioner. House attained world eminence by the masterly feat of keeping the Texas delegation solidly for Wilson at the 1912 convention.

The Warburg-Wall Street draft, superficially revised by Wilson and Senator Carter Glass of Virginia, was simply the Jekyll Island duck hunters' scheme for a central bank, dressed up in fancy toggery. There was some opposition to it from uninformed Wall Street quarters, but it was, significantly, endorsed by the American Bankers Association.

In practice the Federal Reserve Bank of New York became the fountainhead of the system of twelve regional banks, for New York was the money market of the nation. The other eleven banks were so many expensive mausoleums erected to salve the local pride and quell the Jacksonian fears of the hinterland. Benjamin Strong, one of the original duck hunters, son-in-law of E. C. Converse, and Converse's successor as president of the Bankers Trust Company, was selected as the first Governor of the New York Reserve Bank. An adept in high finance, Strong for many years manipulated the country's monetary system at the discretion of directors representing the leading New York banks. Under Strong the Reserve System, unsuspected by the nation, was brought into interlocking relations with the Bank of England and the Bank of France, greatly strengthening the financial fabric of the political *status quo* in the western hemisphere. While Wall Street, during and after the World War, moved on to ever enlarging profits, the farmers, whom the Reserve System was ostensibly created to assist, went from bad to worse.

After the passage of the Federal Reserve Act, Thomas Fortune Ryan commended Wilson in one of his rare public statements: "He is a great man and a great President." [40]

Five days after Wilson's inauguration Henry P. Davison, of J. P. Morgan and Company, and Willard Straight, son-in-law of William C. Whitney, visited the White House to ask presidential approval for American participation in the six-power Chinese loan.[41] Wilson refused, perhaps because at this particular point he was still closely attuned to the more insular views of the banker-industrialists as personified by Dodge and McCormick. Cyrus McCormick, after Dodge, was Wilson's closest adviser throughout.[42]

In May, 1913, James Speyer, of the banking house of Speyer and Company, called at the State Department and confided his anxiety that the Huerta regime in Mexico would default on a $10,000,000 loan maturing in June.[43]

Henry Clay Frick dropped in at the White House to ask that the dissolution suit against United States Steel be quashed; but Wilson decided this heavily publicized litigation would have to take its course.

Lesser government officials were also importuned to bestir themselves for Wall Street. J. P. Morgan appeared personally at the Treasury Department to tell McAdoo that he opposed the shipping bill which provided for government purchase or construction of ships.[44] On July 31, 1914, Morgan telephoned McAdoo to discuss the outbreak of war in Europe.[45]

The biggest problem confronting Wilson when he took office was the situation in Mexico. And it was in this connection that Cleveland H. Dodge, who owned big Mexican copper properties, first functioned significantly behind the scenes.

In 1911 Porfirio Diaz, dictator of Mexico, was driven from an office in which for many years he had collaborated, along mutually profitable lines, with American mining and oil millionaires like Hearst, Doheny, Dodge, and Rockefeller. But it was Standard Oil that dislodged Diaz.

Percy N. Furber, president of Oil Fields of Mexico, Ltd., in 1918 told C. W. Barron that "the [Mexican] revolution was really caused by H. Clay Pierce," who owned thirty-five per cent of the stock of the Pierce-Waters Oil Company, which Standard Oil controlled through a sixty-five per cent stock interest, and was a confidential Rockefeller henchman. "He wanted to get my property," said Furber, who continued: "H. Clay Pierce demanded of Diaz that he should take off the taxes on oil imports" to enable Standard Oil to bring in products from the United States. "Diaz refused. . . . Pierce put up the money behind Francisco Madero and started the revolution . . . neither Clay Pierce or anybody else ever dreamed of what would follow." [46]

Standard Oil's Francisco Madero was ousted on February 18, 1913, and was executed by Victoriano Huerta, pawn of British oil interests. The revolutionary movement deepened. To the north Carranza and his lieutenant, Pancho Villa, took the field against Huerta. The Carranzistas soon obtained backing from Cleveland H. Dodge and his companion magnates. Wilson from the outset refused to recognize Huerta's government.

But Dodge and others with large stakes in Mexico, alarmed by the threat of events, proposed that Huerta be given American recognition if he promised to hold elections, which would give them a chance to install friendly officials. A memorandum to this effect was relayed to Colonel House by Julius Kruttschnitt, chairman of the Southern Pacific Company. House sent it to Wilson. This memorandum, drawn by D. J. Haff, a Kansas City lawyer, was approved, before being sent to Washington, by Phelps, Dodge and Company, of which Cleveland H. Dodge was vice-president, the Greene Cananea Copper Company of Mexico, and E. L. Doheny of the Mexican Oil Company. [47]

Haff then called to confer with Wilson, and was introduced by Dodge, whose "approval always went far with the President." [48]

There was one compelling reason why Huerta should be denied recognition if he refused to take orders from Washington, and he did refuse. The reason was simply that Huerta had been violently installed in place of Standard Oil's Madero by Lord Cowdray, head of the British oil interests in Mexico. [49] Wilson, indeed, in a communication to Sir Edward Grey, the British Foreign Secretary, vowed that he would oust Huerta, whom the British government and various of its international satellites had hastily recognized.[50]

Not until the early part of 1914 did Wilson give up hope of bringing Huerta under the thumb of Dodge, Rockefeller, and the National City Bank. A number of provocative acts by American armed forces disclosed the new temper in Washington. On April 9, 1914, American sailors landed at Tampico, ostensibly to replenish water and gasoline supplies. They were arrested by Huerta's troops, but upon protest from Washington were released. There was some astonishment in the United States when Wilson insisted that Huerta salute the United States flag and apologize. Huerta refused. Under international law the circumstances gave Washington no occasion to demand a formal salute.

On April 21, 1914, American warships, upon instructions from Washington, shelled Vera Cruz to prevent a German ship from landing munitions consigned to Huerta. There was loss of life and great property damage.

On July 15, 1914, Huerta, the odds against him obviously too great, was forced out, and Venustiano Carranza took office on behalf of the National City Bank of New York. When it became clear to Carranza's revolutionary adherents that he, too, had betrayed them, they took the field under Pancho Villa, portrayed in the American press as a common bandit but actually a social revolutionary. In 1915 and 1916 the Wilson Administration tried by armed intervention to pluck this thorn in Carranza's side. Villa's border attacks on American towns were calculated, indeed, to provoke American intervention and thereby to undermine Carranza in the political esteem of the Mexican people.

The story of Dodge's collaboration with Carranza, fortunately, has been left on the record by Frank H. Blighton, a newspaper man whose personal integrity was formally vouched for by former Governor George W. P. Hunt and Senator Henry F. Ashurst, both of Arizona.[51]

Blighton recalled that Dodge had a dubious record. In 1907 Dodge and Louis D. Ricketts were indicted in the Territory of New Mexico for attempting to alienate government mineral lands under fraudulent circumstances. W. H. H. Llewellyn, United States Territorial Attorney, refused to prosecute them, and was for this reason removed by

Attorney General Charles J. Bonaparte. Peyton Gordon, Llewellyn's successor, was just getting ready to draw the legal net around Dodge and Ricketts when Wilson took office. He was precipitately removed by Attorney General James C. McReynolds, a railroad lawyer who entered the Wilson Cabinet on the recommendation of Colonel House and was soon afterward appointed to the Supreme Court of the United States, where he became the most outspoken reactionary of the American bench.

Counsel for Dodge and Ricketts in this action were Albert B. Fall and Thomas B. Catron, both later made United States Senators by the oil and mining interests. Fall, an old school chum of Doheny, is known to history as one Cabinet member caught in venal intrigue with the millionaires—and, mirabile dictu, convicted.

While this New Mexican case was pending Dodge, Ricketts, Arthur Curtiss James, copper and railroad magnate by inheritance and allied by marriage with the Dodge family, and James McLean, vice-president of Phelps, Dodge and Company, were indicted in Globe, Arizona, by a grand jury sitting under J. R. B. Alexander, Assistant United States Attorney General. Grounds of action were similar to those in the New Mexican case.

Soon after Wilson was inaugurated the two Federal indictments were dismissed upon formal order of McReynolds.

Dodge then proceeded to plunge into further illegal adventures; but his operations now concerned Mexico, where he had big properties, and involved gunrunning to the Carranzistas. Dodge was a director and big stockholder of the Winchester Arms Company, the Union Metallic Cartridge Company, and the Remington Arms Company, as well as of Phelps, Dodge and Company, the El Paso and Southwestern Railroad, and the National City Bank.

In May, 1913, the manager of Phelps, Dodge and Company at Bisbee, Arizona, supplied J. L. Perez, a Carranza lieutenant, with ninety thousand rounds of cartridges—this in violation of a munitions embargo proclaimed by Taft on March 14, 1912. As the ammunition was being transported to Mexico it was intercepted by an American border patrol. Perez and his co-workers confessed and pleaded guilty.

United States Attorney Joseph E. Morrison promptly lodged complaints against Dodge, certain of his employees, and Winchester Arms officials, and prepared to ask for their indictment. The Department of Justice thereupon requested Morrison's resignation, which he refused to submit. On October 22, 1913, McReynolds peremptorily ordered Morrison not to indict the Winchester Arms Company. A copy of this interesting message is preserved.[52]

Morrison complied with McReynolds' order. But he brought indictments against two local officers of Phelps, Dodge and Company and others, and not long after this he was removed from office by McReynolds. Morrison thereupon dispatched a long telegram to Washington in which he accused the Attorney General and the Department of Justice of obstructing the course of justice. This message, a copy of which is preserved, gave many details of the case.[53]

On August 7, 1913, President Wilson had appointed W. H. Sawtelle, of Tucson, to the Federal District Court of Arizona. The case against the Dodge employees was tried before him, and, despite a mass of evidence and a host of witnesses, Sawtelle brusquely dismissed the action.

President Wilson, having found it impossible to wean Huerta from Cowdray and the British Foreign Office, on February 12, 1914, lifted the Mexican arms embargo with the pious explanation that conditions had changed since Taft imposed it. Thereupon a stream of cartridges, rifles, and miscellaneous war materials moved steadily to Carranza from Remington Arms and Winchester Arms. And on July 15, 1914, Huerta, his European arms supply cut off by the United States Navy, fled his office before the advancing Carranzistas. Wilson had made good his threat to the British Foreign Secretary.

Representative William A. Rodenberg, of Illinois, on September 6, 1916, formally charged that Dodge was personally responsible for the shipment of one million rounds of cartridges to Carranza. Rodenberg said Dodge had visited the State Department the day before Wilson lifted the arms embargo.

The Dodge ammunition enterprises were to figure significantly but not prominently in the Wilson Administration. After the merchant liner and British naval auxiliary *Lusitania* had been sunk in 1915, and after Wilson had dispatched the indignant note to Germany which did much to crystallize American public sentiment against Germany, Dodge became chairman of the "Survivors of the

Victims of the Lusitania Fund." Dudley Field Malone, Collector of the Port of New York, testified that the vessel was loaded with ammunition and was therefore a legitimate prey of war, although Wilson failed to give due weight to this important fact. The shipping manifests showed, moreover, that the ammunition came in part from Dodge's own Winchester, Remington, and Union Metallic Cartridge companies.

In many ways Dodge, the only one of his close advisers from whom Wilson never was estranged, throws a queer retrospective light upon Wilsonian liberalism. In 1915 Dodge's Arizona miners struck for higher wages and were violently beset by gunmen brought in from city underworlds. Governor Hunt opposed Dodge; the strikers won. Up for re-election, Hunt, Arizona's first Governor, was opposed by Dodge's political machine. He was counted out by thirty-one votes!

## III

Before inquiring into phases of the World War that primarily concerned the American millionaires and multimillionaires, orderly procedure requires brief examination of the 1916 elections wherein Wilson narrowly triumphed over Charles Evans Hughes.

Hughes had long functioned as a Wall Street attorney, although he was widely considered liberal in his leanings; color was lent to this myth by the fact that he had accepted the job of investigating the life-insurance companies when other attorneys were afraid to touch it. Hughes began his career in the firm of Chamberlain, Carter and Hornblower. The latter was chief counsel to the New York Life Insurance Company in the palmiest days of its financial rapine, general counsel to the New York Central Railroad, and deep in the confidence of Depew and the Vanderbilts. In 1894 Hornblower, appointed by Cleveland to the Supreme Court, was rejected by the Senate.

Hughes married the daughter of Walter S. Carter and in 1888 formed the law firm of Carter, Hughes and Cravath. Paul D. Cravath, as we have remarked, succeeded Elihu Root as attorney to Thomas Fortune Ryan, whom he served for more than a quarter century. Hughes' law firm from its inception represented various New York public-utilities companies; after 1901 it acted for the New York, Westchester and Boston Railroad Company, controlled by J. P. Morgan and Company.

In every detail of his life Hughes was joined with the Wall Street freebooters. Even a Baptist Bible class which he led in 1894 numbered among its many wealthy members John D. Rockefeller, Jr., who succeeded Hughes as its leader.

At the beginning of the fight within the insurance companies Hughes was one of counsel to James W. Alexander of the Equitable Life Assurance Society as well as to the Mercantile Trust Company. Yet the magnates felt some trepidation when Hughes in 1906 was proposed for Governor of New York to oppose Hearst and the Democratic ticket; but Cravath is reported to have assured Ryan that Hughes would be "safe." [54] This, indeed, he was. Hughes went so far as to dismiss the weighty charges against District Attorney William Travers Jerome of improper collaboration with Ryan, Brady, and other public-utilities racketeers. Cravath defended Ryan.

The Hughes gubernatorial election fund of 1906 totaled $313,923, and the biggest contributors were J. P. Morgan and Levi P. Morton, $20,000 each; John D. Rockefeller and Andrew Carnegie, $5,000 each; Chauncey M. Depew, John W. ("Bet-A-Million") Gates, J. and W. Seligman and Company, and Kuhn, Loeb and Company, $2,500 each; Charles M. Schwab, Edwin Gould, Jacob H. Schiff, and Adolph Lewisohn, $1,000 to $2,000 each.

After his defeat in 1916 Hughes became chief counsel for the Standard Oil Company, succeeding Joseph H. Choate. He joined Harding's "Black Cabinet" as Secretary of State, later resumed his Standard Oil practice, and in 1930 was named Chief Justice of the Supreme Court by Herbert Hoover. He narrowly escaped being rejected by the Senate, whose insurgent bloc led the fight against his confirmation. As Chief Justice he succeeded Taft (Standard Oil), who had been appointed by President Harding (Standard Oil).

Theodore Roosevelt was in close touch with J. P. Morgan and Company during the preconvention period of the 1916 campaign. To Charles Willis Thompson, of *The New York Times*, Roosevelt said, "As for the financial people, they believe everything is coming their way, and [Henry P.] Davison thinks that if it is necessary to

spend twenty millions it can be done with satisfactory results." [55]
"I knew," wrote Thompson, "that his information was accurate;
George W. Perkins was even then in communication with the Wall
Street people to find out, on Roosevelt's behalf, what their attitude
would be and what they thought." [56] "The financiers," said Roosevelt,
"have an idea just now that they can put Root over. Such men as
Davison, for instance. . . . They want Root because he agrees with
them and they know where they stand. If they can't have him, then,
as Davison says, 'We want a blank sheet of paper on which we can
write.' And if they can't have either, they will be fairly well satisfied
with Wilson." [57] Thompson tells of being present when Roosevelt
had a telephone conversation with Perkins about the candidates.

The Progressive Party, although quite dead, was still on view. The
putrefying corpse merely required the services of Roosevelt as grave-
digger. At Chicago a spurious convention was held at which Bainbridge Colby, also a former lawyer for the Equitable Life Assurance
Society, nominated Roosevelt for the presidency; Hiram Johnson
made the seconding speech. Roosevelt declined the nomination by
telegram, and the party was formally disbanded. George W. Perkins
was, of course, in full control of the convention machinery. [58]

To determine what should be done about the Progressive Party
there had been a political council late in 1915 at the home of Elbert
H. Gary, chairman of the United States Steel Corporation. Present in
the gathering were August Belmont, A. Barton Hepburn (chairman
of the Chase National Bank), Jacob H. Schiff, George F. Baker,
Frank A. Vanderlip, Cornelius Vanderbilt, Daniel Guggenheim,
Clarence H. Mackay, George B. Cortelyou, and George W. Perkins. [59]

Soon after the nomination of Hughes, and after the withdrawal of
Roosevelt from the Progressive ticket, Perkins had dinner with the
Republican nominee and received from him permission to bring
Beveridge back into the fold. [60] This was the least Perkins could do
for the sorely misled Indiana Progressive. Late in 1916 Republican
Governor Charles Whitman, of New York, to indicate that the quar-
rel with the Progressives was ended, proposed Perkins as Mayor of
New York City.

According to *The New York Times* of November 28 and 29, 1916, the largest contributors from the nation's ruling families to the Republican fund of 1916 were as follows:

$92,500

Pierre S. du Pont

$25,000

John D. Rockefeller, Sr., John D. Rockefeller, Jr., Daniel G. Reid, W. H. Moore, Oliver H. Payne, and Frank A. Vanderlip.

$20,000

E. T. Stotesbury and Mrs. E. H. Harriman.

$15,000

J. P. Morgan, J. B. Duke, Galen Stone (public utilities), and Joseph E. Widener.

$11,000

George F. Baker

$10,000

Clarence H. Mackay, Harry Payne Whitney, A. S. Scheuer, Charles O. Pratt (Standard Oil), William H. Childs, Henry P. Davison (Morgan partner), Mrs. Daniel Guggenheim, Mrs. Harry Payne Whitney, Mrs. H. E. Huntington, Edward B. Aldrich, Harry F. Sinclair, Frederic A. Juilliard, Cornelius Vanderbilt, James McLean, Frank E. Peabody, E. V. R. Thayer, Charles Hayden, John N. Willys, William Barbour, H. F. Brown, Bayard Dominick, Hornblower and Weeks (brokers), Thomas W. Lamont (Morgan partner), W. H. Porter (Morgan partner), George D. Pratt (Standard Oil), William A. Reid and Company, J. and W. Seligman and Company, Edward Shearson (United States Steel broker), William Boyce Thompson, and G. E. Tripp.

$7,500

George F. Baker, Jr., and Mrs. Willard Straight.

$4,500

Seward Prosser (Bankers Trust Company).

$2,500

Mrs. Cornelius Vanderbilt, Mrs. W. F. Crocker, Mrs. Felix Warburg, Mrs. Alexander Smith Cochran, Richard B. Mellon, and Andrew W. Mellon.

$2,000

Mrs. T. Coleman du Pont, Arthur Curtiss James, and Edward Hines.
$1,000

Mrs. E. T. Stotesbury, Mrs. Felix Warburg, Mrs. Simon Guggenheim, Mrs. John D. Archbold, Helen Frick (daughter of Henry C. Frick), James N. Hill (son of James J. Hill), Mortimer L. Schiff, and Joseph and W. R. Grace (shipping).

To the fund for the election of Governor Whitman $45,542 came from Perkins and $10,000 from Arthur Curtiss James. Perkins also gave $48,654 additionally to mail Whitman literature to Progressive and Republican Party voters. G. A. Pratt gave the Whitman fund $5,000; Mrs. E. H. Harriman, $1,000; Herbert Seligman and Cornelius Vanderbilt, $500 each; and L. W. Stoesburg, M. J. Dodger, E. S. Whitney, Oscar S. Straus, and H. H. Rogers, $250 each.

To the New York County Republican fund Ogden L. Mills gave $2,000; John D. Rockefeller, $2,000; and Felix Warburg, Louis C. Tiffany, Mrs. Whitelaw Reid, daughter of Darius O. Mills, William K. Vanderbilt, J. P. Morgan, and Henry P. Davison, $1,000 each. The Curran Committee of the Republican and Independent Parties got $5,000 from Willard Straight, $2,000 from George W. Perkins, and $1,000 each from Samuel A. and Adolph Lewisohn.

The Democratic Party was hardly less well provided for. The Wilson Business Men's League collected $2,500 each from S. R. Bertron, broker, and Charles R. Crane; $1,500 from Edward A. Filene, Boston department-store owner, and $1,000 each from Jacob H. Schiff, banker, and Jesse I. Straus, New York department-store owner.

The biggest contributors to the Democratic national fund were Cleveland H. Dodge, $25,000; E. L. Doheny, $25,000;* Roger Sullivan, Chicago Democratic boss, and Thomas D. and David B. Jones, directors of the International Harvester Company, $12,500 each; Alvin Untermyer, son of Samuel Untermyer, Frederick Penfield, Nelson Morris (Chicago packer), Charles J. Peabody, Charles R.

---

* In this instance once again the official record is shown by a private memoir to be too modest by half. Henry Morgenthau writes (*All in a Life Time*, p. 242) that he collected $50,000 from Doheny in 1916 for the Democrats.

Crane, F. X. Peabody, and Bernard Baruch, $10,000 each; Francis P. Garvan, son-in-law of Anthony N. Brady, Martin Vogel, Edwin O. Wood, James Taylor Lewis, Fred Johnson, George S. Mead, F. B. Lynch and Marcus A. Coolidge, $5,000 each.

Frederick Penfield was a wealthy Philadelphia real estate owner. His contribution was understood to include money from Josiah Quincy, a Boston mining-company attorney under Federal indictment for using the mails to defraud.[61] Quincy was subsequently acquitted. Wilson appointed Thomas D. Jones a member of the Federal Reserve Board, but he was not confirmed by the Senate.

Many big Democratic contributions were concealed from the voters by a new technique of delaying campaign gifts until after the election, when there remained a deficit to be liquidated. The first report on the Democratic fund in the *Times* for November 27, 1916, set it at $1,584,548. Notwithstanding that 170,000 persons contributed, under the illusion that Wilson was a great democrat, the campaign, which actually cost $2,500,000, left in its wake a deficit of $600,000, according to the *Times* of February 28, 1917.

In 1916, as afterward, the political parties did not lay all their cards on the table with respect to sources of funds. William Boyce Thompson, partner in the brokerage house of Hayden, Stone and Company, large stockholder in the Chase National Bank and the Sinclair Oil Company, and one of the first directors of the Federal Reserve Bank of New York, lent Will Hays, Republican campaign manager and chief counsel of the Sinclair Oil Company, $1,000,000 in the course of the campaign, which was later repaid.[62]

In 1918 Thompson gave $300,000 to Hays for the expressed purpose of buying control of Congress, in which the Republicans that year gained a majority.[63] In 1919 Thompson became chairman of the Ways and Means Committee of the Republican Party.

## IV

The World War was the overshadowing event of both Wilson Administrations, and marked another stage in the upward march of the American multimillionaires.

The economic royalists offered leadership in bringing the nation into the war; the country—farmers, organized and unorganized labor, the middle classes, professionals, and intellectuals—accepted that leadership. The alternative confronting the millionaires as the world market was torn asunder by the warring nations was domestic economic stagnation, which would have brought down upon them the concentrated wrath of all classes.

The search which historians have made for individuals who caused the war, and who caused America's entry into the war, is probably futile. As some historians have pointed out, the causes of the war were multiple, and operative many decades before 1914.

The question which strikes at the heart of the war situation like a dagger is not, Who caused the war? It is not even, Who brought America into the war? The revealing question is, Who profited by the war, pocketed the profit, and defends the profit? The major portion of the war profits, the fact is, went into the hands of the wealthiest families.

The victorious European powers achieved conquests at the expense of wartime enemies, although the gains did not come anywhere near balancing the cost. But the United States magnanimously refused to participate in the parceling out of economic spoils under the Treaty of Versailles. The Wall Street denizens could afford to underwrite this decision on the part of their politicians, because their conquest took the form of gain at the expense of the American people itself.

The American soldiers fighting in the trenches, the people working at home, the entire nation under arms, were fighting, not only to subdue Germany, but to subdue themselves. That there is nothing metaphysical about this interpretation becomes clear when we observe that the total wartime expenditure of the United States government from April 6, 1917, to October 31, 1919, when the last contingent of troops returned from Europe, was $35,413,000,000. Net corporation profits for the period January 1, 1916, to July, 1921, when wartime industrial activity was finally liquidated, were $38,000,000,000, or approximately the amount of the war expenditures. More than two-thirds of these corporation profits were taken by precisely those enterprises which the Pujo Committee had found to be under the control of the "Money Trust."

Most of the war's cost was financed by pledging the government's credit, i. e., the people's credit; and this pledge at the end of the war amounted to nearly $30,000,000,000, or more than thirty times the prewar national debt. The only way the people could recover some of this money was by taxing the corporations, and the Republican Administrations which held power after 1920 saw that taxes on the rich were sharply reduced rather than increased. What the government did not permit the rich to keep legally they kept by practising wholesale tax evasion, as revealed by various Senate investigations.

The beginning of war was fortunate for J. P. Morgan and Company, sadly involved in the $400,000,000 collapse of the New York, New Haven and Hartford Railroad's financial structure. In 1914, despite the increase in traffic in the two decades during which Morgan had controlled the enterprise, the finances of the New Haven were in ruin. As Charles A. Beard says of this railroad, it "was so loaded with stocks and bonds that it collapsed with an awful crash, spreading ruin far and wide among widows, orphans, and other security holders in New England and giving an awful shock to those who had bought common shares at a high figure in the old days of prudence."

The shambles within the New Haven Railroad would impugn every pretense of J. P. Morgan and Company to social rectitude, if nothing else did. The report of the Interstate Commerce Commission showed that $12,000,000 had been secretly abstracted from the railroad's treasury by J. P. Morgan and Company. C. S. Mellen, president of the New Haven, testified he had warned the New Haven directors that stock of the New York, Westchester and Boston Railroad was not worth ten cents a pound, yet the New Haven graciously relieved J. P. Morgan and his associates of this white elephant for a handsome price. From June 30, 1903, to June 30, 1913, the Interstate Commerce Commission showed, J. P. Morgan and Company, which took control in 1893, had caused the New Haven's capitalization to be increased from $93,000,000 to $417,000,000, of which increase only $120,000,000 was spent on the railroad and the balance on outside speculations through 336 subsidiary companies. The railroad, among other things, bought at fancy prices undesirable traction properties from Senator Aldrich.

The New York *World* of February 1, 1914, observed that the New

Haven stockholders had been "swindled, robbed, and ruined" by "cold, calculated villainy" which had left the railroad "bled white." "Thousands of men," said this newspaper, "are in jail for offenses against society which are picayunish in comparison with this stupendous achievement in respectable robbery."

By midsummer of 1914 the outlook was decidedly black for the House of Morgan, and there were those who predicted it would soon go the way of Jay Cooke and Company. The beginning of the European hostilities, however, found J. P. Morgan and Company fortuitously appointed fiscal agent in the United States for the British and French governments. As such it took charge of the vast war purchases of the Allies in this country. The crisis for the banking house was averted.

As revealed in 1936 by the Nye Senate Committee, Secretary of State William Jennings Bryan on August 10, 1914, less than two weeks after war began, informed President Wilson that J. P. Morgan and Company had inquired whether there would be any official objection to making a loan to the French government through the Rothschilds. Bryan warned the President that "money is the worst of all contrabands," and that if the loan were permitted, the interests of the powerful persons making it would be enlisted on the side of the borrower, making neutrality difficult, if not impossible.

On August 15 Bryan wrote to J. P. Morgan and Company, "Loans made by American bankers to any foreign nation which is at war are inconsistent with the true spirit of neutrality." This statement formally committed the United States against loans to warring Europe. Soon afterward Bryan was constrained to reverse himself, which he did privately.

The ever-facile New York bankers, however, now set about approaching their Washington officials in another way. On October 23, 1914, Samuel McRoberts, vice-president of the National City Bank, informed Robert Lansing, counselor of the State Department, that the bank desired to stimulate trade by assisting foreign governments to buy in the American market but was unable to do so with the available supply of credit.

That evening, with Bryan out of town, Lansing called on Wilson. Between them they drew a Jesuitical distinction between credits and loans: credits were held to be permissible. Then Wilson authorized Lansing to convey his "impressions" to such persons as were "entitled to hear them," upon the express understanding that they would be regarded as Lansing's "impressions" and that Lansing "had no authority to speak for the President or the government."

On the evening of October 24, 1914, Lansing transmitted his "impressions" to a mysterious, unnamed emissary from J. P. Morgan and Company (apparently Willard Straight) at the Metropolitan Club of New York, which had been founded by the elder J. P. Morgan. Two days later, at the State Department, Lansing gave his "impressions" to an agent of the National City Bank. But when Vanderlip, former president of the bank, was asked by the Nye Committee to supply details he suffered a convenient lapse of memory.

Knowing the relations between Dodge and Wilson we may assume that during all these *pourparlers* Dodge was in constant touch with the President. The Nye Committee, unfortunately, did not inquire into the Dodge-Wilson friendship.

Through J. P. Morgan and Company the Allied governments, after the Lansing-Wilson "impressions" had been transmitted, began buying supplies in large quantities on bank credits. All the banks participated in the business, with National City in the forefront of the commercial institutions. It was some time, however, before the new influx of orders was felt.

The financial risk daily became greater, of course, as German military successes piled up in one theater of the war after another.

Meanwhile, in December, 1914, Henry P. Davison, Morgan partner in charge of making financial arrangements with the Allies, assured David Lloyd George, Chancellor of the Exchequer, that the United States within six months would lift the restrictions against formal loans to the Allies.[64] Davison, as a high ranking member of the *de facto* government, knew whereof he spoke; it was only a little more than six months before Wilson secretly gave permission for the flotation of the huge Anglo-French Loan.

To break the ground for this loan in government circles Benjamin Strong, Governor of the Federal Reserve Bank of New York, former official of the Bankers Trust Company (Morgan), wrote on August

14, 1915, to Colonel House, warning that the exchange rate of the pound against the dollar was slipping. This meant, presumably, that England's power to purchase and to pay was diminishing. The Nye Committee tried to establish whether the slump of sterling was not the outcome of a maneuver by the American bankers in collaboration with the Bank of England to frighten the Washington Administration into permitting a loan for the ostensible purpose of rehabilitating the pound.

Then Secretary McAdoo was given a copy of a letter from J. B. Forgan, president of the First National Bank of Chicago (Morgan influence) to F. A. Delano, Vice-Governor of the Federal Reserve Board. Forgan asked what the government's attitude would now be toward an Allied loan, as funds were needed which the banks professed could no longer be supplied by means of open credits. On August 21, 1915, McAdoo wrote to Wilson, "Our prosperity is dependent upon our continued and enlarged foreign trade. To preserve that we must do everything we can to assist our customers to buy. . . . To maintain our prosperity we must finance it. Otherwise we must stop, and that would be disastrous."

On August 25, 1915, Secretary Lansing, who supplanted Bryan, sent Wilson a copy of Forgan's letter, with his own covering opinion that changed conditions must be recognized and that "the large debts which result from purchases by the belligerent governments require some method of funding these debts in this country."

On August 26 Wilson wrote to Lansing: "My opinion in this matter, compendiously stated, is that we should say that 'parties would take no action either for or against such a transaction,' but that this should be orally conveyed, so far as we are concerned, and not put in writing." Wilson, in short, was fearful that evidence of his endorsement of lending to the Allies would leak out. Lansing informed the bankers of this new turn of Wilson's mind.

Now, before coming to flotation of the Allied loans by J. P. Morgan and Company and the National City Bank, let us retrace our steps to April, 1915, when Thomas W. Lamont, partner in J. P. Morgan and Company made a speech before the American Academy of Political and Social Science at Philadelphia. This speech was neither reported in the newspapers nor was it brought to light by the Nye Committee.*

The value of this long-hidden extraordinary speech resides in the fact that it tends to prove the bankers were interested in seeing the European war continue so that they might extract from it maximum profits. After reviewing details of the financial situation since the beginning of the war and after pointing to the great increase in American exports, Lamont dangled before his listeners the prospect of the United States becoming the financial center of the world. Factors pro and con relating to this development were enumerated by Lamont, who continued:

"Another factor, depending upon the duration of the war, is the extent to which we shall buy back American securities still held by foreign investors. . . . If we should continue to buy such securities back on a large scale—and the chances are that if the war continues long enough [*sic!*] we shall do that—then we should no longer be in the position of remitting abroad vast sums every year in the way of interest. . . . We should be paying the interest upon our debts to our own people [banks], not to foreigners. Such a development would be of the utmost importance for this country financially.

"A third factor, and that, too, is dependent upon the duration of the war [*sic!*] is as to whether we shall become lenders to the foreign nations upon a really large scale. I have pointed out that since the war began we have loaned direct to foreign governments something over two hundred million dollars. Yet this is a comparatively small sum. Shall we become lenders upon a really stupendous scale to these foreign governments? Shall we become lenders for the development of private or semipublic enterprises in South America and other parts of the world, which up to date have been commercially financed by Great Britain, France, and Germany? If the war continues long enough to encourage us [*sic!*] to take such a position, and if we have the resources to grapple with it, then inevitably we shall become a creditor instead of a debtor nation, and such a development, sooner or later, would certainly tend to bring about the

* See *Annals of the Academy of Political Science,* Volume 60, July, 1915, pages 106–112.

dollar, instead of the pound sterling, as the international basis of exchange."

After this delineation of the glittering pecuniary possibilities in the war Lamont said, with characteristic histrionic casualness, "These thoughts I have thrown out simply in the way of inquiry and suggestion."

The Lamont document is of first-class historical significance when read in conjunction with the evidence taken by the Nye Committee. It establishes for the first time on the record the conscious economic motivation in J. P. Morgan and Company and the Wall Street bankers in general for inducing the United States government to take the course it did subsequently take, although such motivation has always been publicly denied by the partners of J. P. Morgan and Company.

And it was Lamont who, when the Federal Reserve refused to rediscount English war notes on purchases, advised the Bank of England to discontinue buying, temporarily, thereby frightening the entire business community. Very soon afterward Wilson gave his roundabout permission to the bankers to float Ally loans.

In late 1914, and throughout 1915 and 1916, leading figures of wealth, and their agents in press, pulpit, and rostrum, carried on a vigorous propaganda in favor of the Allies, against Germany. The newspapers particularly did all in their power to insure the success of this campaign.

After President Wilson was maneuvered into permitting loans to the Allies, J. P. Morgan and Company in October, 1915, headed a syndicate of the leading banks which floated the $500,000,000 Anglo-French Loan. The biggest individual subscribers were the Guggenheim brothers (copper), James Stillman, J. P. Morgan, George F. Baker, Andrew Carnegie, Vincent Astor, Otto H. Kahn, Hetty Green, William H. Clark (copper), Charles M. Schwab of Bethlehem Steel, and Samuel Untermyer, New York lawyer. In the first year $620,000,000 and in the next year, up to the fall of 1917, $600,-000,000 was advanced. The leading insurance companies, banks, and corporations as well were induced by their Wall Street masters to stock up with this paper, knitting the nation's finances into the war fabric on the Allied side.

Early in 1917 the Allied governments, which now owed the American bankers and their clients nearly $1,500,000,000, had been brought virtually to their knees by the German armies, and it was believed that the limit of Allied credit had been reached. In March, 1917, the Czar's government, which had also been fighting to make the world safe for democracy, collapsed, threatening to release the German army of the East for duty in France.

On March 5, 1917, Walter Hines Page, American Ambassador to England, sent to President Wilson a long dispatch which Page summarized as follows: "I think that the pressure of this approaching crisis has gone beyond the ability of the Morgan Financial Agency for the British and French Governments. The need is becoming too great and urgent for any private agency to meet, for every such agency has to encounter jealousies of rivals and of sections." Page said that the outlook was "alarming" to America's industrial and financial prospects, but pointed out frankly, "If we should go to war with Germany, the greatest help we could give the Allies would be such a credit. In that case our Government could, if it would, make a large investment in a Franco-British loan or might guarantee such a loan. . . . Unless we go to war with Germany our Government, of course, cannot make such a direct grant of credit. . . ." The alternative to war, Page warned, was domestic collapse.

Within four weeks President Wilson asked Congress for a declaration of war, ostensibly because submarine warfare against shipping had been renewed. Congress, with the exception of a small but gallant band led by Senators LaFollette and Norris, promptly acceded.

Out of the proceeds of the very first Liberty Loan more than $400,-000,000 was paid to J. P. Morgan and Company in satisfaction of debts owed it by the British government! During its participation in the war the United States lent to Europe $9,386,311,178, of which Great Britain got $4,136,000,000 and France $2,293,000,000. American participation in the war made it possible for the government to place the credit of the whole American people behind the Allies, whose fortunes were, early in 1917, at such a low ebb that the American holders of nearly $1,500,000,000 of English and French paper stood to suffer a disastrous loss. The declaration of war by the United States, in ad-

dition to extricating the wealthiest American families from a dangerous situation, also opened new vistas of profits.

Europe got none of the money lent by the Treasury; it received
only materials of war. The owners of American industries got the
money. They employed most of it to expand the industrial equipment of the nation and to increase the size of their fortunes and the
extent of their power. In short, the war debt created by the American
government amounted simply to money transferred from the people
of the country to the richest families, who owned the banks and industries. Wartime profits,* as the Nye Committee showed, were
enormous.

And although Europe has since defaulted on its war and postwar
debts to the United States, it has, except for Russia, Germany, and
Austria, scrupulously paid off every cent owed to the American
banks and bankers. Europe could have liquidated its obligation long
ago, but only in goods. Any settlement of that nature, however, has
been blocked by American bankers and industrialists, working
through their tools in Congress and the White House.

Walter Hines Page, trustee of the Rockefeller General Education
Board and editor of various Wall Street publications, deserves brief
attention at this point. From the moment war broke out in 1914
Page was wholeheartedly committed to the Allied point of view. He
did everything he could to have the United States rake England's
chestnuts out of the fire. So indefatigable was he that he often appeared to be a British agent and he has been flatly accused by many,
notably by H. L. Mencken, editor and critic, of figuring in a treason-
able role.

Such a view of Page is shallow, and scarcely does him justice. Page
was merely playing Wall Street's game, and Wall Street's game happened to be England's. When Wilson in 1913 broached the idea of
the London ambassadorship to Page, the latter held back on the
ground that he could not support himself in proper ambassadorial
style. Wilson thereupon called on Dodge to make up the needed
funds out of his private purse. Dodge agreed to give Page $25,000 a
year during his tenure of the London post.[65] Page was, therefore, as
wartime ambassador to Great Britain, financed by a big stockholder

* See Appendix B: War Profits.

of the National City Bank who also happened to be one of America's munitions magnates.

## V

The wartime emergency found members of the government *de facto* swarming into strategic posts in the government *de jure*. Many of them had long been active, however, in preparing the country for war.

Henry P. Davison who, as a Morgan partner, negotiated the Anglo-French bank loans, in 1915 financed "Aerial Coast Patrol No. 1," a civilian flying unit under the temporary auspices of Yale University. In 1915 General Leonard Wood opened the Business Men's Training Camp at Plattsburg, New York, financed by Bernard M. Baruch, whose initial contribution was $10,000; Baruch spent much time gathering camp funds in Wall Street. The newspapers, of course, gave this project extended attention. With a flourish, Willard Straight, of J. P. Morgan and Company, and Robert Bacon, former Morgan partner, immediately enlisted. Mrs. Cornelius Vanderbilt gave an ambulance train to the New York National Guard. Theodore Roosevelt, Henry Cabot Lodge, Elihu Root, and other faithful servitors of J. P. Morgan and Company were all demanding a declaration of war long before Wilson felt he had the country with him.

There was every reason, of course, for Wall Street to regard the war as beneficent. By the close of 1916 Stock Exchange prices had risen six hundred per cent over the 1914 average. For stockholders and bankers 1916 was until then the most prosperous year in American history.

In 1915 E. I. du Pont de Nemours and Company, for example, through J. P. Morgan and Company, received $100,000,000 of English money to expand the plant capacity of its explosives division; overnight the Du Ponts were lifted from tertiary to primary industrial rank. Crude iron prices, which in 1914 stood at $13 a ton, by 1917 had risen to $42. Whereas unfilled orders of the Bethlehem Steel Corporation at the end of 1913 were only $24,865,000, at the end of 1914 they stood at $46,513,000 and at the end of 1915 at $175,-432,000. Munitions exports in 1914 totaled $40,000,000; in 1915 they were $330,000,000, in 1916, $1,290,000,000. Before America entered the war Wall Street had sold nearly $5,000,000,000 of material to the Allies.

No sooner had the banks shifted the financial risk of their war business to the American people by having the government declare war upon Germany, than the rich families felt it their patriotic duty to take the operation of the government into their own hands; nor did President Wilson oppose them. The government, incidentally, had been secretly preparing for war for six months prior to the actual declaration. According to Franklin D. Roosevelt, then Assistant Secretary of the Navy, the Navy Department began extensive purchasing of war supplies in the Fall of 1916.[66]

By no accident all the strategic government posts, notably those concerned with buying, were reserved for the Wall Street patriots. On the most vital appointments, Wilson consulted with Dodge, who proposed Davison for the head of the American Red Cross.[67] He also recommended the hitherto unknown Baruch, speculator in copper stocks, as chairman of the all-powerful War Industries Board.

Baruch was given his start in the brokerage business by James Keene, a confidential broker for J. P. Morgan and Company; he made his first big money in the Amalgamated Copper manipulation of the National City Bank-Kuhn, Loeb and Company crowd.[68] In 1904 he became a confidential broker for the Guggenheims, and Thomas Fortune Ryan and Henry H. Rogers later became his "business bedfellows." [69]

As head of the War Industries Board, Baruch spent government funds at the rate of $10,000,000,000 annually; aspects of the operations of his department were harshly criticized after the war, and Baruch himself was rebuked, by the Graham Committee of the House of Representatives. Some of the unsavory details of this inquiry's findings are reserved for later exposition.

Baruch packed the War Industries Board and its committees with past and future Wall Street manipulators, industrialists, financiers, and their agents. Some of these were Julius Rosenwald, head of Sears, Roebuck and Company; Daniel Willard, president of the Baltimore and Ohio Railroad; Walter S. Gifford, then vice-president of American Telephone and Telegraph; Howard E. Coffin, president of the Hudson Motor Car Company; Alexander Legge, of the International Harvester Company; J. Leonard Replogle, steel magnate; Herbert Bayard Swope, brother of General Electric's Gerard Swope; Clarence Dillon, of Dillon, Read and Company; Elbert H. Gary, chairman of United States Steel; James A. Farrell, president of United States Steel and son-in-law of Anthony N. Brady; and John D. Ryan, president of Anaconda Copper (Amalgamated Copper), Assistant Secretary of War, and head of the copper-buying committee.

The buying committees in all the war industries were composed of the heads of those industries, who fixed prices on a cost-plus basis and, as subsequent investigations revealed, saw to it that costs were grossly padded so as to yield hidden profits.

With Ryan as an Assistant Secretary of War sat Edward R. Stettinius, partner of J. P. Morgan, who until the United States declared war supervised American war purchases for the Allies. Russell Leffingwell, Morgan partner-to-be, was Assistant Secretary of the Treasury under McAdoo, who appointed Dwight W. Morrow, Morgan partner, as director of the National War Savings Committee for New Jersey. Although without shipping experience, Morrow was also made a member of the Allied Maritime Transport Council, which allocated tonnage among the Powers. Charles M. Schwab, of Bethlehem Steel, took charge of the Emergency Fleet Corporation. Herbert Hoover, promotion agent for various London mining concerns, was made National Food Controller. Frank A. Vanderlip, president of the National City Bank, was given charge of the War Savings Stamp campaign. Samuel McRoberts, vice-president of the National City Bank, became chief of the procurement section of the ordnance division. Paul D. Cravath, Thomas Fortune Ryan's attorney, was made legal adviser to the American War Mission to Europe.

The laxity of the Washington officials is exemplified nowhere better than in the collected letters of Franklin K. Lane, Secretary of the Interior under Wilson. Lane, when war was declared, wrote: "The President ought to send for [Charles M.] Schwab and hand him a Treasury warrant for a billion dollars and set him to work building ships, with no government inspectors or supervisors or accountants or auditors or other red tape to bother him. Let the

President just put it up to Schwab's patriotism and put Schwab on his honor. Nothing more is needed. Schwab will do the job."

This is practically what the President did do in every department of industry. Lane, it is interesting to see, understood that it was auditors and accountants that worried the magnates.

Davison packed the Red Cross with Morgan people. George F. Baker, Jr., of the First National Bank, headed the Preliminary Emergency Commission to Italy. Grayson M.-P. Murphy, vice-president of the Guaranty Trust Company (Morgan), headed the first Red Cross Mission to France, later succeeding Baker in Italy.

Murphy is, perhaps, the most vital minor character in this narrative. Today he is a dominant figure in the Chicago-New York motorbus systems and a director in several Morgan banks as well as the head of his own investment banking house. As an army lieutenant early in the century Murphy, according to Henry Pringle in his biography of Roosevelt, was secretly dispatched by the President to look over the ground in Panama with a view to staging the Panama revolution. So favorably was Murphy impressed with the possibilities that he and a fellow officer considered trying to interest J. P. Morgan and Company in financing the revolution. Late in 1934 Murphy was denounced by Major General Smedley D. Butler as one of the backers of a grandiose scheme, to be financed initially at $50,000,000, in which Butler would lead a militant political movement of World War veterans. After a brief flurry in the press, during which Murphy's scheme was denounced by liberals as fascistic, Butler's grave charge was pushed safely out of public consciousness behind a wall of silence.

With Davison on the Red Cross War Council were Cornelius N. Bliss, Jr., Republican politician; Seward Prosser, now chairman of the executive committee of the Bankers Trust Company (Morgan); John W. Davis, then Solicitor General and now Morgan's chief counsel; John D. Ryan; Harvey D. Gibson, now president of the Manufacturers Trust Company; and Jesse H. Jones, Texas banker and land promoter and now head of the Reconstruction Finance Corporation.

The Russian Mission of the Red Cross was headed by Colonel William Boyce Thompson and Colonel Raymond Robins, Alaska gold prospector. Thompson and Robins in Russia, and Murphy in Italy, used the Red Cross to forward the war aims of Wall Street in a way unsuspected by the American people. The purely political function of the Red Cross is not generally appreciated even today.

Murphy's job in Italy was to bolster shattered morale after the Caporetto disaster. He put the Red Cross to work caring for the homeless and destitute whose mental state was considered dangerously revolutionary. Thompson and Robins, according to their own statements, functioned in Russia as a political arm of the War Department. Their crowning achievement was the purchase of enough delegates to the All-Russian Democratic Congress so that instead of unseating Kerensky, it would support him—and his program of continuing the war. The cost of seducing this congress was $1,000,-000, which Thompson cheerfully paid over. Throughout his stay in Russia, Thompson was at all times in cable communication with Lamont and Morrow at Morgan's, and in intervals paved the way for the grant, by the pre-Bolshevik government, of a mining concession to himself and his friends.

The aim of Thompson and the Red Cross was to prevent the Russian people from making a separate peace with Germany. When the Russians nevertheless made peace, Thompson's revised aim was to prevent them from supplying Germany with materials. The Red Cross gave aid in the form of food and money to anti-German elements and withheld it from pro-German and extreme radical elements. Thompson and Robins, under cover of the Red Cross, carried on espionage to locate supplies suspected of being routed to the German border.

Hoover's postwar European relief commission functioned similarly. Food and supplies were withheld from liberal and radical governments and were given to reactionary regimes.

The end of the war found the political financiers still dogging Wilson's unhappy footsteps. At the Peace Conference Baruch was at Wilson's elbow; Lamont, as a Treasury Department representative, was also present "and wrote the financial part for Wilson's League of Nations," according to William Boyce Thompson, "and was more relied upon abroad in financial matters than was Barney Baruch." [70] Lamont, says another authority, "was one of the few among that admirable body of experts to whom President Wilson lent a willing ear." [71] Confidential copies of the Treaty of Versailles were, incidentally, in the hands of J. P. Morgan and Company long before the United States Senate saw the documents.

All the postwar international financial conferences were dominated by J. P. Morgan and Company, which floated most of the choice postwar international loans, including the two Reparations Loans. The World War easily doubled the power of the clans mobilized around this banking house, as well as of those around the Rockefeller and Mellon banks.

From the personal standpoint of America's richest families the World War was the single most constructive event since the Civil War.

# V

## The Politics of Finance Capital: 1920-1932

THE political ruffians of the Grant era functioned under semirevolutionary sanctions; they were the unconscious midwives of a new industrial society which represented definite material progress. No similar sanctions supported the carpetbaggers of the period following the World War, who had no higher historical mission than common burglars. The robber barons of 1860-1900 accomplished, whatever the means they employed, whatever the waste and losses they inflicted, a vast job of construction. Their heirs and assigns of 1920-1932 were reduced to the practice of empty legerdemain, creating holding companies without end and issuing a complicated tangle of worthless hierarchically graded stocks and bonds.

To such an extent was corruption interwoven with high governmental policies during the postwar years of Republican rapine—years which were, it should not be forgotten, logical continuations of the second Wilson Administration—that this pathological phase must be treated in a following chapter. The White House became, quite simply, a political dive.

Even in their superficial aspects the successive Republican Administrations were suspect. They differed from each other only in the name of the White House occupant. Warren G. Harding was an amiable drunkard who left a legacy of scandal mere allusion to which constitutes a breach of good taste; Calvin Coolidge simply did what he was told by Andrew W. Mellon and by Dwight W. Morrow, his political godfather; Herbert Hoover was an erstwhile vendor and promoter of shady mining stocks who before the war had been reprehended by an English court for his role in a promotional swindle.

"Harding," said Alice Longworth, daughter of Theodore Roosevelt, in a summary that must be considered scientifically exact, "was not a bad man. He was just a slob." [1] Coolidge, according to Senator Medill McCormick, part owner of the rabidly Republican Chicago *Tribune,* was a plain "boob." [2] He was so shunned, as Vice-President, that when he became Chief Executive he made Senator Frank B. Kellogg, the only man in Washington who had spoken a kind word to him, his Secretary of State. The third of the Republican postwar Presidents, in H. L. Mencken's judiciously insulting phrase, was a "fat Coolidge," sweatingly tremulous under the domination of Thomas W. Lamont of J. P. Morgan and Company, whom he invariably consulted over the long-distance telephone before ever announcing any decision of moment. Of Coolidge's ignorance of common affairs, which was transcended only by Harding's, the late Clinton W. Gilbert, long the Washington correspondent for the New York *Evening Post,* related that upon ascending to the presidency Coolidge confounded his advisers when he confided that he believed goods sold in international trade were paid for in actual gold bullion, so much gold for so much merchandise.

The exceptionally low caliber of the Coolidge mentality was never better illustrated than in 1921 when, as Vice-President, he wrote for a woman's magazine a series of articles under the title, "Enemies of the Republic: Are the Reds Stalking Our College Women?" The childish intellect displayed in these writings is sufficient commentary upon the scheming minds that carefully nurtured Coolidge's political fortunes.

Under the Presidents of 1896-1920 the government did little for the people, much for the special interests. But under the three postwar Republican Presidents the government became an actively hostile power, baleful, audacious, and irresponsible, functioning directly against the common interest. The party discipline imposed by Hanna was shattered.

The truly significant thing about the postwar Republican Presidents is that they were installed by banking capital, which in 1920 was just settling itself firmly in the saddle. They were the "blank sheets of paper" that Henry P. Davison craved in 1916. And if they did not participate personally in the looting, they had guilty knowledge of what took place, and for their co-operation were permitted to occupy the highest office within the gift of the American people.

During the early phases of the contest for the Republican nomination in 1920 the main support of the wealthy families was thrown, through their banks, to General Leonard Wood, who in Cuba and the Philippines had functioned as the nation's first imperial proconsul. Premature revelations about the sinister nature of his financial backing squelched Wood's boom at the eleventh hour; he would, in the face of the revelations, have been unable to snare votes. The Wood supporters thereupon flocked to Harding.

Not only had it been recognized after the Republican Congressional victories of 1918 that the Democrats had slight prospect of retaining popular support, but it was also evident that Wilson's "Copper Administration," dominated by the National City Bank, was to be succeeded, no matter what figurehead adorned the White House, by an "Oil Administration." The priority of oil was unmistakably foreshadowed by the brisk wartime development of the automobile industry. Henry Ford's phenomenal success with the popular-priced car indicated that a big market awaited automobile manufacturers, and publications like *The Wall Street Journal* predicted an automobile boom.

During the Wilson Administration the automobile interests had made themselves sufficiently heard to obtain passage of the Federal Aid Road Act under which, ostensibly to help the farmers, $240,000,-000 of public funds were made available for road building. The United States was soon to be crisscrossed by the most elaborate system of roads in the world, constructed at public expense, and worth billions to the infant automobile industry.

Major policy was at stake as well as oil reserves and casual plunder. Finance capital, to retain the dominance won in the war, required certain special governmental policies. These, as they came into view, provided for the nonprosecution of the war profiteers; reduction of wartime income taxes which threatened to recapture a portion of public funds siphoned into private hands; administration of the credit machinery through the Federal Reserve System to facilitate speculation and the flow of surplus capital into an expanding capital-goods industry; a moratorium upon governmental regulation of finance and industry; and the making of empty, but convincing, gestures where the interests of farmers, labor, and consumers were concerned.

The first two policies were readily shaped, but subsidiary objectives remained. As the reduction and remission of taxes on large incomes left national finances in a precarious position, and as the soundness of national finances was integral to the well-being of private wealth, the finances had to be strengthened by some device that would not inconvenience the large fortunes.

The method finally approved involved the flotation of billions of dollars of foreign securities in the domestic market, tapping the savings of thousands of small investors; with the proceeds of these flotations Europe and Latin America continued to buy American goods and, what was important, to make payments upon the adjusted intergovernmental debts. The financial strain which the magnates had imposed upon the government in 1917 to save their own fiscal skins was, therefore, partially eased.

From the beginning all regulation of private wealth was discarded. The government, instead of regulating, collaborated, notably in the use of the Federal Reserve System, by keeping speculative activity at fever pitch and facilitating the proliferation of holding companies, investment trusts, mortgage companies, and stock-market pools.

So gloomy were Democratic prospects in 1920 that there was no genuine contest for the presidential nomination, which was given to James Cox, Ohio politician, newspaper proprietor, and partner, with the Republican Dawes clique of Chicago, in the Pure Oil Company. Franklin D. Roosevelt was the vice-presidential nominee, although E. L. Doheny of the Mexican Petroleum Company sought that honor for himself. Cox was given distinguished backing because he espoused Wilson's League of Nations. Chief among those who spoke for him was J. P. Morgan and Company's Thomas W. Lamont, whose recently acquired New York *Evening Post* led the pro-League newspaper campaign. But even the Morgan camp was split wide open on the League issue, and Cox was opposed by some of Lamont's partners. Cox, like Alton B. Parker in 1904, made sensational charges about a huge Republican slush fund. He could not prove his case, but he precipitated a Senate investigation distinctive chiefly in that it failed to uncover the true situation.

One of the allegations was that Henry Clay Frick had given a private dinner in 1919 in honor of General Wood, with the guests present including George Harvey, George W. Perkins, John T. King (Connecticut Republican boss and Wood campaign manager subsequently indicted in alien property custodian frauds; he died before coming to trial with a co-conspirator who was sentenced to Atlanta Penitentiary), Dan R. Hanna, son of Mark Hanna, E. L. Doheny, Harry F. Sinclair, Ambrose Monell of the International Nickel Company, George Whelan, head of the United Cigar Stores Company of America, H. M. Byllesby, public utilities holding company operator, A. A. Sprague, wholesale grocer of Chicago, and William Boyce Thompson.

Thompson and Harvey took the initiative in bringing about the nomination of Harding after the Wood boom had collapsed under the weight of gold. Harvey, indeed, astutely picked Harding early in 1919 when, a year before the Republican convention, he wrote the name of the candidate he thought would capture the nomination and placed it, before many witnesses, in a sealed envelope. After the convention the envelope was opened. The name inscribed was Warren Gamaliel Harding.[3]

Wall Street, with Will Hays of the Sinclair Oil Company deputized to handle details, began the collection of the Republican slush fund early in 1919. All leading corporation executives were dragooned into giving from $100 to $1,000. As Hays, a Presbyterian elder, had piously spread the tidings that no contribution exceeding $1,000 would be accepted, the leading figures of wealth cautiously made their early offerings only in installments of $1,000 each. Members of the wealthy families who gave $1,000 from two to twelve times (with two to eight members of some families contributing) were S. R. Guggenheim, Murry Guggenheim, William Boyce Thompson, R. Livingston Beekman, Edward H. Clark, C. A. Coffin, Daniel Guggenheim, Percy A. Rockefeller, Thomas Cochran (Morgan partner), George F. Baker, Charles Hayden, John N. Willys, Elisha Walker, Harry F. Sinclair, E. H. Gary, J. Leonard Replogle, James McLean, William H. Woodin, Clarence H. Mackay, Eugene G. Grace, E. C. Converse, W. C. Durant, Charles M. Schwab, Earl W. Sinclair, Theodore N. Vail, Dwight Morrow (Morgan partner),

George D. Pratt, James B. Duke, David A. Schulte, Edwin Gould, Frank J. Gould, Vincent Astor, Mrs. Vincent Astor, Helen Astor, James A. Farrell, H. E. Huntington, George Washington Hill, George J. Whelan, Ludwig Vogelstein (properties seized by Alien Property Custodian and later returned under fraudulent circumstances), Albert H. Wiggin, Dunlevy Milbank, Horace Havemeyer, Ogden Reid, W. K. Vanderbilt, Jr., Henry P. Davison (Morgan partner), August Heckscher, John T. Pratt, Ruth Baker Pratt, T. F. Manville, H. H. Westinghouse, James Speyer, Helen Frick, Walter P. Chrysler, Childs Frick, John D. Rockefeller, John D. Rockefeller, Jr., Mrs. Edwin Harkness, Julius Fleischmann, W. L. Mellon, Andrew W. Mellon, T. Coleman du Pont, Mrs. Otto Kahn, W. K. Vanderbilt, Mrs. T. Coleman du Pont, Eugene Meyer, Felix Warburg, Adolph Lewisohn, Mrs. John D. Rockefeller, Mrs. Henry Seligman, Mrs. Felix Warburg, Mrs. Ogden Mills, Alexis I. du Pont, W. A. Harriman, F. A. Juilliard, Chauncey Depew, Mrs. F. W. Vanderbilt, Miss Flora Whitney, Miss Barbara Whitney, Mrs. Harry Sinclair, Ogden L. Mills, Howard Phipps, Frederick B. Pratt, George W. Perkins, Marshall Field, J. Ogden Armour, F. Edson White, Daniel G. Reid, Mrs. Marshall Field, Mrs. Stanley Field, Mrs. Samuel Insull, Charles E. Mitchell, Harold I. Pratt, Mrs. Harry Payne Whitney, Otto Kahn, and John W. Weeks.

From January 1, 1919, to August 26, 1920, the Republican National Committee collected $2,359,676 for general party purposes, irrespective of contributions on behalf of individual candidates. This was all the Kenyon Committee could find, although in subsequent years vast additional sums were brought to light. According to the final report of the Kenyon Senatorial Investigating Committee, Harry F. Sinclair on May 15, 1919, made two contributions of $1,000 each. Yet, testifying under oath on June 2, 1920, Sinclair made the following answers to questions:

*Q.* You have had nothing to do with political campaigns at all?

*A.* No, sir.

*Q.* Directly or indirectly?

*A.* No, sir.

The Kenyon Committee got no further with its inquiry into the $10,000,000 Republican slush fund of 1920, but it brought about the elimination of Wood by discovering that his preconvention fund totaled at least $1,773,033. William Boyce Thompson in 1922, however, confided to C. W. Barron: "There was no limit on the State contributions or the Senatorial Committee. Every Congressional District and every State had all the money it could use. In all six million dollars must have been spent." [4] As chairman of the Republican Ways and Means Committee which directed Hays, Sinclair attorney and national campaign manager, Thompson presumably knew whereof he spoke. Other committee members were John W. Weeks, of the brokerage house of Hornblower and Weeks, and the United States Senate; William Cooper Procter, head of the Procter and Gamble Soap Company, of Cincinnati; T. Coleman du Pont, William Crocker, and Mrs. John T. Pratt (Standard Oil).

Concealment of campaign contributions is customary. Frank R. Kent, of the Baltimore *Sun*, writes in his authoritative *Political Behavior*: "Indictments for violations of the Corrupt Practices Acts are almost unknown and convictions practically nonexistent. From President down, all elective officers are chosen as a result of campaigns in which both state and Federal laws . . . are evaded and violated. In every campaign for the presidency there is in each party always some man other than the treasurer and chairman, close to the candidate and who knows the game, to whom personal contributions that are never advertised and for which there is no need to account can be made."

Detailed contributions to the Wood fund uncovered by the Kenyon Committee included $731,000 from Procter; $100,000 each from George A. Whelan (United Cigar Stores), Rufus Patterson (tobacco), and Ambrose Monell (International Nickel); $50,000 from Henry H. Rogers (Standard Oil); $25,000 from John D. Rockefeller, Jr.; $15,000 from H. M. Byllesby; $10,000 each from George W. Perkins, William Wrigley, and John C. Shaffer, Chicago newspaper publisher and oil man; $6,000 from G. H. Payne, and $5,000 from Philip de Ronde, sugar importer. John T. King collected $91,-000, but could not remember the donors. His successor as Wood's campaign manager was William Loeb, President Theodore Roosevelt's White House secretary but long before 1920 promoted to vice-president of the Guggenheim's American Smelting and Refining Company and president of the Yukon Gold Company.

The second largest preconvention fund belonged to Frank O. Lowden, son-in-law of the late George M. Pullman, financier of Charles G. Dawes' Central Trust Company of Chicago, a leading spirit in the formation of the American Radiator Company, and wartime Governor of Illinois. Lowden's fund amounted to $414,984, most of which he contributed himself; it was of special interest because the Senate Committee obtained a glimpse of how some of it was used to "finance" two Missouri convention delegates.

Hiram Johnson came third with a fund of $194,393, Herbert Hoover fourth with $173,542, and Warren G. Harding fifth with $113,109. The Coolidge preconvention fund was only $68,375, so far as the record shows, but the Kenyon Committee failed to turn up the names of Dwight W. Morrow and Thomas Cochran although other sources show that these men contributed and were, indeed, the moving spirits behind the Coolidge boom.[5] The largest contributor to the Coolidge fund found by the Kenyon Committee was Frank W. Stearns, Boston department-store owner, who gave $12,-500. Harry M. Daugherty was the principal Harding preconvention contributor.

For eight years after 1920 new disclosures were forthcoming about vast contributions to the Republican slush fund; further inquiry would perhaps disclose additional sums. In 1924 it was brought out that Harry F. Sinclair gave $75,000 in the course of the campaign; in 1928 it was found that he had given $185,000 additionally in Liberty Bonds to defray the campaign deficit. James Patten, wheat speculator, the 1928 disclosures showed, gave $50,000. Andrew W. Mellon gave at least $25,000 more than had previously been admitted. John T. Pratt, brother of Herbert Pratt of the Standard Oil Company, gave $50,000 more than was uncovered by the Kenyon Committee. Edward L. Doheny, contributing $34,900 to the Republicans, also gave $75,000 to the Democrats. T. Coleman du Pont gave the Republicans $25,000 over and above the Kenyon Committee's figures.

In 1928 Hays reluctantly admitted that Daniel G. Reid, member of the board of the United States Steel Corporation, chairman of the American Can Company, president of the Tobacco Products Company, and director of the Bankers Trust Company, Guaranty Trust Company, and numerous other Morgan banks and trust companies, had given $100,000 in 1920.[6] William Boyce Thompson lent the Re- publicans $150,000 and gave $60,000.[7] Perjury was rife in all the hearings. The New York *Herald Tribune,* organ of the Republican Mills-Reid family, gently said of Hays that his "evasion of the law and the truth has been deplorable." [8]

Whereas the known Republican contributions finally came close to $10,000,000, with the usual fat donations under names like Mor- gan, Rockefeller, and Vanderbilt suspiciously absent, the Democratic slush fund amounted to only $2,327,750.

The day before Harding's nomination the room of George W. Harvey at the Blackstone Hotel was the scene of the notorious mid- night conference that was saturated in oil, whiskey, and tobacco smoke. In the light of his earlier prediction that Harding would capture the nomination it is impossible not to see him as the bearer of the highest Wall Street sanction, for as an original deputy of Ryan, who collaborated on equal terms with Morgan, Rockefeller, and Frick, Harvey had handled confidential political missions for all the big financial clans.

Daugherty, who was a purely minor figure in the conspiracy but slated to be Harding's Attorney General, knew enough only to tell newspaper men before the convention that "the nomination would be decided on by twelve or thirteen men 'at two o'clock in the morn- ing, in a smoke-filled room.' " [9]

The political deputies of wealth in Harvey's room were Senators Henry Cabot Lodge (Morgan), Medill McCormick (Chicago *Tribune*-International Harvester Company), James E. Watson of Indiana (Ku Klux Klan), Reed Smoot (Utah sugar interests), James W. Wadsworth of New York (Morgan) and Frank Brandegee of Connecticut (Morgan); the only person in the room who was not a Senator, other than Harvey, was Joseph R. Grundy, chief lobbyist of the Pennsylvania Manufacturers' Association and personal representa- tive of Senator Boies Penrose, who was lying in Philadelphia at the point of death but was nevertheless in constant telephonic com- munication with Harvey's hotel suite.

Although not a delegate to the convention, Harvey "was second to nobody there in influence upon its proceedings." [10] Others on the ground, and in intimate association with the convention managers, were Elbert H. Gary, Henry P. Davison, Thomas W. Lamont, W. W. Atterbury, president of the Pennsylvania Railroad, Richard Mellon, George F. Baker, Frank A. Vanderlip, and F. H. Allen, partner in Lee, Higginson and Company of Boston and New York.[11]

These latter, according to Senator R. F. Pettigrew of South Dakota, actually dictated what went into the hodgepodge collection of evasions that constituted the Republican platform; and "they were willing to take Lowden or Wood . . . They were holding Knox and Hoover, Harding and Senator Watson of Indiana in reserve . . ." [12] The proceedings of the convention were determined each day in advance by the clique around Harvey.[13]

Harding, somewhat incoherent and slightly wilted by heat and beverages, was summoned to Harvey's room at midnight on the eve of his nomination. Solemnly asked if there was anything that would make him unfit for the presidency—a guarded reference to a whisper that Negro blood flowed in his veins—he as solemnly replied in the negative. He was thereupon assured that the finger of destiny had settled upon his shoulder, designating him a successor of Washington, Jefferson, Jackson, and Lincoln. Harding left in a daze to plead unsuccessfully with Senator Hiram Johnson to accept the vice-presidency. Johnson, in bed, haughtily declined the honor and turned his face to the wall.

After Harding's nomination the unseen movers of the convention selected Coolidge as his running mate, a decision disappointing to Stearns but acquiesced in by Morrow and Cochran behind the scenes. Lodge, as convention chairman, adroitly moved the Morgan candidate ahead of Senator Lenroot of Wisconsin.

Like Cox, Taft, and McKinley, Harding was a product of Standard Oil's Ohio. He was, indeed, a product of Mark Hanna's old Standard Oil machine, of which he became a rank-and-file member in his youth while starting out as a small-town newspaper publisher. Ohio State Senator from 1900 to 1904, Lieutenant Governor from 1904 to 1906, Harding formally nominated William Howard Taft in 1912, and in 1914 was sent to the United States Senate. In 1908 Harding had boomed Standard Oil's Joseph B. Foraker for the presidency. Although it was not written upon his brow, Harding was, truth to tell, a Standard Oil man; his regime was, moreover, to be soaked, hardly by accident, in petroleum.

J. P. Morgan's Coolidge was himself no more than a puppet. After astounding his fellow townsmen by capturing the mayoralty of Northampton, Massachusetts, from two abler candidates, he was elected to the Massachusetts Senate as the protégé of the wealthy Senator W. Murray Crane, director of the American Telephone and Telegraph Company and other J. P. Morgan enterprises. In 1913 Coolidge was elevated to the Massachusetts Senate presidency, to the astonishment of outsiders, as a climax to the forehanded intrigue of J. Otis Wardwell, attorney for Kidder, Peabody and Company, close banking associate of J. P. Morgan and Company; a collaborator in this intrigue was Arthur P. Russell, attorney for the New York, New Haven and Hartford Railroad and various other Morgan public-utilities companies.[14] As Senate President, Coolidge exercised power second only to that of the Governor.

In 1915 he was elected Lieutenant Governor, this time with the help of funds from Dwight W. Morrow, whose classmate he had been at Amherst College.[15] Two years later Morrow assisted Coolidge into the governorship, where he was hibernating when the Boston police strike of 1919 goaded conservatives to fury and insensate fear. Before the inept Governor dared to move, the strike fell to pieces, whereupon he issued a resolute proclamation of defiance against the strikers. Coolidge's ostensible forthright action in breaking down the forces of lawlessness, it was argued at Chicago, made him a logical presidential aspirant; but the hard-bitten, booze-soaked delegates were not convinced.

Although keeping himself in the background, the soft-spoken Morrow was present at Chicago, an aspiring President-maker. "Morrow's room at the hotel became the center of intensive lobbying. He expounded, he argued, he cajoled."[16] When Harding was nominated Morrow wrote to Lamont that he did not relish the man, but "nevertheless I feel that there is nothing against him and that there is very much in his favor."[17]

The decisive election victory of Harding and Coolidge at once placed Harvey in a pre-eminent political position. Harvey was, in fact, the real President while Harding occupied the White House. He was offered the post of Secretary of State, but declined and took the London ambassadorship. Harding and Will Hays together telephoned to Harvey in New York from the South to solicit his approval of the Cabinet members. As the names of the men who were to sit in the "Black Cabinet" were read Harvey exclaimed, "Admirable! . . . Perfect! . . . You could not possibly do better." [18]

Until his death President Harding corresponded frequently with Harvey and sought his advice.[19] When Harvey was named to the London post John D. Rockefeller thought it fitting to congratulate him.[20] And even after Harding died Harvey's influence at the White House was scarcely diminished, although it was subordinate to that of Dwight W. Morrow. Harvey and Coolidge corresponded often, and Harvey, resigning his London post to be nearer the scene of action after his political creation had passed into the afterworld, was often at the White House.[21] Harvey, indeed, constantly shuttled in and out to confer with Coolidge.[22] At one time the President wrote to Harvey: "If you get an idea any time, let me have it." [23] Harvey and Coolidge, as a matter of fact, had an "exceptionally intimate and confidential friendship." [24]

On the occasion of one of Coolidge's opaque speeches Harvey and the senior John D. Rockefeller jointly signed a message of felicitation to the President.[25] The dual signature was, perhaps, a delicate way of reminding Coolidge for whom Harvey was the spokesman. So great a political force was Harvey known to be that the pathetically ambitious Herbert Hoover sought and was given his potent aid in the 1928 presidential campaign.[26]

At the instance of Henry Clay Frick, who conveyed his wishes through Senator Philander C. Knox of Pennsylvania, Harding named Andrew W. Mellon Secretary of the Treasury.[27]* Until his appointment Mellon had been virtually unknown to the general public, although he was one of the five richest individuals in the country and since 1871 had been Frick's banker. The appointment of Charles Evans Hughes, Standard Oil attorney, as Secretary of

* Some writers say Daugherty suggested Mellon, but this is highly improbable. Frick was not only the logical man to propose Mellon but George Harvey, an insider, says he did propose him.

State, was probably dictated by Harvey. According to the talkative William Boyce Thompson "Hughes was the connection with John D. Rockefeller." [28]

When Philander C. Knox died, incidentally, he was replaced in the Senate by his law partner, David A. Reed, of Pittsburgh, counsel to the Mellon banks, as Knox had been. The Mellon-Frick Senatorial succession was not permitted to lapse; it was kept alive, however, only by wholesale pecuniary debasement of the electoral processes, as disclosed by a Senate committee.

Hughes and Mellon were the most significant appointees in the Harding Cabinet, the one ruling over the delicate field of foreign affairs, which involved the settlement of war debts and apportionment of postwar markets, and the other over the equally delicate field of domestic finances. It is no wonder that Lodge confided to Barron in 1923 that "Harding is very satisfactory to the financial interests." [29] As to Hughes and the debt settlement, Barron quotes Harding's Secretary of State as saying in June, 1921, "I know Mr. Rockefeller quite well and we are getting the benefit of Mr. Morgan's opinion." [30]

Senator Weeks, Boston broker and Morgan connection, was named Secretary of War. Hays, Sinclair Oil attorney, became Postmaster General for a brief term, resigning to become moral arbiter for the motion-picture industry. Daugherty, a ward politician, was Harding's personal selection as Attorney General. Hoover, about whose connections more will be said later, was named Secretary of Commerce at the bidding of William Boyce Thompson, who probably spoke with the approval of his close friend, Thomas W. Lamont. The pliant Senator Albert B. Fall, protégé of E. L. Doheny, Harry F. Sinclair, and Cleveland H. Dodge, was given the portfolio of the Interior Department, which carried with it custody of the public lands. Edwin B. Denby of Michigan was named Secretary of the Navy. Henry A. Wallace of Iowa became Secretary of Agriculture.

Harding surrounded himself with a motley crew of personal advisers. His "poker Cabinet" included Mellon, Harvey, Will Hays, William Wrigley, Chicago chewing-gum manufacturer, Charles M. Schwab, Harry F. Sinclair, and Walter C. Teagle, president of the Standard Oil Company of New Jersey.[31] The President's private parties soon caused whispering in Washington, so much so that many prominent persons were curious to see the White House room where they took place, although it was not until the Teapot Dome investigation that the mysterious "little green house on K Street" also became widely known as a haunt of the President and his poker-playing friends.

"I had heard rumors and was curious to see for myself what truth was in them," says Alice Longworth of a White House visit. "No rumor could have exceeded the reality; the study was filled with cronies, Daugherty, Jess Smith, Alex Moore, and others, the air heavy with tobacco smoke, trays with bottles, containing every imaginable brand of whiskey stood about [prohibition was a Federal law], cards and poker chips ready at hand—a general atmosphere of waist-coats unbuttoned, feet on the desk, and the spittoon alongside." [32]

Immediately after the Inaugural the piratical poker-playing crew in charge of the ship of state scrambled for the strongbox with the unerring instinct of cracksmen seeking the family heirlooms. Hughes negotiated agreements for the payment of the inter-Allied debts and a general reduction in naval armaments; these were, relatively, "clean" jobs, although of tax benefit to the millionaires. Mellon cheerfully took over the job of manipulating the public exchequer. Fall and Denby, with the President's explicit consent, permitted the ravishment of the naval oil reserves by the Sinclair-Doheny-Standard Oil syndicate. Daugherty quashed prosecutions of war profiteers and other spoilsmen of Wall Street and waged vigorous warfare against labor organizations. Hoover expanded the Department of Commerce at great public expense and used it as a marketing agency for the big industries, which were given its valuable services free of charge.

But, most significantly of all, Hoover used the Department of Commerce to foster monopoly on the most complete scale ever seen outside a Fascist state. The antitrust movement had collapsed completely during the war; even the pretense of enforcing the Sherman and Clayton Acts was discarded. Under Hoover the trust movement took a new form. Approximately four hundred trade associations had come into being during the war, sponsored by the various industries and encouraged by the government.

In 1921 the Supreme Court had held that the pooling of commercial information was in restraint of trade. Daugherty, as Attorney General, contended that the distribution of information and statistics among members of trade associations violated the law. In 1923 the Supreme Court held that the Association of Linseed Oil Producers restrained trade.

"Secretary Hoover then took the final step in using the machinery of his department to circumvent the restraints of the Supreme Court and the Department of Justice. Voluntary committees within the industrial and trade groups sent statistical data to the department. This was combined with data furnished by the Bureau of Census and the Bureau of Foreign Commerce, analyzed, and returned to the associations to be distributed among members." [33]

The Federal Trade Commission protested against this as arrant price-fixing, but the Supreme Court approved. Monopoly and trustification had now reached its highest form: it was carried on through the agency of the government. Up to 1927, no fewer than 243 trade agreements had been arranged through Hoover's Department of Commerce, all having the effect of jacking up prices to the ultimate consumer. It was in recognition of this notable work in improving the mechanism for extracting money from the consumer that Hoover was given general banking support for the presidency in 1928 when Andrew W. Mellon's boom collapsed.

Hoover was not above engaging in even more devious practices to channel money into the hands of the financial lords. Early in his administration of the Commerce Department, for example, he put out a false prediction of a sugar-crop shortage which made possible an increase in prices that netted the Sugar Trust a profit of $55,000,000 in three months.

Hoover's trade associations functioned behind the screen of the highest tariff yet devised, the Fordney-McCumber Tariff Act of 1922, passed by the Republican majority and approved by Harding. Illustrative of the fact that the tariff rates were not arrived at on the basis of abstract principle were the increases on aluminum houseware fixed for the benefit of Mellon's Aluminum Corporation, which in 1921 paid a dividend of one thousand per cent on its original capital and which immediately after passage of the Fordney-McCumber Act declared an additional dividend of five hundred per cent. Other big companies benefited similarly.

The Aluminum Company, to digress momentarily, had been recognized as a monopoly in 1912 by the Federal courts; in 1924 the Federal Trade Commission reported it as an absolute monopoly, and although the Trade Commission filed complaints against it again in 1928 and 1930 nothing was done about it until 1937 when the government again filed suit to break it up. Mellon, in short, enjoyed the immunity reserved for those in possession of money.

But the hub of government, immediately after Harding was installed, became the Treasury Department. Mellon went to work upon the public vaults with a celerity that showed what the election had been about. Under Mellon reductions and remissions of income taxes for wealthy individuals exceeded $6,000,000,000; until he appeared in Washington wholesale tax rebates had been unheard of. The details of Mellon's tax-reduction program were worked out by Assistant Secretary of the Treasury S. Parker Gilbert, who has since become a partner of J. P. Morgan and Company. Gilbert was a protégé of Owen D. Young and Russell C. Leffingwell, Assistant Secretary of the Treasury under Wilson and subsequently a Morgan partner.

Mellon also launched a movement to impose a Federal sales tax upon all articles in retail trade, a barefaced attempt to increase the tax burden of the lower classes. Although repeated efforts to pass the sales tax were made under Harding, Coolidge, and Hoover, with Mellon the individual driving force, it was repeatedly defeated by the Senate insurgents of both parties. The proposed sales tax was applauded by most of the big newspapers, notably by the Hearst chain.

At the time Mellon threw around himself the mantle of Alexander Hamilton the moguls of vested wealth were in danger of losing some portion of their war profits to the public Treasury, whence, indeed, they had come. Upon the declaration of war, Congress had devised an excess-profits tax based on corporation earnings of the 1911-1914 period. The tax amounted to twenty per cent on profits fifteen per cent in excess of the basing figure; to thirty-five per cent on the excess up to fifteen to twenty-five per cent; to forty-five per cent on the excess up to twenty-five to thirty-three per cent;

and to sixty per cent on the excess above thirty-three per cent. Despite these relatively punitive rates the profits taken after payment of taxes were enormous. A wartime surtax of two to three per cent was imposed on individual incomes of $8,000 to $50,000; of twelve to twenty-four per cent on incomes of $50,000 to $100,000; of twenty-seven to fifty-two per cent on incomes of $100,000 to $2,000,000; and of sixty-three to sixty-five per cent on incomes from $2,000,000 upward.

Various ways were discovered by the rich for evading these taxes. One method was to invest in tax-exempt government securities. There were not enough of these to supply the demand from wealthy families, but they were supplemented by tax-exempt securities issued by state and local governments, which the investment bankers stimulated to tap the vast surplus capital resources of Wall Street. Other ways of evading taxes were to invest money abroad; to declare stock dividends and transfer cash earnings to surplus to be held against a day of low taxes for distribution; to build unnecessary plants, hotels, and office buildings; to pay inordinately high salaries to corporation officials; and to resort to technically legal subterfuges such as personal holding companies. Although the income of the wealthy class had risen sharply, in 1922 incomes of more than $300,000 paid only $366,000,000 in income taxes, compared with nearly $1,000,000,000 in 1916 *before* the imposition of the emergency taxes!

Mellon failed to block any of the tax loopholes.

But on the plea of stopping tax evasion the Revenue Act of 1921, drawn by Mellon's Department, eliminated the excess profits tax entirely, saving corporation stockholders $1,500,000,000 a year at one stroke. The maximum surtax on individual incomes was reduced by Congress from sixty-five to fifty per cent, with Mellon calling for a twenty-five per cent surtax. The concession by Congress was not sufficient for the avid Mellon and his supporters, however, for late in 1923 additional measures were enacted that further eased the tax load on the rich. The proposed tax bill of 1924 reduced the maximum surtax from fifty to twenty-five per cent; this was considered so flagrant that the bill could not be stomached even by a subservient Congress. In the substitute bill a surtax of thirty-seven and a half per cent was established and estate taxes were raised from twenty-five to forty per cent on fortunes of $10,000,000 or more. Mellon thereupon advised Coolidge to use the veto, but the President, heeding advice from other quarters, allowed the measure to become law.

Mellon argued that the tax would so operate as to confiscate estates in two or three generations, ending, as he vowed, the existence of private property. Senate liberals, however, pointed to the fact that the Guggenheim, Du Pont, Harkness, and Pratt fortunes had doubled or trebled in the hands of many heirs. Alexis I. Du Pont, who died in 1921 as a member of the fourth generation of a dynasty whose founder left $40,000,000, alone had an estate of $30,000,000; a dozen other members of the fourth generation had fortunes of equal or greater size. Edward S. Harkness left an estate of less than $50,000,000, yet his two sons left $100,000,000 and $170,000,000 respectively.

In 1926 Coolidge signed Mellon's bill that provided for a twenty per cent maximum surtax on individual income taxes; a basic tax rate of 5 per cent; reduction of the inheritance tax; repeal of the gift tax and of the tax on automobile trucks and accessories. Up to this point the Mellon tax reductions had saved wealthy individuals and corporations an officially estimated $4,000,000,000 annually, exclusive of remissions.

Had a halt been called there something might have been saved from the wreckage. But Mellon was coldly savage in his determination to obtain virtually complete tax exemption for the clans of great wealth. The Treasury Department quietly indicated, the moment Mellon took office, particularly to generous Republican Party contributors, that the Internal Revenue Bureau had adopted a policy of "liberal" interpretation of tax laws to allow remissions of taxes paid from 1917 onward. At one time more than twenty-seven thousand lawyers, accountants, and tax experts were handling tax-rebate cases in Washington.

The situation soon caused the launching of a special Senate investigation under the chairmanship of Senator James Couzens of Michigan. One of the cases cited by Couzens concerned a zinc property bought by William Boyce Thompson in 1913 for $10,000 and sold in 1918 for $600,000, upon the five thousand nine hundred per cent profit of which transaction no taxes were collected because, it was said with absurd illogicality, the property had been really worth $600,000 from the first.

The Couzens investigation disclosed other rank favoritism if not criminal intent in the bestowal of public funds disguised as tax rebates; Mellon vindictively retaliated by filing suit against Couzens for the collection of $10,000,000 in taxes allegedly due on the sale in 1918 of Couzens' stock in the Ford Motor Company. Couzens won the case, but at great expense. Before his recent death Couzens enjoyed the distinction of being the only wealthy man ever to sit in the Senate with a keen sense of responsibility to the common welfare. A similar Senator, not so wealthy, was the late Bronson Cutting of New Mexico.

During his first four years in office Mellon gave himself a tax refund of $404,000, second only to one of $457,000 for John D. Rockefeller, Jr. The United States Steel Corporation received a refund of $27,000,000, typical of those to large corporations. It is manifestly impossible to cite all the refunds, for up to December, 1924, the list of tax refunds filled eight folio volumes of ten thousand pages. When Mellon left office the list was more than twice as large.

Mellon on one occasion overstepped the bounds of legality, when a refund of $91,472 to the Mellon banks in Pittsburgh was assailed as improper; it was promptly defended on the Senate floor by Senator David A. Reed, Mellon's lawyer. But the Treasury Department was constrained to admit, in the face of a general outcry from the Senate liberals, that the refund was illegal. It was recalled.

Mellon, of course, fought the disclosure of 1923 and 1924 tax payments brought about by Couzens and the Senate liberals, and he and Coolidge were successful in having this salutary practice discontinued. The Couzens inquiry, unfortunately, did not stop Mellon from ladling out public funds. Indeed, Couzens' committee was not equipped to unravel the tortuous details of all the tax transactions. But the committee made it glaringly evident that virtually every tax transaction of the Treasury Department under the Pittsburgh banker and aluminum monopolist is suspect. During Mellon's tenure a total of $1,271,000,000 of tax refunds were made, of which $7,000,000 were for Mellon's personal account, $14,000,000 for the account of his corporation. In remissions, rebates, and reductions of rates more than $6,000,000,000 was siphoned from the Treasury into private pockets. The Mellon regime therefore had the effect of leaving the national debt larger by this amount than it would have been and of increasing the aggregate of war profits by at least half this amount, since it was capital gains from wartime operations that figured largely in the tax juggling.

Not satisfied with the havoc already wrought in the public finances Mellon and President Hoover in November, 1929, announced a reduction of one per cent on individual and corporation taxes for 1930, of which $100,000,000 accrued to corporations and $60,000,000 to individuals. This reduction was temporary only; since then there has been no fundamental reform in the income-tax schedules, which should never, in the interests of sound public finance, have been changed from the 1919 basis. The Franklin D. Roosevelt Administration, however, closed some tax loopholes, but while it has raised estate and income taxes it has kept a loosely drawn gift-tax law that virtually nullifies estate-tax provisions.

Mellon played politics in many ways with the Treasury Department. During his incumbency he predicted, from time to time, heavy deficits. These predictions had the effect of deterring war veterans and farmers from demanding Federal assistance. In 1921, 1922, and 1924 Mellon predicted deficits in the face of the bonus agitation, and each year there was a substantial surplus. But after 1929, when deficits became the rule, Mellon took to predicting surpluses so that income and inheritance taxes would not be increased by Congress.

As the nation writhed after 1929 in the grip of the crisis, economists criticized the Secretary of the Treasury for having reduced taxes in prosperous years when they might have liquidated the national debt and so left the Treasury in a position to shoulder its proper responsibility to the people as a whole. The conservative Dr. E. R. A. Seligman, McVickar Professor Emeritus of Political Economy at Columbia University, lashed out at Mellon for the "absurdly inadequate" revenues received from the meager inheritance taxes.

The Treasury Department under Mellon was shot through with

scandals, of which the Barco concession deal was outstanding.* The Mellon tax policies were scandal enough, however; they played a big part in fueling the speculative boom of 1924-1929, for the funds released for private use could in many cases find no constructive economic outlet. They were therefore directed into the stock market, into the proliferation of holding companies and investment trusts, and into wild personal extravagances that stimulated luxury trades which later collapsed.

## II

The untimely death of Harding on August 2, 1923, brought no change in government policies. The merry game of plundering continued under Coolidge. The first Teapot Dome revelations in 1924 acted as a slight deterrent upon the process but, on the whole, no change was visible to the naked eye. Coolidge's running mate in 1924 was Charles G. Dawes, Chicago banker and Comptroller of the Currency under McKinley.

* The Carib Syndicate, controlled by Henry L. Doherty and J. P. Morgan, in 1917 bought a Colombian oil concession known as the Barco Concession. It had not been developed owing to high costs, and in 1926 the Colombian government proposed to cancel it. The Mellon's Gulf Oil Company, however, although knowing the facts, on January 5, 1926, paid Doherty $1,500,000 for the concession. Gulf Oil argued against cancellation of the undeveloped concession, and its contentions were upheld by the State Department. American banks instituted an embargo against Colombia, and thus brought about a severe internal political and economic crisis. The National City Bank of New York, appealed to by Dr. Enrique Olaya Herrera, Colombian Minister to Washington, said that nothing could be done about Colombian financing until the confidence of investors was restored. To assist in restoring confidence Herrera was given H. Freeman Matthews, assistant chief of the Latin-American division of the State Department and Jefferson Caffrey, American Minister to Colombia. They recommended the engagement by Colombia of Dr. Edwin Kemmerer, of Princeton University, to revise Colombia's fiscal policies, and of George Rublee, Dwight W. Morrow's aide in Mexico, to advise on legislation. Colombia adopted the petroleum code recommended by these Americans, but only after stormy debate. The new petroleum law gave the Gulf Oil Company a fifty-year concession. Ten days after the law's adoption, the National City Bank advanced to Colombia the final $4,000,000 installment of a $20,000,000 credit earlier contracted for. *The New Republic* expressed astonishment that "an American Secretary of State had used his high office to persuade the National City Bank of New York to grant an unsound bank credit to the government of Colombia as a means of obtaining one of the world's largest oil concessions for a company controlled by the interests of Mr. Mellon, our Secretary of Treasury."

The nomination of Dawes preserved the general low tone and artistic consistency of the Republican ticket. Dawes was a protégé of Mark Hanna, and this was not unknown; but in view of the fact that Davis, in the parlance of the prize-fighting ring, was to "lay down," it made no difference what weakling accompanied the incredible Coolidge. Dawes' chief claim to fame, other than his ostensible authorship of the Dawes Plan of Reparation Settlements, arose from his participation in the William E. Lorimer bank scandal in Chicago before the war.

Lorimer had been elected United States Senator from Illinois in 1910 with the help of a slush fund supplied by Edward Hines, wealthy lumber man. Because Hines was at odds with the Republican faction dominated by the McCormicks, the deal was exposed in the Chicago *Tribune* and Lorimer was refused his seat by the Senate, most of whose members had arrived at their eminence over the very road traveled by Lorimer.

Although a Republican political boss, Lorimer controlled a national bank in Chicago which became involved in difficulties soon after the rejection of its proprietor by the Senate. To avoid a Federal bank examination Lorimer decided to have his national bank charter changed to a state charter. But to get a state charter he had to prove to the State Auditor of Public Accounts that the bank actually possessed $1,250,000 cash as claimed. Unfortunately, Lorimer was even then insolvent. Dawes, head of the Central Trust Company (which he had started after the turn of the century with money obtained from his friend, Frank O. Lowden), without informing his fellow officers or directors, made out to Lorimer's bank a check for $1,250,000 with which Lorimer was to deceive the State Auditor. As soon as a state charter had been issued, the check was returned, uncashed. For his part in the deal Dawes was soundly rebuked by the Supreme Court of Illinois. This court held Dawes' Central Trust Company liable for $110,457.51 in the failure of Lorimer's institution, paring down a liability set at $1,400,000 by the lower courts.

Although thousands of depositors lost money in the Lorimer crash, action against Dawes went no further than the litigation cited, for Dawes was a power in Illinois politics. Moreover, Dawes'

bank did not satisfy the judgment against it until after Dawes'
nomination for the vice-presidency in 1924.

The Democratic contender was John W. Davis, former Congress-
man and Solicitor General, Harvey's predecessor in the London am-
bassadorship, and, above all, attorney for J. P. Morgan and Company.
Davis was chosen by the Democrats as a compromise after a conven-
tion deadlock between the Ku Klux Klan, which backed William G.
McAdoo, and the Roman Catholic Church, which backed Alfred E.
Smith. Davis' running mate was Charles Bryan, brother of William
Jennings Bryan.

With Davis and Coolidge in the field, J. P. Morgan and Company
had the unprecedented distinction of controlling both candidates.

A third ticket was headed by Senator Robert M. LaFollette, with
Burton K. Wheeler of Montana, one of the active figures in exposing
the Teapot Dome swindle, as his running mate. LaFollette polled
five million votes, the most ever garnered by an independent candidate, but Coolidge, supported by a mountain of money, won
handily.

Behind the financial arrangements of the Coolidge campaign
stood Dwight W. Morrow. Thomas Fortune Ryan, as usual, took the
lead for the Democrats. Frank P. Walsh, attorney for the LaFollette
committee, estimated total Republican collections at $15,000,000 and,
considering various special Senatorial contests wherein private stakes
were great, the aggregate may easily have been around this figure.
But the Republican National Committee collected only $4,370,409
as far as a special Senate committee under William E. Borah could
determine. The Democratic National Committee spent only $903,908
for its shadowboxer. The LaFollette campaign cost $221,937.

As in 1904 J. P. Morgan and Company in 1924 took the lead in
scaring up Republican contributions. E. T. Stotesbury collected
$50,000 in Philadelphia; Guy Emerson, now vice-president of the
Bankers Trust Company, did most of the collecting in New York,
although George Murnane, vice-president of the New York Trust
Company (Morgan) collected $77,000. William Wrigley, James A.
Patten, William H. Woodin, and Frederick H. Prince each gave
$25,000; Eldridge M. Johnson, president of the Victor Talking
Machine Company, Mortimer L. Schiff, Arthur Curtiss James, and

Payne Whitney each gave $15,000; J. B. Duke and William Nelson Cromwell each gave $12,500; Julius Fleischmann, Charles Hayden, J. Horace Harding, Andrew W. Mellon, Vincent Astor, Julius Forstmann, John D. Rockefeller, Irénée du Pont, Ogden Mills, Frank A. Munsey, Frank W. Stearns, Arthur W. Cutten, and Charles G. Dawes each gave $10,000; Dwight W. Morrow, Thomas Cochran, Marshall Field, Richard B. Mellon, Helen Clay Frick, Cornelius Vanderbilt, Alfred P. Sloan, Jr., Harvey S. Firestone, William H. Todd, Henry G. Huntington, Archer M. Huntington, and Charles M. Schwab each gave $5,000. Smaller sums in varying amounts were given by other figures of wealth who wanted a word to say in government.

Thomas Fortune Ryan gave the Democrats $55,000, the largest single contribution brought to light. Contributions of $25,000 each were made by Bernard M. Baruch and Jesse H. Jones, Texas banker and land promotor. Henry Morgenthau put up $23,500. Thomas L. Chadbourne, Cuban sugar investor, gave $20,000. Contributions of $10,000 each were made by Norman H. Davis, banker and diplomat, Francis P. Garvan and S. D. Camden. Contributions of $5,000 each were made by Mrs. Jesse H. Jones, John D. Ryan, Percy S. Straus, John W. Davis, Cleveland H. Dodge, Frank L. Polk, Allen Wardwell, Cyrus H. McCormick, Charles R. Crane, and Jesse I. Straus. Smaller contributions came from Ralph Pulitzer, F. B. Keech, Gerard Swope, Edward A. Filene, Richard Crane, and various corporation executives.

A tangle of special interests, analysis shows, was concerned with financing the campaign. Stotesbury, a leading spirit in the United Gas Improvement Company of Philadelphia, was under indictment along with his company; the United States Attorney General dismissed the indictment. More than a score of officials of sugar companies that were under investigation by the United States Tariff Commission contributed; textile men interested in a higher tariff made heavy donations; Charles Hayden, old partner of William Boyce Thompson and special backer of Herbert Hoover, contributed $5,000 and was currently resisting a government claim for a wartime overpayment of $5,267,476 to the Wright-Martin Aircraft Company, of which he was a director. The government soon afterward renounced this claim. Harry M. Blackmer, chairman of the Midwest Refining Company, deeply involved in the Teapot Dome scandal, made a sizable contribution, as did other Teapot Dome defendants. Julius Fleischmann, yeast king, and many others, had pending huge tax claims against the government. Beman G. Dawes, brother of the vice-presidential candidate and president of the Pure Oil Company, gave $5,000; his wife gave the same amount. The Pure Oil Company had a tax-refund claim pending and was a defendant in a suit brought by the government, which charged a conspiracy to control oil and gasoline prices in Ohio. The tax refund was granted, the suit was quashed.

In other words, the old game of purchasing immunity was played. The chairman of the Republican Ways and Means Committee, successor to Thompson, was Joseph R. Grundy, president of the Pennsylvania Manufacturers' Association and one of the Harding conspirators of 1920. Grundy on his own hook collected $300,000 in Pennsylvania.

Harding's "Black Cabinet" had to be reconstituted before the election, but Coolidge was afraid to make a move that would disturb the Republican machine. Against great pressure he held off for some time asking Daugherty for his resignation, and actually commended this arrant spoilsman and expressed regret when he did resign. Coolidge also obtained the resignation of Secretary Denby, who had acquiesced in the alienation of the naval oil reserves. Hughes, his work done, resigned in 1925 to resume his Standard Oil practice; he was replaced by Senator Frank B. Kellogg of Minnesota. There were other new appointments, all dictated by local politicoes, but Mellon remained in the Treasury, the central figure of the Republican regime; Hoover remained in the Department of Commerce.

Reaction gripped the nation. As the result of extensive postwar plotting both houses of Congress were under Wall Street control. William Boyce Thompson in 1922 had said, "The Senate must be controlled and there are Senators from different states who must be looked after." [34] Thompson and Harvey had, events in the Senate showed, wrought well. No bill of any tangible value to persons without wealth was to be passed and signed by a President for many years.

The outstanding new development of the Coolidge Administration was the rise of Dwight W. Morrow to national prominence, giving J. P. Morgan and Company virtually unchallenged jurisdiction over the White House for the first time since 1908. During Harding's incumbency Morrow had been occupied with problems of international finance. In 1921 he made an intensive study of French finances with a view to floating a loan through J. P. Morgan and Company; in the same year he reorganized the Cuban finances on a basis that led to the establishment of the bloody Machado dictatorship and the equally bloody revolt against it. In 1922 he was occupied with floating the Austrian reconstruction loan. Through a misunderstanding, Morrow failed to obtain a desired post on the Reparations Commission, but he succeeded in placing Owen D. Young, head of the General Electric Company, and a nominal Democrat, in his stead. S. Parker Gilbert was appointed Agent-General of Reparations upon the recommendation of J. P. Morgan and Company, which recognized his able services in working out the details of the tax-reduction program.

In 1925 Coolidge appointed Morrow to the Aviation Board; but in 1927 came the most crucial appointment of all. Morrow was named Ambassador to Mexico. This post, at the moment, was of vital interest to Wall Street and Washington; it was, indeed, the most important ambassadorship in the entire diplomatic service at the time, for relations with Mexico, where wealthy Americans owned mineral property worth more than $1,000,000,000, had gone from bad to worse since the first Wilson regime.

Despite close liaison with the overlords of wealth the State Department, its embassy in Mexico City the personal gift of E. L. Doheny, had been unable to obtain substantial concessions for the American millionaires. In 1919 the Rockefellers, the Guggenheims, the Anaconda Copper Mining Company, and E. L. Doheny took matters into their own hands by forming the Association for the Protection of American Rights in Mexico. This organization unloosed wild propaganda for intervention. Prodded by Senator Fall, a Senate committee sat from August, 1918, to May, 1920, hearing about alleged mistreatment of Americans in Mexico and thereby providing an official background for the interventionist propaganda. Wilson, upon listening to representations from Fall, agent in the Senate for the interventionists, reversed Lansing's relatively conciliatory policy and in the closing phases of his term adopted a strong tone toward Mexico. But he refused to accede to the open demands for war.

Harding and Coolidge experimented with Wilson's earlier policy of bullying, and in 1923 Coolidge recognized Obregon, who had ousted Carranza two years before, and agreed to sell him munitions. But after apparent improvement, relations again became very strained with the promulgation of the Mexican land law by the Calles government in 1925. This law replaced perpetual tenure of Mexican mineral and petroleum lands with fifty-year concessions, and so intensified the conflict that in 1927 the Hearst newspapers, their proprietor an owner of Mexican mineral lands, published a series of forgeries involving liberal United States Senators in alleged Mexican radical intrigue and corruption.

Morrow's appointment took effect at this crucial point. The former Morgan partner went to Mexico with conciliatory intentions and succeeded in obtaining a modification, satisfactory to the American interests, of the Petroleum Law. Morrow remained in Mexico until informed during the Hoover regime that he was to be a member of the United States delegation to the London Naval Conference of 1930 which ended in a stalemate. At the same time a movement got under way to make him United States Senator from New Jersey.

Coolidge, like Harding and unlike Theodore Roosevelt, exercised little discretion in catering to organized wealth. He had appointed Harlan F. Stone, Dean of the Columbia Law School and a student at Amherst with Morrow and himself, Attorney General to succeed Daugherty; but when Stone prepared to file an antitrust suit against Mellon's Aluminum Company, he was abruptly elevated to the Supreme Court; the suit was, of course, not brought.

Charles Beecher Warren, for many years an expert in the formation of trusts, was named to succeed Stone as Attorney General; but the Senate could not digest this appointment. Coolidge then appointed John G. Sargent, of Vermont, whose imagination did not encompass suits against great companies. An official of the Pennsylvania Railroad was appointed by Coolidge to the Interstate Commerce Commission to sit in judgment upon the railroads. A prominent sugar lobbyist, Edgar Brossard, who was primarily interested in sugar tariffs, was made a member of the Tariff Commission, which had been transformed into an agency for increasing tariffs instead of reducing them. The Tariff Commission had been empowered by the Fordney-McCumber Act to bring about tariff reforms; on its recommendation the President could raise or lower rates by as much as fifty per cent. In six years Coolidge reduced rates on paintbrush handles, phenol and cresylic acid, millfeed, and bobwhite quail, and increased rates to the maximum on eighteen items, including iron ore (Morgan). In 1928, Edward P. Costigan, later Senator from Colorado, resigned from the Tariff Commission, charging that Coolidge had packed the body and thwarted it in its work.

All effective veterans' legislation was vetoed by Coolidge as by Harding; whatever passed overrode the presidential veto. Both Coolidge and Harding temporized with the pressing farm problem by killing effective bills and approving only joker legislation. Coolidge sabotaged all efforts of liberal Senators to regulate the rampant electric power industry. In short, whatever brought benefit to the nonwealthy was scotched; whatever benefited the wealthy was passed. And the full meaning of it all becomes clear only in the light of the roles Morrow and Harvey, invisible behind the scenes, played as Coolidge's closest advisers. It was no wonder that William Boyce Thompson could say in 1927 that he would be content to have Coolidge for king and Mellon for queen to the end of his days.

Coolidge, a faithful servant, received his pay. Upon his retirement he was elected a director of the New York Life Insurance Company (Morgan) and was made a contributor at the rate of $1 a word to the New York *Herald Tribune* (Mills-Reid) even though what he wrote usually failed to make sense. In 1933 the Senate Banking and Currency Committee brought out that J. P. Morgan and Company in 1929 had Coolidge on its "favor" list. Coolidge was one of those permitted to buy stock far below the market price, the $30,000 difference between the market price and the purchase price representing a flat gift from J. P. Morgan and Company.

### III

The Administration of Herbert Hoover was, in all fundamental aspects, a regime of scandal, like its two predecessors. Hoover's strategy was to do nothing, hoping that the country would remain on an even keel. The economic debacle which overtook the nation under his rule cannot, it is true, be laid to him alone. He did nothing to the situation; rather did the situation catch up with the policy of drift and expediency which had marked all the administrations since 1896. The culmination was poetically logical: Hoover reaped what McKinley and Hanna, Roosevelt and Perkins, Wilson and Dodge, Coolidge and Mellon had sown.

The most serious obstacle to the nomination of Hoover was Andrew W. Mellon who, when Coolidge renounced another term, craftily reached out for the presidency. Mellon was outmaneuvered at the Kansas City Republican convention by the Philadelphia machine of William S. Vare, under control of E. T. Stotesbury and Morgan, Drexel and Company. Hoover had long been a Morgan puppet, and the Republican convention contest was strictly one between Morgan finance capital and Mellon finance capital. Thomas Cochran, partner of J. P. Morgan and Company, was on the ground at Kansas City as Hoover's invisible field marshal.

Long before he became wartime Food Administrator the ambitious Hoover had moved in the Morgan orbit. For more than twenty years he had promoted British mining enterprises in Africa, Australia, and Asia, working in association with British banks that were attuned with Morgan, Grenfell and Company of London; Hoover, according to contracts on the record, drew $95,000 a year salary for his promotional work and $5,000 a year for his engineering advice. In 1909 Hoover reached the turning point in his career when he met in London William Boyce Thompson, then a partner of Hayden, Stone and Company, New York investment bankers. Thompson, a stock-market crony of Thomas W. Lamont of J. P. Morgan and Company, was also primarily interested in mining promotions. He brought Hoover into a number of Hayden, Stone and Company enterprises.

There has been some mystery made of the way in which Hoover

came to the fore as Food Administrator in the Wilson Administration; but there is really no mystery. It was the influential Thompson who introduced Hoover, long absent in foreign lands, to the leading figures of American finance and politics. The Wilson Administration, as we have seen, was in the grip of the "copper crowd," and with the members of this group Thompson was on intimate terms.

Hoover, unknown to the world at large, became Food Administrator after having served as head of the Belgian relief group. In 1920 it was Thompson, when the presidential bee was buzzing seductively around Hoover's head, who turned him into the Republican Party and helped him make valuable political connections in New York, Colorado, and California. Thompson, through his work for the Guggenheims, enjoyed a wide acquaintanceship among politicians, newspaper publishers, and businessmen in the western states; as chairman of the Republican Ways and Means Committee he brought Hoover into close touch with such figures as Charles Hayden, Albert H. Wiggin, Harry F. Sinclair, E. L. Doheny, and Thomas W. Lamont. In 1928 Hayden, Thompson's old partner, was placed in charge of Hoover's campaign finances.

The contest between Republicans and Democrats in 1928 was embittered by the attempts of a young ambitious group gathered around the Du Ponts and Anaconda Copper, to capture the presidency with Alfred E. Smith, Tammany Governor of New York. This group, largely Catholic in composition, introduced a new note in American politics, for it marked the beginning of the functioning of the Roman Catholic Church on a national scale through the political apparatus of financial capital. In the United States the Catholic Church had hitherto concerned itself only with local politics in the large cities.

No fundamental policies were at issue between the two parties. Indeed, the Democratic Party under the leadership of Smith came to resemble more nearly than ever before the Republican Party. It threw overboard, for example, its historic tariff policy. The ostensible issue was Prohibition, with Hoover supporting the drys and thereby gaining the support of the Methodist Anti-Saloon League of America. But not until 1932, under the leadership of the wilful Du Ponts, was Prohibition to become a full-fledged economic issue in national politics.

Smith talked about Teapot Dome and other Republican scandals, but was careful neither to indict the Mellon tax infamies nor the speculative boom nourished by Washington. Yet he attracted the support of certain liberals who were undismayed by his uncouth East Side accent or his Tammany connections. Smith's ostensible liberalism, however, merely reflected the shrewd advice of Mrs. Henry Moskowitz, a social worker who labored in close collaboration with him while he, as Governor of New York, introduced a number of reforms of limited character. When Mrs. Moskowitz later died, Smith's political brain died.

William F. Kenny, Smith's personal friend and president of the W. F. Kenny Contracting Company, who operated, in collaboration with the wealthy Bradys, as a contractor for the New York Edison Company, Brooklyn Edison Company, and Consolidated Gas Company of New York, made the largest individual contribution to the 1928 Democratic slush fund—$125,000. Thomas Fortune Ryan, John J. Raskob, Du Pont deputy and chairman of the finance committee of General Motors Company as well as of the Democratic National Committee, and Herbert H. Lehman of the banking firm of Lehman Brothers, each put $110,000 on the table for the Oliver Street Lincoln. Lehman, who, incidentally, has spent more than $1,000,000 on the various Smith candidacies, in 1932 became Governor of New York. Jesse H. Jones, Texas banker, gave Smith's fund $75,000, and was the moving spirit in bringing the 1928 Democratic convention to Houston.

Smith contributions of $50,000 each were made by Harry Payne Whitney (Standard Oil), M. J. Meehan, Wall Street stock-market manipulator, W. A. Clark, president of the United Verde Copper Company, and Pierre S. du Pont. Bernard M. Baruch put up $37,590. Robert Sterling Clark put up $35,000; William H. Todd, shipbuilder, made an equal contribution. John D. Ryan, chairman of the Anaconda Copper Mining Company, and a director of the National City Bank, put up $27,000. Contributions of $25,000 each were made by Nicholas Brady, Francis P. Garvan, Peter O. Gerry of Rhode Island; Oliver Cabana, president of the Liquid Veneer Cor-

poration and a director in mining companies; Arthur Curtiss James
of the National City Bank and Phelps Dodge Corporation; Edith A.
Lehman, wife of Herbert H. Lehman; George W. Loft, candy manufacturer and stock-market operator; George MacDonald, corporation
attorney; Nicholas M. Schenck, theater and film magnate; B. E.
Smith, president of the Dusenberg Motor Sales Company; Samuel
Untermyer, and William H. Woodin, director of General Motors
and president of the American Car and Foundry Company. These
individuals contributed $1,164,590 of the total Smith fund.

Julius Rosenwald, chairman of Sears, Roebuck and Company,
made the largest known individual Republican contribution—$50,000.
The estate of P. A. B. Widener gave $30,000. George F. Baker, Jr.,
and Richard B. Mellon each gave $27,000. J. R. Nutt, president of
the Union Trust Company of Cleveland and deeply involved in the
Morgan-Van Sweringen promotion, gave $26,000. Contributions of
$25,000 each were made by Walter H. Aldrich of the United Smelting
and Refining Company; W. O. Briggs of the Briggs Body Company;
Edward F. Cary, president of the Pullman Car Company; Walter
P. Chrysler, William H. Crocker, William Nelson Cromwell, George
W. Crawford (Mellon), Clarence Dillon, Alfred I. du Pont, W. C.
Durant, George Eastman, Cyrus S. Eaton, William A. Clark, Jr.,
Harvey S. Firestone, D. M. Goodrich, Daniel Guggenheim, Harry
F. Guggenheim, S. R. Guggenheim, Charles Hayden, E. F. Hutton,
Otto Kahn, S. S. Kresge, A. W. Mellon, Eugene Meyer, Jeremiah
Milbank, John D. Rockefeller, John D. Rockefeller, Jr., Mortimer
Schiff, Charles M. Schwab, Herbert N. Straus, Alfred P. Sloan, Jr.,
Arthur Whitney, Harrison Williams, John N. Willys and George
Woodruff, banker. The Fisher brothers of General Motors Cor-
poration and the Fisher Body Corporation put up $100,000 jointly.
Aggregate contributions of this group amounted to $1,210,000.

These figures by no means exhaust the political contributions of
the wealthy families since 1924. Vast funds were spent during the
1920's in senatorial and gubernatorial contests, because the struggle
for special privileges was intense. Nor do these figures exhaust the
contributions to the national committees; the campaign between
the two parties—to determine who was to enjoy the lucrative privilege of determining governmental policies—began as early as 1926.

The Democratic National Committee had a deficit of $400,000 from 1924 which had to be paid before 1928. The payments to defray the 1924 deficit consisted of $75,000 from Thomas Fortune Ryan; $60,000 from Jesse H. Jones; $30,000 from Thomas L. Chadbourne; $25,000 each from Norman H. Davis and William F. Kenny; $20,000 from John Henry Kirby; $15,000 each from Francis P. Garvan and John W. Davis; $10,000 each from Percy S. Straus and Ralph Pulitzer; $7,500 from Cyrus H. McCormick; $5,000 from Jesse I. Straus; $2,000 each from John D. Ryan and Owen D. Young; $1,000 each from Melvin A. Traylor, Chicago banker, Silas Strawn, Chicago corporation lawyer, and Gerard Swope. Although Strawn was a contributor to the Democratic deficit fund he was chairman of the Illinois Republican Finance Committee, with Julius Rosenwald and James A. Patten, the wheat speculator, as his colleagues.

Most of the 1928 Republican and Democratic contributions of $1,000 to $25,000 came from the wealthy families, as usual, but the special flavor of the contest brought out more money than in 1924. Marshall Field gave the Republicans $15,000. Ogden L. Mills and Ogden Mills, the former's father, gave $12,500 each. F. Edson White, head of Armour and Company, gave $20,000. Republican contributors of at least $10,000 were Edward W. Bok, Philadelphia publisher, Eugene G. Grace, Percy A. Rockefeller, H. B. Rust (Mellon executive), James Simpson, chairman of Marshall Field and Company, Lammot du Pont, T. Coleman du Pont, William H. Crocker, Harold I. Pratt (Standard Oil), J. P. Graham (automobiles), George M. Moffett, Rufus L. Patterson (tobacco), Cornelius Vanderbilt, Murry Guggenheim, Orlando F. Weber (Allied Chemical and Dye), E. T. Bedford (Standard Oil), Dunlevy Milbank, and Ira Nelson Morris. There were, it is clear, Republicans as well as Democrats among the Du Ponts in this as in other years.

Contributors of $5,000 each included Frederic A. Juilliard (insurance), Jules S. Bache (stock broker), Archer M. Huntington (railroads), Mrs. Whitelaw Reid (née Mills), H. L. Stuart (investment banker and backer of Samuel Insull), Sidney Z. Mitchell (Electric Bond and Share Company), Jerome Hanauer (Kuhn, Loeb & Co.), Samuel and Adolph Lewisohn (copper), Mrs. Daniel Guggenheim, Thomas W. Lamont, Thomas Cochran, Mrs. Mary H.

Harkness, J. P. Morgan, Clarence H. Mackay, Dwight W. Morrow, Louis E. Pierson (Irving Trust Company), Mathew C. Brush (stock-market operator), Charles G. Dawes, Harold S. Vanderbilt, Edward J. Berwind, Helen Clay Frick, Mrs. Herbert L. Pratt (Standard Oil), Seward Prosser (Bankers Trust Company), Ogden Reid (Mills-Reid), E. P. Swenson (National City Bank and Texas Gulf Sulphur Company), Mrs. John D. Rockefeller, Jr., and Philip D. Wagoner. G. M. Laughlin, Jr., Irwin B. Laughlin, and J. P. Laughlin, all of the Jones and Laughlin steel dynasty, each gave $4,000; Alexander Laughlin gave $2,000 and his wife gave $5,000. George Whitney, Morgan partner and looked upon in Wall Street as Lamont's understudy as the "brains" of the firm, gave $2,750. Edith Rockefeller McCormick gave $2,000.

Contributions of $1,000 to $5,000 came from Robert R. McCormick, A. Felix du Pont, F. D. Bartow (Morgan partner), Joseph M. Cudahy, Paul D. Cravath, Walter E. Frew (Corn Exchange Bank), Mrs. Marshall Field, Anthony Drexel Biddle, Jr., Albert G. Milbank, Herbert L. Satterlee, Edwin Gould, Walter C. Teagle (Standard Oil), and Alfred H. Swayne of General Motors.

Contributions of less than $25,000 from the wealthy families to the Democrats included $15,000 each from Henry Morgenthau and Rudolph Spreckels (sugar); $10,000 each from Edward S. Harkness and Vincent Astor; $5,000 from John W. Davis; $4,000 from Norman H. Davis; $3,000 each from W. N. Reynolds (tobacco) and Ralph Pulitzer; and smaller amounts from scores of corporation executives. Harry Harkness Flagler gave $5,000.

Not including primary or local expenditures the Republicans spent $9,433,604 and the Democrats $7,152,511 that was admitted to a special Senate investigating committee. Both parties together spent $16,-586,115 nationally. The Democrats were left with a large deficit, and to erase it Raskob, Lehman, Kenny, and August Heckscher, New York realty millionaire, each gave $150,000. William H. Todd, Baruch, T. J. Mara, a partner of M. J. Meehan, James J. Riordan of the County Trust Company of New York, and John F. Gilchrist, each gave $50,000. Pierre du Pont and Daniel L. Riordan each gave $25,000. D. J. Mooney gave $10,000.

In the early days of Hoover's administration preparations were made to continue the swift, silent plundering as of old. The public was still bemused by his campaign references to "a chicken in every pot" and "two cars in every garage," which were soon proved to be as fraudulent as his pretensions to being an engineer (he held no engineering degree) or to being a humanitarian merely because he had administered the disposition of materials to civilian refugees in the World War. Hoover, by his indifference to human misery while in the White House, forever belied his claim to humanitarianism.

Hoover's Cabinet reflected his backing. His choice for Secretary of State was Henry L. Stimson, a relic of the Roosevelt-Taft regime and first cousin of two partners of Bonbright and Company, the public-utility arm of J. P. Morgan and Company. Additional public-utility flavoring was given by the admission of Ray Lyman Wilbur, president of Leland Stanford University, as Secretary of the Interior; Leland Stanford University was distinguished for its big endowment of public-utilities securities. Hoover's Secretary of the Navy was Charles Francis Adams, a director of the American Telephone and Telegraph Company and thirty-two other Morgan corporations, for many years in charge of Harvard University's huge endowment fund, and father-in-law of Henry Sturgis Morgan, son of the present J. P. Morgan.

When Andrew W. Mellon reluctantly relinquished the Treasury portfolio after having his impeachment demanded on the floor of Congress, his place was taken by Assistant Secretary of the Treasury Ogden L. Mills, grandson of Darius O. Mills, gold and silver magnate of the old West, and part owner of the New York *Herald Tribune.* Hoover's Secretary of Commerce was Robert P. Lamont, president of the American Steel Foundries and director of several Morgan corporations; in 1932 he was succeeded by Roy D. Chapin, president of the Hudson Motor Car Company. Upon his resignation Lamont, no relation to the Morgan partner, became president of the American Iron and Steel Institute, protective association of the steelmasters. Walter F. Brown, of the Ohio machine, became Postmaster General, and was to figure prominently in the airplane mail-subsidy scandals of the Hoover regime.

Dawes, supplanted in the vice-presidency by Charles Curtis, former Senator from Kansas and race-horse enthusiast, was sent by Hoover to London as American ambassador, where he remained until Mellon relieved him. The English Ambassadorship had since the 1890's never been out of the grasp of the banking fraternity. John Hay succeeded Joseph Choate (Standard Oil); Whitelaw Reid (Mills) succeeded Hay; Walter Hines Page (National City Bank) succeeded Reid; John W. Davis (Morgan) succeeded Page, and was himself succeeded by George Harvey (Morgan-Rockefeller-Ryan). Hoover's Ambassador to France was Senator Walter E. Edge of New Jersey, brother-in-law of Walter C. Teagle of Standard Oil. Serving as Ambassador to Turkey was Joseph Clark Grew, J. P. Morgan's cousin, who was transferred to the important Tokyo post. John N. Willys, the automobile manufacturer, became minister to Poland; W. Cameron Forbes, a director of the American Telephone and Telegraph Company, gave up the Tokyo post to Grew. Irwin B. Laughlin, of the Pittsburgh steel family, had been Ambassador to Spain since 1928 and was replaced in 1931 by Alexander P. Moore, a Mellon-controlled Pittsburgh newspaper publisher. Hoover's ambassador to Berlin was Frederic M. Sackett, public-utilities operator. Harry F. Guggenheim was sent to Cuba, to co-operate on behalf of finance capital with the repressive Machado regime.

Morrow and Lamont were Hoover's two principal advisers, and shaped the policies of his administration. The essence of Hoover's policy after the stock market tumbled and economic famine stalked the land was to "let the depression take its course." This was also, by a curious coincidence, the policy of J. P. Morgan and Company and its newspapers, for the Morgan banks, alone of the nation's banking institutions, were almost one hundred per cent liquid, i. e., had all their resources in cash or government securities. Every downswing in commodity prices, real-estate values, and securities quotations, enhanced the value of the liquid funds at the disposal of J. P. Morgan and Company, which grew more powerful every day that the nation as a whole became poorer. It was unquestionably the Morgan objective to begin investing at cheap price levels, but the situation passed completely out of Hoover's control in 1932.

In the meantime Morrow and Lamont shuttled in and out of the White House with the regularity of confirmed tipplers visiting their favorite tavern. When Lamont was not in Washington the telephone wire between the White House and 23 Wall Street was in almost constant use.* President Franklin D. Roosevelt was later to refer critically to this arrangement.

Morrow was appointed to the Senate in 1930 by the Governor of New Jersey, to replace Walter E. Edge, who resigned to escape a deserved drubbing at the polls. Morrow was subsequently re-elected by the efficient New Jersey Republican machine of J. P. Morgan and Company, which already had Hamilton Fish Kean, investment banker worth nearly $50,000,000, in the other Senate seat from the state; Kean succeeded his brother, James Hamilton Kean, in the hereditary office.

Morrow, as United States Senator from New Jersey, upheld the best traditions of the Keans and of J. P. Morgan and Company. His conciliatory manners (he would agree to anything verbally) won him the reputation of being a liberal. He voted against the Norris Bill providing for public operation of Muscle Shoals, and on every other measure dealing with the power question he invariably favored the public-utility trust; he sought to block confirmation of three Federal Power Commissioners who had replaced Commissioners friendly to the power trust; he voted to confirm the appointment of a reactionary to the Tariff Commission; he voted against all Federal relief bills for the unemployed; he voted against the veterans' bonus; he voted for all big naval appropriations; and he voted in favor of appropriating War Department funds to foster military training in the schools and colleges. Morrow, in fine, was a typical Morgan partner.

Morrow and Lamont, it is known in Wall Street, put the fearful Hoover up to declaring the moratorium on war debts; Lamont also conferred with Hoover just before Hoover announced the extension of time limits on New York bank credits to Germany. As economic conditions grew steadily worse Hoover resisted all pressure that

* The author was present at a press conference in the offices of J. P. Morgan and Company the day after England suspended the gold standard in September, 1931. Thomas W. Lamont had carefully explained why he thought England's action meant further deflation in the United States. Toward the end of his interview he was interrupted by a page, who slipped a note into his hand. Lamont left the room. Upon returning twenty minutes later, the ghost of a smile flitting over his face, he said drily, "I've just been talking over the telephone with President Hoover. He believes England's action will give prices an upward fillip over here."

he do something; instead, he adopted the Mellon method of issuing false statements to the effect that conditions were improving.

There was more than a breakdown of the capitalistic economy in the Hoover regime; there was a breakdown of common sense. Hoover inherited a situation that not only went back to the war, but to the days of Mark Hanna. The nation's industry was now largely trustified; monopoly ruled through the big commercial and private banks. International trade had gradually been strangled by tariffs set up all over Europe in retaliation against the new American tariff. In 1930 Hoover signed the Smoot-Hawley Tariff Bill, which set duties at the highest level ever seen; it was denounced by hundreds of economists, but was allowed to stand as international trade virtually disappeared and economic crisis, following hard upon the general boosting of tariffs, gripped one nation after the other.

In 1930, just after Hoover had convened a conference of bankers and industrialists for the duly advertised purpose of keeping wages and salaries unchanged, wholesale slashings of pay rates became the rule. They were supplemented by wholesale firings of workers throughout industry in a centrally planned attempt to bring down wages. Formal expression was given to the desire of the rich for the "liquidation of wages" in the annual report of the Chase National Bank for 1930, signed by Albert H. Wiggin, chairman of the board. The biggest corporations led the way, the distinction of instituting nearly two hundred thousand dismissals from 1929 to 1936 going, according to its own annual reports, to the American Telephone and Telegraph Company (Morgan).

Hoover, throughout his term, fought against any governmental action which would benefit the nonwealthy groups, labor in particular. In this he resembled Coolidge and Harding. Like his two predecessors he sought to put over a general sales tax and to increase excise taxes; like his predecessors he reduced income-tax rates; like them he fought war veterans' benefits and saw measures passed over his head by a Congress afraid of the veterans' vote; he temporized with the farm problem, as his predecessors had; and like them he scotched all legislation that would regulate the electric light and power companies.

But the crisis forced Hoover into a position where he seemed much harsher than had either Harding or Coolidge, although Harding and Coolidge would unquestionably have acted as he did. Coolidge from his retirement, indeed, would from time to time step forward to approve some particularly callous action by Hoover. He endorsed Hoover's opposition to Federal unemployment relief.

Two typical Hoover performances served to dramatize for the country the real outlook of the Republican Party. The first was his brutal handling of the veterans' "bonus army," which was driven out of Washington with fire and sword; the second was his evasion of the problem of unemployment relief. Hoover consistently refused to accede to Congressional demands for public funds to aid the millions thrown out on the streets by the industrialists and bankers when it became evident that to retain them on the pay rolls would necessitate tapping swollen corporate surpluses. It was whispered at Washington tea tables after Hoover began ladling out funds to banks and railroads while he continued denying them to the unemployed that his private motto was, "No one who is in actual distress shall be helped by the Federal government." J. P. Morgan and Company co-operated by having the American Red Cross, still very much under its domination, make ineffective gestures, and by sponsoring the ridiculous block-aid program whereby the rich would help the rich and the poor would help the poor.

To seem to be doing something positive Hoover advocated local unemployment relief by states, cloaking his real designs with the invocation of the states' rights shibboleth. Most of the nation's funds had been drawn by absentee owners into a few eastern cities like New York, Boston, and Philadelphia, while in great industrial states like Michigan, Ohio, and Illinois, as well as in lesser states, there were actually no liquid resources available. Local aid therefore meant— no aid.

But in pursuing his Morgan-designed policy Hoover unwittingly incurred the ire of the Rockefellers. Although they remained Republican, the Rockefellers in 1932 gave only nominal support to the Republican Party. But other Standard Oil clans conspicuously backed the Democrats. The policy of allowing matters to take their course was turning out to be disastrous to the Rockefellers, for every decline in the price of oil compromised their position. The Rockefellers had also plunged heavily on their real-estate development at Rockefeller Center, New York, and were seriously embarrassed by the decline in real-estate values. In addition to this, the great Chase National Bank was seriously implicated in various speculative ventures, among which were the Fox Film Corporation, the General Theaters Equipment Corporation, and German credits.

In 1930 Hoover, seeking to placate the Rockefellers, appointed Colonel Arthur Woods to tackle the unemployment problem. Woods, a trustee of the Rockefeller Foundation, had been Police Commissioner of New York City under John Purroy Mitchel, and later became president of the Rockefeller Center Corporation. After conferring with economists Woods reported that a billion-dollar public works program was required, and urged Hoover to recommend such a program. Hoover refused, although Woods reported that at least five million men were unemployed. When Hoover vetoed the Wagner bill providing for a Federal employment agency Woods resigned in anger, and the Rockefellers turned definitely hostile to the President. Hoover then appointed Walter S. Gifford, president of the American Telephone and Telegraph Company (Morgan), to devise a program of community unemployment relief, and until the closing months of Hoover's term Gifford valiantly strove to give the impression that something was being done for the starving millions. In 1932 the Democratic and Progressive congressional blocs laid out a relief program calling for twice the amount of money that Woods had recommended, and passed it over Hoover's head.

# VI

## Intrigue and Scandal

THE very nature of a ruling class requires the existence of special rights and privileges accessible only to its members. This has been historically true of all ruling classes.

In earlier societies, and very familiarly in feudal European society, the special rights of various classes were formally recognized. Law for one class was not law for another. The clergy was served by ecclesiastical courts, the nobility by courts of nobles, and the yeomanry and the artisans, where they had won rights, by their own special courts; the specific rights of each of the lower classes, to be sure, had less substantial content than those of the upper classes.

The American ruling class, to protect and strengthen its favored position, must take serious account of the vestigial democratic apparatus left by the eighteenth century, and must, very often, gain its class objectives by stealth, intrigue, and indirection when it cannot do so by legislative or judicial obscurantism.

Senator George W. Norris went to the core of the issue when, after the acquittal of E. L. Doheny on grave charges in the Teapot Dome case, he said, "We ought to pass a law that no man worth $100,000,000 should be tried for a crime." Such legislation would serve to formalize *de jure* an existing condition, and would at least make for consistency between theory and practice.

The war-profits scandals were covered in an investigation by a special House committee and subcommittee that heard evidence for more than three years under the chairmanship of Representative William J. Graham of Illinois. The evidence and the reports fill twenty-one massive volumes that contain an unparalleled panorama of graft, corruption, extortion, knavery, and incompetence, if not of treason.

The general apology made for the characters involved is that, considering the sudden war emergency, the job done was the best possible. The Graham Committee found, however, that competent persons in certain fields were deliberately removed in favor of incompetents; disinterested persons were shunted aside in favor of persons with a private pecuniary interest in decisions; experts were dismissed in favor of nonexperts; military officers of probity who protested against the plundering and looting were demoted, transferred, and sometimes discredited, and were replaced by officers of dubious inclination; higher bids were accepted in favor of lower; known inferior materials were accepted rather than good, tested materials; and many expenditures, involving huge sums, were made —on the plea of a military necessity that did not exist—solely for the benefit of private entrepreneurs of political influence. Business was not apportioned fairly; discrimination was practised in favor of the politically dominant element of Wall Street finance capital.

The presiding genius over war purchases was Bernard M. Baruch, stock promoter of the Guggenheim camp, and the Graham Committee held him largely responsible, in an individual sense, for much that took place. Supporting Baruch were the National City Bank and the copper elements which had access to President Wilson through Cleveland H. Dodge.

With reference to the copper industry, House Report No. 1400, sixty-sixth Congress, third session, said:

. . . the plan originally was—and which plan has been fully consummated in the subsequent proceedings—that the copper industry, as well as other producing industries should be so centralized that it could be dominated and controlled by one man or a very small number of men, and that this control, once established over the industries, continued throughout the war, was the paramount influence toward price-fixing and price control, and is one of the causes of high-priced commodities at this time. The plan of the Government was to centralize all industries irrespective of the results that might ultimately follow.

To this end the government ignored the antitrust laws. The Graham Committee found:

The various agencies of the Council of National Defense and the War Department not only permitted this violation of the statutes, but encouraged it, and in some cases ordered combinations to be made that were in violation of the law. Every trade and business was consolidated under the directions of the Council of National Defense and its auxiliary bodies; in fact, in most instances the Government agencies refused to transact business with the particular trade or interest until such a combination had been made . . . It is probably exact to say that never in the history of the country was a greater impetus given to illegal trusts and combinations in restraint of trade than was given by the practices above referred to.

The Graham Committee discovered that two weeks before Wilson sent his war message to Congress on April 2, 1917, Baruch and John D. Ryan, president of Anaconda Copper Mining Company (Amalgamated Copper), arranged a combination of copper producers to sell to the government 45,000,000 pounds of copper at 16⅔ cents a pound. The agency of combination was the United Metals Selling Company, of which Ryan was president and William C. Potter, long an executive of many Guggenheim companies and later the chairman of the Guaranty Trust Company (Morgan), a leading executive officer. Stock of United Metals was owned by Anaconda, still directed by the Stillman-Rockefeller clique at the National City Bank.

Twenty-six other companies, mostly under Morgan or Guggenheim dominance, participated with Anaconda in United Metals, from which the government during the war bought 523,338,735 pounds of copper of a total of 592,258,674 pounds purchased in all; 66,846,000 pounds were purchased from the American Smelting and Refining Company (Guggenheim).

Baruch appointed a special government copper purchasing committee consisting of Ryan; W. A. Clark, of the United Verde Mining Company and the Magma Copper Company; Murry Guggenheim; James McLean, vice-president of the Phelps Dodge Corporation; Charles MacNeill, of the Utah Copper Company (Morgan-Guggenheim), the Nevada Consolidated Copper Company, the Chino Copper Company, and the Ray Consolidated Copper Company; and

Stephen Birch, of the Kennecott Copper Corporation (Guggenheim). When protest broke out against the buying of copper for the government by individuals that owned or controlled the selling companies, this committee was disbanded. It was replaced by another that functioned formally as the representative of the copper companies but actually as the first committee had functioned. This new committee was assembled by Eugene G. Meyer, Jr., stock-market operator and Baruch's assistant.

Meyer, later head of the War Finance Corporation and Hoover's Governor of the Federal Reserve Board, was investigated in 1925 by a select House committee, which found that as treasurer of the War Finance Corporation he had bought and sold government bonds through his Wall Street office, charging a commission. Meyer told the committee he had turned over the commissions to other brokers, but while the investigation was going on "it was discovered by your committee that alterations and changes were being made in the books of record covering these transactions, and when the same was called to the attention of the treasurer of the War Finance Corporation he admitted to the committee that changes were being made. To what extent these books have been altered during this process the committee has not been able to determine. . . . The dates of purchase of bonds as given by the Secretary of the Treasury, which would have shown that about $24,000,000 had been paid by the government for bonds in excess of the highest market rate for the various days on which it was alleged that the purchases were made, were found to be incorrect. It was also found that the dates given by the War Finance Corporation and the Federal Reserve Bank of New York City, New York, did not agree and that the records of the former also vary as to dates of purchase. . . . Only a complete audit will disclose how nearly correct is the loss of $24,000,000, which the dates given by the Secretary of the Treasury show."

The second government copper purchase called for 11,595,346 pounds at 23½ cents a pound, as of October 15, 1917. On June 15, 1918, the price was advanced to 26 cents a pound. The average cost of producing copper, the Graham Committee found, was 8 to 12 cents, so that profits ranged from thirty-three to more than two hundred per cent. The Calumet and Hecla Mining Company made eight hundred per cent profit in 1917 and three hundred per cent in 1918.

But, as the Graham Committee reported:

Not all the copper producers shared equally in these profits, it is true. Mr. John D. Ryan, in the first purchase of copper by the government from the United Metals Selling Co., dictated the proportion which each company in that combination should furnish of the copper and this schedule or percentage obtained through the war.

At the time the first sale of copper was arranged at 16⅔ cents per pound, many statements were circulated through the press of the country relative to the very excellent and patriotic work that had been done in this negotiation. The effort was then made to show that because this price was greatly below the average market price, that thereby the Government had made an immense saving and that the copper producers had patriotically turned over the production of their mines to the public for war purposes.*

Owing to the great volume of business involved, prices to the government should have been much lower, as was indicated by the exorbitant profits of the copper companies, notably of the Anaconda group. "Because of the necessity and demands of the Government during the war," said the Graham Committee, "those who operated these copper-producing properties were enabled to make and did make extravagant and extraordinary profits.

"The facts reported and recorded in the evidence speak for themselves, and, in the main, have not been denied or disputed, except by the gloss of rhetoric and a profusion of words intended to cover up the administration of the business affairs of the War Department."

It is difficult to determine in what division of war purchases the commonwealth was most completely betrayed. House Report No. 637, sixty-sixth Congress, second session, related that although more than $1,000,000,000 had been spent for combat airplanes none was ever delivered.

*Mr. Baruch, in various appearances before legislative committees, has stressed that during the war he owned no stock in the companies that benefited from war orders and that he conducted no market operations for his own account. This is true. What Baruch did was to route the lion's share of business into the hands of interests that had been responsible for his rise to financial eminence before the war and that have been associated with him, to his immense personal profit, since the war.

The airplane scandal became so notorious in 1918, indeed, that President Wilson appointed Charles Evans Hughes to investigate. After finding gross inefficiency, incompetence, ignorance, waste, extravagance, and evidence of gross self-interest and improper practises, Hughes recommended that Edward A. Deeds be court-martialed, under sections 95 and 96 of the articles of war. The recommendation was concurred in by the Attorney General and Secretary of War Baker, but Baker then ordered the case re-opened for the hearing of new evidence from two of Deeds' business associates. A special military board thereupon exonerated Deeds.

"Within the sphere of Colonel Deeds' important, if not commanding, influence," said the Hughes report, "his former business associates were placed at once through Government contracts in a position where they had the assurance of very large profits upon a relatively small investment of their own money, and in addition were able to secure generous salaries, which they charged against the Government as part of the cost of manufacture."

Deeds, a vice-president of the National Cash Register Company before the war and one of the National City Bank crowd, came from Dayton, Ohio. He was appointed head of the Equipment Division of Aviation in August, 1917, by Secretary of War Baker, another Ohioan, upon recommendation of Howard E. Coffin, vice-president of the Hudson Motor Car Company and chairman of the Aircraft Production Board. The Graham Committee said:

Nothing appears in any of the hearings of any investigation to show why Deeds was appointed. Justice Hughes' report found that Deeds began his activities by centering aircraft operations at Dayton, Ohio; that he gave large contracts to his business associates . . . although they had no previous experience in such matters . . . that Deeds was largely interested in corporations controlling the Delco ignition system used in the projected Liberty motor, whereas prior to its use on the Liberty, the magneto system had been used on all airplane engines.

The Graham Committee pointed out that Deeds had a doubtful record. In 1912 he was prosecuted in Federal court for alleged bribery and criminal methods in driving competitors out of the cash-register business; he was convicted and sentenced to a year in jail. On appeal the decision was reversed; but the case was never tried again. "The charge, conviction, and court record," said the Graham Committee, "were enough to put any responsible official on inquiry before giving Deeds a place of transcendent importance in charge of matters about which he knew nothing."

Deeds was ostensibly superseded in January, 1918, by Robert L. Montgomery, a bond dealer, but, the Hughes report said, Deeds remained in practical charge. William C. Potter headed the Equipment Division from February to May, 1918, when John D. Ryan became Director of Aircraft Production with Potter as his assistant. None of these men, it was found, knew anything about aviation.

The Graham Committee cited a special report to the Intelligence Department, dated November 23, 1918, to the effect that Ryan, a director of the Chicago, Milwaukee and St. Paul Railroad (in which the Stillman-Rockefeller-National City group had a preponderant interest), was instrumental in giving cost-plus contracts to lumber companies that used this railroad and tapped northwest forest land holdings of the railroad and its affiliates for aircraft timber; that he lent $6,000,000 of government money to such companies; and that he lent them $12,000,000 to construct a railroad spur into forest holdings of the railroad company. The cost of constructing the railroad spur, the Graham Committee found, was double what it should have been. Special officers of the War Department reporting on the same situation had said: "Have unearthed evidence indicating enormous graft, but do not consider the case as yet ready for submission to legal prosecution." The officers were transferred and reprimanded; the advice of lumber experts was rejected in favor of advice from persons who knew nothing about lumber but were interested in fat contracts. Inferior high-priced timber was purchased rather than superior low-priced wood.

Of the $1,051,000,000 disbursed for aircraft which were never delivered, the Graham Committee found that $48,762,826 was spent for spruce supplied by companies with which the Milwaukee road or other National City Bank interests were affiliated. Ryan favored American spruce, though Canada had better spruce at lower prices and had been supplying it for the efficient British Bristol planes.

Although the aviation pioneers had no share in the apportionment

of the government aviation melon of $1,000,000,000, the name of
Wright was purchased by many companies. Deeds bought it, and
so did Charles Hayden; for Wright, first to fly, bore a magical name.
In 1916 Deeds, in association with C. F. Kettering, who since 1918
has been vice-president of the General Motors Corporation, formed
a paper company known as the Dayton Metal Products Company.
This company formed the Dayton-Wright Airplane Company, also
a paper enterprise, which held one thousand shares of the Lincoln
Motor Company, organized expressly to build Liberty engines for
American airplanes and later incorporated into the Ford Motor
Company. The Dayton-Wright Airplane Company, the Graham
Committee found, had no paid-in capital whatever when it obtained
through Deeds government contracts for 3,940 airplanes to cost
$30,000,000. This government money was the first big capital ever
put into the aviation industry.

Deeds was also a vice-president of the United Motors Company,
a participant in the airplane deals, and transferred his stock to his
wife when he became head of the Air Service. He and Kettering in
1908 had formed the Dayton Engineering Laboratories to market the
Delco ignition system that was specified for the Liberty motors. This
company was sold in 1918 to General Motors, of which it is now a
division.

As to the present interlocking of the men concerned in the government aviation contracts, Deeds is a director of the National City
Bank, of which Gordon S. Rentschler, a fellow Ohioan, is president.
Rentschler is a director of the National Cash Register Company, of
which Deeds is now chairman. Kettering is a director of the United
Aircraft and Transport Company, formed by the National City
Bank to consolidate numerous airplane companies on the basis of
government air-mail contracts, and F. B. Rentschler, brother of the
bank's president, is chairman of United Air Lines, Inc., director of
Pan American Airways, and director of the Pratt and Whitney Company. These men, in short, are all kingpins of contemporary aviation.

While the copper and automotive dynasties were exacting their
pound of flesh, the steel industry was far from inactive. The Senate
Committee on Naval Affairs determined in 1916 that the cost of
producing armor plate by the steel companies was $262 a ton, against

prices of $411 to $604 charged the government. Eugene R. Grace, president of Bethlehem Steel and Charles M. Schwab's right-hand man, admitted that the cost did not exceed $315 a ton. While quoting their own country top prices, the United States Steel Corporation and Bethlehem Steel Corporation charged Russia $349 a ton, Italy $395 a ton, and Japan $406.35 a ton for identical plate.

The steel companies, consequently, profited enormously. A Senate Committee found (as related in Senate Document No. 259, *Corporate Earnings and Governmental Revenues*) that profits of the United States Steel Corporation during the war were $888,931,000, or more than the par value of its stock. War profits throughout industry, said the same report, ranged from 25 per cent to 7,856 per cent. House Report No. 998, sixty-sixth Congress, second session, says:

> The committee finds that there has been expended for construction upon the Government's nitrate program to the present time the sum of $116,194,974.37, and that this expenditure produced no nitrates prior to the armistice, and contributed nothing toward the winning of the war. The nitrates program originated with the War Industries Board of the Council of National Defense, and is directly traceable to Mr. Bernard M. Baruch, chairman of the board, who admits that he was the moving spirit in the plans of the government. . . . There was no national necessity at any time which required the War Department to embark upon the vast building program for the manufacture of nitrates for war purposes. . . . The various contracts made for the construction of the nitrate plants of the United States were the ordinary types of contracts made by the Ordnance Department during the war, namely, every interest of the contractor was carefully guarded, and all doubts were to be ultimately resolved against the United States.

Although the nitrate plants were not necessary, as there was an abundant supply of Chilean nitrate, their construction entailed the placing of huge orders for steel, lumber, copper, cement, dynamos, etc. The Du Ponts were given $90,000,000 to build a nitrate plant at Old Hickory, Tennessee, on a cost-plus basis; after the war this plant was sold to the Nashville Industrial Corporation for $3,500,000.

"Theretofore the plants built by the Du Ponts," said the Graham Committee, "had been paid for out of the profits of contracts made with the allied nations before we entered the war." Powder furnished to the United States by private manufacturers was priced at 49 cents a pound, and cost about 36 cents to produce, thus yielding a profit of approximately 13 cents, or more than thirty-three per cent.

Baruch said the grandiose nitrate program was launched in fear that submarines would cut off Chilean nitrate, but the Graham Committee held this fear unjustified. Neither the Old Hickory nor the Nitro plant was necessary, the committee found, and both entailed "enormous waste and extravagant expenditure of public funds" which was "not in any way justified and that the ones primarily responsible for these things very properly merit the disapproval and condemnation of the people of the country in this and the coming days of the Republic."

The Graham Committee discovered a welter of private interests pushing for the nitrate program. The American Cyanamid Company was interested in seeing the government build these chemical plants; the Alabama Power Company and a host of Southern industrialists wanted Muscle Shoals harnessed with the intent, as it became evident after the war, of having the property turned over to private interests for a song.

Directly supervising the explosives and nitrate program under Baruch was D. C. Jackling, head of the Utah Copper Company (Morgan-Guggenheim) and the Nevada Consolidated Copper Company. The Graham Committee found Jackling had no experience whatever with explosives or chemicals.

Leather goods and miscellaneous supplies were purchased by Julius Rosenwald, president of Sears, Roebuck and Company. Although most of these supplies were available in Europe at lower prices for better quality, as the Graham Committee found, purchases were made from American dealers and manufacturers with whom Rosenwald had business relations as head of the big mail-order house. Both Sears, Roebuck and Company and Montgomery Ward and Company (Morgan) had risen, incidentally, on the shoulders of the government, which about two decades earlier, in response to pressure, had instituted the rural free mail delivery without which the mail-order business could not exist. This service has been continued by the government at a loss.

House Report No. 1400, sixty-sixth Congress, third session, tells of huge sums wasted on artillery shells, for whose manufacture by Bethlehem Steel Corporation and its affiliate, Midvale Ordnance Company, an immense amount of material was purchased from leading corporations. The shell orders were placed by the advisory commission of the Council of National Defense, of which Baruch was chairman. Here is the Graham Committee's summary of the shell situation (with the author's italics):

"We had 53 contracts for 37-millimeter shells, on which we expended $9,134,592," said the Graham Committee. *"None of these shells ever reached our firing line.* We had 689 contracts for 75-millimeter shells, on which we expended $301,941,459. Of these shells, we fired 6,000. We had 142 contracts for 3-inch shells, on which we expended $44,-841,844. *None of these shells reached the firing line.* We had 439 contracts for 4.7 inch shells, on which we expended $41,716,051. Of these shells 14,000 were fired by our forces. We had 305 contracts for 6-inch shells, on which we expended $24,189,075. *None of these ever reached the firing line.* We had 617 contracts for 155-millimeter shells, on which we expended $264,955,387. *None of these ever reached the firing line.* We had 301 contracts for 8-inch shells, on which we expended $51,371,207. *None of these ever reached the firing line.* We had 152 contracts for 240-millimeter shells, on which we expended $24,136,867. *None of these ever reached the firing line.* We had 239 contracts for 9.2 inch shells, on which we expended $54,389,377. *None of these ever reached the firing line.* We had 71 contracts for 12-inch shells, on which we expended $9,507,878. *None of these ever reached the firing line.* We had 6 contracts for 14-inch shells, on which we spent $1,266,477. *None of these reached the firing line.* We let 111 contracts, to the amount of $478,828,345, for the construction of artillery of all calibres, guns, howitzers, gun carriages, limbers and recuperators. Of this immense program of expenditures there reached our troops and were actually used in combat thirty-nine 75-millimeter anti-aircraft mount trucks, forty-eight 4.7 inch guns of the 1906 model, forty-eight 4.7 inch gun carriages of the same model, twenty-four 8-inch howitzers, and twenty-four 8-inch gun carriages."

Supplies, although paid for in advance, were never delivered. The government graciously permitted uncompleted contracts to be finished after the war, some by French and British companies which did not want to shut down their factories. There were 17,689,406 shells delivered before the Armistice and 10,211,389, or thirty-seven per cent of the total, after the war ended. The contracts drawn by

Baruch's board, the Graham Committee found, were extraordinary
in that few carried ordinary provisions for cancellation.

The Rockefellers also participated in the grabbing, the Graham
Committee found:

> The operations of some of the "fly-by-night" war corporations that
> sprang up during the war are well illustrated by the Domestic Coke
> Company . . . the capital stock was $2,000,000, none of which, as
> far as the subcommittee could find, was paid in. . . . Some local
> stockholders and persons interested in the Standard Oil Company,
> residing in Cleveland, seem to have been interested early in this
> corporation, and it is probable from what afterwards occurred that
> it was a Standard Oil plan from the beginning. . . . [The company]
> proposed to the War Department to build and operate at Cleve-
> land a battery of sixty by-product coke ovens, which were to cost
> about $50,000 each. On presenting this to the ordnance officers doubts
> were expressed as to their financial ability. Thereupon the Standard
> Oil Company guaranteed the contract on behalf of the Domestic
> Coke Corporation, and from that time forward the Standard Oil
> Company paid all the bills, as work progressed, and the War Depart-
> ment then repaid the advancements of the Standard Oil Company.
> The Domestic Coke Corporation was a mere dummy and did not
> invest a cent in this project. . . .

As we have already seen, the various Standard Oil enterprises
profited enormously from the war through the stupendous volume
of business and the sharp advance in oil prices.*

Leading companies used war orders as a lever to expand plant
capacity and to institute costly improvements at government expense,
and this necessitated, of course, the placing of many orders that were
in no way requisite to war victory. Coke plants costing $250,000
each on a cost-plus basis to the number of 150 units, were built by
Jones and Laughlin Steel (Laughlin family), Domestic Coke Corporation (Rockefellers), Pittsburgh Crucible Steel Company (Mellon-Frick), Birmingham By-Products Company (Morgan), Donner
Union Coke Corporation, Rainey-Wood Coke Company, Citizens
Gas Company, United States Steel Corporation (Morgan), Sloss-Shef-
field Steel Company, Seaboard By-Products Company, and International Harvester Company (McCormick). The new coke-ovens,

* See Appendix B.

which captured by-product oils and chemicals, replaced obsolete bee-hive ovens. Said the Graham Committee:

Large advances were made to some of these companies for con-struction purposes . . . from what has appeared in the hearings, there has been expended by the War Department in claims, construction, and loans in its by-product coke oven program, $28,641,923.18, of which $16,737,932.18 is expended and will not be repaid. It has re-ceived no by-products from any of these plants, either for war or salvage purposes. It may be questioned whether the by-product coke oven program of construction was compelled by the necessities of war.

The war, in brief, provided an unparalleled opportunity for the richest families to grab, at the expense of the public; and, without ex-ception, they made the most of this opportunity. Some of the fami-lies took profits in the stock-market, and hence did not figure directly in the industrial looting. Up to September 1, 1919, the War Depart-ment spent $18,501,117,999, and, judging by the Graham Committee's findings at least one-third of this was dissipated in channels that had no relation to a successful prosecution of the war. The rich families, to be sure, wanted the war to be won, but they took care that the victory was as expensive as possible to the common taxpayers. They uttered no cries for government economy, as since they have done, so long as the public Treasury was at their disposal. Economy became desirable only when government funds were to be expended on war veterans and on the unemployed.

While this plundering was taking place under the direction of sharpers hypocritically posing as patriotic "dollar-a-year" officials, the young manhood of the nation was risking its life in the army at $30 a month.

The basis for many prosecutions was laid by the Graham Com-mittee, and there were indictments of various minor figures. But there were no convictions. By November, 1925, the last of the indict-ments was quashed.

After the war there remained, however, a tangle of claims and counterclaims as between the government and the big corporations. These claims were almost invariably decided in favor of the wealthy. Arrangements were even made to dispose of surplus supplies so as not to embarrass private entrepreneurs. The government, for example, still had 100,000,000 pounds of copper on hand, and agreed with the copper producers to market it gradually at prevailing market prices. As prices sank the government liquidated at a loss, while the copper companies disposed of their surplus 750,000,000 pounds well above cost of production.

Senator John W. Weeks of Massachusetts (Republican) in 1919 virtuously decried the aircraft frauds. He became Harding's Secretary of War, and soon after taking office received a letter from his old Stock Exchange colleague and friend, Charles Hayden, Morgan connection, requesting special consideration for the Wright-Martin Aircraft Company, of which Hayden was a director. This company, it was charged, received $5,267,467 more than its due during the war, and the government claimed the company had extorted profits of 270 per cent. At Weeks' request the Department of Justice, as the Senate investigation of Daugherty showed, shunted the case about and finally quashed it. According to his income tax returns, Daugherty owned two thousand shares of Wright-Martin stock.

The government charged that E. I. du Pont de Nemours and Company had, by various devices, defrauded the government on war contracts. The Du Ponts, according to investigators, had stooped so low as to bill the government $75 for the burial of every worker who died during an influenza epidemic at the Old Hickory Powder Plant, and had sold the bodies for $11 each as well. Industrial alcohol had been illegally withdrawn from the Old Hickory plant, it was also charged, and had been sold to Jess Smith, personal agent of Daugherty, for 30 cents a gallon. Smith resold at $10 a gallon, making a profit of $9.70 a gallon which he shared with persons unknown. A government investigator complained that his report exposing the complicated methods by which the Du Ponts had mulcted the government on a gigantic scale was shown by the Department of Justice to the Du Ponts so that lawyers might prepare a plausible defense. After repeated attempts to bring a voluminous and damning case against the Du Ponts to trial, First Assistant Attorney General John W. H. Crim, blocked at every turn by Daugherty, resigned in disgust. The Du Ponts, politically powerful, arrogant, reactionary, were never prosecuted.

As the Senate investigation of Daugherty proved, his office was a procurement division for persons of wealth. Not only the war fraud cases, but others as well were squelched. A criminal action pending against the United Gas Improvement Company of Philadelphia (Morgan) was nol-prossed. Recommendations of the Federal Trade Commission that the tobacco companies, lumber companies, and the International Harvester Company be prosecuted as illegal monopolies were ignored by Daugherty. The Federal Trade Commission showed that the lumber monopoly had financed a nationwide "Own Your Own Home" campaign, hiring teachers, clergymen, and writers to spread propaganda, and had raised prices when the propaganda became effective.

Daugherty succeeded in setting aside the court order, granted before the war, separating the Boston and Maine Railroad and the New York, New Haven and Hartford Railroad (Morgan). Boston and Maine stockholders were opposed to allowing New Haven directors on the board, but Daugherty arbitrarily reopened the entire case, in defiance of the Public Service Commission of Massachusetts, and after a private conference with Federal Judge Julius Mayer of New York, obtained a decree permitting the New Haven again to penetrate the Boston and Maine.

In September, 1922, Daugherty personally pleaded before Federal Judge James H. Wilkerson of Chicago for an injunction prohibiting railroad shopmen from striking. The court, after hearing Daugherty's arguments, acceded to this denial of the legal rights of labor.

Because Daugherty would not prosecute the war fraud cases, Representative Woodruff on April 11, 1922, said he would demand Daugherty's impeachment unless he began action against the Lincoln Motor Car Company (Ford). But even this threat could not force Daugherty to act.

Daugherty's Washington house was the headquarters for the distribution of special favors in all divisions of the Harding Administration. William J. Burns, private detective long active in antilabor espionage, paid a visit there just before his appointment as head of the Bureau of Investigation. J. Ogden Armour, who once employed Daugherty as an attorney, was a frequent caller, and the Washington branch of Armour and Company was reported to have supplied

Daugherty's house with hams, bacon, eggs, butter, and other products. John Ringling, the circus magnate, came to this house to obtain permission to locate his circus on a piece of Pittsburgh land owned by Andrew W. Mellon. Other frequent visitors were President Harding, Will H. Hays, Secretary Fall, Harry F. Sinclair, and Alexander P. Moore, Pittsburgh newspaper publisher who subsequently became Ambassador to Spain and to Peru. T. Coleman du Pont, a regular caller, was on the best of terms with the Daugherty clique. He was especially close to Alien Property Custodian Thomas B. Miller, who wound up in Atlanta Penitentiary.

The biggest of the postwar scandals in which Daugherty was involved concerned the American Metal Company, a German copper concern taken over by Alien Property Custodian Francis P. Garvan and placed in the hands of an American directorate that included Andrew W. Mellon and Henry Morgenthau. The directors auctioned the company off for $7,000,000 to a syndicate comprising Henry Clay Frick, Jay Cooke, William Randolph Hearst, and some of the original German officials of the company. The money was turned over by the government in 1921 to Richard Merton, of the German family which originally owned the company, after Merton, as he admitted in court, had given John T. King, of Connecticut, a sum which the government contended was disbursed as follows: $224,000 to Attorney General Harry M. Daugherty and Jess Smith; $112,000 to King; and $50,000 to Alien Property Custodian Miller, Harding appointee. All were indicted, but King and Smith died before standing trial, Smith under strange circumstances. King's estate was valued at $1,200,000, and included $50,000 of American Metal Company stock. In Daugherty's case a jury twice disagreed; Miller was sentenced to Atlanta Penitentiary.

The main outlines of the Teapot Dome case are well known. But the extent to which some of the ruling families of wealth and politics participated in it is not generally appreciated. Briefly, the case involved the alienation for relatively slight consideration of a huge reserve of naval oil lands of incalculably great value. The conspiracy, initiated by the Sinclair and Doheny oil companies, was carried out through the medium of corrupt government officials.

Theodore Roosevelt, Jr., an original director of the Sinclair Refining Company, became Assistant Secretary of the Navy under Harding. Archibald Roosevelt, his brother, was a vice-president of the Sinclair company, a position obtained for him by Theodore in 1919 in a personal appeal to Harry F. Sinclair. Theodore Roosevelt, Jr., took Admiral Griffin's qualifying suggestion of a clause providing for Navy Department approval of leases to Secretary of Interior Fall, who subtly modified the clause so as to give the Secretary of Interior full authority to dispose of naval oil lands. Secretary Denby and Assistant Secretary Roosevelt acquiesced in this unusual arrangement.

Roosevelt then took Fall's draft executive order to the White House, where Harding signed it and made it law as of May 31, 1921, three months after the "Black Cabinet" took office.

The swindle became general public knowledge only when the Denver *Post*, owned by the unsavory Bonfils and Tammen, gamblers and promoters, assailed the lease. The *Post's* attack subsided when Harry F. Sinclair gave Bonfils and his partner $250,000. But the St. Louis *Post-Dispatch*, scenting something extraordinary, began to comment editorially, and a Senate investigation was pushed by Burton K. Wheeler and Thomas J. Walsh.

An amazingly large number of influential people played minor or major, direct or indirect, roles in the Teapot Dome case. The first step in this imbroglio had been the appointment in 1918 of William Boyce Thompson, Sinclair Oil and Chase Bank director, as chairman of the Republican Ways and Means Committee in charge of campaign collections. The next step was the appointment of Will H. Hays, attorney for Harry F. Sinclair and protégé of Morgan-partner Perkins, as Republican National Committee chairman. Thompson, late in 1919 and early in 1920, directed a big stock-market pool in Sinclair common, apparently in anticipation of the forthcoming gains of Sinclair Oil under a Republican Administration; Albert H. Wiggin's Chase National Bank financed this pool. Late in 1922 Jesse Livermore, stock-market plunger, ran a pool in Sinclair stock for the account of Harry Sinclair, Blair and Company (of which Elisha Walker, now of Kuhn, Loeb and Company, was then the head), and the Chase Securities Company, affiliate of the Chase National Bank. The various pools in Sinclair, Doheny's Pan-American Petroleum and Transport Company, and the Mammoth Oil Company (which took possession of the Teapot Dome leases) gave opportunity for a wide Wall Street participation in the gains, but the investigation never uncovered the identity of the persons who traded in the stocks.

E. L. Doheny gave Secretary of the Interior Fall $100,000 for his services; Sinclair gave Fall $230,000 in Liberty bonds, $71,000 in cash, and $35,000 for a trip to Russia to negotiate oil leases after Fall resigned his office. In all, Fall received nearly $500,000 that appears on the record, and for taking it he was convicted and sentenced to jail in 1931, the first Cabinet officer ever found guilty of criminal malfeasance.

When Fall resigned under fire Secretary of Commerce Herbert Hoover sent him a note dated March 12, 1923, saying, "This note is just by way of expressing appreciation for the many kindnesses I had at your hands during the last two years in the Cabinet. I know that the vast majority of our people feel a deep regret at your leaving the Department of the Interior. In my recollection, that department has never had so constructive and legal a headship as you gave it. I trust the time will come when your private affairs will enable you to return to public life, as there are few men who are able to stand its stings and ire, and they have got to stay with it." President Harding said he had offered to place Fall on the Supreme Court, but that Fall, a former justice of the Supreme Court of New Mexico, had declined the post.

Sinclair and Doheny, with Fall, were singled out to bear the blame for the conspiracy, but a large number of finance capitalists were also implicated, if not so deeply surely as significantly. The Standard Oil enterprises notably were involved to a considerable degree. The Midwest Oil Company, subsidiary of the Standard Oil Company of Indiana, had presented questionable claims to the Teapot Dome oil lands before Sinclair and Doheny obtained the government leases. J. Leo Stack, a Denver attorney, was retained on contract to get leases on Teapot Dome for this company. But when Sinclair and Doheny got them, Midwest Oil stepped aside, and gladly accepted $1,000,000 from Sinclair for its claim.

This infuriated Stack, who had stood to make $1,500,000 instead of the $50,000 he was now offered by Midwest Oil. Stack testified that Standard of Indiana was willing to relinquish its claim to Teapot Dome because it expected to profit by the pipe line which Sinclair planned to run into Teapot Dome. Senator Walsh opined that Sinclair had bought off Standard Oil in this fashion in order to dispose of powerful potential political competition for Teapot Dome. Standard Oil and Sinclair Oil had joint interests in pipe lines and other properties elsewhere in the West.

Wider participation in the conspiracy was arranged by means of the Continental Trading Company, a secret dummy company set up under Canadian law by Harry F. Sinclair, James O'Neil, president of the Prairie Oil and Gas Company (Rockefeller), and Colonel Robert W. Stewart, chairman of the Standard Oil Company of Indiana. Continental Trading Company was formed in 1921 to purchase 33,333,333 1/3 barrels of oil from Colonel A. E. Humphrey's Mexia, Texas, field. This was at the rate of $1.50 a barrel. Continental Trading Company resold at $1.75 a barrel to the companies headed by the Continental promoters, although the profits were not turned in to their respective companies until later, when the disclosures came out. The Continental Trading organizers, it was presumed, meant to keep this money.

Sinclair made his big mistake in passing around traceable Liberty bonds registered in the name of the Continental Trading Company; the $233,000 of bonds he gave Fall came from this company. And when rumors about Teapot Dome began to circulate he gave $185,000 of bonds to Will H. Hays to help defray the Republican deficit. Incidentally, Hinkle Hays, a brother of the Republican Postmaster General, was still an attorney for Sinclair. Will Hays, his conduct suggests, was afraid to use these bonds openly, so he cashed them surreptitiously with leading Republicans. John T. Pratt, brother of Herbert Pratt, leading Standard Oil official, cashed $50,000 worth. James Patten took $50,000 worth, and testified that he subsequently came to the conclusion that the transaction was "indecent." His conscience bothering him, he donated $50,000 to a Chicago hospital, but made no public disclosure of the "indecent" transaction. Hays offered Mellon $50,000 of the bonds, but Mellon, after keeping them in his safe, returned them, and gave Hays a check for $50,000 instead. Secretary Weeks took $50,000 of bonds and tried to pass them to William M. Butler, chairman of the Republican National Committee in 1924, but Butler was too astute to touch them.

Facts about the sinister Continental Trading Company did not become public until 1928, when Senate investigators independently unearthed the truth. But as early as 1925 Mellon's Treasury Department had known of the Liberty bonds purchased by Continental Trading Company, a special investigation having been made for the government prosecutors of Fall and Sinclair; the wily Mellon, however, said nothing and made no attempt to collect taxes from Continental Trading Company on its enormous profits.

John D. Rockefeller, Jr., testifying at the first Teapot Dome investigation, said he had "the utmost confidence" in Colonel Stewart, who had stormily refused to give the Senate committee information. It was not until 1928, when it became known that Stewart had withheld from the Standard Oil Company stockholders, including Rockefeller, his Continental Trading Company profits and was selling to Standard Oil at a profit petroleum from a company which he personally owned, that Rockefeller turned and ousted him. Stewart had received a salary of $125,000 a year; he was pensioned at $75,000 a year. His son, Robert G. Stewart, was president of Doheny's Pan-American Petroleum and Transport Company, subsequently acquired by Standard Oil of Indiana. James Stewart, another son, was a Pan-American vice-president. Both are now Standard Oil executives.

Doheny and Sinclair won court acquittals. At one of the trials it was disclosed a juror had been led to believe he would get money from Sinclair agents. Sinclair did serve six months in jail—but for contempt in refusing to answer a senator's question.

William G. McAdoo and Franklin K. Lane, Cabinet officers in the Wilson Administration, were retained as attorneys by Sinclair and Doheny. A. Mitchell Palmer was attorney for Edward B. McLean, owner of the Washington *Post*, who tried to help Fall by falsely testifying he had lent Fall money which the Senate investigators believed had come from Doheny and Sinclair. Employment of these attorneys tended to quench the fervor of Democrats who, for partisan reasons, might have wanted to exploit the embarrassment of the Republicans. E. L. Doheny was a Democrat.

Testimony at the investigation of 1928, incidentally, indicated that in a conversation in 1922 between James O'Neil, Harry Sinclair, and two unidentified persons at the Bankers Club, New York, one person said, "Suppose there was some future trouble to come up afterwards, who would take care of it?"

"The Sinclair Oil Company is big enough to take care of that," said Sinclair.

"If the Sinclair Oil Company is not big enough to take care of it Standard Oil is big enough to take care of it," said O'Neil.

John D. Rockefeller, Jr.'s apparent candor and willingness to co-operate made a favorable impression. His ousting of Stewart strengthened that impression. It has been the younger Rockefeller's role ever since the massacre of Rockefeller workers at Ludlow, Colorado, to make favorable public impressions.

Although the original Standard Oil combination was dissolved by a Supreme Court decree, the highly virtuous Rockefellers have not obeyed its mandate. In the late 1920's, under the Coolidge and Hoover regimes, they started piecing together the various parts of the old Standard Oil empire. The Colonial-Beacon Oil Company, itself a merger, was merged with Standard Oil Company of New Jersey. The Standard Oil Company of New York was merged with the Vacuum Oil Company, producing the Socony-Vacuum Oil Company. Then a merger was arranged between the Standard Oil Company of California and the Standard Oil Company of New Jersey, which was to flaunt the name of the General Petroleum Company, but this operation was discarded as the depression disturbed the relationship of stock prices and oil values. The Standard Oil Company of Indiana acquired Doheny's Pan-American Petroleum and Transport Company, and various other Standard Oil companies similarly acquired many independents subsequent to 1911. Standard Oil of New Jersey has absorbed various independents since 1911.

The result today is that, notwithstanding the Supreme Court's decree, the Standard Oil Company of New Jersey, the Socony-Vacuum Oil Company, the Standard Oil Company of Indiana, and the Standard Oil Company of California are each larger than was the entire Standard Oil trust at the time the dissolution order was issued; and the whole Standard Oil empire is six to seven times greater than was the original combination. The intent and spirit of the Supreme Court's decree has, in other words, been clearly violated, and with immunity from challenge. Rockefeller's share in the original Standard Oil Company, was twenty-five per cent; his share in each of the companies created by the dissolution order was twenty-. five per cent.

The Shipping Board after the war, under Albert D. Lasker, Chicago advertising man of potent connections, especially with R. R. McCormick of the Chicago *Tribune*, provided an opportunity for a favored few to add to their hoards. The steamship *City of Los Angeles*, formerly the German ship *Aeolus*, was sold to Harry Chandler, publisher of the Los Angeles *Times* and leading stockholder of the Los Angeles Steamship Company, for $100,000, after prearrangement between Lasker and Chandler to have bids advertised for ten days while the ship was out of port and not available for inspection by outsiders. This was learned in the Senate's investigation of the United States Shipping Board. A year earlier Chandler had offered $250,000 for the vessel, and after the war the International Mercantile Marine had offered $660,000; both offers were refused. Subsequent to the latter offer the government spent $2,816,000 on reconditioning, and according to experts the ship was worth $100,000 for scrap alone when it was released to Chandler.

The Shipping Board also sold seventeen vessels at bargain prices to the Dollar family of California for the Dollar Line. The Dollars themselves had constructed four cargo ships in China at a cost of $2,250,000 each to the government; they later acquired title to them from the government for $300,000 each. Another ship, the *Callao*, which had cost the government $1,619,502.27, was sold to the Dollars for $375,000, although an earlier bid of $825,000 from the International Mercantile Marine was rejected. In October, 1923, the Dollar Line bought seven of its "President" type ships for $550,000 apiece; each had cost the government $4,128,000 to construct.

Extraordinarily liberal terms of payment were given to R. Stanley Dollar, influential Pacific Coast Republican. The aggregate cost to the government of the seven "President" ships was $29,000,000, but Dollar was allowed to make an initial payment on the total purchase price of $3,850,000 in the form of a two-year letter of credit for twenty-five per cent of the amount. The remaining seventy-five per cent was due at the rate of five per cent annually until 1936.

In 1933 a Senate Committee investigating ocean-mail contracts brought out that enormous bonuses and commissions had been voted to Dollar by his stockholders. For purchasing seventeen ships from the government for $13,975,000, Dollar received commissions of $635,493.75 and interest of $73,014.69. From 1924 to 1929 the Dollar Line made a net profit of $6,746,759.33 on the "President" ships, defaulted on its payments to the government in 1933, but went on making payments of commission to Dollar. Although it had liens on the vessels, the government did not reacquire them.

Lasker, while head of the Shipping Board, introduced a merchant-marine bill which a Senate committee found would have subsidized the shipping enterprises of companies like the Standard Oil Company and the United States Steel Corporation in the carrying of their own products. Standard Oil would have received $1,500,000 annually and U. S. Steel $500,000. Enterprises like the Cudahy Packing Company and International Harvester Company were even then protesting that ocean freight rates were higher after the merchant marine had been subsidized than before.

When Hoover became President the airplane industry was still independent, in the pioneering stage. The big interests, after dipping in for the war profits, had temporarily lost their enthusiasm for aviation. But poorer men had done valuable work since the war and Charles A. Lindbergh had electrified the world in 1927 with his flight to Paris. Dwight W. Morrow had just completed the government's aviation program, however, and the wealthy clique was beginning to explore the possibilities of making money in aviation.

Independent manufacturers and operators had to be driven out of the business and their properties taken over, before predatory wealth would have a free hand, and the instrument used to accomplish this was Postmaster General Walter F. Brown, of the Hoover Cabinet. As a Senate committee learned, Brown used the threat of canceling or withholding air-mail contracts to force the independents into undesired mergers with companies especially formed to take them in—companies with strong Republican and Wall Street connections. Major William B. Robertson and his associates, backers of Lindbergh's flight and owners of the Robertson Aircraft Corporation of St. Louis, which operated an airline between Chicago and St. Louis, tried to capitalize Lindbergh's flight to Paris. They approached W. W. Atterbury, president of the Pennsylvania Railroad, with a proposal for a transcontinental air line. Atterbury told them he was involved in a similar scheme with Paul Henderson, of National Air Transport. Robertson and Lindbergh then went to C. M. Keys, New York stock broker. Keys later organized Transcontinental Air Transport in collaboration with the Pennsylvania Railroad, but Robertson was left out. Lindbergh, a heavily publicized figure, was retained, however, and was given twenty-five thousand shares of stock worth $10 each which he was advised to sell immediately. Directors and financiers of T. A. T. included William H. Vanderbilt, Charles Hayden, Richard Hoyt (Hayden, Stone), D. M. Sheaffer, chief of passenger operations of the Pennsylvania Railroad, and Colonel Henry Breckinridge, Lindbergh's personal adviser. The company was dubbed the "Lindbergh Line."

At about the same time Aviation Corporation was formed by William H. Vanderbilt, Cornelius Vanderbilt Whitney, S. Sloan Colt of the Bankers Trust Company (Morgan), Robert Lehman of Lehman Brothers' banking house, D. K. E. Bruce, son-in-law of Secretary of the Treasury Mellon, Richard K. Mellon, brother of Secretary Mellon, Richard Hoyt (Hayden, Stone), and George Mixter of Stone and Webster, Boston investment bankers.

According to a statement by Representative Bulwinkle, these airplane companies retained Lehr Fess, son of Senator Fess of Ohio, and a close friend of Postmaster General Brown, to lobby for the McNary-Watres air-mail subsidy bill, which was passed. For this Fess got $3,000, according to testimony of Paul Henderson. It was also testified by Henderson that he lent $10,000 to Chase Gove, assistant to W. Irving Glover, who in turn was Brown's assistant in charge of air mail. Henderson himself was Second Assistant Postmaster General from 1922 to 1925. He procured a job for Glover with T. A. T., according to the testimony, and tried to get a job for Senator Smoot's son, Harold, with United Aircraft.

Postmaster General Brown called a secret meeting of the big airplane company operators on May 19, 1930, and told them he would like to avoid competitive bidding. After a short talk he left the operators to apportion the air-mail routes among themselves, under the chairmanship of Assistant Secretary William P. MacCracken, Jr. Henderson protested that the conclave was not legal but, according to Senate testimony, MacCracken, who subsequently became a Washington lawyer for the leading airlines, told him he was "crazier than hell." Henderson was so disturbed that he conferred with others and became more firmly convinced, as he told investigating senators, that the meeting was illegal and might cause serious trouble, as it did indeed.

The big lines absorbed the smaller companies by the classic nineteenth-century methods of coercion, threats, and pressure that John D. Rockefeller had used in assembling the original Standard Oil Company. One instance concerned Clifford Ball, an aviation enthusiast, who operated a line between Cleveland and Pittsburgh. Ball testified that Pittsburgh Aviation Industries, a paper company set up by the Mellons, tried repeatedly in 1930 to buy him out. Richard K. Mellon personally telephoned him once to induce him to sell, but Ball refused. While the Mellons were trying to snare Ball's company Postmaster General Brown delayed the renewal of Ball's air-mail contract. Two days before the contract expired Brown appeared and forced Ball to sell out, but he did get Ball a job with the Mellon company at $1,000 a month. As soon as Ball agreed to sell, the mail contract of his company was renewed by Brown until May 6, 1936. The price paid Ball was $137,000, and he received $30,000 in salary before he left the Mellon company.

To a question from a Senator implying that he was not the victim of a hard bargain Ball replied:

"Yes, Senator, I do think it was a hard bargain. You understand I had inaugurated this line with practically no capital; I had devoted from three to four years without any salary of any kind to building it up. I had accumulated considerable prestige, and I had considerable pride in this enterprise, and it was taken from me."

Ball told of various types of coercion used against him. A representative of Pittsburgh Aviation came to his office and in the presence of Ball's employees asked if he was ready to sell. When Ball replied negatively the Mellon man said, "We are going to report you to the Post Office Department for mailing telephone books over your line, and we are going to force you to sell."

"Had you been sending telephone books over?" a Senator asked, and Ball replied, "Never."

"May I ask," said the Senator, "if it is true your route went into the hands of a company that had never flown a plane over it?"

"That is correct."

"And you were the one that had done the pioneering?"

"That is correct."

"And you did object to selling it out?"

"I did, sir."

Another aviation pioneer was Erle P. Halliburton, owner of the Southwest Air Fast Express, operating between Kansas City, St. Louis, Dallas, and Fort Worth. While the Post Office was paying $3 a pound to carry mail on the Atlanta-Los Angeles route, Halliburton offered to carry it for 70 cents a pound over the first thousand miles and 7 cents a pound for each additional mile. His offer was rejected. Halliburton, who owned a fleet of fast, up-to-date ships, was notified he would have to sell out to American Airways, a subsidiary of Mellon's Aviation Corporation of Delaware, of which Pittsburgh Aviation Industries also became a subsidiary.

When Halliburton refused he was threatened with loss of mail contracts. He testified that Glover, Brown's assistant, said to him, "I will ruin you if it is the last act of my life; you have tried to buck this thing all the way through, and you are not going to do it."

When Halliburton saw that the Post Office Department was determined to crush him he sold out to Aviation Corporation for $1,400,000, or slightly more than the cost of his equipment.

Robertson, the financier of Lindbergh's epic flight, was manhandled in similar fashion. Promised mail contracts by Brown in person, he failed to get them and in 1931 was told by William Sacks, member of the Republican State Committee of Missouri, that he ought to contribute to the Republican Party and that he could get a mail contract if he was willing to give Sacks a five per cent participation. Robertson refused to deal with Sacks; and Brown, upon seeing Robertson, remarked that the latter had "given Mr. Sacks a cool reception." This mail contract was awarded to American Airways, Mellon subsidiary, which began competing with Robertson's line on the basis of its government contract and quickly put it out of business. Robertson testified that American Airways was paid $345,000 a year to carry the mail, while he had offered the same service for $175,000 a year. Robertson could not even find buyers for his ships, which he was compelled to junk.

Brown even forced mergers of some big companies. T. A. T., in which the Mellon-Vanderbilt group held stock, was merged with Western Air Express upon Brown's orders, although Western Air executives believed T. A. T. was not soundly organized. Western Air was also ordered by Brown to sell its Los Angeles-Dallas line to American Airways at a loss of $600,000.

The new company, known as Transcontinental and Western Air, thereupon agreed to acquire the Mellon interest in the Butler Airport, Pittsburgh, for twenty-five thousand shares of its stock, although the value of the airport was doubtful. Herbert Hoover, Jr., had an executive position with Western Air Express, and continued with TWA.

"Who first suggested to you the Pittsburgh Aviation Industries should be let in on it?" Senator Black asked a Western Air Express executive.

"Well, the Postmaster General," was the reply.

When the Post Office Department advertised for bids on two transcontinental mail routes in August, 1930, the advertisements contained a provision excluding any company that did not have at least six months' experience in night flying over routes of at least two hundred and fifty miles. This provision, not contained in the McNary-Watres Act, automatically disqualified smaller operators, most of whom had not flown at night.

To qualify for bidding, many small companies merged and formed United Aviation Company, which submitted a bid of 64 per cent of the government postage for carrying mail against a bid of 97½ per cent by TWA. The contract was awarded to TWA, nevertheless, giving the government an estimated loss of at least $833,215 for each

year of a ten-year term. As this estimated loss was predicated upon
one trip each day and as TWA made three trips a day, the actual
loss was greater.

United Aviation brought suit. The issue was put up to Comptroller
General McCarl, who was assisted in his deliberations by Ernest
Smoot, son of Senator Reed Smoot of Utah and hired by TWA to do
this work. While McCarl's decision was pending Senator Smoot, importuned by an official of Western Air Express, wrote McCarl to "ex-
pedite the decision on the Transcontinental-Western Air case."
On January 10, 1931, McCarl decided in favor of TWA, the higher
bidder. McCarl in 1937 resigned his post of guarding the nation's
accounts, and in his valedictory denounced the New Deal for extravagant spending.

From the time of Brown's illegal air-mail conference in 1930 to
the end of the Hoover Administration the government spent $78,-
084,897.09 for air-mail service, more than twice the freight space
actually utilized being paid for with the understanding that the
overpayment was a subsidy. Without the government's funds at
their disposal the big "rugged individualists" behind the new air lines
could not, of course, have paid expenses, much less have shown
profits.

All of the Hoover Administration's air-mail contracts were, fortunately, canceled, as fraudulent and collusively gained, by the Roosevelt Administration on February 9, 1934. The cost of flying the mail
under new contracts was $7,700,238 annually in contrast with the cost
of $19,400,264 in 1933. But, despite the cancelations, and despite sub-
sequent maneuverings, mergers, and reorganizations, the airplane
industry, like the oil, steel, railroad, electric power, aluminum, radio, automobile and chemical industries, had come to rest in the hands
of the Mellons, Morgans, Whitneys, Vanderbilts, *et al.*

The farming out of air-mail contracts to the wealthy groups was
accompanied by stock-market rigging that brought fabulous returns.

Frederick B. Rentschler, brother of Gordon Rentschler, president
of the National City Bank, took a leading part in organizing the
United Aircraft and Transport Company for the bank and its affiliated families. United Aircraft, of which Paul Henderson was also

a director, had a profitable mail contract, and represented a merger of various companies, including the Pratt and Whitney Aircraft Company. Originally Frederick B. Rentschler bought 1,265 Pratt and Whitney shares for 20 cents each, or $253 in all. After the company declared a stock dividend of 79 cents a share he owned 101,200 shares, for which he received in exchange 219,604 shares of United Aircraft. In May, 1929, the shares for which Rentschler had originally paid $253 were worth $35,575,848. He sold $9,514,869 worth and retained the balance.

The National City Company, securities affiliate of the National City Bank, marketed stock of the Boeing Airplane and Transport Company, and directors and executives of United Aircraft were permitted to buy at $25 a share while the stock was offered to the public at $97 a share. The difference represented a gift, and in F. B. Rentschler's case the gift amounted to $92,176.50. National City Company made a profit of $5,895,311 by unloading United Aircraft stock.

When Rentschler acquired his $253 of Pratt and Whitney stock, 200 shares were bought at 20 cents each, or $40 in all, by Charles W. Deeds, son of the Deeds whom Justice Hughes had recommended for court-martial. Young Deeds was made treasurer of United Aircraft, and the stock for which he had paid $40 was worth $5,624,640 in May, 1929. At the time of the Senate air-mail investigation in 1934 young Deeds was thirty-one years old and, like his father when he ran the Aviation Division during the war, had no technical knowledge of aviation. But technical knowledge is not necessary in the realm of high finance, especially when the government can be milked.

Out of the proceeds of the air-mail contracts the executives and directors of the leading airplane companies paid themselves extravagant salaries and bonuses, with the consent of the rich families behind the scenes whom they served.

II

The ruinous speculative boom that collapsed in 1929 was engineered, from first to last, by the wealthy families, and for their personal account. At every stage of the game it was the richest, the most respectable, the most publicized, and the most influential persons who were the prime movers in unloading inflated securities upon a deluded public. None of the truly rich came to grief, although some of their agents like Samuel Insull, Charles E. Mitchell, the Van Sweringens, and Ivar Kreuger had to function as scapegoats.

It has never been properly stressed that these latter were merely deputies for wealthy family blocs, and had little more than a promoter's interest in their own schemes. It was tacitly understood that in the event of mishap the deputies were quietly to defend themselves without attempting to involve their sponsors. They all performed like good soldiers.

The ground work for the postwar speculative orgy that caused thousands of persons of ordinary means a loss estimated at $25,000,-000,000 was laid back in the Harding Administration, with whose Morgan, Rockefeller, Du Pont, Mellon, Vanderbilt, and Whitney backing we are familiar. In order that the speculative boom might attain grandiose proportions it was necessary to alter radically the policies of the Federal Reserve System, for the financial system of the early 1920's would not have accommodated the inflation that came to a disastrous climax in 1929.

President Harding let down the first bar when he failed in 1923 to reappoint W. P. G. Harding, who for nearly a decade had served as Governor of the Federal Reserve System. Governor Harding (no relation to the President) was an experienced banker of unusual probity who studiously held himself aloof from Wall Street influences.

The President replaced Harding with Comptroller of the Currency D. R. Crissinger, a crony from Marion, Ohio. Crissinger, who had dabbled in small business, knew nothing whatever of large-scale public finance and was an impressionable character—just the type the wealthy sponsors of President Harding evidently wanted. Crissinger stepped out as Governor in 1927, and Coolidge replaced him with Roy A. Young, small Louisiana businessman. Young inaugurated no change in policy, and was succeeded in 1930 by Eugene G. Meyer, the stock operator who had held high appointive office from 1917 under Republican and Democratic Administrations alike.

Crissinger came under the influence of Benjamin Strong, a Morgan deputy, who began counseling from the New York Reserve Bank that the Reserve System buy government securities in large volume, thus flooding the banks with liquid funds that demanded profitable release in credit channels. The Federal Reserve Act permitted this, but only as an emergency measure. There was no emergency in 1923 when the Federal Reserve System began buying "governments," so the scheme was obviously predicated upon other considerations. For three years the Reserve System maintained this new policy, and the speculative boom was well started. Between 1924 and 1929 loans, which were enormously profitable to the big banks, increased by ten billion dollars, all of the increase being devoted to stock-market paper; there was little variation in the total of commercial and industrial loans. At the end of 1922, for example, loans to brokers stood at $1,926,800,-000; at the end of 1929 they totaled $8,549,338,979.

From 1922 to 1929 stock averages, according to the Standard Statistics index, soared from $60 to $212, and hundreds of investment trusts, holding companies, and similar dubious enterprises were launched.

Alarm occasioned by the phenomenal increase in brokers' loans was allayed from time to time by reassuring statements from President Coolidge and Secretary Mellon. But in the spring of 1928 the Reserve Board, to disarm critics, authorized an increase in the discount rate from four to five per cent. A much higher rate would have been necessary, however, to quell speculative hysteria. From the spring of 1928 to the spring of 1929 the total of brokers' loans doubled. Early in 1929 a warning from the Reserve Board sent call money up to twenty per cent as the leading commercial banks stepped back hesitantly; but the impasse was broken by Charles E. Mitchell, chairman of the National City Bank, who threw $25,000,000 into the money market and belligerently announced that borrowers could have all they wanted. New York was openly running Washington.

The investigation of Wall Street by the Senate Banking and Currency Committee in 1933 is reported in eight thick, closely printed volumes of more than ten thousand pages. This investigation was preceded by the inquiry of 1932, the report of which fills three thick volumes. The findings of both have been supplemented by exhaustive inquiries of the Federal Trade Commission into the electric utilities companies and the American Telephone and Telegraph Company, by inquiries of the Senate Committee on Interstate Commerce into the looting of railroads by banks, and by special inquiries of the Securities and Exchange Commission. The record throughout is one of wrong-doing. The wrong-doing, indeed, was so complete, so thorough, so pervasive that it had neither beginning nor end, and baffles full comprehension in the lifetime of any single individual. It is, therefore, manifestly impossible to give a complete report. Selections from the evidence are therefore made (1) with the view to showing the general sanction given to the irregularities and intrigue by the rich and (2) with a view to showing that most of the rich were personally and almost exclusively involved, using their political power to confer upon themselves immunity.

Senate Report No. 1455, Stock Market Practices, Banking and Currency Committee, Seventy-third Congress, second session, relates that it was the largest banks and the largest corporations which threw artificially created surplus cash funds into the money market, to act like gasoline upon the speculative fires. The persons in control of these banks and corporations, as officers, directors, or stockholders, were the persons that contributed most heavily to the campaign funds of the two leading political parties. The continuity of policy was insured by the control the dominant elite of wealth exercised over the Federal Reserve System.

According to the Senate Report, in 1929 the thirty-three leading commercial banks, from Chase National and National City down through the list of New York, Philadelphia, Boston, and Chicago institutions, made thirty-four loans of $76,459,550 to stock-market pools and in 1930 they made forty-five such loans of $34,922,750 to pools. On their own account these banks themselves participated, through their securities affiliates, in 454 pools, whose objective was to unload stocks at artificially advanced prices upon a public misled by its newspapers and its political leaders. There were no fewer than 105 separate Stock Exchange issues subject to pool manipulation in 1929, according to the Senate Report.

The origin of bank securities affiliates, it will be recalled, was political. The National City Bank received permission from President Taft to launch the National City Company. The Solicitor General in the Taft Administration, as we have seen, decided that the affiliates were illegal, but he was overruled and his report hidden until the Senate Banking and Currency Committee brought it to light.

Credit from the banks to fuel the stock boom was supplemented by credit from the big corporations. Call loans to brokers in 1929 made by some leading corporations were as follows:

| | PEAK AMOUNT |
|---|---|
| American Founders Corporation | $ 23,629,166 |
| American and Foreign Power (Morgan) | 30,321,000 |
| Anaconda Copper Mining Company (National City Bank) | 32,500,000 |
| Bethlehem Steel Corporation (Charles M. Schwab) | 157,450,000 |
| Chrysler Corporation (Walter P. Chrysler) | 60,150,000 |
| Cities Service Company (Henry L. Doherty) | 41,900,000 |
| Consolidated Oil Corporation (Harry F. Sinclair) | 15,000,000 |
| Electric Bond and Share Company (Morgan) | 157,579,000 |
| General Foods Company (E. F. Hutton) | 3,400,000 |
| International Nickel Company (Morgan) | 500,000 |
| General Motors Corporation (Morgan-Du Pont-Fisher) | 25,000,000 |
| Pan-American Petroleum and Transport Company (Rockefeller) | 8,000,000 |
| Radio Corporation (Morgan-Rockefeller) | 1,000,000 |
| Radio-Keith-Orpheum Corporation (Morgan-Rockefeller) | 8,000,000 |
| Standard Oil of New Jersey (Rockefeller) | 97,824,000 |
| Tri-Continental Corporation | 62,150,000 |
| United Corporation (Morgan) | 3,000,000 |
| United Gas and Improvement Company (Morgan) | 3,600,000 |

The participation of the leading industrial corporations in the money market was unprecedented.

Individuals as well as corporations and banks placed funds in the call-money market. Pierre S. du Pont, for example, had $32,000,000 of cash in the market for his personal account. J. P. Morgan and Company had nearly $110,000,000 in the call-loan market.

For profits to be made on these funds the public had to be induced to speculate, and it was so induced by misleading newspaper accounts, many of them bought and paid for by the brokers that operated the pools. No losses were incurred in lending money, and no losses were possible, for as soon as a speculator's margin was impaired he was sold out and the loan to the broker was liquidated.

Banks and corporations behind the speculative commotion were far from abstract entities. Personalities lay in ambush behind these institutions, and they were—and are—personalities from the richest hereditary family dynasties ever seen in the history of the world.

On the board of the National City Bank, for example, sat Cleveland Earl Dodge, son of the late Cleveland H. Dodge, vice-president of the Phelps Dodge Corporation, and head of a fortune dating back to the Civil War; Cyrus Hall McCormick, chairman of the International Harvester Company and representative of another Civil War fortune; Percy R. Pyne, representative of a fortune antedating the Civil War; Fred J. Fisher, representative of a twentieth-century automobile fortune (General Motors and Fisher Bodies); James A. Stillman, surviving head of a financial fortune dating back to the 1880's; Percy A. Rockefeller, son of John D. Rockefeller's brother; Beekman Winthrop, of the pre-Civil War landed aristocracy; and Nicholas F. Brady, son of Anthony Brady. Among the lesser figures on this board were Sosthenes Behn, president of the International Telephone and Telegraph Company (Morgan), William Cooper Procter (Procter and Gamble), Gordon S. Rentschler, Edward A. Deeds, John D. Ryan (Anaconda Copper), Robert W. Stewart (Standard Oil of Indiana), P. A. S. Franklin (International Mercantile Marine), and Joseph P. Grace (Grace Lines).

On the board of the Chase National Bank sat these representatives of established rich families: J. N. Hill, son of the late James J. Hill, nineteenth-century railroad promoter; Henry O. Havemeyer (American Sugar Refining Company), Jeremiah Milbank (law), Theodore Pratt (Standard Oil), and F. W. Roebling. Sitting with them were agents of dynastic wealth like D. C. Jackling, of the Utah Copper Company (Guggenheim), Charles M. Schwab of Bethlehem Steel, Alfred P. Sloan, Jr., of General Motors, and F. H. Brownell of American Smelting and Refining Company (Guggenheim).

On the board of the Guaranty Trust Company, directing its participation in situations like the Van Sweringen bubble, sat E. J. Berwind, head of a great nineteenth-century coal fortune; Marshall Field, representative of a great nineteenth-century merchandising and real-estate fortune; R. W. Goelet, head of a great nineteenth-century real-estate and banking fortune; W. A. Harriman, legatee of a great nineteenth-century railroad fortune; Clarence H. Mackay, heir to a great nineteenth-century mining and communications fortune; Cornelius Vanderbilt Whitney, scion of two great nineteenth-century fortunes, one in railroads, the other in petroleum; and Harry Payne

Whitney, heir of two great Standard Oil fortunes. There were also T. W. Lamont and George Whitney, Morgan partners, Cornelius F. Kelley of Anaconda Copper, and Grayson M.-P. Murphy, a character whose important confidential role at three stages of recent American history we have observed.

George F. Baker and his son alone sat on the board of the First National Bank as representatives of first-line nineteenth-century fortunes. Directors with them included Myron C. Taylor (U. S. Steel) and Walter S. Gifford (American Telephone and Telegraph). But on the board of the First Security Company, securities affiliate of the bank, were Arthur Curtiss James (Phelps Dodge Corporation and various railroads), L. W. Hill, son of the late James J. Hill, J. P. Morgan, and Thomas W. Lamont.

First-line established dynasties of wealth were represented on the board of the New York Trust Company by Robert W. de Forest (law), Walter Jennings (Standard Oil), and Vanderbilt Webb, descendant of Cornelius Vanderbilt I. Other directors included Charles Hayden and Grayson M.-P. Murphy of the Morgan camp.

First-line fortunes on the board of the Bankers Trust Company were represented by Pierre S. du Pont, Horace Havemeyer, Herbert L. Pratt (Standard Oil), Winthrop W. Aldrich (Rockefeller), and Arthur Woods, Rockefeller executive married to a Morgan daughter. The secondary Altman fortune was represented by Michael Friedsam. Others on the board included John J. Raskob (Du Pont and General Motors), Samuel Mather (steel), Stephen Birch (Kennecott Copper, Morgan-Guggenheim), and James G. Harbord (Radio Corporation).

A wealthy family, but of lesser standing, on the board of the Irving Trust Company was represented by William Skinner (textiles). On the board of the Bank of New York and Trust Company sat Cleveland Earl Dodge, R. C. Hill, W. Emlen Roosevelt, of the late President's family, and Allen Wardwell, of J. P. Morgan's law firm. On the board of the Equitable Trust Company were Otto Kahn, H. R. Winthrop, Bertram Cutler (Rockefeller), and T. M. Debevoise (Rockefeller). The board of the Corn Exchange Bank included Robert Lehman, Philip Lehman, F. D. Bartow (Morgan), W. H. Nichols and C. H. Nichols, both of the Nichols Copper Company and the Allied Chemical and Dye Corporation. On the Chemical National Bank board were Robert Goelet and Philip Roosevelt, a cousin of the late Theodore Roosevelt; and on the Bank of Manhattan board were Stephen Baker, Paul M. Warburg, Marshall Field, Walter Jennings, and Michael Friedsam.

These men and others from the wealthiest families also manned the boards of the leading industrial corporations. The Morgan partners in 1929, for example, held directorates in eighty-nine corporations controlling assets of $18,000,000,000, equivalent at the time to the national debt. The Morgan directorates interlocked with additional directorates of other individuals, giving J. P. Morgan and Company a pervasive influence throughout American industry. In short, the wealthy families stood united behind the disastrous policies, political and corporate, of the 1920's.

Of all these wealthy bank and corporation directors only one, Paul M. Warburg, spoke out, and at a very late date, early in 1929, against the politico-financial speculative scandal. Warburg, to be sure, indicated by his remarks that he was not concerned about the public interest but about the threat of disaster to the Wall Street community. His warnings were generally scoffed at by the newspapers or were given an inconspicuous position that contrasted oddly with the bold display given the provocatively encouraging remarks of Charles E. Mitchell, chairman of the National City Bank, and others.

## III

The individual postwar operations of the wealthy families of finance capital against the background of their absolute control of the government were darkly antisocial in character. Various governmental investigating bodies have heard copious confessions to "mistakes" and "errors of judgment" from the executive representatives of the multimillionaire dynasties. But there were really no mistakes or errors of judgment. Except for the culminating debacle of 1929–33, everything happened according to plan, was premeditated, arranged, sought for.

It is a characteristic of the wealthy families of America that most of them have seen their family spokesmen and heads indicted and

placed on trial at one time or other for serious crimes or misde-
meanors. Unless one takes into consideration certain underworld
circles, in no other social group can one find a parallel. Between
the Civil War and 1910 practically all the highly successful pecuniary
entrepreneurs were indicted by grand juries, and many stood trial
although none was convicted. The rogues' gallery of American finance includes such names as J. P. Morgan, John D. Rockefeller,
E. H. Harriman, Philip D. and J. Ogden Armour, Jay Gould, George
W. Perkins, E. T. Stotesbury, Thomas Fortune Ryan, Anthony
Brady, Harry F. Sinclair, E. L. Doheny, James J. Hill, *et al.* The indictments were sometimes arranged by political, i. e., financial, rivals;
but very often they were returned at the request of public prosecutors
who, sometimes very much against their inclination, had to function
in accord with democratic expectations.

In our own day Mellons and Du Ponts, as well as others, have
been indicted by Federal grand juries and placed on trial, charged
with tax evasion, restraint of trade, or other illegal acts against the
public interest. Such acts in the 1920's, as in no other period, seemed
to become a characteristic feature of national life.

The acquittals of Charles E. Mitchell on charges of income-tax
evasion and of Samuel Insull on charges of using the mails to defraud suggest, however, that the course of justice under the anti-
quated American judicial system is what it has always been: the
poor go to jail, the rich go free.

From the evidence brought before the Senate the National City
Bank, second largest commercial bank in the country, emerged as
the antisocial instrument of its dominant family groups. After the
war, as before and during the war, this bank used the Anaconda
Copper Company, its principal industrial pawn, to inflict grave
injury upon the public interest. In two big stock-market pool manipulations, participated in personally by Percy A. Rockefeller and John
D. Ryan, 1,750,000 Anaconda shares were foisted upon the public,
causing it a loss of $150,000,000.

The bank also operated, illegally, in its own stock through the
securities affiliate, the National City Company.

In September, 1929, National City Bank stock was pushed up to a market price of $579 a share, or $3,200,000,000 in all, while its book value was $70 a share or $385,000,000 in all. High-pressure salesmen sold this stock, and scores of other dubious securities, to a gullible public trimmed right and left for the benefit of the leading stockholders of the bank.

Unknown to small stockholders both the bank and its affiliate had management funds that siphoned twenty per cent of all earnings, after the declaration of eight per cent dividends, to the account of officers. The management fund of the affiliate from 1921 to 1929 was $10,511,670 and of the bank itself $8,490,634, and about a third of both sums was given to Mitchell in addition to salaries and participations in stock-market pools. Special secret stock "melons" were made available to leading stockholders of the bank and to officers, as in Boeing Aircraft and Transport Company and the United Aircraft and Transport Corporation.

The bank directors and big stockholders were permitted, for example, to buy stock units of Boeing, which became United Aircraft, at $590 per unit, while the units were being quoted to the public at $771 in the open market. The differential of $181 per unit amounted to a gift. Percy Rockefeller received 400 of these stock units, James A. Stillman 150 units, Francis Bartow, Morgan partner, 645 units, and Edward A. Deeds 200 units. To make unloading easy, speculative enthusiasm was stirred up by planted newspaper rumors and by sudden sharp advances in price.

Not deeming the presents of stock and of stock dividends from the airplane companies sufficient, the National City group voted itself enormous salaries and bonuses. F. B. Rentschler, for example, in 1929 received $429,999 in salaries and bonuses from United Aircraft, and in 1930 he got $242,150.61. From 1927 through 1933 he received more than $1,250,000 in cash from the United Aircraft Company, in addition to the fantastically huge stock profit realized on an investment of less than $300.

From 1926 through 1932 the government gave this company $40,-174,412, and the company profited by $1,000,000 annually on each original investment of $750. On the other hand the airplane pilots, who daily took great risks, received very low pay, as a Senate committee discovered in the investigation of air-mail contracts.

So much has been said about the indirect value to society of the great fortunes that it is necessary to stress once more in the case of the privately owned airplane industry that it was financed in its initial stages by the government and by pioneer entrepreneurs who have since been frozen out. The Wright brothers received practically nothing; obscure interlopers like Rentschler and Deeds, and the aggregates of private finance for which they acted, reaped the harvest. But this has also been the story in the shipping, the railroad, the automobile, the radio, and other industries. It was Andrew Carnegie who said: "Pioneering don't pay."

The National City Bank participated in the unloading of more than $100,000,000 of Peruvian bonds, although the bank's agents in Peru warned that the country was economically unsound. The bonds soon passed into default. Huge commissions were paid to agents that induced the Peruvian authorities to float these bonds. J. and W. Seligman and Company, participants in the underwriting syndicate, paid Juan Leguia, son of the President of Peru, $415,000 to obtain the bond issue.

During and after the war the bank lent money to Cuban sugar planters on the basis of wartime prices. When sugar prices slumped, the planters were unable to pay $30,000,000 owing to the bank. Federal bank examiners criticized these loans, upon which there was slight possibility of realizing. The bank therefore in 1927 formed the General Sugar Corporation to assume the obligations, and on the day this corporation was formed the bank increased its capital from $50,000,000 to $75,000,000 by selling more stock. The increased capital was turned over to the National City Company, which with this money bought the stock of the General Sugar Corporation. The sugar corporation then gave the National City Bank $23,000,000 of the same money, plus notes for $11,000,000 on $34,000,000 of its obligation. All this was a questionable bookkeeping transaction to expunge the bad debt on the books of the bank, and it remained a secret until the Senate discovered it in 1933.

After the market crash the bank created a fund of $2,400,000 to help officers who had incurred losses in the stock market. The officers were given loans, which they had not liquidated by 1933. Minor employees were not assisted, however, although the bank had encouraged them to purchase stock at inflated prices in the amount of $12,000,000. In 1933 employees were still paying at the rate of $200 to $220 a share for stock then selling at $40 a share.

Among other dubious operations of the bank was the making of a loan of $10,020 to John Ramsey, general manager of the Port of New York Authority, after the National City Company on May 9, 1931, acquired for distribution $66,000,000 of Port Authority bonds. The loan was in cash, avoiding the evidence of a check, and was not regularly issued through the bank but was charged against the syndicate expense of the bond issue. Although ostensibly made for only three weeks, no payment on the principal or interest had been made two years later.

Charles E. Mitchell avoided paying an income tax for 1929, although his net income exceeded $4,000,000, by creating an artificial loss in stock sales to his wife, later repurchasing the stock. Indicted and tried by a Federal jury, he was acquitted. The focusing of public anger upon Mitchell, however, permitted the bigger interests to escape public attention, although Percy Rockefeller, for one, was involved in practically every National City foray of the 1920's, including the Kreuger and Toll swindle.

The Chase National Bank, largest financial institution outside of London, performed similarly, and was, indeed, the direct rival of the National City Bank for shady business. It, too, operated an illegal securities affiliate, through which it managed pools in its own stock and financed pools in other stocks. Insiders among the bank's officials and directors were given preferred positions in stocks and bonds.

Albert H. Wiggin, chairman of the bank, used his personal family corporations to participate in many of the big Wall Street pools financed by the bank and including other bank officers. One pool traded in Sinclair Oil stock in 1928 and made a profit of more than $12,000,000, of which $877,654.25 accrued to Wiggin. The extraordinary ramifications of some of these pools were illustrated in the Sinclair operation, for out of the profits a payment of $300,052 was made to William S. Fitzpatrick, president of the Prairie Oil and Gas Company (Rockefeller), although Fitzpatrick was not a participant in the pool. Harry F. Sinclair could not tell inquiring senators why

Fitzpatrick was given this large sum, but Fitzpatrick testified that the Rockefellers had directed Blair and Company, member of the pool syndicate, to pay him the money as a token of their esteem. Upon receipt of the money, Fitzpatrick testified, he notified Bertram Cutler, agent of the Rockefellers at 26 Broadway.

Wiggin engaged in various market operations of great profit to himself and of great loss to the bank's minority stockholders. He sold stock of the bank short, and by means of various family corporations, one incorporated in Canada, evaded payment of Federal income taxes.

Under his headship the Chase National Bank played an evil role in Cuba, for which the bank wanted to float a $100,000,000 loan on which it could collect commission—despite the fact that its Cuban adviser said conditions on the island were "deplorable." This loan was to finance the building of a road which independent contractors had estimated should cost only $30,000,000. The Platt Amendment prohibited a Cuban loan, so Chase had to circumvent this law to achieve its objective, which was simply to get at the pockets of the Cuban people through the taxgathering machinery of Cuba.

Arrangements were made to build the road and various public improvements, of which an unnecessary, elaborate government house was the major item, at a cost of $60,000,000. The contractors took notes given by the venal Cuban government and discounted them at the Chase Bank, in this way sidestepping the Platt Amendment. Early in 1930 the bank was able to sell $40,000,000 of Cuban bonds, paying off $30,000,000 of the construction notes held by itself and giving itself a commission of $1,404,867.35. The bond prospectus neglected to mention that 1929 Cuban revenues were less than expenditures by $7,440,000, or ten per cent, or that $20,000,000 of public works certificates remained outstanding. The prospectus, in fact, was falsified to indicate that the government had a surplus. In all, the Chase Bank lent Cuba $80,000,000, and paid José Emilio Obregon y Blanco, son-in-law of President Gerardo Machado, a "commission" of $500,-000. The Cuban bonds have since defaulted.

The Chase Bank was very close to President Machado; indeed, it and National City were Machado's main political supports. In 1925, when Machado successfully ran for the presidency, Henry Catlin,

Morgan agent, put up $500,000 for his expenses while other American interests, including the Chase National Bank element and the Guggenheims, put up an equal amount. The brother-in-law of Machado was made notorial attorney for Chase Bank in Havana at a fat salary. Chase Bank lent Machado $130,000 on his personal account.

Machado governed by assassinating all political opponents, including members of parliament, while the Chase Bank was kept informed by its Cuban agents, as revealed in the letters themselves, produced before the Senate Banking and Currency Committee. During part of Machado's term Harry Guggenheim was American Ambassador at Havana; in fact, all American Ambassadors to Cuba since 1900 have represented the Chase or National City interests. Machado was eventually deposed by the populace, and fled with a price on his head.

Another of the many unsavory episodes in which Chase Bank took the leading role concerned the Fox Film Corporation. The first step in the Fox tangle was taken with the launching of General Theatres Equipment Company, whose original assets of less than $2,000,000 were written-up by $38,000,000, after which $30,000,000 of securities were sold to the public by Chase. Then William Fox entered into negotiations for the sale of Fox Film to General Theatres for $55,000,-000, but the negotiations were unsuccessful.

Fox, meanwhile, pursued his own course with Fox Film, contracting to buy working control of Loew's, Inc., for $50,000,000. He found many lenders willing to give him money; the Western Electric Company, subsidiary of the American Telephone and Telegraph Company, which holds the controlling patents on sound films, advanced him $15,000,000, and Halsey, Stuart and Company, investment bankers who were also serving Samuel Insull, raised the balance by selling Fox Film securities and tapping the Fox Film treasury. Because the purchase of Loew's stock did not represent outright control, Halsey, Stuart and Company induced Fox, as he told the story, to commit himself to buy $23,000,000 additional Loew's stock.

Fox had also been encouraged by his bankers to acquire control of the Gaumont Company of England for $20,000,000, committing him in all to the extent of $93,000,000 before the market collapsed. At about this time President Hoover's Department of Justice, conspicuously reluctant to prosecute big violators of the antitrust laws, embarrassed Fox by questioning the legality of the Fox-Loew's arrangement. Threatened by the mysteriously alert Department of Justice, and notes due at various banks, Fox was induced to sell out to General Theatres Equipment for $15,000,000 and a bonus consideration, and was also relieved of his debts. General Theatres and Fox Film were now under the aegis of the Chase Bank and an elaborate arrangement was made to segregate the holdings of Loew's shares; but General Theatres subsequently smashed, entailing a loss of $69,000,000 to the Chase Bank as a consequence of participation in General Theatres stock pools.

Despite these and other disastrous operations Albert H. Wiggin, upon his retirement from the bank in 1932, was voted an annual pension of $100,000. This emolument was approved by the Rockefellers, who have dominated the bank since 1929. Not until the Senate inquiry of 1933 did the news of the pension become public, and Wiggin, who had directed nearly every variety of financial malpractice, then "voluntarily" decided not to claim it. Wiggin, like Mitchell, was uniquely blamed for the policies of the bank; but Wiggin, like Mitchell, acted at all times under warrant from the board of directors whose wealthy members we have already enumerated.

The Guaranty Trust Company (Morgan), third largest commercial bank of the United States, engaged in similar off-color operations. With the National City Company it joined in selling $50,000,000 of Peruvian bonds in 1927, sharing in the huge "spread" of five points that accrued to the underwriting syndicate. With Kuhn, Loeb and Company, which also helped itself in the general scramble for unwholesome profits, it sold between 1925 and 1929 $90,000,000 of Chilean bonds, since defaulted, and failed to mention in the prospectuses that Chile was in the grip of a military dictatorship that ruled over a hostile populace. The chairman of Guaranty Trust was William C. Potter, erstwhile agent of the Guggenheims.

Although implicating itself in various other operations as well, the Guaranty Trust Company, most significantly, was deeply concerned in the Van Sweringen railroad holding-company knavery, functioning in direct collaboration with J. P. Morgan and Company. The two Van Sweringen brothers, Orris P. and Mantis J., before their death were singled out for a good deal of attention in the daily press, but they were no more than deputies of J. P. Morgan and Company, without any real financial status of their own. It was J. P. Morgan and Company which brought them, obscure Cleveland real-estate men, into the capital market, and allowed them to function as they did in the creation of a grandiose $3,000,000,000 holding-company structure in which the public lost millions and the bankers made millions.

There was as much fraud in the Van Sweringen as in the New Haven enterprise. In 1929 and 1930, for example, the Van Sweringen's newly formed Allegheny Corporation unloaded $160,000,000 of stocks and bonds through J. P. Morgan and Company, the Guaranty Trust Company, and affiliated banks. With the assistance of J. P. Morgan and Company, the brothers achieved control, on mere shoestrings, of more than twenty-three thousand miles of railroad trackage, including the Chesapeake and Ohio Railroad, the Nickel Plate Railroad, and others. Public sales of stocks and bonds provided the money with which the brothers cut intricate financial capers.

Although no statement of intention to do so was made, $100,000,000 of the Allegheny money was used to purchase control for Allegheny Corporation of the Missouri Pacific Railroad, giving the Van Sweringens, as obedient agents of J. P. Morgan and Company, virtually a coast-to-coast transportation line. The Missouri Pacific, as the depression set in, proved to be a white elephant.

As early as October, 1930, the Allegheny Corporation floundered in deep water, for it had to make a payment of $10,500,000 for terminal properties it had agreed to purchase on behalf of Missouri Pacific. The company had stripped itself of cash and could not borrow because its preferred stock carried a provision against borrowing in excess of sixty per cent of its assets.

J. P. Morgan and Company thereupon "bought" from Allegheny $10,500,000 of Missouri Pacific five and a half per cent bonds, at a price of 105½, and gave the Allegheny Corporation an option to buy them back. Allegheny, lacking funds, later was unable to exercise this option, but the money given for the bonds enabled it to pay for the terminal properties. In this devious way a loan was in effect projected, contrary to the provisions of Allegheny preferred stock.

Missouri Pacific had borrowed $23,000,000 direct from the Morgan banks, and this debt fell due. As the railroad was not able to repay, it applied to the Reconstruction Finance Corporation for a loan. An Interstate Commerce Commission minority report by Joseph B. Eastman recommended that such a loan not be granted, since it would have no effect other than to relieve J. P. Morgan and Company and its banks of a bad debt. But here the Morgan influence over President Hoover came in handy, and the R.F.C. made the loan in the face of contrary expert opinion. It was subsequently demonstrated that the Missouri Pacific prior to seeking the loan, had falsified its balance sheet, showing cash on hand that it did not have. Soon after the Morgan banks had been bailed out with public funds by the R.F.C., the Missouri Pacific was allowed to slump into bankruptcy.

A memorandum found in 1936 in the files of J. P. Morgan and Company by the Senate Interstate Commerce Committee indicated that this firm knew as of January, 1933, at the very latest, if it did not know earlier, that the railroad's statement to the R.F.C. was false. But the banking house notified neither the government nor the securities holders.

The Guaranty Trust Company underwrote an issue of $30,000,000 of Van Sweringen Corporation notes in 1930. Part of the proceeds of this issue, on which the public lost $15,759,000, was to be used to buy Cleveland real-estate properties. At the time the notes were issued many of the properties were losing money; moreover, the assets of the Cleveland Terminals Building Company, a subsidiary, were written-up by $16,000,000 net prior to the issuance of the notes, thereby making the Van Sweringen Corporation appear more substantial than it actually was.

As to the Van Sweringen's Chesapeake and Ohio Railroad, the Senate Committee on Interstate Commerce reported that, in violation of an order of the Interstate Commerce Commission in 1926 prohibiting a merger, the Virginia Transportation Corporation was

formed to consolidate the Van Sweringen railroads in the East; that
in 1930 Chesapeake and Ohio became a party to a dummy option,
with a dummy intermediary, in order to acquire the Chicago and
Eastern Illinois Railroad "in avoidance of the Interstate Commerce
Commission jurisdiction, and in defiance of the act of Congress";
that Chesapeake and Ohio and the Virginia Transportation Corporation in 1930 and 1931, and afterward, falsified their books to show
cash on hand which they did not possess; that in 1930 C. and O. issued $38,000,000 of stock ostensibly for improvements and used it
to buy stock in other companies in "outright violation of the act
of Congress and a flouting of I.C.C. jurisdiction;" that in 1930 and
1931 C. and O. lent millions of dollars to a stock-market syndicate
which manipulated the Chicago and Great Western Railway and
which established "improper relations between shippers' representatives and the railroad"; that through this syndicate C. and O. obtained dividends which it caused Chicago and Great Western im-
prudently and improperly to declare, necessitating a call by the
Chicago and Great Western upon the R.F.C. for a government loan;
that in 1931 the C. and O. used a dummy to make a secret loan to
the Chicago and Eastern Illinois; that in 1932 the C. and O. caused
the C. and E. I. to obtain a loan from the R.F.C. to reimburse the C.
and O.; that in 1932 C. and O. "entered into a fake option arrangement
with Allegheny for the purpose of acquiring control of Nickel Plate
and Erie without complying with the act of Congress and in defiance of the jurisdiction of the I.C.C."; that the C. and O. then used
false bookkeeping entries to conceal this transaction; that the C. and
O. concealed $50,000,000 used to buy stocks in other companies;
etc., etc.

Certain scattered aspects of the Van Sweringen scandal deserve
brief attention. Flotation by the Guaranty Company of the Van
Sweringen Corporation note issue was characterized in 1937 by
Senator Burton K. Wheeler, chairman of a Senate investigating committee, as "slipshod business" and "purely a wildcat proposition." In
anticipation of the note issue the Van Sweringen Corporation "wrote
up" the value of lands it owned by $25,535,000 gross. Fifteen mem-
bers of the board of governors of the New York Stock Exchange
were permitted to participate in underwriting Allegheny Corpora-

tion stocks and bonds, receiving securities at less than offering price before they were listed. As to whether Allegheny Corporation was sound enough to be listed at all, J. M. B. Hoxey, Stock Exchange listing expert, in a memorandum found by Senate investigators in the Stock Exchange files, wrote: "In commenting upon this type of company I have heretofore called attention to certain possible weaknesses in the financial structure and to the possibility that such corporations may come to be regarded as anti-social and thus to be the object of political attack."

Nine officers and directors of commercial banks that participated in the 1930 rescue loan of $39,500,000 to the Van Sweringens had received personal loans from J. P. Morgan and Company, it was shown. The Senate committee also produced evidence that Chase Bank was envious of Morgan's Van Sweringen toy. E. R. Tinker, vice-president of the Chase Bank, in 1922 wrote to Wiggin: "I am rapidly coming to the conclusion that we will have to put our heads down and go into this railroad financing in the same fashion that we went after the foreign business—in other words, without respect for anybody. . . . The allotments we are receiving from both the Corner [J. P. Morgan and Company] and Kuhn, Loeb in this railroad business are simply a farce. . . ."

A letter in 1920 from a Cleveland investment banker to Tinker, advising him how to proceed in negotiating with O. P. Van Sweringen for securities business, bears out the suspicion that the Van Sweringens were not overly bright pawns of J. P. Morgan and Company, for the writer said O. P. Van Sweringen was not always "facile and clear" about how to get what he wanted done.

At all stages J. P. Morgan and Company played a highly questionable role in the Van Sweringen situation. The firm in February, 1929, underwrote 3,500,000 Allegheny common shares. While market prices were held at $31-$35 a share, 1,250,000 shares were secretly allotted to "insiders" at $20 each, having the effect of creating a hidden pool to which was distributed an immediate market profit of $13,750,000. Most of the pool shares were taken by the Morgan partners themselves, but there was also a wide distribution of stock to clients, corporation executives, Stock Exchange officials, bank and insurance presidents, and political figures. This distribution, as the

Banking and Currency Committee found, was a means of increasing
the influence of the firm, because the stock allotments had a value
tantamount to a gift of money.

Each allotment of 1,000 shares at $20 per share had a differential
value of $11,000 while the market price stood at $31 a share. Among
the political figures who received stock were Secretary of the Navy
Charles Francis Adams, 1,000 shares; former Secretary of War Newton D. Baker, 2,000 shares; former Secretary of the Treasury William
Gibbs McAdoo, now Senator from California, 500 shares; John J.
Raskob, chairman of the Democratic National Committee at the
time, 2,000 shares; and William H. Woodin, in 1933 the Secretary of
the Treasury, 1,000 shares. Mrs. S. Parker Gilbert, wife of the Agent
General for Reparation Payments who is now a Morgan partner
and who in the early 1920's worked out the mechanics of the Mellon
tax-reduction program while serving as Assistant Secretary of the
Treasury, got 500 shares. Members of the wealthiest families who
shared in the stock melon were George F. Baker, 10,500 shares;
Nicholas F. Brady, 2,000 shares; Horace Havemeyer, 1,000 shares;
Arthur Curtiss James, 1,000 shares; Clarence H. Mackay, 1,000 shares;
Richard E. Mellon, 6,000 shares; and Albert G. Milbank, 600 shares.
Charles E. Mitchell and Albert H. Wiggin were each given 10,000
shares, a transfer of value amounting in each case to $110,000. Walter
C. Teagle, president of the Standard Oil Company of New Jersey,
received 1,500 shares. Myron C. Taylor (U. S. Steel) and Alfred P.
Sloan, Jr. (General Motors), each got 10,000 shares.

J. P. Morgan and Company arranged these "preferential lists" for
insiders in other stock issues as well. When stock of Standard Brands,
Inc., was offered in July, 1929, the firm let out 722,600 shares at $10
below the market, or a bonus of $7,226,000 to the recipients. When
United Corporation stock was sold 600,000 units were released to a
favored few at twenty-four points under the market price, a distribution of $14,400,000 before the public bought. When Johns-Manville
stock was offered at $79 a share in 1927 the firm let out 343,450 shares
at 47½ and 56,550 shares at 57½, a total price differential of more
than $13,000,000.

The Standard Brands offering was worth $10,000 per thousand
shares to each insider from the start. It went to persons influential in

the control of national affairs. Among those who got stock were Calvin Coolidge, who had acted under the advice of a Morgan partner while in the White House, 3,000 shares, or $30,000; Bernard M. Baruch, recognized for his war and other services and for his influential position in the Democratic Party, 4,000 shares; Charles D. Hilles, Republican National Committeeman for New York, 2,000 shares; Norman H. Davis, later appointed United States ambassador-at-large and a participant in diplomatic negotiations of immense interest to J. P. Morgan and Company, 500 shares; Mrs. S. Parker Gilbert, 500 shares; William G. McAdoo, 1,000 shares; John J. Raskob, 500 shares; H. Edmund Machold, former New York Republican State Committee chairman, 2,000 shares; William H. Woodin, 1,000 shares; and William Boyce Thompson, 2,500 shares. Members of the wealthiest families who participated were Richard B. Mellon, 5,000 shares; Horace Havemeyer, 1,000 shares; Guggenheim brothers, 5,000 shares; Marshall Field, 2,000 shares; Nicholas F. Brady, 5,000 shares; and Albert G. Milbank, 500 shares. The remaining participants were Morgan partners and strategic corporation, banking, and insurance executives.

While United Corporation stock was offered to the public at $99 in January, 1929, insiders got it for $75 a share, or a bonus of $24,000 per thousand shares. Political figures who were cut in included William G. McAdoo, 250 shares; John J. Raskob, 2,500 shares; Edgar Rickard, personal financial adviser to Herbert Hoover, 400 shares; and J. Henry Roraback, Republican boss of Connecticut, 1,000 shares. The executive heads of many corporations like General Motors, United States Steel, Standard Oil of New Jersey, and Aluminum Company each received substantial blocks of stock. Wiggin and Mitchell received 4,000 and 7,000 shares, respectively, or $96,000 and $168,000. Members of the wealthiest families who participated were Nicholas F. Brady, 3,000 shares; Lawrence P. Fisher, 2,000 shares; Max C. Fleischmann, 1,000 shares; Arthur Curtiss James, 2,000 shares; E. H. Manville, 1,000 shares; Clarence H. Mackay, 1,000 shares; and Richard B. Mellon, 5,000 shares. The Philadelphia office of J. P. Morgan and Company had Drexels, Biddles and Berwinds, as well as two Pennsylvania judges and George Wharton Pepper, former senator, on its United Corporation "favor" list.

There were no persons of influence in the financial markets who did not have the sanction of the wealthiest and most responsible families, and this statement applies to Ivar Kreuger, the Swedish adventurer, as well as to Samuel Insull, the cockney immigrant who started his career as secretary to Thomas A. Edison. Kreuger, for example, had Percy A. Rockefeller among the directors of his hodgepodge pyramid that caused Americans losses of nearly $200,000,000. He gained entrance to the American capital market through Lee, Higginson and Company, ultrarespectable Boston and New York firm that had long maintained close relations with J. P. Morgan and Company. After Kreuger committed suicide in 1932 the unique blame for the failure of his grandiose enterprises was shouldered upon him and it was said that he had "deceived" his collaborators. There was no official inquiry into the collapse; information brought out was developed in a private creditors' investigation. All law enforcement agencies, state and Federal, refused to touch the case, although the creditors' hearings turned up many peculiar aspects involving prominent persons of wealth and standing. It was shown, of course, that Kreuger had had no difficulty in obtaining bank loans, both from the Morgan banks and from Chase National; nobody, it appeared, had troubled to inquire into what he was doing with the money, and when the banks became alarmed they simply called the loans and left the public "holding the bag."

The report of the Senate Banking and Currency Committee (1933) states flatly that "the investment bankers were responsible for the provisions in the Kreuger and Toll bond indentures which occasioned tremendous losses to the American investing public. In 1929, under the leadership of Lee, Higginson and Co., a syndicate composed of that firm, Clark, Dodge & Co., Brown Bros. & Co., Guaranty Co. of New York, National City Co. of New York, Union Trust Co. of Pittsburgh [Mellon], and Dillon, Read & Co., purchased $26,500,000 of the $50,000,000 five per cent secured gold debentures of Kreuger and Toll Co. The price to the syndicate was 96 less three and a half per cent. The indenture agreement covering the $50,000,000 five per cent secured gold debentures of Kreuger & Toll Co., dated March 1, 1929, provided for the deposit with the trustee or depositary of certain bonds specifically designated as security for the debentures. . . .

Under the debenture agreement Kreuger & Toll Co. had at all times the right to withdraw any part of the eligible securities deposited and to substitute for any portion thereof other eligible securities. . . ."

The joker here was that "eligible securities" are defined in financial practice as securities of any community of three hundred thousand persons or more. Under this sanction dubious securities of Balkan and Central European states and cities were substituted for good securities, such as French government bonds.

Samuel Insull has been presented by the newspapers as another individualistic adventurer who worked his way into the confidence of investors without outside assistance. This was not the case. Insull was thrust forward in Chicago by the leading families of the city, and his most distinguished sponsor in the camp of great wealth was the Marshall Field family, owner of Marshall Field and Company and the largest real estate proprietor in Chicago. Since the day of Marshall Field I this family has been especially interested in public utilities, whose operation can seriously affect real-estate values.

Members of the Field family and leading executives of Marshall Field and Company were deeply concerned in the Insull enterprises. Stanley Field, nephew of Marshall Field, was indicted with Insull and others of his collaborators for allegedly using the mails to defraud. After Insull's dethronement, with a pension, the Insull properties fell into the hands of a group dominated by executives of Marshall Field and Company and of banks in which the Marshall Field family has interests. Insull, like Kreuger, had no difficulty getting loans from the leading banks, both of the Morgan and the Rockefeller camps, and of getting the securities affiliates of these leading banks to help in unloading holding company securities upon the public. Like Kreuger and the Van Sweringens, Insull was just an agent who failed to make good. An example of a typical successful agent of a wealthy family, however, is John J. Raskob, of the Du Pont camp, who took the leading part in the General Motors promotion after the Morgan-Du Pont bloc had wrested the company from W. C. Durant. Bernard M. Baruch and the late William Boyce Thompson (died 1932) are other typical examples of the successful financial agent.

The story of the extralegal functioning of the wealthy families has, unfortunately, no beginning and no end. Dipping into the situation at any point, with respect to any dominant family, we find the same story. Electric Bond and Share Company, under Morgan domination, in 1927 consolidated various of its properties and engineered a three-for-one stock split-up. "The investments which were formerly carried by the 'old' Electric Bond and Share Company at $148,501,290.79," said the Federal Trade Commission, "were 'written-up' to $547,703,118.18, the increase representing a 'write-up' of $399,201,827.39, an amount which almost staggers the imagination."

Otto H. Kahn admitted that he engaged in spurious stock transactions with members of his family in order to show income-tax losses. Pierre du Pont and John J. Raskob exchanged with each other $27,000,000 of securities in order to show 1929 "losses," later re-exchanging the securities. Only five Morgan partners out of seventeen paid income taxes in 1930, and none paid any in 1931 and 1932. Thomas S. Lamont, a partner and son of the firm's senior partner, established tax losses of $114,807 for 1930 by selling securities to his wife and later repurchasing them. Another partner set up family trusts in order to be able to show technically deductible "losses" where he had actually made a profit.

But in the late Spring of 1937 J. P. Morgan himself, returning from Europe, showed the jovial contempt of his clan for orderly governmental processes by stating for public consumption that he thought any man was "a fool" not to avail himself of every technical loophole in the tax laws. Blame for tax avoidance he placed upon the shoulders of Congress, which should, he indicated, draw up laws in such a way as to defy the ingenuity of the most subtle, specialized legal minds. Coming on the eve of a government inquiry into widespread tax evasion by the rich, Morgan's statement had the appearance of a preliminary defense of off-color practices by his firm. And, indeed, soon afterward it came out that Thomas W. Lamont had long avoided taxes by means of the Beech Corporation, a personal holding company.

Depredations of the character delineated here were not confined to the 1929 period, however. In 1933 a stock-market pool was formed in stock of the Libbey-Owens Ford Glass Company. Included in it were the Hyva Corporation (family company of Harry F. Sinclair), Walter P. Chrysler, Kuhn, Loeb and Company, Lehman Brothers, and Joseph P. Kennedy, who subsequently became chairman of the Securities and Exchange Commission. Although none of the members of this pool put up any cash, merely trading on stock optioned to them by the company, they made $395,238.12 by dealing in a million shares over a period of five months.

As recently as December, 1936, it was brought out by the Federal Securities and Exchange Commission that David M. Milton, son-in-law of John D. Rockefeller, Jr., and New York lawyer, had engaged in practices that would have delighted Flagler, Rogers, and Archbold, and might have earned a pat on the shoulder from the elder J. P. Morgan. The Securities and Exchange Commission learned that Milton, by the expenditure of $13,000 and the use of stock of an inactive insurance company, had gained control over investment trusts with assets of $218,000,000. David Schenker, counsel for the Commission, characterized Milton as "the Van Sweringen of the investment-trust field." Although John D. Rockefeller, Jr., had apparently nothing to do with the operation, Milton, an obscure lawyer, obtained entry into high finance by reason of the fact that he was married to a Rockefeller and in earlier New York real-estate operations was assisted by his father-in-law. He was forced to admit the impropriety of the investment-trust operations.

Skipping back at random to 1925 we find the Chicago, Milwaukee and St. Paul Railroad in bankruptcy. Leading stockholders had been the William and Percy Rockefeller families, the Ogden Armour family, and the Harkness family. With the exception of the Harknesses, these interests secretly sold out before the collapse. The dominant stockholding interests were, however, responsible for policies that caused losses of millions to stock and bondholders, for the difficulties went back to the expenditure of $180,000,000 for the electrification of the western lines. The electrification program drew its big copper supplies from the Anaconda Copper Mining Company and its power from the Montana Power Company, then a subsidiary of Anaconda. Electrification was of benefit only to Anaconda, on whose board sat William Rockefeller with John D. Ryan, also a director of the Milwaukee road. The I.C.C. in 1928 condemned the electric power contracts of the railroad with the Montana Power Company on the ground that they obligated the railroad to pay for power it did not use. The expenses of the receivership proceedings, handled by lawyers for the controlling interests, were $6,500,000 and were charged against the railroad. The I.C.C. started to investigate the huge receivership fees, but was restrained by an injunction sustained by the United States Supreme Court. Charles Evans Hughes represented the Rockefeller interests in the litigation and John W. Davis represented J. P. Morgan and Company. The wealthy families, it may be remarked, resent investigations of any kind.

More recently we find the manipulation of the Van Sweringen properties continued even while a Senate investigation of railroads was under way. Two obscure groups of men in rapid succession took control of the Van Sweringen (Morgan) railroad empire. In 1935 George A. Ball, glass jar manufacturer of Muncie, Ind., was sold control of the $3,000,000,000 of assets by J. P. Morgan and Company for $275,000. At this rate, as Charles A. Beard wrote in *The New Republic,* an ordinary man could with $92 buy control of $1,000,000 of other people's money. "A workman," Dr. Beard continued, "who has not more than $9.20 to invest could purchase control of $100,000 of other people's money. A schoolboy who cannot put up more than a dime, could buy control of $1,000 of other people's money, and could vote himself into enough emoluments to make out of the use of that $1,000 ten cents for candy every day of the year. . . . It has been estimated that the total wealth of the United States is about $350,000,000,000. On the ratio employed when the Morgan firm sold to Mr. Ball of Muncie, control of all the wealth of the United States could be purchased for some $32,000,000."

Ball vested the controlling interest in a specially created "philanthropic and religious foundation," thereby avoiding tax assessments on a large part of the usufructs of the transaction. Such assessments might very easily have taken all the cash out of Ball's small personal fortune.

In April, 1937, Ball sold control of these $3,000,000,000 of assets to two obscure New York Stock Exchange brokers. One of them, Robert R. Young, had been associated for a long time with the Du

Ponts and General Motors, so that he was not far removed from J. P. Morgan and Company. Young put up $255,000 and his partner, Frank F. Kolbe, put up an additional amount which assured Ball's religious and philanthropic enterprise a profit of thirteen hundred per cent for the trouble of taking temporary charge of $3,000,000,000. From the time Ball took control of the railroad system until he sold it, the book profit on the controlling common stock was seventy thousand per cent, according to *The New Republic,* June 16, 1937. The unusual character of the transaction was indicated by Ball's willingness to relinquish shares showing him a profit of seventy thousand per cent and instead to take a profit of a mere thirteen hundred per cent.

Before Young and Kolbe purchased Ball's controlling stock, Kolbe, as the Senate committee disclosed, discussed the question of control with the Van Sweringen brothers, J. P. Morgan and Company, the First National Bank of New York, and Donaldson Brown, a Du Pont son-in-law, of General Motors Corporation. Both brokers denied, however, that they were interested in control, although they said they opposed any special legislation which would remove control from the shares that J. P. Morgan and Company had placed into the hands of Ball.

The foregoing chapter gives only a very partial account of the malpractices of the rich in the period 1917-1937. The records of the Federal Trade Commission, the Interstate Commerce Commission, the Securities and Exchange Commission, and various Senate investigating committees not cited in this account contain a vast amount of additional material of a nature similar to the data here presented. In brief, the narrative given here is neither overdrawn nor does it represent a one-sided selection of facts designed to prove a preconceived thesis.

Behind all of these practices are people, the richest and, presumably, most responsible people in the country. The wealth they possess confers upon them immunity to carry on irregular but profitable activities which the ordinary person, devoid of wealth and power, might possibly desire to carry on, but cannot. Malpractice itself has become a monopoly.

# VII

## The Press of the Plutocracy

JOURNALISM, which shapes, modifies, or subtly suggests public attitudes and states of mind, morbidly attracts the owners of the great fortunes, for whose protection against popular disapproval and action there must be a constantly running defense, direct or implied, specific or general. The protective maneuvers often take the form, in this plutocratic press, of eloquent editorial assaults upon popular yearnings and ideas.

The journalism of the United States, from top to bottom, is the personal affair—bought and paid for—of the wealthy families. There is little in American journalism today, good or bad, which does not emanate from the family dynasties. The press lords of America are actually to be found among the multimillionaire families.

Newspapers all over the world exist, and have existed, in the service of economic and political power rather than in that of truth and noble ideals. This distinction should clarify at the outset a highly complicated field of human activity, and should indicate at once that America's millionaires have not been guilty, in their journalistic preoccupation, of perpetrating some unusual crime against the ostensible sanctity and purity of the press. Yet, in saying that newspapers do not exist to serve truth, it does not follow that they never serve truth and are never actuated by idealism, although truth in established journalism is always secondary, and very often is incidental, even accidental.

If newspapers print truth, as their proprietors and directors fiercely avow in their understandable endeavor to retain influence over the public mind—then truth has many colors, as one may learn by reading the sharply differentiated accounts of identical events in the world press. If as much difference of opinion about facts and their

244

meanings existed among scientists, if as much difference of opinion about the meaning of language existed among grammarians, as exists among the newspapers of the nations about the events of the day, this would indeed be a fantastic world.

The journalistic differences, however, concern power rather than truth, and only reflect the international differences of economic interest of the dominant classes of the respective nations. And while on the international plane one finds a sharp difference of opinion among the newspapers of the nations (except when their respective Foreign Offices are in agreement), one usually finds a striking uniformity of opinion in the newspapers within each national boundary. This national uniformity of press opinion merely reflects the central control of the national press by the dominant national class.

In Russia the press is controlled by the Communist Party, in Germany by the National Socialist (Fascist) Party, and in Italy by the Fascist Party. And in the United States it is controlled, on the political plane, through the Republican and Democratic Parties, with about seventy-five per cent of the press organs under the tutelage of the Republican Party. As American politics, like English and French politics, is pluralistic in composition, the American press is subject in its political context, like the English and French press, to practical operation by the individual financial groups that support the political parties, although a major part of the press in all three countries is subsidized, owned, controlled, or operated directly by the political parties.

American popular journalism (as distinct from trade, scientific, religious, and fraternal journalism) exists in three broad layers of which sharp account must be taken. The bottom layer consists of the directly controlled and financed political party press; immediately above this lies the layer of "independent" newspaper entrepreneurs, many of whom have been cemented by pecuniary success or political affiliation to the inner circle of great wealth, most of whom operate their newspapers as businesses, and all of whom are dependent for most of their revenue upon the good will of the wealthy families which control the bulk of advertising; and above this layer are the organs, directly owned, of the wealthy families themselves. These latter are, for the most part, the biggest metropolitan newspapers and the great national magazines. These are the personal organs of the sixty families.

As to the politically subsidized bottom layer, which is the rural and small-town press, Frank R. Kent, political editor of the conservative Baltimore *Sun,* writes:

Practically 75 per cent of the county press—the smaller papers of the country, are straight Republican. The remaining 25 per cent are Democratic. . . . Many of the owners and editors of the county press not only depend largely upon party support for the existence of their papers, but are themselves interested and active in party politics. . . . There are approximately 18,000 daily, weekly, and semi-weekly newspapers in the United States. Of this number 15,000 can be classed as strictly party county press. No such thing as fairness in political fights is attempted in these papers.[1]

Sensitively responsive to the two big political parties, but mainly to the Republican Party, this small-town and rural press derives a decisive portion of its revenue from the state and national political committees, and is as attentive to the prejudices of the ruling families which finance the political parties as if the ruling families owned it directly. Large portions of the county press, as we shall see, are actually owned by members of either the first, second, or third group of the rich ruling families.

In the layer of "independent" newspapers just above this one finds many individuals, owners of many large newspapers, who are in the publishing business primarily as professional politicians. Others are publishers for commercial profit, dependent for advertising revenues upon the good will of the corporations controlled by the wealthy families. Very little will be said here, however, about advertising control.

The middle layer of "independent" newspapers, which today includes most notably the Scripps-Howard chain, has been the only socially wholesome feature of the American press. In this division belonged Joseph Pulitzer, the only successful metropolitan newspaper publisher who, in the recent industrial period, consistently criticized the powerful and wealthy figures of all camps.

Since the World War it has been a phenomenon of American journalism that more and more newspapers from this "independent" stratum have gone out of business. Nearly one thousand newspapers have, in fact, succumbed, and this phenomenon has been a logical journalistic accompaniment to the growth and concentration of finance capital, whose spreading influence has obviated the need of various news organs which once existed merely to propagate the special points of view of many commercial or industrial groups.

It is with the top group of newspapers owned directly by the wealthy families, or directly controlled, that we are mainly concerned. Remarks about other newspapers are made solely for the sake of clarification. It is one of the hallmarks of the richest families that they virtually all own, or secretly control, one or more newspapers or magazines.

The ascertainable journalistic connections of the wealthy families are, or have recently been, as follows:

### THE ROCKEFELLER FAMILY

So far as can be learned, the Rockefellers have given up their old policy of owning newspapers and magazines outright, relying now upon the publications of all camps to serve their best interests in return for the vast volume of petroleum and allied advertising under Rockefeller control. After the J. P. Morgan bloc, the Rockefellers have the most national advertising of any group to dispose of. And when advertising alone is not sufficient to insure the fealty of a newspaper, the Rockefeller companies have been known to make direct payments in return for a friendly editorial attitude.

The Rockefellers, however, may still have secret direct interests in various publications, as they had in the recent past. When John D. Rockefeller was faced in the nineteenth century with a press barrage of denunciation he started acquiring newspapers and magazines right and left through hired agents. One of the first papers taken in hand by Rockefeller was the influential Oil City (Pa.) *Derrick,* which immediately changed from his worst foe to his staunchest apologist. This was in 1885. Charles Mathews, a Standard Oil employee, then purchased the Buffalo *People's Journal* and published it on behalf of Rockefeller. Next, Patrick Boyle, Rockefeller's agent in charge of the *Derrick,* acquired for Rockefeller a Toledo newspaper which launched into an attack upon opponents of the grant of natural-gas distribution franchises to two Rockefeller companies.

After this there was formed the Jennings Publishing Company which, as Attorney General Francis S. Monnet of Ohio later found, had contracts with 110 Ohio newspapers under the terms of which they were to publish laudatory articles and editorials about Standard Oil and the Rockefeller henchmen. In 1893 Rockefeller endowed the University of Chicago, which published the *Journal of Political Economy*, edited by Dr. J. Laurence Laughlin. Although the trust question was paramount in American politics of the day, this publication, devoted to politics and economics, never printed a word on the subject. Henry Demarest Lloyd, an editor of the Chicago *Tribune*, in 1894 published his brilliant *Wealth Against Commonwealth*, mainly devoted to an exposition of Rockefeller's antisocial misdeeds, and the precursor by many years of Ida Tarbell's *History of the Standard Oil Company*. Although a masterpiece in its genre, Lloyd's book was severely criticized by Prof. George Gunton in the *Social Economist*. Gunton, in support of his critique, misquoted to opposite effect a letter from Professor John A. Hobson, English economist, and was immediately denounced by Hobson. Gunton later became editor of *Gunton's Magazine* which, as it came out in 1908, was financed by the Rockefellers.

In this period Rockefeller called a conference to discuss his newly launched General Education Board. Among the conferees were Dr. Albert Shaw, editor of the *Review of Reviews*, and Walter Hines Page, editor of *World's Work*. Shaw and Page were made General Education Board trustees, and *World's Work* thereupon began publication, in serial form, of Rockefeller's apologetic memoirs.

Elbert Hubbard, the Industrial Relations Commission learned, was in the pay of Standard Oil, and published, in his influential periodical, *Fra*, eulogies and apologies for Rockefeller and the Standard Oil interests with respect to their Draconian labor policies.

The Rockefellers financed the *Manufacturers Record*, which gave them an audience of businessmen and industrialists who did not know they were being fed propaganda of a certain group. Archbold paid $1,250 to the *Southern Farm Magazine* for a year's subscription. Standard Oil also had entree to *The Outlook*, edited by Dr. Lyman

Abbott, for this publication was secretly financed for many years by James Stillman, president of the National City Bank of New York.

Abbott, to cite an example of how this remote editorial control worked, in 1906 warned his readers when Rockefeller was indicted in Ohio that an indictment was not a conviction. This was very true, although irrelevant. Abbott's attitude, however, is typical of the attitude of the entire American press today, when newspapers and magazines alike wander far afield in seeking at every turn excuses for the wealthy.

Concerning this same prewar period, the Senate Privileges and Elections Committee in 1912 unearthed a letter that Representative Sibley, the Standard Oil pay-off man in Washington, had written in 1905 to John D. Archbold. Sibley said, "An efficient literary bureau is needed, not for a day or a crisis but a permanent healthy control of the Associated Press and kindred avenues. It will cost money but will be the cheapest in the end."

"Apparently something like that was done," says John T. Flynn, Rockefeller's biographer. "An old journalist named J. I. C. Clarke was installed as a publicity man." There followed a perceptible break in the press criticism of Rockefeller. The *Woman's Home Companion* published "How the World's Richest Man Spends Christmas," *The Saturday Evening Post,* owned by the Curtis-Bok dynasty, published an article by Archbold in which he defended Standard Oil.

The United States Industrial Commission, investigating the massacre of Rockefeller workers at Ludlow, Colorado, brought out that Jesse G. Northcutt, attorney for the Rockefellers' Colorado Fuel and Iron Company, owned the Trinidad *Chronicle-News* and the Trinidad *Advertiser*; the company itself owned the Pueblo *Chieftain.* In other industrial regions the Rockefellers also secretly controlled local newspapers through executives and lawyers. Northcutt, incidentally, who was corruptly elected public prosecutor in the Colorado Fuel and Iron region, indicted the strikers. Arms and munitions, the government investigators found, were stored for the strikebreakers in the *Chronicle-News* office.

The same Industrial Commission heard from Ivy L. Lee, Rockefeller's personal publicity man, that the Rockefellers planned to finance to the extent of $250,000 *Nation's Business,* published by the National Association of Chambers of Commerce, forerunner of the United States Chamber of Commerce.

During the Colorado Fuel and Iron Company strike Lee sent the newspapers hundreds of falsifying bulletins, while at the same time the Rockefellers were trying to buy control of the Denver *Rocky Mountain News.* They failed to get it, as they had earlier failed to get the *Ohio State Journal* of Columbus. The critical attitude of the press in general, and especially of the rural press, began to disappear, however, only when the Rockefellers started to advertise. The first widely advertised Rockefeller product was a mineral oil for internal use, said to have been devised solely as a means of placing advertising in hostile newspapers in a day when kerosene, Standard Oil's principal product, did not require advertising and would have excited unfavorable comment had it been advertised.[2] Axle grease was another product used as an advertising instrument.

According to C. W. Barron, Alfred C. Bedford of the Standard Oil Company financed John A. Sleicher's *Leslie's Weekly* to the extent of $300,000, and when Bedford lost interest the magazine abruptly suspended publication. *Harvey's Weekly* during and after the war was financed in turn by J. P. Morgan, James B. Duke, Thomas Fortune Ryan, and John D. Rockefeller at the rate of $100,000 annually, according to a statement by William Boyce Thompson.

And since 1920, according to evidence on the record, the Rockefellers have had more than an academic interest in the press of the nation, although they have cannily left direct ownership to associated Standard Oil families like the Harknesses and Whitneys. The Federal Trade Commission in its investigation of public utilities connected the Rockefeller enterprises directly with one instance of venal press control and indirectly with general control of many newspapers. The direct connection related to the Denver *Post,* in 1927. It was shown by the Federal Trade Commission in 1934 that the Standard Oil Company of New Jersey had sent to J. B. Luse, treasurer of the Colorado Interstate Gas Company, subsidiary of Standard Oil of New Jersey, a check for $350,000 which Luse cashed, turning over the money to the late Fred G. Bonfils, then publisher of the *Post.* The consideration involved was the *Post's* hostile attitude toward the validation of Denver natural gas rates. In return for this payment, the Trade Commission charged, the *Post* reversed its opposition to the gas rates.[3] At the same time, according to the Federal Trade Commission's showing, the Standard Oil Company remitted $50,000 for the mayor of Denver.

In 1929 the Federal Trade Commission revealed that the International Paper and Power Company had taken a sudden large financial interest in important daily newspapers, and as International Power was, and remains, under the aegis of the Chase National Bank group of New York, which the Rockefellers were then entering, the situation lay very close to the Rockefeller bailiwick if it was not indeed engineered primarily on behalf of the Rockefellers. The two largest public-utilities interests in the country are the Rockefeller and Morgan groups, so that the appalling general findings of the Federal Trade Commission in the public-utilities inquiry apply to these two blocs more than to any others. The International Paper Company, apart from the influence of Chase Bank directors over its affairs, included among its directors Herman H. Jennings, Ogden Phipps (Carnegie-U. S. Steel), and Ogden Reid, principal stockholder in the New York *Herald Tribune*. Reid resigned, but was soon replaced by Ogden L. Mills, his cousin and a minority stockholder in the *Herald Tribune*.

International Paper, it was revealed, owned secret interests in the Chicago *Daily News*, the Chicago *Daily Journal*, the Albany *Knickerbocker Press* (Gannett chain), the Albany *Evening News* (Gannett), the Boston *Herald-Traveller*, the Brooklyn *Eagle* (Gannett), the Augusta (Ga.) *Chronicle*, the Spartanburg (S. C.) *Herald Journal*, and the Ithaca *Journal News*, and had endeavored to purchase more than twenty-five additional metropolitan newspapers. After exposure International Paper divested itself of newspaper holdings and gave up negotiations for others.

The Rockefellers are connected very intimately with many of the leading newspaper dynasties. Edith Rockefeller, for example, married a McCormick. Individuals with whom the Rockefellers have close business connections own many newspapers directly. And the Harknesses and Whitneys today, as will be shown, exercise great press influence through direct ownership.

### J. P. MORGAN BLOC

This great private banking house has been as preoccupied with journalism, on behalf of its supporting families, as have the Rockefellers, probably even outranking Standard Oil in its consistent, pervasive, and unbroken interest in the press. More advertising is controlled by the J. P. Morgan junta than by any other single financial group, a factor which immediately gives the banking house the respectful attention of all alert independent publishers.

The first direct journalistic connection of J. P. Morgan and Company appears to have been made in 1887 when William M. Laffan, a drama critic, with money advanced to him by J. P. Morgan the elder, founded the New York *Evening Sun*. In 1897 Laffan acquired the *Morning Sun* from the Dana estate, and switched it to the slavish support of J. P. Morgan and Company. Both *Sun* papers were Morgan spokesmen on all issues. In the Panama Canal steal, for example, they spoke boldly for the Roosevelt-Bunau-Varilla program behind which Morgan and his henchmen lay concealed; and in private fights of Morgan with others of his class for financial and economic prerogatives these newspapers took Morgan's part. Morgan's *Sun*, for instance, opened fire particularly upon Stillman's thriving National City Bank, complaining of Treasury favoritism shown the Stillman-Rockefeller group in the McKinley Administration. Later this newspaper harried E. H. Harriman, as well as all others who dared oppose the Morgan bank.

In 1916 *The Sun* passed into the hands of Frank Munsey, who had long been functioning as a paid tool of Morgan, and Munsey merged it with the *Press* he had acquired in 1912.

Munsey has always been a mystery to rank-and-file journalists because of the way he bought and ruthlessly liquidated newspapers. His biographer, George Britt, who has admirably collected the main facts about his life, unfortunately fails to penetrate this mystery of a sane man who, seemingly for no reason, wrecked valuable newspaper properties. But after one reviews the long list of newspapers whose ruin Munsey encompassed at enormous cost; after one inquires into the policies of those newspapers; and after one takes into consideration Munsey's profitable association with the astute Perkins, there is really no longer any mystery. Munsey put to death newspapers that were inimical, in one way or another, to J. P. Morgan and Company, and founded newspapers that sang the praises of projects in which J. P. Morgan and Company happened to be concerned at a particular time or in a particular locality. Sometimes it was a newspaper opposed to some special public-utility grab of J. P. Morgan and Company which Munsey bought and throttled. Sometimes it was a newspaper that fought some local Morgan political favorite. At other times it was a liberal newspaper operated contrary to the general Morgan philosophy of pelf and plunder. But, always, it was a newspaper whose disappearance benefited J. P. Morgan and Company.

". . . practically, if not verbally, Munsey sold himself to the House of Morgan," says his biographer. "He enjoyed a community of interest, sang Morgan's song, was given an inside position in Morgan deals. Munsey was a Morgan tool."

Munsey, as we have seen, functioned under the direction of George W. Perkins. He first bought the New York *Star* in the 1890's. This paper had been secretly owned by Collis P. Huntington, the railroad magnate, who used it to boost his friends and to damn his foes. Munsey sold the paper back to Colonel John A. Cockerill, Huntington's deputy, and its name was changed to the *Morning Advertiser*; Hearst later bought it.

In 1901 Munsey bought the New York *Daily News* and the Washington *Times,* discontinuing the former in 1904 and selling the latter in 1917 to Hearst. In 1902 he bought the Boston *Journal* and killed it the next year along with the Boston *Evening News,* which he had founded. These acquisitions and discontinuances closely followed the flotation of the United States Steel Corporation and the International Harvester Company by J. P. Morgan and Company, in both of which enterprises the foundation of Munsey's $40,000,000 fortune was laid. The Munsey papers whooped it up for the new Morgan trusts.

In 1908 Munsey bought the Baltimore *News* and formed the Philadelphia *Times,* killing the former in 1915 and the latter in 1914. In 1916 the New York *Sun* was taken in, and in 1920 the two Bennett papers. In 1923 he took in the New York *Globe,* a liberal newspaper with a notable staff. Munsey promptly killed this paper, which had long been a thorn in Morgan's side. In 1924 he purchased the New York *Mail* from Henry L. Stoddard, and merged it with the *Telegram*. One of the *Mail's* leading secret stockholders for many years had been Morgan partner George W. Perkins.[4]

All these and many other transactions involved millions of dollars, garnered by Munsey in various Morgan stock-market pools.

After Munsey's death in 1925 *The Sun* and the New York *Telegram* (founded by the younger James Gordon Bennett) passed to the ownership of the Metropolitan Museum of Art; but as *The New York Times* truthfully commented: "Until the will was opened Mr. Munsey had never been known as a friend of the museum." J. P. Morgan, however, was chairman of the board of trustees of the museum, in the affairs of which his father had taken a leading hand much earlier.

The trustees of the Metropolitan Museum at the time Munsey willed his newspapers to it included Payne Whitney, Elihu Root, Edward S. Harkness, Arthur Curtiss James, Charles W. Gould, George F. Baker, George D. Pratt, George Blumenthal (Lazard Frères), and other representatives of the great families who turn up on every occasion where money or power is involved. Munsey's net estate amounted to $19,747,687, of which $17,305,594 was placed in the hands of J. P. Morgan and the Metropolitan Museum.

It was only logical for Munsey to return his fortune to the keeping of the banking house which had made it for him by methods already scanned. In 1926 *The Sun*, now an afternoon paper, was sold through the Munsey estate's principal executor, the Guaranty Trust Company (Morgan), to *The Sun's* leading executives, headed by William T. Dewart. Through the Guaranty Trust Company, Munsey in 1920 had purchased the New York *Herald* and the *Telegram* from the Bennett estate, whose executor the bank also was, in consonance with the close business and investment relations that existed between Morgan and Bennett; but Munsey in 1924 sold the *Herald* to the Reid-Mills family for $5,000,000, part cash, and it was merged with the *Tribune*.

*The Sun* executives are understood to have obtained the money to buy the paper for a reputed $11,000,000 in the form of a loan, a large part of which is still said to be outstanding, from the Guaranty

Trust Company. This loan does not appear among the admitted obligations of the Sun Publishing Company because it was privately made to the leading stockholders of the publishing company in another corporate guise as Sun Associates. One of these stockholders is Franz Schneider, former financial editor of *The Sun,* who also served as financial editor on T. W. Lamont's New York *Evening Post*; and Schneider is now, while still a big stockholder in the Sun Publishing Company, vice-president of the Newmont Mining Corporation (Morgan). Schneider holds the distinction of being the only journalist to participate in the special 1927–29 stock offerings of J. P. Morgan and Company. He received one thousand shares of Standard Brands, Inc. $10,000 below the market price; one thousand shares of United Corporation $24,000 below the market; one thousand shares of Johns-Manville $20,000 below the market, and five hundred shares of Allegheny Corporation $5,500 below the market. His total realizable profits from this source while on *The Sun* were $59,500. He was on the same road Munsey had traveled. *The Sun* has never, since Dana left it, lost sight of its function as a house organ of J. P. Morgan and Company, which it remains today in all details of its editorial and news policy.

While J. P. Morgan and Company had Munsey and Laffan serving as deputies, it also had other irons in the fire. Harvey on the Morgan financed *North American Review* and *Harper's Weekly* carried out Morgan policies. George W. Perkins, in addition to his relationship with Munsey, maintained exceptionally friendly relations with John C. Shaffer, publisher of the Chicago *Evening Post*, the Denver *Rocky Mountain News*, and the Indianapolis, Muncie, and Terre Haute (Ind.) *Stars.* The Shaffer papers forwarded policies that were, at most times, strikingly like the Morgan policies espoused by Munsey, Harvey, Laffan, and James Gordon Bennett. The latter, like Munsey in his magazines, published eulogies of the United States Steel Corporation while owning the company's stock. And like Munsey, Bennett appointed as his executor the Guaranty Trust Company, with Rodman Wanamaker, department-store magnate, as co-executor. Wanamaker then owned the Philadelphia *Record*; his family had once owned the Philadelphia *North American*. These, too, were pro-Morgan newspapers.

Perkins' successor as the Morgan press contact man was Thomas W. Lamont, of whom we shall have something to say very soon. In 1918 Lamont openly acquired the New York *Evening Post* from Oswald Garrison Villard, but sold it in 1922 to the Curtis family at a reputed loss of $2,000,000.

The *Post* had passed in 1883 into the hands of Henry Villard, promoter of the Northern Pacific Railroad, whose son Oswald inherited it. Under the younger Villard it became a liberal newspaper, quite out of step with the majority of the American press. But Lamont changed that, notably terminating Villard's critical attitude toward Wilson, and under Curtis the paper reverted swiftly to its Hamiltonian reactionism.

Soon after giving up the *Evening Post* Lamont privately financed Henry Seidel Canby, literary editor of the *Post,* in founding *The Saturday Review of Literature,* which has for nearly two decades given J. P. Morgan and Company a strategic foothold in the book-publishing business. As Lamont has continually footed deficits for this publication, which has given utterance to many Morgan theses, Canby must be considered a Morgan literary agent.

Lamont, however, has been less important as a newspaper owner than as a silent manipulator of the press. For many years he was a director of the Crowell Publishing Company, which publishes *The American Magazine, The Country Home, Collier's Weekly,* and *Woman's Home Companion,* all with huge national circulations. Since Lamont's departure the Morgan interest in Crowell has been represented by Director A. H. Lockett, who is also a director of the Newmont Mining Corporation with Franz Schneider; of Lamont, Corliss and Company (Lamont family enterprise); and of *News-Week* (Astor-Harriman-Mellon-Whitney-Cheney), national popular news magazine.

Perhaps the most direct and significant Morgan journalistic connection is with Time, Inc., publisher of the widely circulating *Time,* weekly news magazine of thoroughly reactionary orientation, *Fortune,* chief apologist for the wealthy families, *Life,* largest picture magazine, and *Architectural Forum.* For a brief period Time, Inc., published the now independent *Tide,* organ for advertising men, and Lamont's *Saturday Review of Literature.* According to the statement of ownership in the November, 1936, issue of *Fortune*, the leading stockholders of Time, Inc., are Brown Brothers Harriman and Company, private banking house (W. A. Harriman); J. P. Morgan and Company, (for the account of Henry P. Davison, a partner); F. Du Sossoit Duke; Mrs. Mimi B. Durant; Henry R. Luce, editor, founder, and college chum of Davison; William V. Griffin, trustee of the James C. Brady estate and director of the Bank of Manhattan Company and twenty-four other corporations; the Irving Trust Company (for the account of Elizabeth Busch Pool); the New York Trust Company (for the account of William Hale Harkness, Standard Oil); and the principal editors and executives. Time, Inc. is thus seen to be owned by the inner circle of contemporary American finance, and the policies of its publications down to the smallest detail consistently reflect its ownership.

Through various of its corporations J. P. Morgan and Company has maintained a direct hold over many newspapers, irrespective of any influence which exists by reason of the advertising at its disposal. The most notable example of such Morgan corporation control over newspapers was placed on the record before the war by Louis D. Brandeis in questioning for the government C. S. Mellen of the New Haven Railroad. Mellen admitted that more than one thousand New England newspapers were on the New Haven payroll for about $400,000 annually. As recently as 1920 the New Haven Railroad held at least $400,000 of bonds of the Boston *Herald*.[5]

This editorial influence over newspapers helped the New Haven unload its stock upon unsuspecting middle-class investors. Morgan control of other corporations may carry with it similar sinister influence over newspapers in other regions, although no record of this appears. The newspapers of Pennsylvania, for example, have for long been very cordial toward the United States Steel Corporation in its various skirmishes with public authority.

A current example of a Morgan connection with a great and influential newspaper property, *via* the Steel Corporation, exists with respect to the Chicago *Daily News*. Sewell L. Avery, president of Montgomery Ward and Company (Morgan) and the United States Gypsum Company, and a director of United States Steel, is a director of this big Chicago newspaper, whose principal stockholder is now

Colonel Frank L. Knox, Republican vice-presidential candidate in 1936. The *Daily News* board of directors is composed of men representing every large commercial bank of Chicago and the leading Morgan corporations of the Middle West. Knox, owner of the Manchester (N. H.) *Union-Leader*, in 1931 was introduced to the Chicago *Daily News* board by Charles G. Dawes, who arranged to have Knox and Theodore Ellis, New England textile manufacturer and publisher of the Worcester (Mass.) *Telegram*, acquire the largest equity in the paper from the estate of Walter F. Strong, who was the son-in-law of Victor Lawson, for many years the paper's owner. Strong bought the paper from the Continental Illinois Bank, to which Lawson had willed it in trust for charity. Knox bought Strong's controlling interest and paid off loans of the Dawes Central Republic Bank to Strong. Ellis, however, supplied most of the money.

Family connections, as in other fields, serve to extend the contacts of the Morgan group in journalism. The Lamont family, for example, is closely related to the Gardner Cowles family which owns the Des Moines *Register* and the *Tribune-Capital*, the Minneapolis *Star*, and various radio stations. The Cowles papers are leading Republican organs of the Middle West.

Where the direct, conscious Morgan influence in American journalism ends one cannot tell. It is, quite obviously, very great. Some additional Morgan press connections will be cited at the proper places.

### THE FORD FAMILY

Henry Ford has made only one known direct venture in journalism. This was with the Dearborn *Independent*, which after the war attained a weekly circulation of more than seven hundred thousand copies before it was discontinued in 1927. More than most publications of the magnates, the *Independent* was unspeakably vicious and narrow in its views, specializing in slanderous attacks on the Jews. Ford spent millions on this publication, either to indulge a childish whim or to pursue a policy of spreading dissension among people in order to divide their loyalties. Since the *Independent* stopped appearing Ford has taken to using the radio to spread his highly individualistic social philosophy, which can be classed as anarchistic.

The Ford radio commentator is W. J. Cameron, former editor of the *Independent.* Heavy Ford advertising gives the automobile manufacturer a respectful hearing throughout most of the American press.

## WHITNEYS, HARKNESSES, MELLONS, AND ASTORS

Both the Harkness and the Harriman families, we have seen, own direct interests in Time, Inc., whose *Fortune* lavishly praises from time to time the Harrimans and their enterprises and the Standard Oil families from the Rockefellers down, without neglecting to throw frequent bouquets at J. P. Morgan, J. P. Morgan and Company, and the Morgan partners. The Harrimans are also stockholders, with Vincent Astor and John Hay Whitney (Standard Oil) in the growing *News-Week* magazine, whose policy is straight Wall Street. W. A. Harriman participated with his sister and with Vincent Astor in financing *Today* (1933-36), weekly magazine edited by Professor Raymond Moley. After losing a good deal of money with this early partisan of the New Deal, which subsequently turned against it, Harriman and Astor bought a large interest early in 1937 in *News-Week.* There they joined a group of other important stockholders, which included Ward Cheney, of the Cheney silk family, John Hay Whitney, and Paul Mellon, son of Andrew W. Mellon.

Harriman and Astor put in $600,000 of new money and the original *News-Week* group put up $500,000 in addition to the $2,025,000 its members had already invested. *News-Week* is the rival of *Time* for remote influence over the more literate readers outside of New York, who are unable to find much significant national information in the exceedingly barren and provincial local newspapers. The largest stockholder in *News-Week,* however, is Starling W. Childs, public-utilities investment banker. Another large stockholder is Wilton Lloyd-Smith, Wall Street lawyer and director in various companies.

Although the American Astors have not been conspicuously connected with journalism prior to the past five years, the English branch of the Astor family, its fortune rooted in the United States, is, perhaps, the most influential journalistic family in the world, transcending Rothermeres, Hearsts, Beaverbrooks, and similar press lords in importance. Since 1922 John Jacob Astor has been the largest stockholder of *The Times* of London founded in 1775 by John Walter, coal merchant. The Walter family held the paper through four generations, but in 1908 it was sold to Lord Northcliffe for $1,552,000. After Northcliffe's death this newspaper, representing the highest Empire interests, was sold to John Jacob Astor and John Walter IV for $6,547,500. William Waldorf Astor, upon establishing himself in England late in the nineteenth century, immediately branched into journalism as a means of gaining a peerage. He acquired the *Pall Mall Gazette*, the London *Observer*, and other publications, some of which his family still owns.

The great influence of *The Times* in English affairs makes the Astor family one of the leading newspaper proprietors of the world. Although the policy of this newspaper is conservative, and even socially reactionary, it has never been accused of deliberately twisting facts in news accounts. In this respect it stands unchallenged by any American newspaper, as the *Manchester Guardian* stands without an American equal in the liberalism of its editorial and news columns.

Paul Mellon's ownership in *News-Week* apparently represents the first attempt of the Mellon family to function journalistically on a national scale. But for many years the Mellons have been in control of, and have directly financed, the newspapers of Pittsburgh and environs, notably in concert with the late Henry C. Frick. This was true of all the Pittsburgh newspapers when they were owned by Senator George T. Oliver (Republican), William Flinn, Republican boss, and Alexander P. Moore, Coolidge-Hoover diplomatic appointee.

The only big newspaper today in Pittsburgh that is inhospitable to the Mellon point of view, although not pointedly hostile, is the Scripps-Howard *Press*. The Hearst *Sun-Telegraph* and the Paul Block *Post-Gazette* (confidentially owned by Hearst) might just as well be published by the Mellon family, whose blatant local champions they are.

### THE DU PONTS

The Du Pont's Christiana Securities Company owns the Wilmington *Journal Every Evening* and the Wilmington *Morning News*, the only newspapers in Wilmington. During a wartime split in the

Du Pont family, Alfred I. du Pont bought the *Morning News* to use as a weapon against Senator Henry Algernon du Pont. Pierre du Pont, who was opposed to Alfred I., bought the *Journal* with which to fight back. Alfred I. lost a court decision in the matters at issue, was subsequently helped out by a loan arranged by Pierre through J. P. Morgan and Company, and relinquished the *Morning News* to Pierre. The Pierre du Pont faction also acquired the *Every Evening,* which they combined with the *Journal.* "Ever since," says John K. Winkler in his biography of the Du Ponts, "the newspapers have been operated like a department of the Du Pont company."

The journalistic influence of the Du Ponts is not confined within the borders of Delaware, by any means. Indeed, the indirect Du Pont press influence is very great, and the advertising the family has to bestow, owing to its ownership of twenty-five per cent of General Motors Corporation, of the E. I. du Pont de Nemours Company, and the United States Rubber Company, is vast. In General Motors, of course, the Du Ponts share control with J. P. Morgan and Company and the Fisher brothers of Detroit.

"It is evident that the power to withhold [advertising] contracts of such [great] dimensions must give Du Pont an immense potential influence," says Philip Noel-Baker in *The Private Manufacture of Armaments.* "This influence is the more dangerous, because it can be so easily, so naturally, and so secretly exerted through the routine and unrecorded conversations of the advertising managers on the two sides."

An example of the subterranean manifestation of the Du Pont will in the press was brought to light by the Senate Privileges and Elections Committee under Senator Kenyon in 1920. According to the testimony of Colonel William Boyce Thompson, the American Association of Foreign Language Newspapers was acquired for the purpose of controlling policies of four hundred foreign-language papers of five million circulation by the placing or withholding of advertising of big corporations. Thompson himself put $50,000 into the scheme, and other stockholders who contributed to a $400,000 fund were Cleveland H. Dodge, Andrew W. Mellon, Senator T. Coleman du Pont, John T. Pratt (Standard Oil), Samuel Insull, J. Ogden Armour, Daniel Guggenheim, and Francis Sisson, vice-president of the Guaranty Trust Company (Morgan). The purpose of the group, said Thompson, was to inspire "Americanism" in these newspapers; but suspicious Democratic Senators felt that the purpose of this organization's backers was rather to influence opinion on behalf of their financial interests and the Republican Party.

## McCORMICK DYNASTY

This, one of the industrial dynasties, is also a newspaper dynasty. A quarrel within the McCormick family over claims to Cyrus McCormick's reaper many years ago divided it into two warring factions, one of which retained its hold over the McCormick Harvester Works and the other of which became associated with Joseph Medill's Chicago *Tribune*. Community of interests appear to have healed this breach.

Katherine Medill, daughter of Joseph Medill, married Robert S. McCormick, diplomat; and Elinor Medill, another daughter, married Robert W. Patterson, an editor of the *Tribune*. The issues of the first marriage were Medill McCormick, United States Senator and editor of the *Tribune*, now deceased, and Robert R. McCormick, the present publisher of the *Tribune*. Issues of the second marriage were Joseph Medill Patterson and Eleanor Patterson. Patterson today is the publisher of the New York *Daily News*, which has the largest newspaper circulation in America, and Eleanor Patterson is the chief editor of Hearst's Washington *Herald*. Hearst recently leased the paper to her.

Although the Chicago *Tribune* and the New York *Daily News* are owned by the same group, their policies often differ, in deference to local prejudices and the local requirements of the owners. The *Tribune*, which has the second largest circulation of any American newspaper, was bitterly anti-New Deal in 1936 while the *Daily News* was a New Deal supporter. Some of the differences between the two newspapers stem from the dissimilar personalities of Patterson and McCormick.

Patterson was once a liberal reformer, who turned Socialist after holding office in the Dunne Administration in Chicago, 1905–07. After serving in the World War, from which he emerged as a captain, Patterson settled down to make the *Daily News*, founded in 1919 in order to elude wartime income surtaxes, a paying proposition. McCormick, who was president of the $60,000,000 Chicago Sanitary District from 1905 to 1910, has always been a conformist and reactionary.

So intransigent has McCormick been in Chicago's turbulent journalistic and political affairs that in recent years, fearing assassination, he has been driven like a Chinese war-lord in an armored car between his office and his Wheaton, Illinois, estate. However, this is not extraordinary, as most of the wealthy families surround themselves today with private armed guards. The Chicago *Tribune* from 1900 to 1912, faced by the violent encroachments of Hearst gunmen on its circulation bailiwick, elected to defend its position with hireling guns, and in a period of bloody warfare extending in its phase of climax over more than two years Chicago gang warfare was born.[6] Chicago gangsters were former newspaper gunmen, who learned from the publishers' lawyers how to circumvent the law.

Chicago *Tribune* ownership is vested in two thousand shares of stock, of $100 par value each, of which 1,050 were left in the Medill Trust, founded in 1899 by Joseph Medill, to Robert W. Patterson and Robert S. McCormick and their wives; the four children of both unions have since inherited. Medill McCormick, eldest son of Robert S., married Ruth Hanna, a daughter of Mark Hanna, who was himself a newspaper proprietor and whose family retains social and political status mainly by press ownership; Ruth Hanna now participates, since the death of her first husband, in *Tribune* profits as well as in those of the Rockford (Ill.) *Morning Star* and the Rockford *Register-Republican,* which she owns on her own account.

None of the trust beneficiaries owns any stock (except for ten directors' qualifying shares held by McCormick and Eleanor Patterson), a useful arrangement for evading inheritance taxes. Only income is received, and this will in future be passed on to heirs through the establishment of additional trusts. Medill McCormick in 1925, for example, established for his wife a trust the sole function of which is to relay income received from the Medill Trust.

The next largest slice of the Chicago *Tribune* is owned by the Lloyd family, for whose account five hundred shares exist. Henry Demarest Lloyd, editor of the *Tribune* who wrote the first exposure of Rockefeller and was the first of the "muckrakers," married a daughter of William Bross, who owned the Chicago *Democratic Press*, merged in 1858 with the *Tribune* which Medill founded in 1847. One of Lloyd's sons is William Bross Lloyd, former radical who has been called "Chicago's millionaire Communist" although he is no longer a member of the Communist Party. The Lloyds, and the Cowles family, which owns 305 shares, have nothing to say about the management or the policies of the two papers, but they endorse them.

Patterson and McCormick for a time owned *Liberty Magazine,* on which they consistently lost money. They exchanged this publication with Bernarr Macfadden for the Detroit *Mirror,* a tabloid, which they discontinued after losing $2,000,000 in sixteen months. They could afford to lose, however, as the earnings of the Chicago and New York newspapers were $10,000,000 in 1928 and in 1929, and were $6,700,000 in 1933, when each of the two thousand Chicago Tribune, Inc., shares had a value of $26,800.

The Chicago *Tribune* is the most violently reactionary newspaper in the country and enjoys a virtual monopoly in its local morning field. It shamelessly distorts news, twists facts, and suppresses information in the interests of Robert R. McCormick and his class, as we shall see presently. For antisocial bias no newspaper could conceivably be worse than the Chicago *Tribune.*

### GUGGENHEIM FAMILY

Very little is known of the press interests of the Guggenheim family, and it is probable that this group, like the Bakers, Fishers, Fields, Vanderbilts, Berwinds, Wideners, and others, has been content to string along journalistically behind J. P. Morgan and Company. Yet in localities where the Guggenheims have had mining and political interests they have taken a direct ownership of newspapers. The Guggenheims, for example, owned the Leadville *Herald Democrat* prior to the election of Senator Guggenheim by means of fraud and bribery, according to Harvey O'Connor, the Guggenheims' biographer. As it was the custom for mine proprietors throughout the West to own publications in all the regions where they had profitable titles, it is probable that the Guggenheims have owned or subsidized other publications.

But in recent years the Guggenheims have been content to make their major press influence felt by joining other wealthy families in the financing of propaganda campaigns to which newspaper publishers are hospitable. Congress in 1919, for example, conducted an investigation of the National Security League, which had used the press to make a broadside newspaper attack upon the nation's legislature. It was found that the League was financed by Henry H. Rogers, William K. Vanderbilt, T. Coleman du Pont, Henry Clay Frick, Simon and Daniel Guggenheim, George W. Perkins, J. Pierpont Morgan, Nicholas F. Brady, and John D. Rockefeller. These were the very elements that had drawn huge profits from the war and expected to profit by the maintenance of huge armaments, the issue in question at the moment.

Through Bernard M. Baruch, who gave $47,500, the Guggenheims contributed to the League to Enforce Peace, formed in 1915 to carry on a systematic press campaign for drawing the United States into the war. Other contributors, and the amounts of their contributions, according to the findings of the Kenyon Committee, were Edward A. Filene, $28,100; Mrs. S. V. Harkness, $15,500; Edward S. Harkness, $15,500; Jacob H. Schiff, $11,750; Charles M. Schwab (munitions), $10,000; Adolph Lewisohn (copper), $8,000; Cleveland H. Dodge (copper), $7,000; Felix M. Warburg, $7,000; Arthur Curtiss James (copper), $5,500; James Couzens (Ford Motors), $5,000; and $5,000 each from Edsel B. Ford, Harold F. McCormick, Chauncey H. McCormick, J. P. Morgan, Dwight W. Morrow, and Willard Straight; and $4,500 from Samuel A. Lewisohn.

Most of the wealthy families participate, of course, in these heavily financed press campaigns, which often have as their objective the mobilizing of mass support behind policies which are contrary to the very interests of the majority of the reading public.

### CURTIS-BOK DYNASTY

The Curtis-Bok family, even more than the journalistic branch of the McCormick family, owes the wealth that places it among the sixty first families primarily to journalism. The McCormicks rose on the shoulders of the reaper; the Boks rose solely on the power of the printed word. The secret of the journalistic success of the Curtis-Boks has been that they have catered to ingrained middle-class prejudices, in the service of the wealthiest persons in the land. This propaganda has been conducted specifically for individuals, and generally for a whole class. In its rise to power this family has been very closely associated with Drexel and Company, the Philadelphia branch of J. P. Morgan and Company.

Cyrus H. K. Curtis started *The Ladies Home Journal* in 1875 and in 1897 he bought *The Saturday Evening Post* for $1,000. In 1911 he bought *The Country Gentleman* and in 1913 acquired the Philadelphia *Public Ledger* from Adolph S. Ochs. For many years the Curtis family had a semimonopoly on Philadelphia newspapers. In all, more than seven Philadelphia newspapers passed into the hands of the Curtis family, which in 1922 acquired the New York *Evening Post,* held it for ten years, and sold it to J. David Stern, publisher of the Philadelphia *Record* and the Camden *Courier.* The *Evening Ledger* was started soon after the *Public Ledger* was acquired, and then was merged with the Philadelphia *Evening Telegraph.* The *Ledger* then took over the Philadelphia *North American* and also the *Press.* In 1930 the *Inquirer* was purchased from the Elverson family, was resold to them, and in 1936 was sold for $15,000,000 to Moses L. Annenberg, former general circulation manager of the Hearst publications.

The three widely circulating national magazines owned by the Curtis family give it an enormous influence outside of Philadelphia. Politically, the family has been uniformly Republican; socially, it has been reactionary. The present family head is John C. Martin, son-in-law of the late Cyrus H. K. Curtis.

### LEHMAN FAMILY

Although not conspicuously connected with publishing, this banking family stands close to *The New York Times,* as it is the outstanding interest in the Kimberley Clark Corporation, a paper-making enterprise which, with *The New York Times,* jointly controls the Spruce Falls Power and Paper Company. The latter supplies the *Times* with its enormous newsprint requirements. With Goldman Sachs and Company, Lehman Brothers take an active interest in the Cuneo Press, Inc., and in Condé Nast Publications, Inc., which issues *Vogue* (merged with *Vanity Fair*) and *House and Garden.*

### HEARST, PAUL BLOCK, ETC.

The Hearst family does not belong with the first sixty families in point of wealth, but rather with the ninety families of the secondary group. Hearst, however, has exercised journalistic power far beyond the due of his personal fortune, which is probably less than $30,000,000 net.

The Hearst fortune, unlike the great Curtis-Bok accumulation, which is unique in this respect, was not made in journalism. It originated in the nineteenth-century mining fortune assembled by Senator George Hearst of California. The principal sources of this fortune were the Comstock Lode and the Homestake Mining Company, although there were also other rich mines, notably the Anaconda, which figured in its upbuilding. William Randolph Hearst today, despite the huge aggregation of newspaper and magazine properties he controls, is not primarily a newspaper publisher at all, although popularly regarded as such. The main Hearst financial interest exists in the form of large shareholdings in the Homestake Mining Company, of Lead, S. D., and the Cerro de Pasco Copper Corporation, of Peru. Subsidiary financial interests exist in the form of real estate and newspaper properties, most of the latter mortgaged or pledged against preferred stock issues and bank loans.

Hearst, in short, belongs, by reason of the source and basis of his riches, to the inner camp of great wealth, although up to the end of the World War he functioned as an independent industrialist bludgeoning his way to political and economic power by the ruthless mobilization of his newspapers against all, rich or poor, who opposed him. The expansion of banking capital, however, has involved Hearst in its folds, and today he is obligated to the Chase National Bank and the National City Bank for huge sums, as is shown in recent reports filed with the Securities and Exchange Commission. Without the assistance of the big banks and the families behind them he would be unable to move.

With the Hearst chain, banking capital completes its general envelopment of the American press, although there are many individual cases yet to be surveyed wherein banking capital effects direct contact with the press. The Hearst newspaper chain consists of the following: in New York City, the *Journal*, the *Mirror*, and the *American* (discontinued as a daily in June, 1937, but still appearing in a Sunday edition); in upper New York State, the Syracuse *Journal* and the Syracuse *Sunday American*, the Albany *Times-Union*, and the Rochester *Journal** and *Sunday American;** in Chicago, the *American* and the *Herald-Examiner*; in California, the Los Angeles *Examiner* and the *Herald-Express*, the San Francisco *Call-Bulletin* and *Examiner*, and the Oakland *Post-Inquirer*. Further north on the Pacific Coast the Seattle *Post-Intelligencer* functions as a unit of the Hearst chain. In Pittsburgh the *Sun-Telegraph* and the *Post-Gazette*, in Milwaukee the *Wisconsin News* and the *Sentinel*, in Omaha the *Bee-News*, in San Antonio the *Light*, in Washington (D. C.) the *Herald* and the *Times*, in Boston the *Record* and *Sunday Advertiser*, in Baltimore the *News* and *Post* and the *Sunday American*, and in Atlanta the *Georgian* are links in the Hearst chain.

In the magazine field Hearst controls *Cosmopolitan*, *Good Housekeeping* (circulation more than two million), *Pictorial Review and Delineator*, *Harper's Bazaar*, *Motor*, *Motor Boating*, *American Druggist*, *American Architect*, *Town and Country*, and *Home and Field*. In England he controls *The Connoisseur*, *Nash's*, and *Good Housekeeping*. In the radio field Hearst owns nearly a dozen broadcasting stations.

Paul Block, Hearst's publishing agent for the Pittsburgh *Post-Gazette* and the Milwaukee *Sentinel*, operates, controls, and partly owns the Toledo *Blade*, the Newark *Star-Eagle*, the Duluth *News-Tribune*, the Toledo *Times*, and the Duluth *Herald*. Hearst is thought to have an interest in the last five.

Hearst has illustrated very thoroughly in his career an axiom in the relation of all the magnates to their newspaper properties: it is not necessary, although it is desirable, to show a profit. Hearst has consistently continued publishing many commercially unprofitable enterprises, of which at least ten can be counted. The unprofitable newspapers, however, have provided political influence, and losses have been made up by the profitable properties, by tax deductions in consolidated holding company income-tax returns, and by the revenues from the Hearst gold and copper mines. In short, these un-

* Discontinued, June, 1937.

profitable Hearst newspapers have been subsidized. Munsey, too, in his day purchased for extravagant sums unprofitable properties, but his prime purpose was less to make a profit than to provide an outlet for some Morgan thesis. Although failing to show a commercial profit on its books, a newspaper may be profitable to its owner in its confidential political phases.

The Hearst journalistic domain also includes syndicated news and feature services. Among these are International News Service, Universal Service, and King Feature Service. There is also the *American Weekly*, a magazine with a circulation of more than five million copies, which accompanies Hearst Sunday editions. More than ten million persons read Hearst newspapers or magazines, or more than ten per cent of the adult population of the nation.

Hearst's policies from the beginning, when he was given the San Francisco *Examiner* by his father in 1887, have been reactionary, anti-social, and narrowly selfish. Since the World War the Hearst newspapers have functioned solely on behalf of the camp of big wealth, campaigning for sales taxes, against unemployment relief, etc. In recent years they have become, notably, the special organs for the less literate dupes of the boisterously reactionary Liberty League.

MILLS-REIDS

The Mills-Reid family owns the New York *Herald Tribune,* principal national organ of the Republican Party, and the Paris *Herald.* The New York *Tribune* was purchased in 1872 from Horace Greeley by Whitelaw Reid, editor and diplomat, who in 1881 married a daughter of Darius O. Mills, successful California mining prospector. The male issue of this marriage, now the head of the family, is Ogden Reid, editor-in-chief of the *Herald Tribune.* A minority stockholder is Ogden L. Mills, also a grandson of Darius O. Mills.

The family, among the first sixty families in extent of wealth, is exceptionally influential politically, as was illustrated when Ogden L. Mills succeeded Andrew W. Mellon as Secretary of the Treasury.

Mrs. Whitelaw Reid for many years after her husband's death published the New York *Tribune* at a deficit, subsidizing it with funds from her large personal investment revenues. In 1924 the *Herald* was bought from Munsey for $5,000,000, and the merged combination has since been highly profitable. Partly in consideration of the purchase price, the Reids gave Munsey their personal note for an undisclosed large sum, and upon Munsey's death this note came into the possession of the Metropolitan Museum of Art. It is still outstanding. In the 1928-29 boom period the Reids borrowed additional money from the Metropolitan Life Insurance Company for the building of a newspaper plant.

Upon coming due in 1933 the Metropolitan Museum note placed the *Herald Tribune* under direct obligation to the financial guardian of the Metropolitan Museum, J. P. Morgan and Company. It has been held "open" for a period of more than three years, according to reliable reports, but no announcement has been made of its subsequent history, although it has not been liquidated.

Quite apart from this note, whose existence is not reported in the *Herald Tribune's* statement of ownership, the Reids have always been very friendly with J. P. Morgan and Company, with some of whose interests their extensive investments are interlocked. The *Herald Tribune,* in point of fact, by reason of this note as well as because of other material considerations, must be regarded as a newspaper under strong Morgan influence. Instances of this influence will be cited, but in general the editorial policies of the *Herald Tribune* are always those of the inner clique of finance capital that rules the Republican Party.

### TAFTS, HANNAS, METCALFS, CLARKS, AND GERRYS

The Taft family owns the Cincinnati *Star-Times,* whose chief competitor is the Cincinnati *Enquirer,* owned by the Estate of John R. McLean, public-utilities promoter. Charles P. Taft, half brother of former President Taft and a lawyer concerned in various Morgan transactions and in the affairs of the Republican Party, since 1880 owned the paper, which is now directed by Hulbert Taft. The McLean family, incidentally, also owned the Washington *Post* for many years until its sale in 1932 to Eugene Meyer of the Guggenheim camp. From 1911 to 1930 the McLeans, who were joined by marriage to the Walsh mining fortune, and whose titular head was involved in the Teapot Dome imbroglio, also owned the Cincinnati *Com-*

*mercial Tribune,* which espoused the Democratic Party while the *Enquirer* supported the Republican Party.

The Hanna family owns the Cleveland *News* and the Cleveland *Plain Dealer,* published by Daniel R., Carl, and Mark Hanna, grandsons of Mark Hanna. The *Plain Dealer* has a part interest in two Cleveland radio stations.

Marcus Alonzo Hanna I was a newspaper publisher, like so many other magnates and politicoes of the nineteenth century. Just before the Garfield campaign of 1880 Hanna acquired the Cleveland *Herald,* which had been owned by Richard C. Parsons, a political figure, and William P. Fogg, a crockery manufacturer. These two sold the newspaper to a group composed of J. H. Wade, founder of the Western Union Telegraph System; Henry Chisholm, founder of the Cleveland Rolling Mill; John D. Rockefeller and Henry M. Flagler of the Standard Oil Company; Amasa Stone, father-in-law of John Hay; S. T. Everett; Dan P. Eels, a banker; Elias Sims, part owner of the West Side Street Railway of Cleveland; and Mark Hanna.

The *Herald* lost money and influence, and was eventually given into the sole control of Hanna, who became president of the publishing company in 1880. In order to improve the property Hanna hired away the best members of the Cleveland *Leader* staff. Edwin Cowles, editor and owner of the *Leader,* resenting this maneuver, opened fire on Hanna, and published all the damaging information and rumors about him that he could find. The material published by the *Leader* was made the basis of the later personal attacks on Hanna by William Randolph Hearst. In 1885 Hanna sold the good will and subscription list of the *Herald* to the *Leader* for $80,000, and disposed of the plant to the *Plain Dealer.* The *Leader's* attacks on Hanna, which had been actuated by no principle, abruptly ceased.

The present position of the Hanna family in Cleveland journalism, where its domination is challenged only by the Scripps-Howard publication, has quite obviously an historical basis in nineteenth-century political and financial power, as have so many other contemporary journalistic ventures of the magnates. It is quite logical that this important political family should be connected by marriage both with the Chicago *Tribune* and the New York *Daily News.*

The Metcalfs, wealthy established Rhode Island textile manu-
facturers, own the Providence (R. I.) *Journal* (morning) and the
Providence *Bulletin* (evening). Until March, 1937, the Providence
*News-Tribune* was owned by Senator Peter Goelet Gerry, scion of a
long-established wealthy family whose members today stand in the
forefront of the American plutocracy. It was sold to Walter E.
O'Hara, racetrack promoter and politician who owns the Pawtucket
(R. I.) *Star* and the Rhode Island *Star*. Senator Gerry acquired the
Providence *News* in 1924 and the *Tribune* in 1929, and consolidated
the two publications. The family of the late Senator Nelson Aldrich,
intermarried with the Rockefeller family, owns and publishes the
Pawtucket *Times*. As in Delaware, but also in other states, notably
Montana, every daily newspaper of consequence in Rhode Island is
owned by one of the wealthy families.

The Clark (Singer Sewing Machine Company) family has, like
most other clans of great wealth, been concerned with the direct
operation of newspapers. The Albany *Knickerbocker Press*, founded
in 1842, was acquired in 1911 by Stephen S. Clark, who placed it in
charge of Judge John Lynn Arnold. The paper was sold by Clark in
1928 to Frank E. Gannett, for more than $1,500,000.

### ANACONDA COPPER

The Anaconda Copper Mining Company, dominated by the National City Bank clique (Stillman-Rockefeller-Taylor-Pyne, etc.),
is one of the great newspaper publishers of the country. It owns
nearly every newspaper in Montana that has an Associated Press
franchise.

Under the aegis of the great Anaconda Copper Mining Company
the press in Montana, except for fugitive, independent publications
mostly under labor auspices, has been exceptionally venal, reactionary,
and hostile to the public interest. Directly owned Anaconda Copper
newspapers today, are the Butte *Miner,* the Anaconda *Standard,*
the Butte *Daily Post,* the Helena *Independent,* the Helena *Record-
Herald,* the Missoula *Missoulian,* the Missoula *Sentinel,* the Billings
*Gazette,* and the Livingston *Enterprise.*

The fight waged by the copper interests around the Montana newspapers has been severe for many years. W. A. Clark acquired the Butte *Miner* late in the nineteenth century, and used it chiefly to belabor Marcus Daly, chief promoter of Anaconda Copper after the Hearst interests withdrew in 1895. Daly and Clark had been partners.

Daly replied to the Clark journalistic barrage by hiring a former Syracuse University professor to edit the Anaconda *Standard*, which Daly founded. This newspaper revealed, notably, the facts about Clark's purchase of a United States senatorship, and caused Clark to be rejected by the Senate. Later Clark was reappointed by a subservient Lieutenant Governor. Up to the time of his death Daly was reputed to have spent more than $5,000,000 on the *Standard*.

William A. Clark, Jr., reformist son of the former copper king, became a stern critic of the copper company's methods in his paper, the *Miner*. In 1928, for example, young Clark charged in his newspaper that the copper company had defrauded the state of taxes; had subsidized the state press in general by venal payments and had suppressed news of murders, notably those of dissatisfied or radical workers; had throttled the school system to extinguish liberal ideas; and controlled the entire state government from top to bottom. Anaconda Copper's response to this was surreptitiously to purchase control of the paper from under Clark's nose.

Young Clark thereupon founded the Montana *Free Press* to continue the fight, which hinged upon his desire to elect a Republican to the governorship against Anaconda's Democratic candidate. A damaging advertisers' boycott, engineered by the copper company, forced Clark to sell out.

The United Copper Company crowd under F. Augustus Heinze fought Anaconda Copper through twenty-seven Montana newspapers prior to the debacle of 1907, according to P. A. O'Farrell, editorial agent of Heinze, who told C. W. Barron: "I nearly killed myself writing all the various editorials for these papers but the local readers took them as the views of the local editor and they were law and gospel to them."

Barron's published memoirs also quote John MacGinnis, former Mayor of Butte, Montana, as saying in 1904: "Not one thousand, but many thousands of grafters are on the Amalgamated (Anaconda) pay roll. The Amalgamated loses $500,000 a year in Montana newspapers."

### PHELPS DODGE CORPORATION

The Phelps Dodge Corporation group, also affiliated with the National City Bank in the persons of members of the Dodge and James families, exercises similar remote ownership and control over the leading newspapers of Arizona, where its chief properties are located. Ralph E. Ellinwood, whose father was chief counsel to Phelps Dodge Corporation, owned the Tucson (Ariz.) *Daily Star* and left it to his estate. The Bisbee (Ariz.) *Review* and the *Evening Ore* are owned by the Cochise Publishing Company, a subsidiary of the Phelps Dodge Corporation. Arizona newspapers that are not owned by the copper company are, however, very friendly to it. Notably is this true of the Phoenix (Ariz.) *Republic* and the Phoenix *Dispatch*, owned by Mrs. Dwight B. Heard and Charles A. Stauffer, and the Tucson *Daily Citizen*, owned by Frank H. Hitchcock, Postmaster General in the Taft Administration. All the Arizona newspapers, for example, refused in 1933 to print the account of a scandal concerning a local politician and the construction of a pipe line. The distant Los Angeles *Times*, which published the story, advertised the fact in the Arizona newspapers.

### MISCELLANEOUS

Throughout the United States big newspapers are owned by wealthy men who have no primary interest in newspaper publishing and who are members, by blood relationship or by marriage, of the wealthiest families.

Both the Louisville *Courier-Journal*, formerly an independent paper under Henry Watterson, and the Louisville *Times*, are owned by Robert Worth Bingham, banker and Ambassador to Great Britain. Bingham inherited a large fortune from his wife, who was the widow of Henry L. Flagler (Standard Oil). Flagler, incidentally, upon shifting the scene of his activities from Ohio to Florida, where he acquired and built hotels and railroads, also acquired or founded all the leading newspapers of that state. These Florida publications, however, apparently have since passed out of the hands of the Flagler family.

A half interest in the Kansas City *Journal and Post* was acquired in 1931 by Henry L. Doherty, public-utilities operator and head of the Cities Service Company. Doherty wanted the paper in order to undermine public confidence in local public-utility regulations, which prohibited the sale of Doherty securities.

The Chicago *Journal of Commerce* is owned by the Ames family (Booth Fisheries), which in 1931 acquired the Chicago *Post* from a William Hale Thompson political group. This latter clique had bought the paper in 1930 from John C. Shaffer. Knowlton L. Ames, Jr., was financed in the purchase of the Chicago *Post* to the extent of $500,000 by Samuel Insull's Public Service Trust, a subsidiary of Insull Utility Investments. Ames paid off this note in 1932, after the Insull debacle, at 12 cents on the dollar. The group behind the Insull properties made a practice of exercising indirect press ownership through Insull, and it is difficult to ascertain where such dummy control begins and ends in American newspaperdom. In Maine, where Insull had the leading hydroelectric properties under his control and management, Guy P. Gannett, cousin of Frank E. Gannett, was Insull's journalistic henchman, publishing the Portland *Press-Herald*, Portland *Express*, and Waterville *Journal*, as well as *Comfort*, a monthly periodical with a claimed rural circulation of more than one million copies.

It was partly in order to combat Insull in New England that International Paper and Power acquired two Boston newspapers as well as newspapers in Insull's own western territory in and around Chicago. Many ostensibly independent newspapers from the middle strata are, of course, secretly owned or controlled by larger interests whose dummies the publishers are. One of these conspicuous dummies has been Frank E. Gannett, who acquired the Brooklyn *Eagle*, the *Knickerbocker Press*, and the Albany *Evening News* with money advanced in secret by the International Paper and Power Company. Gannett, exposed, subsequently paid off his obligation to the power company and gave up the *Eagle*, and his chain today includes the *Evening News* and *Knickerbocker Press*,* of Albany; the Beacon

* Discontinued, June. 1937.

(N. Y.) *News*; the *Advertiser, Telegram,* and *Star-Gazette* of El-mira, N. Y.; the Hartford (Conn.) *Times*; the Ithaca *Journal*; the Malone (N. Y.) *Evening Telegram*; the Newburgh (N. Y.) *News*; Ogdensburg (N. Y.) *Journal*; the Plainfield (N. J.) *Courier-News*; the *Democrat and Chronicle* and the *Times-Union,* of Rochester; the *Observer-Dispatch* and the *Press* of Utica; the Danville (Ill.) *Commercial-News*; the Saratoga Springs (N. Y.) *Saratogian,* the Olean (N. Y.) *Times-Herald,* and three radio stations. Although apparently not owned by the wealthy families, the Gannett news-papers ardently support them on all political, social, and economic questions, and either bombard or snipe at all proposals for social amelioration by political action. Gannett was for a time president of the reactionary American Newspaper Publishers Association.

Carson C. Peck, vice-president and treasurer of F. W. Woolworth Company, in 1912 bought the Brooklyn *Times.* In 1932 Fremont C. Peck, his son, bought the Brooklyn *Standard-Union* from Paul Block, and the combined *Times* and *Standard-Union* was more re-cently sold by Peck to the Brooklyn *Eagle,* which is now owned by a corporation headed by Millard P. Goodfellow. This latter corpora-tion took over the *Eagle* from the Gunnison and the Hester families, to whom it had been allowed to revert when International Paper and Power was discovered to have financed Frank E. Gannett in buying it.

Ira C. Copley, chief figure in the United Gas and Electric Com-pany of Illinois, publishes the Aurora (Ill.) *Beacon,* the Elgin (Ill.) *Courier,* and the Joliet (Ill.) *Herald-News.* The Federal Trade Com-mission brought out that he had agreed in 1928 to acquire fifteen units in the Kellogg newspaper chain of California, and that he bought the *Illinois State Journal* of Springfield. The public-utility issue was very keen in the California newspaper area he surreptitiously entered. Copley joined Samuel Insull in supporting the candidacy of Frank L. Smith of Illinois for the senatorship, and he contributed $25,000 to Smith's 1926 campaign.

The Procter (Ivory Soap and politics) family owns seventeen weekly newspapers in Ohio; they belong in the category of the county press and compose the second largest weekly chain in the country. Charles Bond (Two-Pants Suit) joined in advancing $300,000 for the creation of the strategic Procter chain. The largest chain of weekly county papers is owned by the Woodyard brothers, sons of the late Representative Harry C. Woodyard of West Virginia. This enterprise consists of fifteen rural weeklies in Virginia and eight on Long Island's aristocratic North Shore. A leading role in raising the capital for this chain was played by Spruille Braden, scion of the Braden (Chile) copper fortune and a director in the W. A. Harriman Securities Corporation and other corporations.

Joseph F. Biddle, of the Biddle family, owns the Huntington (Pa.) *News*. The Waynesboro (Pa.) *Record-Herald* is owned by the Chalfant (steel) family. The Honolulu *Advertiser,* the only English-language daily in the city, is owned by the Truman (pineapples and sugar) family, which participated in 1897 in the overthrow of the Hawaiian kingdom.

The San Francisco *Chronicle* is owned by George T. Cameron, cement magnate, who inherited the property in 1925 from his father-in-law. The Washington *Post* was acquired in 1932 from the Mc-Lean-Walsh family by Eugene G. Meyer (Allied Chemical and Lazard Frères). The Philadelphia *Daily News,* a tabloid, was founded by Lee Ellmaker, secretary of Boss William S. Vare, for the account of Bernarr Macfadden, who also owns a string of cheap magazines.

The Detroit *Free Press* is owned by Edward D. Stair, director of Graham-Paige Motors, the Detroit Trust Company, and the First National Bank of Detroit, and the leading spirit in the Ann Arbor Railroad. The president of the Christian Herald Association, publisher of the *Christian Herald,* is James Cash Penney, chain-store entrepreneur. Before the Milwaukee *Sentinel* was acquired by Paul Block for Hearst's account it was owned by Charles F. Pfister, meat packer. Before the Omaha *Bee-News* fell into the hands of Hearst in 1928 it was owned by Nelson B. Updike, a merchant, who had acquired it from Victor Rosewater, Republican politician. Charles R. Crane, head of the so-called Bathtub Trust, before the war owned an interest in the Milwaukee *Journal.*

There have been many abortive ventures in journalism by members of the richest families. John Barry Ryan, grandson of the late Thomas Fortune Ryan and son-in-law of the late Otto Kahn, in 1930 bought the Newark *Freie Zeitung* and founded the Newark *Free Press*; both papers soon passed out of existence. Cornelius Vanderbilt in the early 1920's established tabloids in Los Angeles, San Francisco, and Miami; they failed to take hold and were discontinued. Anne U. Stillman, wife of James A. Stillman, now divorced and married to Fowler McCormick, financed magazines called *Panorama* and *American Sketch*; these soon died. Thomas W. Lamont was instrumental in financing the short-lived *Everyweek*, a 3-cent periodical.

The journalistic range of the richest families encompasses all fields. The very successful *New Yorker*, for example, was financed and is largely owned by Raoul Fleischmann, of the yeast and distilling family. It pokes fun, sympathetically, at the foibles of the ruling class and its hangers-on. *The American Mercury*, monthly periodical, was bought in 1935 by Paul Palmer, son-in-law of Adolph Lewisohn, copper magnate. *The Mercury* immediately turned reactionary.

A minor proportion of the metropolitan press is owned by political agents of the two dominant parties. Although not owned directly by the rich families this press, like the subsidized county press, is responsive in the main to their interests. In Buffalo the *Courier and Express* is owned by the family of William J. "Fingy" Connors, Democratic politician of unsavory repute; the Buffalo *Times* was owned by Norman E. Mack, former Democratic national chairman, until it was purchased by Scripps-Howard in 1929. The Doylestown (Pa.) *Intelligencer* is owned by Joseph R. Grundy, lobbyist for the Pennsylvania Manufacturers Association and Republican political secret agent. The Norristown (Pa.) *Times Herald* is owned by Ralph B. Strassburger, wealthy Republican and member of the Liberty League. The Los Angeles *Times* is owned by Harry Chandler, wealthy Republican and promoter.

The Houston *Post-Dispatch* was owned by Governor Ross S. Sterling, of Texas, and only recently was sold. The Houston *Chronicle* is owned by Jesse H. Jones, wealthy Democrat and chairman of the Reconstruction Finance Corporation. The Topeka *Daily Capital* and *Capper's Weekly*, the latter a farm paper with a circulation of more than 350,000 copies, are owned by former Senator Arthur Capper, Republican wheel horse. James Cox, Democratic presidential candidate in 1920, owns a chain of Ohio newspapers consisting of the

Miami *News,* Springfield *News,* Dayton *News,* and Springfield *Sun.* Cox for a period owned the Canton *News,* which he acquired from Henry H. Timken, the roller-bearing manufacturer. Warren G. Harding owned the Marion (O.) *Star,* which functioned as a Republican propaganda sheet. Henry Morgenthau, Jr., now Secretary of the Treasury, owned the *American Agriculturist,* a bimonthly, which he sold in 1934 to Frank E. Gannett.

There remains the "independent" press sandwiched in between the purely political press and the press owned directly by the wealthy families. This independent press is neither very independent nor very numerous, although at one time in American history it was the major support of the national press structure. In this classification belong the Scripps-Howard chain, *The New York Times,* the Baltimore *Sun* papers, the St. Louis *Post-Dispatch,* the Boston *Transcript,* and some of the smaller chains; but very few others. Independence in these newspapers consists largely of bellicosely asserting the right to choose between Republican and Democratic political candidates. On economic and social issues they usually, for reasons which should not seem strange, are found in fundamental agreement with Henry Ford, the Du Ponts, and the Morgan partners. They differ only in detail, mostly of a special developmental character, from the newspapers owned by the magnates or subsidized by the political parties.

The Scripps-Howard chain, which includes nearly thirty newspapers scattered over the continent, and the United Press, the United Feature Service, and the Newspaper Enterprise Association (NEA), was developed as a commercial enterprise by E. W. Scripps, whose two sons inherited majority ownership. Minority interests are owned by leading executives, of whom Roy W. Howard, chairman of the board since 1922, is outstanding. Under the elder Scripps these newspapers, to which some have been added since his death, published a great deal of effective liberal social and political criticism, largely directed at municipal and state affairs. The Scripps-Howard chain has sporadically continued these local crusades, although it is usually careful not to tackle the influential personalities that flit, batlike, behind the scenes. It is a big day now in the Scripps-Howard organization when some grafting judge, unable to strike back, is exposed and rhetorically castigated.

It has been aptly said that since the passing of the elder Scripps the chain has become "progressive only in off-years and on local topics." In 1912 the Scripps press was lined up for Wilson largely through the influence of Charles R. Crane. It accepted the Morgan thesis of the war's origin, and after the war it gradually succumbed almost completely to the blandishments of finance capital. In 1924 the Cleveland *Press* of the chain supported LaFollette for the presidency, and illustrated the power of a newspaper by carrying the city for him. It was the only large city LaFollette captured outside of Wisconsin.

In 1928 the Scripps-Howard organization, apparently taught a lesson by the advertising that was pulled wholesale out of the Cleveland *Press* during the LaFollette campaign (for which the editor in charge was fired), declared in favor of Herbert Hoover on the ground that he was expected to favor a large measure of public-utility operation and control by the government. In 1932 it supported former Secretary of War Newton D. Baker for the Democratic presidential nomination. Baker was the law partner of Thomas L. Sidlo, Scripps-Howard attorney, and was one of counsel for the Van Sweringen brothers (Morgan).

When Franklin D. Roosevelt captured the nomination the Scripps-Howard press espoused him more or less despairingly, as did the Hearst press, but in 1936 it gave very subdued support to Roosevelt's re-election campaign. A number of Scripps-Howard executives argued *in camera* for throwing the influence of the chain behind the incredible Alfred M. Landon; but the Scripps-Howard newspapers contented themselves with reporting the Landon campaign in tones of sacerdotal solemnity. Since the re-election of Roosevelt in 1936 the avowedly liberal Scripps-Howard chain has not only opposed the reform of the thoroughly reactionary United States Supreme Court, but it has also carried on a veiled campaign against the New Deal on all fronts. This campaign has taken the form of poking gentle fun at tragically necessary reform proposals.

Although ostensibly committed to the support of organized labor, and actually printing more news in labor's behalf than any other of the big publications, the Scripps-Howard press let slip no opportunity to sideswipe John L. Lewis in the campaign of the C.I.O. to organize heavy industry. It opposed the efforts of the American

Newspaper Guild to obtain contracts for the Scripps-Howard editorial workers, and from the very inception of this union impeded its work in every possible fashion short of courageously fighting it in the open as did William Randolph Hearst and the Associated Press.

But since Roy W. Howard has become influential in the affairs of the E. W. Scripps Company, its newspapers have shown many contradictions. They have opposed holding companies as a matter of principle, yet they belong to a holding company. While decrying the sale of nonvoting stock by Wall Street, the Scripps-Howard press sold its employees nonvoting stock.

In 1936 the Scripps-Howard papers installed as a daily columnist Hugh S. Johnson, confidential amanuensis to Bernard M. Baruch, and in recent years they have encouraged talented but unsophisticated columnists like Westbrook Pegler to becloud issues by passionate writing on all sides of every social question. On the other hand, the Scripps-Howard press has continued to publish the progressive opinions of Heywood Broun, although individual newspapers in the chain have on occasion suppressed a Broun column that seemed likely to offend wealthy local interests.

Early in 1937 Merlin H. Aylesworth, for ten years president of the National Broadcasting Company, joined the Scripps-Howard newspapers in a general executive capacity. This appointment told a good deal about the drift of these newspapers. Prior to joining the National Broadcasting Company, Aylesworth was, successively, chairman of the Colorado Public Utilities Commission, vice-president of the Utah Power and Light Company, and general manager of the National Electric Light Association. The Federal Trade Commission revealed that his task with the N.E.L.A. was to conduct a heavily subsidized propaganda campaign against public ownership of electric light and power properties. In this capacity Aylesworth ordered payments right and left to college professors and newspaper men who would spread his propaganda, and secretly paid for the writing of textbooks suitable to the public-utilities promoters. At Aylesworth's suggestion Halsey, Stuart and Company hired a University of Chicago professor to plug securities over the radio under the name of "The Old Counselor."

The Scripps-Howard press, the fact is, finds itself in a period of transition, and increasingly exhibits its inability to resist the magnetic attraction of finance capital. Roy W. Howard is personally ambitious and aggressive, and apparently feels that he may succeed in playing a hazardous game where Hearst has failed. Disregarding the injunction of the elder Scripps to stay out of New York, Howard in 1927 bought the Munsey-Bennett *Telegram* from the Metropolitan Museum. In 1931 he acquired the New York *World* and the *Evening World* from the Pulitzer brothers, and forged the *World-Telegram*. All this required financing, which was arranged in avenues that were under the discreet observation of J. P. Morgan and Company. A bond issue of $8,500,000 was floated in 1928 through the Guaranty Trust Company (Morgan), the Chemical National Bank (Goelet), and Sidlo, Simons, Day and Company of Denver. Failure to show earnings on these bonds would place the Scripps-Howard newspapers directly in the hands of bankers, acting for the bondholders.

An arresting feature of the disposal of *The World* papers was that the sale violated the terms of Pulitzer's will, which stipulated that the publications should not be discontinued or transferred. It was necessary to obtain court assent to the sale, but this was procured with a celerity that is usual in financial circles even when apparently unyielding legal formulae stand in the way of a desired objective.

A string of newspaper properties that is operated, like the Scripps-Howard chain, on a straight business basis, but which is directly oriented in its editorial policy toward Wall Street, is Ridder Brothers, Inc. In this chain are the New York *Journal of Commerce,* the New York *Staats-Zeitung,* the St. Paul *Dispatch,* the St. Paul *Pioneer Press,* the St. Paul *Daily News,* the Aberdeen (N. D.) *American,* the Aberdeen *Evening News,* and the Grand Forks (N. D.) *Herald.* Ridder Brothers, Inc., has a minority interest in the Seattle *Times.* The Booth chain in Michigan and the McClatchy chain in California are similar.

The Baltimore *Sun* (morning and evening) is owned by its leading executives, and lays dubious claim to being a liberal newspaper because it is willing to comment harshly on lynchings and similar grossly outrageous affairs. The *Sun* is liberal, but its liberalism is of the Southern agrarian variety that means little or nothing short of reaction in the contemporary social context. The resilient nature of the *Sun's* backbone was clearly indicated in the 1936 national campaign when, although it had been consistently Democratic for decades and found no difficulty in swallowing Cleveland and Wilson, and even Cox and Davis, it came out in opposition to Franklin D. Roosevelt, the first Democratic President since the Civil War to attempt an implementation of the original tenets of the party of Jefferson and Jackson. Although not owned by finance capital, and perhaps not controlled by it, even though stockholders like Henry L. Mencken have fatuously boasted in print of their ownership of stock in United States Steel, the Baltimore *Sun* papers belong in spirit with finance capital, oppose fundamental reform, and are ripe to espouse reaction. The difference between the Baltimore *Sun* and the New York *Sun* is one of degree only.

The St. Louis *Post-Dispatch,* developed into a highly profitable property by Joseph Pulitzer, Jr., in 1936 also turned its back upon its Democratic Party traditions and opposed the re-election of Roosevelt. Although never a performer in the stalwart old Pulitzer tradition, the *Post-Dispatch* has done some excellent things in an era when the press as a whole has functioned as the first line of defense for political and financial rapists. The *Post-Dispatch* alone insisted that the Teapot Dome investigation continue in 1924, it opposed the execution of Sacco and Vanzetti, and it has spoken freely on behalf of the imprisoned Tom Mooney.

The *World* under the other Pulitzer sons could not show such a record, although early in the 1920's it exposed the Ku Klux Klan. This feat was, incidentally, of material value to the paper in catering to New York's large Catholic and Jewish population. In the same postwar period the executive editor of *The World* was Herbert Bayard Swope, stock-market plunger and brother of Gerard Swope, president of the General Electric Company. The earlier trenchant editorials of Frank I. Cobb, which often struck, lightninglike, the richest and most powerful malefactors, gave way to the graceful and pointless vaporings of Walter Lippmann, who plumbed the journalistic depths in 1928 when, plugging for Alfred E. Smith, he presented the country with the "New Tammany"—a reformed semiphilanthropic society. The Seabury investigation of Tammany Hall in 1932

showed how little foundation in fact there was for Lippmann's un-
realistic maunderings.

Two journalistic ventures, committed to the general social welfare
rather than to narrow self-interest, and financed by persons of wealth,
deserve mention before we leave the subject of press ownership. *The
Nation*, founded in 1865 as a weekly periodical, incorporated later
with the New York *Evening Post* and then published separately, was
maintained for many years by Oswald Garrison Villard, son of the
railroad builder. Although the younger Villard is by no means a
person of major wealth, his income is derived from the remnants of a
nineteenth-century fortune. *The New Republic* was founded just
before the war with funds supplied by Willard Straight and his wife,
the daughter of William C. Whitney, and has been subsidized ever
since by Mrs. Straight (now Mrs. Leonard K. Elmhirst).

Both these weekly publications have long represented the best
traditions of American journalism, and have firmly and quietly done
much to awaken social consciousness by spreading liberal ideas of
social, political, and economic amelioration. If there is ever any reform in American journalism, the reform will, in general, follow
paths outlined long ago by *The Nation* and *The New Republic*.
Where these publications have failed has been in missing the opportunity to build large, influential circulations by a dramatic presentation of material in the style which the prewar "muckraking" magazines and the old *World* proved would attract the public. They have
been, perhaps, too academic in a world of rough-and-tumble. In any
case, the subsidy of these publications has been distinctly in the public
interest, and in the long run the ideas which they have spread may
nullify the selfish work of Hearsts, McCormicks, Harrimans, Astors,
Morgans, Rockefellers, Curtises, Reids, Pattersons, Mellons, Harknesses, Davisons, and Lamonts.

The American press, it should be plainly evident from the foregoing, is owned and controlled by the wealthiest families of American finance capitalism. This press is not primarily influenced either
by advertising control or by unconscious plutocratic modes of thought
arising from the established social system. It is directly responsive,
like a shadow, to those individuals that derive the greatest profits

from society. It represents a huge investment, but functions constantly, whether it is commercially profitable or not because it serves a specific class objective.

# VIII

## The Journalism of Pecuniary Inhibition

FREEDOM of the press in the United States is largely theoretic and Pickwickian, consisting, in the main, of the tenuous right of small dissident groups to publish newspapers and magazines of limited circulation for sectarian audiences. Whenever a publication espousing views distasteful to the phalanx of big wealth achieves a great circulation, as some have done, it is merely forced out of business as were the prewar "muckraking" magazines.

Press freedom, about which the publishers talk so much, is largely an historical survival of negative and narrow class significance. It is not meant to be literal freedom of the press from *all* outside restraint and influence; it merely means freedom from governmental restraint and influence. The formal struggle for a free press began in England in the seventeenth century when the commercial classes successfully pitted themselves against the aristocracy and the crown for political power. The subsidized government press in the course of the struggle was overthrown, and was supplanted by the press of the individual commercial and industrial entrepreneur, which insists upon the "natural" right to criticize and even to libel government and other classes in serving its own class interests.

Today nothing would be more resented by the press of the plutocrats than governmental action taken to free it of control and restraint by private pecuniary interests. This press wants no more to be released from the elements that shower it with money and honors than does a courtesan.

The centralized class control over the American press by the very rich has been evidenced most dramatically in the great unified newspaper campaigns which have swept like blizzards over the country at periodic intervals during the past forty years. Careful study of these campaigns would inspire only envy in the directors of the co-ordinated Russian, Polish, Japanese, German and Italian press.

The first of these great unified press campaigns to manifest centralized motivation and direction took place in 1896, when virtually every important newspaper, Democratic as well as Republican, plumped for William McKinley and the gold standard, against William Jennings Bryan and free silver. The Hearst newspapers, numbering then only two, alone of the metropolitan press supported Bryan, but Hearst was interested in silver mines.

The next great national press campaign, wherein practically all newspapers sang the same tune, began in 1915, and had as its successful design the entanglement of the United States in the war. By 1917 few publications opposed entering the conflict. Once war was declared the press was temporarily yoked under a government censorship, but objections were few from publishers, who only when their own pecuniary prerogatives are at stake valiantly espouse press freedom.

In the 1920's virtually the whole of the press, including many outstanding Democratic newspapers like *The New York Times*, swung to the support of the Coolidge "prosperity" nonsense. Perhaps the greatest betrayal by the American press was its failure to warn of the impending debacle, which in private was clearly foreseen by many financial writers. During the depression of 1929-33 there was again a great unified press campaign to conceal from the public the profundity of the disaster.

In 1936 eighty per cent of the American press, according to *Time* (November 2, 1936), and at least seventy-one per cent, according to *The New Republic* (March 17, 1937), opposed the re-election of Franklin D. Roosevelt, and fiercely calumniated him and his supporters.

Virtually the only newspapers outside the subsidized Democratic Party press which supported the Roosevelt Administration were those owned directly by consumer-goods manufacturers, and those owned by department-store magnates or dependent largely upon department-store advertising and consumer well-being for their revenues

These elements were the main financial supporters of the New Deal. Ambiguous Roosevelt support came from *The New York Times* as well as from the Scripps-Howard chain. The attitude of the press as a whole in the election campaign, however, illustrated nothing more completely than the weakness of retail advertisers and of readers with respect to control of editorial policies. In Detroit, St. Louis, Baltimore, and Minneapolis the New Deal had no newspaper support at all, although Roosevelt carried all these cities.

While President Roosevelt was abused as a Bolshevist and Fascist, and his political associates were maligned throughout the American press, the London *Economist*, chief capitalist organ of the world, sympathetically appraised his work and commended him for having brought order out of chaos. *The Economist*, often quoted in America, in this instance was not cited.

It has been assumed by some observers that the Roosevelt landslide of 1936, in the face of a hostile press, proved the impotence of the newspapers in the modern radio age. Such a contention, however, is based on a failure properly to evaluate many complex special factors outside the sphere of journalism.

It has been suggested that "just as the oratory of William Jennings Bryan was defeated by the press in 1896, so the oratory of Franklin D. Roosevelt defeated the press in 1936." There is something in this contention. However, *The New Republic* (March 17, 1937), from which this quotation is taken, pointed out that "nearly two hundred radio stations—one-third of the total number and more than a third in terms of power, listening area and size of audience—are owned or controlled by newspapers." In short, they are largely owned by the very elements that own the newspapers. Moreover, the Republican Party utilized much more radio time than did the Democrats—sixty-nine hours against fifty-six and one-half hours.

Soon after the election the power of the press, and its centralized direction and aim, was illustrated much more thoroughly than during the campaign. If eighty per cent of the press opposed Roosevelt's re-election, then ninety-five per cent of it swung into opposition to the proposed reform of a Supreme Court that since the Civil War has been riding roughshod over the common interest. The Scripps-Howard papers, cool toward Roosevelt's re-election, joined

*The New York Times* in stern opposition to his plan for Supreme Court reform within the provisions of the Constitution. All the radio commentators started blasting.

Evelyn Miller Crowell in *The New Republic* (January 13, 1937) argues that the press is impotent in its campaigns, and cites a good deal of evidence to justify her contention. Her conclusion, however, is based upon inadequate sampling. In 1934 the press, virtually unaided, smashed the proposed Tugwell Pure Food and Drug Act, which provided for more honest advertising. The opposition was openly organized by the various publishers' associations from the American Newspaper Publishers Association down through regional bodies. In the same year the newspapers smashed the San Francisco general strike.

Seldom does the press carry on campaigns for its own vested journalistic interest, but when it does it again shows its power. President Taft said that he received a hostile press because he had not lowered sufficiently the tariff rates on foreign newsprint, which under Wilson were eliminated entirely. Speaker Joseph Cannon said a part of the Republican press turned upon him, when his autocratic powers were assailed by liberals in Congress, because he had supported Taft on the tariff. Although the American press is ardently protectionist as a whole, it insists, inconsistently, upon free importation of newsprint.

The arrogance of the multimillionaires in asserting their journalistic rights knows no limits. The most authoritative statement of the press philosophy of the dominant capitalists was given by *The Wall Street Journal,* central organ of finance capital, on January 20, 1925, as follows:

It is difficult to guess what the editorial writer of the New York *Herald-Tribune* means, or what he thinks he means, when he says "the American newspaper has always been an institution affected with a public interest." That is a legal phrase, in the mouth of a layman, and is ventured with the usual results. It is flatly untrue, but there is much ignorance and hypocrisy about the matter, calling for some plain speaking.

A newspaper is a private enterprise, owing nothing whatever to the public, which grants it no franchise. It is therefore "affected" with no public interest. It is emphatically the property of the owner, who is selling a manufactured product at his own risk. If the public does not like his opinions or his method of presenting news the remedy is in its own hands. It is under no obligation to buy the paper. . . . Without in any way belittling the President's remarks to a recent gathering of editors, it may be said that those editors, except where they own their own newspapers, take their policy from their employers. . . . But for ridiculously obvious reasons, there are many newspaper owners willing enough to encourage the public in the delusion that it is the editor of a newspaper who dictates the selection of news and the expression of opinion. He only does so subject to the correction and suggestion of the proprietor of the paper. . . .

If a newspaper is affected with public interest, then it is a public utility and legally subject to the intervention of government agencies like the Federal Trade Commission or the Interstate Commerce Commission. And conversely, in the reasoning of *The Wall Street Journal*, if a newspaper is not affected with public interest its proprietor may turn it to any use he sees fit within the libel laws.

The attitude of *The Wall Street Journal* is especially important in the light of the influence newspapers exert on the public mentality, which has been molded into almost a counterpart, especially among middle-class readers, of a Wall Street broker's. The press is responsible for a well-established public belief that government operation of railroads during the war was a colossal failure; the fact is, the railroads were never operated more efficiently. The newspapers have impressed most people with the fiction that government operation of public utilities in general is inefficient, whereas it is scientifically demonstrable that it is much more efficient than private operation.

Few newspaper readers are aware that the government operates all enterprises in the Panama Canal Zone on a quasi-socialistic basis, and that the results of government operation are greater efficiency and much lower prices. Bread produced in a government bakery in the Canal Zone, for example, costs only 4 cents a loaf, and is better and more nourishing than is bread sold by the big private baking plants. The Alaska Railroad is operated by the United States Army for military reasons; private entrepreneurs could not be trusted to manage it properly any more than they could be trusted to run the Navy.

Seldom do the newspapers even so much as hint at who is paying the political graft they gabble about. Newspaper readers do not know, for example, that the late John D. Rockefeller probably paid more graft than any other individual in history, and that most of the wealthy families, as shown by Gustavus Myers, founded their fortunes on the cornerstone of graft.

The newspapers, in short, reflect actuality as does a convex mirror at Coney Island. The freedom of the press, under the present dispensation, constitutes merely the freedom to distort and to suppress news.

## II

In 1906 Marshall Field II was fatally shot or stabbed by a Spanish girl in the Everleigh Club, a fashionable Chicago bagnio. The only Chicago newspaper that alluded to this misadventure to one of the city's newsworthy personages was the Chicago *Daily Socialist*. The Associated Press was silent, and the newspapers of the nation were therefore not advised of the happening. Eighteen years later, in 1924, the Chicago *Daily News* incidentally mentioned the affair in another connection, creating a nine-day sensation among Chicago newspaper people.

Andrew W. Mellon sued his wife for divorce under curious circumstances. In order to get a divorce on insufficient grounds he caused to be passed hurriedly by the subservient Pennsylvania legislature a special law, later repealed, depriving a wife of a jury trial in divorce action. The first newspaper to publish the sensational details of the Mellon divorce hearing was the Philadelphia *North American,* owned by the Wanamaker family (Morgan). All other Pennsylvania newspapers, on many of which Mellon's Union Trust Company held mortgages, were silent; the Associated Press remained silent.

In 1924 something happened to Thomas H. Ince, celebrated, newsworthy, motion-picture director, while he attended a party on board the yacht of William Randolph Hearst in Los Angeles harbor. Ince, taken ashore, died suddenly of causes variously reported as liquor poisoning, heart failure, and natural disease. Some Los Angeles newspapers hinted at foul play, and the prosecutor investigated. Whether or not anything extraordinary occurred, all the ingredients of a prime news story were present, including personalities like

Charles Chaplin, Elinor Glyn, Theodore Kosloff, Marion Davies, Hearst, and Seena Owen. Yet the press of the country, prone to inflate to undue proportions the least suggestion of Hollywood scandal, told of Ince's death in briefly perfunctory dispatches.

Happenings of a scandalous tinge relating to persons of great wealth are featured by the newspapers only when the characters concerned obviously desire to have their private affairs written about, as in the Stillman divorce case, or when they are neither so rich nor so powerful as the newspapers represent them to be, as in the Leonard Kip Rhinelander divorce case.

Suppression of personal scandals of the very rich, we may grant, is of slight import. It is symptomatic, however, of secret press control by the rich which extends to socially significant areas. The Mellon family, for example, was able for many years, through its viselike control of the Pittsburgh press and the Pittsburgh Associated Press, to keep secret its status as one of the richest dynasties in the nation. This was a fact of immense social importance, but it did not emerge until after Mellon had been appointed Secretary of the Treasury. Had Mellon's extensive financial interests been known the Senate might have refused to confirm his appointment, which proved so disastrous to the public interest.

In 1917, to touch upon another type of press manipulation on behalf of the vested interests, the Associated Press distorted a statement by Senator LaFollette, wherein he said, "We have grounds for complaint against Germany," into, "We have *no* grounds for complaint against Germany." The Associated Press and its allied newspapers refused for eight years to make a correction; LaFollette opposed entering the war and had to be discredited by means fair or foul. And during the same war period the newspapers, as a whole, also vigilantly protected the vested interests when they declined to carry a single line about an elaborate, heavily documented communication on war profits sent to Congress by Amos Pinchot.

The suppression of news by the press of the ascendant bank capitalists extends even to official findings of government bureaus, and to judicial proceedings which find private wealth guilty of gravely antisocial behavior.

Joseph Bucklin Bishop, the historian, in *Theodore Roosevelt and*

*His Time,* writing about the 1909 period, says, "Through some occult but powerful influences, the local [New York] news account of this trial [of the American Sugar Refining Company] minimized or suppressed entirely the startling evidence of fraud and the prompt verdict against the company." The Havemeyer family, rich, powerful, was directly affected by the decision.

One of the most nearly perfect and most demonstrable cases of plain suppression of significant information that embarrassed vested wealth concerned the 1923 income-tax figures, released to public scrutiny in 1924 by special act of Congress. Newspapers and news associations that flatly refused to carry these figures included the Associated Press, the Curtis papers, the Vanderbilt papers, the New Orleans *Times-Picayune,* the Springfield (Mass.) *Union,* the Philadelphia *Record* (then owned by the Wanamakers), the St. Paul *Pioneer Press* and the St. Paul *Dispatch* (Ridder Brothers), the Portland (Me.) *Express* (Guy P. Gannett), the *Ohio State Journal,* and the Columbus *Dispatch;* and the Star League Newspapers, the Denver *Rocky Mountain News,* and the Chicago *Evening Post,* all then owned by John C. Shaffer.

The New York *World,* managed by the journalistically effete Pulitzer sons, carried the telltale 1923 tax lists in its first edition, frantically struck them out in its second edition, and irresolutely restored them in later editions; the New York *Herald Tribune* (Reid-Mills) took the high-principled position that it was illegal to publish the tax figures, but the very next day began publishing them to meet competition from other newspapers; *The New York Times* published the tax lists but said that the resentment of the rich against release of the figures is "justified but belated" and "should have been aroused more vehemently at the time the bill was pending."

The New York *Evening Post* refused to publish the lists because it was "against the law," and it assailed the *Times* for not publishing the tax returns of Adolph S. Ochs, its publisher. In its first stories the *Times* also omitted the names of Cyrus H. K. Curtis and other publishers, but under the sting of the *Post's* remarks it belatedly published the tax data relating to all newspaper publishers.

In reply to a questionnaire circulated in 1925 by *Editor and Publisher,* trade organ of the publishers, the Omaha *Bee* said it would not publish the figures for 1924 unless obliged to; the Oklahoma City *Oklahoman and Times* said it would not publish all the names; the Cleveland *Times* said the figures were of no more significance than other tax figures and would not be featured; the San Francisco *Bulletin* said it hoped publication of the figures would not be forced upon the publishers; the Portland *Oregonian* said release of the figures was a violation of private rights; and the Cleveland *Plain Dealer* was undecided what to do in the grave crisis. Throughout the press the figures were given equivocal handling, and the subject was dropped as quickly as possible. The newspapers, almost without exception, howled at Congress until release of the tax figures was discontinued.

Again, when the Senate Banking and Currency Committee in 1933 brought to light the fact that J. P. Morgan and Company had given away valuable stock options to political, financial, journalistic, and social leaders in the period 1927–29, the press joined in denouncing the act of revelation rather than the facts disclosed. In New York the newspapers generally, under fire of increasing criticism and distrust, accorded the news adequate display, but the New York *Evening Post,* then owned by the Curtis dynasty, and *The New York Times* and *Herald Tribune,* assailed the committee. Newspapers throughout the country gave the story gingerly treatment, and whenever they could tucked it away in obscure corners.

The *Evening Post* defended the Morgan stock gifts in anguished accents of abject sycophancy. It whined that J. P. Morgan and Company "had tried to help a much-beloved President of the United States to make a little money for his old age," and that "no tar could be spattered upon the name of Morgan."

Another salient example of the anxiety of the press as a whole to suppress, in the interest of the wealthy families, what editors and newspaper men in general considered news of vast import was revealed in the Teapot Dome case. *The Wall Street Journal,* its circulation restricted to brokers, bankers, and speculators, first recorded the distinctly unusual news that naval oil reserves had been leased from the government. The account was headlined on the front page, but no other newspaper saw fit to reproduce it.

For twenty-two months after *The Wall Street Journal's* report Teapot Dome was not mentioned in the newspapers. Then Carl C.

Magee, editor of the Albuquerque (N. M.) *Journal* and an old political foe who had dug up much evidence of Albert B. Fall's venality in
other connections, heard that Harry F. Sinclair had given Fall large
sums of money. Magee put two and two together, published his
suspicions, and went into consultation with Senator Burton K.
Wheeler. After reading Magee's stories, Bonfils and Tammen glee-
fully opened fire in the Denver *Post* on Harry F. Sinclair and the
corrupt leases. They stopped firing when Sinclair hastily paid them
$250,000 and promised $750,000 more. But now Joseph Pulitzer, Jr.,
of the St. Louis *Post-Dispatch,* his attention aroused, began calling
for the investigation sought by the Senate liberals.

As senators got busy the press as a whole maintained silence, except for a few newspapers that fitfully supported and ridiculed the
inquiry by turns. The great press organs, however, uniformly denounced the investigating Senators as blackmailers, mudslingers,
and revolutionary malcontents. The harshest of these voices was that
of *The New York Times,* which was promptly echoed by the New
York *Herald Tribune,* the Chicago *Tribune,* the New York *Sun,* the
Chicago *Daily News,* the Curtis papers, the Hearst papers, and the
rest. It was some time before the Associated Press could bring itself
to send out adequate dispatches. The role of the Rockefeller enterprise in Teapot Dome was soft-pedalled throughout.

The Teapot Dome case provided by no means the last known instance of general suppression of official material. On October 14,
1934, the New York *World-Telegram* published the text of the cable
sent by Ambassador Page to President Wilson in 1917, warning of
internal collapse in the United States if the government did not
extricate J. P. Morgan and Company from the tangle of Allied financing by entering the war. The *World-Telegram* said the cable was to
be made the subject of inquiry by the Nye Munitions Investigating
Committee. Although the sensational message had never previously
appeared in the press, only three out of twenty leading metropolitan
newspapers copied it from the *World-Telegram*: the New York *Post*
(Stern), the Louisville *Courier-Journal* (Bingham-Flagler), and the
Pittsburgh *Press* (Scripps-Howard). The United Press carried the
text of the Page message in its dispatches of the day, but newspapers
receiving the United Press service struck it out. The Associated

Press, the International News Service (Hearst), and the Universal Service (Hearst) ignored the Page cable. Most newspaper readers today are still unaware that such a cable message exists.

The utilization of subtle journalistic technique has become widely resorted to by the plutocratic press to conceal information of grave public concern when the information cannot with expediency be suppressed. Especially has technique been resorted to in reporting labor affairs. There is a very heavy and convincing record of the hostility of the millionaire press in general to labor—a record which has been reinforced more recently by the obvious discrepancy between press reports of labor struggles and the cold record made by the newsreel camera. In Ambridge, Pennsylvania, and San Francisco in 1934, and in Chicago on Memorial Day, 1937, according to newsreel films, police without visible provocation opened fire upon orderly pickets acting under their Constitutional rights. Newspaper reports of all these "clashes" either stated that labor had started the trouble or failed to state who had started it. After the Memorial Day massacre the Chicago *Tribune,* grossly falsifying as it habitually does, flatly said the labor marchers had attacked a heavily armed brigade of police. Seven of the dead strikers were shot in the back and three in the side, although the newspapers carefully failed to report this dramatic fact until it was brought out later in a Washington hearing.

Newspapers as a whole are hostile to organized labor, and the public is therefore suspicious of organized labor whenever it moves to implement its rights. Whether the hostility be open or covert it is nevertheless a notorious fact that all the effective efforts of labor to better its precarious economic position are misrepresented by the newspapers. The average newspaper reader believes that labor starts riots, throws bombs, and is the enemy of law and order. Misrepresentation of union labor is, indeed, fundamental in all newspapers, almost without exception, and is readily understandable since all gains made by labor, although of indirect benefit to the middle classes and to the farmers as well, are gains made at the expense of reduced dividends and management salaries for the rich families that own or control the newspapers.

The news organs of the plutocracy, in misrepresenting organized labor, consciously bid for the support of the farmers and the middle classes, which are the living ballast of the social *status quo*. They do this by playing upon the prejudices of these two blocs, to the detriment of labor. The middle classes, highly individualistic, thrifty, and orderly, are deliberately provoked to resentment by the newspapers' portrayal of labor as disturbing law and order and acting collectively to obtain minimum concessions. There is no attempt in the press as a whole to give an inkling of the deplorable conditions that lead to labor's desperate walkouts. The farmers, small property holders, are impressed by newspaper accounts, usually false, of property damage and pecuniary losses created by strikes. These classes are, as a rule, deaf to protests by labor that the newspapers are filled with wholesale misrepresentation, implicit and explicit.

The farmers and the middle classes, however, have their own interests largely betrayed by the press of the wealthy families. The middle classes, notably in their role as consumers and investors, are duped by the plutocratic press. In 1929, for example, the press consistently refused to give due weight and display to warnings about the collapse of the stock market, in which the middle classes lost heavily. A factual study, *Stock Market Control,* published by the Twentieth Century Fund, shows the press, as a whole, to have been filled with false rumors and misleading "tips" during the period of the boom.

Falsification became especially marked during the period of the 1929-33 depression, when optimistic remarks from persons like Julius Klein, Assistant Secretary of Commerce, Roger W. Babson, promoter of a stock-market service who was regularly billed as an economist, and Leonard P. Ayres, vice-president of the Cleveland Trust Company and self-styled economist, were splashed repeatedly over the front pages. Contrary opinions by reputable economists were "played down."

The instability of the banks was generally concealed. Bank failures were accorded inconspicuous position, and were treated as isolated phenomena. Suggestions by some authorities that the Postal Savings Bank would be safer than many private institutions were derided by the newspapers, to the injury of many of their readers. Obviously spurious rifts in the clouds were, however, given solicitous attention.

*The New York Times,* when the Insull public-utility empire collapsed in 1932, "lost" the story in its financial section, although it was the biggest failure in American history. The New York *Herald Tribune,* closely aligned with the rival International Paper and Power Company, splashed the story on its front page. The *Herald Tribune,* however, refused to publish the facts about defaulted bonds of S. W. Straus and Company, although it possessed such documentary information more than a year before the failure of this firm in 1933.*

The *Herald Tribune* continued to publish S. W. Straus and Company advertisements, and S. W. Straus and Company continued to sell bonds of the defaulted properties. The New York *American* similarly possessed documentary evidence of the S. W. Straus defaults, but did not publish it.

Throughout the depression the alarming growth of unemployment, which affected the middle classes and farmers as well as labor, was concealed by the press as a whole, and the newspapers joined in deprecating reports by the American Federation of Labor on the menacing extent of unemployment. The newspapers rarely found space for news of wholesale layoffs by big corporations like General Motors, Ford Motor, United States Steel, and American Telephone and Telegraph Company, even though announcements of these events were regularly issued over the ticker service of the Wall Street News Bureau. But when the business cycle began an upturn in 1933 the press brimmed with exaggerated reports of wholesale hirings throughout industry. In reading through the newspapers of 1929-33 one is confronted with this apparent paradox: corporations in 1933 suddenly began rehiring employees that had never been laid off!

Although the newspaper offices had the facts, they failed to inform the middle class of the growing number of evictions for nonpayment of rent and mortgage interest. Only when Western farmers, taking the law into their own hands, staged an armed revolt did it become apparent that the big banks and insurance companies were cracking down on delinquents. And not until the Hoover Administration was swept out of office did the full extent of the postwar social damage become known to the country.

* The author, as a Wall Street staff member of the *Herald Tribune,* wrote an account of the Straus defaults more than a year before the firm failed, but the story was never published.

This virtually unbroken co-ordination of the American press would seem a miracle of coincidence if it were not obvious from the previous chapter, that the press is owned by the wealthiest families, who must distort and suppress dynamic news to retain political, social, and economic power.

In the spheres of public health and the retail market the farmers and the middle classes are notably betrayed by the press as a whole. Findings of the Departments of Agriculture and of Commerce—official, factual, and of significant interest—relative to the low grade or harmful character of certain advertised foods, drugs, medicines, cosmetics, clothing and merchandise, are ignored, while the press deliberately helps foist upon the middle classes and farmers harmful, or substandard merchandise, as well as worthless securities and real estate.

Hart, Kingsbury, and Rowe, in a study published in *The New Republic* (October 29, 1930), found only eight newspapers free from advertisements of unsavory or fraudulent medical proprietaries condemned by the Bureau of Investigation of the American Medical Association. The only publications with these perfect records were the *Christian Science Monitor* (institutional), the *United States Daily* (non-commercial), *The New York Times,* the New York *World,* the New York *Evening Post,* the Boston *Transcript,* the Minneapolis *Journal,* and the Milwaukee *Leader* (Socialist).

Just how dangerous, improperly used, the right of the "free press" can be to public health is shown in the comment of *The Journal of the American Medical Association* upon 1924 statistics that proved the United States to have the highest smallpox death rate in the world. The medical journal placed part of the responsibility for the condition upon the "pernicious" influence of such periodicals as Bernarr Macfadden's *Physical Culture,* which constantly preached antivaccination.

George Seldes cites the failure of Chicago newspapers and the press associations to report an outbreak of dysentery during the World's Fair in 1933; the source of the infection was traced at an early stage to a Chicago hotel. There are other cases on record of the failure of newspapers to report epidemics (notably a prewar outbreak of the bubonic plague on the Pacific Coast), when business would have felt the harmful effect of public alarm.

And while the press as a whole withholds crucial information and accepts advertising that facilitates the exploitation of the middle classes in the public market, it refuses, in many cases, to handle advertising of books and agencies that would put its readers on guard. *Time,* for example, refused advertising of Consumer's Research, Inc., an agency that has exposed many pharmaceutical and food frauds. The New York *Herald Tribune* early in 1937 declined to accept advertisements for *False Security,* by Bernard J. Reis, a reputable accountant; the book exposed corporation bookkeeping frauds, naming some of the biggest companies. *The New York Times* has also refused to accept advertisements for literature that disclosed pitfalls of the retail market. It has gone so far as to reject advertisements of novels accurately portraying sordid social conditions.

The class inhibitions that haunt the contemporary press under its multimillionaire ownership are responsible in large measure for the neurotic character of American newspapers. Because so many fields of editorial investigation and exposition are taboo, the press as a whole must confine itself to a relatively restricted "safe" area.

This accounts for the undue measure of attention given to the underworld; to petty scandals involving actresses, baseball players, and minor politicians; to sporting affairs and the activities of the quasi-wealthy. The press, in short, must compensate for enforced lack of vitality in dynamic fields by artificial enthusiasm in static fields. In place of an evenhanded, vital, varied daily news report, the American press as a whole is obliged to present a lopsided news report that is of doubtful reader interest. And in order to recapture the constantly waning attention of readers it must rely upon comic strips, inane "features," contests, gossip columns, fiction, cooking recipes, instruction columns in golf, chess, bridge, and stamp collecting, and similar nonsense. American newspapers, in short, are, paradoxically and with few exceptions, not newspapers at all.

The yearning of the American press for "safe" "stories" to exploit was exemplified perfectly in the Lindbergh career. Lindbergh's flight to Paris was itself an achievement deserving of extended press attention. The prolongation of journalistic interest in Lindbergh, however, was due, very probably, to the fact that some of the wealthiest Wall Street families visualized the great airplane grab of 1928-32. This grab was perpetrated behind the screen of Lindbergh's flight, which stimulated public interest in aviation shares, increased aviation personnel by inducing many young men to take up flying, and made it easy to wheedle huge aviation subsidies from Congress.

Lindbergh, the unwitting pawn in this game, is said to have resented the hysterical behavior of the press, and to have left the United States for relief. But everything he did played into the hands of the aviation propagandists. When he married a daughter of Dwight W. Morrow, chairman of Coolidge's Aviation Board, the newspapers resumed their barrage of adulation; when his children were born the natural events were recorded in giant type that even tired Congressmen studying projected aviation grants could read.

The pecuniary inhibitions that rule the press like a Freudian complex have brought such discredit upon newspapers that they are no longer trusted by informed persons or even by business interests. There has consequently been a phenomenal increase in the number of specialized information and private news services of whose existence the general public is not even aware.

Business interests no longer rely upon newspapers for Wall Street and Washington news. For market news they turn to the publications of Dun and Bradstreet, the *Commercial and Financial Chronicle,* and Standard Statistics Service. From Washington special agencies report on domestic and foreign political events, steering their heavily paying clients around the pitfalls in the daily newspapers. The best known of these Washington news services are the Kiplinger and Whaley-Eaton "letters."

Both were established during the World War to meet the need of businessmen for uncensored information. The wartime government did not object so long as the citizenry in general was kept under illusions. The uncertain political atmosphere at the close of the war, combined with the increasing reticence of the press, made it possible for these news services to expand.

The private Washington news letters are actually miniature newspapers, stripped of ballyhoo. Very often the disparity between the intelligence transmitted in the private news letters and that in the newspaper dispatches is staggering. Large corporations, seeking to cut through the maze of rumors and false reports, have scores of subscriptions to the news-letter services, one for every department head.

The significant aspect of these private letter services, staffed by former newspapermen, economists, statisticians, and other specialists, is this: they could not exist if the newspapers were fulfilling their avowed function of conveying relevant, factual information and measured, sober opinion. Many corporations actually employ former newspapermen in New York, Washington, and European capitals to keep them properly informed by special reports.

The curious situation is, therefore, presented of a select minority kept cognizant of what is taking place by special information services for which high fees are paid, and a vast majority kept in a twilight zone of partial information and misinformation by an informally co-ordinated propaganda press.

Publishers generally deny hotly charges of venality in contemporary newspaper management. In the narrative sufficient instances have been cited to suggest that the millionaire press is a venal press. A few more instances will be cited to clinch the argument.

The Federal Trade Commission, investigating the public-utilities industry, which is dominated by our richest families, found that the General Electric Company (Morgan), the United Gas Improvement Company (Morgan), the Electric Bond and Share Company (Morgan), and the American Telephone and Telegraph Company (Morgan), had subsidized E. Hofer and Sons, operators of a rural press service that placed propaganda in fourteen thousand newspapers. The Darnell Press Service, in the pay of the National Electric Light Association, supplied six hundred newspapers in Alabama, Georgia, Mississippi, and Florida with antipublic-ownership propaganda.

The newspapers, it appeared, did not publish the propaganda merely because they agreed with the propagandists. The newspapers were paid, by the hundreds, to publish specially prepared "canned" editorials and "news" stories. And the Federal Trade Commission, in all instances, traced the paid propaganda to the highest strata of Wall Street—to the Morgans and the Rockefellers.

The principal propaganda agency was discovered to be the National Electric Light Association, trade group for the industry. The president of NELA was George B. Cortelyou, Morgan man from Theodore Roosevelt's Cabinet who had for two decades been president of the Consolidated Gas Company of New York. But when NELA was exposed as a center of journalistic corruption it was dissolved. There was then created the Edison Electric Institute, hailed by the newspapers as an entirely new type of organization. The president of Edison Electric Institute immediately became George B. Cortelyou.

There are, however, innumerable less well-known instances of press corruption on the record. Mrs. Evalyn Walsh McLean sued in 1932 to have her husband, Edward B. McLean, removed as trustee of his father's estate, which included the Washington *Post,* the Cincinnati *Enquirer,* and the Cincinnati *Commercial Tribune.* In the complaint she charged that McLean, on July 10, 1931, "received the sum of more than $100,000 in money upon his agreement to devote the same to the needs of the Washington *Post.*" This sum came, it developed, from Hoover's Secretary of War Patrick J. Hurley. It was ostensibly for the purchase of McLean's Virginia estate, but was actually charged to be in consideration of a "lease on the *Post's* political policy until the end of the Presidential campaign, November, 1932."

In the Senate Shipping Board investigation it was brought out that Albert D. Lasker, Chicago advertising man who headed the Board, inspired widespread newspaper propaganda for government ship subsidies and against nonprofit government operation. The Shipping Board, for example, had not advertised much in the Chicago *Journal of Commerce* (Ames family, Booth Fisheries). In February, 1922, this newspaper suddenly editorialized on behalf of the Lasker Ship Subsidy Bill, and immediately began receiving Shipping Board advertising on a rising scale so that for the year ended June 30, 1923, it received $34,652.52 of such advertising. In return for Shipping Board advertising the farm publication, *Fruit, Garden and Home,* also waged a campaign on behalf of ship subsidies.

Lasker on May 12, 1922, wrote to Robert R. McCormick, of the Chicago *Tribune,* who had suggested that the Paris edition of the newspaper be given more Shipping Board advertising. Lasker said that the Chicago *Tribune* under a new schedule was slated for fourteen hundred lines of advertising a week and that he was sending under separate cover copies of the ship subsidy bill and of the Board's study of subsidies. He suggested that McCormick might want to assign a writer to compose a series on the American merchant marine, and offered to co-operate. The Chicago *Tribune* soon afterward syndicated a series of propaganda articles signed by Lasker himself under the title: "Why the United States Should Have a Merchant Marine." The Shipping Board then gave the *Tribune* the contract for the news service on board its vessels; under this contract the Shipping Board paid deficits and the *Tribune* shared profits.

As the Senate investigators discovered, the American Steamship Owners' Association sent out editorials and articles which were reproduced throughout the nation's press without acknowledgment of their source. This association succeeded, too, in suppressing newspaper material hostile to its aims.

The Chicago *Tribune*, fatuously proclaiming itself "The World's Greatest Newspaper," has functioned under Robert R. McCormick in a way that lays it open to indictment on almost any count. This newspaper has been a wholesale purveyor of bogus news, according to a study made for the period 1925–27 by Professor Frederick L. Schuman of the University of Chicago.[1] Falsifications about Russia were found by Schuman to be frequent, but other falsifications were also noted. Soon after the World War the Chicago *Tribune*, which like the rest of the press was soaked in wartime propaganda, notably falsified with respect to William McAndrew, British-born superintendent of the Chicago Board of Education, on the issue of patriotism.[2] Falsifications by the Chicago *Tribune*, indeed, have been so complete and so flagrant on every conceivable issue that it is impossible to devote more space to them here. From 1933 onward it conspicuously falsified with respect to every significant facet of the Roosevelt Administration's program.

Wherever one touches the American press, for whatever year, the story is the same. In 1921 Senator George W. Norris charged that the packers had paid for advertising in order to inspire certain policies throughout the press; they bought up an unfriendly Texas newspaper.[3] Senator LaFollette in 1923 produced documents which showed the National Coal Association subsidized the press to obtain news stories that falsely indicated a looming coal shortage. The Associated Press was especially co-operative.[4]

In the campaign of Upton Sinclair for the governorship of California on the semiradical EPIC ticket in 1934 the California Newspaper Publishers Association was paid by the California Brewers Association to publish throughout the California press its anti-Sinclair propaganda.[5] The brewing and distilling industries, like the electric-power industry, have for decades found the press open to payments of money.

In 1915, for example, Charles H. Allen bought the Montgomery (Ala.) *Advertiser* with $100,000 advanced by the brewing industry.[6] Christian Feigenspan, Newark brewer, advanced from time to time $150,000 to keep the Newark *Ledger* under control on the liquor question.[7] The brewers boasted in 1911 that "every newspaper in the State of Texas of any consequence . . . is on our side." [8] In 1917 they raised a national advertising fund of $535,000 for the purpose of controlling editorial views.[9]

German-American brewers, it was brought out by a Senate Committee, in 1917 advanced $500,000, unsecured and with no note to evidence the money as a loan, to Arthur Brisbane, Hearst's right-hand man. Brisbane used the money to purchase the Washington *Times* from Frank Munsey; it was a moot point whether Brisbane was to operate the paper as an antiprohibition publication or as a pro-German organ.

The Hearst newspapers have been involved in many known venal transactions. In 1898 it was revealed that six years earlier Hearst had signed contracts with the Southern Pacific Railroad, agreeing for a monthly consideration of $1,000 not to be unfriendly. And in 1934, to mention a recent instance, the Hearst newspapers agreed to supply the Hitler press bureau with American news dispatches for the sizable consideration of $400,000 annually. (Germany had previously been receiving dispatches of the Associated Press in free exchange for dispatches of the Wolff Bureau of Germany.) After this arrangement with the Hitler regime the Hearst newspapers began beating the drum for the Third Reich.

According to James Rorty in *Our Master's Voice: Advertising,* seventy-five per cent of newspaper revenue comes from advertising, so that it would be unusual if newspaper policies were never affected by promised or withheld advertising. But advertising, as this analysis should indicate, is secondary to ownership by the very rich in influencing newspapers. Were there no advertising, newspaper policies would remain very much what they are, with only minor variations of emphasis.

Newspapers, especially those directly controlled by members of the inner circle of wealth or by their deputies, have often resisted attempts of advertisers to dictate policies, and, on the whole, the bigger publications have refused to subordinate policies to the requirements of advertisers. To permit advertisers to dictate would simply be to surrender press control—something the wealthy families will never do willingly.

Publishers often boast of the way they have resolutely protected "freedom of the press" by rebuffing a big advertiser, but their zeal in this direction means usually that they have other uses for the press in consonance with the needs of more powerful interests. In 1895, for example, R. H. Macy and Company, New York department store, asked James Gordon Bennett to support Nathan Straus, an owner of the store, for Mayor of New York because the store was a big *Herald* advertiser.[10] Bennett refused, publicized the attempt to coerce him, and was applauded by Pulitzer; whereupon Straus organized most of the large department stores and induced them to withdraw advertising from *The Herald* and *The World*.[11] Pulitzer and Bennett stuck fast, however.

In short, when the interests of an advertiser conflict with the class interests of the individual or group publishing a certain newspaper, it is impossible for the advertiser to influence editorial policies. Even the Chicago *Tribune* has publicly rebuked brash advertisers that sought to influence editorial policies.

J. David Stern, who publishes three lively New Deal newspapers that have probably the most vigorous editorial pages in the country, supported an anti-Hitler merchandise boycott in New York in the face of hostility from some advertisers. But Stern's militant liberalism on various contemporary questions was actuated by the self-interest of his financial backers as much as was the reactionary policy of the Chicago *Tribune*. Related by marriage to the Lit Department Store family, of Philadelphia, Stern numbered among the financial backers of his New York *Post* Albert M. Greenfield, Philadelphia realtor; Governor George H. Earle of Pennsylvania, former head of the Pennsylvania Sugar Company; Senator Joseph F. Guffey and Samuel Untermyer, both wealthy lawyers; William Fox, former film magnate; Samuel Fels, soap magnate; Warner Brothers, film entrepreneurs; and Vincent Astor, recent large-scale publisher and the largest owner of real estate in New York City after the Goelet family. These people were all hard hit financially during the Hoover regime; they have since been interested in sponsoring policies of benefit to their properties. The Hoover deflation, for example, smashed a Philadelphia bank owned by Greenfield, and the Astor realty values ebbed greatly at the same time, so it was not extraordinary that the three Stern newspapers should espouse New Deal easy money policies and other measures for the rehabilitation of consumer purchasing power. But, although fighting on behalf of reformist proposals of all shades and varieties, the New York *Post* refused in 1934, as disclosed by Don Wharton in *Scribner's Magazine*, to feature widespread criticism of Astor's New York slum properties. This led to the resignation of Ernest Gruening, the managing editor, who, as an independent publisher in Maine, had waged unceasing war against the Insull interests.

Stern, however, has never been accused of venal dealings. And he did nothing journalistically unusual in protecting Astor. Most publications blatantly boost their backers and friends both in editorial and news columns.

*The Saturday Evening Post* and other Curtis publications, for example, have always automatically jumped to the defense of the rich. After Upton Sinclair exposed conditions in the Chicago stockyards the *Post* invited J. Ogden Armour (Editor George Horace Lorimer's former employer) to enter a denial, which it printed. In a postmortem eulogy of J. P. Morgan, written for the *Post*, Elbert H. Gary said, "It was not generally known that he was deeply religious." The *Post* invited Philander C. Knox to defend "dollar diplomacy" in its pages. And during the boom of the 1920's the magazine lived up to its traditions by obliging Lee, Higginson and Company in permitting

Isaac Marcosson to write a laudatory series about Ivar Kreuger, master swindler.

For more than twenty years *The American Magazine* of the Crowell Publishing Company has excelled in the publication of articles romanticizing individuals who have made or inherited money. After the 1929 smashup *Fortune*, published by Time, Inc., entered this field, but aimed at a more sophisticated audience. *Fortune,* no less than *The American Magazine,* has done nothing to invalidate the charge that it is a propaganda organ for the pecuniary motive in all its devious ramifications.

Time, Inc. is ruled by Henry R. Luce, Yale classmate of Harry P. Davison, Morgan partner, who contributed original capital to the enterprise in concert with E. Roland Harriman, the late Dwight W. Morrow, Harvey Firestone, and various members of the Harkness family.

In view of the identities of its stockholders detailed in the preceding chapter, it is not strange that *Time, Fortune's* sister enterprise, should have assailed the Senate Banking and Currency Committee for presuming to inquire into the operations of J. P. Morgan and his partners, and that it should similarly have assailed the Nye Munitions Investigating Committee, although *Fortune* (March, 1934) published an ostensible exposure of the munitions traffic. Most of the exposure, however, was devoted to European munitions makers; out of ten thousand words only three hundred and fifty were devoted to American munitions makers, and out of these three hundred and fifty words only fifteen were devoted to the Du Ponts, perhaps the biggest munitions fabricators in the world. Of the Nye Committee, *Time* (October 19, 1936) said, "The Nye Committee had spent months blackguarding the Du Ponts, Britain's late George V, a handful of Latin American dignitaries, Woodrow Wilson, and the House of Morgan." One may readily imagine about whom in this collection *Time* was really distressed. The sinister facts elicited by these two Senate committees were, however, passed over lightly.

From its inception in 1924 *Time* has consistently performed as the journalistic champion of the wealthiest families. In January, 1925, *Time* used three oddly assorted news items about John D. Rockefeller as an excuse for a sermon on the camel and the needle's eye, proving that the younger Rockefeller would surely pass through. A disgusted subscriber wrote to protest against the "sweet eulogy of this saint that would make a dog sick."

But obvious as has been the adulation lavished on the Rockefeller clan—until it made a hostile move against Morgan—it is delicate by comparison with *Time's* elephantine capers around John Pierpont Morgan. *Time* had a field day when reporters, eager to know whether she was engaged to Colonel Lindbergh, burst into the stateroom of the late Elizabeth Morrow, returning on the *Olympic* "in the personal charge" of J. P. Morgan. As the photographers got ready, in "strode a tall, heavy man of magnificent carriage, instantly recognizable as John Pierpont Morgan. At his word reporters fled." *Time* writers have apparently stayed up nights to invent new ways of presenting Morgan. The issue of February 11, 1929, carried a classic entitled "Le Monsieur Embarks" (for the Young Commission), which began: "Parisians were especially delighted, last week, by a sly little story which came clicking over the cables." The story was merely that a square porthole had been left open at the pier level so that "America's greatest Monsieur" could go aboard unseen.

In a beatific account of Mr. Morgan's return, "[Newsmen] told how, after a gentle suggestion from a bold photographer, the strikingly handsome Banker Morgan shifted to a more advantageous position. . . . Perhaps never had so great a banker appeared in so happy a light."

Although Morgan and Rockefeller have claimed much of *Time's* spotlight, many other names in the cast of great wealth have come in for breathless attention. When the Elbert H. Garys acquired Henry Clay Frick's box at the Metropolitan Opera House *Time* gushed: "At them steelworkers in the topmost gallery will point with pride." Speaking of F. Trubee Davison, brother of stockholder Harry P. Davison, *Time* (August 24, 1935) said, "He is not of the ordinary run of local politician. He is in politics more after the old British fashion—by which a distinguished family sends one of its sons into public life. What is more, he is able. He ought to be. Look at his father." His father started life as an upstate bank clerk.

*Time* waited many months to sink a rapier into Winthrop W.

Aldrich of the Chase National Bank, after Aldrich, during the bank holiday of 1933, anticipated criticism of the Chase Securities Company by suggesting that the underwriting and deposit functions of banks be separated by law. Aldrich's defensive maneuver struck directly at J. P. Morgan and Company in its complex deposit-underwriting business.

In 1934 came *Time's* opportunity to punish Aldrich, for it went far out of its way to make an exceedingly frank report of a survey junket taken around the country by Aldrich, several Chase bank officials, and two Rockefeller sons in a private car that, said *Time,* cost $75 per day plus railroad fares. The costliness of the trip was stressed, and just at a time when Chase Bank minority stockholders were criticizing officers for extravagant handling of the bank's funds. *Time* contrasted the Chase tour with one made by James H. Perkins, new chairman of the National City Bank, who, it was slyly pointed out, ensconced himself ascetically in a lower berth.

*Time* let several big Aldrich cats out of the bag. It charged that "in St. Paul local newspapers were asked to play down the Chase junket," and that a speech critical of President Roosevelt made by Aldrich to Los Angeles bankers and businessmen was, at Aldrich's order, left out of Harry Chandler's *Times,* E. Manchester Boddy's *Illustrated Daily News,* and the two local Hearst papers. Since this episode *Time* has let slip few opportunities to pinprick the Rockefellers.

*Fortune* (November, 1934) called Pierre du Pont, backer of the reactionary Liberty League, a man of liberal ideas. And while admitting that the Du Ponts ruled Delaware politics and that Delaware politics were venal, *Fortune* nevertheless insisted that the Du Ponts were a good influence in the state. Owen D. Young is another "liberal," although "he is too well versed in the age-old organisms of human trade to offer specious nostrums for their sudden improvement or the cure of such ills as they have developed" (March, 1931). Of Bernard M. Baruch, in October, 1933, *Fortune* said, "Baruch is perhaps the only specimen of that brilliant type of public figure which is best represented by his good friend, Winston Churchill."

*Fortune,* like *Time,* seldom forgets distinctions in distributing accolades. In an article on Vincent Astor, after he had identified himself with the New Deal, which Morgan opposed, *Fortune* patronizingly implied that Astor had overcome his earlier intellectual lassitude; but *Fortune* has never yet brought itself to admit that the reigning J. P. Morgan is far from being esteemed as an intellectual heavyweight.

*Time* and *Fortune* have unkind things to say only about governments that are, coincidentally, on bad terms with J. P. Morgan and Company. Soviet Russia has been consistently misrepresented; the rise of a left-liberal government in France was met with scorn by *Time* which, by word, radio, and film boosted the Fascist Croix de Feu; the defense of a legally elected democratic regime in Spain brought quick sneers from *Time*, in whose pages the Madrid citizens' army was intemperately alluded to as "flat-footed mobsters." That social bias has little to do with some of these attitudes, and that pecuniary bias has much, is revealed in the fact that Hitler's rightwing Germany—a financial defaulter and proud of it—has been handled without gloves. Right-wing Italy, like Germany a land of castor oil, the bastinado, and the dagger, is, on the other hand, recurrently flattered. Italy, however, has not defaulted on Morgan loans.

As with politics abroad, so with politics at home. *Time* has let pass no opportunity to ridicule the New Deal. Hostile to Roosevelt, hostile to his light-industry program throughout, it was still hostile in 1936; but as election day approached, it became, with typical opportunism, less stridently pro-Landon—because the *Fortune* poll showed that Roosevelt would win by a great majority.

The enterprises of Time, Inc., were subjected to notably acute analysis by Dwight MacDonald, former *Fortune* editor, in *The Nation* (May 1, 8, and 22, 1937). Liberals, he observed, object to *Time's* "habitual distortion or suppression of labor and radical news, the constant pooh-poohing of all movements for social progress."

"In 1930," said MacDonald, "*Fortune* published a eulogy of Albert H. Wiggin, in 1931 of Samuel Insull, Jr. In 1931, the present J. P. Morgan, whom only *Fortune* takes seriously, was the subject of a tenderly respectful biography. In March, 1934, the Van Sweringens were whitewashed (and their critics rebuked) in some 15,000 words. The most gruesome of the many skeletons in *Fortune's* closet is probably the amazing article on Pittsburgh (December, 1930) from the hand of Luce himself. 'Pittsburgh,' Luce pronounces, 'is a gentle city.' (The Mellons are gentle, too; for example, R. B. Mellon's whimsical remark, which Luce doesn't quote: 'You couldn't run a coal mine without machine-guns.') As for living conditions, Luce reports: 'Windows of Pittsburgh homes are washed once a week—by the maid, not by some window-cleaning concern.'" *Fortune*'s whitewashes have extended even to the financial affairs of Hearst, in which the banks are concerned, although Hearst himself many times has been spoken of slightingly in *Time*.

In a pseudoscientific search for typical American families, *Fortune* ignored the preponderance of Southern sharecroppers, city slum dwellers, and unskilled laborers, and found, as MacDonald notes, that "the typical Midwest farmer owned a farm worth $100,000 and made a *net* income of $4,000 in 1934. The typical white-collar worker got $58 a week."

*Time* and *Fortune* have on their staffs a notable array of liberal and radical writers, chosen because of their sensitivity to social and political phenomena. But, as MacDonald testifies, their writings are subject to careful revision and distortion—and suppression—by the executive editors. Articles about personalities and enterprises in *Fortune* are, moreover, often submitted for approval or "correction" to their subjects.

Few readers are able to see through the spurious claim of objectivity behind which *Time* and *Fortune* class-consciously maneuver, for both employ a highly refined and deceptive journalistic technique wherein a brief adjective or adverb may slant a whole series of facts. This technique belongs to Henry R. Luce, the spiritual heir of Frank Munsey, whose Morgan-inspired *Sun,* a joke to newspaper people, was once saluted by *Time* as "a great newspaper."

Thomas W. Lamont is probably the single most influential individual in contemporary American journalism. He began his career as a financial reporter on the old New York *Tribune*.

Lamont's duties as a Morgan partner and apostolic successor to George W. Perkins are varied, but among them journalistic concerns have played a very large part. Perkins and Lamont have, each in his respective period of ascendancy, been the pacemakers of the Morgan banking house—the trouble shooters, the business getters, the schemers, the diplomats, and the apologists.

Lamont, like Perkins, has been adept in getting Morgan theses presented by the newspapers, which have not failed to keep confidential the source of their inspiration. Perkins was, indeed, so skilled at manipulating newspapers (as witness his profitable use of the *Times* in 1907) that at an early semiofficial wartime gathering of Charles Evans Hughes, Thomas L. Chadbourne, Willard Straight, John Purroy Mitchel, Henry E. Morgenthau, and others, Frank Munsey argued that Perkins should be given charge of government censorship. Munsey, as Morgenthau relates, apostrophized Perkins as "one of the great experts in the securing of publicity."

Perkins' only disciple became Lamont, who became the only peer of the Rockefellers' late Ivy L. Lee.

To Lamont's desk at 23 Wall Street newspapers, magazines, and books from all over the world are brought immediately after publication, relevant passages marked by a staff of readers, works in foreign languages translated. Lamont reads and evaluates praise and dispraise of J. P. Morgan and Company; then the material is filed. Sometimes he enters into personal correspondence with writers and editors; sometimes he sends out a letter for publication; sometimes he suggests that a third party make denial, emendation, affirmation.

At least half of Lamont's contact with the surrounding world is with publishers, writers that cater to mass audiences, newspapermen, and editors. Among the many Lamont literary and journalistic friends are Walter Lippmann*, who went with him on a trip to the Near East in 1931 and who has forwarded in his nationally syndicated columns many theses that Wall Street financial writers had previ-

---

* Walter Lippmann is coming to be more and more clearly recognized as spokesman for the rich. Professor T. V. Smith, of the University of Chicago, speaking on August 29, 1937, before the Institute of Human Relations at Williamstown, Massachusetts, said: "Plutogogue is the voice of the wealthy when they can no longer speak for themselves, the successor of the plutocrat of other days. He is not Allah, but Allah's public relations counsel. You will hear his soft-spoken message in the columns of our sophisticated Walter Lippmanns and our unctuous Glenn Franks. You will see or gently feel his gloved hand in the eulogistic releases of our late Ivy Lees and our ever present Edward Bernays." And to these Professor Smith might have added Westbrook Pegler, Hugh Johnson, David Lawrence, and Mark Sullivan.

ously heard, often similarly phrased, from the lips of Lamont; B. C. Forbes of the Hearst organization; William T. Dewart and Franz Schneider of the New York *Sun*; Henry R. Luce, of Time, Inc.; Arthur Hays Sulzberger, of *The New York Times*; Sir Willmott Lewis, Washington correspondent of the London *Times* and son-in-law of Frank B. Noyes, a leading spirit in the Associated Press and publisher of the Washington *Star*; Henry Seidel Canby; Charles Seymour, president of Yale University; Edwin L. James, managing editor of *The New York Times*; and Mrs. Ogden Reid of the New York *Herald Tribune*. Lamont has even made a pilgrimage to the California ranch of William Randolph Hearst.

Writers of standing and repute not personally acquainted with Lamont will, sometimes, receive an invitation to lunch with him, and will learn from him wherein they have erred in reviewing a certain book, in writing a preface, or in composing an essay that mentions J. P. Morgan and Company or one of its many enterprises or friends. They will be asked to retract, and, failing to comply, they may count upon Morgan hostility to manifest itself invisibly in various parts of the magazine- and book-publishing world.

Writers to whom Lamont is friendly unquestionably have their paths smoothed toward pecuniary success. For example, the New York *Evening Post* under Lamont included the following staff members who have since achieved rapid promotion: Henry Seidel Canby, Franz Schneider, and Arthur Pound, editor of Barron's memoirs and author of a series of articles on corporations which were published by *The Atlantic Monthly* in 1935 as part of a paid advertising program (although this fact was not at first told to readers). Ellery Sedgwick, editor of *The Atlantic Monthly*, is, incidentally, a Lamont contact, and lunches occasionally at 23 Wall Street and at the First National Bank of New York.

Unpublicized dinners frequently given by Mr. and Mrs. Lamont are usually graced by writers, foreign as well as American, and by editors and publishers. Among European writers recurrently entertained are H. G. Wells, André Maurois, and John Masefield, British poet laureate; all have big American audiences. None of them ever touches upon practical concerns of J. P. Morgan and Company, but their general attitudes are, beyond question, of more than academic interest to the banking house.

Lamont's journalistic and literary peregrinations have perceptible effect. In 1933 he served notice on New York publishers that the Guaranty Trust Company, the Bankers Trust Company, the First National Bank, and the New York Trust Company were no longer to be referred to as "Morgan banks." In the uncritical boom period such references, frequently made, were of distinct advantage to J. P. Morgan and Company. Since the order to discontinue was given, only the New York *Post* (Stern) has mentioned the "Morgan banks." Similarly, the Hearst newspapers, after Lamont's visit to Hearst in California, stopped blaming all the ills of the country upon the bankers, as they had been maliciously doing for several depression years.

Long before the Van Sweringen bubble burst Lamont was able to keep mention of the looming catastrophe out of the newspapers, although as early as 1931 the New York financial writers knew what was happening. In that year the *Herald Tribune*, whose Reid family held some Van Sweringen securities and was more than passingly interested, sent a reporter to Cleveland to check on rumors of difficulties. Cleveland bankers, shocked at the familiarity with the Van Sweringen "secrets" displayed by a strange newspaperman, immediately telephoned J. P. Morgan and Company. The *Herald Tribune* reporter was peremptorily recalled, his suspicions verified but his mission uncompleted; he was not permitted to write his report.

In 1933 another *Herald Tribune* reporter obtained information that the Van Sweringen railroad interests were headed for drastic reorganization. The story he wrote was submitted, at the insistence of the *Herald Tribune* management, to Lamont, who rewrote it to indicate that the crisis was being handled by J. P. Morgan and Company to the satisfaction of Washington. An entirely misleading and soothing story, anonymously authored by Lamont, was published on the front page of the *Herald Tribune,* February 9, 1933.

*The New York Times* subsequently featured on its first page a long account of a Van Sweringen loan default to J. P. Morgan and Company; but after receiving a midnight telephone call from Lamont or an associate the *Times'* editors hastily wrote a substitute story for an inside page. The next day the bankers denied that the loan had been defaulted, although interest due had to be deferred for another year!

Dwight MacDonald, in his valuable *Nation* series, wrote that after *Fortune* prepared an article on the United States Steel Corporation which attributed responsibility for many abuses to Myron C. Taylor, "Thomas W. Lamont, of J. P. Morgan and Company, went to work on the editors of *Fortune*. He scored a diplomatic victory which must have amazed even so seasoned a strategist as Lamont. Not only was an abbreviated and emasculated version of the article printed, but an objective (hence unflattering) biography of Mr. Taylor was excised completely and replaced by a full-throated burst of lyrical eulogy which the editor in charge took care to write himself."

About another build-up for Taylor in connection with the capitulation of the United States Steel Corporation to the C.I.O.—a build-up in which *Fortune* presented Taylor as a great industrial statesman, MacDonald remarks: "Did not Mr. Lamont possibly sell Mr. Luce's editors another bill of goods?"

Lamont is accustomed to such successes; very probably he is only astonished on those rare occasions when he fails to bring an editor to "understand" his point of view.

Lamont's *Saturday Review of Literature* published a review of Professor Jerome Davis's *Capitalism and Its Culture*, which gets down to mentioning cases disagreeable to J. P. Morgan and Company. Canby, then the editor in charge, found the seventy-six words of the review too much. He later admitted having edited the eulogy out of these brief remarks, which were written by an eminent political authority, Professor Harold J. Laski. Contributors to the *Saturday Review*, incidentally, have been asked to delete sharp remarks relating to J. P. Morgan and Company and to Thomas W. Lamont in reviewing histories of railroads and industrial corporations.

The New York *World-Telegram* (April 7, 1936) revealed that Canby had admitted turning over to Lamont the proofs of *M-Day*, by Rose M. Stein. The book discussed war preparations, past and present, and criticized J. P. Morgan and Company. Canby said he gave the proofs to Lamont merely so that he might suggest a competent reviewer. Lamont suggested Charles Seymour, Yale professor who has since become the university's president. Seymour was associated with Lamont at the Versailles Peace Conference and has since promulgated far and wide the Morgan thesis that the United States was brought into the war by the German submarine warfare. Seymour, himself under fire from historians, attacked the Stein book.

Canby, however, far from having received the book in the usual routine, had gone out of his way to obtain advance proofs from Harcourt, Brace and Company, the publishers. The situation was brought to the attention of the *World-Telegram* by a curious exchange of letters in *The Nation* between Miss Stein and Walter H. Millis, *Herald Tribune* editorial writer and author of *The Road to War*, who had reviewed *M-Day* for *The Nation*. Miss Stein charged that Millis's objections to her book were identical with those made by Lamont who, she asserted, had tried unsuccessfully to induce Harcourt, Brace and Company to change portions of the book to which Lamont took exception. Lamont obtained his advance information from the proofs supplied by Canby.

Millis, in reply to Miss Stein, disavowed Lamont's having had anything to do with his critical position. Miss Stein's point recalled to other observers, however, that Millis's *The Road to War* was criticized by C. Hartley Grattan in *The New Republic* for having omitted the dramatic Page-Wilson cablegram of 1917.

This cablegram is a tender subject for J. P. Morgan and Company, and the pro-Morgan newspapers, as we have seen, did not carry it when Senator Nye alluded to it. Something that neither Grattan nor Miss Stein knew, however, was that Lamont had been tipped off in advance, possibly again through *The Saturday Review*, that Millis's war book was about to appear, and had effected a meeting with Millis.

Millis volunteered to the author, when asked about the curious absence of the Page cablegram, that it had been included, but was deleted, in the interests of a shorter text, while the book was in manuscript. *The Road to War*, however, contained material of a less significant nature. The omission of the revealing Page cablegram marred an otherwise fine piece of work.

Bernard De Voto, novelist and critic, has replaced Canby as editor of *The Saturday Review*, and although a more independent thinker than Canby, he has yet to show where he stands on social and economic problems.

Lamont is virtually ubiquitous in the American press. Usually when the New York newspapers, in editorial or news columns, chastely allude to "prominent banking opinion," "impressions in financial circles," and "the consensus among bankers," they refer only to Lamont. The newspaper accounts, rewritten by the Associated Press and the United Press, then blanket the country. But when newspapers refer to "a conflict of banking opinion" or to "an alternative view held by other well-posted financiers," they mean only that Winthrop W. Aldrich at the Chase Bank has taken issue with Lamont.

The newspapermen who "cover" Wall Street are (a) instructed by their offices to see Lamont regularly and are (b) referred to Lamont or to Aldrich by other bankers in Wall Street, who usually fear to speak even anonymously on general affairs.

There are certain things which Lamont cannot, however, depend upon financial reporters, shackled though they are, to write. In such instances he has been known to telephone the newspaper editors after the financial men have gone home, and inquire innocently whether anyone has telephoned him. Assuming that someone on the financial staff has actually called Lamont and that the subject is important, the editor has eagerly listened while Lamont audibly supposed what the unknown inquirer wanted to know. The editor has then rushed Lamont's version of some affair into print, to appear the next day with no mention of Lamont's name. This has happened a number of times.

Among the many Lamont theses that have found their way into the nation's newspapers through the writings of the Wall Street financial reporters are: (a) "the stock market break [1929] is purely local and has no relation to general business or economics"; (b) "the situation is well in hand [1930] and should improve"; (c) "the depression [1931] must take its course"; (d) "Japan [1931] will maintain the gold standard"; (e) "there is no danger [1931] of a German collapse"; and (f) "the banking system [1932] is fundamentally sound."

As one who has unwillingly played a part in relaying these fraudulent theses to the public consciousness, the writer takes this oc casion to divulge their common source.

More recently, Lamont has been instrumental in feeding the coun· try the theses that New Deal "spending" is paving the road to ruin and that there is no danger of a European War. This last was released immediately after Lamont's return from Europe in 1936; marvelous to relate, he signed it. Soon afterward many of the Lamont journalistic connections began sounding off in their columns and books on the novel theme that fears of war were exaggerated, thereby disarming public opinion.

The general effects of Lamont's work are much more far-reaching than anything ever undertaken by the late Ivy Lee for the Rockefellers. Where Lamont's shadowy journalistic power begins and where it ends could be determined, very probably, only by a government investigation. Walter Lippmann is, of course, Lamont's most important editorial outlet, although Lippmann also turns to Russell C. Leffingwell at Morgan's for ideas.

Lippmann, however, once was forced to maneuver awkwardly by reason of his Morgan friendship. When J. P. Morgan and Company was investigated in 1933 by the Senate, which found evidence of so much irregularity, Lippmann wrote a column for the *Herald Tribune* and syndicate newspapers in which he put in a soothing word for the banking house. Such a false atmosphere did his essay throw around the investigation that a number of persons connected with the Senate committee said Lippmann would be called to tell of his Morgan affiliations. Word to this effect was relayed to the *Herald Tribune* office.

Four days later, on May 31, 1933, Lippmann in his column gave the Senate committee support which, for him, was strong. Reversing himself completely, he said: "The most discouraging aspect of the testimony of Mr. Morgan and Mr. Whitney is the assumption that all of these transactions can be explained away and that no important reforms are necessary or desirable." Making it look good, he said:

"The great [Morgan] power is almost entirely unregulated by law . . . the possession of such great power by private individuals who are not publicly accountable is in principle irreconcilable with any sound conception of a democratic state."

# IX

## Philanthropy, or Noncommercial Investment

*"They . . . were supporters of such charitable institutions as might be beneficial to their sick domestics."*
JOHN GALSWORTHY, *The Forsyte Saga*

THE field of contemporary philanthropy, or noncommercial investment, is a labyrinth of mirrors, flashing lights, fitful shadows, and pervasive ballyhoo. One can be sure of little in this maze, for everything superficially perceptible is an illusion multiplied to infinity.

Practical philanthropy, so-called, centers largely about the foundations. E. C. Lindeman, the outstanding authority on the internal functioning of foundations, states in his monumental *Wealth and Culture*, published in 1936, that his "first surprise was to discover that those who managed foundations and trusts did not wish to have these instruments investigated. Had it occurred to me then," he continued, "that it would require eight years of persistent inquiry at a wholly disproportionate cost to disclose even the basic quantitative facts desired, I am sure that the study would have been promptly abandoned."

The reader, then, should prepare to enter in this chapter a subterranean cavern of modern capitalism, discarding at once all preconceptions about munificent donations by the economic barons for the welfare of mankind. Fostered by the newspapers and the publicity bureaus of the millionaires, these preconceptions have little justification in objective fact.

But have not the Rockefellers given away from $500,000,000 to $700,000,000, as the newspapers have plainly stated? Have not all the American multimillionaires given away huge sums? Do not gifts from the wealthy support most scientific research? Are not vast artistic and cultural enterprises—symphony orchestras, operas, universities—largely supported by gifts from the wealthy to which there are no personal strings attached?

Unfortunately, the answer to all these questions is no.

What, then, has been taking place to justify all the publicity?

There has, it is quite true, been some disinterested philanthropic activity, but the philanthropies, so-called, have to the grandiose descriptions they inspire the relation that a pebble has to the pool on whose surface its impact brings countless momentary ripples. For very little money—a trivial amount, in fact—has' been given away by the wealthy of fabulously rich America, and most of that has been given since the income tax took effect in 1913. The word "gift" might properly be discarded in this connection in favor of more precise words like "allocation" and "transfer."

All gifts and donations to institutions in the period 1909–32, by rich, well-to-do, moderately circumstanced, and poor, according to Robert R. Doane, in *The Measurement of American Wealth*, aggregated only $27,888,000,000, or less than two per cent of total incomes for persons of *all* classes.

From 1860 to 1932 social expenditures, philanthropic and nonphilanthropic, by rich and poor, according to the same authority, amounted only to $65,533,000,000, or about twenty-five per cent of the $233,628,000,000 expended by the government in social avenues.

"The total gifts of all who filed income tax returns has never amounted to as much as two per cent of their incomes, even in our prosperous years," according to Ryllis A. and Omar P. Goslin, *Rich Man, Poor Man*. "Our 3,000 richest families with average income of $300,000 and over gave an average of only $25,400 each in 1928. After the depression set in they found it necessary to reduce their gifts to $12,900 each. The 248 very richest families with incomes of over a million dollars gave an average of $30,100 each in 1928. This includes all gifts to churches, colleges, endowments, or relief."

The total philanthropic budget for 1928, according to The John Price Jones Corporation, was $2,330,600,000, and Lindeman found that of this all the foundations and community trusts, instruments of the rich, contributed only 9.16 per cent.

Professor Lindeman explodes the newspaper-fostered notion that much money is willed to philanthropy. After a scientific study of wills filed in New York City in 1927–33, Lindeman concluded that ninety-four per cent of the wills transferred ninety-four per cent of the wealth to relatives and friends. As the greatest ownership of wealth is concentrated in New York City, this distribution of $11,500,000,000 of private property in seven years must stand as the authoritative indication of the disposition of wealth by wills in the United States.

"The bulk of the wealth thus distributed," Lindeman remarks, "flows into the treasuries of churches, hospitals, and conventional charities. In short, the cultural importance of redistributed personal wealth is slight." Lindeman, it may be pointed out, uses the word "culture" to connote those activities of men which have collective meaning in terms of value; to him, culture implies ways for organizing emotional experience, experiments in tone or quality of living; thus, culture cannot be merely something which conserves but must, as he insists, become dynamic.

Has not philanthropic activity been greater, however, during the post-Civil War ascendancy of the industrialists and bankers than it ever was before?

Again, unfortunately, no. Henry Demarest Lloyd, in *Wealth Against Commonwealth*, quotes the Committee of the United Hospitals Association of New York as saying in 1893: "The committee have found that, through the obliteration of old methods of individual competition by the establishment of large corporations and trusts in modern times, the income of such charitable institutions as are supported by the individual gifts of the benevolent has been seriously affected."

The trend of giving to philanthropic and charitable enterprises, in relation to all income and all other expenditures, is still downward. According to the Golden Rule Foundation, national income in 1936 was $48,718,000,000 more than in 1932, representing an increase of sixty-one per cent. In the same interval earnings of 105 of the largest industrial corporations increased by 3,975 per cent, while contributions to colleges declined eighteen per cent, to community chest's twenty-four per cent, to general benevolences twenty-nine per cent, and to churches thirty per cent.

Abraham Epstein, distinguished sociological investigator and re-

former, says in *The American Mercury* (May, 1931), that "the benevolences of a dozen individuals, such as Carnegie, the Rockefellers,
Harkness, Rosenwald, and a few others account for a considerable
proportion of existing foundations." The supposed benevolence of
even these persons is questionable; but if we grant that Epstein has
veritably isolated the true philanthropists, we can say he has about
exhausted the list. Among the powerful, rich families that have no
reasonable claim to significant philanthropic inclination at all are the
Mellons, Fords, Du Ponts, Fishers, Fields, Phippses, Berwinds,
Bakers, McCormicks, Reynoldses, Metcalfs, Greens, Fricks, Morgans,
Stillmans, Ryans, Tafts, Goulds, Bradys, Guggenheims, Vanderbilts,
Goelets, Astors, and most of the others.

"An examination of organized philanthropy in the United States
at once reveals," says Epstein, "the parsimoniousness of the many
rather than the largesse of the few. Even a casual study shows that
the myth of our unparalleled generosity has no firmer base than
the benevolences of a very few men who have distributed small
parts of their extraordinarily large fortunes. Among the masses of
the well-to-do not many give anything to charity, even in the most
generous city, New York. A negligible proportion of rich individuals
support all of the charities. The vast bulk of the wealthy contribute
to none.

"In the cities in which money is raised through community chests
or welfare federations the contributors never exceed 17 per cent of
the total population. The 360 American community chests, in spite of
the energetic trumpeting, cajolery, and high-pressure salesmanship
that go with them, do not raise more than $80,000,000 a year—less
than half of the sum now spent through workmen's compensation
laws alone." Fewer than eight hundred persons and corporations,
Epstein says, donated $250 or more at one time to become life mem-
bers of the Association for the Improvement of the Condition of the
Poor in New York City.

"That the slackers in the United States are not the poor people but
the richest and most respectable is well known to persons engaged
in the business of raising money for charitable purposes," Epstein
says. "In many cities the charitable agencies spend far more upon
relieving the distress of the workers of certain local corporations

than these firms contribute. A Detroit attorney recently testified before a United States Senate Committee that while over 36 per cent of the city's expenditures on unemployment relief go to unemployed Ford employes, Mr. Ford even pays no taxes to the city. Edsel Ford's contribution to the Detroit Community Chest of $130,000 amounts to about 15 per cent of what the city spends monthly on unemployed Ford Company men. A number of heads of community chests blamed the failure of their recent drives entirely on the richer groups. At the same time, they commended the generosity of the poorer classes, who have been giving more than ever before."

Private philanthropy, Epstein warns, "will never be able to relieve the growing difficulties inherent in the industrial order, and it is also seriously objectionable for another reason. Under this system the burden of social ills falls almost entirely upon the few generous rich and the bulk of poor wage-earners, who cannot refuse to give to charitable appeals when the boss asks them to contribute. It is altogether contrary to the modern principle of fair proportional distribution of the burden. The bulk of the well-to-do escape entirely from paying their share."

But are there not, then, vast sums concentrated in philanthropic foundations?

There is, alas, actually much less than $1,000,000,000 in philanthropic foundations, or less than 1/350th of the tangible wealth of the United States. The twenty largest foundations, according to a study published as of 1934 by the Twentieth Century Fund, account for $622,066,308, or 88.6 per cent, of all effective foundation capital, and the records of *The Foundation Study* show 258 foundations and 73 additional funds that may be classified as foundations.

Total foundation *capital* of substantially less than $1,000,000,000 compares with recurrent annual *income* of substantially more than $1,000,000,000 accruing to the five hundred richest individuals, whose personal capital resources exceed $20,000,000,000; and it compares with recurrent annual *income* of more than $5,000,000,000 (estimated) for all members of the five hundred richest families.

Total grants out of investment income by the twenty largest foundations in 1934, according to the Twentieth Century Fund study, amounted to $30,968,778—90.5 per cent of all foundation grants.

In previous years the grants ranged up to about $50,000,000, equiva-
lent to slightly more than 40 cents per year for every man, woman,
and child in the United States. Lindeman discovered that eighty
foundations and twenty community trusts made grants of $83,743,490
in 1928, the maximum for any year in the postwar period.

When it is observed that the appropriations of two men—Rockefeller and Carnegie—account for nearly sixty per cent of all capital in
123 foundations studied by the Twentieth Century Fund—an organization financed by Edward A. Filene, Boston department-store
owner, it becomes clear that institutional philanthropy is, on the
whole, a shoestring proposition. However, the shoestring, while it
means little to society in a constructive sense, confers immense social
power on those who hold it, as does the shoestring control by the rich
of the big corporations and banks as described by Berle and Means.

The twenty largest foundations, according to the Twentieth Century Fund study (1934), are as follows:

|     |                                                                 | Capital |
|-----|-----------------------------------------------------------------|--------:|
| 1.  | Carnegie Corporation of N. Y.                                   | $157,553,073 |
| 2.  | Rockefeller Foundation                                          | 153,609,942 |
| 3.  | General Education Board (Rockefeller)                           | 45,822,414 |
| 4.  | Commonwealth Fund (Harkness)                                    | 43,430,252 |
| 5.  | W. K. Kellogg Foundation (Kellogg cereals)                      | 41,592,087 |
| 6.  | Carnegie Institution of Washington                             | 34,611,416 |
| 7.  | Carnegie Foundation for the Advancement of Teaching            | 30,821,545 |
| 8.  | Russell Sage Foundation                                         | 15,457,575 |
| 9.  | Buhl Foundation (Henry Buhl, Jr.)                               | 13,120,850 |
| 10. | Carnegie Endowment for International Peace                       | 11,127,415 |
| 11. | Milbank Memorial Fund                                           | 10,449,862 |
| 12. | Children's Fund of Michigan (Couzens)                          | 10,177,137 |
| 13. | Maurice and Laura Falk Foundation (Maurice Falk)              | 10,000,000 |
| 14. | New York Foundation (Warburg, Lehman, Lewisohn, and numerous others) | 8,646,011 |
| 15. | New York Community Trust (numerous donors; Rockefeller management) | 8,024,688 |
| 16. | Spelman Fund of New York (Rockefeller)                          | 6,542,421 |
| 17. | Cleveland Foundation (numerous donors)                          | 5,906,751 |
| 18. | Carnegie Hero Fund Commission                                   | 5,750,000 |

| | | |
|---|---|---|
| 19. | John Simon Guggenheim Memorial Foundation | 5,049,437 |
| 20. | Committee of the Permanent Charity Fund (numerous donors) | 4,900,000 |

Not many of the sixty richest families, it is readily apparent, are included in the tabulation. It is also clear that many persons who do not rank among the wealthiest—Kellogg, Falk, Couzens, and Buhl—have made relatively large contributions. The second largest accumulation, that of Carnegie, does not represent a surviving dynasty, nor does the Sage fund. All of the sixty families, however, as the Twentieth Century Fund study clearly shows, are associated with some organized philanthropy or pseudo-philanthropy; all find it expedient to carry on some ostensible philanthropic activity.

Some of the foundations are established, it appears, merely as imitations that confer prestige; the lesser rich, striving for status, imitate the greater rich, although the foundations of the former are practically moribund, consisting merely of desk room in some office, a small bank account, and stationery with an impressive letter-head. We will not concern ourselves with these.

Size of capital, however, does not always determine the size of annual grants, for some of these foundations plow part of the income back into the capital fund. In the distribution of income other foundations, having no connection with the sixty richest families, figure outstandingly. Income distribution of the twenty most active foundations in 1934 was as follows (Twentieth Century Fund data):

| | | Grants |
|---|---|---|
| 1. | Rockefeller Foundation | $11,840,719 |
| 2. | General Education Board | 5,465,225 |
| 3. | Carnegie Corporation | 4,738,022 |
| 4. | Carnegie Foundation | 1,919,962 |
| 5. | Commonwealth Fund | 1,720,515 |
| 6. | Cranbrook Foundation (Booth family, Michigan) | 668,296 |
| 7. | Spelman Fund | 537,250. |
| 8. | Horace and Mary Rackham Fund (Horace H. Rackham, Michigan) | 527,110 |
| 9. | Children's Fund of Michigan | 507,249 |
| 10. | Julius Rosenwald Fund | 505,691 |

11. John and Mary R. Markle Foundation (donor:
     John Markle; J. P. Morgan management) ......... 420,656
12. New York Foundation ............................................. 413,913
13. Russell Sage Foundation ...................................... 267,255
14. W. K. Kellogg Foundation .................................... 252,465
15. Carnegie Hero Fund Commission ........................... 216,285
16. Carnegie Endowment ............................................. 205,032
17. New York Community Trust ................................. 199,493
18. Committee of the Permanent Charity Fund ......... 197,333
19. Cleveland Foundation ........................................... 190,179
20. Buhl Foundation ................................................... 176,128

The Rosenwald Fund appears among the ten largest distributors
of grants but not among the twenty largest foundations because the
late Julius Rosenwald stipulated that the capital should be distributed
in twenty-five years rather than maintained in perpetuity as are the
Carnegie and many of the other foundations. Originally capitalized
at about $20,000,000, the Rosenwald Fund is now down to about
$13,000,000; largely devoted to the erection of school buildings for
Negroes in the South, for Negro health and other forms of aid to
Negroes, this fund has been one of the most judiciously utilized
from the standpoint of human welfare. In 1931 the M. and L. Guggenheim Foundation granted $707,158 and in 1932 it granted $401,-
608, but in 1934 neither it nor the John Simon Guggenheim Memorial
Foundation figured in the twenty largest grants.

Except for the contributions of the skeptical Carnegie, Mrs. Russell
Sage, and Julius Rosenwald, none of these relatively modest capital
sums has been "given away." Control of the foundation investment
portfolios, consisting of stocks and bonds of corporations dominated
by the respective donors, has been retained by the donors, in virtually
all cases, through special, complicated charter provisions; the donors
sit among the trustees and officers, and direct the affairs of the foundations. What has actually happened in the "giving away" process
is that title to capital has been transferred to foundations; the foundation income, instead of being paid to the donors in dividends and
interest, has then been employed, to the material advantage of the
donor, in philanthropic, social, semiphilanthropic, quasi-philan-
thropic, and even antiphilanthropic and antisocial avenues.

By allocating funds to philanthropies, it should also be noticed, the persons that retain control over these philanthropic funds have evaded payment of inheritance and income taxes. One is permitted a deduction of fifteen per cent from net taxable income if this proportion of income has been transferred in a given year to a philanthropic enterprise, even though the money is capitalized instead of expended by the philanthropy. Where the ostensible philanthropist has been faced by the prospect of reduced financial strength through the incidence of taxes he has, in taking advantage of the provisions of the tax laws, actually increased his financial power by placing income as well as capital in personally controlled philanthropic funds.

Not only has the public been given an exaggerated conception of the total of endowment funds, but it has also been given an exaggerated conception of the so-called benefactions of various individuals. Carnegie, who had no son, allocated to his foundations $350,000,000, or eighty per cent of his fortune, of which $62,000,000 went to Great Britain and $288,000,000 to the United States. As Carnegie attached no personal strings to the allocations other than to prescribe their fields and to stipulate their "perpetual" existence, his must be considered a unique contribution although in the Carnegie foundations there has been, as in all the other foundations, much misdirected activity. Upon analysis it appears that the bulk of appropriations by the Carnegie Corporation has been expended upon library buildings, museums, college buildings, and conventional educational enterprises. In recent years this foundation has made to adult education fairly large contributions, which may seem to be culturally progressive, but here again it appears that most, if not all, of this money is distributed through the agency of the American Association for Adult Education, the chief officer of which is a former Carnegie Corporation employee; consequently, it cannot be expected that the variety of adult education thus promoted will have true cultural significance; as a matter of fact, the above Association expends most of its funds on salaries for its officers, on publications, and on researches.

The size of Rockefeller allocations to so-called philanthropic uses has been particularly exaggerated by newspapers and even by some rather critical commentators, because the Rockefeller publicity bureaus have, from time to time, made repetitive announcements of identical allocations which have emerged to public view in different forms at different times. Funds initially announced as received by the General Education Board and the Rockefeller Foundation have later been announced as received from Rockefeller personally by the University of Chicago and the Rockefeller Institute for Medical Research, although these latter have actually received the funds from the two big foundations.

Outside observers have increased the confusion by failing to distinguish between the original capital endowment and the recurring grants from the foundation income; the consequence has been that estimates of Rockefeller transfers to foundations range from $550,000,-000 to $700,000,000. *Fortune* (December, 1931) set Rockefeller endowments at $445,556,183 and total Rockefeller "benefactions" at $574,155,789. *The New York Times*, on the occasion of the elder Rockefeller's death in May, 1937, set the endowments at $420,754,335 and total Rockefeller benefactions at $530,853,632; although this computation was made six years after *Fortune's*, it was lower, thus indicating that a different result is produced by each different approach. John T. Flynn gives the total of the elder Rockefeller's "gifts" as $508,921,123.01 as of 1928 (no "gifts" have since been made); "gifts" of the younger Rockefeller he computes at $65,234,606.29, bringing the total for the family to $574,155,729.30, or very nearly the same as the *Fortune* total. But "gifts" is an all-inclusive word, and does not connote philanthropies; the elder Rockefeller, as we know, made to United States senators and representatives "gifts" which some persons have been unkind enough to term bribes.

One would have to be uncritical to accept these computations. *The New York Times* as well as *Fortune* supplied partial breakdowns of the items entering into their respective computations, thus enabling us to evaluate the merits of some Rockefeller "philanthropies." A Rockefeller philanthropy, according to the *Times*, was an item of $510,042 given to the Anti-Saloon League, which opponents said functioned as a Rockefeller political arm and opposed even "drys" when they were hostile to Standard Oil. The *Times* also included as a benefaction $118,000 presented by Rockefeller to the Republican National Committee! An item of $5,962,839, said the *Times*, covered undesignated Rockefeller "gifts" in amounts of less than $100,000.

Among the individual gifts unquestionably were donations to churches, whose philanthropic character some students might dispute, and whose reactionary social role other students might proclaim, and to individuals whose friendship was of great profit to the Rockefellers. Also included may have been other contributions to the Republican National Committee. The Rockefellers, to be sure, have no apparent reason to regard the Republican Party as other than a philanthropic enterprise; it has, at any rate, been charitable to them.

Both the *Times* and *Fortune* included among the individual Rockefeller "benefactions" $250,000 given to the American Petroleum Institute—trade association of the petroleum industry whose chief function is lobbying for tariffs and arranging marketing agreements among oil companies! Both publications included many other dubious items, and appear also to have included grants out of foundation income as contributions of additional Rockefeller capital to philanthropy.

Flynn sets forth the philanthropic allocations of the elder Rockefeller up to 1928 as follows:

| | |
|---|---:|
| Rockefeller Foundation and Laura Spelman Memorial | $256,580,081.87 |
| General Education Board | 129,197,900.00 |
| Rockefeller Institute for Medical Research | 59,778,141.14 |
| University of Chicago | 45,000,000.00 |
| Miscellaneous | 18,365,000.00 |
| | $508,921,123.01 |
| By John D. Rockefeller, Jr. Various gifts | $65,234,606.29 |

The first two items of the elder Rockefeller's gifts may stand as unchallengeable; Rockefeller transferred approximately that much to his two foundations. However, not more than $11,501,000 of the University of Chicago item or more than $8,000,000 of the Institute item may be designated as given by Rockefeller, for most of the University and Institute funds came from the Foundation or the General Education Board. Very probably all of the Institute fund came from the Board and from the Foundation. The total of Rockefeller capital transfers has been approximately $400,000,000.

Up through 1902-03 Rockefeller appears to have given the University of Chicago ¹ $11,500,000 directly. The General Education Board, formed in 1902, was thereafter Rockefeller's main instrument of transfer until the Rockefeller Foundation swung into action in 1913. From the fact that he reserved the right to allocate a certain portion of the funds of the General Education Board and the Foundation himself, confusion arises in totaling Rockefeller's transfers. He did not give up this privilege until 1917, before which a good part of the funds received by the University of Chicago and the Rockefeller Institute came from the Board, and, after its formation, from the Foundation, although the reports of the University and of the Institute attributed the allocations to Rockefeller personally.

Included in the total Rockefeller gifts to the $129,000,000 fund of the General Education Board, for example, is a transfer of $32,000,000 made in 1907. According to *The General Education Board: An Account of Its Activities, 1902-1914*, published by the Board itself in 1916, $13,554,343.99 of this was earmarked immediately for the University of Chicago and $10,267,022.10 for the Rockefeller Institute. Rockefeller gave to the Board $1,000,000 in 1902, $10,000,000 in 1905, $32,000,000 in 1907, $10,000,000 in 1909, $20,000,000 in September, 1919, and $50,438,768 in December, 1919, or $123,438,768 in all. Anna T. Jeanes gave this fund $200,000, and some smaller additional Rockefeller transfers were also made.

As the General Education Board total obviously included $13,554,343.99 earmarked for the University of Chicago this amount must be deducted from the total of $45,000,000 indicated by Flynn as an additional benefaction for the University. The annual report of the University of Chicago, 1910-11, noting Rockefeller's "final" endowment gift of $10,000,000, published Rockefeller's letter wherein he said: "I have this day caused to be set aside for the University of Chicago, from the funds of the General Education Board which are subject to my disposition, income-bearing securities of the present market value of approximately $10,000,000. . . ." Rockefeller stipulated that the University was to receive this fund in equal installments over a period of ten years. It was a fund obviously in addition to the 1907 fund, which had already been transferred to the University, so that we are justified in subtracting $10,000,000 more from the $45,000,000 ostensibly given by Rockefeller as new capital to the University.

In acknowledging the 1910 bequest the University added to the confusion when it remarked that it had received $35,000,000 in all from Rockefeller, but failed to explain that nearly $25,000,000 of this came from funds of the General Education Board subject to Rockefeller's personal disposition. Since 1910 the University has received something over $10,000,000 more from the General Education Board and the Rockefeller Foundation, so that we are justified in taking away this amount from the $21,445,656.01 gained by above deductions. The resulting $11,445,656.01 is very close to the $11,500,000 personally given by Rockefeller to the University up through 1902-03.

Similar misinterpretation of Rockefeller Institute benefactions has also taken place. On the basis of the reports of the Rockefeller Institute (1911 and 1934) it becomes doubtful if Rockefeller personally allocated to it more than $200,000 in 1901 and some land in New York City in 1902. The 1911 report of the Institute indicates that Rockefeller gave it $2,620,610 as an endowment in 1907, $500,000 for a hospital and $170,015.20 for general uses in 1908, $3,650,000 in 1910, and $925,-000 in 1911. This made $7,865,625.20 apparently transferred by Rockefeller to the Institute, which reported that as of October 14, 1911, its endowment aggregated $7,186,554.11. But, as we have seen, $10,267,-022.10 was earmarked by the General Education Board for the Institute in 1907, or more than had already been transferred to it up to 1911. Reports of the Rockefeller Foundation subsequent to its formation in 1913 indicate that the later Institute funds have been derived from it as well as from the General Education Board.

We are therefore justified in eliminating all except $11,500,000 of the University of Chicago money and all of the $59,778,141.14 of Institute money which Flynn and others treat as philanthropic capital additional to the capital already reported by the General Education Board and the Rockefeller Foundation.

This writer also eliminates the "miscellaneous" item of $18,365,000 because he does not regard as philanthropies the contributions of the elder Rockefeller to the Republican Party, the Anti-Saloon League, church organizations, propaganda associations, magazine editors, and similar recipients.

A word of further explanation is in order as to why this writer does not concede the philanthropic character of the $18,365,000 handed out by the elder Rockefeller. It is not to be doubted that this money was given away. From the very beginning Rockefeller gave away some of his earnings—to churches, to individuals—in consonance with the religious teachings of his mother. As Rockefeller was an individual mainly intent upon increasing his personal power (his whole life proves this), we must infer that he gradually discovered the transforming effect of such gifts upon individuals. He learned that loyalty, or at least silence, could be bought. He therefore, as he grew wealthier, increased his gifts to churches, to hospitals, to schools, to politicians, in time utterly silencing all general criticism of his business methods which, incidentally, were no worse than those of many other men. Rockefeller, however, had gained such a fundamental position in the nation's industry that he simply had more than others to "give away."

Should any gift, whatever its nature, be considered a benefaction to humanity? To argue that it should would leave oneself open to crushing rejoinders. Rockefeller, in all his miscellaneous "giving," was not really giving at all: he was buying. One can purchase a good many friendly observations for $1,000,000; patents of nobility have been acquired for much less. For $18,000,000 one can very nearly purchase sainthood.

To what extent have the individual "miscellaneous" allocations of the younger Rockefeller out of his vast income been philanthropic? Let us look at one salient and, perhaps, debatable example. John D., Jr., allocated $14,000,000 to reconstruct Williamsburg, Virginia, as it stood in colonial days. The undertaking looks to this observer like part of a combined advertising stunt, playing upon the patriotic susceptibilities of the sentimental multitude, and a method of reducing income-tax liability. However, young Rockefeller showed in the Williamsburg project that he was willing to reconstruct the past; he and his family have not been so willing to reconstruct the present. The money given to perpetuate a useless though agreeable historical monument might better have been used to build a much needed free

hospital in the Harlem area of New York City or livable dwellings
in the share-cropper region of the South.

A more dubious Rockefeller "philanthropy" consisted of $22,-
500,000 allotted by the Foundation to war work in the period 1914-18,
of which money a little more than $8,000,000 went to the Red Cross.
The only one of the Central Powers that was given assistance was
Turkey, which got a mere $55,504. Because it concentrated relief and
assistance on one side, although many were suffering on the other
side, the expenditure represented less of a contribution to the welfare
of humanity than a means of bolstering the war morale of one group
of belligerents.

What, if anything, have the Rockefellers given to indisputable philanthropic uses?

They have given some of the income of their funds; but not all
the income. Computations based upon the published reports of the
Rockefeller foundations lead to the conclusion that not more than
$225,000,000 of income has been granted. As about $100,000,000 of this
income has been recapitalized by the University of Chicago, the
Rockefeller Institute, the China Medical Board, and other organizations under Rockefeller control, it seems that not more than $125,000,-
000 has been given in the sense that control over its disposition has
been relinquished. However, the Rockefellers, like the other philanthropists, have stipulated the uses to be made of these "gifts," so the
gift aspect itself is subject to severe qualification. The "gifts" usually
control behavior in the interests of the donor.

Not only has the amount of initial capital allocated by the Rockefellers to so-called philanthropy been exaggerated but, as previously
remarked, capital has been added together with income. John T.
Flynn, whose thorough biography of Rockefeller is otherwise very
valuable, has unfortunately given currency to this grievous error.
After totaling the elder Rockefeller's "benefactions" to $508,921,123.01,
Flynn goes on to say:

"For many years in addition to grants out of the principal of these
endowments, immense sums in interest have been dispersed which
would add not less than $175,000,000 to the above, so that it may be
reasonably [*sic*] stated that various public philanthropic enterprises
have received from the Rockefellers a sum equalling seven hundred

and fifty million dollars." As if this were not bad enough, Flynn continues: "After which most of the principal was still intact."

Reduced to everyday terms, this is like saying, "Years ago I put $100 in the bank and designated it for charity; the interest on this has amounted to $100, which has been paid out to various benevolences; and, to cap it all, the original $100 is still intact. I have therefore given $300 to charity."

The giver in this hypothetical case has allotted $100, the income, to charity, and no more. And if he stipulated that starving vagabonds use the money for fad diets, he has been less of a benefactor than a dictator of behavior.

As the Rockefeller family retains its foundations under its control, subject to its own disposition after listening to the counsel of "experts," the capital funds have in no sense been given away or alienated from Rockefeller dominance. Under the present arrangement Rockefeller, Jr., strangely enough, could transfer to his foundations all his personalty that carries working control of corporations and banks, and still suffer no diminution in his industrial and financial authority; for he would still decide how these securities might be voted in the various Rockefeller companies, and he could determine what salaries the companies should pay him, or what salaries the foundations should pay him in lieu of dividends he relinquished to them.

## II

There is a double aspect perceivable in the use of the noncommercial foundations, although this dualism is only apparent, not actual; the foundations really function as wholes under the dispensation of a loose integration which is not externally apparent; all their separate aspects blend into a unifying perspective, a general sense of direction: they function, in brief, on behalf of the *status quo*.

It is convenient, however, to study the workings of the foundations from a dualistic, or double-aspect, point of view. In this dualistic frame-work we find that the foundations function intensively as well as extensively; specifically as well as generally; and, stated in psychological terms, sentimentally, personally, and emotionally as well as coldly and impersonally. The dichotomy might also be outlined thus: in their intensive, specific, and emotional aspect the foundations and their directors are "soft"; in their extensive, general, and impersonal aspect they are "hard." In the good they accomplish—and they unquestionably do accomplish a restricted amount of good—the foundations serve truth; in their extensive, general, and impersonal aspect—the aspect which contains the real reason for their existence, they serve personal pecuniary power as much as do the political machines and the newspapers.

There is, therefore, no inconsistency in the fact that the men who direct these "philanthropic" enterprises are (a) contributors to political slush funds, (b) controllers of newspapers, and (c) men accustomed to "bargain" with their employees under cover of machine guns. Before leaving the power-serving aspect of the foundations for a brief interval it is instructive to note the names of men who direct foundation affairs. Some trustees of the Rockefeller endowments are Rockefeller, Jr., Winthrop W. Aldrich, John W. Davis, Harold H. Swift, and Owen D. Young. Some Carnegie trustees are John W. Davis, Herbert Hoover, Howard Heinz (pickles), Frank O. Lowden, Andrew W. Mellon, Walter S. Gifford, Edward L. Ryerson, Jr. (steel), Silas H. Strawn, corporation lawyer, Robert A. Taft, and Thomas J. Watson, head of International Business Machines Corporation. Some Guggenheim trustees are Francis H. Brownell, head of American Smelting and Refining Company, Simon Guggenheim, and Charles D. Hilles, New York Republican boss. A trustee of the Falk Foundation is Ernest T. Weir, ultrareactionary steel manufacturer. The trustees of all the foundations are, it is evident, persons whose careers have identified them less with benefactions to humanity than with the exercise of power for private pecuniary satisfaction.

Lindeman's penetrating study revealed that more than fifty per cent of the trustees of the seventy leading foundations belonged to the power-serving rather than the truth-serving area of society. Fifteen per cent were lawyers, ten per cent were corporation officials, nine per cent were bankers, nine per cent were university and college administrators (i. e., plain corporation executives), and five per cent financiers. Of the 186 trustees remaining out of four hundred, no fewer than fourteen were manufacturers, eight were merchants, seven were editors, seven were judges, seven were railroad officials, four were United States senators, four were publishers, three were real-estate brokers, three were bishops, two were capitalists, and two were ambassadors, politicians, cardinals, priests, and brokers, respectively.

Illustrations will be chosen throughout from the Rockefeller institutions, both because so many illusions are cherished about them and because they lend themselves readily to full exposition. Here and there, however, illustrative examples will be cited of other philanthropies when they serve to bring out a general condition.

What are the philanthropic foundations used for on their intensive, specific, emotional, quasi-truthserving side?

Lindeman, after studying the operation of one hundred of the largest foundations over a decade, concluded that expenditures upon work in education were largest, upon work in health and medicine next largest, and upon "social welfare" third largest.

Not at all oddly, the greatest emphasis in the educational field was in higher education, which produces engineers, doctors, lawyers, scientists, and the like, who are employed profitably by the big corporations and whose increasing oversupply constantly tends to reduce scales of remuneration. Overproduction of technicians, it should be plain, increases the profits of the owning class.

Educational grants by the foundations, says Lindeman, aggregated $223,000,534.21 for the decade 1921-30. Of this sum 60.9 per cent went into higher education, which relatively few persons can afford even with scholarship and fellowship grants, and only 4.1 per cent went into adult education, on which the public itself spent from $10,000,-000,000 to $15,000,000,000 in the decade 1926-35. Only two foundations, neither of which is heavily publicized, assisted with grants for the education of labor leaders in the problems of their own class. Elementary and secondary school education received only 14.8 per cent of the grants.

As it is only the relatively well-to-do that can afford to finance themselves up to the threshold of higher education, the grants in this field have had the effect of supporting the lower fringe of the well-to-do in completing their studies. In the following chapter on education, as we shall see, most of the foundation allocations of funds go to fewer than a dozen institutions of the upper class—Harvard, Yale, Princeton, and so on.

In medicine and health, which took 33.2 per cent of all disbursements in the post-war boom decade, as contrasted with 43 per cent of disbursements for education, an aggregate of $173,141,129.55 was expended. Here again the emphasis fell upon areas that included the personal problems of the rich. Dental hygiene, of crucial concern in a nation the bulk of whose people is afflicted with grave dental disorders but of little concern to a wealthy class able to pay privately for the best personal dental attention, received only seven-tenths of one per cent of foundation grants. Mental hygiene, another field wherein the rich are little concerned personally but of ever greater importance as social and economic disequilibrium is increasingly reflected in widespread mental disequilibrium, received less than five per cent of disbursements. According to Albert Deutsch, in *The Mentally Ill in America*, there were 480,000 inmates in American mental hospitals in March, 1937; the population of mental hospitals is increasing by fifteen thousand persons a year; and the rate of increase is five times that of half a century ago. Public health, of deep concern to the body of the populace but of little concern to the rich, received only 28.3 per cent of foundation health grants. But physical health, directly related to diseases and maladies with which the rich as well as the poor are inevitably afflicted, received no less than 61.1 per cent of the combined foundation budget.

The controllers of the foundations determine what use medical men engaged in research shall make of the money. According to well-grounded reports in New York medical circles, the Rockefeller Institute is prompted in the inquiries it undertakes by Rockefeller, Jr. It is a matter of cold record that many persons who transfer specific sums to medical work designate fields restricted to diseases with which they or members of their families are or have been afflicted rather than fields in which there is the most pressing public need for help. A great many examples could be cited.

In 1925, for instance, Mrs. Aida de Acosta Root (now Mrs. Henry

S. Breckinridge), wife of Wren Root, traction magnate and nephew of Elihu Root, endowed a fund in honor of Dr. William Holland Wilmer, surgeon who had saved her eyesight; she enlisted the aid of the General Education Board and offered $1,500,000 if an equal sum were raised by others. J. P. Morgan, George F. Baker, Sr., and George F. Baker, Jr., each gave $100,000, and Munsey, Harriman, Rosenwald, and Widener also contributed. The outcome was the creation of the Johns Hopkins Eye Hospital.

In 1927 J. P. Morgan gave $200,000 to equip and maintain an entire floor at the Neurological Institute of New York, for treatment of sleeping sickness. Two years previously his wife had died of the malady.

In 1932 William H. Donner, steel magnate, gave $2,000,000 for research on cancer, with the stipulation that none of the money be used to construct buildings; three years earlier his son had died of cancer. There is, incidentally much to-do about cancer, but the editors of *Fortune* issued a survey in 1937 which showed that only $700,000 annually is spent upon cancer research, or less than Harold S. Vanderbilt and his associates spend to equip and maintain each America Cup yacht defender. The largest single yearly expenditure for cancer research—$140,000—is made by the United States government. Soon after the appearance of the *Fortune* survey Starling W. Childs, utilities man, announced the allotment of the annual income on $10,000,000 for cancer research, bringing the total up to slightly more than $1,000,000, or still under the cost of an America Cup defender.

The Rockefeller Foundation gave Cornell University $42,500 to study diets as a means of prolonging life—a subject in which the elder Rockefeller, who lived nearly 100 years under the care of a personal medical staff, was keenly interested.

A one-for-one personal gain or satisfaction can be shown in almost all the medical "benefactions" of the rich. The Rockefeller Institute, for example, has done much work in seeking control over tropical diseases. Helpful as this work is, it must be observed that it is of material assistance in the economic exploitation of tropical Latin America, where the Rockefellers have vast oil holdings.

Discoveries of cures for obscure diseases are, unquestionably, valuable; but cures for many diseases that afflict mankind are already known and yet these cures are not "distributed." There is the same lag in medicine between the capacity to produce and the facilities to distribute that there is in commerce and manufacture, and this is illustrated in the case of a disease like pellagra, spread over a good part of the South. Pellagra sufferers merely require food. Heart disease, to cite another example, leads in the causes of death today; its causes are well known, and among them are overwork (industrial speed-up), malnutrition (unemployment), and worry over economic instability. Research is not required for the control of most heart ailments; social reconstruction, however, which could take place only at the expense of the present "philanthropists," is required.

Public rather than private funds have supported movements to control tuberculosis, diphtheria, smallpox, and typhoid fever. Although cures for a disease like syphilis are known, five hundred thousand Americans contract it annually, according to Dr. Herman N. Bundesen, health commissioner of Chicago; and one out of five Americans is said to be affected by syphilis in some form. Significantly, the recent movement to "distribute" the cure for syphilis was launched under public auspices.

The rich in their medical benefactions concentrate rather extensively, it is instructive to see, upon research laboratories. These are economical to operate, and discoveries obtain the maximum of publicity. It would be infinitely more expensive to underwrite wide distribution of medical services.

However, the rich, individually and through their foundations, are very devoted to hospitals, and reports of this devotion have a pleasant sound to the misinformed multitude, which supposes these hospitals to be maintained for it. The private hospitals, however, in no ascertainable cases are wholly free institutions except when operated in conjunction with some big manufacturing industry, in which case they are merely adjuncts to the profit-making machinery. Hospitals endowed by the rich operate on a strictly commercial basis as far as the majority of patients is concerned but, like all hospitals, they have some free wards and clinics. The expensive laboratories, operating rooms, and general equipment, however, are always ready for use by the "donors" and their friends, and medical advances made in clinical work naturally accrue to the advantage of the "donors" as well. In no case does it appear that any rich family has endowed free institutions like the huge government-operated Cook County Hospital of Chicago or the Bellevue Hospital of New York.

Yet the restricted number of hospitals established by the rich, and in large part supported by paying patients, are as good as neighborhood hospitals to all members of the wealthy class although of little importance to the citizenry in general outside the immediate hospital area. It is instructive to note this. The facilities of specialized, remotely located hospitals are at the disposal of the rich wherever they may be. In an emergency a wealthy man can be rushed to such hospitals by airplane or by train; and if he is unable to move a specialist may be dispatched to him by ship, train, or plane. The distant poor, and even most members of the middle class, cannot except rarely avail themselves of these specialized hospital services. Medical advance, therefore, means less than it seems to mean contemporaneously to the ordinary man.

Not a few of the hospital benefactions present curious personal aspects. The huge, commercially operated Medical Center of New York at One Hundred and Sixty-eighth Street and Broadway, largely created by the Harkness family, has often provoked curiosity as to the reason for its location. The twenty acres on which it stands were acquired by the Harknesses many. years ago when the region was virtually rural.

At the close of 1935 the assets of the Medical Center, including the Presbyterian Hospital, the Vanderbilt Clinic, and the Sloane Maternity Hospital, stood at $41,687,323.77. The land was valued at $1,418,-213.72 and the buildings at $13,271,376.50. Stock, bond, and real-estate investments were valued at $23,194,846.42, and current assets, including cash, had a certified valuation of $2,165,960.08. Radium, furniture and fixtures, and equipment comprised the remainder of assets.

Balanced against this, as *liabilities,* or obligations of the establishment to the donors, were the endowment funds—the income from which alone accrued to the Center. These endowments totaled $25,-158,947.45, and most of the remainder of liabilities consisted of the capital account, which was $16,315,605.51, offsetting the value of land and buildings. Among the liabilities were the Edward S. Harkness Endowment Fund, $6,188,794.01; the Mary S. Harkness Fund for Convalescent Care, $1,000,000; the Russell and Margaret Oliver Sage Memorial Fund, $878,061.64; the Edward S. Harkness Research Fund, $500,000; the Alice M. Flagler Fund, $226,751.54; and about a dozen other funds.

Income in 1935 was derived from the following sources: $1,718,691 from patients who paid $7 to $25 a day for private rooms, $6 a day for semiprivate rooms, $4 a day for beds in wards, $65 for obstetrical services in wards, and varying fees for clinical and X-ray treatment; and $999,037 from the endowment funds, donations, and the United Hospital Fund (generally contributed to by New Yorkers). The total money value of free treatment was only $1,334,735, or the price of three or four Park Avenue "coming-out" parties. According to the Medical Center's own report, the Vanderbilt Clinic treated 456,279 patients in 1935, but refused admission to 28,544 applicants "for lack of facilities."

Similar curious unphilanthropic features were disclosed in the 1933 report of the New York Hospital-Cornell Medical College center—another monolithic medical establishment. The assets of nearly $60,-000,000 were composed of buildings and realty valued at $32,815,100 and securities and cash valued at $24,309,529. The liabilities mainly comprised $56,897,415.21 of securities. Three Payne Whitney endowment funds aggregated slightly more than $17,000,000, and three George F. Baker funds came to a little less than $3,000,000. A J. P. Morgan fund amounted to $2,092,914, a James Buchanan Brady fund to $783,067, and an Alice M. Flagler fund to $228,154.

The majority of the New York Hospital patients also appear to pay liberally for services. Both the New York Hospital and the Medical Center reports indicate that their individual hospital units are never more than sixty-seven to seventy-five per cent occupied, yet every public hospital in the New York area suffers from chronic overcrowding.

Neither the Medical Center nor the New York Hospital, in short, is a philanthropy, although both are referred to as such by the newspapers. Among the trustees of the Society of the New York Hospital are Henry W. de Forest, Cornelius N. Bliss, William Woodward, Arthur Iselin, Robert Winthrop, Joseph H. Choate, Jr., F. Higginson

Cabot, Jr., John Hay Whitney, Vincent Astor, George T. Bowdoin, and Henry R. Stürgis. George F. Baker was a trustee. Edward S. Harkness is a vice-president of the Medical Center. Among the trustees for 1937 were Henry W. de Forest (interlocking with his New York Hospital trusteeship) and Dunlevy Milbank. Trustees for 1938 include Johnston de Forest and S. H. Fisher (Chase National Bank and the Harkness-controlled Commonwealth Fund). Other trustees include officials of the Rockefeller, Harkness, and Carnegie foundations.

We are confronted here with another paradox. Just as we find in charge of the "philanthropic" enterprises in general men who have dedicated their lives to grinding out profits, here we find presiding over establishments of mercy men whose corporations in many instances rule their workers by machine guns and labor spies, men who dictate when the country shall go to war.

Many instances could be cited to show how these establishments, and others like them, utilize the doctors and scientists in their pay on strictly upper-class errands having nothing whatever to do with medicine or science. But one example will suffice. In Thomas W. Lamont's *Saturday Review of Literature* (July 31, 1937) appeared a review of two distinguished books dealing with the menace of syphilis and the need for coping with it through government agencies, as private treatment was obviously inadequate. The review was written by Thomas J. Kirwin, M.D., urologist with the Brady Foundation for Urology, New York Hospital. Dr. Kirwin wrote:

The very idea of free treatment for those who can afford to pay violates the inherent principles upon which the government of this nation was founded.

And he continued, with a particularly revolting chauvinistic turn:

We have no means of knowing whether the blood from the unprotected feet of the Continental Army which stained the snows of Valley Forge carried a syphilitic taint or not. But we do know that that blood was shed in defense of our liberties, chief among which is our right to bear to the extent of our rightful share of the country's responsibilities while at the same time we enjoy the protection of a just and equitable government. This does not mean paternalism; it does not mean that when we have perhaps spent our all in riotous living we have a right to demand from the government the treatment or other measures which we must have administered to us, in order to overcome the physical effects of our folly..

Dr. Kirwin, it is clear, saw the government campaign against syphilis, which affects even innocent children, as an insidious invasion of the field of "private enterprise," which might set a precedent for other "invasions."

Perhaps the most elaborate hospital in the country—if not in the world—is Doctors' Hospital, New York City, to the creation of which one hundred and eighty of New York's wealthiest families contributed. Exclusively for the rich, its appointments rival those of the Waldorf-Astoria Hotel; a temperamental patient may have a suite specially decorated. This hospital boasts a small clinic for free "emergency" treatment of neighborhood patients.

There is much more to be said about the strictly class character of the medical benefactions of the rich, but enough has been said to suggest that these benefactions are tinged to a large degree with self-interest.

The vague field of "social welfare" took $74,776,259.84 of foundation grants, or 14.4 per cent, in the decade 1921-30, according to Lindeman's findings. This is a wholly static field, wherein activity does little to modify the social causes of public distress. Work in this field at most absorbs a fraction of the shock of social dislocation. Community organization took 25.4 per cent of the "social welfare" budget, Lindeman found, and "relief" took 18.8 per cent. With decreasing emphasis the grants then ranged down through items classified as "club work, dependents, settlements, maladjusted, counsel, surveys, training, pensions, administration and standards, handicapped, unclassified, defectives, and preventive." In a world standing on its head for more than twenty years this distribution of funds in the name of philanthropy was obviously insane.

Expenditures in these three broad fields of education, health, and social welfare accounted for 90.6 per cent of all foundation grants in 1921-1930. All are, under the present social dispensation, socially static fields.

What of a constructive nature could the wealthy do with their foundation grants? They might follow the example of the Russell Sage Foundation, established by the widow of a big stock-market operator. This foundation makes social studies, interprets its findings, and disperses the information through publications and conferences with a view to helping people to help themselves. Or they might follow the example of a small fund which, according to *Wealth and Culture,* has accorded decreasing emphasis to individual philanthropy, conventional relief, and conventional education; and has increasingly emphasized the arts, experimental learning and cultural interaction, international action, the social application of science rather than its prostitution for private profit; social planning, social legislation, and movements for freedom and justice.

A rich family could establish a great daily newspaper, supporting it as Willard Straight and Mrs. Leonard K. Elmhirst have supported *The New Republic* and as Mr. Villard supported *The Nation.* Such a newspaper, if endowed and placed in the absolute control of a board of trustees consisting of undisputed truth servers like Dr. John Dewey, Dr. Charles A. Beard, the late Dr. James Harvey Robinson, and Dr. Carl Becker, would increase general enlightenment and thereby make possible intelligent social and political action. Such a newspaper, however, would be, from the standpoint of special privilege, "subversive" in character.

Many curious examples could be cited of the manner in which the rich, seeking to earn distinction as philanthropists and yet desiring to avoid upsetting the social *status quo* which has served them so well, select fields of so-called philanthropic activity which will not affect existing social relationships. They often want to do good, it cannot be doubted; but not so much good that their own interests will be affected adversely. Walter P. Chrysler recently entered the field of philanthropic activity by underwriting a study of child camping, into which he intended to put some money. This philanthropy will have a pleasantly sentimental sound, but the area of possible social good embraced in it is so small as to be negligible.

We can conclude, therefore, that in their intensive, specific, sentimental, truth-serving aspect the philanthropies of the rich, so far as the health of society is concerned, are hopelessly warped and almost wholly misdirected and inutile.

Lindeman summarizes this very aptly in *The New Republic* (December 16, 1936) as follows: "Although foundations are often referred to as philanthropies or charities, it is apparent that only a small portion of their gifts is directed toward specifically charitable ends. ... only the slightest fraction of foundation money ever finds its way into the hands of economically dependent persons. ... The basic purpose of foundations is to support existing institutions."

## III

In their power-serving aspect the great so-called philanthropic enterprises are most significant and, perhaps, most impressive. That portion of activity just surveyed provides merely their excuse for existence.

One may lay down generalizations about the operation of the philanthropic enterprises, but it must be pointed out that all these enterprises are designed to serve the special needs of certain families. The special personal needs account for differences in size of philanthropic allocations and for differences in philanthropic incidence and emphasis. The Rockefeller philanthropies will continue to be relied upon as a central point of reference.

*I. Very little philanthropic activity, so-called, is carried on unless the ostensible philanthropist has been under sharp political attack or public criticism: the philanthropies are in the nature of good-will offerings to public opinion and must therefore be accompanied by a maximum of publicity.*

*II. Virtually all so-called philanthropic activity has a direct relationship to the tax structure of the nation or of a particular locality at the time it is instituted. Philanthropies provide means for escaping taxes and of retaining, or expanding, industrial control.*

*III. Philanthropic foundations in themselves confer upon their promoters a vast amount of concentrated social power which can be, and is, exercised on behalf of the general social status quo.*

*IV. Many philanthropies come into being simply because the philanthropist has no progeny or no male progeny.*

Rockefeller announcements of "gifts" to the public have always

followed some outburst of public or political hostility against the
Rockefeller family, or some change, or proposed change, in the basic
tax laws. Rockefeller announced his first small donation to the University of Chicago in 1889, when the political onslaught against the
Standard Oil "octopus" threatened to become disastrous. Chicago
was located in the Middle West, where sentiment against Rockefeller
was strong.

Until 1902 Rockefeller made gifts almost annually to the University. Thereafter, as we have seen, annual gifts came from the
General Education Board, although made in Rockefeller's name.
Rockefeller could easily have given in the beginning the whole
amount he did give up to 1910, but in that case he would have received only one salvo of acclaim. He knew that the memory of the
public was short, and set out to refresh it from time to time.

In June, 1901, was announced Rockefeller's allocation of $200,000
to the Rockefeller Institute, and up to this point he had given less
than $10,000,000 to the University, to the Institute, and to all chari-
ties, although he was, by all odds, the richest man in the country. He
had, of course, been feverishly distributing money privately, for
reasons already suggested.

In September, 1901, President McKinley, a Rockefeller creation,
died. And in 1902, with Theodore Roosevelt publicly and privately
manifesting virulent hostility to Rockefeller for real or imagined
political opposition, Rockefeller announced the formation of the
General Education Board, capitalized at $1,000,000. In 1905, with
Roosevelt still harrying him, Rockefeller announced that he had
turned over $10,000,000 to the General Education Board. Just at this
time, too, Standard Oil was frontally attacked by suits in many
states, some of which issued warrants for Rockefeller's arrest.

Late in 1906 Roosevelt sent to Congress findings of his Bureau of
Corporations, and in his message of transmittal the President said:
"The Standard Oil Company has benefited almost up to the present
moment by secret [railroad] rates, many of these secret rates being
clearly unlawful."

At this time Standard Oil was indicted in Indiana for violations of
the Elkins Act, which prohibited secret freight rebates, and in Missouri for violation of the Sherman Antitrust Act. Another threat

appeared in the form of a sly proposal by Roosevelt on December 3, 1906, that an inheritance tax be made operative.

Reeling under these blows, Rockefeller in February, 1907, announced the allocation, "for the benefit of mankind," of $32,000,000 to the General Education Board. On July 7, 1909, Rockefeller gave the Board $10,000,000 more. Unquestionably Rockefeller was thoroughly scared, but he was not so scared that he failed to retain control over the funds he "gave away." The allocation of the $32,000,000, it was observed, preceded by a few days the imposition of a $29,000,000 fine by Judge Landis in one of the railroad rebate cases; the decision was upset on appeal.

The next allocation came in 1910, a few days before Standard Oil attorneys filed briefs in the Supreme Court on the antitrust suit, and was disclosed in the statement that $10,000,000 was to be given to the University of Chicago. As this amount of money had already been appropriated to the General Education Board and as the new contribution was to come out of the Board's income, it represented no new capital. Rockefeller was merely noisily shuffling over his earlier "benefactions."

A new reason soon developed for the allocation of further funds to philanthropy. The transfer of about $60,000,000 had already succeeded in quelling public hostility, and Rockefeller "benefactions" among newspaper editors and publishers played no small part in the improved public temper.

On July 12, 1909, Congress submitted to the states the income-tax amendment to the Constitution which Pulitzer had long been demanding. On March 2, 1910, with various states approving the amendment, Rockefeller asked Congress to issue a special charter for his foundation; but the stipulations laid down by Congress were so rigid that Rockefeller instead procured a New York charter on May 14, 1913. The Rockefeller Foundation was precipitately endowed with $100,000,000. On May 31, 1913, the sixteenth amendment to the Constitution, authorizing income taxes, took effect. But Rockefeller had reduced his tax liability.

Rockefeller, as we have observed, was a tax dodger. He was, in fact, the biggest tax dodger ever seen and probably the possessor of the most highly developed power complex on view in the United

States of our own day. As the Rockefeller family possessed more money than it could conceivably use for itself, it is clear that multiplication and retention of power for power's sake was at the root of all the Rockefeller pecuniary maneuvers. Rockefeller neglected no device—not even that of controlled philanthropies—that would help him, nor has his son.

It was hardly an accident that the contest of the first income-tax law should have been handled by Joseph H. Choate, Rockefeller's principal attorney for many years, and that Choate should have prevailed on the Supreme Court in 1894 to hold the law invalid. Rockefeller, as the man with the largest income, stood to lose more by such a law than any other man.

The Rockefeller Foundation, like the General Education Board, put a good deal of money—and voting power—beyond the reach of any proposed income or inheritance taxes, and the gentle veil of philanthropy was drawn around it all. Is saying this an injustice to Rockefeller? Did he really want the money put to effective public use? If he did why did he not merely turn it all over to Congress and permit Congress to allocate it?

The next conspicuous Rockefeller benefactions were not announced until 1917, 1918, and 1919, when the profits from Standard Oil became greater than ever as a consequence of war business (see Appendix B) and when income-tax rates had been scaled up to relatively punitive levels. The income-tax rates have been mentioned earlier, but a word is necessary on the novel inheritance taxes. A tax of ten per cent on estates above $5,000,000 was passed by Congress in 1916; the next year this rate was increased to twenty-five per cent on estates of more than $10,000,000. Then Rockefeller, terrified, began transferring the bulk of his fortune to his son, betraying that it was really taxes he was worried about. When Rockefeller died his personal fortune had been reduced to $25,000,000.

In 1917 Rockefeller retained control of $13,000,000, which the income-tax bureau would have taken, by allocating it to the Foundation. In 1918 by creating the Laura Spelman Rockefeller Memorial he retained control of $73,000,000 of war profits otherwise destined for the tax bureau. In 1919 he gave the Board $50,000,000 and the Foundation $70,000,000, retaining control of the funds at the same time that he escaped heavy tax assessments. On the basis of the reports of the General Education Board, the Rockefeller Foundation, the University of Chicago, the Laura Spelman Rockefeller Memorial, the Rockefeller Institute, and the China Medical Board we can conclude that the Rockefeller family, by reason of war profits and avoidance of income taxes, possessed more voting power in American industry in 1920 than ever before.

But as the Republican postwar administrations progressively reduced upper-bracket income and inheritance tax rates the frantic Rockefeller transfers of capital to philanthropic funds ceased. Nothing was given for more than twelve years except by the younger Rockefeller, who was able to reduce his tax liability by an amount equivalent to fifteen per cent of his income if such an amount was distributed in the broad, ill-defined field of "public philanthropy." In the upper brackets it is often more profitable to "give away" fifteen per cent of one's income than to retain it and pay taxes on it.

In this period, however, the Rockefeller publicity bureaus kept up a barrage of announcements about various gifts, which were the grants out of income from the funds set up much earlier.

Especially has it become more profitable to give away certain sums since the passage of the 1935 and 1936 tax laws. The Cornellian Council *Bulletin,* addressing alumni in 1936, pointed out that persons with net taxable estates of $1,000,000 could save $4,350 in estate taxes and $350 in administrative costs by giving the University $15,000; and that persons with net taxable annual incomes of $100,000 could save $8,650 in Federal income taxes and $1,000 on the average in state taxes by giving the University $15,000 out of income.

Under the New Deal tax laws gift taxes range from one and one-half per cent on all individual personal gifts of $5,000 to fifty-two and one-half per cent on gifts of $50,000,000 or more. Estates of $20,000,-000 to $50,000,000 are taxed sixty-nine per cent, in contrast to sixty per cent under the tax law of 1934, forty-five per cent under the law of 1932, and twenty per cent under the law of 1926. There are, of course, additional taxes imposed by various states.

As soon as the tax laws of 1934 and later began coming out of the legislative hopper the Rockefeller family, displaying its old solicitude about its power, once more began restlessly moving funds about.

The new Securities and Exchange Act also impelled some of the transfers.

In November, 1934, Rockefeller, Jr., announced that he had "disposed" of enough Standard Oil of New Jersey and Standard Oil of California shares to bring his holdings under ten per cent of the two companies' outstanding stock aggregates. What form the "disposal" took was not indicated, but Rockefeller has six children; if the "disposal" was made in the form of six gifts it would incur a relatively modest gift tax.

In August, 1936, the Securities and Exchange Commission revealed that nine days after President Roosevelt asked Congress for higher taxes Rockefeller, Jr., "gave away" 2,100,000 shares of Socony Vacuum Oil stock, worth $27,000,000. As no announcement was made that the shares were going to "philanthropy," they were presumably given to members of the family. If they were split six ways among the children the total gift tax incurred amounted to no more than thirty-two per cent of the full amount. If they were made in the form of one gift the tax incurred amounted to fifty-one and three-quarters per cent. If Rockefeller had retained them in his estate, and if he had died under the 1935-36 tax dispensation, they would have been subject to a Federal estate tax of sixty-nine per cent, less credit for payment of state taxes. And if Rockefeller had retained them the income at five per cent would have been subject to an income surtax of seventy-three per cent.

As the distribution of these shares served to bring his holdings of the stock below ten per cent of those outstanding for Socony Vacuum, Rockefeller was no longer obligated under the law to report changes in his holdings to the Securities and Exchange Commission. The distribution, therefore, also regained secrecy for the family.

There are some persons, ever on the alert for innocent interpretations, who would call this juxtaposition of tax laws, philanthropies, and gifts coincidental. But they would not be in agreement with an authority like Frederick P. Keppel, president of the Carnegie Foundation, who was quoted by The New York Times (November 9, 1936) as saying that doubts and fears concerning taxation spur "giving." Only by "giving" in a period of relatively high estate and income taxes can the wealthy retain control over a maximum of assets;

and control, as many know, is worth more than ownership and is not fraught with many of the responsibilities of ownership.

Before 1800 there was only one foundation, according to Lindeman's figures; from 1801 to 1900 there were established only five foundations, although men like Astor, Vanderbilt, and Rockefeller already had huge fortunes. From 1901 to 1905 five more foundations were established, two of which were the General Education Board and the Rockefeller Institute. From 1906 to 1910 seven foundations were established. The vogue of foundations, however, did not really set in until the income-tax amendment was passed and the estate tax was instituted, and in the period 1911-15 no fewer than twelve foundations were formed. In the period of high taxes and high profits from 1916 to 1920 twenty-one foundations were launched. The usefulness of the device having been demonstrated, we find no fewer than forty-nine foundations being born in the decade 1921-1930. (In 1924 Federal estate taxes were raised from twenty-five to forty per cent on accumulations exceeding $10,000,000; the tax rate was reduced to twenty per cent in 1926.) In this decade there was a great deal of tinkering with all the tax laws, which were steadily revised downward. However, special tax problems existed in many states, and even in a period of declining national taxes the foundation, like the family holding company, is useful as a device for manipulating income and capital in such a way as to reduce tax liability.

As to the increased industrial and financial power conferred by the foundations we find an excellent example of the use of these funds in the Rockefeller endowments. Robert W. Stewart was ousted as chairman of the Standard Oil Company of Indiana in March, 1929, by John D. Rockefeller, Jr., who voted against Stewart the shareholdings of the Rockefeller Foundation, the General Education Board, and other Rockefeller endowments, as well as the shareholdings of the Harkness, Pratt, and Whitney families. The foundation funds, in brief, are a factor in controlling industry while escaping taxes. Although the rich forego some personal income in setting up foundations, they forego no power.

As to the social power conferred upon their creators by the foundations, Lindeman points out that most of the foundation grants go into salaries. If control over an individual's livelihood confers any control over the individual, then the foundations exercise a decisive degree of power over many highly placed, influential persons who enjoy public confidence. Lindeman continues, in *Wealth and Culture*:

Foundations do not merely exercise power and control over those who accept their money. Such influence is obvious even when the foundations making grants insist to the contrary. A more subtle and much more widespread control comes about by reason of the multitude of indirect relationships in which foundations play a part. Those who accept foundation grants often turn out to be radical critics, in private, of the control which has been exercised over them and their programs. Those who live in anticipation of receiving foundation grants are the more servile.

Another device for projecting foundation control has become popular in recent years: foundations frequently supply the initial funds for a new project, these funds to be used for exploratory and conferencing purposes. In many cases the foundation acts as host for such preparatory groups. By the time the final project is formulated it becomes clear that nothing will be proposed or performed which may be interpreted as a challenge to the orthodox conception of value which characterizes foundations as a whole. Very few important cultural projects of any size are consummated in this country without having experienced either the direct or indirect impact of foundation philosophy and influence.

Lindeman's observation that those who merely anticipate foundation grants are often more servile than those already in receipt of grants is especially illuminating. The power of the foundations is so insidiously refined that without expending any money they can influence the attitudes of professional and technical people who need money to go on with their work. These people, hoping that the lightning of a foundation grant will strike them, consciously or unconsciously shape their attitudes so as to please potential donors, who passively achieve their objective of inducing these prospective recipients to speak out in defense of the social *status quo* or to maintain silence about features of the *status quo* that they would otherwise be obligated to challenge.

This subtle extension of the power of foundation grants far beyond the immediate money payment accounts for the otherwise mysterious fact that many presumably independent, freethinking scholars, scientists, and professional people give public utterance to opinions that differ in no way from those of a Wall Street banker. In private these persons may differ among each other profoundly; but in public their utterances are as uniform as those of newspaper editorial writers. A number of *obiter dicta* by such persons will be cited in the chapter on education to follow. Here there is room for only one, typical of many.

On the first page of *The New York Times* (October 20, 1936), under the headline "High Taxes on Wealthy Crippling The Hospitals, Surgeons Are Told," appeared the remarks of Dr. Frank E. Adair of the Memorial Hospital of New York. Dr. Adair spoke before the annual Clinical Congress of the American College of Surgeons, in Philadelphia. The gist of his remarks was adequately summarized in the headlines; it apparently never occurred to Dr. Adair that the public tax reservoir could do more for hospitals than the undependable, haphazard, egocentric benefactions of the rich.

The ordinary reader could not be expected to remember that the *Times* (April 28, 1936, page one) told that the General Education Board had given the Memorial Hospital $3,000,000 for the erection of a new building. The *Times* accompanied this particular announcement with a rewrite of the same eulogistic editorial it has published recurrently for years whenever some new "philanthropy" is announced by a rich family.

The outflow from foundations inspires shallow thinking like that of Dr. Adair in a multitude of professional and technical people, who are quicker to spring to a defense of the prerogatives of the rich —feeling themselves to be champions of the truth—than are the rich themselves. These professional people are not familiar with the fact, disclosed by Doane, that the much-maligned government has allocated to social uses since the Civil War more than four times as much as private persons. Nor are these professionals conscious that their first allegiance should be to the race in general, which has handed down to them their skill and knowledge.

"It seems to me entirely reasonable and clear," says Lindeman, "that independent scholars, artists, writers, and critics should have some voice in determining the ends for which vested wealth is used. They cannot make an effective contribution, however, if they become subservient to foundation officials or trustees. If there is to be in our society a reservoir of wealth which is not needed for material purposes, or if it is conceived that cultural aims are necessary, if economic progress is to lead toward true social progress, then it seems clear that the use of such a fund should devolve upon persons who are culturally minded in a valid sense."

At this point Lindeman touches upon the crux of the entire problem, saying, "Nothing, it seems to me, is so repugnant as the arrogance of those who presume to impose cultural norms upon a society on no basis of warrant other than their pecuniary success under the dispensation of a competitive economy."

In his *New Republic* article Lindeman indicated (a) that the foundations exert a controlling influence in research and (b) that they act as a drag upon American cultural development by conservative selectivity and "the tendency to neglect or to stereotype creative movements."

The Rockefeller philanthropies have been singled out in this chapter. Let us, however, clearly understand that a similar critical approach to almost all the other foundations would yield very similar conclusions. The Rockefeller contribution, if such it may be called, is larger than the others because the Rockefeller ownership is larger and because Rockefeller had only one son to whom to transmit his fortune. Where there are no sons, or daughters, the tendency is to leave the entire fortune to public uses. The two big nineteenth-century fortunes of Stephen Girard and Leland Stanford were, for lack of progeny to leave them to, given to the public. But where there are many children—as in the Du Pont, Vanderbilt, Mellon, and other families—there is little need to resort extensively to the device of foundations to escape either income or inheritance taxes, since tax liability can be spread among many persons. It is observable that the younger Rockefeller, who has six sons, in his 1934 and 1936 transfers did not allocate the taxable surplus funds to one of the foundations under his control.

The Guggenheims, a numerous tribe, have set up two small foundations, which must be regarded (from the standpoint of the Guggenheims) as devices to bring about favorable publicity. Awards of less than $200,000 a year by the John Simon Guggenheim Memorial Foundation to writers, scholars, scientists, and other professional workers, inspire a recurring torrent of publicity. Each recipient, distinguished in his field, continues work and goes through life identified as a former Guggenheim scholar. The socially and culturally sterile name of Guggenheim is thus associated, in a never-ending stream of echoes, with art, science, progress.

## IV

Brief attention must be given to the more extreme pseudo philanthropies, although most of those we already have observed are themselves of that category. Nevertheless, along with the self-biased social, financial, and industrial control exerted by units like the Rockefeller funds, there has accrued some good to the human race. Through the Rockefeller and Rosenwald funds a number of Negroes in the South have learned, at least, to read. Through Rockefeller's endowments some people have escaped the ravages of disease. They have, it is also true, been saved from physical death very often only to prolong what might be called their social death; but that is another matter. And somewhere along the line one of these funds may unwittingly have helped to preserve a Beethoven, a Lincoln, a Darwin, a Newton. Private philanthropy is most easily justified, perhaps, in the field of medicine.

There is a lower plane of so-called philanthropic activity where chicane is much more obvious than in the branches already surveyed. In contrast with some so-called philanthropists the Rockefellers, Guggenheims, Harknesses, and a few more take on the appearance of human saviors. It is, however, not only these who, upon dying, are proclaimed in simple newspaper headlines as a "capitalist and philanthropist," or even, more simply, as a "philanthropist." In passing, it may be observed that in modern journalistic jargon "capitalist" and "philanthropist" have become synonymous. One cannot, in the contemporary inversion of values, be a philanthropist without being a capitalist, or vice versa.

Lindeman, as we have observed, found few evidences of philanthropy in wills. Let us look at a few of the big wills. They are peculiarly interesting illustrations of the psychology of the rich.

When Henry Clay Frick died in 1919 the fortune he left, after earlier personal bequests and gifts to individuals, was $75,000,000. Of this total $20,000,000 went to a daughter, $5,000,000 to the widow, and the balance to educational institutions. Harvard was ostensibly given $10,000,000, Princeton an equal amount, and the Massachusetts Institute of Technology $5,000,000, while similar sums went else-- where. Frick was hailed by the newspapers, of course, as a great bene- factor of the human race. There was a fly in this ointment, though, and it was pointed out to C. W. Barron by Frederick H. Prince, wealthy Boston railroad promoter. Prince said that Frick's will ac- tually stipulated that the inheritance tax, then twenty-five per cent, was to be paid entirely out of the philanthropic bequests; after this was done the philanthropic items were all reduced by more than eighty per cent, and some were reduced by ninety per cent.

James B. Duke, the tobacco king, distributed his property before his death, thus avoiding inheritance or estate taxes. One-third went to his wife, one-third to his daughter, and one-third was kept under Duke control by segregation in the Duke Endowment, for the bene- fit of Duke University. Controlling blocks of tobacco and public utility stocks were given to the Endowment, to be used in the domi- nation of certain companies. Furthermore, the nature of the endow- ment included the University in the privately unhappy consequences of any regulation of public utilities or increases in tobacco taxes.

The greatest secrecy surrounds the Duke Endowment. The Twen- tieth Century Fund reported in its 1934 study that the Endowment had failed to respond to requests for information, and therefore was not included either among the twenty largest capital funds or among the twenty largest donors of income. In its study for 1931, however, because the Duke Endowment made grants of $3,754,592, or the fourth largest total for the year, the Twentieth Century Fund capital- ized these grants theoretically at five per cent, or $75,091,840. For reasons which do not appear, the Duke Endowment does not want its inner operations scrutinized.

Richard B. Mellon, brother of Andrew W. Mellon, died in 1933, and left an estate officially appraised at $200,000,000. A headline in *The New York Times* called him "a noted philanthropist" and also reported: "Many gifts to charity in testator's life." The only charitable items reporters could find to tell about, however, concerned the erec- tion at Mellon's expense of a $3,000,000 Pittsburgh church and the giving of "hundreds of thousands of dollars to the unemployed."

Even so, Richard B. Mellon was considered the "philanthropist" of the radically unphilanthropic Mellon clan; and the profundity of his philanthropic inclinations is, perhaps, best illustrated by his own remarks: "You couldn't run a coal mine without machine guns."

Mellon's will, however, carried out the fiction of the philanthropies by saying with laudable reserve: "I have always been interested in religious, charitable, and educational institutions, and particularly in those which I felt had an especial call upon me." The testament did not explain to be sure that this "interest" was largely academic. The will itself best indicated how philanthropic the deceased had been: $1,100,000 was left to the personally profitable Mellon Institute, $250,000 was left to servants, and $198,650,000 was left to Mrs. Mellon, to Richard K. Mellon, a son, and to Mrs. Alan M. Scaife, a daughter. The executors, moreover, entered into prolonged litigation with the state of Pennsylvania over taxes, and after nearly four years agreed to accept an assessment of about $13,000,000. Prolonged wrangling was also carried on with the Federal government, the final outcome of which has not been announced at this writing. Under the 1932 Revenue Act the estate was subject to a tax of forty-five per cent, or $90,000,000, including the payment to Pennsylvania. The net value of the estate left to the wife and two children was, therefore, about $108,650,000.

The Mellons have established in Pittsburgh the Mellon Institute, which a wide public fondly supposes is devoted to scientific advancement of general benefit. The Institute cost $80,000 to establish, was designed solely for industrial research, and has already produced so many privately profitable discoveries that it has been greatly expanded at no genuine expense to the Mellons. Patents are taken out on the discoveries and inventions of its workers, and the patents are exploited in the market. The Institute endorses products, some of dubious merit, which are sold in the retail market. Much of its income is paid by manufacturers for permission to put their research men to work in the Institute's laboratories.

Very recently the wide and subtle uses to which foundations and charitable trust funds may be put have been borne in upon the consciousness of many wealthy persons. What many now realize, the Rockefellers, always farsighted, long ago understood.

When George Ball, Muncie, Indiana, glass-jar manufacturer, purchased control of $3,000,000,000 of Van Sweringen railroad assets for $275,000 from J. P. Morgan and Company, sophisticated observers suspected something unusual. When Ball placed the controlling Van Sweringen stock in a "religious and philanthropic foundation" informed observers surmised there was something even more unusual, and watched to see what would be the outcome of this transaction. When Ball's foundation within two years gave up the control, which already showed the enormous potential profit indicated in Chapter VI, to gain a much smaller profit by selling out to two New York brokers, the transaction became even more extraordinary. Charity and religion would have benefited tremendously had Ball left the entire Van Sweringen railroad system behind them. As it was, Ball's foundation took the lesser profit offered by the two New York brokers. What was behind all this is not yet plain. One thing, however, is certain; a goodly amount of capital-gains taxes was avoided.

Very probably the future will bring forth many more of these tax-saving philanthropic foundations to act in similar odd transactions.

George F. Baker, Jr., died in May, 1937, and his will set up a philanthropic fund that showed he had learned well from the elder Rockefeller that it is more profitable to give than to receive. Baker inherited from his father $73,000,000 of assets in 1931, the valuation being at extreme depression lows. In 1929 the elder Baker's assets had a reported market value of $200,000,000. Between the deaths of the father and the son there had been a great rise in market values, but as no announcement was made of the value of the son's estate, and as he had previously transferred a good deal of wealth both to his wife and to his four children, as his will stated, it is impossible to tell precisely what he left.

The New York Times set the estimated value of the estate at $60,-000,000, after the gift of $5,000,000 of First National Bank stock to his wife in 1934 prior to the increase in the still modest gift-tax rates and after uncomputed transfers to two sons and two daughters. Assuming this to have been the size of the estate (the Times said its value may have ranged up to $80,000,000), we find from that pessimistic analysis that the Baker family would have been left only $20,000,000 after payment of state and Federal estate taxes. The *Times'* analyst construed the Revenue Act of 1935 to mean that taxes of seventy per cent are levied on estates above $50,000,000, whereas the Act says that amounts above $50,000,0000 are taxable at seventy per cent after $32,-362,600 has been paid on the first $50,000,000.

The Bakers, however, had no intention of turning over even this amount to the Treasury; moreover, the Federal law allows a credit for the payment of state taxes in the amount of eighty per cent of the estate-tax liability under the 1926 Federal law. The *Times* conveniently assumed that Baker had arranged it so that his estate would pay the government the maximum possible.

On June 24, 1937, the *Times* published some of the provisions of the Baker will under the typically misleading headline:

## G. F. BAKER WILLED
## PUBLIC $15,000,000

Baker was one of the group behind the Republican Party that stormed against high taxes in the 1936 election campaign. Here, then, was a paradox: he did not want the government to get his fortune; yet he wanted to leave one-quarter of it to the public. Let us see how this worked out.

If Baker's net estate was $60,000,000, as it may have been after the earlier transfers to his wife and to his sons of what the will termed "substantial property," then the philanthropic "bequest" reduced its net taxable value to $45,000,000. In effecting this reduction the estate rid itself of the $10,000,000 surplus above $50,000,000 which, taxable at 70 per cent, would have yielded the Federal government $7,000,000.

The hypothetical $45,000,000 remaining would apparently yield New York State $7,500,000 at its tax rate of sixteen and one-half per cent on fortunes exceeding $10,000,000. The Federal credit against this would be $7,200,000 under the terms of the 1935 Revenue Act. The Federal tax on the remaining $45,000,000 amounts to $11,662,600 on the first $20,000,000 and to sixty-nine per cent, or $17,250,000, on the remaining $25,000,000.

Instead of the $40,000,000 tax which the *Times* had indicated the estate would pay, much to the anguish of readers who sent in letters, the actual payment would be approximately as follows (assuming always that the estate amounted only to $60,000,000):

| | | |
|---|---|---|
| New York state tax at 16½% on $45,000,000.. | | $7,500,000 |
| Federal estate tax............... | $28,912,600 | |
| Less credit for payment of state tax ...................... | 7,200,000 | |
| Net Federal tax................ | $21,712,600 | 21,712,600 |
| Total tax ...................... | | $29,212,600 |

On the first $10,000,000 of his charitable bequest Baker saved $7,000,000 and on the second $5,000,000 he saved $3,450,000 in Federal taxes—$10,450,000 in all, or more than two-thirds of the sum left to "charity." The cost to the Baker family of the philanthropic fund that controls $15,000,000 of First National Bank stock is, therefore, slightly more than $4,000,000.

Taxes, then, have reduced the Baker estate only to $30,787,400, in contrast with the $20,000,000 reported by the *Times*. However, even this figure does not represent the assets left in the control of the Baker family. It actually appears that the family, on the basis of the modest $60,000,000 estimate of the fortune and the earlier intrafamily gifts, retains control of at least $40,000,000 of assets, or twice as much as was indicated by the *Times*.

Baker's will stipulated that his philanthropic fund should be placed in charge of his family, his two sons taking it over upon attaining their majority. In this fund is immobilized enough First National Bank stock to keep in Baker control the twenty-two per cent of stock they have always controlled. Only income on the seventy-five hundred shares allotted to philanthropy goes to philanthropy, and only to such philanthropies as the Bakers may select, thereby increasing their power over persons far removed from the world of finance. Baker, incidentally, in obvious anticipation of the 1935 tax law, increased the bank stocks he had allotted to the philanthropic fund from five thousand to seven thousand five hundred shares.

However, even after all this, it is quite a come-down to see the vaunted fortune of George F. Baker, of a market value of $200,000,000 in 1929, reduced to a paltry $40,000,000 odd. Let us, therefore, examine it more closely.

Baker Jr., as we have seen, inherited from his father an estate valued at $73,000,000, on which a state and Federal tax of about $13,000,000 was paid. Not only had the younger Baker before his death transferred to his wife and two sons about eleven thousand First National Bank shares, but he also had settled an unannounced amount of property on his two daughters, Mrs. John M. Schiff and Mrs. T. Suffern Tailer.

The will, significantly, did not appraise the assets. And even after the assets are appraised there will be no real indication of what the family is worth, for it would be necessary to know what intrafamily gifts have been made over a term of years, and among how many persons they had been apportioned, before one could estimate its true worth.

Harking back to the 1924 income-tax returns we find that both George F. Baker and his son paid approximately the same tax each on the income from an indicated joint fortune of $210,000,000. In short, back in 1924 the junior Baker was already in receipt of half the family revenue. As no disaster has engulfed the Baker properties, whose market values were only temporarily reduced in 1931, it cannot be argued that the payment of the Federal taxes already surveyed would do much to reduce the fortune. However, if the Baker who died in 1937 had in his own name much of the family property above the value of $50,000,000, it would be subject to total taxes higher than here indicated. But if the property had been distributed to a "substantial" extent among his wife, two sons and two daughters, as appears to have been the case, his death, contrary to *The New York Times*, brought no tax disaster to the estate.

The income, estate, and gift-tax laws, especially the latter, are so drawn as to give the rich a premium for having numerous progeny. This aspect will be touched upon in our final chapter. The tax laws only make it necessary for the rich to maneuver their wealth in sections to escape effective taxation. Newspapers like the *Times*, however, reporting that Cyrus McCormick's 1936 estate of $22,000,000 bore a tax liability of $11,680,000, that Henry H. Rogers' 1935 estate of $16,255,440 bore a tax of $11,600,000, and that James Couzens' estate of $30,000,000 faced a tax liability of $21,000,000, fail to make clear the antecedent preservative role of multiple, low-taxed gifts and of philanthropic foundations and joint-stock family corporations.

Milton S. Hershey, the chocolate king, in 1918 endowed the Hershey Industrial School at Hershey, Pa. The stock he gave was valued at $60,000,000, the stock he kept at $1,000,000. Hershey, however, retained personal control over the tax-free endowment, the income of which was to be devoted to healthy, white, orphan children. Work went on as before at the Hershey factory, where there was so little manifestation of philanthropy that labor disputes took place. The workers, on strike, were subdued by police and vigilantes in classic fashion. Surveys made of the community, which is almost entirely dominated by the Hershey endowment, suggest that the endowment is nothing more than an instrument of power wielded by a few men. Benefactions there have been, such as agreeable housing for workers, parks, swimming pools, concerts, etc., but paralleling all this has been an autocratic control over the lives of all citizens. The educational program in the school is rigidly prescribed along manual-training lines and, according to some observers, completely unfits the "beneficiaries" to enter other fields of work. The average 1936 weekly wage in the Hershey plant was $17.30.

Charles Hayden, banker, left an estate in 1937 valued unofficially at $50,000,000. The income of this fund was given over to the establishment of a charitable foundation for boys and young men—thereby eluding estate taxes. The organization will be known as the Charles Hayden Foundation. Hayden, unmarried, had no children, it is instructive to note. It is no less instructive to reflect that this vast fund was left in the keeping of Hayden's business associates and that through it they will exercise wide industrial and social control. Had Hayden left the estate to these individuals personally it would have been subject to a seventy per cent Federal tax, minus credits for payment of the New York State tax. As the estate carried with it more than sixty industrial directorships, it was worth preserving.

The establishment of philanthropic funds has, indeed, become a fine art, and the danger seems to be that capitalism under the impetus of its tax laws will metamorphose itself entirely into a "philanthropic" enterprise, controlling not only the economic apparatus but the very soul of humanity.*

At least a brief look at the great art collections bequeathed to "mankind" is advisable, for the public is frequently gratified to read that some financial freebooter has left a valuable collection in the hands of public agencies.

The artistic interest of the magnates, who have not been esthetes, has been almost wholly pecuniary. Works of art, under competitive private bidding, have attained a high scarcity value; but, this apart, relationships are traceable between the purchase of objects of art abroad and various tax schedules, fluctuations in foreign exchange

* The menacing extremes to which the establishment of philanthropic foundations have gone were nowhere better illustrated than in the terms of the late Andrew W. Mellon's will, a reading of which leads one to the conclusion that there is a tacit conspiracy among the lawyers of the millionaires to keep the fortunes out of the hands of the public while seemingly devoting the fortunes to the public. Mellon died late in August, 1937, and a fortune of $200,000,000–$400,000,000 was left to the A. W. Mellon Educational and Charitable Trust, but under the trusteeship, irrevocably and perpetually, of his son Paul, his son-in-law David K. E. Bruce, his attorney, and their self-designated successors. As the *Herald Tribune*, August 29, 1937, remarked, the announcement "came at a time when officials of the United States Treasury . . . were anticipating a windfall in taxes from the Mellon estate. So did the tax collectors in Harrisburg, where already eager functionaries had announced that the Mellon estate was expected to yield at least $28,000,000 for the State of Pennsylvania." Prior to his death Mellon made substantial provision for his son and daughter, according to the will, but as he had only two children to whom to distribute his fortune, he would have incurred heavy gift taxes had he given it to them before he died. Mellon's will discloses that it is control rather than ownership that the rich are seeking to preserve, if they cannot have both, in their philanthropic benefactions; for Mellon's family will retain control, under the terms of his will, of the vast Mellon properties which in an ordinary transfer would have incurred a Federal tax of seventy per cent. If control can be preserved by philanthropic foundations in a period of tangled taxes, perhaps at a later date, under more benign political auspices, the controllers of the foundations can have them restored to private status. Indeed, the very existence of so many privately controlled foundations will in time provide a very weighty motive for the rich to instigate a revolution of the Right in order that private ownership of the foundation funds may be restored to their private trustees. The establishing of a philanthropic fund by Mellon reduces the word philanthropy to an absurdity in current practice, for Mellon was never philanthropically inclined and always did everything in his power to evade taxes. After his death his attorneys said he had given more than $70,000,000 to philanthropy in his lifetime, but they neglected to add that the philanthropies consisted largely of gifts to the personally profitable University of Pittsburgh, Mellon Institute, and Carnegie Institute of Technology—all more or less subsidiaries of the Mellon industrial empire

rates, and tariffs. As to the first, it must be remembered that the tax system is extremely complicated. In addition to Federal income, estate, and gift taxes, there are also state income and estate taxes and local personal-property and real-estate taxes. Art works, furthermore, lend themselves readily to pecuniary manipulation because the values set upon them are usually arbitrary, and are seldom subject to pricing in the open market. As the private bookkeeping that covers the purchase and sale of art is very slack, not subject to investigation by Federal Trade Commissions and Interstate Commerce Commissions, almost any juggling is possible; foreign art dealers, for example, often permit American buyers to exaggerate reported purchase prices, if an exaggerated value best fits into the tax scheme, or to minimize reported prices, if a minimum figure is desired.

If the art is to be held as personal property a low valuation is desirable. If it is to be housed in a private museum, as part of a real-estate project, a low valuation is also often desirable. However, if it is to be used to reduce income tax liability, an overvaluation is preferable. For example, if $75,000,000 of money, representing profits on business abroad, perhaps, that may be subject to repatriation transfer taxes or even to income taxes, is put into a collection that is subsequently valued at $25,000,000, a total of $50,000,000 is hidden. The art works, of course, enter the country tariff-free. If the collection is housed in a quasi-public museum, local real-estate tax exemption may be claimed for a sizable piece of property being held in

comprising the Gulf Oil Company, the Aluminum Company, the Koppers Coke Company, etc.

There is no new law needed to cope with these pseudo-philanthropic foundations, although, in order to spin out the issue, some legislative agent of the big fortunes will soon be seen to arise and suggest that special laws be framed to cope with philanthropies; such futile shutting of the barn door will drag the issue out for ten or twenty years, in which interval much may happen. There is already enough law on the books to hold such "bequests" of 1937 as were made by Baker, Mellon and Hayden essentially unphilanthropic devices for insuring continued industrial control in few hands; a great deal of discretionary power rests with the legally constituted tax officials in judging the philanthropic character of these so-called charitable funds. And only a refusal by the tax officials to recognize the philanthropic character of these funds will prevent the big fortunes from preserving themselves and working their selfish will upon the commonwealth. The Mellon "bequest" merely proves anew that the philanthropic funds are tax-dodging schemes, as the wily Rockefeller discovered long ago.

anticipation of a rise in land values that may, in time, offset the entire cost of the art collection.

The foreign art-works market is, according to private accounts, crisscrossed with a system of rebates, drawbacks, and confidential concessions that serve to obscure precise costs and values, and in this shadowy atmosphere pecuniary maneuvers that are practically undetectable can take place. Undervalued art, while concealing assets, also enables the owner to transfer wealth virtually tax-free to friends and to relatives if the transfer is carried out in piecemeal fashion. Concise illustrations are lacking because of the secrecy enshrouding this field. Moreover, foolproof hypothetical illustrations in relation to the tax structure at any given time are not possible without a knowledge of the specific inner tax problems of a given family.

In the multiple tax structure of the United States different localities have different ways of taxing art works. Although the Federal law is uniform, state laws are not, nor are municipal real estate and personal-property laws.

Again, the fluctuation of European exchange rates has enabled Americans to acquire works of art, very often, for next to nothing. If these works were resold or retransferred in the United States with the admission of the huge profit involved, the profit would be taxable. Seldom are huge profits admitted, however, although we know the American money lords are mainly interested in profits, as their visible careers show. Citing a hypothetical case, we may say that an American millionaire has Art Agent A go into a certain country, whose currency is temporarily badly depreciated, to buy various works of art. These, let us assume, cost $100,000 of American money. Art Agent A then "resells" to Art Agent B (also an employee of the art-minded millionaire), who resells to Art Company C (privately retained), which resells to Art Company D (also privately retained) located in Paris. At each resale the price is advanced, but as the millionaire behind the scenes is always reselling to himself through dummies the cost of the art to him is still only $100,000. Art Company D then may place the works of art up for auction, where they are bid in at top prices by Art Agent E, working in the open for the American millionaire. The auction price paid, let us say, is $5,000,000, and this is reported in the newspapers.

The collection is repatriated, tariff-free, and in due course, requiring cash, the millionaire sells it for $4,000,000. Here he has a capital loss of $1,000,000, which he may deduct from his income-tax return. As his hidden purchase price was $100,000 and his resale price was $4,000,000, he has actually made a profit of $3,900,000, subject only to cost of handling, and fees and commissions to the agents, and he has escaped taxes on $1,000,000 of income for which deduction has been claimed.

Many millionaires, especially in the nineteenth century, unquestionably paid top prices for art works. Others, more recently, have not been so foolish. Lacking a public record, one cannot separate the sheep from the goats, but before conceding the esthetic motive in the gathering of art works by money-minded men each case would have to be rigidly scrutinized on its individual merits.

That there is pecuniary motivation behind the big art collections is, however, attested by the public record. The elder Morgan, chairman of the Metropolitan Museum board, turned his collection over to it; the public believed that he had "given" the collection away. But when he died it became obvious that he had merely "lent" the collection, and his son sold it for about $25,000,000 cash. The Metropolitan Museum, art center of the nation, has been used by the Morgan firm, as we have seen, in newspaper deals in which J. P. Morgan and Company did not want directly to be concerned. Munsey left his estate and newspapers to the museum, having garnered the estate in the stock market under Morgan auspices; the museum sold *The Sun* to a Morgan group and the *Telegram* to Scripps-Howard. Munsey himself had sold the *Herald* to the Reid-Mills family. In the latter case the museum inherited a note in part payment, with more than $1,000,000 of it still outstanding, undevoted to art. Whether the museum was paid off entirely in the *Sun* sale is not clear from the record.

The Metropolitan Museum, beloved of art connoisseurs, is, therefore, a device for holding newspaper properties. It is controlled by its trustees, whose names we have scanned. The New York *Sun*, incidentally, carries more advertising of art dealers than any other newspaper, although the average newspaper reader does not as a rule contemplate purchases of objects of art.

The Morgan family, still pursuing its credo of art for money's sake, built a big library adjoining its town house on Madison Avenue. After inaugurating a policy of allowing a few public visitors admission by card to look at costly illuminated manuscripts and other literary works, J. P. Morgan claimed real-estate tax exemption from the city. As the assessed tax liability of the land exceeded $500,000 annually, giving effect to the library improvement, this was an item worth considering. The land is in the heart of Manhattan, surrounded by big skyscrapers, and its value has increased yearly. The Morgan Library, however, was not open except to closely supervised and limited public inspection. And in the evening (when the public is not admitted), it reverted to its status as a private Morgan palace.

Henry Clay Frick, also interested in taxes, made his Fifth Avenue town house into a private art museum which was later thrown open to the public. Taxes on these private city demesnes can, in time, exceed their value. However, if taxes are held down in a period of high rates, perhaps, after a political overturn by which taxes are reduced, the properties may be restored to their strictly private status, for legal title is retained by the heirs and assigns.

In 1936 Andrew W. Mellon announced the outright gift of his $50,000,000 art collection to the government. Under the 1935 Revenue Act this collection in the Mellon estate would have been liable for taxes of $32,362,000, payable in cash. Mellon, therefore, paid $32,362,000 into his estate by giving up this art.

However, if the collection cost Mellon $50,000,000, as it apparently did, must it not be regarded nevertheless as a bona fide gift? One cannot say that the collection represents a gift in any sacrificial or praiseworthy sense until one has had the opportunity to estimate its pecuniary role in the inner history of the Mellon fortune. Granting the cost of $50,000,000, the collection may have represented a great pecuniary convenience to Mellon at a time when he possessed much surplus cash, or possessed the cash abroad and was unable to repatriate it by reason of currency or other restrictions. Cash alone is often a nuisance to a multimillionaire; when deposited in large amounts in banks it seldom draws interest. Safe investment vehicles may be sufficiently scarce to make it impossible to invest $50,000,000 at a particular time with any feeling of security. Immortal works of art, however, which can be insured against theft, fire, or other forms of destruction, do represent relative stability of value.

Could not a multimillionaire achieve equal security, however, by keeping his funds in the form of noninterest-bearing cash? Cash, however, often depreciates in value, and the depreciation is evidenced by a rise in prices. United States funds after the war, for example, were quoted at eighty per cent of par on the Stock Exchange. In 1918 the gold-exchange rate of the dollar in Madrid was below 30 cents. In 1933 its gold value was reduced by 40.4 per cent.

A multimillionaire takes all these factors into consideration, and seeks to diversify the forms in which his wealth is held. Works of art provide a special form for holding wealth and for giving extra diversification. Wealth is diversified not only through a multiplicity of stocks, bonds, and cash, but through real estate, art works, jewels, life-insurance policies, etc. After the national possibilities of diversification have been exhausted, there is the international field of many national currencies and securities, as well as of foreign real estate. Once all these have been utilized there remain the tax-exempt philanthropic foundations.

A huge collection of art, like a big insurance policy, is a form of insurance for the fortune against a depreciation in currency and against many other types of financial fluctuation. Works of art are actually an international currency much like gold. Governments, in time of emergency, have confiscated private works of art, as well as gold and holdings of foreign securities and currencies.

The Mellon family, therefore, has derived steady pecuniary benefit from its great art collection. Assuming that it has been held substantially in its present size for twenty years, the cost of $50,000,000 figures down to $2,500,000 annually. This is relatively cheap insurance for a huge fortune. Faced at the present time by an estate-tax rate that makes this particular form of insurance potentially costly, the Mellon family merely wafts the art collection away.

Until estate taxes made it expensive, Mellon's art collection, for example, assured him that he would always have from $25,000,000 to $50,000,000 no matter what happened to United States money, no matter what regulatory measures were taken against his companies.

If he could not realize upon the paintings in America, Europe would have repurchased them at a substantial price.

To the outsider these considerations may seem farfetched. They seem farfetched only to those who have not come in contact with wealthy people, whose minds are in a perpetual turmoil about alternative employments for their wealth which will (a) yield the highest return, (b) avoid a maximum of taxes, (c) assure a maximum of diversification, and (d) guarantee the greatest possible permanence. The wills themselves attest that this preoccupation with the internal distribution of the fortunes extends beyond the portals of death. Like Carnegie, most of the multimillionaires want their hoards held intact through eternity.

The uninformed often complain that men of wealth are only interested in "dead" art, are seldom interested in modern art, and rarely are interested at all in subsidizing living artists. The fact should be plain, however, that the wealthy men, concerned only with exercising and retaining their own power, are not really interested even in "dead" art. They are drawn to it only because of its status as a highly developed international pecuniary medium.

Illustrative of the indifference of the rich as a class to the realm of art is the fact that the Federal government in recent years has had to support some fifty thousand artists on the relief roll; that the artists of America, some of whom already belong to an immortal company, have no audience save in a few large cities among esthetic-minded foreign born. Had it not been for Federal intervention after the crisis, the theater, too, would have passed out of existence as a field of artistic expression. The wealthy, for whom the drama means only a succession of "first nights," evinced no interest in the dying stage, nor in the plight of thousands of destitute actors and actresses. The Federal Theater has sponsored virtually the only vital and original productions of the past few seasons.

Music has fared no better at the hands of wealthy "patrons." As with opera, dependence upon rich sponsors had, until the government took a hand, kept music in its higher forms well out of the reach of the populace. Federal Music Project concerts, with admissions scaled down to twenty-five and thirty-five cents, and not limited only to the biggest cities, did more to stimulate public attendance at musical performances than had fifty years of privately patronized orchestras.

There is, in conclusion, much piecemeal charity carried on, but most of it can successfully be called into question as tinged with pecuniary self-interest. For many years, to give a glaring example, New York's wealthy families posed as patrons of the Metropolitan Opera. When the opera ran upon evil days during the depression of 1929–33, it was brought out that it leased its quarters from the Metropolitan Opera and Realty Corporation, a profitable enterprise controlled by the box holders. Computation showed that the "contribution" of these "patrons" over a period of years actually amounted to slightly more than $8 a box seat per performance, or only slightly more than the price to the public of a main-floor seat. Not only was the tangible value of these patron-monopolized boxes far higher than the money paid for them by the "patrons" over whom the newspapers periodically gushed, but the value of the boxes to social climbers was enormous.* Fabulous prices have been privately offered for an opera box—with no sellers in sight. Had the box seats been thrown open periodically to general bidding the opera would have received a return far in excess of the $8 per chair paid by the "patrons." When Rockefeller, Jr., offered the opera more adequate housing in Rockefeller Center, where the tier boxes were to be supplanted by revenue-producing balcony seats, his offer was refused by the "patrons" who enjoyed such munificent personal returns from the old opera house. And when the Metropolitan Opera faced financial crisis in the depression of 1929–33 it was saved by public subscription.

Philanthropies and benefactions, so-called, are carried on by certain wealthy families in an apparently sporadic, unsystematic fashion because their personal pecuniary requirements are different from those of a family like that of the Rockefellers. All the families get their names into the newspapers at least once a year by some contri-

---

* Miss Georgine Iselin during the season 1920–21 sub-let her box for forty-seven performances, for which she received $9,525. Her assessment of $4,000 left her a profit of $5,025; the average price she received was $33.77 a chair. She got $550 for opening night and $3,025 for 11 subsequent Mondays; $300 for the Prince of Wales "gala" (one performance); $2,200 for an additional eleven Monday nights; and $3,450 for twenty-three Friday nights.

bution, however small, to one of the general charitable or church funds. Most of them have some pet hospital, school, park, or playground which they use to gain good repute and, in prosperous years, to reduce tax liability. Each of these benefactions should, however, be carefully studied on an individual basis before its philanthropic character is conceded; the author has scrutinized many and has found, almost invariably, that the family could preserve for itself more tax money by engaging in the philanthropy than by not engaging in it.

Have not the Fords and Du Ponts been great philanthropists, as newspapers have suggested? Let us see.

The Du Ponts have financed the construction of most of the elementary schools in Delaware; they have built most of the paved Delaware highways; they have constructed the principal hospitals of the small state. They and their relatives by marriage are, however, the only persons of any considerable pecuniary well-being in the state, and they would have paid for all this, anyhow, through taxes. Rather than pass the money through the political sieve, the Du Ponts decided to spend it themselves for public improvements, thereby assuring minimum costs and, very probably, giving their own companies a profit in the supplying of materials. Thus, having built roads, schools, hospitals, and other buildings for a presumably sovereign state—which might better be named the duchy of Du Pont—the Du Ponts have earned distinction as philanthropists. Small towns near which particular branches of the Du Pont dynasty maintain residences have also been "given" hospitals, which the Du Ponts and their guests, of course, may also use.

Henry Ford has put money into hospitals at Detroit and at Dearborn Michigan, largely devoted to caring for injured workers who turn out profits for Ford. This writer does not regard this as philanthropy, but merely as business. The Hearsts, Guggenheims, Dodges, and others also maintain hospitals in the mining centers to care for men injured in the mines. This, too, is not philanthropy.

Ford has earned distinction as a "philanthropist" mainly by an attempted physical reconstruction of the American past at Greenfield Village, Michigan. Inns, spinning wheels, harpoons, candlesticks, schools, and the like have been transported and made into a museum, the value of which is highly doubtful. Eccentric though Ford's expensive schemes are, however, they seem to win the acclaim of many people—and a design is thereby achieved. Ford has been unusually successful in turning white into black in the public consciousness. He is, for example, considered an exponent of high wages because, in order to create a surplus of labor in Detroit, he once proclaimed the doctrine of $5-a-day pay. Few people realize that a large proportion of Ford workers are laid off much of the time and that the Ford pay scales are not computed on a yearly basis.

It is true that there has been some disinterestedness shown by the rich in contributions to art, music, and the sciences, but the clearly disinterested contributions have been so trivial as not to merit mention. The critical reader, unversed in the ways of philanthropy, may exclaim: "What possible personal value could one ascribe to the creation of the magnificent Field Museum of Natural History in Chicago, erected by the Field family?" The building of this splendid monument on the Lake Michigan water front not only reduced tax liability in a period of relatively high income taxes and brought public acclaim for the Fields, but, along with other nearby improvements, it enhanced the value of the downtown Chicago real-estate holdings of the Field family. The will of Marshall Field I stipulated that a portion of income was always to be reinvested in improved Chicago real estate. Old Field, like old Astor, was real estate mad, and even joined in giving to the University of Chicago land that abutted on a greater amount of land whose ownership he retained. The peculiar provisions of the Field will have nearly driven its executors and trustees frantic to find suitable outlets for the estate's surplus income, and the heirs have, without avail, tried to upset the testament. Like the mill in the fable that ground out salt in the sea, the Field estate continues to grind out buildings, buildings, buildings —and the only hope of respite lies in the fact that all the structures will in time make each other mutually unprofitable.

In conclusion, the paradox is this: the rich grow richer and more powerful by the practice of philanthropy—as it is loosely defined.

# X

# Education for Profit and Tax Exemption

CLASS consciousness is, perhaps, nowhere more clearly or more amusingly manifested by the rich than in education. In no other sphere of pseudo-philanthropic activity is it more apparent that the rich, in escaping taxation by the expedient of creating tax-immune endowments, are merely transferring the money from one of their many capacious pockets to another.

Most private money earmarked for higher education is given, in the first place, to schools that belong rather exclusively to the rich. Albert N. Ward, president of Western Maryland College, in 1930 surveyed the endowments of four hundred privately supported institutions of higher learning and reported the conclusion that ten belonging to the very wealthy, catering to seventeen per cent of the national student body, held forty-three per cent of the recorded educational endowment; ninety belonging to the upper middle class, catering to forty-two per cent of the national student body, held thirty-eight per cent of the recorded endowment; and three hundred belonging to the lower classes, catering to forty-one per cent of the national student body, held only nineteen per cent of the recorded endowment.

Left out of consideration by Dr. Ward were state and municipal institutions, the so-called public colleges and universities. With very few exceptions these institutions are indirectly controlled, through the medium of the political machines whose phantom directors we have observed in furtive action, by the same persons that control the private institutions. The backbone of education in the United States is the tax-supported public school system, of course; the rich become active in educational affairs only when it comes to taking the product

374

of the public secondary school and forging it for special uses in the privately endowed or politically controlled college and university.

According to Federal government figures, in the school year 1933-34 there were 20,880,120 students in public elementary schools compared with 2,382,251 in private elementary schools (largely parochial); there were 5,715,608 students in public secondary schools compared with 380,880 students in private secondary schools (in part parochial); but there were only 529,931 students in public higher educational institutions compared with 525,429 in private higher educational institutions (of which few were parochial). If we exclude those training to be teachers, there were vastly more students in the private higher educational institutions, 518,578 to 400,598.

The public universities and colleges will not concern us here, however, although the general remarks applicable to the social bias of private schools are applicable in only slightly less degree to the politically controlled public schools.

The twenty universities and technical colleges with the largest endowments (accounting for more than seventy-five per cent of the entire private higher educational endowment of more than seven hundred institutions), and their managing and donor groups, are as follows:

| School | Managing group and principal donors | Endowment (latest figures) |
|---|---|---|
| 1. Harvard University | J. P. Morgan management. Largest donor: Standard Oil (Whitney, Harkness, Rockefeller); various other wealthy donors, including George F. Baker, Sr. ............... | $129,000,000 |
| 2. Yale University | Morgan-Rockefeller joint management. Largest donor: Standard Oil (Harkness, Whitney, Rockefeller), also Sterling, Stillman, *et al.* ........ | 95,838,568 |

| School | Managing group and principal donors | Endowment (latest figures) |
|---|---|---|
| 3. Columbia University | National City Bank management. Largest donors: Baker, Dodge, Gould, *et al.* Also Havemeyer, Schermerhorn, and various others. ........ | $69,576,915 |
| 4. University of Chicago | Rockefeller management and principal donation. Smaller donors: Field, Ryerson, Swift, Yerkes, *et al.* ............................... | 65,389,498 |
| 5. University of Rochester | George W. Eastman (kodaks), donor. .................. | 58,008,103 |
| 6. University of Texas | Various donors. ........... | 33,642,546 |
| 7. Massachusetts Institute of Technology | Du Pont management; Eastman-Du Pont donors. ...................... | 33,000,000 |
| 8. Stanford University | Southern Pacific Railroad and California public-utilities management; Leland Stanford donor. | 32,000,238 |
| 9. Duke University | Duke management and donation (tobacco and public utilities). ............... | 30,880,031 |
| 10. Cornell University | Rockefeller management; various wealthy donors. ............................ | 30,311,743 |
| 11. Princeton University | National City Bank management; Taylor, Pyne, McCormick, Dodge donors. ............... | 26,929,810 |
| 12. Johns Hopkins University | Morgan influence predominant on board; various wealthy donors. ...... | 26,934,827 |
| 13. Northwestern University | Methodist Church management; Deering family (International Harvester) largest donor; other donors Patten, McCormick, Ward. ........ | 21,782,482 |

| School | Managing group and principal donors | Endowment (latest figures) |
|---|---|---|
| 14. Washington University (St. Louis, Missouri) | Various wealthy donors. Robert Brookings, main donor. | $20,911,986 |
| 15. University of California | Crocker, Giannini, Fleischacker, Hearst, and Doheny donors and management. ................. | 20,228,414 |
| 16. Vanderbilt University | Vanderbilt donation plus some smaller donations. | 20,000,000 |
| 17. University of Pennsylvania | J. P. Morgan management; Morgan, Drexel, Widener, Clothier, *et al.*, donors. ............................... | 18,998,279 |
| 18. Oberlin College | Various donors. .............. | 18,149,822 |
| 19. Dartmouth College | Various wealthy donors. | 17,239,839 |
| 20. Carnegie Institute of Technology | Mellon management; Carnegie donation. ......... | 16,369,382 |

All the foregoing are upper-class schools in that they (a) cater to the offspring of the upper classes or (b) aim to turn out graduates that will be, regardless of their class origin, of pecuniary value to the upper class in the economic exploitation of American society: lawyers, accountants, physical scientists, engineers, salesmen, business executives, etc. It is noteworthy that the private schools, as a rule, have little interest in training teachers.

A review of this list of leading endowed institutions of higher learning readily brings to mind their importance in contemporary life. With the exception of a few publicly supported institutions like the University of Wisconsin, the University of Michigan, and the University of Minnesota, these listed are the top-ranking institutions of learning of the United States.

The direct management and support, by wealthy private families, of institutions of higher education extends, to be sure, far beyond the confines of the list just given. The University of Pittsburgh (endowment $2,314,225) is under Mellon control; Colgate University (endowment $6,700,000) is under control of the shaving-cream and toothpaste family; Drexel Institute (endowment $3,330,730) is under the

Drexel family (Morgan); Lehigh University (endowment $5,400,000)
is supported by various steel and industrial interests; and both the
more and the less opulent of the rich families subsidize and dominate
an assortment of institutions that includes Brown University, Amherst College, Williams College, Rensselaer Polytechnic Institute,
Oglethorpe University, Case School of Applied Science, Rutgers
College, Antioch College, California Institute of Technology, St.
Lawrence University, Syracuse University, Stevens Institute of Technology, Worcester Polytechnic Institute, and many others.

All these schools are adjuncts, or departments, of the big corporations and banks, and are more or less openly operated as such. This is
evidenced in many ways, but mainly (a) by the identities of trustees,
most of whom are men engaged in pecuniary pursuits as deputies
of the great fortunes or are in person the ruling heads of the great
fortunes; (b) by the composition of the investment portfolios of the
institutions themselves; (c) by the curricular emphasis upon studies
of direct pecuniary value to the wealthiest estates, studies embracing,
in the main, the physical sciences and problems of business administration as well as the professional pursuits; and (d) by the recurrent
official pronouncements of the presidents of the institutions on behalf
of the political, economic, and social *status quo.*

Professor Jerome Davis, surveying the occupational status of the
trustees of the twenty-seven institutions of higher learning with endowments of $10,000,000 or more, brought out that of 659 trustees,
254 are bankers, 141 are merchants, 111 are public-utilities operators,
63 are railroad operators, 153 are professionals (whose presence af-
fords protective coloration), 22 are judges, representatives of the two
dominant political parties, and 7 fall into miscellaneous classifications.
Seventy-two are classifiable in more than one category.

The breakdown of the occupational status of college trustees, given
by Professor Davis (*Capitalism and Its Culture*), for these twenty-
seven institutions with endowments of $10,000,000 or more follows:

| | Endowment | Trustees | Bankers | Mfrs., Merch. | Pub. Util. | R. R. | Prof. | Judges |
|---|---|---|---|---|---|---|---|---|
| Harvard | | 33 | 12 | 6 | 4 | 4 | 9 | 2 |
| Yale | | 20 | 10 | 5 | 5 | 2 | 8 | 1 |
| Columbia | (See pages 373-377) | 23 | 9 | 5 | — | 3 | 4 | — |
| Chicago | | 30 | 11 | 5 | 2 | 2 | 6 | 1 |
| M. I. T. | | 48 | 21 | 23 | 20 | 8 | 10 | — |
| Rochester | | 25 | 10 | 6 | 4 | — | 2 | — |
| Stanford | | 31 | 14 | 4 | 11 | — | 5 | 2 |
| Texas | | 10 | 3 | — | 2 | 1 | 6 | — |
| Johns Hopkins | | 18 | 8 | 3 | 6 | 3 | 3 | 1 |
| Princeton | | 34 | 17 | 5 | 2 | 5 | 12 | — |
| Cornell | | 30 | 12 | 5 | 10 | — | 6 | 2 |
| Northwestern | | 10 | 7 | 4 | — | — | — | — |
| Duke | | 36 | 5 | 5 | — | — | 9 | 1 |
| Vanderbilt | | 31 | 14 | 4 | 3 | 9 | 10 | 2 |
| Washington U. (St. Louis) | | 18 | 5 | 7 | 3 | 3 | — | — |
| Oberlin | | 24 | 2 | 3 | — | — | 14 | — |
| California | | 17 | 11 | — | 3 | 2 | 1 | — |
| Carnegie Institute | | 36 | 15 | 16 | 10 | 3 | 1 | 2 |
| Dartmouth | | 12 | 8 | 2 | — | — | 4 | — |
| Pennsylvania | | 40 | 10 | 6 | 6 | 4 | 17 | 3 |
| Western Reserve | 11,468,225 | 24 | 10 | 8 | 2 | 5 | 3 | 2 |
| Minnesota | 10,681,421 | 12 | 3 | — | 2 | 1 | 1 | — |
| Brown | 10,630,797 | 49 | 16 | 10 | 5 | 3 | 15 | 2 |
| California Inst. of Tech. | 10,500,000 | 15 | 5 | 3 | 6 | 1 | 3 | — |
| Virginia | 10,311,996 | 10 | 5 | 2 | 1 | 2 | 1 | 1 |
| Tulane | 10,060,052 | 17 | 7 | 2 | 3 | 2 | 3 | — |
| Rice Inst. | 10,000,000 | 6 | 4 | 2 | 1 | — | — | — |
| | | 659 | 254 | 141 | 111 | 63 | 153 | 22 |

The aggregate endowment of these institutions is slightly more than $800,000,000, as compared with $1,150,000,000 approximate total endowment of all private colleges and universities; but a great deal of wealth is also held in the form of untaxed land, buildings, and equipment. The total value of endowment and other property of all the private colleges and universities is about $2,500,000,000.

The predominance of bankers and other money-motivated persons on the boards of trustees does not seem unusual to the average unsophisticated American, who is accustomed to the situation. But in no other civilized country is this barbarous phenomenon observable. In England, for example, the universities are autonomous, self-governing bodies.

J. McKeen Cattell, in his authoritative *University Control*, says:

The historic English universities, Oxford and Cambridge, have been primarily groups of independent colleges. The masters and fellows are the college; they own the buildings and endowment and divide the income among themselves. They elect their colleagues and successors and of course their head. The headship is an honorary and social position with but few executive powers or duties. Government is by town meeting and committee. There have been abuses of the monastic system, and perhaps even now too much time is spent on details of management. But high standards of scholarship and conduct have on the whole been maintained. From among the resident fellows and from the students great men have been forthcoming in every line of activity. Probably half the leaders of England in statesmanship, scholarship, science, poetry, have come from its two universities, having together no more students than one of our larger institutions; and England has produced more great men than any other nation.

The universities of Oxford and Cambridge, as distinguished from their colleges, have long had a few endowed professorships and have conducted libraries, but until recently they were essentially degree-conferring institutions. They are administered by councils elected by the resident teachers, but the ultimate control is vested, as is becoming, in the masters of art. The Church of England clergy have perhaps had more influence than is desirable, but their interference has in the main been confined to prescribing the conditions for the degree. In any case it is only a temporary phase, and a certain amount of conservatism is not so bad for a university. It would seem quite absurd to invest the ultimate control of Oxford and Cambridge in a self-perpetuating board, consisting of a score or larger crowd of business and professional men. The chancellorship is an honorary office, without executive power or influence. . . . The professors are usually nominated by boards of electors, consisting of men of distinction in the subject or in related subjects, partly from the university and partly from outside. I have never heard of the expulsion of a fellow or professor. That a professor's salary should depend on the favor of a president or that he should be dismissed without a hearing by a president with the consent of an absentee board of trustees is a state of affairs not conceivable. . . .

As control of the colleges and universities in America slipped from the hands of the clergy after the Civil War, the pecuniary element eased itself into dominance. The overwhelming presence of bankers as trustees and regents became only logical, however, once the inner pecuniary motivation of the American university was granted, because the endowments, in combination with the philanthropic foundations and church endowments (supervised by essentially the same persons), conferred upon the trustees a large amount of industrial control and voting power as well as strategic supervision over research and studies. The university endowments are really instruments of industrial as well as social control; and, like other endowments, are tax-exempt, making possible an ever-enlarging concentration of authority in the hands of the rich.

The philanthropic character of the privately endowed institutions is, however, doubtful. One can raise the issue in many ways, but at this juncture let it merely be noted that, according to Federal statistics for 1933-34, no less than 47.2 per cent of the income of private establishments came from student fees in contrast with 16.7 per cent of income from student fees in public universities and colleges. Endowment produced only 22.7 per cent of income for the private institutions. Gifts and grants brought in 11.2 per cent of income. In the case of the public institutions grants from state and municipal governments accounted for 56.8 per cent of income.

Among the overseers of Harvard University are Henry Sturgis Morgan, son of J. P. Morgan; George Whitney, Morgan partner; Charles Francis Adams, Boston banker, director of various properties and father-in-law of Henry Sturgis Morgan; Walter S. Gifford, president of the American Telephone and Telegraph Company (Morgan); Elihu Root, Jr. (Morgan); George R. Agassiz, copper magnate; Albert A. Sprague, head of Sprague, Warner and Company, wholesale grocers; Gaspar G. Bacon, son of a former Morgan partner; and Walter Lippmann, exponent in journalism of various approved Morgan themes.

Among the trustees of the Yale Corporation are S. H. Fisher,

director of the New York Trust Company (Morgan), various Rockefeller companies, and the Commonwealth Fund (Harkness); Howell Cheney, member of the silk family; Mortimer N. Buckner,
president of the New York Trust Company (Morgan); F. Trubee
Davison, son of a former Morgan partner and brother of a current
Morgan partner; and Edward L. Ryerson, Jr., of a Chicago steel
dynasty.

Among Columbia University trustees are Marcellus Hartley Dodge
(copper and munitions); Stephen Baker, chairman of the board of
the Bank of Manhattan; Joseph P. Grace, Grace Lines (shipping);
Clarence M. Woolley, chairman of the American Radiator and
Standard Sanitary Corporation; Thomas J. Watson, president of
International Business Machines Corporation; and Everett W. Gould.

Trustees of the University of Chicago include Edward L. Ryerson, Jr. (interlocking with his Yale trusteeship); James H. Douglas,
Jr., partner of Marshall Field in the investment banking house of
Field, Glore, Ward and Company; Albert L. Scott, trustee of Spellman College, Atlanta (Rockefeller) and the Riverside Church, N. Y.,
(Rockefeller); Harold H. Swift, meat packer; Eugene M. Stevens,
investment banker; Cyrus S. Eaton, steel magnate; John Stuart,
president of the Quaker Oats Company (also a trustee of Princeton
University); and Sewell L. Avery, director of the United States
Steel Corporation and managing head of Montgomery Ward and
Company and the United States Gypsum Company.

Among the Johns Hopkins University trustees are Walter S. Gifford; Daniel Willard, president of the Baltimore and Ohio Railroad;
Newton D. Baker, Van Sweringen attorney (Morgan) and former
Secretary of War. Among the Leland Stanford University trustees
are Harry Chandler, publisher of the Los Angeles *Times* and a
trustee of California Institute of Technology; Paul Shoup, vice
chairman of the Southern Pacific Railroad; and Herbert Hoover.

University of Pennsylvania trustees include E. T. Stotesbury, Morgan partner and Republican political-campaign fund collector; George
Wharton Pepper, Morgan political figure; Joseph E. Widener; Morris L. Clothier; John E. Zimmerman, president of the United Gas
Improvement Company (Morgan); Robert C. Hill, chairman of
the Consolidation Coal Company; Edward Hopkinson, Jr., Morgan

partner; A. Felix du Pont; and Eldridge R. Johnson, former owner of the Victor Talking Machine Company. The president of the University of Pennsylvania is Thomas S. Gates, former Morgan partner; the president of Rutgers College is a member of the Clothier family.

On the board of Cornell University sits Charles M. Schwab, creator of the Bethlehem Steel Corporation and personally involved during his lifetime in numerous unsavory episodes such as the selling of defective armor plate to the government, the drawing of extravagant bonuses from his stockholders, and profiteering on war contracts. With Chandler on the board of the California Institute of Technology are Louis D. Ricketts, mining engineer close to the Phelps Dodge interests and once under Federal indictment with Cleveland H. Dodge for attempted alienation of government land, and Henry M. Robinson, Los Angeles shipping magnate and banker. Among the trustees of the University of California are William H. Crocker, descendant of a member of the lawless Crocker-Huntington-Stanford railroad group; Mortimer Fleischacker, San Francisco banker and shipping magnate; John F. Neylan, attorney for the Hearst properties; and A. P. Giannini, leading California banker and largest stockholder of the National City Bank of New York.

On the one hundred per cent reactionary board of the Massachusetts Institute of Technology are Gerard Swope, president of the General Electric Company (Morgan); W. Cameron Forbes, Boston investment banker and director of the American Telephone and Telegraph Company; Edward S. Webster, of the banking-engineering combination of Stone and Webster; Pierre S. du Pont; Lammot du Pont; John E. Aldred, investment banker; Albert H. Wiggin, former chairman of the Chase National Bank; Alfred P. Sloan, Jr., president of General Motors Corporation and director of E. I. du Pont de Nemours and Company; Philip Stockton, Boston banker; and J. J. Pelley and Alfred E. Loomis, railroad presidents.

Similar personalities dominate virtually all the private university and college boards, and select the academic presidents who dragoon the faculties and give utterance as well to reactionary pronouncements under the ostensible sanction of science and learning, enlightenment and progress. Without readily perceptible exception, the university presidents are the drudges of the money lords that lurk behind the boards of trustees.

The American Telephone and Telegraph Company appears to hold more university trusteeships through its directors than any other big corporation; J. P. Morgan and Company appears to hold more than any other banking house; the Rockefeller philanthropic endowments control more than any other so-called philanthropic enterprises. The coalitions of wealth which exercise the greatest direct influence in American higher education are the Morgan, Rockefeller, Du Pont, and Mellon groups.

The University of Wisconsin, of all first-class institutions, alone has resisted, until recently, the domination of finance capital. It has been unique in its refusal of contributions from the Rockefeller foundations, on the ground that such contributions conferred influence over the recipient. It has more recently begun to accept Rockefeller money.

The university trustees of the United States have placed the endowments in the following composite portfolio, which represents seventy-four per cent of the combined investments of all American universities and colleges having more than $5,000,000 of assets (report compiled in 1932 by Wood, Struthers and Company):

| | | |
|---|---|---|
| Real estate | $146,931,510 | 27.4% |
| Public utilities | 125,646,750 | 23.4 |
| Railroads | 99,586,800 | 18.5 |
| Industrials | 87,779,010 | 16.4 |
| Miscellaneous | 30,907,910 | 5.8 |
| U. S. governments | 17,757,150 | 3.3 |
| Foreign bonds | 13,274,240 | 2.5 |
| Bank and insurance | 9,698,160 | 1.8 |
| U. S. municipals | 5,024,560 | 0.9 |
| | $536,606,090 | 100. |

The point of chief interest in this tabulation is that holdings of government securities comprised only 4.2 per cent of investments. This might seem strange were it not for the fact that (a) the universities do not need gilt-edged government bonds to escape taxes, since all their income is tax-exempt, and (b) one of the prime purposes of university endowments is to achieve a foothold in industry through

the massed voting power of stocks and bonds and through the interlocking of boards of university trustees and boards of corporation
directors.

As the bulk of their income from investments is derived from private
industrial and mercantile enterprises, there is strong economic motivation for the running fire of criticism the universities direct through
their presidents against the government on those rare occasions
when government moves to hamper bold exploitation of society by
the bank-controlled corporations. Their investment portfolios also
give the universities an economic motivation for keeping silent at all
times when one of the big corporations is exposed as an overtly antisocial force.

The rise of the universities as great financial institutions has closely
paralleled the appearance of income, estate, and gift-tax laws. From
1906 to 1928 the property assets of American universities and colleges,
including land, buildings, and endowment, rose from $554,000,000
to $2,400,000,000; in the same period endowments rose from $250,-
000,000 to about $1,150,000,000. Most of the increase came after the
war, and represented the plowing back of war profits into tax-
exempt areas; the process resembled the huge Rockefeller philanthropic activities of 1917, 1918, and 1919.

The wealthy, in making educational "gifts," have obtained triple
value for their money, for usually they have stipulated (the Rockefellers notably so) that the favored institutions raise double or treble
the amount of the "gift" before it has become effective. This stipulation has sent academic officials scurrying about to raise money among
thousands of less wealthy people in order that the universities might
obtain the big single gifts; and the consequence has been to bring
extra funds into the endowment from many sources to be represented,
of course, only by trustees designated by the biggest donor.

It may be pointed out here that wherever money coagulates in
society, and whatever its source, one finds members of the wealthiest
families stepping in to assume control by making some additional
contribution. This is true whether the purpose of the fund be ostensibly philanthropic, charitable, or artistic. The inner pecuniary motivation is discovered in the nature of the investment vehicle of each
particular fund or in the mode of its expenditure. Merely to be able

to designate depositary banks and investment vehicles is highly
profitable, even though the directors of a fund do not own it. To be
able to purchase materials from companies of one's own choice is also
profitable.

Control over the universities has been assured to the rich in many
ways, but one effective way has been to space the gifts. Few are the
wealthy men that have given to the universities single lump sums;
only those who have not sought to perpetuate a dynasty of wealth
through heirs—men like Stanford, Eastman, and one or two others—
have given very large sums at one stroke. University officials, in the
knowledge that more money may be forthcoming after one gift,
have been careful that the institutions under their direction should not
become involved in social or political controversies distasteful to the
donors. Few also have been the gifts the employment of which has
been left to the discretion of the educators. The funds given have
usually been earmarked for some pecuniary purpose dear only to the
donor and irrelevant to a sound educational program. Buildings have
often been presented for academically superfluous purposes, and even
their location on the campus has been designated by the donors. To
obtain certain vast sums the universities have had to create departments in subjects only vaguely related to higher education, but
closely related to commercial and industrial profit-seeking.

## II

What reason have the wealthy families for intruding as they do in
the sphere of higher education? What is their objective?

Since the founding of the colonies the educational system has been
a matter of prime importance to the wealthiest citizens of each community, but it was not until nearly fifty years after the War of Independence that free elementary schools for the public were even
dreamed of. The free schools came into being largely as the consequence of agitation by urban labor groups; free secondary schools
were later won from the dominant elite, and, still later, the free
university of the western states.

The rich, however, were always solicitous about educating the
young of their own class, and Harvard University, oldest of American institutions of higher learning, was from the first a rich man's

school. Yale and Princeton were similarly rich men's schools from their earliest days. But shortly after the Civil War the faculties of theology, central in the old American college, were gradually undermined by the new departments of physical science, which were invaluable in the spheres of mining and industrial technology. Then the college became the university. The first American university, incidentally, was Johns Hopkins, established in 1876 through the bequest of a Baltimore merchant.

The new industrialists, less fastidious than the predecessor land and mercantile capitalists about the class origins or religious beliefs of students, flung money into higher education and opened wide the gates to young men of ability. They established scholarships to support the discernibly brightest intellects of the poorer classes. Then, as now, the prime interest of the new rulers of America was only in technology, and this was evidenced by the opening of the School of Mines at Columbia College in 1864, and by the founding of the Massachusetts Institute of Technology in 1861, Worcester Polytechnic in 1865, Lehigh University in 1866, Stevens Institute in 1871, the Case School of Applied Science in 1880, Rose Polytechnic in 1883, and Brooklyn Polytechnic Institute in 1889. Soon there were added Armour Institute of Technology in Chicago (later absorbed by Northwestern University), Rensselaer Polytechnic Institute in Troy, and more recently the California Institute of Technology in Los Angeles. The drive for technology led to the creation of elaborate physical-science departments at Harvard under Charles W. Eliot and to the inauguration at Yale of the Sheffield Scientific Institute. Mechanical techniques which would serve the profit motive were in universal demand.

The contemporary university president has made shrewd use of the technological appeal in fund-raising campaigns directed toward men of wealth. Walter Dill Scott, president of Northwestern University, for example, while soliciting contributions in 1924, pointed out that Newton, Watt, Faraday, Maxwell, Huxley, Pasteur, and Lister were all university professors. He drew attention to the fact that Professor Armstrong of Columbia had originated the "feed-back" radio circuit; that Professors Winchell of the University of Michigan, and White of the University of Wisconsin, had evolved the theory of oil and gasoline deposits which made tremendous expansion of the petroleum industry possible; and that other professors as well had done work of immense profit to the ruling industrialists and financiers.

Dr. Scott could have gone a good deal further and said that all those features of contemporary life styled "progressive" originated in the brains of university professors, whose work has been seized upon by promoters and turned into profits. He could also have said that it had been the dream of many scientific men, especially of Professor James Watt, Scotch inventor of the modern condensing steam engine, that their discoveries would free the human race of hard labor but that, perverted by the promoters, the discoveries had instead intensified hard labor. The raising of these considerations, however, would not have brought in funds.

While the utmost intellectual freedom was given to faculty members preoccupied with the physical sciences and mechanical techniques, and with the law, business, and medical schools, the new industrialists were not long in becoming aware of the menace to themselves of the social sciences, and in moving to protect themselves. Glutted as they were by easily obtained wealth, the industrialists saw no need to criticize, to analyze, or to explore the society that had given them riches. With the problems of farmers, laborers, and middle classes they were not concerned. Their attitude was perfectly expressed by George F. Baker, Sr., during the Pujo inquiry when he said he thought society was pretty good as he found it. More recently the inner attitude of the industrialists and moneyed elite toward the social sciences themselves was expressed by Henry Ford, who from profound conviction said, "History is bunk."

It was in the 1890's that there began a quiet campaign of terror against those members of the university social-science departments whose speculations were considered too bold for the comfort of the profit-making coterie. Earlier, under the theological dispensation, the physical scientists had often been subjected to similar intimidation, but they were now freed, except in backwoods regions, by the new industrial dispensation.

The campaign of the industrialists and bankers against the social scientists—men preoccupied with economics, sociology, history, and political science—found Richard T. Ely, distinguished economist, placed under fire at the University of Wisconsin and at Johns Hopkins University. John R. Commons, outstanding historian of the American labor movement, was ousted from Syracuse University, which was financed by Standard Oil through John D. Archbold, who recognized the existence of no "labor movement." At Brown University E. B. Andrews was cashiered for espousing "free silver," but by avoiding immediate issues Lester F. Ward, dynamic sociologist, managed to retain his position at the same school although he was, perhaps, the most subversive of all the nineteenth-century American social scientists—subversive, that is, from the point of view of the wealthy beneficiaries of the chaotic *status quo.*

In 1906 the University of Chicago, academic subsidiary of the Standard Oil Company, ousted Thorstein Veblen, perhaps America's most original social thinker, on the pretext that he had been party to an unsolemnized love affair. Only two years earlier Veblen had published his suavely corrosive *Theory of Business Enterprise,* and it was obviously this work, and the antecedent *Theory of the Leisure Class,* that provoked his dismissal. Professor Edward W. Bemis, an economist, who had criticized methods of the railroads, also failed to be reappointed. J. Laurence Laughlin, head of the economics department, publicly professed to have found hidden virtues in John D. Rockefeller and in the established order. At Yale, William G. Sumner expounded *laissez-faire* economics and at Columbia John Bates Clark taught that the by-product of unfettered capitalism was a rough-hewn justice. Schools and departments were founded in many instances with an expressed ulterior purpose; a wealthy manufacturer, for example, in 1881 founded the Wharton School of Finance at the University of Pennsylvania simply to uphold the theory of the protective tariff.

To attempt an enumeration of the hundreds of professors and instructors ousted from the social-science departments of the American universities and colleges since the 1890's would require too extensive cataloguing. Practically every institution of higher learning, including the pseudo-liberal Harvard, has joined in the witch-hunt, ferreting out nearly every vital thinker in the social sciences. The liberalism of Harvard, it may be remarked, is purely historical and relative in character, an echo of the day when Eliot enthroned the physical sciences in defiance of Fundamentalist churchmen. In the contemporary social context the attitude of Harvard University cannot be called liberal unless the policies of J. P. Morgan and Company and the attitudes of Ogden L. Mills and Herbert Hoover are defined as liberal. Mills and Hoover really believe themselves to be liberals, although they fail to explain that they are liberals of the eighteenth-century Manchester school whose basic doctrine was *laissez faire*. This doctrine in the mouths of big capitalists has become merely a justification for Jack-the-Ripper tactics upon the body of society.

The universities proceed against the independent social thinkers on two broad theories. One is that professors should have no concern with questions of the day outside the campus, and the other, that the offending professors are social revolutionaries. It is highly doubtful if any of the ousted professors have ever been social revolutionaries, but it is clear that the issues of the day in which they have "meddled" concern taxation, labor policies, economic policies, public-utility rates, and the general rough conduct of the rich toward the rest of society. The professors, in short, have been reformists, and they have embarrassed special vested interests by pointing to the furtive hand in the public coffer.

However, the argument of the university trustees that the professors are wandering far afield in taking up problems that lie outside the campus is dishonest, for no objection is raised when professors of physical science address conventions of engineers or bankers about technological and industrial problems, or when professors of surgery leave the campus to perform some difficult operation. The universities object to off-campus professorial activity only when it is directed in some fashion against the *status quo* or the privileges of some vested interest.

The dictum that the academic mind should not concern itself in practical affairs is, furthermore, called into question by the behavior of the university presidents themselves, who never fail to throw all the prestige of their office and their assumed intellectual attainments both behind the *status quo* and behind the aims of certain selfish vested interests.

A typical example of a university president who is always making pronouncements on questions of the day, and who is always given flattering attention by the newspapers, is Nicholas Murray Butler of Columbia University. There is apparently nothing that Dr. Butler feels himself incompetent to discuss in public at a moment's notice. It is difficult, after surveying the long record, to believe that Dr. Butler functions so fortuitously at crucial moments without external prompting from nonacademic quarters.

Dr. Butler makes upward of fifty speeches every year, an enormous output for a septuagenarian. If it were not that his speeches, although cloaked in academic language, advance the theories of certain special interests, one might justly describe him as America's greatest busybody.

Like other university presidents Dr. Butler in his secular talks has wandered very far from the academic groves. In 1935 and 1936 he busied himself with issuing blasts against passage of the proposed child-labor amendment to the Constitution, defending the "right" of children to work. In September, 1936, he decried the "terror" in Seattle during a strike conducted by the American Newspaper Guild, although the competent local authorities denied the existence of any terror and no evidence has since been forthcoming to indicate that there was any. Both in his pro-child-labor and his anti-Newspaper Guild crusade, Dr. Butler appears to have been speaking for the vested estate of newspaper publishers, but as usual he professed to speak on behalf of immutable and universal principles. Of fewer than one million minors employed outside of agriculture, approximately five hundred thousand are employed in the delivery of newspapers.

During the depression of 1929–34 Dr. Butler, now only too obviously a propagandist of social obscurantism, addressed himself to the task of proving that the economic crisis was greatly exaggerated —an imaginative product of the mind; and that reports of the unemployment total by agencies like the Federal government and the American Federation of Labor were several times too great. Scientific findings relative to the maldistribution of wealth he termed radical talk and sheer invention.

Since the advent of an antibanking Administration in Washington, Dr. Butler has consistently decried government "spending," obviously with unemployment-relief expenditures in mind; he has gone so far as to charge that New York City retains on its pay roll twenty per cent too many workers, but he has not suggested what should be done with this surplus if it were lopped off. His calls for reductions in governmental expenditures have been reflexes to the demand of the rich for lower taxes. At all times he has given voice to opinions on public affairs differing in no wise from those of an editorial hack or a class-conscious, intelligent Wall Street broker.

In all of Dr. Butler's public speeches, it is noticeable, he has invariably defended property rights. If he has ever defended purely human rights the fact is not disclosed by an examination of *The New York Times* files, 1913-37. But in conducting himself in this fashion, rarely if ever adverting to purely intellectual questions, Dr. Butler has behaved as have all university presidents. If any president of an American college in the past three decades has ever spoken out in denunciation of human exploitation, or in defense of judicially persecuted social dissidents, it does not appear on the record. Most have spoken frequently, however, in defense of vested property rights.

Karl T. Compton, distinguished physicist who is president of the Massachusetts Institute of Technology, while not so prolific a speech-maker as Dr. Butler, in his few appearances has not scrupled to perform similarly under the cloak of disinterested science. In October, 1936, for example, when President Roosevelt suggested that engineers and scientists co-operate in the work of social reconstruction Dr. Compton seized this occasion to launch a partisan and oblique assault upon unemployment-relief expenditures, which were a matter of sore concern to the prosperous M.I.T. trustees. Dr. Compton voiced the convenient fear that "the attention and money devoted to relief and regulation should interfere with simultaneous adequate attention and support to the basic contribution which our sciences can certainly make if given a chance." The newspapers gave these opinions of a ranking scientist prominent display. Speaking before the American Bankers Association in December, 1936, this eminent physicist felt himself qualified to declaim against government ownership of public utilities, a question one might suppose to be outside his scientific province; but twenty out of forty-eight M.I.T. trustees are public-utility operators.

Another reactionary among American university presidents has been James Rowland Angell of Yale, who since his retirement in 1937 has chosen to inflict the doctrines of his preceptors upon the public through the medium of his new position as educational director of the National Broadcasting Company. His daughter is married to one of the Rockefeller-McAlpins, and he was formerly on the faculty of the University of Chicago.

Dr. Angell was another of the university presidents who professed to see the long-dead American democracy endangered by Franklin D. Roosevelt, although he saw no menace, any more than did his colleagues, in Warren G. Harding, Calvin Coolidge, or Herbert Hoover. Angell, anesthetic to the manipulation of the Treasury by Mellon and the wartime conspiracies of the Wilson regime, after the re-election of Franklin D. Roosevelt discovered a menacing shadow in a government supported by a mere numerical majority.

Democracy was jeopardized, Dr. Angell pontificated, by pressure groups, of which the veterans' bonus bloc was the example he cited; by the sit-down strike; and by unwillingness to submit to rule by the judiciary. "Real and lasting progress can come only by slow and thoughtfully considered measures," said Dr. Angell, "which, resting on those elements in the existing order that are sound, seek one by one to eliminate those which are evil and replace them with such as are wholesome and just." He stood, in short, against any change.

The university president in America, it should be clear, is a brigadier general of reaction, as President A. Laurence Lowell demonstrated by his behavior in the Sacco-Vanzetti case.

And while the university presidents may meddle in public affairs to their trustees' content, and while the professors may also do likewise provided only that they support the *status quo*, especially in its more evil phases, it goes hard, as we have remarked, with any faculty member who espouses an unorthodox point of view. The American Civil Liberties Union has in its files hundreds of reports on cases wherein the holders of unorthodox views have been discharged. The number of dismissals does not mean, unfortunately, that there is consistent rebellion against the trustees, for there is not. The instructors in the social sciences are taught circumspection by the mishaps of outspoken colleagues. Those who remain often become, to all intents and purposes, social as well as academic eunuchs.

The two most prominent recent instances of punitive measures taken against independent faculty members have occurred at Harvard and at Yale. At the former two economics instructors, popular with the students and unquestionably in full grasp of their subject, failed of reappointment because they had concerned themselves sympathetically with labor problems off the campus. Their cases are still pending at this writing.

At Yale, Professor Jerome Davis failed of reappointment, on the spurious ground of incompetence discovered only after he had published the highly critical *Capitalism and Its Culture*. Many independent organizations of professors, teachers, and liberals investigated the case, and uniformly found that Davis had been fired in flagrant disregard of Yale's pretensions to academic freedom. It was brought out that, owing to his outspoken utterances, he had been in almost constant conflict with the university administration. In 1931, for example, he denounced the Insulls as "higher racketeers," and was reprimanded after Samuel Insull, Jr. (Yale, '21) protested. He was also reprimanded for inviting Senator Gerald P. Nye, munitions-industry investigator, to speak on the campus.

Yet a character witness at the trial of young Insull after the crash of the Insull properties was President Robert M. Hutchins of the University of Chicago. Early in 1937 Hutchins was fervidly denounced by John Dewey, dean of American philosophers, for attempting to revive the principle of blind authority in teaching—an attempt in which Dewey discerned fascist tendencies. There is, in brief, class logic behind the superficially aimless actions of the university presidents.

The locus of authority at Harvard was eloquently illustrated in July, 1936, when an alumni committee brought in a report "exonerating" the department of economics of the charge of spreading radical propaganda. The significance in this committee is to be found in the identity of its members, who were Walter Lippmann; Walter S. Gifford, president of the American Telephone and Telegraph Company; Winthrop W. Aldrich, chairman of the Chase National Bank;

George F. Baker, Jr., president of the First National Bank; Barklie McK. Henry, New York investment banker; Richard Whitney, brother of a Morgan partner, himself a Morgan broker, and former president of the New York Stock Exchange; Orrin G. Wood, Boston financier; Charles M. Storey, Boston attorney; and Representative Christian A. Herter.

Among a few of the distinguished social investigators discharged or induced to leave under pressure by universities since the World War have been Professor Harold J. Laski (Harvard), Professors J. McKeen Cattell, James Harvey Robinson, and Henry Mussey (Columbia), Dr. Alexander Meiklejohn (Amherst), Professor Scott Nearing (Pennsylvania), Professor John E. Kirkpatrick (Olivet College), Professor Ralph E. Turner (Pittsburgh), Granville Hicks (Rensselaer Polytechnic), Professor Wesley Maurer (Ohio State), Professor James N. Yard (Northwestern), Professor M. F. Meyers, and H. O. De Graff (Missouri).

During the war, because he espoused free speech even though he supported the war aims of the Allies, Dr. Charles A. Beard found life made so uncomfortable for him at Columbia, where he was head of the department of American politics, that he soon resigned with the declaration that "the status of a professor in Columbia is lower than that of a manual laborer." He decried the "few obscure and willful trustees who now dominate the university and terrorize young instructors."

## III

The clans of wealth gain many things from the universities in addition to endorsements by the university presidents of reactionary policies, the discoveries in the physical sciences, and the proliferation of a huge backlog, or labor reserve, of skilled technicians. Although the newspapers did a good deal of jesting about a "Brains Trust" when the national administration of the second Roosevelt sought advice from professors in the social sciences, they have not called attention to the extent to which the big corporations and banks utilize the services of former university faculty members.

Owen D. Young, chairman of the General Electric Company, was once a professor of law at Boston University. Jackson E. Reynolds, chairman of the First National Bank of New York, was associate professor of law at Columbia University until 1917. His successor as president of the bank was Leon Fraser, one-time instructor in history at Columbia who later became president of the Bank for International Settlements. Thomas I. Parkinson, president of the Equitable Life Assurance Society, is the former dean of the Columbia University Law School. The list could be extended indefinitely.

The newspapers present professors as crackpots only when the owners of the newspapers, who are also the controllers of the political parties and the trustees of the universities, are opposed to the specific objectives of the professors. Until the Roosevelt Administration took office professors had been regular government advisers to successive national administrations and legislative committees. William Z. Ripley of Harvard had frequently testified and given advice on railroads. Professor Irving Fisher of Yale was a "brain truster" of the Coolidge-Hoover era. Professor O. M. W. Sprague of Harvard was a monetary adviser and was "lent" to the Bank of England, where he functioned as a liaison officer between the British central bank and the Federal Reserve Bank.

But at Yale, under the "New Deal," President Angell suddenly discovered a grave intellectual menace in having professors engage in government work, although while Professor Fisher was commuting between Washington and New Haven and was active in the Prohibition struggle Angell had nothing to say.

The powerful coalitions of wealth are also amply rewarded by the endowed technical schools in the graduates these schools turn out. Massachusetts Institute of Technology, for example, has graduated the following: Willis R. Whitney, vice-president in charge of research of the General Electric Company; William D. Coolidge, chief of the General Electric research laboratories; Edwin S. Webster and Charles A. Stone, of Stone and Webster; Gerard Swope, president of the General Electric Company; Paul W. Litchfield, president of the Goodyear Tire and Rubber Company; Arthur C. Dorrance of the Campbell Soup fortune; J. Howard Pew, president of the Sun Oil Company; Francis R. Hart, president of the United Fruit Company; Philip R. Stockton, president of the First National-Old Colony Bank of Boston and director of A. T. & T.; the late Charles Hayden, of

Hayden, Stone and Company; Alfred P. Sloan, Jr., president of General Motors Corporation; William C. Potter, chairman of the Guaranty Trust Company; Elisha Walker, partner of Kuhn, Loeb and Company; and six Du Ponts: the late T. Coleman, Alfred I., Pierre, Henry Belin, Irénée, and Lammot.

M.I.T. is to the field of technology what the law schools of Harvard, Columbia, and the University of Chicago are to politics. The latter supply figures like Charles Evans Hughes, Joseph H. Choate, and William Howard Taft, who are never at a loss for legal justification of the most antisocial acts and policies of the wealthy families.

With golden returns such as these coming from the class-centered schools, it is no wonder that the trustees and administrators of the private institutions look with deep hostility upon the growth of free colleges and universities supported by taxation. Before his retirement as president of Cornell University, Dr. Livingston Farrand warned the Association of Colleges and Universities of the State of New York against the competitive growth of publicly supported colleges. The development of these latter, to be sure, might in time make it impossible for the purely upper-class schools to continue functioning on the old highly profitable basis. If the United States ever sees Fascism it will surely see the end of the free public college and university.

## IV

Most graduates of American universities fall into two broad classifications. One is the specialist, an expert in a certain field—law, physics, chemistry, engineering—but with little intellectual curiosity outside that field; the other is the typical anti-intellectual college product whose mental horizon appears to be limited to sports events, bridge games, *The Saturday Evening Post,* stock market quotations, and formulae for cocktails.

This latter type is by all odds the more numerous, and for a livelihood generally turns to stock brokerage; the selling of real estate, bonds, insurance, or automobiles; or the management of bank and corporation departments where a not too bright intelligence is requisite. The former type emerges as a thoroughly trained technical research man, a hired inventor, an engineer, or a lawyer. There are now so many of these in relation to available jobs, however, that they are relatively as numerous as typists or stenographers.

It was quite by political design, incidentally, that the present glut of technical workers was brought about. Business and manufacturing interests appealed to Congress in 1917, for example, to introduce vocational courses in high schools. The United States Chamber of Commerce joined in getting a bill passed that provided that the Federal government would give an amount equal to amounts appropriated by the states for this purpose. Secondary schools today are often little more than training grounds for prospective book-keepers, clerks, stenographers, bank tellers, and similar low-paid, intellectually undeveloped robots.

Although the specialists graduated by the universities may be magnificently trained, they are seldom intellectually equipped to understand human affairs in a broadly sympathetic fashion. They are also unable to comprehend their own role in society, and often privately confess to feeling "lost" and impressed by the "futility" of their work.

The explanation for this state of affairs is found in the emphases demanded in higher education by the donors of funds, who always give for specific purposes and rarely with a view to developing integrated intellects ready to play a creative role in society. In the order of their greatest emphasis allocations to universities by the rich appear to be made for (a) the physical sciences and techniques, (b) the development of schools of business and commercial administration and related departments of modern foreign languages and literature, and (c) sports stadia, dormitories, clubhouses, and other adjuncts of campus sociability.

Very few donors have made provision for the creation of a complete institution, and among the few have been Johns Hopkins, Leland Stanford, John D. Rockefeller (Chicago), and George Eastman (Rochester). Other donors have preferred to make gifts with personal or class interests less covertly attached to them.

What would have been the nature of the educational allocations if they had been designed to serve the general public interest? Had the university donors been devoted to the public interest they would surely have done more to encourage the development of the social sciences along the traditional avenues of free thought and would have given social-science scholarships equivalent in value and number to the physical-science scholarships. They would, if serving the public interest rather than their own narrow designs, have encouraged the interrelation of all the university departments through a progressive, experimental social philosophy as outlined by John Dewey instead of insistently segregating the various departments. To escape indictment as servitors of their own interests in their educational "philanthropies" wealthy donors would, moreover, have had to contribute to the scientific study of agriculture, of labor problems (not problems in labor relations), and of the inherent deceits of the public market.

Instead of sending forth scientists and engineers imbued with the idea that they are creatively participating in a developmental process, the universities have sent them forth with the idea that they are to work in a fixed, static, supremely well-balanced society that merely requires a few additional embellishments in the way of new inventions, discoveries, and products like cellophane, celanese, and radios that can readily be marketed. While developing specific branches of science to the utmost, the universities have prostituted the ultimate aims of science which, in the best thought of the greatest scientists, should serve the whole of mankind rather than a few stock promoters of companies like General Electric, General Motors, American Telephone and Telegraph, and United States Steel Corporation.

Let us, however, examine a few of the "philanthropic" contributions to the institutions of higher learning with a view to disclosing their purely class and personal character. George Eastman, childless kodak-maker who committed suicide in 1932, during his lifetime allocated some $75,000,000 to educational and technical purposes. As he had no family he, like Carnegie, who had no son, felt no need to hold on to the money. Some Eastman money went into the erection of free dental clinics here and abroad, for Eastman was beginning to realize that it was not so much a case of making new discoveries as of putting old discoveries into circulation. When he died his will disposed of an additional $20,000,000, most of which went to technical education.

Eastman, like many other wealthy men, was hypnotized by the

profit-producing power of science. For many years the Eastman Kodak Company had been hiring chemists and physicists who made many notable—and profitable—discoveries. Eastman, upon investigation, learned that a large number of his men came from the Massachusetts Institute of Technology. In 1912, under the pseudonym of M. Smith, he started giving money to this school—one of the few cases in which an alias was used in the giving of money, although the newspapers are prone to say, without producing any evidence, that much money is given away anonymously by the rich.

In 1920 Eastman revealed himself as the donor of the mysterious large sums to M.I.T. Up to 1932 he had given this institution a little more than $20,000,000 to which there were no strings attached, although the nature of the school assured that the money would all be used in developing technicians who might be of service to the Eastman Kodak Company. During his lifetime Eastman gave approximately $35,000,000 to the University of Rochester, and additional posthumous bequests guaranteed for Rochester the fifth largest endowment in the country. And in addition to dental clinics Eastman encouraged the creation of a great music school at Rochester, and financed from scratch a symphony orchestra and a local opera and dramatic company.

In Eastman's case these bequests were obviously not part of a tax-reduction or self-advertising scheme, for he gave everything away. Very probably there was no conscious pecuniary motive behind his gifts, either, but it is interesting to observe that he could not completely transcend the limitations of the technical field in which he had worked all his life.

For purposes far less disinterested than Eastman's the numerous Du Pont clan, most of whose prominent members are M.I.T. graduates, have lavished large sums on the school. T. Coleman du Pont as early as 1910 gave the institution $500,000, and at frequent intervals since then Pierre, Irénée, and Lammot du Pont have given money. In all probability, the Du Ponts have put up as much as Eastman did. There is, however, a close relationship between M.I.T. and the chemical and automotive enterprises of E. I. du Pont de Nemours and Company, many of whose products have been developed by M.I.T. technicians and most of whose technicians are M.I.T.

men; the Du Pont-Fisher-Morgan General Motors Corporation is
also filled with M.I.T. men. From one tenable point of view, M.I.T.
can be regarded as a department of General Motors and E. I. du Pont
de Nemours and Company.

Outside of M.I.T. the Du Ponts have done little in education other
than to construct Delaware elementary and secondary schools for
which they, as virtually the only large taxpayers, would in any case
have been taxed. Some Du Pont money has gone to the University
of Pennsylvania and about $2,000,000 has gone to the University of
Delaware. Pierre du Pont is said to have put $5,000,000 into educa-
tional enterprises, and he may well have done so in his hysterical
attempts to reduce his postwar tax bills. But for every dollar the
Du Ponts have put into schools they have obtained, in addition to
lowered taxes, a hundredfold personal pecuniary return.

The elder George F. Baker chose to regard himself as a supporter
of education, and there are those who therefore consider him a great
human benefactor. He gave $6,000,000 with which the Harvard
Graduate School of Business Administration constructed elaborate
buildings along the Charles River; but what advance in knowledge
or human betterment was represented by this contribution to the
production of more efficient business executives and more scientific
ways of marketing and, in general, of extracting greater profits from
a bedeviled public is not clear. Baker also gave $2,000,000 to Cornell,
and $1,000,000 to Dartmouth for a library. He bestowed $700,000 on
Columbia University for a football stadium. As the Baker gifts were
made in the postwar boom era their donor probably saved more in
taxes by "giving" than if he had not "given."

In addition to making educational contributions to certain profit-
producing fields, the rich in general reserve their heaviest contributions for a small group of institutions in the East, to whose general
regional problem of dominating the farmers of the West and South
and the workers of the industrial areas these institutions zealously
address themselves. The preparatory schools that feed these favored
colleges and universities are themselves located in and around New
England. They, too, are the recipients of huge sums, although their
benefactors are not otherwise visibly interested in the broad field
of secondary education.

When it becomes more generally understood that the educational
apparatus of the rich functions as a regional as well as a class instrument of domination, other sections of the country will be less inclined
to accord to the rich fatuous admiration for so philanthropically holding them in subjection. Class lines in the United States, it may be remarked, are to some extent obscured by regional particularism, so
that where an individual does not perceive himself as exploited by
another class he often sees himself exploited by another region. It is
all too obvious in studying school gifts and endowments that the rich
have largely passed over the people of the South, the Southwest, and
the Northwest, who must, after profits have been siphoned away by
absentee owners, struggle along with whatever educational facilities
they can afford. Indeed, about seventy-five per cent of educational
"gifts" go to the East.

The reciprocal functioning of the endowed Eastern universities
and colleges in the forwarding of class and regional aims was perhaps
never better illustrated than during the general fight of predatory
wealth and its press against the proposed mild reform of the Supreme
Court. According to *The New York Times* (April 15, 1937), the
presidents of Massachusetts Institute of Technology, Dartmouth,
Brown, Wellesley, Bowdoin, Wesleyan, Williams, Tufts, Boston
University, Yale, and Harvard joined in decrying any "tampering"
with the sacred court. It should, of course, be obvious by now that
the private universities and colleges are hotbeds of political intrigue.
Sometimes their presidents aspire to or attain high political office, as
Wilson attained the presidency, and as Butler dreamed of attaining
the same eminence.

For illustrations of the class and regional character of educational
contributions by the rich we will concentrate, as the donors have done,
on Harvard, Yale, Phillips-Andover and Phillips-Exeter Academy.

No less than $60,000,000 has been poured in recent years into new
buildings at Yale University. The contributors included Edward S.
Harkness, the heirs of the late Payne Whitney, and John W. Sterling,
corporation lawyer who served as the confidential adviser of Jay
Gould, James Stillman, and William Rockefeller, and who was the
brains behind the Amalgamated Copper swindle. The Yale building
group comprises seven great quadrangles amid eight colleges, each

college containing within itself a separate kitchen, dining room, squash courts, library, and a master's house, and each catering to 150-200 boys from the three upper-school classes. Here, in the words of *Fortune* (March, 1934), they live "together in elaborate ease as though such things as classes never were."

Seven colleges are Gothic in style; the eighth is Georgian. The plan is carried out, too, in additional buildings that include the Sterling Memorial Library, the Payne Whitney Museum, the Sterling Graduate School, and the Sterling Law School. The layout is styled the "Oxford plan," as though it were the intention to bring the English university system to America. Unfortunately, there is more to the English university than physical appurtenances; underlying it is the democracy of the intellect from which the progeny of oil barons automatically exclude themselves by devoting their major energies to preserving their inheritances.

The essentially undemocratic character of the Yale colleges is most prominently indicated, perhaps, by the interiors whose elegance may well inculcate in the undergraduate, if he has not previously been so conditioned at home, a lasting taste for luxurious surroundings. This taste can be satisfied only by means of pecuniary pursuits after leaving college.

The new Payne Whitney Gymnasium at Yale contains a huge exhibition swimming pool, to which a number of practice pools may be joined; a basketball amphitheater convertible into exhibition tennis courts; two additional basketball courts; wrestling, fencing, boxing, and gymnastic rooms; two golf galleries, two polo cages, a rifle range, a solarium; an outdoor running track on the roof; three rowing tanks; eight hand-ball courts, and twenty-eight squash courts. Yale also has facilities for outdoor sports, including nine football fields in addition to the Yale Bowl, soccer, lacrosse, and polo fields, forty-four tennis courts, an eighteen-hole golf course, and three boathouses, as well as the Armory Riding Hall and the Coxe Memorial Field Gymnasium.

All other equipment is similarly elaborate in this Hollywood of higher education.

Harkness contributed about $13,000,000 to the Yale building program. Sterling, who died in 1918, left $20,000,000 to the university, but before Yale could get around to utilizing the fund it had multiplied in the stock market. Though Yale has expended $41,000,000 of the bequest to date, there is still much of it left, and this remainder is constantly increasing in value.

Harkness equaled his Yale contribution with a gift to Harvard on the stipulation that the house plan be adopted. Harvard had at first balked, but reconsidered after Harkness turned to Yale; today Harvard has the same elaborate pseudo-English college system. Phillips-Exeter Academy received $7,000,000 from Harkness for a similar house plan.

Praise has been showered on Harkness for giving vast sums to the wealthiest and most exclusive class schools in the country, but in view of the crucial need for educational facilities in other parts of the country his gifts look more and more like a scheme for transferring money from one class pocket to another. The press is responsible for the general—and erroneous—conception of Harkness as a benefactor of education in general.

It is true that Harvard and Yale, as well as other upper-class institutions, offer free tuition, some cash scholarships, and nominal paid employment to the highest-ranking graduates of accredited secondary schools without regard for the social class origins of these students. One can, it is true, meet a coal miner's or a farmer's son at Harvard, although it is a rare experience. The task of Yale and Harvard, however, is to mold these bright youngsters into unconscious servitors of the ruling class—as lawyers, as corporation scientists, as civil servants, as brokers, bankers, and clergymen—and the enforced "democratic" mingling effected by the new house plans assures this result more positively now than ever, for in the past many students were made to feel like pariahs by their exclusion from the quasi-aristocratic clubs.

The Harkness, Whitney, and Sterling money represents only a small portion of the vast sum that has been given to Yale, Harvard, and Princeton by many wealthy individuals. Harvard's total endowment represents ten per cent of the endowment of more than seven hundred private universities and colleges. The combined endowment of Harvard, Yale, Columbia, and Chicago represents about thirty-three per cent of the endowment of all private universities and colleges. None of these institutions concerns itself in the normal university program with the problems of any class except the wealthy; none has made any substantial contribution toward the solution of the social and economic problems facing farmers, industrial and white-collar workers, the foreign born, or Negroes.

The heavily endowed colleges and universities have very evidently left a wide section of the populace out of consideration in their prescribed courses of study. At Yale, Harvard, Columbia and the University of Chicago one can, however, study stock-market trends, advertising layouts, the mail-order business, office management, etc. In view of the linkage of the physical science departments with the big corporations, and the schools of journalism and of business with general capitalistic enterprise, and in view of the exclusion from these universities and colleges of branches of study concerned with the problems of the lower income groups (except as those problems become problems of the ruling families as well), one can say that they are upper-class schools in all their phases.

At both Yale and Harvard the social science departments are so weak as to draw comment from savants at universities like Columbia, Chicago, Johns Hopkins, and Wisconsin, which are somewhat more cosmopolitan in character.*

Phillips-Exeter has received large sums in addition to the $7,000,-000 Harkness gave for its house plan, which prepares students for easy living at Yale and Harvard. William Boyce Thompson presented it with $1,000,000 for a gymnasium. Thomas W. Lamont and the late Thomas Cochran of J. P. Morgan and Company both gave it large sums and helped it and Phillips-Andover to raise funds among other wealthy men. But contributions to Exeter and Andover, like those to Harvard and Yale, can hardly be classified as contributions to the intellectual advance of mankind, even though some product of one of these schools may some time take the bit in his teeth, confound the trustees, and turn out to be a Copernicus, a Darwin, a Marx, or a Veblen.

Both Phillips-Exeter and Phillips-Andover have separate endowments of $6,000,000 each, greater than those of institutions like the

* See "Harvard Starves the Social Sciences," by Robert Keen Lamb (*The Nation,* May 15, 1937).

University of Alabama, Beloit College, the University of Buffalo, Carleton College, Colby College, Colorado College, Cornell College (Ia.), Creighton University, Denison University, University of Denver, Depauw University, University of Idaho, Kenyon College, Knox College, Ohio Wesleyan, Wabash College, Wittenberg College, or the College of Wooster.

In short, while money is lavished on a few Eastern preparatory schools, higher education in the West and the South is being starved. The private preparatory schools, moreover, have a class function only; they do not fill a genuine need, for the public high-school system is extensive.

Andover and Exeter are only two of the Eastern preparatory schools patronized by the rich families. Groton has an endowment of $1,500,000; Lawrenceville, $500,000; St. Mark's, $600,000; Taft, $500,000; and St. Paul's, $3,059,018. Andrew W. Mellon gave Choate School a library and the Archbold family gave an infirmary; Clarence Dillon, banker, gave Groton an auditorium, William A. Gardner gave a $500,000 chapel, while various large gifts were also made by the late Payne Whitney; Edward S. Harkness contributed to the Hill School endowment of $2,340,187, as did the late T. Coleman du Pont; Charles G. Dawes, Lammot du Pont, and Mortimer B. Fuller (International Salt) made big gifts to Lawrenceville; Paul Block gave a chapel to Hotchkiss School, whose endowment is $400,000. Middlesex School was founded by W. Cameron Forbes, Henry Lee Higginson, Francis Lowell, and Dean Briggs of Harvard, all of whom gave it money and buildings. The Armour family and August Belmont contributed to St. Mark's. James Simpson of Marshall Field and Company and H. E. Manville contributed to St. Paul's. Benefactors of the Taft School have been Mrs. William Rockefeller, who gave Rockefeller Field, Edward S. Harkness, who gave $500,000, and Harry P. Bingham, who gave Bingham Auditorium.

This is only part of the story, for there are also the Eastern girls' "finishing schools." These expensive and strictly upper-class institutions, where the tuition fee ranges from $1,000 to $3,000 a year, include Foxcroft, Brearley, Miss Chapin's, Spence School, Rosemary Hall, Ethel Walker's, Farmington, Westover, Miss Hall's, and Dobbs School. The education of women, whose occupations hold forth little promise of great monetary profit such as derives from the work of chemists, engineers, lawyers, and market manipulators, has aroused among rich families somewhat less enthusiasm than has the education of men. The big Eastern universities have excluded women, and the Eastern women's colleges have been far less successful in wheedling funds out of their wealthy connections than have the big profit-producing men's colleges. Vassar College, for example, has an endowment of less than $10,000,000. Smith College and Bryn Mawr have endowments of only slightly more than $6,000,000. Wellesley College has less than $9,000,000 of endowment. The greatest progress in the education of women has been made by the co-educational Western universities supported by public taxes, although Oberlin College first instituted co-educational training.

Most of the wealthy families have, nevertheless, made some contribution to the Eastern schools for women, and the campuses of the women's colleges, like those of the universities, are strewn with towers, lecture halls, libraries, dormitories and gymnasia that bear such intellectually significant names as Rockefeller, Harkness, Havemeyer, Drexel, Carnegie, Stillman, Whitney, *et al.*

These examples, and many others that for lack of space are not cited, provide the data for the statement that the rich in making their contributions to education are merely serving their class and individual interests. Strictly viewed, the private schools are oases of aristocracy amid an embattled democracy, which President Angell of Yale has eloquently termed an incipient "bastard democracy."

# XI

# Danse Macabre: Extravagance Amid Poverty

## I

"At a dinner eaten on horseback," says the historian Beard of the Gilded Age of the 1890's, "the favorite steed was fed flowers and champagne; to a small black and tan dog wearing a diamond collar worth $15,000 a lavish banquet was tendered; at one function, the cigarettes were wrapped in hundred-dollar bills; at another, fine black pearls were given to the diners in their oysters; at a third, an elaborate feast was served to boon companions in a mine from which came the fortune of the host. Then weary of such limited diversions, the plutocracy contrived more freakish occasions—with monkeys seated between the guests, human goldfish swimming about in pools, or chorus girls hopping out of pies.

In lavish expenditures as well as in exotic performance, pleasures were hungrily sought by the fretful rich delivered from the bondage of labor and responsibility. Diamonds were set in teeth; a private carriage and personal valet were provided for a pet monkey; dogs were tied with ribbons to the back seats of Victorias and driven out in the park for airings; a necklace costing $600,000 was purchased for a daughter of Croesus; $65,000 was spent for a dressing table, $75,000 for a pair of opera glasses. An entire theatrical company was taken from New York to Chicago to entertain the friends of a magnate and a complete orchestra engaged to serenade a new-born child. In a burst of sentimental benevolence a family of destitute Negroes in the South was suddenly dowered with riches, garbed in luxury, and placed in a gorgeous house."—*The Rise of American Civilization*

The plutocracy of the Mauve Decade was ascetic by comparison with the plutocracy of the present Black Decade. Point by point the most fantastic of the earlier extravagances, entailing the carefully studied waste of wealth produced by the people, are being duplicated or exceeded by the infinitely more monstrous extravagances of today.

408

But in the 1890's the wholesale dissipation of wealth took place in mansions of the newly rich strung along Fifth Avenue, in plain view of journalists from the Populistic and semiradical press, or in relatively free and open Newport. Today the plutocracy is more cloistered in country estates and luxurious hostelries, and the newspapers, all owned or controlled by the millionaires, are no longer interested in holding the private life of the rich up to public scrutiny. First-class reporters are seldom sent to Newport any more; only society editors and sports writers go there.

Where once one had merely to refer to Pulitzer's *World* to learn what the latest expensive inanity of the leisured class might be, today one has to search publications that circulate in a much more restricted area: *House and Garden, Town and Country, House Beautiful, Spur, Vogue, Vanity Fair* (recently merged with *Vogue*), *Harper's Bazaar, The New Yorker, Fortune, The Connoisseur, American Kennel Gazette, Arts and Decoration, Horse and Horseman, Yachting, Motor Boat,* etc. Sources of contemporary material are also to be found in the sycophantic "society" pages of the metropolitan newspapers, which more or less unconsciously from time to time make significant sociological revelations about the misuse and abuse of wealth. Many of the readers of these publications are, of course, merely vicarious participants in wasteful spending.

Judged by the way they squander money on vapid personal amusement and bizarre decoration, the rich are a psychopathic class, waltzing obliviously toward a hidden precipice and, apparently, dragging the nation along. Whom the gods would destroy they seemingly first make rich. Yet the personal expenditures, great though they seem to the ordinary onlooker with the needs of society in mind, are small in relation to the unprecedentedly vast incomes that accrue to the families of the plutocracy. Less than twenty-five per cent of the income of multimillionaires, according to Robert R. Doane, is expended in personal channels; for try as a multimillionaire family may, it cannot spend its swollen income. To make appreciable inroads upon it there would have to be wholesale giving, and this is not *de rigueur*, as we have seen in the survey of the philanthropic field.

Before examining systematically the personal extravagances of the rich, an impressionistic survey will, perhaps, gradually prepare readers' minds for more colossal examples of wilful waste and egocentric indulgence, and will at the same time show the purple 1890's to have been but the overture to what is now taking place. It would be well, however, if the reader reminded himself from time to time that the money represented by these personal outlays is social credit which might better be utilized in agricultural reconstruction and in the building of needed clinics, hospitals, schools, colleges, low-cost residential housing, laboratories, workers' clubs, parks, playgrounds, etc. It is, in short, money that might better be taken over by the government through taxation, with a view to relieving upward of two million Southern sharecroppers, ten million industrial unemployed, and five million submarginal farmers from chronic destitution.

To depict the extravagances of the rich families in their proper perspective let us briefly turn back to 1929—the last highly prosperous year of record in the United States. In fateful 1929 no more than 513 Americans had a total income of $1,212,099,000, while the gross price (not profit) received by more than two million farmers for all wheat and cotton produced in 1930 was only $1,191,000,000. The 513 plutocrats could, with their 1929 income, have purchased these two basic crops, and have had enough remaining to cover the expenses of living on an extravagant scale. In 1929 no more than 14,816 Americans had taxable incomes of $100,000 upward, aggregating $4,368,-152,000—the cost of operating the national government, including the Army and the Navy, for the fiscal year. This volume of revenue, going to persons sufficient in number to populate only a very small town, was thirty-eight per cent of the $11,421,631,000 earned by 8,742,761 factory workers and, according to the census of manufactures for 1929, equaled the aggregate wages of 3,339,634 factory workers. The wages of 781,830 iron and steel workers for the year aggregated only $1,239,499,000; of 737,840 food manufacturing workers only $781,736,000; of 511,667 automobile workers only $828,420,-000. In the same year 428,128 cotton-goods workers received $322,-389,000, or $753 each, while the thirty-eight richest persons took $360,644,000, or an average of $9,490,600 each.

While the income of the rich was reduced by twenty-five to fifty per cent in the ensuing depression, the incomes of ten to twenty million working-class citizens disappeared entirely for varying protracted periods. And in the "recovery period" the nation has gradually moved back to an approximation of the 1929 period, although it possesses at this writing about ten million certified paupers in contrast with approximately two million in 1929.

To obviate the need of placing a reference note after every line relative to the source of information, only occasional allusion to sources will in this chapter be made. In general, the sources are the relevant public prints since the World War.

Beard tells of a "dinner eaten on horseback" in the Gilded Age. In September, 1931, Joseph E. Widener was given a "testimonial dinner" at the Biltmore Hotel, New York City, by some wealthy turfman friends. The ballroom was transformed into a replica of Belmont Park, a race track named after the Belmont family but the major owner of which is Widener; a part of the ballroom was given over to a detailed reconstruction of a corner of the park, complete to turf, a stretch of straightaway, white-painted railing, de luxe box stalls, gayly painted water buckets. As the guests sat dining in the boxes there performed before them prize mounts of the New York City Police Department, of blue-ribbon artillery and cavalry regiments, and of wealthy private owners. The palatial room resounded with the thud of hoofs, neighing of steeds, popping of champagne corks, and laughing chatter, while on the street corners outside the unemployed were selling apples.

Banquets for dogs are still given among the wealthy who make a hobby of keeping kennels, and a number of wealthy persons have established expensive canine cemeteries filled with elaborate tombstones and mausoleums. The Eleanor Speyer Hospital for dogs and cats in New York was erected by James Speyer, the banker.

As to fantastic—and expensive—parties, they are so numerous that they bewilder the inquirer. The Dorrance family (Campbell Soup) makes a regular practice of taking over the ballroom, the Clover Room, and the entire second and third floors of the Bellevue-Stratford Hotel, Philadelphia, for parties to which Wideners, Stotesburys, Dukes, Drexels, and Biddles are invited. *Fortune*, ecstatically describing one of these pretentious affairs, said, "There would be rare flowers and foliages, and hundreds of live macaws and toucans and cockatoos and parakeets and birds of paradise in cages, and showers of rose petals falling pinkly on the dancers out of an electrically activated sky." Newspapers estimated the cost per function at from $75,000 to $150,000. But these were really rather small parties.

In December, 1930, Mr. and Mrs. Henry L. Doherty arranged a coming-out party for Helen Lee Eames Doherty, daughter of Mrs. Doherty by a former marriage. This debut took place at the May-flower Hotel, Washington, and guests were brought from New York in a special chartered train paid for by Doherty. Several floors of the hotel, in addition to the public entertaining rooms, were rented by the Dohertys for their entourage of guests, servants, and entertainers. The newspapers estimated the cost of the function at no less than $250,000. Senator Norris, citing the prevalance of unemployment, said the next day in the Senate chamber, "I don't know how they had the heart to do it."

Doherty's Cities Service Company earned distinction during the boom period by unloading huge quantities of nonvoting stock at $40 to $50 a share in a nation-wide door-to-door selling campaign. The price range of this stock in 1937, after three years of rising prices, was $2.62½ to $5.37½ per share.

About the time of the quarter-million-dollar Doherty debut Mr. and Mrs. Franklyn L. Hutton gave a party for their daughter Barbara in the Crystal Room of the Ritz-Carlton Hotel, New York. The vast interior was stage-set by Joseph Urban, famed scenic designer, to represent a moonlit garden. There were, according to the public prints, two thousand cases of champagne for one thousand guests; the aggregate cost was given as $100,000.

At the close of 1936 Mrs. Evalyn Walsh McLean, the proud pos-sessor of the $2,000,000 Hope diamond, heiress to a mining fortune, and married into a newspaper and Cincinnati public-utilities fortune, renewed her custom of staging a lavish New Year's Eve party in Washington. The newspapers set the cost of this function, tendered to her son, John R. McLean II, at $50,000, which seems rather low in view of the details. There were 325 guests at dinner and 650 at the ball which followed. As the house on the McLean estate, Friendship, was not large enough to accommodate the guests and their equerries and footmen, Mrs. McLean ordered constructed a special wing, which was torn down after the party was over. Two orchestras played for the dancers; the cost of beverages alone was, according to the New York *Herald Tribune,* $9,000. The liquid refreshments comprised 480 quarts of champagne, 288 bottles of Scotch whiskey, 48 quarts of cocktails, 36 bottles of liqueurs, and 40 gallons of beer. The menu included several tons of tomato stuffed with crabmeat, cream-of-mushroom soup, breast of guinea hen, spinach, potatoes, ices, fruits, and coffee.

Mrs. McLean, presiding in the turmoil, wore the Hope diamond, the Star of the East (another large stone), and six diamond bracelets. She was closely guarded, as befitted a walking fortune, by fifteen private detectives and a company of Washington police, who kept vigilant eyes as well on the scintillating jewelry of the guests.

When Mrs. Marjorie Post Close Hutton married Joseph E. Davies, Washington corporation lawyer and later Ambassador to Russia, her huge apartment was bedecked "with 5,000 chrysanthemums that had been dyed blush pink at a cost of $2,000 to match the icing on the 300-pound wedding cake which the establishment's twenty-five servants, assisted by three caterers, served to fifty wedding guests." The flowers themselves cost $6,000. When the Hutton-Davies menage removed to Moscow it was reported that it ordered transported several carloads of specially prepared foods as well as furniture, ice-boxes, electric fans, and other equipment. Several hundred quarts of frozen cream were brought along, to the astonishment of Russians who pointed out that the country still had cows. During the summer of 1937 Mrs. Davies ordered two tons of frozen foods sent to Moscow for a cruise she and her husband were taking. Mrs. Davies happens to own the major interest in the General Foods Corporation, which specializes in frozen fresh products that are preserved indefinitely.

Mrs. Hutton-Davies likes to transport things long distances. She makes a practice, according to Helen Worden's *Society Circus,* of sending exotic plants from her Long Island hothouses down to her Florida estate. The plants, wrapped in cotton batting, are moved in heated railroad cars.

To celebrate her twenty-second birthday in Paris in November, 1934, the Princess Barbara Hutton Mdivani, now the Countess Haugwitz-Reventlow, gave a modest little party costing only $10,000. "We didn't think it fitting," her husband apologized, "to spend too much in these times." Among the guests journalists discerned two princes, one duchess, three barons, thirteen counts, one earl, and one hundred lesser personages.

The plutocracy has traveled a long way since Mrs. Potter Palmer of Chicago dazzled Carlton Terrace, London, in 1909 with a puny $10,000 party and a $100,000 season. The cost of a really fashionable party is now at least $100,000, and such affairs are the rule, not the exception. It is no longer, however, the item of cost but the occasion of the cost that attracts the attention of the newspapers. At Newport throughout the summer season, in Florida during the winter, the rich families by turns entertain extravagantly with garden parties, yachting parties, costume parties, and dances, the cost of which ranges from $50,000 to $100,000 each. During a recent study at Columbia University it was discovered that a doctor's career at its outset might be capitalized for its bank-loan value at a little more than $100,000. The cost of the main party of the season given by one of the sixty wealthiest families would support an ordinary American family of five for a lifetime in relative luxury.

The ninety second richest families ape the personal expenditures of the sixty top-ranking families for the status and reflected glory conferred upon them; and the three hundred and fifty families of lesser wealth in turn ape their pecuniary superiors. The consequence is that there is an eternal round of lavish personal expenditure throughout the three strata of extreme wealth.

According to Beard, in the 1890's "cigarettes were wrapped in hundred-dollar bills . . . fine black pearls were given to the diners in their oysters . . . a necklace costing $600,000 was purchased for a daughter. . . . An entire theatrical company was taken from New York to Chicago . . . a complete orchestra engaged to serenade a new-born child."

As to the last, we may remark that the late Joseph Pulitzer habitually had the New York Symphony Orchestra transported to his Maine estate, there to soothe himself and his guests. Clarence Mackay, more recently, upon marrying Anna Case, opera singer, ordered the whole Philharmonic Symphony Orchestra brought out to his Long Island estate to accompany the ceremony. The largest contributors to the deficits of symphony orchestras and opera companies frequently summon the magnificent artistic organizations to appear and dazzle guests at private parties, a *quid pro quo* that is seldom referred to by the newspapers when they talk about "patrons" of the arts.

As to cigarettes wrapped in $100 bills, we cannot discover a precise contemporary counterpart, although at private functions the cigarettes may now be wrapped in $1,000 bills or government bonds. But *Time* (June 6, 1932) informs us, upon the occasion of a suit won by Tiffany and Company for $75,005 claimed on items charged to his account in fourteen months, that John Barry Ryan, struggling along on $29,000,000 left to him by Thomas Fortune Ryan, regularly "showers his friends with presents—diamond roosters, coral monkeys, ox-blood coral Buddhas, zodiac charms, brooches, bracelets, a hand-bound copy of the encyclical on marriage of Pope Pius XI. . . . Absent-minded, poetic, he forgets his bills (haberdashery accounts totaling $3,160.75 were also judged against him last week)."

Christmas parties at the home of the late George F. Baker, Jr., regularly attended by two hundred to three hundred relatives and friends, saw, according to Helen Worden's *Society Circus,* the presentation to each guest of expensive baubles like gold vanity cases, silver flasks, first editions of books, rare perfumes, and platinum jewelry.

As to the trivial item of a $600,000 necklace given to a daughter of the Gilded Age, we may note that in the more recent Jazz Age Mrs. Horace E. Dodge, widow of the automobile man and now Mrs. Hugh Dillman of Detroit, Palm Beach, and Grosse Point, bestowed upon her daughter Delphine a pearl necklace valued at $800,000 and once the property of haughty Catherine II of Russia. Delphine was first married to James H. R. Cromwell, son of Mrs. E. T. Stotesbury, who is now the husband of Doris Duke; after her divorce Delphine married Raymond T. Baker, previously the husband of Margaret Emerson (Bromo Seltzer), who in turn had been the wife at an earlier date of Alfred Gwynne Vanderbilt.

On the subject of jewelry and gewgaws, it may be noted that Jessie Woolworth Donahue owns the priceless Romanov crown jewels and is credited with the possession of a $75,000 sable wrap. According to *Fortune,* she lost $10,000 in eight months at Bradley's gaming tables in Palm Beach, while her husband, according to the same source, lost $900,000. Mrs. Donahue owns one of the largest emerald collections in the United States, although Mrs. E. T. Stotesbury is credited with owning the finest collection, valued at considerably more than $1,000,000. Other emerald collectors are Mrs. Forsyth Wickes, Mrs. Harrison Williams, wife of one of Bernard Baruch's "dollar-a-year" men who is now a big public-utility operator, Mrs. Felix Warburg, and Mrs. Marjorie Post Close Hutton Davies. Mrs. Williams owns a necklace and bracelet, worth many hundreds of thousands, composed of 129 square-cut sapphires, 144 square-cut emeralds, 762 small round diamonds, and 79 pearls. Their peers can be found only among the Romanov-Donahue jewels.

Whole new fields of extravagant expenditure have been opened up since the horse-and-buggy days of the 1890's. Bathrooms, swimming pools, and stamp collections take up a good deal of surplus money, while some tens of thousands of American citizens dine out of garbage cans. *Fortune* (January, 1931) summarizes the bathroom fad. The Ralph Pulitzer family of New York, among the ninety second richest clans, have their most prized bathroom embellished in a jungle motif, "walls decorated with monkeys swinging from palm trees, gaudy flamingos, and yawning crocodiles, all painted on gold canvas. . . . The tub is soft yellow, faced with black and gold marble." Continuing, "Mrs. William Stern's bath is found to be silver and green, the wall above the tub offering intimate glimpses into submarine life. . . . Just as impressive is Mrs. Seton Porter's [National Distillers' Products], with its black and white marble floor, jade ceiling, and mirror rising from the edge of the tub, framed in black glass." Stuart Chase, in *The New Republic,* May 25, 1927, refers to a jade-and-gold Park Avenue bathroom that cost $35,000 but he does not give the name of its owner.

The most recent champion in the bathroom sweepstakes, however, appears to be W. C. Grunow, radio manufacturer, who owns "a tub made from a single slab of Mexican onyx marble, costing $12,000 and equipped with fixtures of twenty-four carat gold plate." The gold plating, although a definite feature, has its duplicates in the fixtures of many other aristocratic bathrooms. In Mrs. Hugh Dillman's Palm Beach *palazzo,* for example, all the faucets except those in the kitchen and butler's pantry are of gold, says *Fortune*;

and gold is indeed so common that much of the hardware—door hinges, knobs, metal trimming in general—in the various châteaux of the wealthy is now made of it.

The bathroom in a wealthy American's home is not, of course, synonymous with the bathroom of ordinary usage. It is usually a large vaulted chamber, with a sunken tub that may in some cases very easily be used as a swimming pool. Some of the bathrooms of the plutocracy are equipped with gymnastic paraphernalia; all have as standard equipment such things as quartz lamps, rubbing tables, unusual lighting arrangements, and strange decorations.

Nor is the American millionaire's bathroom noteworthy for its rococo style alone. Its frequent incidence also deserves attention. Taking into consideration all the private residences and large apartments of the wealthiest families, it emerges as a fact that each family possesses at least one hundred bathrooms for the use of its own members, its guests, its servants, and its entertainers. This particular inquiry managed to isolate 723 bathrooms in the various Du Pont establishments, at which point, with much ground remaining to be covered, the quest was regretfully terminated. The Du Pont baths are plain and fancy, somber and gay, for chauffeurs and maids, for engineers and aviators, and for ladies and gentlemen.

Bathing is a frequent ceremony in upper-class life, and the member of the average wealthy family is apt to spend much time in the bath— telephoning, transacting business with secretaries and housekeepers, reading, listening to the radio or the phonograph, visiting with friends. The psychologist Freud has a theory that frequent washing of the hands marks a betrayal of a subconscious feeling of guilt. Frequent bathing, by the same token, must then mark a betrayal of an even deeper feeling of subconscious guilt.

The subject of bathing among the rich would not be complete without some mention of swimming pools. The newspaper rotogravure sections frequently regale the public with photographs of the pools of Hollywood actors, but theirs are really modest affairs. William Randolph Hearst on his San Simeon estate has an outdoor pool of Carrara marble, connected with an indoor pool for use in inclement weather. Although all the standard equipped estates have their pools, perhaps the prize of them all is to be found on the estate of the late Henry H. Rogers at Southampton. This pool cost $250,000, and was designed in Pompeian style by Architect John Russell Pope. The interior housing arrangement is lined with colored mosaic; the lighting is indirect, and there is an outdoor counterpart. Walter Chrysler owns a "handpainted" swimming pool. The pool on the average estate is usually merely a regular part of other sports equipment. On the Long Island estate of Mrs. Dodge Sloane, for example, a separate glass building, which can be opened at will to the elements, contains an elaborate swimming pool, tennis court, and billiard and backgammon rooms. Helen Worden's *Society Circus* informs us that "the soil used for the court is tile pink, imported from France."

Upward of a thousand private pools are to be found on the estates of the wealthy.

All of the rich, to be sure, have their expensive little hobbies. The hobby of the recently deceased E. H. R. Green, son of Hetty Green, was the collecting of postage stamps. Green paid a Washington office boy $18,000 for a sheet of stamps merely because the illustration was printed wrong side up. Retaining the choicest specimens for himself, Green sold the balance; and the Scott Coin and Stamp Company is reported to obtain $3,300 upward from wealthy collectors for each of these stamps.

Complicated litigation is often an expensive pastime of the rich. The seven heirs of the late George Gould, for example, tied up the estate in a snarl of suits, the cost of which was estimated in 1924 by the lawyer for the estate at $2,500 an hour throughout the protracted period of the dispute.

## II

It is in their palatial country estates that the rich families, niggardly in philanthropies, really extend themselves, for in these places they are sheltered from the prying eyes of the sweat-stained, fatigue-racked proletariat and the ever-trusting, infinitely gullible middle class.

It has become the recent fashion to point to the four estates and many apartments of William Randolph Hearst as representing the apogee of contemporary extravagance; but Hearst is merely "keeping up with the Joneses," and is doing it very noisily. We must disagree with Dixon Wecter when he writes in *The Saga of American Society*: "The greatest attempt ever made to achieve lordly splendor in America is William Randolph Hearst's 240,000 acre estate at San Simeon, California, with its estimated cost of $15,000,000 for furnishings and antiques alone. Its great dining-hall hung with Sienese banners and a magnificent Gothic chimney piece from the Château du Jour, its sixteenth-century refectory tables, Flemish tapestries, seventeenth-century Spanish candlesticks and old English silver, six Gobelin tapestries costing $575,000, a notable collection of armour, and Cardinal Richelieu's own bed are witnesses to the spoliation of Europe." Mr. Wecter is impressed by the fact that Hearst once transported a castle from Spain to New York in packing cases, that he purchased St. Donat's Castle in Wales, and that at San Simeon he owns a private railway spur and three cars and a diner to transport his guests to the main *palazzo*. Overlooking an entire Bavarian village that Hearst has constructed at Wyntoon, California, Mr. Wecter also overlooks the fact that all this is merely the minimum standard equipment of the contemporary American multimillionaire.

Several decades ago George Vanderbilt's Biltmore château in North Carolina cost $6,000,000, and to duplicate it today would probably cost three times as much. But neither Hearst nor this lone Vanderbilt fully indicates what has taken place in the accumulation by the rich of the appurtenances of mere living. It is only when the subject is approached on a family basis that one discerns the true picture.

The Du Pont clan, because of its many members, probably owns more personal possessions than any other American family of the plutocracy, although the Vanderbilt group runs it a close second and the Rockefellers probably come third. A careful survey indicates that the Du Ponts own more yachts, more pipe organs, more swimming pools, more ducal estates, and more bathrooms than any other family in the world today. They employ more servants than the royal family of Great Britain, not excluding the King's Own Life Guards.

In a broad but very real sense the Du Ponts own the whole state of Delaware and parts of adjoining Pennsylvania. Delaware itself is the private fief of the Du Ponts, who have constructed its schools and roads, collect its taxes—Pierre du Pont is the Delaware tax commissioner for the fourth term at this writing—and, in general, supervise every detail of Delaware life.

Owing to the many elaborate Du Pont estates, Delaware and the immediately contiguous territory might aptly be termed the American "Château Country." Should other regions dispute Delaware's right to this designation, regions such as the North Shore of Long Island, and Newport, the Du Ponts have only to assert their unchallengeable right to be recognized as ruling over an entire province of châteaux.

Near the environs of Wilmington there are precisely two dozen Du Pont country estates, four of which are of the first magnitude. There is, for example, Winterthur, the ducal 150-room residence of the Henry F. du Ponts, boasting forty bedrooms, each with a radio installation, each replete with costly antiques; the cost of the building alone was $2,000,000, and including the grounds, trappings, furniture, and fixtures, the cost of the whole establishment easily touches $10,-000,000.

Then there is Longwood, residence of Pierre du Pont, surrounded by 1,000 carefully tended acres which include six acres of glassed-over tropical gardens; in these are orangeries and separate orchard houses for the growing throughout the year of peaches, nectarines, and exotic fruits. The house has nearly two hundred rooms, and more than one hundred servants, including the gardeners who are employed there. A feature of the establishment is an organ of ten thousand pipes to transport which required fourteen railroad freight cars. According to *Fortune*, the volume of this regal instrument is sufficient to fill three cathedrals. The building was especially constructed to contain the apparatus, whose attendant is Firmin Swinnen, former organist at the Antwerp Cathedral; underlying the organ are large 72-horsepower blowers that required installation of special power lines. The organ pipes give out into the indoor gardens, to which the public is admitted occasionally at a small charge which goes to local charities and helps reduce Du Pont taxes. The conception behind the arrangement is that one may wander with one's guests in tropical gardens, enjoying the perfumes of rare plants as one is beguiled by the music.

Another feature of Longwood, perhaps the chief residence of the

Armorers to the Republic, is an authentic Norman tower, in which is an old carillon that, when played, fills the countryside for many miles around with melody. Still another is an open-air theater, seating twelve hundred. To dwell here at greater length on the costly wonders of Longwood and on the details of its many great rooms is, of course, inadvisable. There are too many other Du Pont estates. The value of the entire Longwood plant, however, is at least $15,-000,000.

There is a friendly competitive spirit among the Du Ponts in thinking up distinctive residential features. At Winterthur, as if to rival the organ and the carillon at Longwood, Henry F. du Pont, instead of installing a private pipe organ, gave one to a neighboring church and has its music brought to the château by a special loud-speaker system with outlets at the swimming pools, the tennis courts, and in various chambers. He also caused the construction outdoors of the world's largest loud-speaker, whose outlet is ten by twelve feet, so that hunting songs and Christmas carols can be sent echoing over the countryside. In Delaware, as on the battlefield, one can readily see, there is no escaping the Du Ponts.

Notable points of interest at Henry I. du Pont's princely Nemours are its entrance gates. One is from a palace of Catherine the Great and another from Wimbledon Manor; the estate also contains sunken gardens that are considered by connoisseurs among the foremost in the world even after taking into consideration those at Versailles and Schönbrunn. Nemours is justly celebrated for its magnificent stables and mounts.

To enumerate the wonders of the regal palaces of all the Du Ponts would, perhaps, be repetitious. Most of them have swimming pools, tennis courts, private telephone switchboards with from fifty to more than one hundred outlets, elaborate music rooms, libraries, salons, and guest chambers furnished with antiques, tapestries, paintings. Many of the rooms have been taken bodily out of famed European châteaux and palaces.

William du Pont has two imperial palaces near each other; one, Bellevue, is in Delaware, and the other is in Newtown Square over the state line in Pennsylvania. S. Hallock du Pont rules over Henry Clay, named after the parliamentary apologist for chattel slavery;

Bessie Gardner du Pont over Chevannes; Eugene du Pont over Owl's Nest; Francis I. du Pont over Louviers; Victor du Pont over Guyencourt; Irénée du Pont over Granogue when he is not absent at his vast Cuban plantation outside Havana; and Edmond du Pont over Centerville. There are other near-by Du Pont estates, smaller than these and not quite so lavish, but grandiose enough to make the casual wayfarer believe he has stumbled upon a motion-picture set; and these are owned by Eugene E. du Pont, Ernest du Pont, Mrs. William K. du Pont, A. Felix du Pont, and Mrs. Philip du Pont. There are, too, the estates of Du Pont women married to outsiders— Copelands, Lairds, Schutts, Meeds, Bayards, Carpenters, Sharps, Rusts, Greenewalts, and Mays.

Aside from these ducal palaces a good many of the Du Ponts maintain houses or apartments in New York, Philadelphia, Washington, London, and Paris. The clan also has its "poor" relations, some of whom hold executive positions in various Du Pont enterprises and live humbly in secluded $50,000 and $100,000 homes. A few are looked at askance by the main branch of the family, having married Irish barmaids or English nurses, and these glumly plow the Seven Seas in their steam yachts or clip gilt-edged coupons in St. Cloud.

All in all, the residential establishments of the Du Ponts, taking into consideration land, buildings, furnishings, and equipment, may be conservatively estimated as costing at least $150,000,000, or more than ten per cent of the total university and college endowment of the nation.

The Vanderbilt family exhibits a similar inclination toward conspicuous residential display, although its palaces are somewhat more scattered. And when we come to the Vanderbilt and other families a difficulty interposes; intermarriage has made it problematical which family may be said to own an estate. Biltmore, a towering pile of French architecture in North Carolina, is, perhaps, the Vanderbilt family prize. It is large enough to take into its folds all the Hearst châteaux in California, with sufficient room left over in which to have a hunt ball. At Newport alone there are the palatial villas of the late Dowager Mrs. Cornelius Vanderbilt, Brigadier General Cornelius Vanderbilt, William H. Vanderbilt, and Mrs. Henry D. Phelps, the Dowager's grandniece. Until the Dowager built The Breakers, the

$9,000,000 Marble House of her sister-in-law, Mrs. W. K. Vanderbilt, was a show place of the clan at Newport. Cornelius Vanderbilt Whitney, scion of the railroad and the oil family, owns a whole town, Obregon City, in Mexico, which he operates as his private estate; a large New York apartment; a horse farm in Kentucky; an elaborate hunting lodge in Canada and another in the Adirondacks; the Wheatley Hills mansion of his father, Harry Payne Whitney; a château in Newport; a town house in New York City—and he shares the marble *palazzo* of his grandmother, Mrs. Cornelius Vanderbilt, at 1 East Sixty-seventh Street, New York City. All this is pretty much for a single Vanderbilt; but taking all the Vanderbilts into consideration one can isolate nearly thirty separate residences of the family, most of them very ornate.

Mrs. Gertrude Vanderbilt Whitney has a six-hundred-acre estate at Old Westbury, Long Island, and magnificent houses in New York and at Newport. Mrs. Payne Whitney has an eighty-five-hundred-acre estate, possessing one of the finest stables in the country, near Thomasville, Georgia.

The probable aggregate cost of all the Vanderbilt dwelling places is not less than $125,000,000, with the cost of three alone exceeding $25,000,000; all, of course, boast such appurtenances as pipe organs, numerous bathrooms, swimming pools, private motion-picture theaters, antique furniture, tapestries and paintings, private telephone switchboards, gymnasia, ballrooms, trophy rooms, sitting rooms, salons, cardrooms, etc.

In surveying the residential seats of the Rockefeller family it is also difficult to know to which family one should assign each mansion and estate, as the Rockefellers are intermarried, as we have seen, with Stillmans, Carnegies, McCormicks, Aldriches, Davisons, Dodges, etc. We will, however, concentrate on the two main Rockefeller lines of descent, observing first, however, that the Rockefeller publicity men, geniuses of a sort, have admirably succeeded in suggesting that this imperial family lives rather ascetically; seldom are descriptions of the Rockefeller residential interiors permitted to leak out, so that one must reconstruct them mentally from fragmentary suggestions just as a paleontologist reconstructs the framework of a dinosaur from a few scraps of bone.

There is, first, the great family duchy of thirty-five hundred acres at Pocantico Hills, Tarrytown, New York. On this estate stand five separate family mansions, for as each child marries a house is constructed for separate occupancy. Like the Standard Oil Company, the estate has been assembled with guile and force against the will of neighbors. In Cleveland the Rockefellers had a town house on Euclid Avenue and a regal estate in Forest Hill, now turned into an expensive suburban real-estate development; but in the 1890's the family moved to Pocantico Hills. This estate at the turn of the century comprised only about sixteen-hundred acres, which have since been added to by purchase and by persuasion. The first brush the elder Rockefeller had with the local authorities, who are now the family's most ardent servitors, was occasioned by his desire to have Tarrytown construct a road around Croton reservoir, the property of New York City. Rockefeller offered to pay for the road, which would connect his place with his brother William's; but local officials pointed out that to build the road one would have to condemn a number of private homes whose owners had, cannily (they thought), raised prices when they visualized Rockefeller as a potential purchaser. Rockefeller apologists have pointed with indignation to the attempt of the local burghers to make the oil baron pay fancy prices, and have applauded Rockefeller's refusal to do so, even though it was by unfairly, dishonestly, and illegally contriving to raise and fix oil prices that he made his fortune. Rockefeller, however, was determined to have his road, and his workmen proceeded in defiance of the law until they encroached on the private property of John Weber, the village president. When the chief of police mysteriously refused a request to protect the property Weber and his sons, acting on their constitutional rights, attempted to stop the Rockefeller men. At a signal, the latter were reinforced by a near-by gang of Rockefeller roughnecks, armed with picks and shovels, who pummeled and drove the village president away.

In 1929 Rockefeller, Jr., paid the town of Eastview $700,000 for the privilege of ousting forty-six families so that the main line of the Putnam division of the New York Central Railroad might run along what was Eastview's main street instead of through the gradually swelling Pocantico Hills estate. Preserved against encroachment, however, was the summer home of James Butler, chain-store operator. The assessed valuation of the Rockefeller demesne in 1928 was $5,588,050, calling for a tax of $137,000, but by dint of litigation and argument the assessment has since been scaled down by about $2,000,-000. Either valuation seems rather modest in view of all the improvements that have been installed. Trees, shrubs, and plants have been brought from all quarters of the globe. The grounds are traversed by roads and bridle paths over which private police course in radio cars. John T. Flynn describes a three-story stable on the estate, containing elevators, grooms' quarters, and room for twenty-two blooded horses.

According to *The New York Times* (May 24, 1937), the elder Rockefeller's fifty-room mansion at Pocantico, surrounded by carefully nurtured gardens, alone cost $2,000,000 to build and $500,000 a year to maintain, while the estate itself requires the services of three hundred and fifty employees and thirty teams of horses the year round, making a monthly pay roll of $18,000. Included in the standard equipment of the house are private elevators and air-conditioning units to preserve even temperature throughout the seasons; and all of Rockefeller's mansions, according to the *Times,* "contained elaborate medical equipment for checking his condition. There were machines for taking his basal metabolism, fluoroscopes—the equipment of a small hospital. He always had on hand, for special circumstances, small tanks of oxygen and he carried them with him when he traveled."

Thanks to all this equipment Rockefeller outlived twenty personal physicians, according to the New York *Post* (May 24, 1937); for Rockefeller realized that money was often equivalent to life, lack of it to virtual death, and that the struggle over money in the world was really a struggle over life and death. Money, Rockefeller also unquestionably realized, has the power to expand the effectiveness of a single life span so that it is equivalent to many ordinary ones. Everything else being equal, a man with $1,000,000 lives many times longer in an effective sense than a man with no money, for the former is able, with the help of servitors and technicians, to accomplish in minutes and hours what it takes the penniless man weeks, months, and, perhaps, years to achieve.

The New York *Herald Tribune* (May 24, 1937) in part described
the Rockefeller estate as follows:

From the village of East View the estate extends northward three
miles over soft, pleasant countryside to the boundaries of Ossining,
where it joins the estate of the elder James Stillman, former president
of the National City Bank. It averages two miles in width. . . . At
the southern tip of Pocantico on a high knoll two miles from the
Hudson stands the massive Georgian house of Mr. Rockefeller. It
lies in the center of the estate's only enclosure area, 350 acres surrounded by a high fence with two gates. . . . Thirty watchmen—
twenty in the winter when the families are living in town—patrol the
enclosure in eight-hour shifts to keep out unwelcome visitors. . . .
Within the enclosure live five Rockefeller families. A sixth, that of
Mrs. David W. Milton, the former Abby Rockefeller, only daughter
of Mr. and Mrs. Rockefeller, Jr., live in their home a half mile away
to the northeast. . . . The [central] house has fifty rooms, most of
them very large, beginning with two anterooms, an enormous central hall, a living room and a dining room on the first floor. All are
furnished with furniture of the Georgian period. Two floors of ex-
pansive bedroom suites above are topped by quarters for the fifteen
servants required to run the house. Floodlights on the roof can light,
the entire area surrounding Kijkuit whenever the two watchmen
stationed there see fit to use them. More as a part of the house than
a separate adjunct is its rather formal combination rose and Japanese
garden with statuary (mostly copies) by George Gray Barnard. . . .
    The house occupied by Mr. and Mrs. John D. Rockefeller, Jr., is a
rambling country residence, roomy and plain. Wings have been
added to it casually from time to time until it has lost all function as
an architectural medium. Along the coach road that rims the southern edge of Pocantico rest the homes of three of their sons, Nelson,
Laurance and John D. Rockefeller, 3rd. Nelson converted a 200-
year-old Dutch farmhouse into a comfortable home where he is
forever erecting his own stone walls and rearranging his rock garden.
John also reconverted a local farmhouse and Laurance put up a pre-
fabricated Georgian house put out by a steel company in 1937.
    On a flat knoll to the west of the five family homes is the playhouse,
built in 1926 for Mr. Rockefeller's grandchildren and great-grandchildren. It is a faithful copy of a large, rambling Normandy farmhouse with its ascendant tower. It was designed by Duncan Candler,
architect, of New York City, and cost $250,000 [The New York
*World* (September 19, 1926), said the cost of this house was $500,000].
The ground-level floor houses a Grecian swimming pool opening on

to two tennis courts, locker rooms and showers. Close by is the nine-hole golf course where Mr. Rockefeller played. . . . On the oak-panelled first floor are a bowling alley, a squash court, a large living room, card room and kitchen for light suppers. In the tower is a billiard room. . . .

Both superintendents live in houses just inside the Pocantico Hills gate. A new building outside the gate houses offices, shops, a garage and sheds for supplies. Under the impetus of Mr. Rockefeller, Jr., there is no end to new construction projects. More than fifty miles of roads, and the bridle paths, with over and under passes to avoid high-ways, have been completed to date. . . . The Rockefeller farm, two miles north of the village, is home for a herd of thirty-five blooded dairy cattle. . . .

In New York City are the two principal Rockefeller town houses, at 4 and 10 West Fifty-fourth Street. Both mansions are now being given up, however, as Rockefeller, Jr., is taking a large Park Avenue apartment. The married children have separate apartments or houses in town.

The elder Rockefeller shifted southward with the seasons. His first stop would be at Lakewood, New Jersey, where Golf House domi-nates a regal estate that includes a private golf links, dairy farm, etc. Winter would find him at The Casements, his ornate Ormond Beach, Florida, estate. Although Pocantico Hills was as far north as the elder Rockefeller ever got in his later years, his son for many years has taken his family to a private summer estate at Seal Harbor, Maine. This residence enables him to contribute to the Maine Re-publican State Committee as well as to the New York Republican State Committee. On the basis of residential addresses the Rockefel-lers may contribute to state political campaigns in six states.

The late Edith Rockefeller McCormick, daughter of John D. Rockefeller, had two ornate places in and near Chicago. At 1000 Lake Shore Drive stood her great town house, a bridal gift from her father. At Lake Forest, Illinois, was the Villa Turicum, built of Italian marble at a cost of $2,500,000, and filled with costly rugs, marbles, and objects of art. Mrs. McCormick never entered the place after 1913. Then there is the Mount Hope estate of Mrs. E. Parmalee Prentice, the former Alta Rockefeller, at Williamstown, Massachu-setts. This country seat comprises fifteen hundred acres and had an assessed valuation of $715,000 in 1931. The Prentices have, too, town houses, and their children, as they come to maturity, are setting up households of their own.

The Cuevas family was left Golf House and the Lakewood, New Jersey, estate by the elder Rockefeller's will, and this may now be regarded as their center of activity when they are neither in town nor in Europe.

There remains the William Rockefeller line of more than one hundred persons. William had six children, two of whom were daughters. One daughter—Mrs. Marcellus Hartley Dodge, wife of the board chairman of the Remington Arms Company—has her country estate, Geralda Farm, at Madison, New Jersey, and it is the annual scene of a much-heralded dog show, for Mrs. Dodge is one of the foremost dog breeders in the world. William G. and Percy A., the only two of William's sons to reach maturity, had their separate estates and town houses. Mrs. David Hunter McAlpin, who is William's daughter Emma, also has her separate residences.

As we have seen, the will of William Rockefeller provided that at least fifty great-grandchildren will be millionaires in their own right by 1950, so by that date there will have been a vast increase in the number of separate Rockefeller menages. All in all, it can be estimated that existing Rockefeller establishments, including the thirty-two-thousand-acre Adirondack estate of William which was offered at a sacrifice price of $1,000,000, have a total valuation, including furnishings and equipment, of $50,000,000 to $75,000,000.

Like the Rockefellers, the Pratts have the country seats of their clan all bunched together, at Glen Cove, Long Island. The Bedfords concentrate on Connecticut and adjacent New York State. On the one-thousand-acre Pratt estate, the assessed value of which is $5,865,-130, there reside in neighboring residences one hundred and thirty members of the family when they are not dispersed among their town houses and apartments. The Pratts were the first to install private police patrol cars, radio-equipped, to guard the children and grandchildren from kidnapers who might invade the winding roads and woodlands.

The country estates exhibit various special features. Some are grouped by families; some represent self-incorporated villages established to reduce taxes for a number of families; and others are merely units in an international chain of residences.

The Morgan family, with town houses and apartments in New York City, also owns East and West Island, off the North Shore of Long Island near Glen Cove. Junius Morgan shares West Island with Mrs. William Harkness, whose country seat occupies one side. This island is joined by a private bridge to East Island, where J. P. Morgan's American country estate stands, surrounded by elaborate gardens. After prolonged litigation Morgan got $1,000,000 pared off the island's tax assessment of $2,256,000; his son failed in an attempt to have his assessment of $625,000 reduced.

The Morgan town house in New York adjoins the Morgan Library, valued at $7,000,000 and provided with an endowment of $1,500,000, which makes it, theoretically, a philanthropy. It is filled with ancient Bibles, Assyrian and Babylonian seals, Egyptian and Greek papyri, Coptic texts, illuminated manuscripts, Blake drawings, and manuscripts by Shelley, Swift, Scott, Napoleon, and others. The title to this property is vested in Mr. Morgan, which makes it a part of his household.

In London the banker owns a great four-story mansion at 12 Grosvenor Square, Mayfair, which is occupied as often as is the Madison Avenue house. He owns the whole of the village of Aldenham, Hertfordshire, where his great Wall Hall castle and estate stands. Only the village church is not owned by Morgan. All the villagers are his employees. In Scotland he has Gannochy, a stone hunting lodge of thirty rooms, serviced in the hunting season by forty servants.

A fair valuation on the residences of the various members of the Morgan family, including the library in New York, would seem to be at least $30,000,000.

To reduce taxes a number of wealthy families, owners of estates covering three square miles whose assessed valuation is $7,000,000, have formed the village of Lattingtown, Long Island. The incorporators included J. P. Morgan, the late George F. Baker, Harvey D. Gibson, S. Parker Gilbert, Clarence H. Mackay (whose place is said to have cost $6,000,000 to build), J. E. Aldred, and William D. Guthrie. With a separate village these men can now impose their own local taxes.

Vincent Astor owns an estate at Rhinebeck, New York, adjoining
Franklin D. Roosevelt's Krum Elbow, one at Newport, and one in
Bermuda. Frederick H. Prince has an establishment at Pau, France.
Mrs. Moses Taylor has her home estate in Marrakech, Morocco, but
also has a Newport house (said to require more than one hundred
servants) and an estate in France. Most of her time, however, is
spent on her yacht or in New York apartments.

The gardens on some of the estates cost a king's ransom. Pierre
du Pont, according to *Fortune* (August, 1933) spent $25,000 to have a
single bush brought to Longwood. The same issue of the magazine
relates that the late Rodman Wanamaker spent $1,000,000 to have
his estate decorated with especially fine specimens of small-leafed
box. The house and twelve gardens covering one hundred and fifty
acres of the Oyster Bay estate of Charles E. F. McCann (Woolworth)
cost $3,500,000, says *Fortune*. According to C. W. Barron, Samuel
Untermyer, the lawyer, has 167 men constantly tending the vast gardens on his Yonkers estate; the same authority relates that the late
James B. Duke employed forty men simply to tend the lawns on his
New Jersey place, where the fountains ran with filtered water. Duke
had four houses which he left to his family: the principal residence
at Somerville, New Jersey, another in the south, one in Newport, and
a fourth on Fifth Avenue. Doris Duke Cromwell is now mistress of
the Somerville place.

The sixty-acre estate of Henry H. Rogers at Southampton was
improved with two *palazzi* at a cost of $2,800,000. The Deepdene
estate of C. Ledyard Blair on Bermuda cost $550,000. Samuel Insull
poured $9,000,000 into his forty-two-hundred-acre Hawthorne Farm
near Chicago which was put on forced sale for $780,000; features of
the establishment were gold-plated bathroom fixtures and rooms
imported from European castles. The late Alexander Smith Cochran
spent more than $1,000,000 on his eight-thousand-acre Rocky Moun-
tain estate outside the Garden of the Gods. The late Edmund C.
Converse, Morgan factotum in charge of the Bankers Trust Company, put $3,000,000 into his Greenwich, Connecticut, estate.

Henry Carnegie Phipps owns an Italian palace on Long Island's
north shore, valued at more than $1,000,000. The biggest estate on
Long Island, however, belongs to Marshall Field, whose former wife

owns a two-thousand-acre place at Huntington, Long Island, with six acres of landscaped garden valued alone at $400,000. The main Marshall Field estate at Lloyd's Neck, Long Island, is said to be worth $15,000,000. It comprises landscaped gardens, special airplane and boat landings, the best pheasant-shooting grounds in the country with specially bred birds, indoor and outdoor tennis courts, private guest apartments in the house, a large garage, and all the other embellishments a modern Croesus can command.

Some of the biggest gardens in the country, valued at from $500,000 to $1,000,000, are owned by Arthur Curtiss James, Clarence Lewis, Horatio Gates Lloyd (Morgan partner), Cyrus McCormick, Charles Schweppe, William G. Mather, and William West Frazier.

Owners of large Newport places, other than those already mentioned, are Mrs. Hamilton McK. Twombly, Mrs. Harry Payne Whitney (also several town houses and other country residences), Perry Belmont, Arthur Curtiss James, Herman Oelrichs, Mrs. Oliver Harriman, Frederic Rhinelander, the Berwind family, Mrs. Henry Clews, Robert Walter Goelet, Mrs. William Goadby Loew (daughter of the senior George F. Baker), Anthony Biddle, and Mrs. Edward V. Hartford (Great Atlantic and Pacific Tea Stores). The Newport colony numbers no more than three hundred persons, and all the Newport houses are enormous show places.

Mr. and Mrs. E. T. Stotesbury live in retirement at Whitemarsh Hall, their Philadelphia estate, which has gardens arranged in replica of the gardens at Versailles. The house contains 145 rooms, forty-five baths, fourteen elevators, thirty-five house servants, and sixty-five outside employees. The Stotesburys inhabit Wingwood House, Bar Harbor, in the summer; El Mirasol, Palm Beach, in the winter.

The Nicholas F. Brady house, Inisfada, on Long Island, contains eighty-seven rooms, according to *The New Yorker* (May 1, 1937). Its cost was $3,000,000, and it contains a great hall eighty feet long and fifty feet high, an Aeolian organ, a dining room in which fifteen hundred guests have been served at once, chambers for forty-five overnight guests with a *prie-dieu,* crucifix, and holy-water font in each room, a private chapel where masses may be said by special dispensation of the Pope (for Brady was a papal duke), and a house telephone switchboard with eighty-seven extensions. The Brady bedchamber holds an eight-foot-square Spanish Renaissance canopied bed. The vast kitchen contains thirty feet of stoves and a special butcher room that will accommodate entire beeves, boars, stags, and a wide variety of game. A wine cellar "stretches endlessly" under the lawn. A separate ice plant supplies refrigeration. Only twenty-five servants were required to operate this place, which was recently given to a Catholic order.

Most of the persons who own residences at Newport also have establishments in Florida, but these latter will not be enumerated. Before abandoning the estates, however, it may be interesting to observe that others beside the Morgans own islands over which they rule like Neptunes. Naushon Island, near Martha's Vineyard, is owned by the Forbes family of Boston, whose six power boats and two cruising schooners connect them with their mainland homes. A dozen branches of the family have summer homes on this island. The clan includes W. Cameron Forbes, former Governor General of the Philippines, head of J. M. Forbes and Company, and director of American Telephone and Telegraph Company; Allan Forbes, president of the State Street Trust Company, Boston; J. Grant Forbes, investment banker; Edward Waldo Forbes, director of the Fogg Art Museum at Harvard; and Dr. Alexander Forbes, member of the faculty of Harvard Medical School.

Harvard University owns Bumkin Island, off the Massachusetts coast, and has leased it for ninety-nine years to Albert C. Burrage, copper magnate and associate of H. H. Rogers in the Amalgamated Copper coup. Once the president of the American Orchid Society and the present owner of the 260-foot yacht *Aztec*, Burrage organized the Chile Copper Company in 1913. It was sold to Anaconda in 1923.

Sapelo Island, off the Georgia Coast, is owned by Howard E. Coffin, Detroit automobile magnate (Hudson Motors). A famed hunting ground, it boasts a large Spanish-mission residence and a blue-tiled, glass-domed swimming pool. Both Presidents Coolidge and Hoover were visitors to Sapelo, and Coffin had easy access to them at the White House.

The neighboring St. Catherine's Island is largely owned by C. M.

Keys, aviation executive, although Coffin and J. C. Wilson, aviation man, also have an interest in it. Karl Adams, son of Melvin O. Adams, onetime owner of the Boston, Revere Beach, and Lynn Railroad, owns Brewster Island, near Boston. Independent of the United States, it was seized by the government during the World War; later it was returned to Adams.

Perhaps the most ambitious island purchase was made by the late William Wrigley, Jr., Chicago chewing-gum man and sportsman, who bought Santa Catalina Island, off the California coast, for $2,000,000. Wrigley put an additional $2,000,000 into constructing a large hotel, a golf course, tennis courts, a theater and dance pavilion, and an airplane landing field. He invested $1,000,000 in a steamer to connect Santa Catalina with the mainland.

Two hundred of the wealthiest families joined before the war in founding the Jekyll Island Club, on Jekyll Island, off the Georgia coast. Among the founders were Morgans, Drexels, Bakers, Goulds, Rockefellers, Carnegies, and Du Ponts. The natural yacht basin and sweeping beaches make it an attractive spot in which to rest after grappling with the problem of squeezing more money from the world markets. Not given to associating much with his pecuniary peers, Henry Ford has spent a good deal of time there.

## III

While the foregoing sheds some light on how the rich manage to dissipate a part of their income in personal indulgence, only a fraction of the story is told. In conclusion the exposition will center briefly upon expenditures for yachts, pipe organs, horses, private railways, private railroad cars, airplanes, and a few unique extravagances.

### Yachts

After the country estate and garden, the yacht seems to be the most compelling item of expense in the multimillionaire's domestic budget. More than thirty yachts are owned by the Du Pont family, which seems to be the greatest collective private yacht owner in the world. According to *Lloyd's Register of American Yachts* (1935), Irénée du Pont owns the *Icacos* (60' 10"); Lammot du Pont owns the *Nemea* (76'); Pierre S. du Pont III owns the *Barlovento* (50'); the estate of

Alfred I. du Pont owns the *Gadfly* (101' 6"), the *Mummy* (44'), and the *Nenemoosha* (125' 5"); A. Felix du Pont owns the *Orthia* (73' 2"); E. F. du Pont owns the *Bob-Kat* (24' 10"); E. Paul du Pont owns the *Theano* (58' 6"); Ernest du Pont owns the *Edris* (74') and the *Ponjola* (38' 8"); Eugene E. du Pont owns *High Tide* (50'); F. V. du Pont owns *Tech Jr.* (84' 2"); Henry Belin du Pont owns *Nor' Easter* (54'); Henry F. du Pont owns the *Sea Urchin* (35'); R. R. M. Carpenter, married into the Du Pont family, owns the *Galaxy* (121' 8") and the *Harmony* (95'); W. C. Carpenter, Jr., owns the *Grey Gull* (65' 4"); and Donaldson Brown, vice-president of General Motors Corporation and a Du Pont son-in-law, owns the *Oceania* (149' 2").

The Forbes family of Boston is credited by Lloyd's with the ownership of thirteen yachts, of relatively moderate sizes. George W. C. Drexel of Philadelphia owns five yachts: the *Ace* (48'), the *Akbar* (56' 8"), the *Alcedo* (175'), the *Atrypa* (62' 6") and the *Aztec* (40'). The Vanderbilt family owns ten yachts, not including the America Cup defenders. Brigadier General Cornelius Vanderbilt owns the *Winchester* (225'); F. W. Vanderbilt owns the *Leander* and the *Vedette* (82' and 148'); Harold S. Vanderbilt owns the *Prestige* (54'), the *Vagrant* (80'), and the *Vara* (149'); Harold S. Vanderbilt and Associates own the *Rainbow* and the *Ranger*, international cup contenders; William H. Vanderbilt owns the *Arrow* (73'); William K. Vanderbilt owns the *Alva* (259' 2") and the *Ara* (213'). The Whitney (Standard Oil) family has three yachts: the *Adventure* (57' 6"), the *Aphrodite* (72'), and the *Captiva* (101' 9"). Frederick H. Prince owns three yachts, the *Aide de Camp* (102'), the *Lone Star* (161' 9"), and the *Weetamoe* (83'). The Pratt family has four yachts; the Reynolds and Rogers families have two yachts each; Winthrop W. Aldrich has four, including the 102-foot *Wayfarer*; the George F. Baker family has three, including the *Viking* (217' 6"), thirteen-hundred-ton vessel on which the younger Baker died in the Pacific; the Baruch and Bedford families have four each; the Blumenthals own three; Barron Collier, advertising promoter, owns seven, including the 147-foot *Florida*; the De Forests have four; the Donahues have two; the Fisher family has five, including the 196-foot *Nakhoda* and the 105-foot *Margaret F. III*; Edsel B. Ford has two, including the 114-foot

*Onika*; the Guggenheims have three, including the 204-foot *Trillora* and the 105-foot *Leonie;* the Harknesses have three, including the 179-foot *Cythera*; the Huttons have three, including the 254-foot *Hussar*; the Jennings family has five; A. Atwater Kent also has five, including the 169-foot *Whileaway*; the Lippincotts, Philadelphia publishers, have six; the Charles E. F. McCanns (Woolworth) have three, including the 206-foot *Chalena*; the Mellons have two, including the 187-foot *Vagabondia*; the Metcalfs have four, including the 134-foot *Felicia* and the 109-foot *Sachem*; the Reynolds have two, including the 113-foot *Zapala*; and great cruisers that are really small transatlantic liners, luxuriously equipped, are owned by others.

Some of the biggest yachts, their owners, and their estimated costs exclusive of the luxurious furnishings and fittings, are as follows:

| | Steam Yachts | | |
|---|---|---|---|
| Owner | Name | Length in feet | Original cost |
| Mrs. Richard M. Cadwalader | *Savarona* | 408 | $2,500,000 |
| J. P. Morgan | *Corsair* | 344 | 2,000,000 |
| George F. Baker | *Viking* | 272 | 1,225,000 |
| Mrs. Anna Dodge Dillman | *Delphine* | 258 | 2,000,000 |

Displacement of these four ships is 1,200 to 4,700 gross tons

| | Diesel Yachts | | |
|---|---|---|---|
| Owner | Name | Length in feet | Original cost |
| Julius Forstmann | *Orion* | 333 | $2,000,000 |
| Mrs. William Boyce Thompson | *Alder* | 294 | 1,800,000 |
| Eldridge R. Johnson | *Caroline* | 279 | 1,000,000 |
| William K. Vanderbilt | *Alva* | 264 | 1,250,000 |
| Vincent Astor | *Nourmahal* | 264 | 1,250,000 |
| Bertha M. Fisher | *Nakhoda* | 235 | 1,250,000 |
| Walter O. Briggs | *Cambriona* | 235 | 1,250,000 |
| Alfred P. Sloan, Jr. | *Rene* | 235 | 1,250,000 |
| Mrs. Mary L. C. Bok | *Lyndonia* | 230 | 450,000 |
| Julius Fleischmann | *Camargo* | 225 | 850,000 |
| Frederick H. Prince | *Lone Star* | 172 | 575,000 |
| David C. Whitney | *Sumar* | 160 | 550,000 |

To operate the *Corsair* for a year is said to cost $250,000 to $500,000, one trip to England costing $50,000. Although the *Corsair* cost $2,000,000, it probably represents an investment of double that amount owing to the expense of periodic reconditioning. The cost of operating the *Alder* is reported to be $175,000 a year. Once included in its equipment was a $25,000 pipe organ, installed by the former owner, Mrs. Cadwalader of Philadelphia; it is still fitted with antique rugs and tapestries, gold-plated bathroom fixtures. The interior fittings of all the big yachts, truth to tell, often cost as much as the ships themselves.

Vanderbilt's *Alva* is equipped with an airplane cradle on the afterdeck and the $75,000 plane carried is half the size of the *China Clipper*. The ship's equipment also includes motorboats and express cruisers which can be rapidly launched.

Some other famous large yachts are Colonel Edward A. Deeds' *Lotosland*, a 2,500-horsepower Diesel ship 203 feet in length, the Doheny family's 293-foot *Casiana*, Allison V. Armour's 220-foot *Utowana*, E. L. Cord's 175-foot *Virginia*, Arthur Curtiss James' 165-foot *Aloha*, William B. Leeds' 162-foot *Moana*, H. E. Manville's 215-foot *Hi-Esmaro*, Ogden L. Mills' 161-foot *Avalon*, Mrs. Moses Taylor's 258-foot *Iolanda*, Harrison Williams' 210-foot *Warrior*, and George Whitney's 108-foot *Wanderer*.

Although many yachts are owned at one time by a rich family, in serial order the families acquire and dispose of whole fleets of vessels, much as the man of ordinary means buys and discards shoes. The Vanderbilts in their time have worn out more than fifty yachts of various sizes, mostly large. According to *Fortune*, one builder has delivered fourteen vessels to the Fisher brothers, seven to John N. Willys, seven to Walter P. Chrysler, and twenty-four to General Motors officials.

Richard J. Reynolds, Jr., who inherited $20,000,000 from his father and $100,000 a year from a trust fund, was attracted to yachting by a stipulation in the will that for every dollar he earned two more should be paid him by the estate. Young Reynolds bought a Norwegian freighter, christened her the *Harpoon*, and set her to work as a tramp steamer. The Hartford family (Great Atlantic and Pacific Tea Stores) acquired the four-masted schooner *Joseph Conrad* from Allen

Villiers, the author, and use it as a yacht. James A. Farrell, Brady son-in-law and former president of the United States Steel Corporation, owns the *Tusitala,* largest windjammer extant, which alternates as a yacht and a cargo vessel.

## Pipe Organs

Although the wealthy families are not perceptibly musical they plunge heavily on expensive pipe organs, which are an honorific badge of the ability to dissipate funds and at the same time serve to impress country cousins, servants, and business acquaintances. The pipe organ, it may be observed, is virtually an obsolete instrument, and survives largely because of its medieval religious associations. In flexibility of range it has been superseded by the piano; in sonority and volume it has been superseded by the modern symphony orchestra, the faithful recordings of which may be played by anyone on the phonograph. But both recorded symphonies and pianos are within the reach of the lower classes; they do not confer honorific pecuniary distinction upon their owners.

While it would be about as expensive to maintain a private string quartet as a pipe organ, few of the wealthy families have seen fit to do so; for there is not much to display in four musicians holding fiddles of various sizes. The late E. J. de Coppet, Swiss-American broker, subsidized for many years the famed Flonzaley Quartet, named after his Swiss residence, and enjoyed its music in private when the organization was not on tour. John W. Garrett, of Baltimore, former Ambassador to Italy, in part financed the Stradivarius Quartet, which played for him in his Baltimore home and at the Embassy in Rome. Elizabeth Sprague Coolidge has done much for chamber music. The late Paul M. Warburg played the violin and hobnobbed a good deal with string-quartet players, and one of his nephews is a prominent cellist. But such evidences of a truly refined musical taste among members of our wealthiest families are seldom encountered.

The most expensive privately owned pipe organ in America is Pierre du Pont's Longwood instrument, which cost $250,000. The organ in Charles M. Schwab's Riverside Drive New York château would cost $200,000 to duplicate today. Pipe-organ installations have been made by Aeolian or Wurlitzer for Felix M. Warburg, William K. Vanderbilt, John D. Rockefeller, Sr., John D. Rockefeller, Jr., Mrs. H. McK. Twombly (who is a Vanderbilt), Andrew W. Mellon, and Edsel Ford. The Skinner Organ Company has made installations for Arthur Curtiss James, Dudley S. Blossom, and Robert Law. Estey pipe organs have been installed for Henry Ford, Harry F. Sinclair, and for Mrs. Cadwalader on her yacht. These, of course, are only a few of the rich individuals who can astound dinner guests with a salvo of Bach fugues.

### Private Railway Cars and Railroads

The private railroad car, once an indispensable adjunct to ostentatious display, is gradually giving way to the private airplane cruiser, but among the magnates of modern democracy who still own their own railroad cars are Albert Burrage, the estate of Nicholas F. Brady, Charles Clark, Herbert Coppell, Richard Crane, Jr., J. P. Donahue, Max C. Fleischmann, Henry Ford, the estate of E. Palmer Gavit, Eugene G. Grace, Edward Harkness, William Randolph Hearst, E. F. Hutton, Edward B. McLean, John Raskob, Jacob Replogle, John Ringling, Walter J. Salmon, Mrs. Elmer Schlesinger, Charles M. Schwab, Harry F. Sinclair, Paul Block, John A. Vietor (factoring), Harry Payne Whitney estate, Mrs. Payne Whitney, Joseph E. Widener, and John D. Rockefeller. Some corporations maintain private railroad cars so that officials and their guests may travel about in privacy, and among them are the Anaconda Copper Mining Company and the General Motors Corporation.

The cost of each car, depending upon interior furnishings, ranges from $85,000 to $125,000; the annual maintenance runs from $35,000 to $50,000. Wealthy travelers who do not own a private railway coach find it less troublesome to rent one from the Pullman Company at $75 per day plus twenty-five regular fares for the distance traveled and ten per cent of the prescribed surcharges.

Much has been made of the fact that a railroad spur penetrates the Hearst San Simeon ranch; it is not generally known that many of the big estates, including the Rockefellers', have these railroad sidings. Vincent Astor, indeed, has an entire miniature steam railroad, with five locomotives, on his place at Rhinebeck, New York. Henry Huntington also has a steam railway for travel about his New York estate. Boies Penrose, nephew of the late politician, has a mile-long railway on his estate outside Philadelphia. There are hundreds of these expensive little passenger-carrying railroads, some electrified, on estates throughout the country.

## Horses

Horses absorb a good deal of a millionaire's money, although the racing stables, representing investments of $1,000,000 to $5,000,000, are often a source of profit. The horses of Harry Payne Whitney in the 1926 season, for example, won $407,139 in prizes. Gallant Fox, owned by Joseph E. Widener, alone won $308,275 in 1930. Most of the publicized racers are, of course, owned by the wealthiest families, who take naturally to the "Sport of Kings."

Belmont Park and $1,750,000 Hialeah Park, the latter in Miami, are largely owned by Widener, and many other rich turfmen are also coming to look upon the sport, tied up as it is with betting, news syndicates, and communications systems, as a source of revenue. The Du Ponts, for example, just recently built a public racing track in Delaware. All the big tracks are owned by syndicates of the plutocracy.

The big stables, too, are owned by the richest families. Mrs. Henry Carnegie Phipps owns the Wheatley Stable with her brother, Ogden L. Mills. Mrs. Graham Fair Vanderbilt owns the Fair Stables. The Whitney stables at Brookdale Farm, which cost about $2,000,000, are perhaps the most famous; sometimes there are Whitney horses racing at as many as sixteen different tracks. The stables of Isabel Dodge Sloan (automobiles) are valued at $1,000,000 and her horse, Cavalcade, was the outstanding performer of the 1934 season. Mrs. Edward V. Hartford (chain groceries) specializes in steeple-chasers, of which she possesses perhaps the finest string in the country. An indication of the cost of operating the big stables may be gleaned from the annual cost of the Whitney stable, which is said to run up to $100,000, excluding transportation charges for the horses.

Among the fifty members of the exclusive Jockey Club, which rules American racing, are Perry Belmont, Raymond Belmont, Marshall Field, Robert L. Gerry, W. A. Harriman, Pierre Lorillard,

Clarence H. Mackay, Ogden L. Mills, H. C. Phipps, Herbert L. Pratt, John Sanford, Cornelius Vanderbilt ("Sonny") Whitney, John Hay ("Jock") Whitney, Richard Whitney (former president of the Stock Exchange, brother of the Morgan partner, George Whitney, but not a member of the Standard Oil family), George D. Widener, Joseph E. Widener, P. A. B. Widener, and William Woodward, president of the Central Hanover Bank and Trust Company.

Polo, upon which is expended an estimated $5,000,000 annually, is dominated completely by about forty players from seventeen of the richest families, although about 5,000 persons are currently believed to play the game in some form. Each serious polo player requires a whole string of tough ponies, for the game is exceedingly wearing on the mounts. Quite fittingly, the game was introduced in the United States by the late Harry Payne Whitney.

Leading polo players of America are Devereaux Milburn, son of a corporation lawyer, polo protégé of the late Harry Payne Whitney, and husband of Nancy Steele, who is a daughter of Morgan-partner Charles Steele; Francis Skiddy von Stade, husband of Kathryn N. Steele, another of Charles Steele's daughters; Louis E. Stoddard, son of a banker and married first to the daughter of a wealthy Pittsburgh distiller and then to the daughter of an early associate of the elder Rockefeller; Robert E. Strawbridge, Jr., of the Philadelphia department-store family, who married a granddaughter of the late George F. Baker I; D. Stewart Iglehart, president of W. R. Grace and Company (Latin American shipping) and his sons; Thomas Hitchcock, Jr., grandson of William W. Corcoran, Washington banker, and associated in Wall Street with Lehman Brothers; Cornelius Vanderbilt Whitney and John Hay Whitney; James Watson Webb, grandson of Cornelius Vanderbilt I and husband of Electra Havemeyer; William A. Harriman, son of E. H. Harriman and brother of Mrs. Robert L. Gerry; Winston and Raymond Guest, grandchildren of Henry Phipps—Winston is married to Helena McCann (Woolworth); three sons of John S. Phipps; three Bostwicks, descended from Jabez Bostwick, early associate of the elder Rockefeller (Dunbar Bostwick married Electra Webb, daughter of James Watson Webb and Electra Havemeyer); James P. Mills, great-grandson of Anthony J. Drexel and husband of a granddaughter of Francis G. du Pont; and Stephen Sanford.

The show-horse field, representing an investment of about $50,000-000, is also dominated by the wealthiest families through the Association of American Horse Shows, two of whose directors are H. E. Manville and William du Pont, Jr., and some of whose past directors have been Oliver Harriman, Pierre Lorillard, Jr., and William H. Vanderbilt.

### Automobiles

Since instalment buying and second-hand marts have enabled even relatively poor people to own some sort of motor-car, the rich families can achieve the distinction of honorific display in this field only by sheer quantity. The richest families, therefore, own from 25 to 50 automobiles, with some families in possession of several hundred. The automobile license records in the Atlantic seaboard states suggest, for example, that the Du Pont family alone owns more than 500 private passenger automobiles. The Vanderbilt family also seems to have more than 500.

Helen Worden in her impressionistic *Society Circus* says that William Leeds has had as many as one hundred Lincolns in his garage at Oyster Bay, that Lorraine Manville owns a "fleet" of cars, and that the Edward T. Stotesbury garage at Palm Beach holds forty cars. She is authority as well for the statement that Pierre du Pont keeps cars in New York and Paris, and chauffeurs, too, merely for the use of his friends.

In 1934 Doris Duke owned nine cars, one of them a $14,000 Dusenberg, according to *Time* (September 17, 1934). The $18,000,000 estate of Mrs. Elizabeth Mills Reid, widow of Whitelaw Reid, in 1934 included sixteen private automobiles as well as a $300,000 pearl necklace. *Time* (September 9, 1929) reports that E. H. R. Green, recently deceased son of Hetty Green, owned twenty-five automobiles. An invalid, he used only an old electric car on the grounds of his estate until he procured a specially built machine from the General Electric Company. This car had no clutch or gear-shift, only a brake and an accelerator. Pleased with this conveyance, he ordered a limousine like it.

The cost of these special cars was not indicated, but Walter P. Chrysler in 1934 presented his son with a $20,000 custom-built automobile that boasted such features as a built-in cocktail bar, a special rack for holding glasses, and silverware for use at emergency picnics. A $3,000 leopard-skin robe—its cost exceeding the price of the average car—was thrown in for good measure.

Cornelius Vanderbilt, Jr., spent part of the season 1936–37 touring Europe in an expensive custom-built trailer that contained a cocktail bar, electric kitchen, and various other engaging features. The trailer was the scene of many a gay party in the courtyards of castles en route, and in England especially it served to introduce a fresh note into upper-class life.

The multimillionaire's estate is not, of course, complete without station wagons, agricultural trucks, trailers, motorcycles, and various other utilitarian vehicles in addition to the fleet of limousines, sedans, roadsters, broughams, cabriolets, and touring cars. If the estate adjoins a body of water, the boat-house, in addition to canoes, dories, and rafts, will contain from five to ten launches and speed-boats, in which to convey parties to the distant anchored steam yacht or auxiliary sailing schooner.

### Airplanes

The rich have discovered a new pastime and a fruitful avenue of expenditure in air transport. They are beginning to acquire air yachts, and some wealthy air enthusiasts have even equipped their ocean-going yachts with auxiliary planes. The largest estates, too, now have their private airplane landing fields, while at Port Washington, Long Island, there are already two big millionaires' hangars. At Hicksville, Long Island, the Aviation Country Club has been opened with 200 wealthy members whose names appear in the *Social Register*. *Fortune* (August, 1937) relates that Robert R. McCormick, E. R. Harriman, and Marshall Field have purchased $47,000 twin-engine Grumman amphibian air yachts which seat six, attain a speed of 170 miles per hour, and have a cruising range of 1,000 miles. New York City, using Works Progress Administration funds, has built sea-plane ramps at the foot of Wall Street and of Thirty-first Street for millionaire commuters from Long Island estates; Henry P. Davison,

Jr., of J. P. Morgan and Company, daily flies to town in a Stinson. Other regular commuters in their private airplanes are Marshall Field, Franz Schneider, Jr., and Arthur M. Anderson, Morgan partner.

## Children

In upper-class circles minors may prove as expensive as divorced mates, who often take a goodly fraction of the absentee revenues. Little Gloria Morgan Vanderbilt, who was worth $3,667,814.79 in her own right as of December 27, 1935, incurred rather strange living expenses while her custody was disputed by her mother and her aunt. Pending settlement of the case, the mother was allowed $34,500 for the child's household expenses and $9,000 for her own personal needs. Among Gloria's childish expenses for 1935 were $175.79 for soda water and ginger ale; $125 for the medical treatment of a cat from November, 1935, to January, 1936; $30.75 for the rental of a motion picture projector so that she would not run the risk of catching cold in a theater; $415 for toys; $153 for a single dress; $1,000 for a month's rent of a summer house; $125 for a French tutor for a month (the equivalent of the ailing cat's medical care); $30 for one hat; $1,391 for dental and medical care from March to November, 1935; $1,995 for detectives' hire; $11,515.39 for servants' hire; and $12,000 for legal expenses. Lucy Cotton Thomas, nine-year-old heiress, was allowed the following expenses pending settlement of her estate: $1,500 per month for a non-housekeeping apartment; $70 a week for groceries; $150 a month piano rental; $71 a month for toys; $24 a month for massage; $55 a month for drugs; $37 a month for telephone calls; and $350 a month for a chauffeur and a maid.

The average cost of a delivery at Doctors' Hospital, where most of the rich babies are born, is $10,000, according to Helen Worden. The price may run higher if the mother is ensconced in one of the suites on the tenth floor and has it decorated by her personal household decorator, but the mother will always have the satisfaction of knowing that J. P. Morgan was chairman of the board of directors during the trying period, and the cost may therefore be well worthwhile.

*Clothes*

Wealthy women notoriously spend a king's ransom on their clothing, but it is not, perhaps, generally known that rich men often spend more on their clothes in a year than a professor earns. The men, to be sure, still do not begin to compete with the women. *Fortune* (November, 1932) tells us that Clarence Mackay spends $7,000 a year on his wardrobe, and that in 1929 men like Herbert Bayard Swope, H. F. du Pont, and Frederick Rentschler paid $225 per custom-tailored suit at Twyeffort's. Shoes cost the wealthy man up to $50, and he may own several dozen pairs. Schedules of estates reveal that wealthy men often leave several hundred suits of clothes, several hundred shirts, dozens of pairs of shoes, etc.

Stuart Chase, in *The New Republic,* May 25, 1927, cites an analysis of the composite Park Avenue budget for 1927 which was made by the Park Avenue Association. Placing its figures arbitrarily at 25 per cent below actual findings in order to be safely conservative, the Park Avenue Association said that 4,000 families residing on Park Avenue had an annual composite budget of $280,000,000. Of this sum 4,000 women and their daughters spend $85,000,000 annually on their clothes, or $21,000 for each mother and one daughter, while the fathers and sons spend $19,000,000 or $4,500 per year on clothes. Apartment rentals average $1,500 per room annually, with $11,500 paid for a ten-room apartment and $23,000 for a twenty-room establishment. Decorations alone cost $100,000 on the average for each apartment, and the average rental of each apartment was $15,000. Food for the 4,000 and their servants cost $32,000,000, or $8,000 per family; jewelry cost $20,000,000, or $5,000 per family; automobiles cost $16,000,000, or $4,000 per family; travel cost $15,000,000; beauty shop expenditures, $8,000,000; yachts, $7,000,000; amusements, $5,000,000; flowers, candy, and small gifts, $10,000,000; and charity, $5,000,000. *The World,* commenting on these data, estimated that liquor expenditures were $15,000,000, or $4,000 per family annually. As the foregoing figures applied to a period before the peak of the "prosperity" boom devastated the land, they may be assumed to apply approximately to 1937 as well.

All these wasteful expenditures of the rich, only a few of which have been briefly enumerated, are extenuated by hired apologists on the ground that they give many people work—in the luxury trades, in domestic service, in the garages, stables, and gardens, and on board the yachts. It is not realized, it seems, that if the money wasted by the rich in personal indulgence were taken in taxes and put into the building of needed hospitals, schools, playgrounds, clinics, low-rent apartment buildings, farm homes, sanatoria, rest homes, and recreation clubs for the mass of Americans, the persons now given employment by the wealthy would obtain work of a more constructive character in these other fields.

But so firmly convinced are some of the rich that their expenditures are a boon to mankind—because collectively they keep 400,000 to 700,000 persons directly or indirectly employed—that a wealthy man like E. F. Hutton during the depth of the depression in 1931 urged wealthy yachtsmen, in the cause of unemployment relief, to keep their yachts in commission instead of hiding them in drydocks out of fear of provoking the poor. Mr. Hutton pointed out that it costs $100,000 to keep the average two-hundred-footer in commission for five months, and he seemed to feel that if all the big boat-owners would follow his suggestion the nation might yacht its way out of the depression.

Marine observers, however, were quick to charge that Mr. Hutton and his friends invariably had their ships built in Germany, effecting a saving of $500,000 per vessel through the wage-differential of 48 cents an hour, and so were depriving American shipyard workers of employment. It was estimated that the philanthropic-minded Mr. Hutton had to pay an import duty of $375,000 on his *Hussar* II, and this sum alone would have provided wages for many workers.

Man has such a capacity for rationalization that when he finds himself affluent and able to spend as he pleases he is quick to justify his most indefensible expenditures on the ground that they give some people employment. There is probably no rich person who upon quaffing a glass of champagne does not experience a happy glow of pleasure at the thought of all the vintners, bottlers, freighters, and servants to whom his simple act has given livelihood. But the same sort of reasoning could be employed by the burglar who, to prove that his occupation was economically constructive, could cite the great number of police, judges, bailiffs, wardens, prison builders, criminologists and detective story writers to whom his activities gave remunerative employment.

# XII

## The "New Deal"—and After

### I

NOTHING would be more gratifying than to be able to say at this juncture that the swashbuckling administration of Franklin D. Roosevelt, with all its war cries against "the money-changers in the temple," the "economic royalists," and the "gold-plated anarchists," had succeeded in placing a checkrein and halter on the restless, powerful, self-centered clans of great wealth. But such a conclusion would not, unfortunately, be justified by the facts.

Roosevelt's "New Deal" at its inception in 1933 was denounced by the Communists as semi-fascist, was hailed by the Socialists as semi-socialistic, and was quietly welcomed by apprehensive Democrats and Republicans alike as their salvation. J. P. Morgan, for example, stepped forward with indecent celerity and publicly blessed the abandonment of the gold standard; this rite was a clear signal to conservatives to remain calm.

But, as events unfolded, the Communist Party came to look more and more tolerantly, albeit skeptically, upon the "New Deal," and the Socialist Party turned away from it, professing to discern portents of a budding fascist authoritarianism, while conservative Democrats and Republicans soon came to regard it with more or less feigned alarm as bolshevistic.

These were all acutely partisan reactions, predicated upon the shifting political and economic needs of each faction, but they illustrated concretely that the "New Deal" was born of crisis and has had its existence in a period of confusion and transition.

Yet in the face of all the hostile partisan cries the Western progressive Republicans and Farmer-Laborites as well as liberal Democrats found the "New Deal," on the whole, to their liking; and millions

of people, saved from downright starvation, and returned by the
Federal government to their pre-Hoover condition of chronic malnutrition and insecurity, were pathetically grateful to it. It was these
latter, overjoyed at having their immediate needs met by an un-
expectedly and mysteriously benign government, that returned
Roosevelt to office in 1936 by an overwhelming plurality. However,
the Administration, in succoring the pauperized millions, acted from
motives that were not primarily benevolent.

The final verdict on the "New Deal" is, of course, impossible to
formulate, for it is still evolving. But certain conclusions may be
tentatively ventured on such factual evidence as is available, and
these conclusions are here sought in a frankly critical spirit in the
hope of avoiding those mistakes in judgment made by sentimental
observers during the administrations of Wilson and the first Roosevelt.

The "New Deal," while subject to discriminating criticism, certainly, has not been without progressive ingredients that deserve the
support of liberals and humanitarians in a world where nothing is
perfect; and such support has been merited more especially by reason
of the fact that political leaders of the Left—Communists, Farmer-
Laborites, Socialists—have thus far been unable to develop a common, practical program of action that would attract the adherence
of wide sections of the electorate.

The first conclusion drawn from the facts to be reviewed in this
chapter is that the "New Deal" is not revolutionary nor radical in
any sense; on the contrary, it is conservative. Its mild, tentative
reformist coloration is but a necessary concession in the face of widespread unrest. In its basic tenets and practical aims the "New Deal"
is well within the American political tradition. It is a stanch exponent
of Jackson's maxim that "to the victor belong the spoils." It believes
in punishing its enemies and rewarding its friends, especially those
that have contributed generously to its campaigns. And Franklin D.
Roosevelt, like Wilson and the first Roosevelt, has been an adept in
concealing group economic objectives under a gloss of pleasant
rhetoric.

Circumstances have contrived to lend some support to President
Roosevelt's forensic assertion that his program is actuated by purely

philanthropic motives; yet those among the economically disinherited who believe the "New Deal" will lead them into a promised land of social security and "the full life" are probably due for a rough awakening. It is safe to predict that when the "New Deal" is over the poor will be no richer, the rich no poorer.

This observation could be buttressed by citation of many facts, of which the most salient one will be cited here. *The New Republic* (August 11, 1937) published, on the basis of figures obtained from reports of the Securities and Exchange Commission and the Department of Labor, a study of the yearly salaries of officials and average weekly wages of workers of 133 leading corporations in 1936. The wage averages, of course, did not prevail throughout the year. The salaries of corporation officials varied from $25,000 to $260,000, and were received in return for standardized, often perfunctory duties. Weekly wages of workers as of December, 1936, ranged from $15.86 to $38.25. The low of $15.86 prevailed throughout the tobacco industry—American Tobacco Company, Consolidated Cigar Corporation, General Cigar Company, P. Lorillard, R. J. Reynolds Tobacco Company, and United States Tobacco Company—all sturdy "New Dealers" and contributors to the Roosevelt campaign funds. George W. Hill, president of the American Tobacco Company, on the other hand, drew $246,173, and two of his associates received $125,000 each. Hill, a gusty innovator of advertising slogans, was rewarded at a rate twenty times greater than such epochal intellects as Professor Albert Einstein or Professor John Dewey.

The "New Deal," in brief, is not by any means a "people's coalition" directed against the vested interests that have seized everything of pecuniary value in the land. It is only in the remarks of the President and of his supporters that it is made to appear as such. In essence the "New Deal" represents one faction of great wealth—the light-goods industrialists—pitted in bitter political struggle against another faction—the capital-goods industrialists. Roosevelt, addicted as he is to verbal castigation of the wealthy, was supported in 1932 and again in 1936 by some of the richest families of the country. But because the juntas of the rich against which the presidential barbs were directly aimed were better publicized than those which stood behind him, the belief became prevalent that the "New Deal" was hostile to great aggregates of wealth. Some of its tax policies lent color to this misconception, which will not be eradicated until it is generally realized that the "New Deal" merely represents an unfamiliar though orthodox way of dealing with problems within a capitalistic context.

From its beginning the "New Deal" was underwritten by those wealthy individuals whose revenues derive primarily from direct exploitation of the retail market—department-store owners, textile fabricators, cigarette manufacturers, independent industrialists, processors and distributors, and big real-estate operators. Excepting the latter, these comprise the light-industries group. And because the task of the "New Deal" was to restore prosperity to these beleaguered capitalists by restoring purchasing power to the populace, it succeeded in rallying around itself organized labor and the farmers; for in expanding popular purchasing power certain immediate small benefits accrued to these latter. The "New Deal's" big public works program, combined with unemployment relief, operated further to spread purchasing power and at the same time solved the immediate economic problem of millions of paupers, who thereafter became its grateful supporters.

Candor is, perhaps, the most effective form of deceit in politics, and President Roosevelt has frequently been very candid about the aims of his administration, knowing that his frankness would cost him nothing, since his partisan critics were bound to scoff at whatever he might say. He has constantly reiterated that the basic aim of the "New Deal" was to revive purchasing power, and that in so doing it was following a middle-of-the-road course. It has been no part of the strategy of the Republicans to disclose what the actual "New Deal" aims are, because to do so would disclose the political essence of the Republican as well as of the Democratic Party: special favors for wealthy supporters. The Republicans have perforce been obliged to criticize the "New Deal" unrealistically as a radical regime that is undermining the sacred, blood-hallowed structure of American society. The deliberately false accusations of radicalism have, ironically, gained supporters for the "New Deal" among the economically disinherited and have failed to frighten middle-grounders.

The heavy industries, including the banks, which are bound inextricably to heavy industry by the latter's constant need for new capital, ran the country as they pleased during the Harding, Coolidge, and Hoover Administrations. Aiming always at monopoly control of industry, the banks were committed under Hoover to the policy of allowing the depression to "take its course." Further deflation would, indeed, have brought the sinking light industries and merchandising enterprises under the dominion of the banks, and monopoly centralization of America's economic apparatus would have been virtually completed. The banks and heavy industries, of course, did not want to see popular purchasing power wiped out completely, although in retrospect it may seem that they did. They were simply committed to reviving purchasing power on a lower price level, with all of industry under their control.

The light-goods industrialists and merchants, seeing in this course their virtual extinction so far as their independent status was concerned, were quick to take advantage of Hoover's unpopularity to install the "New Deal," espousing policies for which the Democratic Party has always more or less stood. So-called economic reforms under the "New Deal" have all, it is pertinent to observe, been engineered at the expense of the big banks and the heavy industries. The 1936 measure taxing corporate surpluses, for example, was directed only at the heavy industries and banks, which had built up big surpluses in the 1920's and had preserved them by dropping millions of workmen from their pay rolls during the depression. The discharge of these millions and their consequent loss of purchasing power had the effect of cutting into the surpluses of the light industries, consisting in the main of inventories which had to be turned over several times annually in order for profits to be made. The "New Deal" light industrialists, to protect themselves against a recurrence of such destruction of the retail market by general layoffs throughout heavy industry, have encouraged the unionization program of John L. Lewis and the Committee for Industrial Organization. This program has been directed to date only against the citadels of heavy industry— steel, oil, chemicals, coal, and automobiles—and although the C. I. O. will in time probably take light industry under its jurisdiction this will be a matter of little concern to light industrialists, secure in the knowledge that the employment policy of heavy industry is locked in a vise.

The "New Deal," in short, has represented one side of a grave split in the camp of the big capitalists, and although fundamental questions relating to capitalism and its basic theory have not really been in dispute, the method of coping with capitalist crisis has very definitely been in violent dispute. The "New Dealers" are those who, consciously or unconsciously, are working to smash the synthesis of finance capital completed under Harding, Coolidge, and Hoover. They are trying, by the political methods of finance capital itself, and by novel political forms inspired by communism, fascism, and liberal democracy, to return to the capitalism of the individual industrial and mercantile entrepreneurs who were free of the overlordship of banks and banking alliances. By drawing upon the forms of the future, they hope to resuscitate the political past.

It has, however, been no part of the "New Deal's" intention to crush heavy industry and banking. The aim appears to have been merely to bring them into parity with the light goods and merchandising enterprises. But the details of the reforms which have whittled down the power of heavy industrialists and bankers are interesting, and will be touched upon.

## II

There was nothing in the prepresidential career of Franklin D. Roosevelt which would have led anyone to surmise that he would espouse such ameliorative social principles as many observers believe he stands for and as he himself professes to stand for. Yet President Roosevelt is not, it must in fairness be admitted, hostile to reform—unless the reform threatens one of his powerful partisans.

Son of a wealthy aristocratic family intermarried with the Astor and other great clans, now including the Du Ponts, Roosevelt was educated at Groton and Harvard. Before the World War he was a member of the New York State Legislature, and was named Assistant Secretary of the Navy (1913-1920) because he supported the campaign for Wilson's nomination in 1912. In 1920 he was given the Democratic vice-presidential nomination apparently only for the reason that his name was Roosevelt, and his campaign speeches then were notable chiefly for their callow militaristic bias. He advocated, among other things, universal military training in the schools. Early in his presidential career he revived some of these sentiments in a saber-rattling speech before the American Legion in Chicago.

After an unfortunate illness, from which he recovered, Roosevelt in 1924 and again in 1928 advanced himself politically by placing Alfred E. Smith in nomination for the presidency at two Democratic conventions. In 1928 Roosevelt was rewarded with the second highest office in the nation when Smith, recognizing the potency of the Roosevelt name in building up a vote-getting Democratic ticket, procured for him the Democratic gubernatorial nomination in New York. Roosevelt captured the governorship, while Smith lost the state.

As Governor of New York Roosevelt's only noticeable departure from the Smith gubernatorial policies related to electric power. Whereas Smith had advocated the building of state-owned power generators and no more, Roosevelt came out for state transmission of power as well, where satisfactory contracts could not be negotiated with private companies. This embellishment gained for him many influential supporters among liberals, who are accustomed to expect little in a world where tougher personalities habitually take all.

The oratorical passion for the underdog which Roosevelt later exhibited as President was not to be found in any of his words or deeds as Governor, although it may well be, as friends have said, that his illness aroused in him a profound sympathy for the problems of the helpless throughout society.

His bid for the presidency in 1932, it is significant, was not reinforced by an espousal of any of the dynamic social issues abroad in the land. Candidate Roosevelt contented himself with criticizing the Hoover Administration for its ineptitudes and for its extravagant expenditures, which he promised to curtail by consolidating government bureaus. The campaign strategy was obviously to take advantage of the unpopularity of President Hoover, and to promise as little as possible. In the speeches of Roosevelt and his partisans there was no foretaste whatever of the heady brew to come, and it was the consensus of political observers that the country voted less for

Roosevelt, who stood for nothing in particular at the time, than against Hoover.

Victory for Roosevelt on the fourth ballot at the Chicago Democratic convention was contrived through a typically American political deal between William Randolph Hearst, William Gibbs McAdoo, John Nance Garner, and Mayor Anton Cermak of Chicago. In return for the votes of the California, Texas, and Illinois delegations, controlled by the Hearst coalition, Garner received the vice-presidential nomination, and from the vantage point of that office he was afterward to do everything in his power to sabotage progressive proposals of the "New Dealers." Failing in his attempt to corral for himself the presidential nomination, Alfred E. Smith, in concert with John J. Raskob, Bernard M. Baruch, and Hugh S. Johnson, tried to procure the nomination for Newton D. Baker, upon whom Walter Lippmann had placed a Morganatic blessing in his syndicated column. But the Smith-Du Pont-Guggenheim-Morgan forces were unsuccessful.

In his 1928 campaign for the New York governorship Roosevelt had been supported by the same faction of finance that tried to place Smith in the White House. In 1930 Roosevelt's campaign was financed by Vincent Astor, Edward S. Harkness, Bernard Baruch, Percy S. Straus (R. H. Macy and Company), Owen D. Young, and Jesse H. Jones. Except for Astor and Harkness, these were all Democratic stalwarts.

Virtually the same individuals helped reduce the heavy Democratic deficit left over from 1928. At the end of 1931 the Democratic National Committee still owed Raskob $345,250 and the County Trust Company of New York $433,766. Toward liquidation of this indebtedness during 1931 Astor gave $25,000; Pierre S. du Pont, $12,500; Percy S. Straus, M. F. Reddington, and Potter Palmer, $5,000 each; Charles H. Sabin, $2,000, etc. Early in 1932 the deficit was still further reduced by a contribution of $125,000 from Raskob and $27,000 from Pierre S. du Pont.

The largest known contributions from the camp of wealth to Roosevelt's presidential campaign fund in 1932 were as follows:

| | | |
|---|---:|---:|
| Bernard M. Baruch | $45,000 | |
| Additional for Senatorial funds | 15,000 | |
| | —— | $60,000 |
| Vincent Astor | | 35,000 |
| William H. Woodin (American Car and Foundry Company) | | 35,000 |
| Percy S. Straus (R. H. Macy and Company) | | 30,000 |
| William Randolph Hearst | | 25,000 |
| John J. Raskob | | 23,000 |
| Peter Goelet Gerry | | 22,000 |
| Morton L. Schwartz | | 20,000 |
| Jesse I. Straus (R. H. Macy and Company) | | 20,000 |
| James W. Gerard, former Ambassador to Germany | | 17,528 |
| Edward A. Guggenheim | | 17,500 |
| W. N. Reynolds | | |
| Bowman Gray | | |
| James A. Gray ⎬ R. J. Reynolds Tobacco Company | | 16,000 |
| S. Clay Williams | | |
| Joseph P. Kennedy, banker and stock market operator | | 15,000 |
| Francis P. Garvan (Brady) | | 15,000 |
| Edward S. Harkness | | 12,000 |
| Potter Palmer (Chicago real estate) | | 5,000 |
| Harry Warner (motion pictures) | | 5,000 |
| Robert Goelet | | 5,000 |
| Mrs. Harry Payne Whitney | | 5,000 |
| Herman B. Baruch | | 5,000 |
| Mrs. Sumner Welles, wife of the diplomat | | 5,000 |
| Charles R. Crane | | 4,000 |
| Cyrus H. McCormick | | 4,000 |
| Arthur Curtiss James | | 2,500 |
| Eleanor Patterson | | 2,000 |
| William K. Vanderbilt | | 1,000 |
| Harold F. McCormick | | 1,000 |
| Edward A. Filene, Boston department-store owner | | 1,000 |
| | | —————— |
| Total | | $408,528 |

Other members of these families also contributed, with the result that about $1,000,000 of the Democratic fund appears to have come from the wealthiest families. The remainder was collected by professional politicians from the host of aspirants to political berths in the new administration.

A great deal of additional financial impetus was given the Roosevelt candidacy by his espousal of the "wet" cause in the Prohibition issue; and when one includes the contributions of the wealthy families to the Association Against the Prohibition Amendment, its members primarily interested in the tax yield of a revived distilling and brewing industry, the Democratic Party funds exceeded those of the Republicans. Sums of money ranging from $10,000 to more than $100,000 were given to the anti-Prohibition organization over a period of three years by Lammot du Pont, Pierre S. du Pont, John J. Raskob, Edward S. Harkness, Richard T. Crane, Arthur Curtiss James, Eldridge R. Johnson, Marshall Field, Samuel Mather, Frederic A. Juilliard, and others.

Contributions of $5,000 to $50,000 were made in 1932 to the Republican Party by John D. Rockefeller, Sr., and Jr., Eldridge R. Johnson, Ogden L. Mills, Andrew W. Mellon, Richard B. Mellon, William Nelson Cromwell, Edward F. Hutton, Felix M. Warburg, John M. Schiff, Hallam Tuck, G. A. Tomlinson, Harvey S. Firestone, Mrs. Edward S. Harkness, Mrs. Andrew Carnegie, Mrs. John T. Pratt, Jeremiah Milbank, Alfred P. Sloan, Jr., Edward E. B. Adams, Julius Fleischmann, George M. Moffett, Herbert N. Straus, Harrison Williams, Myron C. Taylor, George D. Pratt, Harold I. Pratt, Herbert L. Pratt, Mrs. Ruth Baker Pratt, H. H. Timken, George W. Crawford, Frederick B. Pratt, Mrs. George F. Baker, L. K. Thorne, Alfred H. Loomis, Mrs. Daniel Guggenheim, Thomas W. Lamont, Murry Guggenheim, S. R. Guggenheim, Simon Guggenheim, J. P. Morgan, Josuah D. Armitage, Charles Hayden, Percy A. Rockefeller, Mr. and Mrs. Childs Frick, Howard Heinz, W. L. Mellon, Albert H. Wiggin, Clarence Wiggin, R. R. M. Carpenter (Du Pont), Silas Strawn, Archer M. Huntington, Howard M. Hanna, E. T. Weir, Robert W. Goelet, Walter E. Frew, Henry Ford, Edsel Ford, William Cooper Procter, Mortimer Fleishacker, Sidney Z. Mitchell, Lawrence C. Phipps, E. T. Stotesbury, Jasper E. Crane, Max E. F.

Fleischmann, Thomas Cochran, Anne S. Davison, George F. Baker, and Sewell Avery.

Families that contributed both to the Republicans and to the Democrats included the Du Ponts, Harknesses, Vanderbilts, Fleischmanns, McCormicks, Goelets, Whitneys, Strauses, Guggenheims, and Bradys. Where identical estates did not contribute to both parties on a family basis they often did so on a corporate basis. Many corporation officers in the lower brackets of contributors gave funds to the party formally opposed by the head of a particular clan. In this way the avenue of approach was kept open to the key men, the financial managers, in each party.

The Wall Street banks, incidentally, while Republican in politics, make a regular practice of keeping a few outstanding Democrats among their chief officers. Jackson E. Reynolds, chairman of the First National Bank, and S. Parker Gilbert and Russell C. Leffingwell, both of J. P. Morgan and Company, are all sturdy Democrats.

## III

Roosevelt upon taking office had initially to address himself to a grave emergency, for the nation was in the throes of one of those disastrous collapses which Karl Marx had predicted would one day mark the melodramatic end of the capitalist system. Banks were toppling by the hundreds all over the country, and the crashes in Detroit brought the situation uncomfortably close to New York, Chicago, Boston, and Philadelphia.

A "bank holiday" was therefore proclaimed, and the government went to work during the general shutdown to salvage the existing banking system and to repair it where it was most severely damaged. The President unmistakably betrayed his bias toward the *status quo* when he failed to propose, as he could have with exploded banks on every hand, that the government, to avoid a recurrence of the situation, take the banking system into its own hands, where it properly belonged.

But the new President's task, as he envisioned it, was merely to restore the faltering economic system to operation and then to revive popular purchasing power. Although various "New Deal" measures have been sorted by critics into "reform" and "recovery" categories, every one of them, without exception, was designed to induce recovery of the export and domestic retail markets before all else. This policy played directly into the hands of merchants and light industrialists, who were further accommodated by the government's stringent measures against heavy industry and the banks.

No part of this program was consciously formulated at first, and it is highly doubtful if any individual had the entire plan *a priori* in mind. But the economic interests of the President's closest supporters and advisers, each one of whom came forward with some pressing personal problem, made the ensuing pattern inevitable. And as time went on, the design becoming more and more conscious, those advisers that were inspired principally by their stake in heavy industry or banking dropped away, while certain other groups that had opposed Roosevelt in 1932, suddenly seeing their needs catered to in unexpected fashion, came forward to lend their counsels to the Washington gatherings. Roosevelt, in short, did not concoct the "New Deal." Rather was he made by the "New Deal" to stand for something he had never, as recently as January 1, 1933, given any sign that he intended to espouse.

Aside from the suspension of the gold standard (the first and most important price-lifting measure) and the closing and reopening of the banks, the most spectacular early measures of the "New Deal" were the Agricultural Adjustment Act and the National Industrial Recovery Act. Both were nullified by the Supreme Court which, by these very decisions, contributed greatly to the outcry for judicial reform. The AAA gave subsidies to farmers for taking land out of cultivation, and did much to raise farm-purchasing power in consonance with the basic aim of the "New Deal." An unusually severe drought in 1934 provoked a storm of criticism, much of it insincere, of the Administration's program of destroying crops and farm animals in order to achieve higher prices; the same critics had not been perturbed by the sabotage of industry practiced by the banks and heavy industrialists when they shut down factories and laid off workers in 1929-33. Farm production had declined only about five per cent in four years, but industrial production had been reduced by 48.7 per cent. Within one year the AAA increased farm income by thirty-eight per cent and farm purchasing power by an estimated twenty-five per cent through the inauguration of the very production-control method that was originally used by the industrialists. The cost of the farm subsidy was met by a $1,000,000,000 processing tax, in effect a sales tax imposed on the consumer.

The increased farm-purchasing power redounded to the immediate benefit of the group which had financed Roosevelt. The McCormicks of the International Harvester Company benefited from increased sales of farm implements. Mail-order houses and manufacturers of clothing, cigarettes, and household products profited as well.

The National Industrial Recovery Act, approved June 16, 1933, concealed some very questionable aims under cover of Section 7A, which guaranteed to labor its already legally established right to bargain collectively through agents of its own choice. The Act closely resembled a plan that had long been advocated by Gerard Swope of the General Electric Company, and it bordered, indeed, upon fascism. President Roosevelt himself is said to have been greatly perturbed by the operation of certain features which had been written into the measure by many hands during the confusion attendant on the NIRA's creation. As cogently summarized by Professor Dwight Lowell Dumond in *Roosevelt to Roosevelt,* perhaps the most complete economic and social history of the United States for the period 1900-1936, the act "intended (1) to legalize those voluntary trade associations which President Hoover had encouraged by removing the restraints of the antitrust laws; (2) to make them effective by bringing the recalcitrants into line through compulsion; but (3) to bestow these privileges upon trade and industry in return for an acknowledgment of their social responsibility in the form of concessions to labor and the consumer."

The act, in short, sought to restore industrial stability by guaranteeing the *status quo* of worker and employer, one in possession of little, the other in possession of much. As those industries which assented to the codes were exempted from the operation of the antitrust laws, the government was underwriting monopoly more flagrantly than it had ever done before. In most instances the codes were merely the existing agreements of the monopolistic trade associations, with the government underwriting and agreeing to enforce them; in some cases they were precise copies of these agreements. In almost every instance the authorities responsible for enforcing each code were simply the leading executives of the trade associations.

Washington in 1933 and 1934 was once more flooded with the same crowd that had inundated it in 1917 and 1918. The "dollar-a-year men" were back, wrapped in the banner of high patriotism, with the stiletto of narrow self-interest concealed in its folds.

Most of the code provisions required the establishment of a forty-hour week and minimum weekly wages of $12 to $15 as well as the elimination of child labor. Section 7A, which avowed the right of workers to buttress these guarantees with unions of their own choosing, was immediately violated by the big industrialists, who formed company unions, turned loose an army of labor spies, and devised complicated schemes for evading even the wages and hours provisions. As voting control of all the code authorities was vested in the big industrialists, these latter utilized the provisions of the codes not only to war upon labor but also upon small, independent enterprises. A majority report of the NRA Board of Review, signed by Clarence Darrow and Charles Edward Russell, found on the basis of voluminous evidence that the Act was being used to foster monopoly. Senator William E. Borah made the same ugly charge.

"Here was a case," as Professor Dumond scathingly observes, "where the sovereign powers of self-government were handed over to private businessmen, whose trade and industrial association regulations were clothed with the authority of Federal statutes and, although they were written for private gain, without thought for the welfare of society as a whole, they were presented to the people as economic planning—the policies of the nation as determined by the considered judgment of Congress."

The controversy over Section 7A, however, did much to stimulate public thinking about the problems of labor. The cold-blooded, ruthless fashion in which the industrialists consciously moved to vitiate those provisions of the section that were beneficial to labor perhaps did more to educate the country about the socially irresponsible character of the big proprietors than had all the preachments of radicals for years. Moreover, the pathetic eagerness with which a vast multitude grasped at pay of $12 a week, and the outcry from the Southern industrialist against such "high" wages, drove into public consciousness the fact that labor in the United States, excepting its aristocracy in the American Federation of Labor crafts unions, had long been fiercely exploited at coolie pay. Details of the farm situation, highlighted in the debate around the AAA, also had a similar educative effect, so that if the "New Deal" did nothing else it succeeded, in these and other of its efforts, in implanting a deep suspicion in the public mind about the motives and methods of the big feudalistic proprietors, who habitually masquerade as simple "businessmen."

The gigantic program of unemployment relief embarked upon by the "New Deal" was of direct aid to retail trade and to the farmers in that the money paid out to the unemployed went immediately into the purchase of necessities. Several government agencies were created to handle the projects, but the Works Progress Administration, launched on May 6, 1935, finally consolidated all the divisions of relief. Works Progress funds were allocated to naval building, to municipal improvements and construction where local governments shared part of the cost, to reforestation, and many other ends; the principal aim, however, was to get money into circulation. In connection with the building and construction phases of this program there was, of course, a demand for cement, stone, machinery, steel, and lumber, which was of benefit to heavy industry; but the benefit was neither so great nor so immediate as that conferred upon industries more closely aligned with the retail market.

Meanwhile, various measures designed to hamper the banks in their domination of heavy industry were passed under presidential authority. The first of these was the Banking Act of 1933, which divorced commercial and investment banking, provided for insurance of deposits, and vested in the Federal Reserve Board the right to control loans entering speculative channels. The separation of the deposit and underwriting functions of the banks was a blow directed consciously at J. P. Morgan and Company, and measurably weakened the power of that and other private banking houses. Not at all strangely, this action was sought and approved by Winthrop W. Aldrich, chairman of the Rockefellers' Chase Bank. Weakened under Hoover, the Rockefellers were strengthened for a time by the "New

Deal"—by the sharp rise in oil prices and by the improvement of the real estate market; and although John D. Rockefeller, Jr., outwardly maintained his Republicanism the Standard Oil clans helped the "New Deal" at many points and manifested cordiality to its acts. The "New Deal" reciprocated by doing nothing, in its early stages at least, to disturb or injure the Standard Oil empire.

After passage of the Banking Act J. P. Morgan and Company immediately set up Morgan, Stanley and Company for handling securities issues, but as this branch was effectively segregated from the central house the firm could no longer function as freely as of old. Extension of the powers of the Federal Reserve Board by giving it control over the so-called "open market committee" and over the reserve requirements of the member banks also weakened Morgan power in finance, for under the old dispensation the Federal Reserve System, dominated by the New York money market and the Morgan banking bloc, was as effectively under Morgan control as if J. P. Morgan and Company owned it. Symbolic of the new regime Marriner S. Eccles, small banker and mining entrepreneur from Utah, was made Governor of the Reserve Board. Control of the money market, transferred to Washington, was thereafter to be wielded by whoever controlled the government.

There was an immediate outcry, to be sure, against "political control" of the Reserve System, but it had always been under "political" control. It was only a question of which political faction should control it. The method of control made little difference.

The next big blow against the finance capitalists of Wall Street by the independent industrial and mercantile capitalists came with the passage of the Federal Securities Act, signed by the President on May 27, 1933. Its provisions required the registration of securities with the Federal Trade Commission, but did not require its approval, and gave purchasers the right to recover losses incurred by misrepresentation. A campaign against this Act, fiercely waged by Wall Street for more than a year, resulted in passage of the new Securities Exchange Act, in June, 1934. This measure established the Securities and Exchange Commission and gave the Federal Reserve Board enhanced power to regulate the money market. It forbade the operation of pools or other devices for manipulating market values, required the registration but not approval of securities, and penalized promoters for making false statements in the sale of securities. This was, without doubt, an intolerable handicap to the finance capitalists, who had long been accustomed to raking in the money of investors under cover of the most unbridled misrepresentation.

Another severe blow directed against banking capital was the Wheeler-Rayburn Act, passed in August, 1935. This measure directed the Federal Power Commission to supervise the interstate transmission of electric power and the Federal Trade Commission to supervise interstate transmission of gas. Significantly, the Act prohibited officers of banks, and of brokerage or investment houses, from serving as officers or directors of public-utilities companies—an obvious attempt to divorce the profitable utilities industry from the banks. The Securities and Exchange Commission was given the power to determine depreciation write-offs, to pass upon dividend rates, and to require public-utilities lobbyists to register with it. An amendment by Senator Borah abolishing all except the holding company immediately above the operating companies, referred to in the press as the "death sentence," was defeated in Congress after an intense and spectacular campaign waged by the public-utilities companies. The Securities and Exchange Commission was, however, empowered to eliminate all holding companies that were proved to be acting against the public interest. Intercompany transactions, which had been so profitable to the holding companies, were forbidden under the new law.

As to the source of opposition to this and other legislation, Professor Dumond justly observes about the opponents of the Federal Securities Act: "For the most part, it was those financiers who had been responsible for the stock and bond swindles and those corporation directors and lawyers who had always opposed social legislation who led the attack and who, there is some reason to believe, delayed refinancing with the fixed purpose of bringing pressure to bear upon Congress for modification of the act."

The effectiveness of all these measures in keeping the banking clans out of the industrial picture in the future will be determined to a large extent by the severity of their enforcement. A rightist Republican or Democratic government succeeding the "New Deal" would unquestionably relax the enforcement of many of these measures on the ground that they were retarding "business," *i.e.*, the flow of profits to the richest families.

The "New Deal" tax measures were aimed specifically at the biggest clans of wealth, although they significantly left loopholes for its own clans to slip through. There has been some protest that the tax base was not broadened enough, that lower incomes were not brought into the tax net; but such a blighting assault upon popular purchasing power, already siphoned away by steadily rising prices, was carefully avoided. The tax measures of the Roosevelt Administration are interesting, and deserve analysis.

Congress in 1932, with the authority of President Hoover and the Republican Party weakened, engaged in some writing-up of tax schedules. The Revenue Act of 1928 had imposed a regular tax of five per cent on incomes of more than $8,000; the Act of 1932 set the regular tax at eight per cent. Whereas the Act of 1928, the last one to be sponsored by Mellon, had levied a flat surtax of twenty per cent on all incomes of more than $100,000, the Act of 1932 set a rate of forty-eight per cent on incomes of $100,000 to $150,000, of forty-nine per cent on incomes of $150,000 to $200,000, of fifty per cent on incomes of $200,000 to $300,000, of fifty-three per cent on incomes of $500,000 to $700,000, and of fifty-five per cent on incomes of more than $1,000,000. The Revenue Act of 1934 raised the surtax on incomes of $100,000 to $150,000 to fifty-two per cent, on incomes of $150,000 to $200,000 to fifty-three per cent, on incomes of $200,000 to $300,000 to fifty-four per cent, on incomes of $500,000 to $700,000 to fifty-seven per cent, and on incomes of more than $1,000,000 to fifty-nine per cent.

There were further sharp write-ups of the rates in the Act of 1935, which levied fifty-eight per cent on incomes of $100,000 to $150,000, sixty per cent on incomes of $150,000 to $300,000, seventy per cent on incomes of $500,000 to $750,000, seventy-three per cent on incomes of $1,000,000 to $2,000,000, seventy-four per cent on incomes of $2,000,-000 to $5,000,000, and seventy-five per cent on incomes of $5,000,000 or more. The Revenue Act of 1936 left these relatively high rates unchanged, and, on the whole, the "New Deal" may be said to have wrought well thus far.

As to the estate taxes, the Act of 1928 levied only three per cent on estates of $100,000, and the Act of 1932 levied nine per cent; the Act of 1928 levied eight per cent on estates of $1,000,000, and the Act of 1932 levied nineteen per cent; the Act of 1928 levied fifteen per cent on estates of $5,000,000, and the Act of 1932 levied thirty-five per cent; the Act of 1928 levied twenty per cent on all estates of $10,000,000 and above while the Act of 1932 levied forty-five per cent. For these same net estates the Act of 1934 respectively levied twelve per cent, twenty-eight per cent, fifty per cent, and sixty per cent. The Act of 1935 instituted further write-ups in the estate levies, $100,000 paying seventeen per cent, $1,000,000 paying thirty-two per cent, $5,000,000 paying fifty-six per cent, $10,000,000 paying sixty-five per cent, $10,-000,000 to $20,000,000 paying sixty-seven per cent, $20,000,000 to $50,-000,000 paying sixty-nine per cent, and $50,000,000 and more paying seventy per cent. The Revenue Act of 1936 left these rates undisturbed.

The Revenue Act of 1932 instituted a gift tax to stop the widespread practice among the rich of giving away, tax free, their fortunes to relatives prior to death. Gifts of $1,000,000 were required to pay $92,125, plus fourteen per cent on additional gifts up to $1,500,000. Gifts of $5,000,000 were required to pay $862,125, plus twenty-six per cent up to $6,000,000. Gifts of $10,000,000 were required to pay $2,-312,125, plus 33⅓ per cent on any excess. The Revenue Act of 1934 lifted these rates to a flat twenty-one per cent on $1,000,000 to $1,500,-000, to 37½ per cent on $5,000,000 to $6,000,000, to forty-five per cent on $10,000,000, to 50¼ per cent on $10,000,000 to $20,000,000, to 51¾ per cent on $20,000,000 to $50,000,000, and to 52½ per cent on $50,-000,000 and more. The Revenue Act of 1935 raised the rate to twenty-four per cent on gifts of $1,000,000 to $1,500,000, to forty-two per cent on $5,000,000 to $6,000,000, to 48¾ per cent on $10,000,000, and retained the rates of the 1934 Act in the higher brackets. These rates were not changed by the Revenue Act of 1936.

The Act of 1936, however, blocked an important loophole through which the wealthiest taxpayers had escaped the provisions of the law. It placed a tax of fifteen per cent on corporation income of more than $40,000 and established a graduated tax scaling up to twenty-seven per cent on undivided corporation profits. The rich owners of corporations, instead of disbursing profits in dividends, had been plowing them back into surplus, to be drawn upon at some future date after they had been successful in getting income-tax rates reduced; this untaxed surplus stood behind the stockholdings, and was as good as money in the bank. Indeed, it was reflected in the advanced market prices of the stocks of those corporations which had large cash surpluses. Under the Act of 1936 it became more profitable for the rich to distribute this surplus in the form of dividends, and many corporations did. It was this item of legislation, incidentally, which Republican presidential nominee Alfred M. Landon in 1936 called "the most cockeyed piece of tax legislation ever imposed in a modern country."

That there was nothing quixotic or haphazard in President Roosevelt's tax reform proposals was indicated clearly when, at a press conference in July, 1935, he discussed with reporters some interesting features of the 1932 tax returns of which he had just made careful study. In that year 58 persons had reported incomes of $1,000,000. These individuals who, the President remarked, deserved to be called "the 58 thriftiest people in America," had paid no tax at all on $21,000,000, or thirty-seven per cent of their aggregate income, which was derived from tax-exempt securities. The President further revealed that in 1932, when gift-tax legislation was on its way through Congress, one man transferred about $100,000,000 in tax-free gifts, and another transferred about $50,000,000. One estate, the President reported, was reduced, to avoid estate taxes, from $100,000,000 to $8,000,000 within two years of the owner's death.

In the course of this press conference Roosevelt aimed at very big game when he said that one family in 1932 had divided its holdings into 197 separate trust funds which could easily be demonstrated to have been designed for tax evasion. Although he did not name the family, nor did subsequent tax investigations reveal it, the Rockefellers were generally conceded to have been the family in question. It is, incidentally, a fact verifiable on the public record that Rockefeller, Jr. began, a few days after these revelations, hastily transferring parts of his fortune to relatives to escape the higher gift and estate taxes which Roosevelt had just recommended to Congress.

Stringent though the Roosevelt tax measures may have seemed, they left many loopholes. Some of these have been disclosed, and provision made for their closing; but the most important loophole has not been discussed at all, and it concerns the gift-tax rates. As the law governing gift taxes is drawn, the tax is levied on each individual gift. Actually it operates to penalize the wealthy man who has a small family and to make avoidance of heavy taxes possible for the man with a large family. By making multiple gifts a rich man may spread among his many sons and daughters a huge fortune, and incur only a small tax. As we have already mentioned, John D. Rockefeller, Jr., in 1935 "gave away" $27,000,000 of stock at one stroke, and he has been making "gifts" of large blocks of securities regularly since 1933. If the $27,000,000 stock gift was made to one person, it incurred a tax of 51¾ per cent; but if it was distributed among his six children it incurred a total tax of only thirty-two per cent. If any grandchildren were included in this stock distribution, then the percentage of tax paid was even lower, perhaps less than twenty-five per cent. By doling out his fortune in this way among his many children and their offspring Rockefeller will be able, even under the "New Deal" tax laws, to give away most of his fortune, incurring only an approximate 25 per cent tax upon it rather than the flat 70 per cent to which he would otherwise be liable under the estate-tax law as it stands.

Where there are few children, as in the case of Andrew W. Mellon, or no children, as in the case of Hayden, the obvious course of tax avoidance is to leave the bulk of the estate to "charity," under control of the children or of business associates. Although both Mellon and his brother have died, the Aluminum Company and the Gulf Oil Company remain in control of the Mellon family, unaffected by the most stringent tax laws. It remains for the authorities to pass upon the validity of these "charitable" endowments, whose central purpose is to retain industrial control and power, and if the law is properly interpreted the charitable character of the endowments will be denied, for it was the plain intent and expressed purpose of Congress in writing these tax laws that they should so operate as to dismantle the largest of the mammoth estates even though they do not seriously affect the smaller ones.

The gift-tax loophole should be stopped up by a statute making a

flat levy on the total of gifts over a period of five years at the rate
that the estate-tax schedule provides in its present form—with the
additional provision that taxes shall be collectable retroactively after
death at the same rate that would apply had the gifts not been made
and as though their sums were still a part of the estate.

This statute should also be applied to gifts to family-controlled
charitable foundations, and the income-tax laws should be made to
apply to the income of all these foundations, including the privately
controlled university and church endowments, which are all merely
instruments for the concentration of pecuniary power in the hands
of the wealthy individuals that supervise them. Closure of the multi-
ple-gift loophole, the philanthropic gift loophole, and the founda-
tion-income loophole would effect an appreciable reduction in the political and social power of the very rich.

A further necessary measure for blocking avenues by which the
wealthiest citizens escape taxes designed to encroach upon their
dictatorial social and political power should be a law that would for-
bid the filing of separate returns by members of a family jointly drawing unearned income in excess of $50,000 annually. The filing of
many income-tax returns by a family in receipt of more than $5,000
annually tends to reduce the tax rate, and the greater the amount
of income the more sharply the tax rate is reduced. Where many
members of a family are in receipt of earned income from professional or business sources it would obviously be unjust to force these
individuals to file a consolidated family tax return. But where unearned income is drawn by several individuals solely by reason of
the fact that they are members of a family group it is obvious that
the income tax should be levied upon the *family* rather than the
*individual*. The Rockefeller sons draw unearned income not because
they are individuals with some talent or ability to contribute to society
but because they are members of the Rockefeller family. The family
should therefore be required to file a joint tax return, incurring a
higher levy, with first cousins, nephews, and nieces of the main branch
of each family included. In circles of great wealth the family itself
becomes a pecuniary device, to be manipulated at will, and primarily
valuable in evading taxes levied upon individuals.

There are so many ways in which the very rich can evade taxes that it is doubtful whether all the legal loopholes can ever be closed. Much can be done, however, to whittle down the largest estates. In such an undertaking the less wealthy among the rich, with fortunes ranging from $10,000,000 to $20,000,000, might well collaborate, for in the very competitive character of contemporary private enterprise the biggest estates are a menace to them as well as to poorer people. Few among the lesser rich, for example, are given a share of the vast "melons" that from time to time are divided among the richest elements—melons like the Panama Canal swindle, the initial United States Steel pool, the Tennessee Coal and Iron grab, the Teapot Dome grab, the life-insurance racket, the government-subsidy racket, the Morgan "favor list," etc.

The "New Deal" government made a genuine contribution by disclosing many of the more novel means used by the rich to evade taxes, although it should be clear that the fundamental ways of escaping taxes have naturally not been called into question by an administration that is supported by one faction of great wealth. Secretary of the Treasury Henry E. Morgenthau on June 17, 1937, listed the following devices for evading income taxes: formation of foreign personal holding companies, foreign insurance companies, domestic personal holding companies; the incorporation of yachts and country estates (expenses of operation being charged off against income); creation of multiple trusts for relatives and dependents; establishment of family partnerships, and pension trusts. Scores of wealthy taxpayers employed such devices as these.

Alfred P. Sloan, Jr., chairman of General Motors Corporation, was shown to have incorporated his yacht *Rene* under the name of the Rene Corporation. Operating "losses" on this pleasure vessel for 1931–36 were $278,474, which Sloan deducted from his income of $2,140,563 for the period. This neat trick enabled him to avoid payment of $128,528 in taxes—an amount which he was then free to invest in a bathtub, a pipe-organ, or a hunting lodge. Sloan and his wife, according to data adduced on June 29, 1937, by the Treasury Department, also avoided payment of $1,921,587 in taxes in 1933–36 by the personal-holding-company device. Others who gained large tax savings through personal holding companies were Henry L. Doherty, Mrs. Helena A. Raskob, Mrs. Wilhemina du Pont Ross,

Ailsa Mellon Bruce, William Randolph Hearst, Horace Havemeyer, Pierre du Pont, F. V. du Pont, R. C. du Pont, O. D. Fisher, O. W. Fisher, D. R. Fisher, Roy W. Howard, Robert P. Scripps, E. W. Scripps, William Dewart, Paulina du Pont, Mrs. H. Ethel du Pont, Charles F. Kettering, Charles Hayden, Thomas W. Lamont, Jacob Ruppert, Frederick H. Prince, Edward A. Cudahy, Jr., Jeremiah Milbank, and others. Eighty incorporators of personal holding companies, according to the Treasury Department, evaded an aggregate of $2,500,000 of taxes for 1936.*

Some very peculiar devices were brought to light, illustrating the desperate lengths to which the rich are willing to go to preserve from public use their huge accumulations. Myron C. Taylor, chairman of the United States Steel Corporation, incorporated his various residences and personal properties, on which he claimed an "operating loss" of $354,083 during 1931-35, charging it against income. John Hay ("Jock") Whitney incorporated his magnificent stables at $1,325,940 and for the years 1932-35 saved $396,125 in taxes. Alfred I. du Pont incorporated his Wilmington residence at $1,000,000, saving taxes of $200,000 from 1931 to 1935. Mrs. Emily R. Cadwalader of Philadelphia, daughter of John A. Roebling, incorporated her big yacht and saved taxes of $220,183 in six years. Mrs. Wilhelmina du Pont Ross incorporated her stables and farms, saving $172,469 in taxes.

Abe Fortas of the Yale Law School, testifying in Washington as an expert, explained how the rich also evaded taxes through the incorporation of airplanes, automobiles, and miscellaneous possessions. The rich tax dodgers, in their eagerness to retain every last cent of the money under their control, appear to have stopped short only of incorporating their children and mistresses. *The New York Times* and other newspapers of reaction stressed that the personal holding company and other devices were all perfectly legal, and so they were. Legality, it may be said, is often the last refuge of a scoundrel.

Following these disclosures, Congress set to work on measures

* Wilbur K. Potter, secretary to the late Edward H. R. Green, testified on May 26, 1937, during a court struggle over the estate of Green, that his employer had paid no state income taxes at all from 1929 through 1929 on an annual income of $20,000,000. Green avoided these local income taxes, as not a few of the rich do, by failing to maintain any permanent address, thereby achieving the status of a multi-millionaire vagabond.

for preventing further evasions; but as Congress concentrated on rather superficial evasions and as the significant loopholes had not even been discussed, the tax laws as they stand will still enable most of the rich families to resist the plain intent of Congress and the people that the big fortunes be seriously reduced. For it is coming more and more widely to be recognized, even among many very capable businessmen who find the big corporations impeding them at every step, that huge fortunes confer entirely too much power on a few individuals in what is sedulously advertised as a great democracy.

And while one can say that the "New Deal" tax measures, directed though they are mainly against finance and heavy industry (the tax on corporation surplus was especially directed against heavy industry, which had saved its surplus by throwing out its workers in 1929–33), represent a great step forward—they by no means solve the problem. Much remains to be done, especially in focussing public thought on the new ways of tax-dodging behind the beautiful tapestry of philanthropic, religious, and educational bequests.

The root of the tax-dodging dilemma is to be found in the fundamental law itself and in fewer than a dozen of the eminent law firms of New York and Washington. These firms are an integral part of the apparatus of finance capital, and while they will not be discussed further here, they do merit an increased amount of attention from social critics, who should be able to show in detail how these firms function in harmony with local and national political machines, philanthropic and educational bodies, banks and corporations, and the exclusive millionaires' clubs.

In encroaching upon the prerogatives of the socially inimical bank capitalists and in making it less difficult for ordinary businessmen to operate, the "New Deal" has been fairly conventional and altogether in harmony with the American political tradition. But these conventional political accomplishments have been, unfortunately, mere stop-gaps in an exceedingly complicated and menacing situation. Where the "New Deal" has distinguished itself to the greatest degree in an historical sense has been in its unconventional anticipations of the future, in its so-called experiments. These have been, it is all too true, rather tentative, but collectively they provide a body of experience and form a framework around which later economic and social development may concentrate in an orderly fashion.

Among the measures looking to the future has been the creation of the Tennessee Valley Authority to provide seven southern states with electric power and fertilizer, and to supervise reforestation, control of floods and soil erosion, the erection of subsistence homesteads, educational institutions, etc. Funds for this vast project were supplied by the protean Public Works Administration as part and parcel of the scheme to get the nation back to work and to rehabilitate the domestic market by spreading purchasing power; but it was, too, more than this—it was a partial unveiling of the future. Under the TVA was created the Electric Home and Farm Authority to inaugurate the use of electric appliances and equipment in the region served by TVA—a great step forward in an area that has been culturally, economically, and socially backward since the Civil War.

The National Housing Act of 1934, which helped home owners refinance and make repairs and improvements, was also a forward step in that it made provision for the building in cities of model apartment homes and for the resettling of agrarians in villages abutting on farm areas. This agency has been seriously hampered in its progress by the political intrigue of real-estate speculators who for many decades have profited heavily from the exploitation of city-dwellers in slum areas, but work has proceeded at a cost of more than $200,000,000 on about fifty separate projects scattered all over the country. The Resettlement Administration has been concerned with the erection of four model villages, and while the result of its work, like that of the city division of the Federal Housing Authority, has not been entirely satisfactory and has been impeded and sabotaged at every step by hostile political forces, it nevertheless provides valuable experience for the future.

The Social Security Act was also forward-looking in its provision for Federal aid to states that instituted old-age pension laws, for Federal old-age pension annuities, and for unemployment insurance. As it stands, this plan, as President Roosevelt himself admitted, is by no means perfect; but a beginning has been made, especially in the education of the public.

The "New Deal" has also been alive to the inability and refusal of private agencies to face the cultural crisis of the great depression. As wealthy men, long hymned by newspapers as patrons of the arts, indifferently turned their backs, musicians, actors, painters, writers, impresarios, designers, and their helpers and assistants stood in breadlines and subsisted on meager charity. Divisions of the Works Progress Administration established cultural projects for all these workers, projects that have attained, on the whole, an amazingly high degree of excellence. Although attacked by newspapers like *The Sun,* which deliberately belittled the activities in which unemployed adults were finding a creative outlet, and although at first it provided for many non-professional interlopers that should merely have been on other projects, a genuine public service was rendered by this nation-wide program. *The Sun,* its nominal publisher the beneficiary of a tax-dodging personal holding company, one of its leading stockholders a Morgan agent, its editorial and news columns redolent of the stench of special interest, was, to be sure, the logical foe of "boondoggling." The WPA cultural projects, above all else, provided a body of experience upon which the future can build.

Thus far throughout this study, it may be remarked, critical attention has been focussed upon the selfish activities of the rich in catering to their own sterile whims and needs, but it must be admitted that the wealthy would be unable to function as they do if they were confronted along a wide front by an enlightened public opinion. The "New Deal" has done much to stimulate public thinking, however, and it may be that the future historian will conclude that its greatest public contribution lay in this alone, even though it was probably no part of the original intention of the "New Dealers."

The "New Deal" has been active progressively in so many other fields that all its work cannot be touched upon in a single chapter. It attacked the tariff snarl which had ruined foreign trade, and which, since the enactment in 1930 of the Smoot-Hawley Act, had played a major role in keeping the world in a state of economic stagnation. In an attempt to break the deadlock, the State Department set about painstakingly negotiating reciprocal tariff agreements with many nations. The Administration also addressed itself to the vital related problem of neutrality, at least insuring that the American people will, if called upon to participate in the next general war, join the belligerents with their eyes open. It formally disavowed the old policy of armed intervention in Latin America, and to prove its pacific intentions abrogated the vicious Platt Amendment. It renewed diplomatic relations with Russia, which had remained severed for more than a decade and a half only because certain special interests like the National City Bank of New York, the Singer Sewing Machine Company, the International Harvester Company, and the Metropolitan Life Insurance Company had various individual grievances against the Soviets arising out of the Russian revolution.

Most universally popular of "New Deal" accomplishments was the repeal of the Eighteenth Amendment, and, while the "liquor problem" remains, the situation marks a vast improvement over the Harding-Coolidge-Hoover bootleg era when the master collaborator in the obstruction of the law-enforcement agencies was the Treasury Department under Andrew W. Mellon. That the prohibition law could have been enforced, there is no longer any doubt. Prohibition enforcement was sabotaged by the inner circle of the Republican Party even as it genuflected publicly to the Anti-Saloon League and the Methodist Board of Temperance, Prohibition, and Public Morals.

But full approval of the "New Deal" as an instrument of popular or semi-popular welfare must be qualified. The "New Deal" has not been nearly so progressive as it has tried to appear. Students of the sports pages are familiar with the pugilistic ruse of making a rigged boxing match look "good" when its outcome has been determined in advance. Students of labor affairs know the technique of the old Industrial Workers of the World in seeming to be busily at work while actually soldiering on the job. This technique of seeming to do much while actually doing little has been borrowed from politics, and the "New Dealers" have been political adepts.

Documentary evidence may some day be forthcoming to prove that some of the measures President Roosevelt espoused in public he failed to champion in the crucial legislative arena. One of these was the Tugwell Pure Food Bill, emasculated in Congress by lobbyists for the pharmaceutical and proprietary interests who have otherwise been stanch "New Dealers." Another measure was the Child Labor Amendment which, approved by more than thirty states, reached the Legislature of the President's home state and, despite the patronage club at the disposal of the White House, was allowed to go down to defeat under the joint onslaught of Cardinal Hayes and a horde of newspaper and sweat-shop proprietors. This stopped, for the time being, the drive to get thirty-six states to endorse the amendment, which had been before the nation since 1924. There were many such rhetorical fights for "New Deal" progressive measures that were signally lacking in the practical political organization needed to put them into effect.

Yet despite his failure to translate many of his promises into action, it cannot be denied that President Roosevelt has on a number of occasions stepped far to the forefront of his advisers and has even alienated some of the most influential of them by his advocacy of reform. He has done this at times without regard for political expediency, which explains the cry of "Dictator" raised by conservatives against him. The rich clans can understand a President that favors one group of special privilege, even though it is not their own; they see something menacing, however, in a President moving to implement a generalized public interest.

Marked Rockefeller hostility, for example, dated approximately from the July, 1935, press conference already referred to at which the President brashly stigmatized rich tax-dodgers before proposing the hotly assailed Revenue Act of 1935. The Rockefeller interests had earlier shown a willingness to collaborate with the Administration, notably in formulating the NRA petroleum code. But in 1936 the Rockefeller family was the third largest contributor to the Republican campaign fund, a factor which served to throw many votes to Roosevelt. It is also from the date of this press talk that Vincent Astor is said to have begun turning against the "New Deal," whose virile supporter he had been. Astor, one of the biggest Democratic campaign fund contributors in 1932, does not appear in the lists of contributors for 1936.

Further evidence that President Roosevelt, unlike many preceding Presidents, is not given to deferring to the rich merely because they are rich, is to be found in the Treasury Department's challenge of the pretensions of the A. W. Mellon Charitable and Educational Trust. In this the Administration is establishing an important

precedent for a general future assault on the fake philanthropic
enterprises of the wealthy families.

The accomplishments of the Roosevelt Administration through
1936 were achieved at the relatively small cost of a Treasury deficit
of about $14,000,000,000 or less than half the cost of our participation
in the World War. The Hoover Administration left a deficit of
nearly $6,000,000,000, with nothing to show for it but a record of
having salvaged the privately-owned railroads, banks, and insurance
companies that supported the Republican Party.

Not the least of the items that must be set to the credit of the "New
Deal" has been its relative friendliness to labor. It is the first administration in American history that has even attempted to deal
fairly with labor. In this departure, as in others, it has not, however,
been actuated entirely by ideals; the "New Deal" labor policy has,
like its other policies, been forced upon it by necessity.

After the early melancholy experience with the dubious NRA,
which labor was soon to characterize as "The National Run-Around,"
it became plain to the light-goods industrialists and merchants around
the President that stern measures would be required if heavy industry were not to depress wages again to the jeopardy of the retail
market. Not only were the heavy industrialists taking bold advantage
of the chaotic situation, but many fly-by-night operators in the light-
goods and mercantile fields were following their example. It was the
plan of the President's advisers not only to deal with these latter,
but to strike the first blow at heavy industry and its fat war and
post-war surpluses.

The industrial unions of the American Federation of Labor thereupon broke away and formed the Committee for Industrial Organization under John L. Lewis. Since the heads of all these unions, including Lewis, had been the President's close collaborators in labor
affairs, it is safe to assume that the entire movement was practically
inspired by the Administration, whose light-goods industry advisers
saw clearly that the old crafts-union policy of the American Federation of Labor had for years been of assistance only to the banks and
to heavy industry in their domination of the national economy. The
crafts-union policy had made it impossible for labor to organize heavy
industry, although the A. F. of L. had succeeded in fastening a noose

around certain of the light industries, making it difficult for them to compete with heavy industry for their share of the national income.

Banking capital and its allied newspapers immediately opened fire on Lewis, called the CIO a revolutionary organization and succeeded in building up a certain amount of public distrust that was by no means helpful to the Committee's orderly progress. Lewis, however, was far from being a social revolutionary. He had once backed President Harding and for years had fought the radicals in the United Mine Workers union. Although the Communists applauded the aspirations of the CIO, they did so only because it organized hitherto unorganized workers. That the "New Deal" also looked benignly upon the CIO was explainable on quite other grounds. The CIO, by organizing workers in heavy industry, was making it impossible for heavy industry and the banks during the next downswing of the business cycle to institute arbitrarily the wholesale lay-offs which had robbed the mercantile houses of their customers during the years 1930–33.

While the CIO was swinging into action on the industrial front, the unionization campaign was implemented by the passage on July 5, 1935, of the Wagner-Connery Labor Dispute Bill which established a permanent National Labor Relations Board to "promote equality of bargaining powers between employers and employees and to diminish the causes of labor's disputes," and declared collective bargaining to be a national policy. Commonly known as the Wagner Labor Relations Act, this law was intended to succeed Section 7A of the NIRA. Of almost equal importance to labor was the passage, in the same year, of the Guffey Coal Bill, although it, like the NIRA, was found unconstitutional by the Supreme Court. The Wagner Act, however, stood the test of the courts, and was significant chiefly for the fact that it encouraged workers to organize in the knowledge that the Administration was behind them. It has since been recognized that there are elements in the Wagner Act which are susceptible of modification, so that at some future time labor courts might be set up to function against labor. Any changes, interpretations or amendments of this law will bear careful scrutiny on their individual merits by the leaders of the labor movement.

With the heavy industries organized the government can, during the next decline, accelerate its housing and general construction program while the corporations involved debate with the CIO the merits of laying off workers and reducing their wages. The government, given notice by the formally declared intention of the steel, automobile, chemical, and oil industries to curtail operations, will be able to allocate appropriations to those "experimental" fields it has already marked off. If the procedure is orderly—though it is probably too much to hope that it will be—the government during each of these downswings should enlarge the field of its activity until greater and greater areas are gradually brought under the same auspices that now efficiently operate the Army and Navy, the Panama Canal, the Post Office, the rivers and harbors, the Coast Guard, the Alaska Railroad, etc.

The "New Deal" has not, the fact is, been socially revolutionary at any stage, and in substantiation of this conclusion one can refer to analyses of its work in *The Economist*, of London, chief theoretical organ of world capitalism. The "New Deal" merely represents enlightened capitalism at work, doing the best it can with a bad, almost hopeless, contradictory situation. Except for those unconventional features of its work which look to the future, none of its accomplishments has been more than part of a transitional phase of historical development.

But although one can, and should, criticize it in the interests of a realistic approach, it must be admitted that the "New Deal" represents without doubt the most enlightened government the United States has had in the post-Civil War industrial age. It is, indeed, a better government than the people by any concerted political action of their own have earned. It has been the one alternative, in a time of profound crisis, to government by machine-gun.

## IV

The "New Deal" has not been above according special favors to powerful interests in consonance with the old tradition of power-politics. Such favors have been an integral part of its strategy and, although no attempt will be made here to outline them in detail, a few may be mentioned. In 1934 President Roosevelt personally intervened to set aside a decision of the National Labor Relations Board requiring William Randolph Hearst, then one of his supporters, to reinstate an illegally discharged employee. There is also good reason to believe that President Roosevelt personally intervened early in 1937 to have the CIO terminate the strike at the Chrysler automobile plant; Walter P. Chrysler had, after 1932, become an ardent "New Dealer." But the General Motors Corporation strike was bitterly fought out to the end, with the company losing the decision and the White House holding aloof.

It has been President Roosevelt's unusual faculty for nice discrimination in the parceling out of special favors within the framework of his general economic program that has given him his political strength and that has, indeed, raised the Democratic Party to the peak of its power. That the "New Deal" has not cracked down indiscriminately upon the wealthy, that it has given special favors, and that it is far from being radical, was clearly indicated in the personalities that rallied to support President Roosevelt's re-election in 1936.

The lines divided, it will be observed, rather strictly between light and heavy industry, with most merchants in the former group and all the bank capitalists in the latter group. After 1932 there had been some defections in the "New Deal" ranks, but most of them may be explained on the basis of the division between the banks and heavy industry on one hand and light industry and the merchandising clans on the other. The chief defection was represented by the Democratic wing of the Du Pont family, which turned Republican. Another important defection was that of William Randolph Hearst, who had been checkmated by the "New Deal" tax stipulation that inter-company transactions within holding company systems might not be used to reduce income-tax liability, *i.e.*, that the losses of one company in a loosely held holding-company structure might not be deducted from the profits of other companies in a consolidated holding-company income-tax return. Hearst, moreover, was heavily in debt to the Wall Street banks, a factor that made his turn against the "New Deal," which his papers had once extolled, entirely logical. The Scripps-Howard newspapers, their leading proprietors enmeshed in tax-dodging personal holding companies, the papers themselves part of a holding-company system that was embarrassed by the new tax laws, remained loyal, but lukewarm, to the "New Deal."

The heaviest individual contributions to the Roosevelt re-election campaign came from the following, mostly identified with light manufacturing enterprises and businesses dependent upon the retail market:

| | | |
|---|---|---|
| Walter A. Jones | Oil lands | $102,500 |
| James W. Gerard | Former Ambassador to Germany | 51,000 |
| Henry L. Doherty | Cities Service Company | 50,000 |
| Mrs. Doris Duke Cromwell | American Tobacco Company | 50,000 |
| Mr. and Mrs. Joseph E. Davies | (Post-Hutton) General Foods Corp. | 26,500 |
| Joseph and Nicholas Schenck | Theatrical and amusement enterprises | 26,000 |
| Curtis Bok | Curtis Publishing Company | 25,000 |
| Lucius B. Manning | | 25,000 |
| Mary Drexel Biddle | | 25,000 |
| Joseph Medill Patterson | Publisher, New York Daily News | 20,000 |
| Nathan and Percy S. Straus | R. H. Macy and Company | 20,000 |
| R. J. Reynolds Tobacco Company | Through Richard S. Reynolds, W. N. Reynolds, James A. Gray, and S. Clay, Williams | 28,500 |
| Jesse H. Jones | Texas banker and promoter | 16,000 |
| W. L. Clayton | Texas | 15,000 |
| Mark Eisner | | 12,200 |
| Emil Schwartzhaupt | | 11,510 |
| Fred Pabst | Premier-Pabst Corporation, brewing | 10,000 |
| Robert W. Bingham | Diplomat and Louisville publisher | 10,000 |
| Cameron Morris | North Carolina | 10,000 |
| Bert Fish | | 10,000 |
| Arthur Mullen | | 10,000 |
| F. W. Burford | | 10,000 |
| Fred J. Fisher | General Motors Corporation | 10,000 |
| John T. Turtletaub | | 10,000 |
| A. Phelps Dunham | | 10,000 |
| Laurence C. Steinhardt | | 10,000 |
| Floyd Odlum | Atlas Corporation, investment trust | 10,000 |
| Cornelius Vanderbilt Whitney | Vanderbilt-Whitney family | 10,000 |
| Lewis S. Rosenthal | | 7,500 |
| Frank L. Crocker | | 5,000 |
| James D. Mooney | President, General Motors Export Corp. | 5,000 |
| Samuel S. Fels | Soap manufacturer | 5,000 |
| Margaret B. Biddle | Biddle family, Philadelphia | 5,000 |
| Jacob Ruppert | Brewer | 5,000 |
| W. A. Harriman | Banking | 5,000 |
| Henry E. Morgenthau | | 5,000 |
| Mrs. Henry Morgenthau | | 5,000 |

| | | |
|---|---|---:|
| Albert A. Hovell | | $5,000 |
| George H. Johnson | | 5,000 |
| Charles Harwood | | 5,000 |
| Paul V. Shields | | 5,000 |
| James Roosevelt | | 4,293 |
| Donald R. Richberg | Chicago lawyer | 4,000 |
| A. B. Klepper | Brooklyn | 3,500 |
| Harold F. McCormick | International Harvester Company | 3,000 |
| Augustus A. Busch, Jr. | Brewing | 2,500 |
| Thomas E. Wilson | Wilson and Company, packing | 2,500 |
| Christian Feigenspan | Brewing | 2,500 |
| Mrs. Gaspar Whitney | | 2,000 |
| Herbert Bayard Swope | Radio-Keith-Orpheum Corporation | 1,000 |
| Sosthenes Behn | International Telephone and Telegraph Corporation | 1,000 |
| Fowler McCormick | | 1,000 |

$719,003

William Hard, Republican radio commentator, in August, 1936, stated quite truly that 400 persons identifiable as "economic royalists" gave money to the Democrats. Among them he listed Russell Leffingwell and S. Parker Gilbert, partners of J. P. Morgan and Company; Walter E. Frew, head of the Corn Exchange Bank (Lehman); Walter Dunnington, trustee of the Central Hanover Bank and Trust Company; P. A. S. Franklin, head of the International Mercantile Marine; Arthur Curtiss James; William K. Vanderbilt, Frederick H. Prince; Walter P. Chrysler, Vincent Bendix, airplane entrepreneur; Jesse I. Straus, Cyrus and Harold McCormick, Vincent Astor, and A. P. Giannini.

The New York Times, December 2, 1936, listed Mr. and Mrs. E. C. McCann, of Oyster Bay, heirs of the Woolworth fortune, among the largest Democratic contributors, although they apparently made their major contribution through some agency not reported in the press. Their names, however, can be found in a number of places credited with amounts like $1,000, and presumably they made many contributions of this size.

Scores of professional politicians contributed from $500 to $5,000 on their own account. Committees in each state busily collected from $5,000 to $50,000 each from unidentified individuals, so that many of the persons in the foregoing tabulation may have contributed additional funds that do not appear upon the national record. In any event, the funds collected by state committees were obtained from merchants, manufacturers, and professional men.

In order to cope with the avalanche of money turned loose against it by finance capital and heavy industry, the Democratic Party cleverly made use of a number of new, and possibly illegal, devices for raising money. Advertisements in a souvenir handbook of the Philadelphia convention were sold to almost all the leading corporations, netting $385,525; many of the "advertisers" also contributed heavily through their chief officers to the Republican Party. Advertisers included Armour and Company, Firestone Tire and Rubber Company, Bethlehem Steel Corporation, etc. Large quantities of this handbook were then sold to wealthy individuals that did not want to contribute directly to the Democratic Party. This sale brought in $142,711.07.

Mrs. A. J. Drexel Biddle, Jr. bought $20,000 worth. Walter P. Chrysler gave $12,600 to the literary cause; the American Radiator and Standard Sanitary Company gave $15,000; the Automatic Voting Machine Company, $3,000; the Cuban-American Sugar Company, $1,250; John Bass, $1,200; the Bethlehem Steel Corporation, $5,000; Ellsworth Bunker, $2,700; the Chilean Nitrate Educational Bureau, $2,500; Colonel Edward A. Deeds, $2,750; George F. Trommer, brewer, $1,500; the National Gypsum Company, $1,250; the Trico Products Company, $3,900; C. J. Devine and Company, $6,000; Remington Rand, Inc., $1,250; Oliver Cabana, $1,000; Gruman Aircraft Engineering Corporation, $1,000; Robert R. Young, $3,750; James D. Mooney, $2,500; S. Klein, department-store merchant, $1,000; William Gaston, $2,500; Collins and Aikman Corporation, $1,000; etc., etc.

Another money-raising device was the Roosevelt Nominators, which sold dollar memberships that totalled $237,390.68. Jackson and Jefferson Day dinners were also given under Democratic auspices throughout the country, netting large sums over and above costs.

The light-goods and mercantile interests behind the Democratic Party received unprecedented support from labor organizations, which contributed the following extraordinary amounts:

| | |
|---|---|
| United Mine Workers of America | $469,668 |
| American Labor Party | 133,534 |
| International Ladies Garment Workers Union | 5,000 |
| Amalgamated Clothing Workers Union | 5,000 |
| International Brotherhood of Electrical Workers | 1,000 |
| Brotherhood of Locomotive Firemen and Engineers | 1,000 |
| Order of Railroad Telegraphers | 1,000 |
| International Alliance of Theatrical Stage Employees and Moving Picture Operators | 10,000 |
| Miscellaneous labor | 144,016 |
| | $770,218 |

The story of the "New Deal's" struggle for re-election would not be complete without an enumeration of the Democratic Party loans outstanding at the end of the campaign. The party owed Joseph P. Kennedy, Boston banker, former head of the Securities and Exchange Commission, and now chairman of the Maritime Board, $36,876; Richard J. Reynolds, $10,000; Samuel Kramer, $25,000; Walter Jones, of Pittsburgh, $50,000; the United Mine Workers, $50,000; the Manufacturers Trust Company of New York, $100,000, and the Chase National Bank of New York, $100,000.

It was well that the Democratic Party had the labor unions with it financially, for otherwise it would have been unable to shield itself against the onrush of hostile money. It may be conservatively estimated that the Republican campaign absorbed at least $50,000,000, although the cost is set officially at less than $10,000,000. In this latter total are included only direct contributions, although a dozen subsidiary agencies, including the Liberty League, the Crusaders, the Independent Coalition of American Women, the Landon-Knox Clubs, the Pennsylvania Protection Bureau, the Women Investors of America, the National Civic Federation, the Sentinels of the Republic, the Minute Men and Women of Today, the Southern Committee to Uphold the Constitution, the Economists' National Committee on Monetary Policy, the Farmers Independent Council, fought shoulder to shoulder with the Republican Party, and collected funds throughout the East. More than direct contributions are involved in campaign costs, however; William Randolph Hearst, for example, gave the Republicans $50,000 in cash, but the thousands of pages of Republican propaganda printed in the Hearst newspapers represented a contribution on their proprietor's part of several million dollars. R. R. Mc-Cormick, of the Chicago *Tribune,* made no visible contribution in cash, but he spent millions of dollars for the Republicans in his newspapers. His wife gave $10,000.

The identities of the "New Deal" opponents were an important source of strength to the Democratic ticket, for they comprised all the heavily publicized clans whose selfish activities have tormented the American people for many years. A few of the heaviest contributions placed upon the record (and what the *sub rosa* contributions were will perhaps never be known) were as follows:

| | | |
|---|---|---|
| 18 Du Ponts | E. I. du Pont de Nemours | $855,520 |
| J. Howard Pew family | Sun Oil Company | 514,102 |
| 5 Rockefellers | Standard Oil Company | 187,000 |
| 8 Mellons | Aluminum Company and Gulf Oil | 130,775 |
| Ira C. Copley | Public utilities | 103,011 |
| Ernest T. Weir | National Steel Corporation | 97,300 |
| 2 Whitneys | Standard Oil Company | 77,625 |
| Max C. Fleischmann | | 76,156 |
| 3 Morgans | J. P. Morgan and Company | 67,706 |
| 2 Milbanks | | 59,000 |
| 5 Guggenheims | Copper mining and smelting | 59,500 |
| George F. Baker | First National Bank | 55,000 |
| William Randolph Hearst | Mining | 50,000 |
| 3 Heinzes | Pickles | 35,000 |
| Harold F. Pitcairn and family | Pittsburgh Plate Glass Company | 30,175 |
| Frazier Jelke | Wall Street broker | 25,000 |
| Harold S. Vanderbilt | N. Y. Central Railroad | 25,000 |
| J. A. Hartford | Great Atlantic & Pacific Tea Co. | 25,000 |
| J. A. Roebling | | 25,000 |
| 2 Harknesses | Standard Oil Company | 23,000 |
| Ogden L. Mills | Mining | 20,000 |
| W. R. Coe | Turfman | 17,000 |
| A. Atwater Kent | Radio manufacturer | 15,000 |
| L. H. Young, Detroit | | 15,000 |
| Dr. Victor C. Thorne | | 15,000 |
| Mrs. Anna Dodge Dillman | Automobiles | 14,000 |
| Mrs. Mabel L. Kent | | 13,550 |
| Mrs. W. Bayard Cutting | | 12,500* |
| Charles S. Dewey, Chicago | | 12,200 |
| Mrs. Hugh D. Auchincloss | | 11,900 |
| Chauncey McCormick | International Harvester Company | 11,000 |
| E. T. Stotesbury | Morgan, Drexel and Company | 11,000 |

* Also gave $1,500 to Socialist Party, according to *The New York Times,* December 22, 1936.

| | | |
|---|---|---|
| Harvey S. Firestone | | $10,000 |
| Hariss Dunn | | 10,000 |
| Julius Forstmann | Textiles | 10,000 |
| William M. Potte | | 10,000 |
| Frederic A. Juilliard | | 10,000 |
| Joseph E. Widener | | 10,000 |
| Eugene G. Grace | Bethlehem Steel Corporation | 10,000 |
| Lester Armour | Armour and Company | 7,000 |
| Frank Jay Gould | Railroads | 6,350 |
| Eleanor M. Chalfant | Chalfant Iron and Steel Company | 6,200 |
| Mrs. Anne Archbold | Standard Oil Company | 6,200 |
| Albert Bradley, Greenwich, Conn. | | 6,150 |
| Walter E. Edge | Standard Oil politician and former Senator | 6,060 |
| William B. Bell | | 6,025 |
| J. W. Kieckhofer | | 6,000 |
| Edward G. Seubert | President, Standard Oil Company of Indiana | 6,000 |
| Dwight F. Davis | | 6,000 |
| Frederic M. Sackett | Public utilities | 6,000 |
| William Ewing | Partner, J. P. Morgan and Company | 5,737 |
| George Blumenthal | Lazard Freres | 5,250 |
| Mrs. C. W. Henry, Philadelphia | | 5,050 |
| Keith Dunham, Chicago | | 5,000 |
| A. B. Dick, Jr., Chicago | | 5,000 |
| Duncan D. Sutphen | | 5,000 |
| Alfred Busiel | | 5,000 |
| James Norris | | 5,000 |
| Mrs. G. B. Dryden | | 5,000 |
| S. Sloan Colt | President, Bankers Trust Company | 5,000 |
| Harriet L. Greenway | | 5,000 |
| Joseph Wilshire | President, Standard Brands, Inc. | 5,000 |
| William Woodward | President, Central Hanover Bank and Trust Company | 5,000 |
| George Whitney | Partner, J. P. Morgan and Company | 5,000 |
| H. H. Timken | Timken Roller Bearing Company | 5,000 |
| John M. Schiff | Kuhn, Loeb and Company | 5,000 |
| Frederick M. Warburg | Kuhn, Loeb and Company | 5,000 |
| Mrs. John T. Pratt | Standard Oil Company | 5,000 |
| Harry Payne Bingham | | 5,000 |
| William H. Crocker | San Francisco banker | 5,000 |
| Philip K. Wrigley | | 5,000 |
| Alden B. Swift | Swift and Company | 5,000 |
| Paul Moore | American Can Company | 5,000 |
| E. P. Crawford | President, McKeesport Tinplate Company | 5,000 |
| Sewell Avery | President, Montgomery Ward and Company | 5,000 |

| Henry P. Davison | Partner, J. P. Morgan and Company | $5,000 |
| Edward F. Hutton | Broker | 5,000 |
| George A. Ball | Container manufacturer | 4,500 |
| F. T. Bedford | Standard Oil Company | 4,400 |
| Philip D. Armour | Armour and Company | 7,000 |
| H. E. Manville | Johns-Manville Company | 3,800 |
| Thomas Wilson | | 2,500 |
| John Stuart | Quaker Oats Company | 2,500 |
| Stuart R. Douglas | Quaker Oats Company | 2,500 |
| John D. Archbold | Standard Oil Company | 2,500 |
| Edward L. Ryerson, Jr. | Ryerson Iron and Steel Company | 2,500 |
| Dexter Cummings, Chicago | | 2,000 |
| Edward H. Clark | Hearst mining executive | 2,250 |
| Mrs. Lorraine Manville | | 1,000 |
| Mrs. Pierre Lorillard | Tobacco | 500 |
| Elihu Root, Jr. | | 1,000 |

Total    $3,001,992

The Independent Coalition of American Women collected $102,721, the Union League Club, $48,260, and the Liberty League more than $500,000 in addition to an approximately equal amount collected and spent in 1935 in preparation for the mutually slanderous campaign of 1936. Individual contributions to all these agencies, and to various others, ranged from $500 to $50,000.

The Harkness, Vanderbilt, Whitney, McCormick, and Hutton families gave to both parties, and the subsidiary political agencies made it possible for many individuals to contribute in virtual anonymity to both parties. Walter P. Chrysler, for example, contributed to the Crusaders and was also an ardent purchaser of Democratic convention literature.

The extraordinarily large outlay of the Du Pont family, perhaps the most spent by any clan in any election, was inspired by a personal grievance against President Roosevelt. Although one wing of the Du Pont bloc gave him support in 1932, his administration was to prove the most disastrous ever experienced by the munitions lords, for the President himself supported the Nye Munitions Investigating Committee which brought to view much Du Pont knavery. Apparently the Du Ponts felt that Roosevelt should have soft-pedalled this damaging inquiry early, as he subsequently did when it seemed likely to involve important British interests. The Du Ponts undoubtedly realized full well that no high principle actuated the "New Deal" leadership in permitting the Nye Committee to reveal them in as ugly a light as any rich family has ever been placed. They must have known, for example, how President Roosevelt terminated the Senate Banking and Currency Committee investigation of Wall Street as soon as it had successfully impugned "New Deal" foes and was logically ready to begin investigating the Wall Street machinations of high-ranking Democrats. This investigation, largely driven through at the behest of William Randolph Hearst, who obtained the appointment of Ferdinand Pecora as the committee investigator through the efforts of Bainbridge Colby, was supplied with inside Wall Street information by the financial staff of the New York *American*. It was, moreover, information damaging to Hearst's financial foes of the moment, and the Senate investigation succeeded notably in making hard-hit J. P. Morgan and Company rather friendly to Hearst.

Among the names of the Republican slush-fund contributors of 1936 will be found certain light-goods industrialists and merchants, but their presence does not affect the interpretation of the "New Deal" policies laid down in this chapter. These persons uniformly represented companies that had long ago been taken under the wing of finance capital, which dragooned them into opposing the "New Deal" even though it had been very profitable to them. Automobile interests were almost uniformly in opposition to the "New Deal." The automobile industry does not, however, contrary to popular conception, really belong to the retail market. It cannot, for example, sell its product over-the-counter for cash; it must finance its essentially uneconomic sales by means of an elaborate installment system that utilizes a great amount of bank credit. Furthermore, it is closely bound in with heavy industry in that it is one of the hungriest outlets for steel, copper, nickel and chemicals. The automobile industry, in short, belongs to heavy industry and finance capital.

Henry Ford's name does not appear in the foregoing list of Republican contributors, but Ford, in 1936 as in 1932, made his contribution to the Republican Party by conducting advertising for it in newspapers and over the radio. In 1932 he paid the Republican radio bill outright.

After his re-election Roosevelt more and more perceptibly began wooing the banks and heavy industries, for the "New Deal" had pushed corporation profits in general up to fantastic levels and there was danger to the "New Dealers" in a heavy industry that was falling out of line. As this is written, all signs point to the achievement of a coalition between many "New Dealers" and their recent foes. Frederick H. Prince, of Boston, wealthy capitalist, publicly gave expression to this notion in the early part of 1937 when questioned about the "danger" of Roosevelt seeking re-election again in 1940. Prince replied that by 1940 the entire business community might be united in trying to return Roosevelt to office to head off a coalition of disillusioned farmers and industrial workers under the leadership of John L. Lewis or someone else.

President Roosevelt in 1937 disclosed that he was cooling toward the CIO movement just as it was preparing to launch organizing campaigns in textiles, tobacco, and merchandising industries. His historic rebuff of Lewis during the strike in "Little Steel" was, it may be remarked, as fine an example of political dodging as recent American chronicles can present. For without the labor forces under Lewis supporting him as they did, Roosevelt might have been beaten in 1936; at any rate, he would not have won by so impressive a majority. Evidently feeling that he had made sufficient use of the lusty CIO in furthering the program designed to accommodate his supporters, and desiring to nip the Lewis presidential boom in the bud, Roosevelt spoke out sharply again when Lewis called him to account.

But although apparently forsaking the CIO, the "New Deal" in 1937 maintained its affection for the light industrialists. This was illustrated outstandingly when President Roosevelt in the closing sessions of Congress approved the Tydings-Miller price-maintenance bill which was attached as a "rider" to the appropriations bill for the District of Columbia. Four months earlier the President had warned Congress against passing such a measure, designed merely to insure a high retail price level, but his approval of the appropriations bill, which he could easily have vetoed in the full knowledge that Congress would soon see to it that the District of Columbia received necessary funds, contradicted his first reassuring warning and even nullified government suits against price-fixers. As *The New*

*Republic* remarked, "We should certainly not entrust the job of deciding what prices are to be fixed, and at what levels, to a few private manufacturers of trademarked products. In all history they have demonstrated that their interest is not in the welfare of the community but, oddly, in the welfare of the manufacturers of trademarked products."

Unfortunately, these were the persons that, with organized labor, had supported Roosevelt for re-election.

The limitations of the Rooseveltian liberalism were perhaps never opened to better view than in his plan for enlarging the membership of the Supreme Court. Without consulting anyone, Roosevelt announced his scheme, the success of which would have made possible merely the placing of Roosevelt measures on the statute books and would have wrought no constructive change in the court's status. To the extent that the "New Deal" measures forced through an acquiescent court might have been progressive, the enlargement plan would have been progressive. But had enlargement of the court meant a resuscitation of the National Industrial Recovery Act, which many "New Dealers" have recurrently demanded, the change in the court would have been reactionary. Had President Roosevelt, on the other hand, intended to bring about a genuine liberalization of the high bench, he would have seen to it that his court-reform plan provided for majority or unanimous decision in the nullification of legislation and for the over-riding of a court decision by repassage of rejected congressional legislation. It was, quite evidently, not the President's intention to curtail the power of the court to sabotage legislation. He merely wanted the court recomposed so that legislation sponsored by his own group might be approved.

At the beginning of this chapter it was pointed out that various political groups have discerned fascism, communism, and bolshevism interlarded in the "New Deal" with some liberalism, progressivism, and good old-fashioned American political greed. Observers whose gaze has met these apparitions have not been myopic; they have, it is all too true, seen accurately, even though they have told about only a fraction of what they saw. For the "New Deal" has been a mixture of many ingredients, and little more than a transitional jerry-built contrivance marking the end of one period in American history, and the inception of a new, perhaps more chaotic, period.

It is certain, for one thing, that the rich family blocs will stop short of nothing to reduce the "New Deal" tax-rates and to smash all the projects in which the "New Deal" has gingerly anticipated a future collectivized economy under an industrial democracy. It is entirely possible, moreover, that President Roosevelt, as "recovery" gains impetus, will accede to the strident demands that a retreat be called in these very sectors.

The further "recovery" proceeds, the more will President Roosevelt probably come to resemble President Hoover in his public attitudes, for the "New Deal" recovery has yet to enter that phase of its logical development which means acute hardship to the masses. The heavy-industry and finance program which the "New Deal" succeeded required mass suffering in its primary stage before an upturn of the business cycle was possible. The light-industry program of the "New Deal" had as its initial requisite easy money and relative well-being of the masses, but with the squeeze to follow. This later phase of the "New Deal" is already beginning to manifest itself in sharply rising commodity prices, rising rents, and diminishing real wages. High finance fears this phase, for with a heavily increased national debt it will no longer be easy to fasten the tax burden on the masses; high finance may itself be called upon to shoulder a large portion of the tax burden. It may decide, in such an event, to govern by force.

Orderly democratic development for the future requires the forwarding, either by the "New Deal" or by some other political coalition, of the progressive legislative trends of 1933–37, the closing up of the wide tax loopholes in the upper-bracket income categories in the interests of reducing the national debt, and the extension of the legislative gains made by organized labor and the farmers. But to realize even such a minimum and far-from-visionary program, a widespread conscious participation in politics will be required of the people. And the danger of a dictatorship of the Right was never more real than at the present moment, with many of the wealthy already stung in their pocketbooks and worried about possible future stingings. The country must seriously address itself to the task of dealing with the historically unprecedented huge fortunes growing like cancers on American society, without having any illusions about the difficulties of the problem. Merely to toy with the fortunes of the wealthy, in which their entire psychologies are bound up from birth to death, is very much like toying with a high-tension electric wire.

# APPENDIX A

## The Public-Utilities Background
## of Wilson's Backers

AN EXCEEDINGLY rich field in the most densely populated area of the country was controlled by this group of utilities lords before 1912. Included in this field were the Consolidated Gas Company of New York (Rockefeller), the constituent parts of what are now the Brooklyn Edison Company (Brady), the New York Edison Company (Brady), the Third Avenue Railway Company (Rockefeller-Ryan), the New York Railways Company (Ryan), the Brooklyn Rapid Transit Company (Brady), the Interborough Rapid Transit Company (Belmont-Morgan), the developing Brooklyn-Manhattan Transit Company (Brady-Rockefeller), and the Queens Electric Light and Power Company (Morgan-Baker). There were also scores of outlying, unconsolidated gas, electric, and traction companies controlled by the same group and later consolidated.

The same bloc controlled, either as individuals or collectively, the local public utilities in practically every other large city of the United States where there was not municipal ownership. And it was this bloc that surreptitiously fought public ownership through newspapers and political tools during the early years of the century. Individuals like Hearst, striving to gain a personal foothold in the same field, supported the public-ownership element and mobilized liberal and radical sentiment for it in order to bring the dominant interests to private terms.

The Metropolitan Securities Company, through which Ryan, Brady, and the Rockefellers manipulated traction companies, functioned in collaboration with Tammany Hall. As it was brought out by a grand jury in December, 1907, Ryan, P. A. B. Widener, William L. Elkins, of Philadelphia, and William C. Whitney bought from

493

Anthony N. Brady for $250,000 the unused franchise of the Wall and Cortland Street Ferries Railroad Company. This franchise was then sold to the Metropolitan Securities Company for $965,607.19, yielding Ryan and his associates a profit of $692,292.82 and Metropolitan Securities a loss equal to the purchase price. Another operation by Ryan and his associates was the purchase for $1,600,000 of the franchises of the People's Traction Company, a paper enterprise, and the New York, Westchester and Connecticut Traction Company. Shortly before this transaction the franchise of the latter company had been sold in bankruptcy proceedings for $15,000.

In 1907 the Public Service Commission learned that $16,000,000 in cash had disappeared from the treasury of the Third Avenue Railway Company, controlled by the Metropolitan Securities Company, and that the books had been destroyed. Through tactics such as these, resorted to in connection with scores of franchises, the investing public lost more than $90,000,000 in the Metropolitan Street Railway Company.

Ryan and his cronies escaped prosecution for their misdeeds through the collaboration of the authorities. The foreman of the grand jury which heard the charges was, according to later revelations, a director in Ryan's Equitable Life Assurance Society. And according to the opinion rendered by Judge Otto Rosalsky in General Sessions on January 27, 1908, District Attorney William Travers Jerome had so examined Ryan before the Grand Jury as to invalidate the state's case. Ryan's attorney was Paul D. Cravath.

Jerome admitted before an investigating commission that he had improperly asked leading questions of Ryan and Brady. Yet removal proceedings instituted against Jerome were dismissed by Governor Charles Evans Hughes, Cravath's law partner.

The escape of Jerome, as well as of Ryan and his friends, was all the stranger in view of the fact that William N. Amory, former official of the Third Avenue Railway Company, charged that while he was a state's witness a former law partner of Jerome offered him $200,000 to drop the accusations against Brady and Ryan. It was also brought out that Samuel Untermyer, counsel to Hyde in the insurance scandal, was a contributor to Jerome's political campaign fund.

The Metropolitan Street Railway Company had extensive political connections. State Senator Patrick H. McCarren of Brooklyn, real-estate operator and race-track entrepreneur, acted in Albany for Brady and Whitney, and was known to function as well for H. H. Rogers, J. P. Morgan, August Belmont, and William K. Vanderbilt. In 1910 it was brought out in an official inquiry that ten members of the New York State Legislature were on the confidential pay roll of Metropolitan Securities.

In New York City today virtually all the gas and electric companies have been combined into the Consolidated Edison Corporation (Morgan-Rockefeller). The traction companies, losing propositions because of the indoctrination of the public mind with the politically useful slogan of the five-cent fare, are now being offered to the city at stiff prices.

Ever since the first franchises were issued to its own favorites by Tammany Hall immediately after the Civil War the operation of the New York public-utility companies has constituted an uninterrupted scandal. As to the gigantic Consolidated Gas Company and the New York Edison Company, now constituent parts of the Consolidated Edison Corporation, their history has been dispassionately summarized by Judge Samuel Seabury in these words:

"Their record has been one of extortion. Their privileges were conceived in fraud and political corruption and throughout their existence they have been a constant source of temptation to corrupt officials. Both of these corporations exist in violation of the law and both enjoy absolute monopolies in the necessaries of life. Both have violated the law of the State, both have made false reports to avoid the payment of their just taxes, and both have entered into a close and friendly alliance with public officers whose duty required that they should protect the public from extortion."

# APPENDIX B

## War Profits

WHAT the war and Woodrow Wilson did for Wall Street is shown briefly by a few random figures.

At the end of 1913 the assets of the Du Pont company were $74,817,826; at the end of 1918 they were $308,846,297. Gross revenues in 1914 were $25,179,948. In 1915 they were $131,142,015, in 1916 they were $318,845,685, in 1917 they were $269,842,465, and in 1918 they were $329,121,608. Du Pont war dividends equaled 458 per cent on the par value of the original stock.

The Standard Oil Company of New Jersey until 1918 carefully concealed its profit, but in that year it reported net income of $45,125,569, or as much as all the constituent Standard Oil Companies annually earned before the dissolution decree of 1911. Net profits of the Standard Oil Company of New York were $7,735,919 in 1914; in 1915 they jumped to $36,638,495, in 1917 to $30,000,673, and in 1918 to $28,642,388. Net profits of the Standard Oil Company of California in 1914 were $10,058,388; in 1916 they had risen to $17,605,304, in 1917 to $18,649,630, and in 1919 to $31,062,768. In 1914 the Standard Oil Company of Indiana had net profits of $6,590,924; in 1916 the profit was $30,043,614, in 1917 it was $43,808,930, and in 1918 it was $43,263,877. The other Standard Oil units experienced similar gains; each of the largest splinters of the old Standard Oil Trust were turning in greater earnings than the parent company before 1911. Profits of the thirty-two constituent units of the old Standard Oil Company in 1918 were about $450,000,000.

But the cream of this jest appeared after the war, when the biggest Standard Oil profits were still to come; for the automobile was now coming into general use and Standard Oil was in a strategic position to take advantage of the new vehicle. Before the war the

Rockefeller profits came mainly from sales of kerosene; during the war they came from the sale of crude petroleum; after the war the biggest profits of all were to come from the sale of gasoline drawn from regions that had been, of course, once a part of the public domain.

The industrial enterprises of J. P. Morgan and Company followed the upward wartime course of its many banks. Profits of United States Steel, which in 1914 were $23,496,768, in 1916 stood at $271,531,730, in 1917 at $224,219,565, and in 1918 at $137,532,377. Assets in 1914 were $1,765,257,492; in 1918 they were $2,571,617,175. There had been a deficit for the common stock in 1914, but in 1915 the common stock earned 9.96 per cent, in 1916 it earned 48.46 per cent, in 1917 it earned 39.15 per cent, and in 1918 it earned 22.09 per cent. From 1915 to 1919 inclusive the United States Steel Corporation paid dividends of $355,000,560.

The activities of J. P. Morgan and Company—and its profits—were not confined to United States Steel, however. The American Telephone and Telegraph Company completed the job of acquiring almost all the telephone companies of the nation; during the war it was saved serious embarrassment when the government gave permission to raise telephone rates. The International Telephone and Telegraph Company, the Radio Corporation of America, and the American and Foreign Power Company were launched, and preparations were made for further coups in the roaring twenties. The wartime gains of J. P. Morgan and Company and its associated families were, indeed, so vast as to defy proper description.

The copper industry, its executives buying copper for the government, were not behind the procession. Anaconda Copper, successor to Amalgamated Copper (its three leading directors still were Nicholas F. Brady, son of Anthony, William Rockefeller, and Henry H. Rogers) saw its assets rise from $141,400,798 in 1914 to $254,194,633 in 1919. In 1914 its net income amounted to $9,198,420, or 7.86 per cent on the common stock. In 1915 net income was $16,695,807 or 14.27 per cent; in 1916 it was $40,828,476, or 43.61 per cent; in 1917 it was $25,203,751, or 21.74 per cent, and in 1918 it was $20,802,870 or 18 per cent.

The assets of the Phelps Dodge Corporation, successor to Phelps,

Dodge and Company, in 1914 stood at $59,236,053 and in 1918 at $241,432,427, representing an increase rivaling that of the Du Pont Company. In 1914 net income was $6,664,839, or 14.8 per cent on the common stock. In the next four years, respectively, the company earned 21.6, 48.8, 37.6, and 22.8 per cent on the common stock.

Assets of the Morgan-Guggenheim Utah Copper Company were $39,557,108 in 1914 and $89,354,917 in 1918. Profits were $8,678,491 in 1914, $17,913,481 in 1915, $39,738,675 in 1916, $32,000,000 in 1917, and $24,750,000 in 1918. The 1917 earnings were 200 per cent and the 1918 earnings 150 per cent on the capital stock.

According to a Congressional report, *Expenditures in the Ordnance Department* (Sixty-sixth Congress, Report No. 1400), "The Calumet and Hecla Company in 1917 made a profit of $9,500,000, or 800 per cent of its capital stock, and in 1918 $3,500,000, or 300 per cent of its capital stock. The Inspiration Consolidated Copper Company in 1917 made a profit of $12,260,000, or 55 per cent of its capital stock, and in 1918 $9,250,000, or 40 per cent of its capital stock. The Kennecott Copper Company in 1917 made a profit of $11,826,000, or 70 per cent of its capital stock and in 1918 $9,390,135.90, or 60 per cent of its capital stock. . . ."

Professor Scott Nearing analyzed the earnings of other companies and found that the Republic Iron and Steel Company had an average profit of $2,500,000 in the three years before the war compared with $17,899,163 in 1916; the American Sugar Refining had an average profit of $2,000,000 for three years before the war compared with $6,000,000 in 1916; the Central Leather Company had a three-year average annual prewar profit of $3,500,000 compared with $15,500,000 in 1916; the General Chemical Company had an average annual three-year prewar profit of $2,500,000 compared with $12,286,826 in 1916; the International Nickel Company had an average annual three-year prewar profit of $4,000,000 compared with $73,500,000 in 1916.

Assets of the International Harvester Company, which stood at $126,341,792 in 1914, aggregated $283,218,992 in 1918. Profits rose from $4,262,595 in 1914 to $24,395,696 in 1917 and to $26,713,326 in 1918.

The Mellons cannily neglected to place upon the record wartime earnings of their Gulf Oil Company and Aluminum Company; but that their rate of growth was similar to that of other corporations cannot be doubted.

The United States government, like the majority of its people, found its financial position hopelessly compromised at the end of the war. Unlike the dominant families, it was not richer; it was poorer. In 1914 the national debt was $967,953,000, or $9.88 per person. At the end of the war it stood at $24,061,000,000, or $228 per person. Although the direct cost of the war in round numbers was $36,000,-000,000, this was not the full cost; for the costly and profound social derangement that took place in the years after 1929 must be assessed as part of the war cost. Including the expense of rehabilitation in the 1930's, the cost of the war was approximately $75,000,000,000 to the people of the United States. About half the direct war expense was contracted in making loans to the Allied governments so that they could buy materials through J. P. Morgan and Company, which profited by an admitted $30,000,000. Today the total of this indebtedness stands in default, repudiated by the sovereign governments of England, France, and Italy. This money, amounting to $13,736,000,-000, it is well to stress, is not in European hands; it belongs to Morgan, Rockefeller, Du Pont, Mellon and similar groups.

In 1914 the total estimated wealth of the nation was $192,000,000,000; under the stimulus of the war and the postwar period this estimate rose to $362,000,000,000 in 1929, a year when 2,000,000 citizens were totally unemployed. In 1900 labor, according to government computations, received seventeen and one-half per cent of the value of the products it produced; but in 1929, notwithstanding fifteen preceding years of extravagant industrial and financial development, it received only sixteen and one-half per cent. Whereas industrial output rose by fifty per cent from 1920 to 1930, the total paid in wages rose only thirty per cent, meaning that the rate paid went down.

And by 1929 the situation had become such that, according to no fewer than six surveys by conservative economic agencies, three-fifths of the nation's material wealth was owned by two per cent of the citizens. And more than half the corporate wealth was owned by two hundred companies. *No survey of the many undertaken has shown any different result.* In 1900 similar surveys indicated that two per cent of the people owned slightly more than fifty per cent of the nation's wealth.

In other words, as the nation multiplied in riches its people as a whole became poorer. And this was not the result of chance. It came about according to a design similar to that which is found in T. W. Lamont's 1915 analysis with respect to the economic effects of the war on the wealth of the Wall Street community.

# APPENDIX C

THOMAS FORTUNE RYAN secretly contributed $500,000 in a lump sum to the Democratic Party in 1900, according to his own testimony in the New York insurance investigation of 1905. This fact alone throws a curious light upon Bryan's "radicalism". Ryan later broke with Bryan.

# BIBLIOGRAPHY

Abbott, Willis J., *Watching the World Go By*. Little, Brown and Company, 1933.

Ackerman, Carl William, *George Eastman*. Houghton Mifflin Company, 1930.

Adams, James Truslow, *Our Business Civilization*. A. & C. Boni, 1929.

Allen, Frederick Lewis, *Only Yesterday, An Informal History of the 1920's*. Harper and Brothers, 1931.

—*The Lords of Creations*. Harper and Brothers, 1935.

Allen, Robert S., and Pearson, Drew, *Washington Merry-Go-Round*. Horace Liveright, 1931.

—*More Merry-Go-Round*. Liveright, Inc., 1932.

American Civil Liberties Union, *The Gag On Teaching*. Published by the American Civil Liberties Union, 1936.

*Annals*. The American Academy of Political and Social Science, Vol. 60, July, 1915.

Anonymous, *Mirrors of 1932*. Harcourt, Brace and Company, 1931.

Anonymous, *Mirrors of Wall Street*. G. P. Putnam's Sons, 1933.

Ayer, N. W., and Sons, *Directory of Newspapers and Periodicals*.

Baker, Ray Stannard, *Life and Letters of Woodrow Wilson*, 4 vols. Doubleday, Page and Company, 1927-1931.

Barron, Clarence W., *They Told Barron*; Notes of Clarence Walker Barron, edited by Arthur Pound and Samuel Taylor Moore. Harper and Brothers, 1930.

—*More They Told Barron*, Harper and Brothers, 1931.

Barry, David S., *Forty Years in Washington*. Little, Brown and Company, 1924.

Bates, Ernest Sutherland, *The Story of Congress*, Harper and Brothers, 1936.

—*The Story of the Supreme Court*. The Bobbs-Merrill Company, 1936.

Beard, Charles A., *The Devil Theory of War*. The Vanguard Press, 1936.

—*The Economic Basis of Politics*. Alfred A. Knopf, 1922.

Beard, Charles Austin and Mary Ritter, *The Rise of American Civiliza-*
*tion.* The Macmillan Company, 1927.

Beard, William, *Create the Wealth.* W. W. Norton Company, 1936.

Beer, Thomas, *Hanna.* Alfred A. Knopf, 1929.

—*The Mauve Decade,* Garden City Publishing Company, 1926.

Bemis, Samuel Flagg, *A Diplomatic History of the United States.*
Henry Holt and Company, 1936.

Bent, Silas, *Ballyhoo: The Voice of the Press.* H. Liveright, 1927.

—*Strange Bedfellows: A Review of Politics, Personalities and the*
*Press.* H. Liveright, 1928.

Berle, Adolf A., and Means, G. C., *The Modern Corporation and Pri-*
*vate Property.* Commerce Clearing House, 1932.

Bishop, Joseph B., *Theodore Roosevelt and His Time.* Charles Scribner's Sons, 1920.

Bleyer, Willard Grosvenor, *Main Currents in the History of American*
*Journalism.* Houghton Mifflin Company, 1927.

Blighton, Frank H., *Woodrow Wilson & Co.* Pamphlet. The Fox
Printing House, 1916.

Bok, Edward, *The Americanization of Edward Bok.* Charles Scribner's
Sons, 1923.

Bowers, Claude G., *Beveridge and the Progressive Era.* Houghton Mifflin Company, 1932.

Brandeis, Louis D., *Other People's Money.* National Home Library
Foundation, 1933.

Britt, George, *Forty Years—Forty Millions: The Career of Frank A.*
*Munsey.* Farrar and Rinehart, 1935.

Browne, W. R., *Altgeld of Illinois.* B. W. Huebsch, Inc., 1924.

Bryce, James, *The American Commonwealth,* 2 vols. The Macmillan
Company, 1922-1923.

Burke's *Peerage,* E. P. Dutton and Company, 1936.

Burr, Anna Robeson, *The Portrait of a Banker, James Stillman.* Duffield and Company, 1927.

Butt, Archie, *Letters.* Doubleday, Doran and Company, 1924.

Busby, L. W., *Uncle Joe Cannon.* Henry Holt and Company, 1927.


Carnegie, Andrew, *Autobiography.* Houghton Mifflin Company, 1920.

Cattell, J. McKeen, *University Control,* Science Press, 1913.

Chamberlain, John, *Farewell to Reform.* The John Day Company, 1933.

Chambers, Walter, *Samuel Seabury—A Challenge.* The Century Company, 1932.

Chase, Stuart, *Prosperity, Fact or Myth?* A. & C. Boni, 1929.

Clark, Champ, *My Quarter Century of American Politics.* Harper and Brothers, 1920.

Clark, George T., *Leland Stanford.* Stanford University Press, 1931.

Clarkson, Grosvenor B., *Industrial America in the World War.* Houghton Mifflin Company, 1923.

Cochran, Negley D., *E. W. Scripps.* Harcourt Brace and Company, 1933.

Corey, Lewis, *The House of Morgan.* G. Howard Watt, 1930.

Cortissoz, Royal, *The Life of Whitelaw Reid.* Charles Scribner's Sons, 1921.

Croly, Herbert D., *Marcus Alonzo Hanna.* The Macmillan Company, 1912.


Daugherty, Harry M., *The Inside Story of the Harding Tragedy.* Churchill Company, 1932.

Davenport, Walter, *Power and Glory, Life of Boies Penrose.* G. P. Putnam's Sons, 1931.

Davis, Elmer, *History of The New York Times, 1851-1921.* The New York Times, 1921.

Davis, Jerome, *Capitalism and Its Culture.* Farrar and Rinehart, 1936.

Davis, Oscar K., *Released for Publication.* Houghton Mifflin Company, 1925.

Dawes, Charles G., *Notes as Vice-President.* Little, Brown and Company, 1935.

Debrett's *Peerage.* Dean & Son, 1936.

Depew, Chauncey M., *My Memories of Eighty Years.* Charles Scribner's Sons, 1922-1925.

Dewey, Davis R., *Financial History of the United States.* Longmans, Green and Company, 1934.

*Dictionary of American Biography.* Charles Scribner's Sons. 1928-1932.

Doane, Robert R., *The Measurement of American Wealth.* Harper and Brothers, 1933.

Dorfman, Joseph, *Thorstein Veblen and His America.* The Viking Press, 1934.

Dumond, Dwight L., *Roosevelt to Roosevelt.* Henry Holt and Company, 1937.

Dunn, Arthur W., *From Harrison to Harding*. G. P. Putnam's Sons, 1922.

Dunn, Robert W., *American Foreign Investments*. The Viking Press, 1926.

Duffy, Herbert Smith, *William Howard Taft*. Minton Balch and Company, 1930.

Emerson, Edwin, *Hoover and His Times*. Garden City Publishing Company, 1932.

Fay, Sidney B., *Origins of the World War*. The Macmillan Company, 1928.

Flexner, Abraham, *Universities, American, English, German*. Oxford University Press, 1930.

Flynn, John T., *God's Gold*. Harcourt, Brace and Company, 1932.
—*Graft in Business*. The Vanguard Press, 1931.
—*Investment Trusts Gone Wrong*. The New Republic, 1930.
—*Security Speculation*. Harcourt, Brace and Company, 1934.

Foraker, Mrs. Joseph B., *Notes of a Busy Life*. Stewart and Kidd Company, 1916.

Forbes, B. C., *Men Who Are Making America*. B. C. Forbes Publishing Company, Inc., 1926.

Gardner, Gilson, *Lusty Scripps*. The Vanguard Press, 1932.

General Education Board, *Annual Reports*.

Gibbons, Herbert A., *John Wanamaker*. Harper and Brothers, 1926.

Gilbert, Clinton W., *Behind the Mirrors*. G. P. Putnam's Sons, 1922.
—*Mirrors of Washington*. G. P. Putnam's Sons, 1921.
—*You Takes Your Choice*. G. P. Putnam's Sons, 1924.

Gilbert, Mort and E. A., *Life Insurance: a Legalized Racket*. Farrar and Rinehart, 1936.

Gilfond, Duff, *The Rise of St. Calvin*. The Vanguard Press, 1932.

Glasscock, C. B., *War of the Copper Kings*. The Bobbs-Merrill Company, 1935.

Gosnell, Harold F., *Boss Platt and His New York Machine*. University of Chicago Press, 1924.

Grattan, Clinton Hartley, *Why We Fought*. The Vanguard Press, 1929.

Hacker, L. M., and Kendrick, B. B., *The United States Since 1865*. F. S. Crofts and Company, 1932.

Hagedorn, Hermann, *Brookings*. The Macmillan Company, 1936.

—*Leonard Wood*, 2 vols. Harper and Brothers, 1931.

—*The Magnate, The Life and Time of William Boyce Thompson*. Regnal and Hitchcock, Inc., 1935.

Hallgren, Mauritz, *The Gay Reformer*. Alfred A. Knopf, 1935.

Hansbrough, Henry C., *The Wreck: An Historical and Critical Study of the Administrations of Theodore Roosevelt and William Howard Taft*. Neale Publishing Company, 1913.

Hansl, Proctor W., *Years of Plunder: A Financial Chronicle of Our Times*. Smith and Haas, 1935.

Hapgood, Norman, *The Changing Years*. Farrar and Rinehart, 1930.

—*Professional Patriots*. A. & C. Boni, 1927.

Hapgood, Norman, and Moskowitz, Henry, *Up From the City Streets: Alfred E. Smith*. Harcourt, Brace and Company, 1927.

Hard, William S., *Who's Hoover*. Dodd, Mead and Company, 1928.

—*Raymond Robin's Own Story*. Harper and Brothers, 1920.

Harding, T. Swann, *The Degradation of Science*. Farrar and Rinehart, 1931.

Harvey, George, *Henry Clay Frick, the Man*. Charles Scribner's Sons, 1928.

Heaton, John L., *Cobb of "The World."* E. P. Dutton and Company, 1924.

Hendrick, Burton J., *The Life of Andrew Carnegie*. Doubleday, Doran and Company, 1932.

—*The Life and Letters of Walter Hines Page*. Doubleday, Page and Company, 1922-1925.

—*The Story of Life Insurance*. McClure, Phillips and Company, 1907.

Hibben, Paxton, *The Peerless Leader: William Jennings Bryan*. Farrar and Rinehart, 1929.

Hoover, Irwin Hood, *Forty-Two Years in the White House*. Houghton Mifflin Company, 1934.

Houston, David F., *Eight Years with Wilson's Cabinet*. Doubleday, Doran and Company, 1926.

Howe, M. A. de Wolfe, *George von Lengerke Meyer; His Life and Public Service*. Dodd, Mead and Company, 1920.

Huntley, Theodore A., *The Life of John W. Davis*. Duffield, 1924.


Johnson, Hugh, *Blue Eagle From Egg to Earth*. Doubleday, Doran and Company, 1935.

Johnson, Willis Fletcher, *George Harvey: 'A Passionate Patriot.'* Houghton Mifflin Company, 1929.
—*The Life of Warren G. Harding.* The John C. Winston Company,
1923.
Josephson, Matthew, *The Robber Barons.* Harcourt, Brace and Company, 1934.

Kennan, George, *E. H. Harriman.* Houghton Mifflin Company, 1922.
Kent, Frank R., *The Democratic Party.* The Century Company, 1928.
—*The Great Game of Politics.* Doubleday, Doran and Company, 1930.
—*Political Behavior.* William Morrow and Company, 1928.
—*Without Gloves.* William Morrow and Company, 1934.
—*Without Grease.* William Morrow and Company, 1936.
Kerney, James, *The Political Education of Woodrow Wilson.* The Cen-
tury Company, 1926.
Keynes, John Maynard, *Economic Consequences of the Peace.* Har-
court, Brace and Howe, 1920.
Kirkpatrick, J. E., *Academic Organization and Control.* Antioch Press,
1931.
—*The American College and Its Rulers.* The New Republic, 1926.
Klein, Henry H., *My Last Fifty Years.* Isaac Goldmann Company,
1935.
—*Dynastic America and Those Who Own It.* Isaac Goldmann Com-
pany, 1933.
—*Politics, Government and the Public Utilities in New York.* Isaac
Goldmann Company, 1933.
Kohlsaat, Herman H., *From McKinley to Harding.* Charles Scribner's
Sons, 1923.
Kolodin, Irving, *The Metropolitan Opera.* Oxford University Press, 1936.

Laidler, Harry W., *Concentration in American Industry.* Thomas Y.
Crowell Company, 1931.
LaFollette, Robert M., *Autobiography: A Personal Narrative of Political
Experience.* Robert M. LaFollette Company, 1913.
Lamont, Thomas W., *Henry P. Davison: The Record of a Useful Life.*
Harper and Brothers, 1933.
Lane, Franklin K., *Letters.* Houghton Mifflin Company, 1922.
Lawson, Thomas W., *Frenzied Finance.* Ridgway-Thayer Company,
1904.

Lee, James Melvin, *History of American Journalism*. Houghton Mifflin Company, 1923.

Lehr, Elizabeth Drexel, *King Lehr and the Gilded Age*. J. B. Lippincott Company, 1935.

Lindeman, E. C., *Wealth and Culture*. Harcourt, Brace and Company, 1936.

Lindley, Ernest K., *Halfway with Roosevelt*. The Viking Press, 1936.
—*The Roosevelt Revolution*. The Viking Press, 1933.

Lloyd, Henry Demarest, *Wealth Against Commonwealth*. National Home Library Foundation, 1936.

Lloyd's *Register of American Yachts*. Lloyd's Register of Shipping, 1936.

Lodge, Henry Cabot, *Letters of Theodore Roosevelt to Henry Cabot Lodge*. Charles Scribner's Sons, 1926.

Longworth, Alice, *Crowded Hours*. Charles Scribner's Sons, 1934.

Lowenthal, Max, *The Investor Pays*. Alfred A. Knopf, 1933.

Lowry, Edward G., *Washington Close-Ups*. Houghton Mifflin Company, 1921.

Lundberg, Ferdinand, *Imperial Hearst*. Equinox Cooperative Press, 1936.

Lynch, Dennis Tilden, *Criminals and Politicians*. The Macmillan Company, 1933.

McAdoo, William G., *Crowded Years*. Houghton Mifflin Company, 1931.

McCaleb, Walter F., *Theodore Roosevelt*. A. & C. Boni, 1931.

McCombs, William F., *Making Woodrow Wilson President*. Fairview Publishing Company, 1921.

McElroy, Robert M., *Grover Cleveland*. Harper and Brothers, 1923.

McLean, Evalyn, *Father Struck It Rich*. Little, Brown and Company, 1936.

Martin, E. S., *The Life of Joseph Hodges Choate*. Charles Scribner's Sons, 1920.

Merz, Charles, *The Dry Decade*. Doubleday, Doran and Company, 1931.

Millis, Walter, *The Martial Spirit: A Study of Our War with Spain*. Houghton Mifflin Company, 1931.
—*The Road to War*. Houghton Mifflin Company, 1935.

Mitchell, Edward P., *Memoirs of an Editor*. Charles Scribner's Sons, 1924.

Mitchell, Ewing Young, *Kicked In and Kicked Out of the President's Little Cabinet*. Andrew Jackson Press, 1936.

508   BIBLIOGRAPHY

Moody, John, *The Masters of Capital.* Yale University Press, 1919.
—*The Truth About the Trusts.* The Moody Publishing Company, 1904.
Moody's *Corporation Manuals.*
Morgenthau, Henry, and Strother, French, *All in a Life Time.* Double-day, Page and Company, 1922.
Muzzey, David Saville, *The American Adventure.* Harper and Brothers, 1927.
Myers, Gustavus, *History of the Great American Fortunes,* 3 vols. Charles H. Kerr and Company, 1909-1911.
—*History of the Supreme Court.* Charles H. Kerr and Company, 1912.
—*History of Tammany Hall,* Charles H. Kerr and Company.
Myers, William S., and Newton, W. H., *The Hoover Administration.* Charles Scribner's Sons, 1936.

National Bureau of Economic Research, *Economic Tendencies in the United States: Aspects of Pre-War and Post-War Changes.*
*National Cyclopedia of Biography.* J. T. White, 1924.
Nearing, Scott, and Freeman, Joseph, *Dollar Diplomacy: A Study in American Imperialism.* The Viking Press, 1925.
Neuberger, Richard L., and Kahn, Stephen B., *Integrity: The Life of George W. Norris.* The Vanguard Press, 1937.
Nevins, Allan, *The New York Evening Post.* Boni and Liveright, 1922.
The New Republic, Special Section, *Yale On Trial: Two documents in the case of Jerome Davis.* The New Republic, November 18, 1936.
Nicolson, Harold, *Dwight Morrow.* Harcourt, Brace and Company, 1935.
Noyes, Alexander Dana, *Forty Years of American Finance.* G. P. Putnam's Sons, 1925.
—*The War Period in American Finance.* G. P. Putnam's Sons, 1926.

Oberholtzer, Ellis Paxon, *A History of the United States Since the Civil War,* 5 vols. The Macmillan Company, 1926.
O'Brien, Frank M., *The Story of* THE SUN. D. Appleton Company, 1928.
O'Connor, Harvey, *Mellon's Millions.* The John Day Company, 1933.
Odegard, Peter H., *Pressure Politics: The Story of the Anti-Saloon League.* Columbia University Press, 1928.
Ogg, F. A., *National Progress: 1907-1917.* Harper and Brothers, 1918.
Olcott, Charles S., *Life of William McKinley,* 2 vols. Houghton Mifflin Company, 1916.

Overacker, Louise, *Money in Elections*. The Macmillan Company, 1932.

Palmer, Frederick, *Newton D. Baker*. Dodd, Mead and Company, 1931.
Peel, Roy V., and Donnelly, Thomas C., *The 1928 Campaign*. Richard R. Smith, 1931.
—*The 1932 Campaign*. Farrar and Rinehart, 1935.
Perry, Bliss, *Henry Lee Higginson*. The Atlantic Monthly Press, 1921.
Pettigrew, R. F., *Imperial Washington*. Charles H. Kerr and Company, 1922.
Platt, Thomas Collier, *Autobiography*. McClure's Magazine, 1910.
Pollock, James K., *Party Campaign Funds*. Alfred A. Knopf, 1926.
Pringle, Henry F., *Big Frogs*. The Vanguard Press, 1928.
Poor's *Corporation Manuals*.
Poor's *Directory of Directors*.
President's Research Committee on Social Trends, *Recent Social Trends in the United States*. McGraw-Hill Book Company, 1934.
Pringle, Henry F., *Alfred E. Smith: A Critical Study*. Macy-Masius, 1927.
—*Theodore Roosevelt*. Harcourt, Brace and Company, 1931.
Pyle, Joseph G., *The Life of James J. Hill*. Doubleday, Page and Company, 1917.

Raup, Bruce, *Education and Organized Interests in America*. G. P. Putnam's Sons, 1936.
Raushenbush, H. S., *The Power Fight*. The New Republic, 1932.
Ravage, Marcus E., *The Story of Teapot Dome*. The New Republic, 1924.
Regier, Cornelius C., *The Era of the Muckrakers*. The University of North Carolina Press, 1932.
Rhodes, James Ford, *The McKinley and Roosevelt Administrations*. The Macmillan Company, 1922.
Ripley, William Z., *Main Street and Wall Street*. Little, Brown and Company, 1927.
Rochester, Anna, *Rulers of America*. International Publishers, 1936.
Rockefeller Foundation, *Annual Reports*.
Rockefeller Institute for Medical Research, Occasional Reports.
Rogers, Cameron, *The Legend of Calvin Coolidge*. Doubleday, Doran and Company, 1928.
Rorty, James, *Our Master's Voice: Advertising*. The John Day Company, 1934.

Rosewater, Victor, *Backstage in 1912*. Dorrance and Company, Inc., 1932.

Rugg, Harold Ordway, *Culture and Education in America*. Harcourt, Brace and Company, 1931.

Russell, Charles Edward, *Bare Hands and Stone Walls*. Charles Scribner's Sons, 1933.

Ryllis A., and Goslin, Omar P., *Rich Man, Poor Man*. Harper and Brothers, 1935.

Sage, Russell, Foundation, *Bulletin 1-92*.

Salmon, Lucy M., *The Newspaper and the Historian*. Oxford University Press, 1923.

—*The Newspaper and Authority*. Oxford University Press, 1923.

Sears, J. B., *Philanthropy in the History of American Higher Education*. United States Department of Education, Bulletin No. 26, 1922.

Seitz, Don C., *The Dreadful Decade, 1869-1879*. The Bobbs-Merrill Company, 1926.

—*Horace Greeley*. The Bobbs-Merrill Company, 1926.

—*Joseph Pulitzer*. Garden City Publishing Company, Inc., 1927.

—*The James Gordon Bennetts*. The Bobbs-Merrill Company, 1928.

Seldes, George, *Freedom of the Press*. The Bobbs-Merrill Company, 1935.

Seldes, Gilbert, *Years of the Locust*. Little, Brown and Company, 1933.

Seymour, Charles, *The Intimate Papers of Colonel House*, 4 vols. Houghton Mifflin Company, 1926-1928.

—*Woodrow Wilson and the World War*. 1921.

Shukotoff, Arnold, *The College Teacher and the Trade Union*. Local 5, American Federation of Teachers, 1936.

Shultz, William J., *Taxation of Inheritance*. Houghton Mifflin Company, 1926.

Shultz, William J., and Caine, M. R., *Financial Development of the United States*. Prentice-Hall, Inc., 1937.

Sinclair, Upton, *The Goose-Step*. Published by the author, 1923.

Slosson, Preston W., *Great Crusade and After, 1914-1928*. The Macmillan Company, 1930.

Smith, Alfred E., *Up to Now*. The Viking Press, 1929.

Smith, Arthur D. Howden, *Commodore Vanderbilt*. Robert M. McBride and Company, 1927.

—*John Jacob Astor*. J. B. Lippincott Company, 1929.

—*Men Who Run America*. The Bobbs-Merrill Company, 1936.

*Social Register,* New York, 1936.

Standard Statistics Company. *Standard Corporation Records.*

Steffens, Lincoln, *The Autobiography of Lincoln Steffens.* Harcourt, Brace and Company, 1931.

Stein, Rose M., *M-Day.* Harcourt, Brace and Company, 1936.

Stephenson, Nathaniel W., *Nelson W. Aldrich: A Leader in American Politics.* Charles Scribner's Sons, 1930.

Stoddard, Henry L., *As I Knew Them.* Harper and Brothers, 1927.

Straus, Oscar S., *Under Four Administrations.* Houghton Mifflin Company, 1922.

Stoneman, W. H., *Life and Death of Ivar Kreuger.* The Bobbs-Merrill Company, 1932.

*The Strange Career of Herbert Hoover Under Two Flags,* by J. Hamill. William Faro, 1931.

Strong, Theron G., *Joseph H. Choate.* Dodd, Mead and Company, 1917.

Sullivan, Mark, *Our Times.* Charles Scribner's Sons, 1927-1935.

Symposium, *Democracy at the Crossroads.* Harcourt, Brace and Company, 1932.

Tarbell, Ida M., *The History of the Standard Oil Company,* 2 vols. The Macmillan Company, 1925.

Taussig, F. W., and Joslyn, C. S., *American Business Leaders: A Study in Social Origins and Social Stratification.* The Macmillan Company, 1932.

Thirty-Thirty-two, *High Low Washington.* J. B. Lippincott Company, 1932.

Thompson, C. D., *Confessions of the Power Trust.* E. P. Dutton and Company, 1932.

Thompson, Charles Willis, *Presidents I've Known and Two Near Presidents.* The Bobbs-Merrill Company, 1929.

Tucker, Ray, and Barkley, Frederick R., *Sons of the Wild Jackass.* L. C. Page and Company, 1932.

Tumulty, Joseph P., *Woodrow Wilson As I Knew Him.* Doubleday, Page and Company, 1921.

Turner, Frederick Jackson, *The Frontier in American History.* Henry Holt and Company, 1920.

Twentieth Century Fund, *American Foundations and Their Fields, 1932-1934.*

University of Chicago, *Annual Reports,* 1893-1930.

Unofficial Observer, *The New Dealers*. Simon and Schuster, 1934.

Vanderlip, Frank A., and Sparkes, Boyden, *From Farm Boy to Financier*. D. Appleton-Century Company, Inc., 1935.

Veblen, Thorstein B., *The Theory of Business Enterprise*. Charles Scribner's Sons, 1936.

Viereck, George Sylvester, *Spreading Germs of Hate*. H. Liveright, 1930.

—*The Strangest Friendship in History*. Liveright, Inc., 1932.

Villard, Oswald Garrison, *Prophets True and False*. Alfred A. Knopf, 1928.

—*Some Newspapers and Newspaper Men*. Alfred A. Knopf, 1928.


Winkler, John K., *John D., A Study in Oil*. The Vanguard Press, 1929.

—*Morgan the Magnificent*. The Vanguard Press, 1930.

—*The First Billion*. The Vanguard Press, 1934.

—*The Du Pont Dynasty*. Reynal and Hitchcock, 1935.

Waldman, Seymour, *Death and Profits*. Brewer, Warren and Putnam, 1932.

Warburg, Paul M., *The Federal Reserve System*, 2 vols. The Macmillan Company, 1930.

Warshow, Robert Irving, *The Story of Wall Street*. Greenberg, 1929.

Washburn, Watson, and De Long, Edmund S., *High and Low Financiers*. The Bobbs-Merrill Company, 1932.

Watson, James E., *As I Knew Them*. The Bobbs-Merrill Company, 1936.

Wecter, Dixon, *The Saga of American Society*. Charles Scribner's Sons, 1937.

M. R. Werner, *Bryan*. Harcourt, Brace and Company, 1929.

—*Privileged Characters*. Robert M. McBride and Company, 1935.

—*Tammany Hall*. Doubleday, Doran, 1931.

*Who's Who.*

White, William Allen, *Masks in a Pageant*. The Macmillan Company, 1928.

—*Woodrow Wilson*. Houghton Mifflin Company, 1925.

Wickwire, A. M., *Weeds of Wall Street*. Newcastle Press, 1933.

Willis, Henry P., *The Federal Reserve System*. The Ronald Press Company, 1923.

Worden, Helen, *Society Circus*. Covici, Friede, Inc., 1936.

# REFERENCE NOTES

1 *Fortune*, IV, No. 3 (September, 1931), p. 52.

2 *Fortune, loc. cit.*, p. 108.

3 *The New York Times*, December 5, 1936, pp. 3, 6.

4 Harry W. Laidler, *Concentration in American Industry;* Anna Rochester, *Rulers of America;* Adolf A. Berle, Jr., and Gardiner C. Means, *The Modern Corporation and Private Property, passim.*

5 *Fortune*, XIV, No. 5 (November, 1936). *"Richest U. S. Women."*

6 Pitrim Sorokin, "American Millionaires and Multi-Millionaires," *The Journal of Social Forces*, May, 1925.

1 Clarence W. Barron, *They Told Barron*, notes of the late Clarence W. Barron, p. 353.

2 Rochester, *Rulers of America*, pp. 39–40.

3 *Ibid.*, p. 57.

4 *Ibid.*, pp. 69–70.

5 *Ibid.*, p. 76.

6 Berle and Means, *The Modern Corporation and Private Property*, p. 19.

7 The selection of 1924 as "normal" is not arbitrary. The period 1924–26 has come to be so treated by economists because it is the only interval in the postwar period, when the United States emerged as a creditor nation, that was devoid of extreme depression or abnormal boom. To select any other period of the postwar years would be to take a period replete with distinctly abnormal data, and to revert to prewar years in search of normality would be to encounter data based upon the nation's status as an international debtor.

8 Robert R. Doane, *The Measurement of American Wealth*, p. 120.

9 *Ibid.*, p. 32.

10 The general thesis that at least seventy-five per cent of Americans own nothing except clothing and a few chattels is supported by a large number of conservative studies. See President's Committee on Unemployment, *Recent Economic Changes in the United States*, II, p. 478; *The Survey*, November 1, 1928, pp. 61, 120; Leven, Moulton, and Warburton, *America's Capacity to Consume*, Brookings Institute, pp. 55–56; Prof. C. Wesley Mitchell, *Mechanical Engineering*, February, 1931; Federal Trade Commission, *Report on National Wealth and Income*, 1926; The National Industrial Conference Board, *The Economic Status of the Wage Earner in New York and Other States;* and Robert R. Doane, *The Measurement of American Wealth, passim.* Specific examples of economic degradation are cited even in *Fortune*, organ
513

of the Wall Street banks, VI, No. 6 (December, 1932), p. 49; XII, No. 4 (October, 1935), pp. 56–57.

## CHAPTER III

[1] Charles A. Beard, *An Economic Interpretation of the Constitution of the United States*, pp. 152–188.

[2] John Chamberlain, *Farewell to Reform*, p. 211.

[3] Henry Demarest Lloyd, *Wealth Against Commonwealth*; Gustavus Myers, *History of the Great American Fortunes*; Charles Edward Russell, *Stories of the Great Railroads*; Claude G. Bowers, *The Tragic Era*; Don C. Seitz, *The Dreadful Decade*; Ida Tarbell, *The History of the Standard Oil Company*; Henry Adams, *Chapters of Erie*; Matthew Josephson, *The Robber Barons*; etc., etc. *passim.*

[4] David Saville Muzzey, *The American Adventure*, II, 443.

[5] John T. Flynn, *God's Gold*, p. 254.

[6] *Ibid.*, p. 254.

[7] Herbert Croly, *Marcus Alonzo Hanna*, p. 143.

[8] John T. Flynn, *op. cit.*, p. 383.

[9] *Ibid.*, p. 353.

[10] *Ibid.*, p. 257.

[11] Don C. Seitz, *Joseph Pulitzer*, p. 162.

[12] Robert McElroy, *Grover Cleveland*, II, 21, 999.

[13] Clarence W. Barron, *More They Told Barron*, p. 9.

[14] Croly, *op. cit.*, pp. 51, 59–61, 267–268, 269.

[15] *Ibid.*, p. 170.

[16] *Ibid.*, pp. 146–147.

[17] Flynn, *op. cit.*, p. 360.

[18] *Ibid.*, pp. 255, 206.

[19] Croly, *op. cit.*, p. 219.

[20] James K. Pollock, *Party Campaign Funds*, pp. 23, 51–56; Charles E. Merriam, *The American Party System*, p. 335.

[21] Croly, *op. cit.*, p. 220.

[22] United States Privileges and Elections Committee. Hearings before a sub-committee on compaign contributions, 62nd Congress, 3rd session, 1913, p. 453 (hereafter referred to as the Clapp Committee).

[23] New York Legislative Insurance Committee, 1905, X, 62.

[24] Gustavus Myers, *op. cit.*, III, 270–272 (Kerr edition).

[25] Croly, *op. cit.*, p. 326.

[26] *Collier's*, February 7, 1931, *"Power & Glory,"* by Walter Davenport, cited by Walter F.McCaleb, *Theodore Roosevelt*, pp. 115–116.

[27] Walter Millis, *The Martial Spirit*, pp. 63, 112.

[28] John K. Winkler, *The First Billion; A Biography of James Stillman*, p. 106.

[29] Louis Hacker and B. B. Kendrick, *The United States Since 1865*, p. 280 (1934 edition).

[30] *Ibid.*, p. 281.

[31] George Harvey, *Henry Clay Frick, The Man*, p. 290.

[32] *Ibid.*, letter, pp. 290–291.

[33] Don C. Seitz, *op. cit.*, p. 226.

[34] Henry Pringle, *Theodore Roosevelt*, p. 237.

[35] C. W. Barron, *More They Told Barron*, p. 80.

[36] Pringle, *op. cit.*, pp. 202–203.

[37] *Ibid.*, p. 208.

[38] *Ibid.*, p. 201.

[39] *Ibid.*, p. 208.

[40] *Ibid.*, pp. 211–212.

[41] Croly, *op. cit.*, p. 314.

[42] *Ibid.*, pp. 309–310.

[43] Pringle, *op. cit.*, p. 227.

[44] *Ibid.*, p. 244.

[45] *Ibid.*, p. 350.

[46] *Ibid.*, p. 256.

[47] *Ibid.*, p. 263.

[48] Walter F. McCaleb, *op. cit.*, p. 148.

[49] Pringle, *op. cit.*, p. 304.

[50] Walter F. McCaleb, *op. cit.*, p. 147.

[51] *Ibid.*, p. 157.

[52] Pringle, *op. cit.*, p. 333.

[53] Don C. Seitz, *op. cit.*, p. 338.

[54] *Ibid.*, p. 356.

[55] Pringle, *op. cit.*, p. 350.

[56] McCaleb, *op. cit.*, p. 251.

[57] Don C. Seitz, *op. cit.*, pp. 300–303, Letter in full.

[58] Clapp Committee, *op. cit.*, p. 128.

[59] Clarence W. Barron, *More They Told Barron*, p. 166.

[60] Don C. Seitz, *op. cit.*, p. 269.

[61] Clapp Committee, *op. cit.*, pp. 1073–1090.

[62] *Ibid.*, p. 454.

[63] *Ibid.*, p. 59.

[64] *Ibid.*, p. 1102.

[65] Ibid., pp. 1038–1039.

[66] Clarence W. Barron, *op. cit.*, p. 51.

[67] Pringle, *op. cit.*, p. 368.

[68] McCaleb, *op. cit.*, p. 261.

[69] *Ibid.*, p. 254.

[70] *Ibid.*, p. 255.

[71] *Ibid.*, p. 256.

[72] Pringle, *op. cit.*, p. 437.

[73] *Ibid.*, p. 437.

[74] Stanley Committee, p. 1687.

[75] McCaleb, *op. cit.*, p. 246.

[76] *Ibid.*, p. 249.

[77] *Ibid.*, p. 324.

[78] George Kennan, *E. H. Harriman*, pp. 215–216.

[79] Clarence W. Barron, *They Told Barron*, p. 33.

[80] Flynn, *op. cit.*, p. 436.

[81] John Chamberlain, *op. cit.*, p. 93; McCaleb, *op. cit.*, p. 241.
[82] Flynn, *op. cit.*, p. 449.
[83] *Ibid.*, p. 449.
[84] Claude G. Bowers, *op. cit.*, p. 374.
[85] Clapp Committee, *op. cit.*, p. 1581.
[86] Flynn, *op. cit.*, p. 449.
[87] Pringle, *op. cit.*, p. 531.
[88] John K. Winkler, *op. cit.*, p. 207.
[89] Muzzey, *op. cit.*, p. 435.

CHAPTER IV

[1] George Britt, *Forty Years—Forty Millions, The Career of Frank A. Munsey*, p. 177.
[2] *Ibid.*, pp. 147, 149.
[3] *Ibid.*, p. 145.
[4] *Ibid.*, p. 283.
[5] William G. McAdoo, *Crowded Years*, p. 115.
[6] Henry L. Stoddard, *As I Knew Them*, p. 421.
[7] *Ibid.*, pp. 305–307.
[8] *Ibid.*, pp. 305–307.
[9] *Ibid.*, p. 400.
[10] Britt, *op. cit.*, p. 178.
[11] Henry H. Klein, *Politics, Government and the Public Utilities in New York City*, p. 125.
[12] Claude G. Bowers, *Beveridge and the Progressive Era*, p. 438.
[13] *Ibid.*, p. 431.
[14] *Ibid.*, p. 423.
[15] *Ibid.*, p. 441.
[16] *Ibid.*, p. 444.
[17] John K. Winkler, *The First Billion*, p. 210.
[18] Frank A. Vanderlip and Boyden Sparkes, *From Farm Boy to Financier*, pp. 225–226.
[19] *Ibid.*, p. 226.
[20] Ray Stannard Baker, *The Life and Letters of Woodrow Wilson*, IV, 397.
[21] *Ibid.*, I, 40.
[22] *Ibid.*, IV, 210, 247, 332, 379, 465.
[23] Edward P. Mitchell, *Memoirs of An Editor*, p. 387.
[24] *Ibid.*, p. 387.
[25] Baker, *op. cit.*, I, 277.
[26] Clinton W. Gilbert, *Mirrors of Washington*, p. 53.
[27] Willis Fletcher Johnson, *George Harvey, "A Passionate Patriot,"* p. 138.
[28] William F. McCombs, *Making Woodrow Wilson President*, p. 30.
[29] Baker, *op. cit.*, III, 249.
[30] *Ibid.*, III, 250–251.
[31] Willis Fletcher Johnson, *op. cit.*, p. 213.
[32] *Ibid.*, p. 213.
[33] *Ibid.*, p. 211.
[34] Gustavus Myers, *History of Tammany Hall*, p. 390.
[35] McAdoo, *op. cit.*, p. 75.

[36] *Ibid.*, p. 503.

[37] McCombs, *op. cit.*, pp. 41–42.

[38] Thomas W. Lamont, *Henry P. Davison, The Record of A Useful Life*, p. 97, and Frederick Lewis Allen, *Lords of Creation*, p. 198.

[39] Frank A. Vanderlip and Boyden Sparkes, *op. cit.*, pp. 210–219.

[40] Baker, *op. cit.*, IV, 206.

[41] *Ibid.*, IV, 60, 70.

[42] *Ibid.*, IV, 210.

[43] *Ibid.*, IV, 245.

[44] McAdoo, *op. cit.*, p. 305.

[45] *Ibid.*, p. 290.

[46] *They Told Barron*, p. 141.

[47] Baker, *op. cit.*, IV, 245–246.

[48] *Ibid.*, p. 247.

[49] *Ibid.*, p. 347.

[50] *Ibid.*, pp. 292–293.

[51] Frank H. Blighton, *Woodrow Wilson & Co.*, pamphlet, 1916, New York Public Library classification, IAG. p. v. 169, No. 2.

[52] *Ibid.*, p. 25.

[53] *Ibid.*, pp. 28–35.

[54] Gustavus Myers, *History of the Supreme Court*, p. 756.

[55] Charles Willis Thompson, *Presidents I've Known*, p. 202.

[56] *Ibid.*

[57] *Ibid.*

[58] Bowers, *op. cit.*, p. 488.

[59] *Ibid.*, p. 488.

[60] *Ibid.*, p. 489.

[61] William McCombs, *op. cit.*, p. 70.

[62] C. W. Barron, *They Told Barron*, p. 12.

[63] Hermann Hagedorn, *The Magnate, The Life and Time of William Boyce Thompson*, p. 279.

[64] Thomas W. Lamont, *op. cit.*, p. 190.

[65] Baker, *op. cit.*, IV, 33–34.

[66] *The New York Times*, April 7, 1937, 20:6.

[67] Lamont, *op. cit.*, p. 267. The name of Davison was brought to Wilson's attention by this route: Dwight W. Morrow, Morgan partner, suggested it to Cornelius Bliss, Jr., son of the former Republican Party treasurer, who suggested it to Dodge, who suggested it to Wilson. J. P. Morgan and Company, in short, wanted Davison in this job. *See* also *The Intimate Papers of Colonel House*, III, 16.

[68] *Fortune*, October, 1933, p. 109.

[69] *Ibid.*

[70] *They Told Barron*, p. 327.

[71] Harold Nicolson, *Dwight Morrow*, p. 237.

CHAPTER V

[1] Alice Longworth, *Crowded Hours*, p. 325.

[2] Duff Gilfond, *The Rise of St. Calvin*, p. 124.

[3] Willis Fletcher Johnson, *George Harvey, "A Passionate Patriot,"* p. 279.

[4] *They Told Barron,* p. 251.

[5] Harold Nicolson, *Dwight Morrow,* p. 232.

[6] *The New York Times,* March 2, 1928

[7] *Ibid.*

[8] Henry F. Pringle, *Big Frogs,* p. 196.

[9] Charles Willis Thompson, *Presidents I've Known,* p. 326.

[10] Willis Fletcher Johnson, *op. cit.,* p. 274.

[11] R. F. Pettigrew, *Imperial Washington,* p. 399.

[12] *Ibid.,* p. 399.

[13] *Ibid.,* p. 398.

[14] Duff Gilfond, *op. cit.,* pp. 47–51.

[15] Harold Nicolson, *op. cit.,* p. 368.

[16] *Ibid.,* p. 233.

[17] *Ibid.,* p. 234.

[18] Willis Fletcher Johnson, *op. cit.,* p. 282.

[19] *Ibid.,* pp. 348–362.

[20] *Ibid.,* p. 286.

[21] *Ibid.,* pp. 400–404.

[22] Irwin Hood Hoover, *Forty-Two Years in the White House,* p. 170.

[23] Willis Fletcher Johnson, *op. cit.,* p. 403.

[24] *Ibid.,* p. 399.

[25] *Ibid.,* p. 401.

[26] *Ibid.,* p. 418.

[27] George Harvey, *Henry Clay Frick, The Man,* pp. 292–293.

[28] Clarence W. Barron, *They Told Barron,* p. 251.

[29] *Ibid.,* p. 252.

[30] Clarence W. Barron, *More They Told Barron,* p. 214.

[31] Irwin Hood Hoover, *op. cit.,* pp. 249–250.

[32] Alice Longworth, *op. cit.,* p. 324.

[33] Dwight Lowell Dumond, *Roosevelt to Roosevelt,* p. 335.

[34] *They Told Barron,* p. 251.

### CHAPTER VI

There are no reference notes for this chapter. Sources acknowledged in text.

### CHAPTER VII

[1] Frank R. Kent, *The Great Game of Politics,* p. 210.

[2] The writer was told by the late Holland Reavis, founder of the *Oil and Gas Journal* and numerous other petroleum trade publications and a successful oil share operator, that Nujol was created to give the Rockefellers a product to advertise in the rural press.

[3] *The New York Times,* October 30, 1935, 6:2.

[4] Oscar K. Davis, *Released for Publication,* p. 270.

5 William Z. Ripley, *Railroads, Finance and Organization*, p. 432.
6 *See* Ferdinand Lundberg, *Imperial Hearst*, pp. 139–173.


## CHAPTER VIII


1 Cited by Davis, *Capitalism and Its Culture*, p. 301.
2 Silas Bent, *Ballyhoo*, p. 109.
3 George Seldes, *Freedom of the Press*, pp. 114–115.
4 *Ibid.*, p. 115.
5 *Ibid.*, p. 120.
6 Peter Odegard, *Pressure Politics*, p. 263.
7 *Ibid.*, p. 263.
8 *Ibid.*, p. 252.
9 *Ibid.*, p. 258.
10 Don C. Seitz, *The James Gordon Bennetts.*


## CHAPTERS IX TO XII


Sources acknowledged in body of text.

# Index

Abbott, Lyman, 248–249
Aberdeen (N. D.) *Herald*, 282
Academic freedom, 388–390, 393–395
Adams, Charles Francis, 43–44, 183, 236, 381
Adams, Edward E. B., 456
Adams, Karl, 433
Adamson Law, 120–121
Advertising industry, 247, 252, 256, 261, 289, 305–306
Agassiz, George R., 381
Agricultural Adjustment Act, 458–459, 461
Aircraft Production Board, 194
Air-mail contracts, 196, 211–217, 226
Alabama Power Co., 198
Alaska Railroad, 290
Albany *Evening News*, 251, 275
Albany *Knickerbocker Press*, 251, 272, 275
Albuquerque (N. M.) *Journal*, 295
Aldred, J. E., 429
Aldrich, Edward B., 131
Aldrich family, 28, 272
Aldrich, Nelson W., 10, 61, 69, 88–90, 109–110, 121, 122, 135
Aldrich, Walter H., 180
Aldrich-Vreeland currency bill, 89
Aldrich, Winthrop W., 10, 43, 223, 310, 336, 394, 461
Alexander, James W., 78, 129
Allegheny Corp., 232–235, 255
Allen, Charles H., 305
Allen, F. H., 158
Allied Chemical and Dye Corp., 27, 42, 181, 224, 277
Aluminum Co. of America, 7, 26, 53, 175, 163–164, 237, 365 *f.n.*, 467, App. B.
Aluminum industry, 42, 163
Amalgamated Copper Co., 86, 91*ff.*, 144
*American Agriculturist*, 279
American Airways, 214, 215
American and Foreign Power Co., 44, 221, App. B
American Assoc. for Adult Education, 328
American Assoc. of Foreign Language Newspapers, 261

American Can Co., 44, 84, 112, 156
American Car and Foundry Co., 455
American Civil Liberties Union, 393
American Cyanamid Co., 198
American Founders Corp., 221
American Iron and Steel Institute, 183
American Locomotive Co., 85
*American Magazine, The*, 256, 308
*American Mercury, The*, 278
American Metals Co., 204
American Museum of Natural History, 19
American Newspaper Guild, 280–281
American Newspaper Publishers Assoc. 276, 289
American Petroleum Institute, 330
Amercan Radiator and Standard Sanitary Co., 482
American Radiator Co., 156
American Red Cross, 144, 146–147, 187, 334
American Smelting and Refining Co., 26, 156, 191
American Steamship Owners' Assoc., 304
American Steel Foundries, 183
American Sugar Refining Company, 11, 54, 63, 69, 99, 104, App. B.
American Telephone and Telegraph Co., 32, 42–44, 63, 104, 144, 159, 186, 230, 302, 384, App. B
American Tobacco Co. 26, 27, 88, 101, 449, 480
Ames family, 275, 303
Ames, Knowlton L., Jr., 275
Amherst College, 378
Amory, William N., App. A
Anaconda Copper Mining Co., 41, 91, 145, 174, 191*ff.*, 221, 225, 241, 438; press of, 272–274, App. B
Anaconda *Standard*, 272, 273
Anderson, Arthur M., 443
Andrew, Piatt, 121
Angell, James Rowland, 393, 396
Angell, Marion, 11
Anglo-French Loan, 137–138, 140, 143
Ann Arbor Railroad, 277
Annenberg, Moses L., 266
Antioch College, 378

521